Fredrick B. Pike is Professor of History, University of Notre Dame. Among his previously published works are *Spanish America, 1900-1970* and *The Modern History of Peru*.

The American Foreign Policy Library
Edwin O. Reischauer, Editor

Peru, Bolivia, and Ecuador

The United States and the Andean Republics: Peru, Bolivia, and Ecuador

Fredrick B. Pike

Harvard University Press
Cambridge, Massachusetts
and London, England
1977

Library of Congress Cataloging in Publication Data

Pike, Fredrick B
    The United States and the Andean republics.

    (The American foreign policy library)
    Includes bibliographical references and index.
    1. Andes region—Social conditions. 2. Andes
region—Economic conditions. 3. Andes region—
Politics and government. 4. United States—Foreign
economic relations—Andes region. 5. Andes region
—Foreign economic relations—United States.
I. Title. II. Series.
HN260.A5P54   309.1'8   76-55314
ISBN 0-674-92300-6

Foreword

by Edwin O. Reischauer

Among the many and diverse regions of the world, Latin America might appear to be one of the easiest for Americans to understand. A shared location in the New World and a common heritage as cultural offshoots of Europe would seem a basis for shared interests and understanding. In the early days, the new republic of North America was indeed an inspiration and often a model for the founders of the many republics of Latin America. In the decades on either side of the turn of the century, it seemed likely that some of the lands of Latin America would follow the path of development the United States had already taken. But they never did, going instead in their own varied ways. In place of a warm sense of fellow feeling, Latin Americans have tended to view the United States with resentment and hostility, while Americans have usually shown more bewilderment and disdain for the lands of Latin America than understanding or empathy.

One of the problems may have been the condescension with which Americans have lumped some twenty diverse lands together under the rubric of Latin America. Each is a distinctive nation, worthy of study in its own right. If generalizations are to be made, rather than taking Latin America as a whole, the various countries might best be grouped into regional blocs of states sharing somewhat similar geographic conditions, histories, and societies. One such regional grouping is clearly formed by the three Andean republics of Peru, Bolivia, and Ecuador.

A series of factors, all growing out of their high mountain setting, set the three Andean republics off from the rest of Latin America. These high mountains were the home of Inca civilization, which, like the Aztec civilization of Mexico, attracted the conquering Spaniards. They in turn made this region a center for prerepublican Spanish rule, while the relatively advanced culture and heavy populations of the Incan empire left behind a large Indian component in the racial makeup of these lands. Somewhat the same configuration of factors appears in only one other, but far distant, region in Latin America— namely, Mexico and parts of Central America. These historical factors seem to have determined the development of the three Andean nations more than their natural endowments, such as the mineral resources of Bolivia or the rich fisheries of Peru.

Professor Pike, in seeking to make the three Andean republics understandable to American readers, has centered his interpretation around their basic value systems and their cultural patterns. These contrast sharply with those of the United States. Americans glorify individual independence and the right and possibility of almost unlimited achievement by any individual. Rising expectations are taken for granted, and progress seems unlimited. By way of contrast, the peoples of the Andean republics, drawing on both their Indian and Spanish heritages, assume a more limited world and a society of closely intertwined dependence. In place of egalitarianism and rugged individualism, one finds a ubiquitous patron-client relationship. Higher organizations tend to be corporative rather than democratic.

Within this broad framework, Professor Pike presents a careful analysis of the historic development of each of the three countries. He devotes more than two thirds of his book to the long history before World War II, and he pays particular attention to intellectual trends. He has told a rich and complex story, but he has given it overall shape by his interpretation of the underlying nature of Andean society. Some readers may have doubts about his suggestion that the Andean concept of an unequal and limited world may prove more viable in our present age of recognized global limitations than the American emphasis on individualism and the dream of unending progress. Some may wonder why the Andean countries are so unlike some other societies that have also minimized individualism and emphasized patron-client relations. For example, if one were to contrast the Andean republics with the lands of East Asia, one would be struck by the multiracial foundations of Andean society, the pervading elitism of Hispanic culture, and the weakness of the drive for education on the part of the masses. But for the American reader, the contrast Professor Pike draws between Andean and American values throws a particularly revealing light. He has, I believe, made a great contribution to our understanding of these three culturally distant neighbor lands.

Preface

Shaped by reinforcing Hispanic and Indian influences, Andean society continues to this day to function in a manner calculated to blunt the individual egotisms of a great majority of the populace. Crucially important in accomplishing this objective are networks of intermediate groups. Encapsulated within these groups, constantly seeking peer-group reinforcement and ever sensitive to peer displeasure, the individual develops basic attitudes of dependence and deference. Generally, the closer to the bottom of the social pyramid the individual is, the more pronounced are the dependence-deference characteristics. Moreover, these characteristics are manifested not only in relationships with the group to which the person is most intimately tied, be it functional, local, or regional, but also in relationships with more powerful personages located at higher levels within the vertically structured society. Having learned to subordinate private desires to group pressures, individuals are predisposed to sacrifice self-reliance in any number of interpersonal associations. Above all, they are predisposed to expect the allocation of goods and services by power domains lying beyond their control.

Such, at least, has been the great ideal of Andean elites from preconquest times up to the present. Like any great ideal, this one has at best been no more than approximated in reality. But the hard facts of reality have never dimmed the appeal of the ideal; and except for several brief moments in the nineteenth and twentieth centuries when a few Andean leaders were beguiled by the rival charms of liberalism, elites have clung to their traditional ideal, no matter how sorely divided on other issues. Nor have nonelites waged any consistent challenge to this ideal. In their moments of protest it has not been the ideal to which they object. Rather, they have protested the failure of the system as currently functioning to bestow security in exchange for dependence and deference.

The term corporativism is used in this book to designate the type of social-political structure prevalent in and apparently natural to Andean America. Many North Americans might prefer to use the implicitly pejorative terms primitive and premodern. In twentieth-century Andean countries, however, political leaders from virtually all positions on the ideological spectrum are convinced that the corporative society offers the best means for attaining modernity—without sacrificing the stabilizing and disciplining mechanisms of the traditional order.

Bolivia embarked on its version of a twentieth-century modernizing, corporativist revolution in 1952, after having flirted, along with Ecuador, with a similar transformation in the 1930s. Then in 1968 Peru began its widely publicized revolution under the direction of the military. In all these instances, corporativist movements of national regeneration were justified ideologically on the grounds that they offered the best means for combining the most desirable features of premodern and modern life, while avoiding the undesirable aspects of socialism on one hand and capitalism on the other.

As 1976 drew to a close, Andean corporativism was functioning poorly, particularly in Peru, the country that had been the most aggressive in attempting to adapt the system to contemporary needs. At the end of 1976, in fact, the prospects for Peru's revolutionary corporativism seemed decidedly dimmer than when the year began and when the manuscript of this book was completed. It is possible that by the time this book appears in print the death knell for the most recent specimen of Peruvian corporativism will have sounded. It is further possible that the demise of revolutionary, military corporativism will have been hastened by the dictates of international bankers under circumstances suggesting that dependence on private capitalists (what I refer to in chapter 12 as the privatization of dependency) may be more onerous than traditional dependence on the State Department and other arms of the U.S. government. Even if corporativism in its latest guise escapes extinction in Peru and elsewhere in the Andes, it will hardly have contributed to one of its most heralded objectives: attainment of economic, political, and cultural independence.

However dim its immediate prospects, Andean corporativism will survive as a great ideal. It has already assumed mythic qualities that place it in the company of the two other systems whose myths and mystiques also guarantee longevity regardless of the failures of human beings to live in accordance with their respective myths. I refer, of course, to capitalism and socialism.

Capitalism has promised to raise the human condition to almost unimaginable splendors by means that are primarily material and quantifiable—hence its claim to modernity. That it has not yet perfected human existence to a degree even remotely approximating what has been promised does not dismay true believers. They contend that capitalism has not had the chance to show what it can deliver because it has never been properly practiced. Nor have the failures of socialism to achieve development—while at the same time avoiding the alienation assumed to be associated with the capitalist pursuit of progress—caused abandonment of the socialist myth. Socialism's true believers await one more opportunity to apply their belief system, confident that this time the blunders of the past can be avoided. With good reason Robert G. Wesson has given to his recent book on Marxism the subtitle: *The Continuing Success of a Failed Theory.*

Peter Berger, in *The Public Interest* (summer 1976), attributes the indestructibleness of the socialist myth to its promise to synthesize features of modernity and premodernity. (Neither Berger nor I use the term myth in a pejorative sense or necessarily question the truth content of the visions and ideals of myths.) According to its myth, socialism will bring about development without destroying the sense of community associated with the middle ages and with many primitive societies. Even as it is accomplishing prodigies of progress, socialism allegedly will nourish fraternity, persuading people happily to subordinate their desires to group interests and decisions of national leaders.

Just as much as socialism, corporativism promises to weave the warp of modernity with the woof of traditionalism to produce a new social fabric. And corporativists, at least of the contemporary Andean variety, have at their disposal certain lures denied to socialists. These corporativists promise to weave a cloth ample enough to encompass private capitalists. Thus the bourgeoisie does not experience with Andean corporativism the difficulties they encounter with socialism.

With problems of crime, alcoholism, drug abuse, and family breakup becoming ever more menacing in the United States, the corporativist myth takes on an added attractiveness in the lands to the south. Only corporativism, the believers of the myth profess, will foster the mental-spiritual habits of obedience and abnegation needed to check the excessive concern for individual gratification said to cause social disintegration in capitalist countries. At the same time corporativism will purportedly avoid the complete crushing of the human will presumed to occur in socialist nations. With a common denunciation of many aspects of modernity and a common assurance as to the feasibility of tempering modernity with traditionalism, corporativism and socialism have far more to share than do corporativism and capitalism— a fact that is bound to color Andean attitudes toward the United States.

In yet another significant way corporativism reveals greater affinity to socialism than to capitalism. For capitalists of ideological purity, if any exist, the sole source of political legitimacy must be the ability of the system to get things done, in other words to accomplish material progress. Socialists, however, are able to hedge. They can rest their claims to legitimacy on the ability of the system to get things done and also to preserve for citizens the contentments of social belongingness and group participation within a style of life that does not equate pursuit of happiness with gratification of the acquisitive instincts of possessive individualism. Corporativists also can hedge. Like socialists, they can justify their regime, whenever indices of material development falter, on the grounds that it provides certain essential nonmaterial rewards. It is as difficult to hold such claims up to verification as it was to substantiate the claims of the priestly class in premodern societies that they and their allies of the secular aristocracy were creating circumstances most conducive to the eternal salvation of the masses. What matters is that for decades and centuries the masses believed the priestly assertions, a lesson that has duly impressed modern socialists and corporativists.

In premodern societies with their conditions of physical adversity myths helped make life bearable. And they are just as important in modern times, especially in those areas where adversity stubbornly refuses to yield to the exorcisms of prophets of progress. Corporativists share with socialists a sense of awe before the power of nonmaterial forces and an appreciation of what myths can accomplish in mobilizing those forces in support of a political regime. In this they enjoy a certain advantage over capitalists. Their advantage lies in a broader view of human existence. Their political vision encompasses a world far more vast than the physical features that tend to blind archetype capitalists, inordinately proud of their demythologizing modernity, to all other facets of the human condition.

The tendency of the United States to see in a modern sense contrasts with the Andean habit of seeing in a traditional, medieval manner that takes in the real world of spirit as well as the real world of matter. From the contrast ensues a great deal of the incompatibility between the two regions. Prospects for reducing the incompatibility are slight, precisely because it has been formed by circumstances far more basic than the heedless or vicious acts of individual fools or knaves on either side. But if reduction should occur, it probably will not be because Andeans narrow their vision so as to see in the same way as most North Americans. More likely the day of greater compatibility waits upon the ability of North Americans to broaden their vision of human existence, as indeed they may very well be forced to begin to do in a postmodern era. So, at least, it seems to me, and the reader will find my explanation for this assumption in the final chapter.

Among the satisfactions afforded by writing this book has been the opportunity to rectify some of the mistakes of judgment and interpretation that have made me regret some earlier forays into the field of Andean history. For their aid in rescuing me from some old errors I am grateful to those whose research and writing, especially during the past ten or fifteen years, have expanded my understanding. My debt to them is acknowledged in the dedication of this book. But for them, and for the patient encouragement of my wife, Helene, this book could never have been written.

F.B.P.
South Bend, Indiana

Contents

Contents

Contents

Contents

Maps

The United States
and the Andean Republics

1

Perspectives of Cultural Contrasts

Concepts of national character may belong more to the realm of myth than of reality. But people live more by myth than facts. Thus the prevailing conviction that there is a U.S. national character and that individualism is—or has been—a principal ingredient deserves careful consideration in any study intended to explain North American relations with other countries, such as those of Andean America, which have rejected society-wide individualism. In the 1970s, when shortages of resources and concern about environmental pollution counsel greater state control over private conduct, individualism is increasingly under criticism in the United States. No matter: individualism still remains one of the favorite yardsticks of North Americans for measuring their own virtue and that of foreign peoples.[1] In fact, even as they become increasingly unattainable, the ideal of individualistic self-determination and the desire to be masterless grow ever more hallowed.

Individualism and the determination to be masterless have "expressed the universalism and idealism most characteristic of the [American] national consciousness."[2] And, far more than in most countries, these qualities have been nourished from a tender age within the typical family. Erik H. Erikson demonstrates that children in the American family are brought up to value their freedom of choice, rather than to seek security and emotional support through dependence on parents. "The American family . . . tends to guard the right of the individual member . . . not to be dominated." This type of family situation, Erikson contends, breeds "undogmatic people, ready to drive a bargain and then to compromise."[3] All of this is

1

associated with the American dream to be free from subordination and to bargain, as equals, with those whose authority to command (that is, parents, employers, and so forth) is calmly accepted in other cultures.

Associated with individualism, from which basically they all derive, have been such other American characteristics, commented upon by virtually all observers of the national scene, as compulsive competitiveness, the need for private achievement,[4] and intolerance of economic failure.[5] Also associated with individualism has been basic suspicion of government, arising from the conviction that individual men in their immediate situations could always act best in their own interests and thereby best serve the common good.[6] Understandably, the great American dream has envisioned a final stage of human progress that would be achieved "in a spontaneously cohesive society of equal individual rights."[7]

Ironically, it was an Englishman, Herbert Spencer, who was to provide—especially in his book *Man Versus the State*—one of the most complete rationales of American individualism and of the paramount characteristic sired by it, suspicion of the state. Spencer maintained, at least with regard to the economic phase of social life, that men "have been blest with an automatic, self-regulating mechanism which operated so that the pursuit by each individual of his own self-interest and private ends would result in the greatest possible satisfaction of the wants of all. All that was necessary was to remove the obstacles to the operation of this mechanism."[8] Convinced that the state did not have to intervene to assure a harmony that was self-assured, Spencer urged each man to dedicate himself to his own maintenance through his own work, free from "the direction of society in its totality." What is more, he believed that the social regulatory role of the state would grow "narrower and narrower, for it would have no other object than that of keeping individuals from disturbing and harming one another."[9]

The price that Americans have had to pay for their devotion to individualism has been enormous, as a large number of social commentators have recognized. In the quest of individualism Americans have snuffed out the desire for community, "the wish to live in trust and fraternal cooperation with one's fellows." Also sacrificed has been the desire for dependence, "the wish to share responsibility for the control of one's impulses and the direction of one's life."[10] Summarizing the case against the national trait lauded uncritically by most

American liberals only a few years ago, Richard N. Goodwin wrote in 1974:

> We live under the domination of an individualism whose conquest has been so complete that it has torn the thread of individual life from the fabric of humanity. We have been sundered from the wholes which gave us life ... For the ideology of individualism is so powerful that we still look on bonds as restraints; values as opinions or prejudices; customs as impositions. The remaining structures of shared existence, the restraints which make it possible for people to live with, and through, and not merely alongside one another, are assaulted as unjust restraints on liberty, impediments to the free assertion of self.[11]

Individualism has been pursued also at the cost of self-delusion and hypocrisy. Those who seek escape from the crushing competitiveness of freedom try to mask the fact, for acceptance of dependence on others is regarded somehow as un-American, as unmanly, and today also as unwomanly. The psychological strains resulting from not being able to admit openly the need for dependence are enormous.

As much opposed to the individualistic credo as the open acceptance of dependence is the overt attempt to dominate others. Thus the ambition to command and dominate is carefully disguised and even the means used to persuade others must be hidden from the public gaze. North Americans, it has been written, no longer curtail and conceal their sexual urges but instead their "inner drives for power and status. They can never be mentioned or acknowledged without shame or embarrassment. Just as the Christian prohibitions were the source of innumerable hypocrisies about sex and individual conduct, so our new ethic gives rise to endless hypocrisies in politics and social life."[12]

INDIVIDUALISM AND RISING EXPECTATIONS

American individualism stems from "strong confidence in self, or reliance upon one's own exertion and resources"; it stems also from belief in "the strife of all our citizens for wealth and distinction of their own, and their contempt of reflected honors."[13] Making feasible the competition for distinction of their own and their insistence upon "parity in competition"—which has been the real essence of the American belief in equality,[14] at least until the late 1960s when certain writers began to urge parity of results—has been the great abundance of the United States. This abundance, present in the frontier in the nineteenth century but even more in evidence in the cities which provided greater opportunities for mobility than the wilderness, can be viewed as the true wellspring of U.S. attitudes.[15] Only unique abundance, combined with a small population, made it possible for persons to compete for ever greater wealth and distinction without destroying all mechanisms of social and political control.

Dealing with these themes, Stuart Bruchey refers to "a quality of alertness to the possibility of material betterment" that either inheres or fails to inhere in a cultural value system. He argues persuasively that that quality "came with the first Americans to these shores, . . . and that with the progressively greater market opportunities provided by both government and private business during the late eighteenth and early nineteenth centuries, it seems increasingly to have permeated the American people."[16]

At the heart of Bruchey's analysis lies the conviction that the United States has fostered a belief in unlimited material progress, both for the individual and the nation. Certainly the belief in progress seemed well justified in the early nineteenth century. Between 1800 and 1840 real per capita domestic product increased about 60 percent.[17] To men of religious fervor, abundance and unparalleled progress indicated that God had singled out the people of the United States: they were his chosen people, destined to effect the sort of temporal progress that would result in the highest degree of human virtue and perfection that mankind could achieve. In short, progress as achieved by the American people would complete the work begun by the Reformation and usher in the millennium. No less a person than John Adams was among those caught up in belief in the providentially ordained role of the United States to bring about the millennium through temporal progress.[18]

To those inspired by this belief, achievement in the City of Man pointed to high rank in the City of God; for material progress automatically brought with it moral progress. From its infancy, then, the United States was acquiring the "spirit of capitalism," that is, a set of attitudes that strongly endorsed "the acquisition of money and the activities involved in it."[19] Earlier societies in their formative periods had tended to regard materialistic, acquisitive instincts as a necessary evil. In contrast, the United States exalted the spirit of capitalism, which accords approbation to acquisitive activities, holding them up as both the result and the source of virtue.

4

In the United States, persons entertained rising material expectations, initially at least, because fulfillment of such expectations brought them not only comfort and security in this life but constituted in addition an augury of salvation in the next world.[20] Any number of beliefs, values, and prejudices originate in religious convictions, and then are retained long after the religious origins have been forgotten. And so, long after secularism suppressed religiously inspired concern with the millennium the acquisitive instincts remained, undiminished in strength, to guide America's business society.[21]

Given this background, it is understandable that success in America has been judged not so much in terms of the wealth or position one possesses but rather by what one has gained.[22] The all-important determinant of success is how far one progresses from the starting point. Owing to these values and attitudes, social and political stability has depended upon the ability of a fairly high percentage of people—an ability that is either real or imagined, it doesn't really matter which so far as consequences are concerned—to fulfill their ever-rising expectations.[23]

How is it that the United States has managed in the perception of most citizens, at least in the past, to provide sufficient fulfillment of rising expectations to maintain stability? The question is particularly significant in view of the abundant literature that questions whether there has been any significant redistribution of income at all in the twentieth century.[24] One answer points to the American standard of living, "higher than that of any other country for many generations." This standard of living "has permitted the large majority of the population greatly to improve their living standards from one generation to the next, and has narrowed the gap in consumption standards among the classes,"[25] without occasioning the need for a more equalitarian distribution of income.

PATRONALISM-CLIENTALISM, CORPORATIVISM, AND ANDEAN CULTURAL PATTERNS

The cultural patterns of Andean America have permitted the desire to be masterless to extend only to a tiny segment of the population. Historically, only this minority has exhibited the traits of individualism. In contrast, the vast majority has hoped to attain security through dependence upon some more powerful personage. Those in positions of dependence did not take part in the individualistic pursuit of happiness; rather, they solicited happiness, along with security, from those patrons to whom they acknowledged ties of subordination.

Andean America of the colonial period, and even of the nineteenth and twentieth centuries, affords a classic example of a patronalist-clientelist society. Within this type of society there exists an endless variety of asymmetrical relationships (relationships between nonequals) characterized by the relative power of patron elements on one hand, the deference and dependence of clients on the other. Patrons are those persons who because of their authority, prestige, status, and wealth, or a combination of all these elements, can fulfill their will against the resistance of others. In fulfilling their own will, they can defend not only themselves but also those who are dependent upon them. In contrast, clients are those who, recognizing their inability to shift for themselves, seek out others to provide protection.[26]

The social structure under discussion may be described in terms of a continuum. At one end is the pole of most complete independence and power, and about this pole cluster the tiny minority of individuals who neither defer to nor acknowledge dependence upon any persons more exalted than they. At the opposite extreme of the continuum is the pole of unattenuated dependence, and here are assembled those members of society who rely exclusively on more exalted beings for their security and subsistence and who can claim no clients who are dependent upon them. In between the two poles there stretches an endless number of vertical, asymmetrical relationships involving those who are patrons for certain individuals of lesser status while in turn the clients of persons outranking them in status. In the patronalist-clientelist setting, the status that society ascribes to the individual is determined to some degree by how closely he approaches the patron pole of the continuum, and by the number of clients who acknowledge dependence upon him. In these circumstances, the lust to dominate others, regarded as antisocial behavior in the United States, is the normal determinant of conduct for society's upper sectors.

Patronalist-clientelist ties often are based upon kinship, whether created by blood or by the spiritual bonds of *compadrazgo* or co-parenthood. In many instances those who lack the resources to maintain themselves independently are related by blood to their patrons. In addition, many who feel inadequate to protect their own interests seek out someone more powerful as their *compadre* or co-parent. In the resultant relationship of *compadrazgo* the more powerful person becomes the godfather of the child of the less powerful, and in return for the ties of deference which the child's father assumes toward him, he assumes obligations to protect both the child and the child's father, who has become his *compadre*. This situation is one of "vertical *compadrazgo*," in contrast to the "horizonal *compadrazgo*" that exists when *compadres* are social equals.[27] Through vertical *compadrazgo*, social hierarchy acquires added legitimacy because it is "dressed in spiritual rhetoric and ritual."[28]

For its harmonious functioning, the patronalist-clientelist system requires acceptance by the overwhelming majority of their inability to initiate action on their own and recognition of the need to appeal to patrons to initiate desired actions. Attempts to obtain action, however, are seldom confined to relations between just one patron-client unit. More often than not a patron cannot himself initiate the action desired by his client; instead, he can only appeal to someone more powerful than he, someone who is his patron, to take the desired action. Thus the role of the intermediary, acting as a broker between the more and the less powerful, has been all important and all pervasive in society.

What was true of the temporal order was true also of the relations of humans with God. Only the most audacious mystic could conceive of going directly to God with a request to bring about some desired action on earth. For the vast majority of persons, God could only be approached through the brokerage of saints or of the Virgin. In the process, religious beliefs and practices reenforced the conviction that human beings, on their own, were generally incapable of mastering their destiny. Action was not the result of the individual's willing it or of coalition and alliance among subordinates; instead, it resulted from an appeal to a superior being.

The supernatural reenforcement of the belief that it was necessary to rely on others in seeking the means of survival derived not only from Spanish Catholicism and the place of honor accorded by it to the saints and the Virgin. Reenforcement derived also from preconquest Indian faiths. In Inca times, Indians had recourse to numerous gods from whom they sought the temporal conditions they felt powerless to bring about on their own. In more recent times, an Indian with a problem is likely to seek out a witch because of the latter's presumed power to influence or control supernatural forces.[29]

Acceptance through the years of the patronalist-clientelist society in Andean America has rested in no small part upon the harmony in the relationships between those who dominate and those who are dependent. There has existed, at least as the great social ideal, a give-and-take relationship beneficial both to patrons and clients. Whether

7

animated by considerations of Christian charity, or simply by enlightened self-interest and the desire to preserve social stability, patrons have, in return for their clients' performance of duties to them, assumed with some degree of willingness the burdens of paternalism. Moreover, if clients may occasionally feel frustrated in their dependence upon a patron, they can, in the vast majority of instances, find compensation in the fact that they in turn are patrons over others less powerful than they. Those in society who have absolutely no one to dominate are relatively few. Even those males toward the very bottom of the class structure have, more often than not, a woman whom they expect to command, while the women have children to dominate, and the children often have a dog to dominate and abuse—in vivid contrast to the U.S. family which is an association of equals and in which the dog is often accepted as a family member almost on a basis of equality.

A basic prerequisite through the years for a harmonious relationship between patrons and clients has been, in addition to paternalism, the universal belief that a state of dependency by no means detracts from human dignity or impedes realization of human potential—a belief that in Andean America goes back even beyond the Spanish colonial period to the great pre-Columbian civilizations. One of the most striking indications of this belief is the prevalence of Marianism (*Marianismo*, or the cult of the Virgin Mary), not only in Andean America but in other parts of Latin America as well. Marianism entails belief in the spiritual superiority of women, specifically upper-class women. To a very considerable degree, Marianism finds its origin in the concept that persons liberated from competitive, individualistic struggle for survival can attain to the highest degree of human perfection. In Andean culture the upper-class woman is expected to accept dependence upon her husband as the family patriarch who must concern himself with providing materially for all its members. Freed from material concerns, the woman can dedicate herself to the life of the spirit, while the husband-patron must allow himself, for the well-being of the family, to be distracted by material pursuits, succumbing inevitably to temptations of improper conduct. Quite possibly it is owing to the superior virtue ascribed to her, in her role of dependence, that the upper-class Latin American woman shows greater acceptance of her role in society than does her U.S. counterpart.[30]

The role of lower-class women in Andean society, and the roll assessment made by their social superiors, is an altogether different

8

matter. Women of lower social circumstances often avoid marriage, recognizing it as more often than not an institution that simply enables men to exploit women while giving little if anything in return; and they are resigned to making their way through their own initiative and competitive hustle. According to the standards that society has set for the poor in general, lower-class women are guilty of deviant behavior because of their individualism. This is one of the reasons they are so often dismissed by respectable society as *sin vergüenzas* (without shame), or shameless hussies.

The poor who accept their dependence on others are regarded by society as virtuous, and from this very fact originates some considerable degree of the self-satisfaction and dignity which can brighten the lives of social underlings. Dependence is widely recognized as conducive to moral progress, and from this stems the belief that poverty, which is always associated with dependence, is one source of virtue in this life and of salvation in the next.

In the cultural setting shaped by U.S. liberalism, dignity has inevitably been viewed as unattainable by those lacking freedom. Andean Americans, however, see no necessary connection between dignity and freedom. Thus they find it perfectly natural to assume that even in the status of slavery a person was not necessarily altogether deprived of human dignity.

In the ante-bellum south of the United States, largely unaffected—like Andean America—by liberalism's view of the human condition, certain defenders of the "peculiar institution" insisted that a social organization of domination and subordination was natural to and inevitable in human existence, and that dependence did not deprive a person of dignity. One of these southerners, Henry Hughes, tried to persuade northern capitalists of the advantages of establishing what amounted to patronalist command domains over their workers in the interest of rationalizing employer-employee relationships. Southerners, of course, failed ignominiously to win northern converts to their belief in the need for a society dichotomized between those who were dominant and those who were subordinate. The spirit of independent, individualistic capitalism in the north, as well as the absence of a large nonwhite labor force, doomed the southern arguments.[31]

The southern slaveocracy desired, in effect, to establish a dual society throughout the United States. Increasingly motivated themselves by an individualistic, bourgeois, capitalist ethic, they hoped to prevent the spread of this ethnic among slaves; and they doubted their ability to achieve this purpose unless northern capitalists could

9

also be enlisted in an effort to snuff out individualistic, self-reliant competitiveness among their laboring classes. What the southerners desired was a society based on self-reliance for those at the top, dependence for those below. Northerners did not go along, and they won the Civil War. In Latin America, however, as Richard M. Morse has observed in one of the most profound sentences ever written about that area, "The 'South' seems always to have won the 'Civil War.' "[32]

In order to provide a broader structural framework which would encompass and rationalize the countless dyadic relationships throughout society between patrons and clients, Spain introduced in its American colonies a system of corporativism based on models developed in Castile. The breakdown of the body politic into semiautonomous corporations or guilds provided an institutional basis for bringing together into one vertically structured association all those patrons and clients concerned with performance of a particular function in society, or all of those occupying a particular, narrowly circumscribed geographic area, such as a municipality. Each corporation was in turn linked through bureaucratic apparatus to the central government mechanism. While joined to a central government, corporations were not connected to each other.[33] Consequently, class consciousness at any level of society was virtually impossible to achieve, and no general sense of citizenship could develop.[34] Instead, all persons saw themselves as patrons, or as clients, within a particular functionally or geographically determined community.

In spite of all attempts in the postindependence era to eliminate corporativist structures, corporativism has retained its appeal in Andean America and was clearly reemerging in new guises during the 1960s and 1970s. Helping to explain the enduring strength of corporativist traditions in Andean America is the fact that they are the products not just of the Spanish but also of the Indian heritage. Preconquest Inca society was divided into *ayllus*, or agrarian communities whose members originally at least were related and who worked in common the land they held in usufruct, and also into various functional associations such as those of the silversmiths, the weavers, and the like. This corporative division of Indian society, discussed more fully in the following chapter, impeded social mobility, and consequently parents could calculate at birth their children's life chances. Moreover, Inca corporativism, even as its Spanish counterpart, placed a decided curb on the thrust of dynamic individualism and bred in most members of society a sense of dependence and reliance upon the collectivity to which they belonged.

The great French sociologist Emile Durkheim has provided, indirectly at least, one of the most compelling rationales for the type of corporativism that has prevailed in Andean America since pre-Hispanic times. According to him, a nation can be maintained "only if, between the State and the individual, there is intercalated a whole series of secondary groups near enough to the individuals to attract them strongly in their sphere of action and drag them, in this way, into the general torrent of social life."[35] The great advantage that Durkheim recognized in corporative organization is that functional associations "subordinate . . . private utility to common utility" and attach a moral character to individual subordination by necessarily associating it with "sacrifice and abnegation."[36] The corporative association was seen as having a further advantage in that from it "comes a warmth which animates its members, making them intensely human, destroying their egotisms."[37]

Down through history, the ultimate objective of Andean corporativism—whether shaped by Indian or Iberian traditions—has been, in effect, to combine the individualism hailed by Spencer with the collectivist spirit lauded by Durkheim. Within each corporation patron elements, although hedged about by commitments of paternalism to client segments, have behaved to some degree in accordance with the value and goals of competitive individualism. The directing or patron groups represent their particular corporation in the rest of society that exists outside the corporate confines; and they compete for maximum advantage in that outside world. What is more, within their own corporation, their exalted status, resulting from wealth, prestige, and authority, provides the basis for some element of self-reliance. Above all, the patrons, in the exercise of their individual wills, set the collective policies of each corporation. Also present within each corporative entity is a clientelist sector, made up of collectivist beings whose egotisms are curbed by unmitigated dependence upon their group and also upon the patrons who command it. Thus the corporative society is a projection of the basic social unit, the patronalist-clientelist extended family—just as U.S. society is, or at least used to aim at being, an extension of the family of bargaining equals.

In Andean corporativism the disciplining mechanism which attaches a moral character to subordination applies, obviously, mainly

11

to the client sector. Subordination to the group represents, in fact, the basic source of the dependency mentality of the masses. With the instincts of dependency once firmly established among the collectivized majorities, in consequence of their group consciousness, the more individualistic patron sectors can proceed to forge the interpersonal links of domination-subordination between themselves and clients. Corporativist collectivism, therefore, is not only the means for providing the broad structural framework necessary to rationalize the myriad relationships throughout society between patrons and clients; corporativist collectivism is also the origin of the dependency attitudes of the masses, of their willingness to be dominated, that is the bedrock of the patronalist-clientelist society.

PATRONALIST-CLIENTELIST CORPORATIVISM AND THE IMAGE OF THE LIMITED GOOD

In the interpersonal relationships between patron and client, harmony depends to some measure, as has been noted, upon the willingness of the patron to assume the burdens of paternalism. Similarly, within each corporation solidarity depends upon the willingness of patron segments to shoulder responsibility for the security of underlings. The paternalism practiced by society's better-off elements was inspired and also frequently augmented by an institution that cut across all corporative boundaries and was omnipresent in society, the Catholic Church.

In addition to paternalism, harmony in the corporative society depended upon what anthropoligist George Foster has described as the image of the limited good.[38] There existed, that is, within this society the well-nigh universal agreement that the available amount of wealth, goods, and resources was relatively fixed and that it was beyond human power vastly to expand the total. This being the case, persons acted not in response to motivations of rising expectations; rather, their actions were guided by the assumption that those with power and those dependent upon them had always to interact in harmony, for stability could not endure in the face of competitive drives that threatened to bring about any basic reallocation of the limited good.

Although challenged on some occasions, the limited good image has endured in Andean America through the ages—pre-Hispanic, colonial, and post-independence. Its survival explains why the person who has progressed notably from his or her point of departure in the accumulation of worldly goods is regarded as immoral; for whoever

12

augments wealth is thought to do so by depriving others of their former share of goods. In the society where the limited good image prevails, the person who succeeds too spectacularly in the City of Man offers proof thereby of alienation from the City of God.

The concept of the limited good throws much light on the dramatic differences that distinguish Andean heroes from U.S. heroes. In the history of Andean America one looks almost in vain for heroes of the Horatio Alger type. One finds instead heroes of failure, beginning with Rumiñavi, the commander of the Indian forces who conducted opposition to the Spanish conquerors engaged, under Francisco Pizarro, in subjugating the Inca empire. In the end, Rumiñavi was captured and executed in the main square of Quito. It was the same with Manco Inca, "the Great Rebel," who led a vain uprising against the Spaniards in 1536, and with Túpac Amaru I who some thirty years later took up the same cause, and with Túpac Amaru II who according to popular myth assumed the form of the sacred bird, the Condor, following his execution by the Spaniards in 1781. The heroes of failure continue through the years: with Simón Bolívar, the Venezuelan-born Liberator of much of Andean America who died convinced he had ploughed the sea; with the Ecuadorans Gabriel García Moreno who died at the hands of assassins, Juan Montalvo who died of cancer in poverty and self-imposed exile convinced like Bolívar of the failure of his life-long struggle to improve the worldly ambience, and Eloy Alfaro who was lynched by a once-adoring populace; with the Peruvians Miguel Grau and Francisco Bolognesi who despite their astonishing valor met death in the course of military defeat administered by Chile; with the Bolivians Andrés Santa Cruz who died in exile and ill repute, Manuel Belzu who although the idol of the masses was gunned down by an alcoholic rival, Germán Busch who committed suicide in the face of overwhelming adversity, and Gualberto Villarroel who was hanged from a lamppost. In general, the heroes of Andean America have shown Seneca-like resignation before hostile circumstances they could not possibly master. Their lives provide useful examples for impressing upon the masses the folly of seeking personal, material success. Andean American heroes have also been, most generally, kind, generous, affectionate father-symbol types, men who have shunned the quest of personal wealth in the desire to allocate fairly and equitably among their fellow citizens (often referred to as their children) the limited good available to the nation.[39]

There have been successful, Horatio Alger types in Andean history, men who on the basis of entrepreneurial skill, daring, vision, and hard work, and sometimes on the basis also of vicious, individualistic competitiveness, have accumulated vast personal fortunes as they advanced spectacularly beyond their starting points. In this connection, one thinks especially of the Bolivian tycoon Simón Patiño. Such persons, however, have never become national heroes. Instead, they stand as examples of the bad aristocracy, of the "oligarchy," whose members are characterized by their individualism, their refusal to be burdened by paternalistic ties to clients, and, in consequence of all of this, by their heedless upsetting of the delicate balance in the distribution of the limited good.

The difference between U.S. and Andean hero types extends even to contrasting views on the "good" Indian. In the United States, once the Indian menace had been dealt with by extermination and by confining the relatively few surviving Red Men to reservations, there began to enter into folklore the legendary, heroic Indian hunter who symbolized the virtues of resourcefulness and self-reliance, who lived in accordance with the "free exercise of natural impulses and power of men," and who refused steadfastly to accept fetters other than those imposed by his own nature.[40] In Andean America, on the other hand, the Indian most commonly glorified—at least by mainstream, establishment society—is the collectivized Indian, liberated, because of his dependence on group and state, from the socially disruptive drive of the individual will, patiently resigned to an environment whose adversity can be no more than slightly mitigated, and developing inward, spiritual strength as a result of his stoicism.

Understandably, in light of the preceding material, Andean Americans have traditionally viewed the businessman with suspicion. In a society that subscribes to the limited good concept, the businessman is seen as a predatory exploiter who amasses wealth not by creating it, but by bringing about a redistribution of wealth to the disadvantage of others. Throughout most of Andean America's history, moreover, religion has sanctioned and reenforced the hostility to businessmen.

The preconquest Indian past and also the colonial past were ages of faith, during which it was assumed that supernatural forces had fixed the amount of wealth and resources available to mankind. By their own efforts, mortals could not increase this wealth. However, by appealing to the deities they might gain an increase in overall wealth in such manner that should they thereby be benefited they would not at the same time damage the interests of their fellow beings. Therefore, appreciable increase in one's material well-being could be obtained legitimately only by "the favor of the saints . . . ,

14

certaintly not by thrift, work and enterprise."[41] In order to remain socially acceptable within this sort of cultural environment, a person who inclined toward the deviant behavior patterns of seeking wealth through thrift, hard work, and enterprise had to do all in his power to disguise this conscious pursuit of material success and to pretend that good fortune had come about unexpectedly, altogether fortuitously, and could only be attributed to providence. The callous businessman who did not take pains to disguise his activities was, at best, merely tolerated by elites because of his sheer usefulness. But the greater his success, the more of a pariah he became. Little wonder that during much of the colonial period applicants to the University of San Gregorio in Quito had to prove that none of their ancestors had engaged in trade.[42]

In stark contrast to the situation in Andean America, cultural values in the young United States were influenced by a deistic concept of the relationship of God to mortals. The almighty, it was assumed, left persons alone to pursue in their own way the expansion of the means originally entrusted to them—permitting these mortals all the while to enhance sanctity by means of augmenting the resources placed in their care. In this society the successful businessman was originally a saint and later, as the age became more secular, a culture hero. Undoubtedly, the dimensions of the U.S. development experience would have been far less dramatic had it not been for the nearly universal interest in and admiration of business that permeated the social structure.[43]

Faith that the good was not limited, but could be endlessly expanded through the actions of man, particularly the businessman, helped create a situation which amazed an English mission sent in 1853 to study the sources of U.S. industrial success. The mission concluded: "the real secret of American productivity is that American society is imbued through and through with the desirability, the rightness, the morality of production. Man serves God in America, in all seriousness and sincerity, through striving for economic efficiency."[44]

The outlook observed by the English mission also accounts for the premium that the Americans attached to science and technology. Obsessed with increasing their already bountiful wealth and resources, Americans were interested in ideas that would produce practical, tangible results in the physical environment, results that could be measured in terms of increased affluence, private and national. For Americans, it soon became axiomatic that ideas led to action and produced results in the real world.

15

In Andean America, ideas were less directed toward producing actions and quantifiable results in the physical environment; for the environment was regarded as a fixed good that man could not decisively alter. As a result, ideas were seen mainly as a source of inward gratification. Ideas were nonetheless terribly important, for inward realms were widely regarded as more important than the outer world —a situation which materialistic societies have always regarded condescendingly as typical of primitive people. In addition to being terribly important, ideas in Andean society also became the playthings of the upper classes; and their display served to increase prestige just as much as did the conspicuous flaunting by rich North Americans of their material playthings.

Because ideas were not associated with producing actions in the temporal order or changing the environment, society in Andean America became accustomed in the postindependence era to tolerating bizarre and even subversive ideologies. At least until quite recent times, those who propounded such ideologies were generally engaging in the conspicuous display of harmless playthings; they seldom expected their ideas to produce concrete social results, in spite of the bombast with which they propounded these ideas. Tolerance of ideas markedly at odds with mainstream consensus has been a characteristic of Andean culture. In contrast, North Americans, accustomed by their attitudes toward science and progress to associate ideas automatically with action and results in the social order, have been little inclined to put up with "un-American" ideologies.

THE NATURE OF GOVERNMENT

American individualism, as already noted, has fostered an ingrained suspiciousness of government. For a society that placed its faith in individualism, logic demanded that interference with the private bargaining process be kept to an absolute minimum. Americans came to believe that theirs was a "self-maintaining" social and political system;[45] and in this they were one with John Locke, to whom it never occurred that "public good might not always be compatible with ... the [private] rights of property ... A century later the possibility did occur to Adam Smith, and was waived aside by his 'harmony of interests' theory."[46]

By the time of the immediate post-World War I era, faith in uncurbed private bargaining had given way to a new faith, no less firm, in the miraculous results of collective bargaining and interest-group pluralism.[47] According to the new faith, the public interest is determined through the unchecked competition of interest groups. Given the fact that the country's roots were sunk deep in individualism, it is scarcely surprising that interpretations of political processes based on collective bargaining, countervailing forces, and interest-group pluralism proved totally "congenial to national sentiment."[48]

Pluralist theories of politics, even as the earlier creed of Spencerian individualism, narrowly circumscribed the role of government. In fact, the "zeal of pluralism for the group and its belief in a natural harmony of group competition tended to break down the very ethic of government by reducing the essential conception of government to nothing more than another set of mere interest groups." In the view of the pluralists, government was not an entity distinct and separate from the countervailing group forces that determined the public interest; instead, "government was nothing but an extension of the 'political process.' "[49]

Always, just outside the mainstream of American political ideology, there has existed a significant group of thinkers and leaders who have challenged the optimistic faith in the working of the "unseen hand." These persons have been fearful "that man's weakness would betray the nation," and they have sought a balance between liberty and order that stresses the second element.[50] Certain observers of the social and political scene have remained pessimistic about the ability of the self-regulating system to find, spontaneously, the public interest and they contend that there has always been present a far greater degree of planned control than is commonly recognized. They point to the president as virtually an uncrowned monarch and to his power, rather than to an unseen hand, they attribute what success the American political system has enjoyed.

Especially since the 1950s, a growing number of thoughtful persons have drawn attention to the failure of interest-group pluralism to achieve what they construe to be the true objectives of democracy. In their view, important political decisions have long ceased to be the result of free competition among a vast number of roughly equal groups. Instead, a few corporate giants are said to control the system and in the process to deny to the citizenry in general any meaningful participation.[51] Yet, despite the broadening perception of the weaknesses of the political system, Americans, who are perhaps more than most people the products of their past because all of that past is so recent, remain peculiarly loathe to seek to cure the failures of democracy through government intervention. In few areas is the contrast

17

between the political cultures of the United States and Andean America so glaring.

Basically ill-disposed toward "unseen hand" theories, Andean Americans do not regard as best a government that intervenes the least. To them, it seems natural for the state to "impose its power upon individual wills, in order to serve as the mobilizing force within a responsible, obedient, and at times passive people." The Andean political theorist "tends to separate, analytically, the command from above from the spontaneous initiatives and pressures from below, and to proclaim the virtues of the former." Consequently, he is "suspicious of attempts of the civil sectors to define themselves in spontaneous action."[52] To him, "the idea that the existence of a plurality of competing interests could lead anywhere except to anarchy is almost beyond comprehension."[53] The roots of these attitudes must be sought not only in the Spanish but also in the Indian background.

Among the higher preconquest civilizations of Andean America, government was something altogether apart from the people, something that totally transcended them because, at the very highest level, the powers of government were wielded by rulers who were divine as well as human. At the top, for example, of the Inca Empire of Tahuantinsuyo was the "Sapa Inca, head and heart of the empire, God himself, made man, absolute sovereign, with total political, administrative and legislative powers."[54] Not only for the Incas but for all of the high pre-Columbian Andean civilizations there existed a "religiopolitical system." Government was headed, that is, by a personage assumed to be endowed with divine attributes; and from the divinity of the ruler, government derived its legitimacy.[55]

Certain of the features of a religiopolitical system were continued, perhaps even strengthened, during the Spanish colonial period. More than the popes, the Spanish kings were the administrative heads of the Catholic Church throughout the Hispanic world. As such they were enveloped in an aura of divinity, and the interpenetration of religion and politics was evident in virtually all phases of temporal existence. Sovereignty was conferred upon the ruler not by the people, directly (as in the Lockean view), but only by the people as the instrument of God. And, once the people had conferred sovereignty, it passed altogether from their possession unless the king should prove himself to be an unmitigated tyrant. As a result, royal power rendered its holder superior to the community of citizens. In the words of the Spanish Jesuit Francisco Suárez (1548–1617), one of his country's most important political theorists: "Once power has been transferred

18

to the king, he is at once the vicar of God and by natural law must be obeyed ... the transference of power from the community to the prince is not a delegation but almost an abrogation, that is, a total grant of power which was formerly in the community."[56]

Until the very end of the colonial period, Spanish kings were secure in their legitimacy because they possessed charisma, in the sense in which Max Weber used the word: "It [charisma] is the quality which attaches to men and things by virtue of their relations with the 'supernatural,' that is, with the nonempirical aspects of reality in so far as they lend theological meaning to men's acts and the events of the world ... Legitimacy is thus institutional application or embodiment of charisma."[57] Accustomed by the colonial experience to obey their ruler because of his charisma or sacredness, Andean Americans retained intact, on the very eve of independence, a traditional religio-political system.

If democracy is to take root, the assumption must prevail that truth and proper norms of conduct can be discovered by citizens, largely on their own. According to the Lockean analysis that was so influential in shaping U.S. values, each person was capable of acquiring individually, through the use of his or her own reason, a knowledge of the natural law. However, in the Hispanic colonial world, the cradle in which Andean America developed its political culture, the natural law was strange and mysterious, in part because it was inseparably interwoven with the divine positive law which was incomprehensible to all save those trained in theology and canon law. Thus the intelligentsia, a group apart, separate from and above the masses, had to advise and consult with rulers in order to assist them in applying the interpenetrated divine and natural laws to any particular situation. In these circumstances, justification for monarchy derived from what has been termed "transcendental metaphysics."[58]

Even after monarchy came formally to an end with the attainment of independence, it remained latent in Andean America's political attitudes. Governments continued to concern themselves with transcendental metaphysics, the only difference being that now, as the age became more secular, the sources of transcendent truth ceased to be the revelations found in the writings of saints and doctors of the Catholic Church and became instead the pronouncements of such prophets and lawgivers as Bentham, Saint-Simon, Comte, and Spencer. Later, for those who were seeking to topple incumbent governments, the sources of transcendental metaphysics came to be such prophets as Bakunin, Marx, and Lenin.

Belief that law had necessarily to proceed from a highly complex and mysterious fusion of divine and natural sources and could only be formulated and interpreted by specially trained groups set apart from ordinary mortals contributed to the reverence in which the legal profession was traditionally held in the Spanish-speaking world. In Andean America, as elsewhere in that world, the masses turned to the lawyer as an absolutely essential mediator before a higher power. Popular attitudes and the need for government bureaucracies to be staffed by persons trained in law, given the incredible confusion arising from the existence of numerous corporative entities each with its own legal immunities and court of law, contributed to the enormous prestige of legal study. The law faculty became from the very outset the heart of the university structure in colonial Andean America. And it retained this status at least until the post-World War II era when suddenly the demand for development began to transfer reverence to another breed of persons apart, the technicians.

In notable contrast, the people of colonial English America and of the young United States "cherished . . . an ingrained hostility to the law as a profession." Lawyers were accepted, if at all, only on the premise that they might have a kind of nuts-and-bolts expertise acquired through practice, but never in the belief that they had through long training somehow gained initiation into a world that the common man could not hope to enter. For this reason law schools made their way in the United States "against widespread popular suspicion."[59]

Within the framework of Andean American political attitudes, shaped by the conviction that government and even its legal advisers are removed from the people by possession of charismatic qualities, the interventionist, omnipresent state is taken for granted. The corporativist traditions of the colonial past contribute strongly to this outlook. Within the colonial corporativist structure one of the most important prerogatives attaching to the ruler's sovereignty was the exercise of a moderating power.[60] Through this power, the ruler could regulate activities both within and among the various functional and local compartments into which society was divided. Traditionally, the political ideology of corporativism has denied to the vast majority the right to share in the exercise of the moderating power. Their energies absorbed and their interests confined by their local and functional groups, average persons could not—the reasoning goes—see society in its totality. It followed that only the ruler and the ruler's advisers who were removed from and above the rest of society could acquire the overall view necessary for the rational pursuit of the common welfare.

Within Andean America's political culture, it has proved extremely difficult to introduce collective bargaining. Instead of by this process, labor relations are shaped by what has been termed political bargaining. In political bargaining, labor appeals directly to government for protection of its interests. Frequently labor resorts to violence in order to dramatize its appeal. This violence may be misinterpreted by foreign observers as a challenge to the government. Actually, at least in many instances, it is simply a part of the ritual by which labor, accepting its role of dependent clientelism, brings its pleas before the state.[61]

Democracy in the United States may be viewed as based upon the conflict of laterally interacting organized groups as they compete first for the backing of other groups, then for concessions from government, and ultimately, if need be, for the support of the electorate. In the patronalist-clientelist, corporativist setting of Andean America, where the important social ties are vertical rather than lateral and where government is something apart and transcendent, organized groups compete for the benevolent attention of those in power. This is the ultimate weapon in their arsenal, short of revolution. What passes for justice is determined by direct relations between government, the superpatron, and the petitioning group. The number of people supporting the petitioning group is often irrelevent. It would be demeaning to the group and insulting to the patron to suggest that matters of justice should be influenced by the viewpoint of the half plus one.

OBSTACLES TO U.S.-ANDEAN UNDERSTANDING

At the conclusion of an influential book, Louis Hartz asks: "Can a people 'born equal' ever understand peoples elsewhere that have to become so?"[62] If slightly rephrased, this question probes at some of the most basic aspects of U.S. relations with Andean America. Can a people born affluent and equal ever understand peoples elsewhere that are poor and unfree and, with the exception of minorities in their midst, not terribly interested in becoming rich and free?

Comparing themselves to Andean Americans, the people of the United States traditionally have seen the contrast of modernity (good) with traditionalism (evil). Modernity they have equated with technology, industrialism, democracy, secularism, individualism, progress, and equalitarianism. For them the modern society, being the good society, merits the adjectives civilized and developed. In contrast, traditionalism—in the eyes of the North Americans who pride themselves on their modernity—is characterized by backwardness and primitivism which in turn derive from excessive concern with kinship and honor, from the sacred or religious view of life, from corporativism, hierarchism, localism or particularism, and the like.[63]

From the U.S. viewpoint, Andean America has remained mired in traditionalism.[64] All the more disconcerting in North American eyes is Andean rediscovery and unabashed glorification in the twentieth century of the historical tradition of corporativism, associated not only with the Spanish past but also with the pre-Hispanic background.

Erikson tells us that for every positive identity, both for individuals and for nations, there must be a negative identity, embodying all the opposite values—all of the objects of the positive identity's scorn and derision. The positive identity "must ever fortify itself by drawing the line against undesirables, even as it must mark itself off against those negative potentials which each man must confine and repress, deny and expel, brand and torture, within himself."[65]

Prominent among the traits of the U.S. positive identity has been devotion to society-wide equalitarianism. The contrasting negative identity, that is, commitment to corporativism, is perceived as the badge of uncivilized people. For other aspects of the negative identity, even stronger revulsion obtains. Lack of concern with progress, for example, was actually attributed by many nineteenth-century North Americans to the influence of satan.[66] Thus North America's quarrel with the life style of its Andean neighbors initially rested in some measure on religious grounds.[67]

Also conspicuous among the features of the U.S. positive identity has been the already-alluded-to need to achieve. Francis G. Grund, a German observer who lived in the United States in the early 1830s, noted the general contempt for a person who remained poor and who was not animated by the desire to attain success. Such demeanor was taken as a sign of irresponsibility and bad character.[68] The same judgment has been assessed against the Andean Americans who, in this instance, exhibit yet another trait of the negative identity.

The struggle of the positive identity always to triumph over the negative was involved in the attitudes shown by the dominant culture toward the counterculture that surfaced in the United States during the 1960s. One author suggests that the virulence manifested by defenders of the dominant culture may have sprung from inner misgivings about the cult of individualism and achievement, and from fear of finding something to admire in the counterculture.[69] Perhaps inner misgivings and fear have often been present as North Americans observed in Andean Americans the personification of their negative identity.

Heaping opprobrium on those who personify the negative identity is by no means a one-sided undertaking in hemisphere relations. Through the years, the majority of cultured Andeans seem to have been in agreement with the assessment that the renowned Peruvian intellectual José Carlos Mariátegui made of human liberty. For Mariátegui, individual liberty was the root cause of the evil that had befallen mankind in modern times. In the quest of individual liberty, human beings had set themselves against one another; and, in the obsessive pursuit of private material gain they had suffered alienation.[70] Although Mariátegui stood far to the left in the ideological spectrum, his views on the effects of obsession with individual liberty have been shared by most right-wing Andean ideologists. For left and right alike, negative identity is embodied in North Americans.

If U.S. opinion has generally shown concern and even dismay over Andean Americans as they are perceived to be, hope has sprung eternal that they could be transformed and uplifted. Thus Americans have always been encouraged when they detected, as the U.S. minister assigned to La Paz thought he detected among Bolivians in 1879, signs that their neighbors were moving "as fast as possible" to fashion "their form of government after our own."[71]

However much North Americans have grasped at the hope that Andeans were eager to embrace new and allegedly better ways and beliefs, the truth is that Peruvians, Bolivians, and Ecuadorans have clung to their traditional modes of existence with remarkable tenacity. Their identity has, after all, been shaped by factors reaching far back into their history. To begin to understand how Andeans have been formed in an identity that encompasses many of the traits of the U.S. negative identity, it is necessary to consider the cultural matrix of their Indian and Spanish colonial past.

2

The Social Matrix
of the Andean Past

Notwithstanding their claims to great antiquity, the Quechua-speaking Indians of highland South America who eventually came to be popularly known as the Incas (the term Inca had originally been reserved for the supreme and absolute ruler over the Empire of Tahuantinsuyo, or Four Corners) could actually point to a history, maintained through the generations by word of mouth,[1] that stretched back only to about A.D. 1100. After first rising to prominence among other tribes inhabiting the *altiplano* (highland plateau) region around Lake Titicaca, these Indians began to expand the territory under their control and founded Cuzco, probably not much earlier than 1300, as the capital of their empire. By the eve of Spanish conquest, the Quechua-speaking imperialists had established their sway over most of the area included in the present-day republics of Peru, Ecuador, and Bolivia, and over a vast amount of contiguous territory as well.

Many aspects of pre-Columbian Indian history are shrouded in mystery, a situation that has engendered conflicting interpretations and sparked long-lasting disputes among anthropologists and historians. Even on such a fundamental matter as population numbers, widely divergent opinions are advanced. The low estimate has been generally in the neighborhood of 2 million, but some have claimed a population reaching to and perhaps even exceeding 30 million. John Heming, author of the best overall treatment of the conquest of the Incas, places the population of the area controlled by the Empire of Tahuantinsuyo at 6,300,000.[2]

When it comes to evaluating the cultural level of pre-Hispanic civilization, differences of opinion are even more striking and more

24

passionately argued. The debate over the true nature of the Andean Indians and of the type of civilization they had developed began at the time of Spanish conquest and became, if anything, more bitter in the ensuing centuries. This is hardly suprising, for the debate over the nature of pre-Hispanic civilization is inseparably linked to the destiny that Peruvians, Ecuadorans, and Bolivians envisage for their republics. Some of the intellectuals and statesmen of these countries foresee a future in which assimilated, acculturated Indians will play a decisive role in bringing about national progress and development. In their view, then, the Indians possess a potential for the accomplishment of great tasks. In order to justify their view of national destiny, champions of the Indians, or Indianists (*Indigenistas*), turn to history, their minds to a large extent already made up as to what they must discover by studying the past. What they are determined to find through the study of preconquest aboriginal history is proof that the Indians had lived wisely and virtuously, thereby demonstrating for all time their high capacities and natural endowments.

In opposition to the Indianists, numerous Andean intellectuals and statesmen have dismissed the Indians as altogether lacking in potential. For them the achievement of a proud national destiny depends upon the gradual disappearance of the Indians, to be achieved through a combination of factors including downright exploitation and also miscegenation. Many of the anti-Indian spokesmen, moreover, have sought to encourage the massive immigration of purportedly superior peoples so as to replace the Indian as the basic population stock.

Those who discount the role of the Indian in the future of their countries also turn to history to find evidence to justify their views of national destiny. Their concern with Indian history is to discover evidence that points to the basic inferiority of the aborigines. The anti-Indian school gained its first spokesmen at the time of Spanish conquest; for many of the first conquerors, in order to excuse their deeds, found it necessary to establish the bestiality of those whom they sought to dominate. In more recent times, the use of history to establish the inferiority of Indians has been enthusiastically taken up by persons seeking a rationale for maintaining the Indians in a marginal status on the outer fringes of society and subject to unrestrained exploitation.

Early in the twentieth century the polemic over Indian nature took on a new character. At this time Indianists began to make more and more use of a new ideological weapon: Marxism. Rejecting altogether the liberal criteria, according to which the inferiority of Indians was clearly established by their lack of competitive individualism and capitalist spirit, Marxist Indianists found in the natives' traditional collectivism and absence of individual achievement orientation the proof of aboriginal superiority.

In turning what liberals had regarded as Indian vices into virtues, the Marxists were, even though they may not always have been aware of it, building upon some well-established interpretations, and misinterpretations, originating in the colonial past. The sixteenth-century Spanish Jesuit José de Acosta, for example, had praised the Incas for their acceptance of what was essentially a noncapitalist way of life. In particular, the Jesuit took the alleged absence of private property among the Incas as proof of their virtue and freedom from greed.[3] Similarly, numerous sixteenth-century Franciscan missionaries in Andean America and also in Mexico praised the Indians because of their docile, Franciscan-like acceptance of proverty, their lack of competitive instincts and greed. In fact, a wide variety of sixteenth-century Spaniards from all walks of life, accustomed to criticizing the purported acquisitiveness of Jews, Moriscos, and the Genoese, as well as of the Dutch, French, and English, were in many ways predisposed to find virtue in the noncapitalist approach of the Indians.

Catholicism, in its medieval, Hispanic form, had shaped the early anticapitalist values that permitted some Spaniards of the conquest generation to form a favorable assessment of Indians; and Marxism had provided the basis for the favorable assessment that appeared between three and four centuries later. In this instance, traditional Catholicism and Marxism were mutually reenforcing in casting the United States in the role of Andean America's negative identity; for the criteria that caused Catholicism and Marxism to extol the Indian led automatically to a rejection of the United States because of its ostensibly acquisitive, competitive, individualistic style of life.

Despite what the predilections of missionaries and Marxists led them, at different times, to read into the past, preconquest Inca civilization was not one of universal or society-wide socialism. Within the Empire of Tahuantinsuyo there existed a dichotomized society, with one life style for the masses and quite another one for elites. Among the masses, collectivism prevailed. Protected as much as was humanly possible against adversity of every type by an elaborate system of bureaucratized paternalism, the masses were not allowed to accumulate the surplus value of their labor. The state took from them according to their abilities, while giving to them according to their needs. In contrast, an Inca elite was to a considerable degree economically independent. Moreover, in the late stages of the empire, elites were coming increasingly to hold private property and to engage in practices of conspicuous consumption. Thus, Inca society was cast in a two-culture mold.[4]

Inca society was also compartmentalized or corporativist in nature, for a good number of its members were divided into various crafts associations; and many more were dispersed among the thousands of *ayllus*, areas of land collectively utilized by ostensibly tribally related families. The social system based on *ayllus* consisted of "a series of nested units defined in terms of kin, whether real or mythical. At each level of the society, a person made his claim on goods and resources on the basis of his membership in one of these units."[5] As a result of this institutional arrangement, individualism was virtually eliminated—among the masses.

Within the Empire of Tahuantinsuyo a highly differentiated bureaucracy provided a linkage between the collectivist world of the masses and the more individualistic and even incipiently capitalistic world of the elites. To a remarkable degree Spaniards, in the wake of conquest, built upon these Indian traditions in fashioning their colonial apparatus for ruling Andean America. Grouping the natives of the sierra into *comunidades* that bore resemblance to the *ayllus*, the conquerors permitted the heirs of the Indian *kurakas* (lords or chiefs) a wide degree of power within their particular area of jurisdiction. In addition to exercising political, social, and economic control over Indian comunidades, the *kurakas* represented these settlements in the outside world, frequently selling the goods produced by Indians in Spanish markets and also disposing of European goods among their Indian constituency. Enjoying a secure status within the Spanish world, frequently the holders of university degrees and even titles of nobility, the heirs of the Inca *kurakas* constituted a bridge between the European, partially capitalist economy that developed during the colonial period and the vast masses of rural Indians who continued to lead collectivist lives.[6]

By the eighteenth century, not only the *kurakas* and descendants of lesser Inca chieftains but also a large number of the wealthier members of Indian society were increasingly involved in commercial transactions on the European pattern. "They had converted the land and goods they once held as part of the Andean community into private possessions, and traded these in the Spanish markets for goods that they resold to the Indian villagers." This local merchant sector in native villages was made up of Indians called *principales* (important people). Functioning as middlemen, the *principales* carried on "private business activities for their individual gain."[7]

Andean America's Indian culture of the colonial period was neither capitalist nor collectivist, but combined features of both life styles. It symbolizes the system of capitalism for the upper classes matched by collectivism for the masses that many mid-twentieth-century Andean leaders have in mind when they reject both U.S. and Soviet models and insist that they will forge a political culture in keeping with their own authentic national traditions.

The clash of cultures provoked by Iberian conquest was less cataclysmic than it might otherwise have been—much less so, for example, than had the conquerors been Anglo Saxons—owing to the degree to which Spanish and pre-Hispanic traditions coincided. Within the Iberian corporativist structure, patrons had developed some degree of self-reliance, while clients had undergone the diminution of individual egotisms as they accepted dependence upon the collectivity. In the New World, ethnocentric Spaniards succeeded in their endeavor to fit Indians into life styles that combined capitalism and collectivism in a dual society because these life styles were in many ways in harmony with preconquest, aboriginal customs and values. To the similarity in Spanish and Indian cultural values and even sociopolitical organizational patterns is owing a great deal of traditionalism's staying power, out of which comes Andean America's ability to reject U.S. models.

INDIANS, THE HACIENDA, AND THE FRONTIER EXPERIENCE IN THE COLONIAL ERA

In the seventeenth and eighteenth centuries creoles (*criollos*, or persons of pure Spanish extraction born in the New World) and even mestizos (persons of mixed, Spanish-Indian origins) encroached on lands of Indian comunidades in the attempt to carve out private estates. In consequence, Indians came increasingly to live and to labor on haciendas (the large estates of the emerging creole aristocracy). Living at little above the subsistence level, with what scanty capital surpluses they might accumulate drained from them by the annual need to invest in the conspicuous consumption of religious festivals,[8] hacienda Indians—theoretically, at least—were protected through the paternalism and charity of the estate owner (*hacendado*) and the church, which was represented on the hacienda by one or more chaplains. Internally, the hacienda was a largely self-sufficient collectivist unit; but through the linkage to the external world provided by the *hacendado*, it did participate in outside, marketplace transactions. The *hacendado*, then, even as the *kuraka* and *principales* of an Indian *comunidad*, played the role of a capitalist patron. Furthermore, just as with *kurakas* and *principales*, the ability of the *hacendado* to exercise internal domination over the collectivized labor force of his land unit necessitated to some degree his own dependence upon an external marketplace over which he enjoyed very little control.[9]

Like the Indian *comunidad*, the hacienda affords a clear example of collectivism for the client class but capitalism for the patron sector. On this situation a Peruvian scholar has written: "The hacienda remained located on the border of two economies, and of two social sectors ... capitalistic business toward the outside, semifeudal social system on the inside. The hacienda thus coordinated two formally contradictory systems."[10] What is more, the "hacienda system of recent years has retained this ambivalent character."[11]

The culture of the hacienda stands in obvious contrast to the liberal society toward which the United States was evolving in the nineteenth century. Furthermore, the manner in which the hacienda was formed served to widen cultural differences between North America and Andean America. This fact is demonstrated in the contrasting frontier experiences of the two regions.

Andean Americans settled their frontier largely through the formation of the hacienda. For them, the frontier was an area already occupied by Indian *comuneros* (residents of *comunidades*); and expansion into the frontier resulted in the establishment of additional bonds of domination over vassals. The essential features of a patronalist-clientelist society were strengthened, and more than ever prestige came to be construed according to the number of vassals a patron held under his sway. Just as "respectable people were expected to hold [African] slaves"[12] in coastal Peru of the colonial era, so also respectable residents of the sierra were expected to hold Indian vassals under their domination.

The U.S. frontier experience, resting mainly on the expansion into unoccupied or sparsely inhabited territory, had precisely the opposite effect, nourishing the values of self-reliance and at the same time intensifying dislike of asymetrical relationships. The frontier in the United States also led its settlers to become killers of "inferior" people. The Andean frontier, in contrast, encouraged its settlers to become masters of "inferior" people.

In dealing with the founding of such new societies as the United

States, Canada, and Australia, Seymour Martin Lipset writes: "Many important European strata, values, and institutions, usually those associated with the privileged classes, never reached the 'new societies' ... Each left behind in Europe an ancient source of conservative ideology in the form of the traditional class structures."[13] In stark contrast, the element Spaniards left behind as they colonized Peru was the agricultural working class. People who had been peasants in Spain ceased working the land once they arrived in viceregal Peru because of the presence of Indian labor and later because of the relative abundance of slave labor.[14] The utilization by Spaniards of a native labor force as they expanded the frontier and their far greater reliance on imported Africans, in comparison to their Anglo-American counterparts, contributed enormously to divergencies in cultural values between the United States and Andean America and also to vast differences in patterns of race relations.

RACE RELATIONS AND CORPORATIVISM

In the society of viceregal Peru, which along with colonial Spanish American society in general can be described as a "pigmentocracy,"[15] the darker-skinned masses, the Indians, Africans, and mixed-bloods, formed the great base of a social pyramid; the higher the social status, the lighter the skin color was likely to be. Society, however, was to a considerable extent open, providing opportunities for the exceptional person of color to rise. Still, when the exceptional dark-skinned person did rise, the process frequently involved simply passing from the subordinate (client) into the dominant (patron) culture with a particular corporate entity—as in the case of Indians who rose from the collectivized masses of a communidad to the status of *principales*. As often as not, the corporative entity was rather close to the bottom of the hierarchical structure, and when the dark-skinned individual rose into the dominant sector within it, he or she continued to receive rights and privileges accorded that particular corporation and to receive justice from its separate tribunal. The person thus elevated did not receive the rights and privileges pertaining to the corporations that were higher in the social hierarchy; nor did he receive justice from the law courts of more exalted units.

So long as the corporative structure functioned properly, the great masses of the darker-skinned elements within the subordinate culture of each corporation were content to remain within their dependent status. This was because within their status of dependency they were at least assured of security through the operation of various paternalistic devices. Moreover, they were under no pressure from society to "improve" themselves. No liberal success myth which attached virtue to upward social mobility and the attainment of personal independence was operative in the corporative society of the Spanish American colonial world. Instead, society regarded the masses as most virtuous when they remained docile and subservient in whatever station they had been born to. Because they were spared exhortations to improve themselves, it was possible for the masses to derive some sense of dignity; and this was an important nonmaterial reward that helped assure harmony in the relationship of the subordinate to the dominant culture.

When the truly exceptional man of the lower, subordinate sectors did advance upward, he could, regardless of skin color, anticipate some degree of acceptance by society, precisely because his rise was exceptional and did not pose the threat of the rise of underlings en masse. Moreover, the exceptional man was not likely to ascend to the very top of society, for there were all kinds of compartments to trap him in a station still quite far from the truly aristocratic level. There was no general fear on the part of accommodated sectors that persons newly risen in status would play an influential role in society as whole, because there was no society as a whole; there were only compartments.

Beyond the corporative apparatus, there existed any number of asymetrical relationships through which the generally whiter patron sectors of society could dominate the darker-skinned client elements. This situation permitted the frequent manumission of slaves in colonial society and made it relatively easy for Andean society in the post-independence period to absorb slaves once manumission was universally extended at mid-nineteenth century. The liberated black man became at once attached to a white or "whitish" patron upon whom his dependence was subtler but scarcely less complete than upon his former owner. Within such a society virtually all persons, most particularly those toward the bottom of the pigmentocracy, saw security as deriving from a relationship to a patron, not from any collective bargaining process carried out by self-reliant persons. Moreover, once they escaped slave status, blacks were likely to pass into a racially integrated functional community and to identify henceforth more with this group than with blacks in general.

The toleration of upward social mobility on the part of exceptional persons of the dark-skinned subordinate culture played an important part in preserving the two-culture, patronalist-clientelist corporative society: for the recently risen persons at once identified with the higher status into which they had climbed and, in effect, turned their backs on the lower status from which they had just emerged. Consequently, the natural leadership class of the subordinate culture was co-opted into the world of the dominant culture. Noting the manner in which this process operated in regard to manumitted Africans, Frederick P. Bowser writes:

> Intelligent free Afro-Peruvians who had accumulated modest fortunes were quick to see that racial solidarity was all very well, but that "whitening" and "passing," culturally if not racially, was the key to socioeconomic advancement. Any sense of community the free coloreds possessed was constantly eroded by their recognition of the value of having ties to those who are lighter or wealthier or better connected than themselves.[16]

As this process continued through the years, the persons of pure African blood gradually disappeared as a result of racially mixed unions. Although whitish society did not seek to conceal its disdain for persons of color, be they free or slave, "the Afro-Peruvian and his descendants were . . . allowed, slowly and painfully, generation by generation, to lay to rest the burden of race" as they went through the "whitening" procedures. Whitening, already well under way in the seventeenth century, continued during the postindependence period. In 1792, Afro-Peruvians apparently accounted for over 7.5 percent of the entire viceroyalty's population, with free persons of color slightly outnumbering slaves. According to Peru's 1876 census, there were only 44,224 persons judged to be of pure African background, and they represented 1.94 percent of the total population of 2,704,998. By 1940, the percentage had declined to 0.47. "The remainder of the descendants of Peru's once-numerous colored population had joined the ranks of the nation's 'mestizos.' "[17]

In the United States, if exceptional persons of color moved upward, they rose in a society that—in theory, and as it was generally perceived—was open and neither divided into corporative compartments nor pervaded by patronalist-clientelist relationships. Thus there was nothing to prevent them from gaining full civic equality. Accordingly, the upward-bound dark-skinned individual was more resented than in the Hispanic world, where there were so many traps within the social and political system to stop the ascendant person at a safe distance from the top. In racist Spanish America, therefore, it was less necessary than in racist Anglo America to discriminate against the dark-skinned person purely on the basis of skin color. Moreover, within the U.S. political culture, which placed a premium on social ascent and the acquisition by all of self-reliance and which—until well into the twentieth century—frowned upon extending charity to the indigent lest their moral fiber be weakened, there were few means, outside of overt discrimination, to deter dark-skinned lower classes from seeking to rise en masse if any one from their ranks was permitted to move upward.

The corporativist, hierarchical, patronalist-clientelist, multiclass society has enabled Spanish America's upper classes to present the appearance of being racially open and tolerant. It has facilitated the co-optation of leadership groups from the darker stations of society into the whiter, while keeping the great masses of the dark-skinned at the base of the social pyramid. The appearance of racial openness and tolerance is, of course, deceptive. For the societies of Peru, Bolivia, and Ecuador, dark skin color has, since colonial times, been associated with stupidity or evil. Indians, for example, by the mid-sixteenth century were generally labeled *gente sin razón* (not fully rational persons) while by the end of that century mestizos and Africans were seen as members of a *mala raza* (bad race), as people who possessed intelligence but were basically inclined to abuse that intelligence by opting for vice rather than virtue.

Attitudes toward race have influenced attitudes toward political goals, leading to a rejection of democratic values and a commitment to domination-subordination ties. In a manner altogether typical among Andean American leaders, a one-time president of Ecuador gave expression to the interconnected attitudes on political forms and race when he wrote that democracy can exist only in countries "where the white population clearly predominates."[18] Had the social matrix of the United States been one in which the dark-skinned were numerically preponderant, its white populace undoubtedly would also have resorted to permanent asymetrical relationships as the foundation of society.

The Spanish American system of race relations has resulted in a society that is to a large degree racially mixed, even at its higher levels. And this fact has contributed to the disdain with which so many in the United States, accustomed by long-standing prejudices to abhor racial mongrelization or what Latin Americans refer to as *mestizaje*, regard their neighbors to the south; for, especially in the Andean region, "*mestizaje* . . . is the most interesting, significant and enduring contribution of Latin America to a world poisoned by deeply rooted racism."[19]

U.S. racial attitudes have resulted in fairly constant friction with Andeans and have contributed to the North American tendency to cast Andeans in the negative identity role. The leading, whitish classes of Andean America, while accepting it as natural that they should disdain and dominate the darker skinned, are in turn outraged to discover that they themselves are likely, in the United States, to be dismissed contemptuously as inferior mestizo types. In the nineteenth century the Ecuadoran liberal Juan Montalvo refused to set foot in the United States, although he admired many of the country's liberal values. Himself a mestizo, Montalvo feared that in the United States he would be treated with the discourtesy he heard had been accorded a certain dark-skinned Brazilian diplomat. Criminals from Europe, he bitterly observed, will be accepted in the United States if they have a white skin, whereas the most respectable persons from Ecuador would suffer enormous affronts if their skin showed the slightest color. In Venezuela, Peru, and Ecuador, he added, a person of dark skin could have ambitions to rise and to become important, and could fulfill those ambitions; but in the United States, it was necessary to have a white skin to be accepted as a human being.[20]

A trip to the United States in the early 1940s evoked from the Peruvian intellectual Luis Alberto Sánchez reactions similar in some ways to Montalvo's. He complained that if Spaniards had "disdained us as creoles, the new democratic power holds us no less in disdain as mestizos."[21] In particular, Sánchez was distressed to discover that in the United States anyone with even the slightest portion of African blood was held to be a Negro. This meant that according to "Yankee terminology," all of the mixed bloods of Andean America who had even a miniscule admixture of African blood "are Negroes, and only Negroes." The same was true in regard to Indians, Sánchez observed. "Who is an Indian in the United States? Anyone with even a drop of Indian blood. For the United States, mestizos do not exist. Persons who for us would be white (if they had economic position) are for them Indians." With us, the Peruvian added, "race depends as much on economic status as ethnic considerations; a mestizo who acquires culture and money becomes white."[22] The United States, however, did not allow for this, and where in such a setting, Sánchez wondered, could one find democracy.

The Peruvian visitor stressed the obvious when he noted: "from our point of view as South American mestizos" the racial attitudes of the United States have built "a bad road for achieving permanent solidarity between the two parts of America." And, he sounded a warning to the United States: racial discrimination, by making it impossible for the dark-skinned to rise, would lead to their radicalization and encourage turning to communism.[23] Clearly, he was smugly confident that the racial policies of Andean America had eliminated this danger.

EDUCATION, LETTERS, AND THE PATRONALIST-CLIENTELIST, CORPORATIVE SOCIETY

In the traditional and largely medieval society that Spain established in the viceroyalty of Peru, education was considered appropriate only for the power-wielding groups within the dominant culture. Accordingly, within each corporation education, beyond the level of vocational training, was offered only to a small minority. Moreover, within the corporative structure only an infinitesimally small elite might be expected to become associated in an advisory capacity with the supreme executive arm of the government that, sharing in the prerogatives of the crown, exercised a moderating power in the viceroyalty. Only to this elite was it proper to impart the sort of education that would enhance wisdom and understanding so as to enable the recipient to see beyond the confines of his or her particular compartment in society and to take into consideration broad, overall imperial considerations. For the fragmented masses, who were expected to be dependent upon the decisions reached by those above them, there seemed little purpose in developing intellectual capacity beyond the most rudimentary stage or in sharpening and enlarging powers of deduction and analysis.

Probably Martin Carnoy is correct when he maintains in his book *Education as Cultural Imperialism* (1974) that the function of schooling in every country of the world for hundreds of years has been to serve the interests of dominant groups in society. In Andean America's society of patrons and clients, the interests of the first group were served by not educating the second. In the industralized, achievement-oriented setting of the United States, however, an educated labor force was clearly to the advantage of the employer-entrepreneur class.

Within the context of the seventeenth-century Hispanic world, both in the Iberian peninsula and America, not only education but also artistic creativity and aesthetic appreciation were expected to serve elite interests by maintaining and broadening the gulf between the two cultures, dominant and subordinate. This fact is illustrated in a work published in 1694 by the mestizo Juan de Espinosa Medrano who held a professorial chair at the University of Cuzco from the time he was sixteen. In this work, referred to by one twentieth-century authority as possibly the most interesting piece of literary criticism produced in the entire colonial period,[24] Espinosa defended the Spanish poet Luis de Góngora (1561–1627) and praised the convoluted, baroque literary style which had come to be known as *gongorismo*. According to Espinosa, art should be strange and uncommon; and those engaged in artistic creativity should strive to make art "acquire mystery through its form."[25] This defense of baroque literary style struck a responsive chord among the cultured elements of the Peruvian viceroyalty, and understandably so. In their view, artistic creativity and aesthetic appreciation required the exercise of the most exalted abilities and as such were reserved to the upper classes. Art, therefore, which could be nourished and enjoyed only by the initiated and the exceptional, should be strange and uncommon so as to set the upper classes further apart from the masses.

The concept that education and the ability to create and appreciate works of art should serve to separate elites from commoners is reflected in a saying that was widely voiced in the Spanish-speaking world of the seventeenth century: *las letras y las armas dan nobleza*, which translates as "letters and arms confer nobility." Precisely how did one acquire nobility through letters? In Spain one could do so by obtaining an advanced degree from the prestigious universities of Alcalá, Salamanca, or Valladolid. Possession of these degrees brought most of the perquisites reserved to the nobility.[26] In Spanish America as well as in Spain, an advanced university degree was extremely useful to one hoping either to acquire or to enhance the prestige of aristocratic status.

What sort of letters did one pursue in the university as a means of setting himself apart from the common classes and gaining nobility? Letters in the Spanish-speaking world came, in effect, to mean theology, jurisprudence, and the sort of philosophy that derived from theology, not from rational analysis or empirical observation.[27] The pursuit of letters, moreover, consistently took place within an academic ambiance pervaded by scholasticism. According to the essential tenet of scholasticism, God was the source of all truth; and "in His wisdom, this truth, or portions of it, was divinely revealed to chosen individuals as the human agencies of transmission. Their writings were revelation and hence the final authority on all learning.[28]

Indian concepts of knowledge were strikingly similar to those of scholasticism. Among the native civilizations of preconquest Andean

America, knowledge was held to be initially revealed; and, once revealed, it was surrounded by religious ritual.[29] Here is one other instance in which Indian and Spanish traditions have, in their similarities, been mutually reenforcing—and mutually at odds with the U.S. heritage.

The study of science was also widely eschewed by Spain's American colonists who hoped to acquire or demonstrate nobility through the pursuit of letters. This has been explained in varying ways by different writers. The views of one important group are expressed succinctly by the Peruvian writer and diplomat Felipe Barreda Laos. According to him Spanish repression accounted for the dominance of scholasticism and the lack of concern with science and its methodology. Barreda, writing in 1909, insisted that tyrannous Spanish administrators had forced the unwilling colonists into intellectual strait jackets and impeded altogether the development of individual intellectual freedom. "There was no intellectual freedom," Barreda contends. "Afraid to express their ideas as to how to improve society, men kept their thoughts to themselves, never employing them as means to accomplish practical ends."[30]

Barreda overlooks the possibility that intellectuals in the Peruvian viceroyalty may have chosen the style of scholasticism and rejected rationalist philosophy and science because of their free and voluntary commitment to values most generally described as medieval. His whole argument is, in fact, rendered suspect by scholarly studies which demonstrate that colonists in viceregal Peru, in spite of the legal framework of imperial regulations, exercised the powers of self-rule to a truly remarkable degree—at least until the second half of the eighteenth century.

Peru's eminent historian-statesman Raúl Porras Barranechea put his finger on the real situation when, writing in 1951, he described his country's colonial culture in these terms: "The Spanish people always, . . . have maintained their inward freedom of thinking; they have always clung to interior liberty. And thus it was with colonial education, out of which gradually emerged a unique and Peruvian culture, whose culminating expression would be the independence movement."[31] In clinging to their freedom of thinking, men of letters in viceregal Peru chose, as a conscious exercise of that freedom, to pursue letters—and by means of letters, status, dignity, and prestige —in accordance with the dictates of the scholastic method. Not until the end of the eighteenth century did serious opposition to this method develop among even a small minority of intellectuals; and when this opposition did appear, the crown, despite its best efforts, was powerless to curb it.

Nineteenth-century liberals in Peru, Bolivia, and Educador assumed that their ancestors, had they not been subjected to tyranny, would have acted in an enlightened or liberal manner. That is, they would have used education and art forms to bring the classes together, not to further separate a dominant from a subordinate culture; and concerned with progress, they would have relegated religion to a low intellectual status and taken up the scientific, empirical, rational, inductive search for truth. The falseness of this liberal assumption—an assumption that contributed for generations to the blackening of Spain's image both in Spanish America and the United States—accounts in part for the failure of liberalism to attain a lasting triumph and to alter the traditional culture and society, fundamentally and permanently, in the three republics. In the postindependence period, a substantial number of articulate and politically participating Andean Americans continued to opt freely for the same values that had set the tone of intellectual, social, and political life during the colonial period; and liberal politicians and caudillos, often bolstered by the moral backing of the United States, were powerless to change this situation.

MERCHANTS AND LANDOWNERS

According to a prodigiously researched study, the first conquerors of Peru were motivated, on the whole, by the desire to gain sufficient wealth to enable them to purchase land and then to settle into the seigniorial way of life; they wanted to become gentlemen and to be able to bequeath honor and a handsome patrimony on their families and heirs. The 168 conquerors who participated in the seizure of the Inca Atahualpa at Cajamarca in 1532 included a good number of merchant-entrepreneur types. However, the booty obtained by these men from Atahualpa's ransom enabled them to take up the more respected seigniorial life style. A few apparently did continue to be active in commerce, but now that they had achieved what they regarded as a higher status they sought to camouflage their business activities. "After having been at Cajamarca, . . . no man with an ordinary sense of propriety would openly use that label [of merchant]."[32]

The desire to avoid giving the impression of being actively engaged in the direct and single-minded pursuit of money or of using capital to generate more capital constitutes, in the opinion of numerous historians, one of the key cultural legacies bequeathed by Spain to its portion of the New World. Some observers have attributed the origins of anticapitalist prejudices to the obsession of Spaniards with avoiding identification with pursuits associated with the peninsular Jews prior to their expulsion in 1492. Whatever their origin, the prejudices against the capitalist life style—that initially evoked favorable assessment of Indian culture by various missionaries—seem to have been deeply ingrained in Hispanic, especially Castilian, culture. Furthermore, by the time the viceroyalty of Peru was officially created in 1542, the social values of Castile were already firmly established within its territory. Already within the viceroyalty, the highest social position was reserved for the landowner. Also, as in Castile, the landownership system provided few incentives to the seignior to maximize production.

Despite the fact that business activity did not convey the highest ascribed social standing, an industrious group of successful merchants and entrepreneurs came into being in viceregal Peru, its members occupying a position just beneath the top level of prestige. Their success owed much to the fact that from a point even as early as the late sixteenth century, Spain, because of its economic decline and constant involvement in wars, was unable to control the colonial economy in line with mercantilistic principles. As a result, colonists were free to develop an economy that had few ties with the metropolis.[33] As Spain's official presence in the viceroyalty's economic structure declined, the vacuum was filled not only by enterprising colonists but also by a host of foreign traders and ambitious *peninsulares* (Spaniards born in Spain), the latter often anxious to find in business profits the means of obtaining land and with it a stake in the seigniorial life as well as the security conferred by economic diversification. Thus the penetration of private capitalists from abroad—either from Spain or other European powers—became as distinctive a feature of the viceroyalty's economy as its relative independence from control by an imperial bureaucracy.

These developments contributed to a suspiciousness on the part of interior landowning and mining interests toward the coastal merchant class, a suspiciousness that has underlain a good deal of the regionalism surviving to the present day in Andean America. The coastal merchants depended upon foreign markets and frequently engaged in contraband trade with nations officially at war with Spain; and this was enough to cause many figures of the interior to develop toward merchants the same attitudes that were widespread in Europe during the middle ages. "From the outset the merchant represented a peculiar social type. The more he depended on his international relationships, the clearer it became that he was not a citizen of his community like other people."[34] These attitudes, gaining intensity in the twentieth century often under the stimulus of Marxism, would help foster the image of merchants and bankers as *vendepatrias* and *entrequistas* —men who sold out and delivered the national interests to foreigners. In the seventeenth and eighteenth centuries, however, despite evidence of friction, merchants and interior—as well as coastal—landowning interests were most generally able to compose their differences and to constitute a fairly cohesive class.

As the noneconomic operations of agricultural estates during the colonial period gradually rendered precarious the financial position of the landowners, they often sought an infusion of new capital by marrying into successful urban, business-class families. Through such unions the landowner acquired money, without demeaning himself by having to work for it, while the bourgeois family gained not only economic diversification but also the social recognition reserved to landownership and often, beginning in the seventeenth century, the added prestige of maintaining armies—thereby acquiring *nobleza* through *armas*. The entreprenurial family that had acquired higher social status might at once abandon commercial enterprise, or it might continue in commerce, even if in a less dedicated fashion, for a generation or more. Sooner or later, though, the general rule seemed to be that it would take up the aristocratic life style of the family it had married into and which by the infusion of fresh capital it had temporarily saved. As a result, within two to five generations the family, in which there were united bourgeois and old-line aristocratic elements, would find itself facing the need for liquid capital and hence anxious to arrange a marriage with creoles or *peninsulares* who had more recently gained fortunes through business enterprise. Here was an ongoing process in which landowning, traditional elements absorbed and "civilized" merchants, with society thereby escaping the sort of bourgeois revolution (*embourgeoisement*) that helped usher in the industrialization of Europe and that also helped set the values of many of the English colonists in America.

In the process of social change under way in colonial Andean America, creole families with their wealth shrinking were often locked into a cycle of downward mobility, while newly rich *peninsulares* were ascending. Not only were the latter's capital resources mounting; they also had the prospect of marrying into a local landowning family and thereby acquiring the respectability that would subsequently enable them, should they so desire, to purchase a title of nobility. This situation understandably nourished creole resentment against the outsider capitalists from the Iberian peninsula.[35] But, such resentment was assuaged through the frequent marriages that took place between *peninsulares* and creoles and, until the late eighteenth century, through permitting creoles to acquire an increasing number of high administrative posts once reserved to *peninsulares*.[36] After independence, however, the outsider capitalists who replaced the banished *peninsulares* continued to present the appearance to local elites of becoming ever more prosperous, while they, the local elites, seemed doomed to a precarious situation of dependence on the foreigners and to relative downward mobility. The resulting tensions and resentment were no longer resolved, with any degree of regularity, by marriage or even friendly contact; indeed, the foreign capitalists often did not even set foot in the countries whence they derived profits. As a result the frustration of local elites as they regarded foreign capitalists—a frustration that when focused on *peninsulares* had contributed to the Spanish American independence movement—led to economic nationalism that was directed against outside capitalists, who in the twentieth century were more and more likely to be U.S. businessmen. The new capitalists were even more unpopular than their peninsular predecessors because of their apparent immunity to the efforts of local elites to wean them away from their bourgeois traits (that is, to "civilize" them).

In yet another way, U.S. capitalists in the late nineteenth and early twentieth centuries began to inherit the ill will directed against others during Andean America's colonial period. Ever in need of ready cash, colonial aristocratic families had often entered into borrowing transactions with the Catholic Church. These circumstances yielded steadily mounting resentment on the part of civilian elites against the creditor, ecclesiastical institution that was omnipresent in society. Once independence was achieved this resentment impelled the elites toward repudiation of their debts. Beyond this, in all-inclusive programs of anticlericalism, they sought in many instances to strip the church of every vestige of temporal influence. In this post-independence period foreign capitalists, rather than the church, became the principal suppliers of capital to local elites whose preferred life styles were often counterproductive to capital formation. Eventually the debtors would come to resent their new creditors. Thus by the twentieth century antiforeign, and especially anti-U.S., sentiments paralleled the anticlericalism of the previous century.

The Ideological Background to the Andean Independence Movement

Whether or not the Enlightenment as an intellectual movement in Spanish America prepared the way for the independence movement is an issue that has long divided scholars.[37] Whatever its impact on independence, there can be little question that the Enlightenment brought considerable ferment to the Spanish American intellectual ambiance beginning at mid-eighteenth century. Moreover, in its extremely late manifestations, when it began to merge with liberalism and to draw inspiration increasingly from non-Hispanic sources, the Enlightenment helped set the stage for postindependence civil strife because of its challenge to some of the basic tenents of traditional society.

Authoritative scholarship has begun to establish that the Enlightenment in Spanish America, until its very late stages almost at the beginning of the nineteenth century, was shaped primarily by Spanish influences which, in their political and social objectives, were generally quite conservative.[38] Spanish American intellectuals acquired Enlightenment ideas through such Spanish intellectuals as the priest-professor of the University of Oviedo Benito Feijóo and the statesman-scholar Pedro Rodríguez de Campomanes. Exhibiting virtually nothing of the pagan aspect that scholars have identified in the movement elsewhere in Europe and especially in France, Spain's Enlightenment had its roots in Catholicism. Feijóo and Campomanes, and virtually all their fellow devotees of the new thought in eighteenth-century Spain, were convinced that a secular spirit and a concern with scientific, utilitarian knowledge in the quest of progress could be reconciled with the traditional faith. They most definitely wanted a society that would continue to be based on faith—and one faith, exclusively, at that. In Ecuador a typical disciple of the Enlightenment as conceived by Feijóo and Campomanes was Francisco Javier Eugenio Santa Cruz y Espejo (1747–1795), the offspring of an Indian father and a mulatta mother. Although he denounced intellectual reliance on Aristotle, demanded economic reforms, and criticized some clergymen, he staunchly defended the Catholic faith and also preached a type of economic protectionism that was diametrically opposed to the free trade policies championed by many leaders of the non-Spanish Enlightenment.

Leading spokesmen of the Enlightenment in the Spanish-speaking world stressed the importance of the natural law and of the natural rights that emanate from it for all members of the body politic. They insisted, in the Thomistic tradition, that the natural law could be discovered through the use of human reason without recourse to revelation. The natural law doctrine, however, did not imply anything revolutionary in its impact on the social and political order. After all, reason was to be exercised, it was assumed, by a small elite. Even in Spain the use of reason, at least insofar as it might influence decision-making at anything above the grass-roots level, was not expected of the lower classes. In Spanish America, where the Indian masses were regarded as not fully rational, still less would the natural law philosophy have a revolutionary impact on the sociopolitical structure.

Many of Spain's and Spanish America's Enlightenment thinkers used the natural law to justify their advocacy of subsidiarity. In its political ramifications, subsidiarity required that society be divided into its natural, functional associations and that each of these be, as far as possible, free to govern itself in those matters of most immediate and direct concern. In the name of subsidiarity, colonial thinkers, even as many peninsular Spaniards, spoke out against the centralizing efforts of the eighteenth-century Bourbon dynasty. What they desired was a return to Habsburg traditions (Spain and its empire had been ruled by the Habsburg dynasty or House of Austria from 1516 to 1700), which had left to numerous corporative entities, both in the motherland and the colonies, a broad degree of self-government.

The Bourbon rulers appeared intent upon depriving the colonists of the considerable economic independence they had enjoyed since the seventeenth century. They seemed further intent upon snuffing out the political self-government that had developed under the Habsburgs.[39] Bourbon policies, as implemented by intendants introduced late in the eighteenth century and a generally enlarged bureaucracy made up more and more of *peninsulares*, naturally aroused the opposition of creoles and predisposed them to grasp at any ideological arguments that might provide a rationale for their discontent.

Representative figures of the Enlightenment in the Peruvian viceroyalty at first proved extremely reluctant to advocate a move away from the hierarchically structured society characterized at all levels by the domination-dependence dichotomy. But the Enlightenment, as embodied in the truly radical ideas of Rousseau, the Encyclopedists, and other French as well as English and even U.S. thinkers, did have an influence in Spanish America at the beginning of the nineteenth century—particularly after 1808.[40] From that time on these ideas were used to justify an independence movement that had been provoked by much different causes—most immediately by Bourbon imperial policies.

Although the more radical aspects of the Enlightenment and of the general intellectual revolution in evidence in much of the Western world began to attract adherents in the Peruvian viceroyalty, the forces of conservatism easily retained the upper hand. In part this was because, as a Peruvian historian has put it, even those intellectuals who had their "heads filled with Encyclopedist ideas" had their hearts "rooted in the *ancien régime*."[41]

Creole upper classes in Andean America had their heads filled with Encyclopedist ideas because on the basis of these ideas they could condemn the abuses and limitations on freedom they felt they were suffering at the hands of the motherland. They demanded treatment from the metropolis that accorded with advanced Enlightenment principles. But they had no intention of applying these principles universally within their own society. Instead, they insisted overwhelmingly upon maintaining within their lands the traditional hierarchical, multiclass, corporativist society. Thus their hearts remained rooted in the ancien régime.

Looking on the independence struggle to the south, some North Americans were deceived by the rhetoric with which its leaders often justified their struggle. Perhaps Thomas Jefferson was among those misled, for in 1813 he referred to a unity of the American peoples that extended to all "their modes of existence."[42]

Any important movement produces its self-justifying propaganda which often serves to mask rather than to reveal reality; and it would be foolish to expect the Andean American bid for independence to depart from this norm. Nevertheless, the resort by the independence seekers to the more radical principles of the non-Hispanic Enlightenment has spread confusion and misunderstanding which persist to the present time; for it has fostered a mistaken belief in the basic similarity between the independence movements in Anglo and Hispano America.

Despite the existence of Negro slavery, which caused guilt feelings among many fathers of U.S. independence, a sizable number among those who engineered the break with England genuinely hoped to bring about a situation in which citizens would be freed of the domination of others. Their faith ran high that they could fashion a world "where authority was distrusted and held in constant scrutiny; where the status of men flowed from their achievements and from their personal qualities . . . and where the use of power over the lives of men was jealously guarded and severely restricted." Above all, men of this faith believed that it was only where there prevailed "the refusal to truckle and the distrust of all authority, political or social, that institutions would express human apirations, not crush them."[43]

Although the details of the new age expected to dawn in America had not been thought out, the faith that a freer and therefore better world could be shaped by a chosen people contributed enormously to the ideological origins of the North American revolution against British rule. A similar faith, while not totally lacking, was far less important in preparing the way for independence in Andean America. Differing in their colonial backgrounds, the two regions remained different in the goals they sought through independence.

The racial heterogeneity of the Andean population is one of the many factors helping to explain the divergence between the independence struggle there and the one waged by North Americans. The English colonists had in their midst a tiny minority of dark-skinned subjects about whose fitness for the exercise of liberty and sovereignty they were dubious. But the Andean populace consisted overwhelmingly of nonwhites about whose capacity the whitish minorities entertained profound doubts. Despite this, intellectual currents of Indianism (*Indigenismo*, or glorification of Indians) became noticeable in the latter part of the eighteenth century and were soon incorporated into the ideological justification of the Andean independence movement.

Beginning to experience the first feelings of self-awareness, of being a new and different people in new and different lands, certain creole intellectuals of viceregal Peru developed an interest in their local environment and in its preconquest traditions. In this frame of mind they rejected in high dudgeon the theories of the Comte Buffon (1707–1788) concerning the inferiority of the New World environment. The Ecuadoran Jesuit Juan de Velasco (1727–1792) evidenced a strong feeling of incipient nationalism in his *La historia del Reino de Quito*, written during his Italian exile following the expulsion of the Society of Jesus from Spain and Spanish America in 1767. In it Velasco glorified the accomplishments of the Kingdom of Quito's Indian civilization. A similar note of Indianism was struck by the Peruvian intellectual José Baquíjano y Carillo in a 1781 address of welcome to a new viceroy. In this celebrated discourse, Baquíjano spoke in glowing terms of Inca antiquity.[44] Furthermore, even as early as the first three decades of the eighteenth century, Bartolomé Arzáns de Orsúa y Vela, born in and a lifetime resident of Potosí, the fabled

45

silver-mining city, had written with considerable empathy of the Indians of his native region.[45]

Undoubtedly, the victims of peninsular oppression who were of most concern to thoughtful creoles were creoles themselves. To disguise their self-interest, however, they found it convenient to allege Spanish exploitation of Indians, picturing *peninsulares* as cruel oppressors who had snuffed out the potential of the gifted aborigines. But, envisaged reforms did not involve better treatment for the Indians so much as creole acquisition or reacquisition of political power. Thus it is not surprising that when they succeeded in gaining that power by winning the wars of independence and ousting the old peninsular elite, creoles by and large set themselves against the reforms for the Indian masses that seemed to be mandated by the more radical Enlightenment principles they had ostensibly espoused.

In the days immediately preceding and following independence, however, a tiny minority of innovative, out-of-the-mainstream creole upper classes—and in the Andean political setting it took no more than a tiny minority to produce far-reaching consequences—launched an attack against certain basic features of the traditional society. Some of those joining in the attack had lived in the United States and sincerely desired the universal application in their lands of the more extreme and libertarian aspects of Enlightenment ideology, particularly as found in the North American Declaration of Independence and the writings of Jefferson, Paine, and Franklin. In the pronouncements of this small group of atypical Andean intellectuals many North Americans found the basis of an optimistic appraisal as they contemplated the prospects of regeneration in the lands to the south.

3

Prelude to Chaos: The Implications of Independence

Only in the eighteenth century did Spaniards seriously take up the debate that had shaken other European countries in the seventeenth century: the debate between the traditionalists and the modernists. This heralded the arrival of a national crisis, one that sprang from, in the words of Ortega y Gasset, a dual existence. On the one hand was the old life, which still persisted, while on the other hand was the "obscure germination of a new life."[1] In Spain, and in Spanish America as well, the struggle between the two ways of life was destined to produce more than two hundred years of instability and civil discord.

Despite the prominence they gained in the reign of Charles III (1759–1788), the Bourbon ruler most sympathetic to reform, the proponents of a new life of progress remained a small minority in Spain.[2] Defenders of the status quo waged a spirited resistance to the innovators and the fortunes of the two hostile camps often shifted rapidly. Reformers who had gained the upper hand under Charles III fell into disrepute in the 1790s; for events of the French Revolution dismayed many Spaniards who had toyed with ideas of renovation and led them to close ranks with the opponents of change. Then in 1808 came the Napoleonic invasion of Spain, and with much of the country occupied by French troops, reformers gained a majority in the Cortes that assembled at Cádiz in 1812 and pushed through this legislative body a constitution that pronounced a death sentence against traditional Spain. The triumph of the liberals, as the ideological heirs of the Enlightenment's reform advocates were coming to be known, was short-lived, for by 1814 King Ferdinand VII, restored to the throne after the defeat of the invading French armies, scrapped the constitution, declared himself an absolute monarch, and in most of his policies followed the advice of Spain's traditionalists. Liberals gained the upper hand once more in 1820, this time through a military uprising, only to relinquish control to their adversaries in 1823. And so it went through much of the remainder of the nineteenth century, with the Carlist civil wars of the 1830s and 1870s being but the more spectacular manifestations of an identity problem that had swelled to crisis proportions.

Spaniards concerned with reforming their own country had turned their attention also to the colonies in America, particularly during the reign of Charles III. If they were to carry out the sort of massive changes in America that they desired for Spain, it was of course first necessary for them to establish a far firmer control over the colonies than the metropolis had exercised in the past. Thus the rule of Charles III produced the attempt to effect what has been described as a second conquest.[3] Suppressing the very considerable rights of regional and corporative autonomy that the colonists had come to take for granted during the late stages of Habsburg rule, the Spanish government dispatched to the New World an ever-growing number of peninsular officials and bureaucrats whose purpose was to fashion a centralized political structure that might be rigorously controlled from Madrid.

In the endeavor to create a more efficient political machinery, Spain's imperial reformers during the eighteenth century created two new viceroyalties, one (Nueva Granada) with its capital at Santa Fe de Bogotá, another (La Plata) with its capital at Buenos Aires. Each was assigned part of the territory once governed by the viceroyalty of Peru: the Kingdom of Quito (today Ecuador) went to the viceroyalty of Nueva Granada, and Upper Peru (today Bolivia) to La Plata. Of more immediate concern in the Peruvian viceroyalty than the loss of territory was the commercial realignment effected by Bourbon reformers in the interest of rationalizing economic relations between metropolis and colonies and making the American holdings more profitable to the mother country.

Attacking many of the trade monopolies in existence since the sixteenth century, Spain's reformers liberalized commerce and especially in the 1770s opened ports both of Spain and Spanish America to relatively unencumbered commercial traffic. Almost over night the trade handled by Buenos Aires soared to unprecedented levels. European goods that had once reached the mining regions of Upper Peru through the carefully controlled monopolistic apparatus manipulated by Lima-Callao merchants now began to pour into Chuquisaca (today Sucre), Potosí, and even Cuzco, from Buenos Aires. Silver from the highland mines that had once passed through the ports of coastal Peru on its way to Spain, nourishing on its journey through the viceroyalty any number of business activities, now passed through Buenos Aires on its way to Spain.[4]

Until the mid-seventeenth century Potosí, with the richest silver deposits in the world and its very name synonymous in Europe with vast wealth, had been a bustling, brawling boom city and the center of a thriving highland economy that also brought prosperity to scores of coastal merchants. Despite its extreme elevation and rarified air to which Europeans adjusted with extreme difficulty, Potosí, with its estimated 160,000 inhabitants, was reputed to be the third most populous city in the Christian world. More than five hundred *potosinos* were registered mine owners, and the city also included between seven hundred and eight hundred gamblers and some 120 prostitutes —among them Doña Clara, said to be the highest paid practitioner of her profession in the world. On several occasions the region's fabled wealth had so fired the imagination of residents or passers-through as to lead them to plot for independence from Spain. But, in the second half of the seventeenth century mining output entered upon a steep and steady decline, many of the city's dance halls and gambling houses (estimated at fourteen and thirty-six, respectively, in the boom days) closed, and fewer Indians were pressed into the inhuman conditions of mining labor. Before long the economic malaise of the highlands began to enervate the business life of the coast.

Bourbon trade regulations therefore delivered further blows to a Peruvian economy already in decline. Peru now sank into a deep depression from which it would not fully emerge until the 1840s, when the age of large-scale guano exports began.[5] Meantime, just as abundance had once nourished independence schemes, so now economic adversity, attributed by some to faulty administration from the metropolis rather than to natural causes, played a part in fostering new thoughts of freedom.

Along with Buenos Aires, Guayaquil benefited from the commercial liberalization about which Peruvians tended to grumble. Despite complaints, however, in some years the volume of trade handled in Callao was actually higher than in the days before the easing of restrictions.

But the commercial structure was now so ordered that the merchants who gained the lion's share of profits as the level of transactions rose were Spaniards (*peninsulares*) rather than creoles.

In the economic restructuring now underway, numerous artisans of the interior, who had previously earned a livelihood by selling the goods they produced to local markets, faced ruin because of the mass of European goods suddenly introduced into America. The owners of textile mills (*obrajes*) also found it impossible to compete in local markets against the European cloth that had begun to appear in unprecedented abundance. The artisans and textile interests of highland Peru were threatened especially by goods introduced through Buenos Aires; and their counterparts in Quito and the surrounding region were victimized by European products entering not only through Guayaquil but, more notably, through the ports of the Nueva Granadan viceroyalty. In Cuzco, many of the *obrajes* were forced out of existence; and in the Ecuadoran region of Riobamba alone it is estimated that in the second half of the eighteenth century fifteen of twenty *obrajes* were eliminated by the new competition.[6]

Highland artisans and textile producers directed their wrath not only against the merchants of Buenos Aires and of the ports of Nueva Granada. Increasingly, hard-pressed Peruvians grew resentful of the Spanish and the surviving creole merchants of Lima–Callao who were directing expanding streams of manufactured goods into the interior. More and more the demands of interior Peruvians centered upon "freedom from Lima."[7] Similarly, speaking in behalf of the economic interests of the Ecuadoran highland, Santa Cruz y Espejo, the *quiteño* exponent of Enlightenment, declared in 1786 that the Guayaquil merchants were extracting "the vital juices" from Quito, Riobamba, and the surrounding territory. Guayaquileños, he charged, are "irreconcilable enemies of the *serrano*." (A *serrano* is an inhabitant of the sierra or highland area.) And he expressed his disgust that recent laws had aided only the *guayaquileños*. As a result of these laws, "cloth made in the interior no longer has a market, being undersold by goods brought in from abroad."[8]

Resented increasingly by white and mestizo *serranos*, coastal creole merchants in turn nourished growing animosity toward Spain and its new commercial system. Many Lima-Callao merchants who had previously made a lucrative living through contraband with foreigners, especially the English, now faced hard times; for Spain, in the interests of a so-called free trade that actually went no farther than giving to Spaniards in Spain freedom to trade with Spaniards in America, had moved resolutely to suppress illegal commerce between colonial merchants and the non-Spanish countries of Europe.[9] In the eyes of some discomfited creole merchants, a bright economic future lay only in trade that was genuinely free, based upon unfettered commercial relations with all the countries of the world. The economic future would be brighter still for Lima–Callao merchants if they could limit the entry into Upper Peru of goods shipped through Buenos Aires, and for Guayaquil merchants if they could restrict the entry into the highland area of goods from Nueva Granada's ports. At issue also was control over trade. Some merchants found that Spain's trade liberalization had resulted in saturation of the market and mounting stockpiles of unsold goods. They could see no decent future for themselves unless they were allowed to regulate the volume of imports.[10]

In seeking the advantages of a free trade with foreign lands that they could control, in its domestic effects, in their own interests, and in coveting the additional benefit of restrictions against Buenos Aires and Nueva Granadan ports, creole commercial interests of coastal Peru and Ecuador had their eyes always on the interior markets. Their hopes lay in gaining control over the exports of coastal agricultural surpluses through which they could finance the large-scale importation of finished goods that were needed if they were to capture interior markets. Success for them lay in clamping upon the interior the sort of outside commercial domination that the interior interests were ever more insistent upon escaping.

Two rival camps had appeared in viceregal Peru. The members of one camp, residing mainly in the interior, desired economic self-sufficiency or autarky. Attainment of their goal depended upon re-establishing the economic isolation of Habsburg times. As their quarrel lay with change and innovation, the label of conservative is in many ways a fit one for those belonging to this camp. In some ways, though, they were reactionary, for they wanted a return to the pre-Bourbon status quo. To members of the opposed camp, neither the Bourbon present nor the Habsburg past was acceptable. The prosperous future they envisioned could result only from the creation of a massive export-import trade which inevitably, by its own dynamic, would destroy the obstinate "obscurantists" who were willing to settle for the past.

All the while, animosity between the two camps was exacerbated by the issue of race relations that actually lay at the heart of some of the reforms that Spanish imperial officials and their creole allies,

among whom coastal creole business interests figured most prominently, sought to introduce. These men had awakened to the economic benefits that could result from stimulating the material appetites of the lower classes of the interior and then of giving them,
through such means as vocational education, the means of satisfying
those appetites. The lower classes of the interior were, of course, overwhelmingly Indians and mixed bloods. This fact had not deterred the
innovative zeal of Spaniards and some *costeño* creoles, and in the late
eighteenth century certain steps were taken to help the Indians acquire the know-how through which they could accumulate more
capital that could then be spent on imports. Moreover, the Cortes
that had produced the 1812 constitution had, under the urging both
of Spanish and creole liberal delegates, the latter representing primarily commercial interests in America, abolished Indian tribute and
forced labor (known in Peru as *mita*). The motivation had not been
purely humanitarian. If Indians were freed from tribute obligations,
then they would have at hand the economic means for additional
purchase of imported goods. And if they were freed from obligation
of forced labor, then they could earn wages which might go to the
purchase of consumer goods.

Upper class *serranos* were dismayed by these measures, which inter-
fered with the traditional patterns through which they had maintained
control over Indians. Because of tribute requirements, Indians had
had to work for white landowners in order to raise the money to
satisfy the demands of the tax gatherer. Liberated from these demands, Indians would be able to work in their own behalf and to
acquire some degree of financial independence which would make
them henceforth reluctant to assume the role of humble dependency
in their relations with landowning patrons.

In the interest of progress and modernity, certain self-styled reformers had begun to interfere with the relationships that white upper classes had relied upon to keep the Indians dependent upon them.
There was no telling where such interference, once begun, might end.
White and mestizo *serranos* were convinced that reformers living in
isolation from the Indians, either in Spain or in coastal America,
could not comprehend adequately the inferiority of the Indians and
the fact that the only way in which superior elements could maintain
control over such unreasoning hordes was through unmitigated domination. So far as upper class *serranos* were concerned, attempts by
outsiders to arouse the acquisitive instincts of Indians and to hold out

to them the prospect of increasing their consumption of goods by means of income earned in free labor portended social revolution. The issue was in every way momentous, and easily capable of contributing to an independence movement from Spain and, following it, to civil discord within the new republics. Comparable efforts, after all, by northern would-be reformers to interfere in what southerners regarded as the only feasible processes for keeping allegedly inferior dark-skinned laborers in a status of dependency would help touch off the Civil War in the United States.

At first, each side in Andean America's escalating controversy appealed to the Spanish crown for protection of its vital interests. Each group enjoyed varying success in these appeals, depending upon which side, traditionalist or reformist, happened at the moment to hold the upper hand in Spain. Given the uncertainty of the political situation in the peninsula, both sides came eventually to realize they could not rely on Spanish intervention for their well-being. Developing self-confidence and discarding a colonial mentality, creoles, locked in their own bitter polemic, issued what in a way was the first Spanish American ultimatum of nonintervention. Throwing down the gauntlet to Spain, they declared their determination to resolve their differences on their own.

Independence was only an incident in the traditionalist-modernist struggle that extended throughout the Hispanic world. In discarding the ties to Spain, Spanish Americans were simply preparing for the uninhibited confrontation between the two irreconcilable forces that had carried out their initial skirmishing through the mediation of the Spanish crown. And in losing their colonies, Spaniards were freed from distractions and enabled to throw all of their passions and energies into resolving the differences that divided them at home.

Instability in nineteenth-century Andean American came not because the colonists gained independence before they were ready for it or because they were inexperienced in self-government. Spanish Americans had been allowed a remarkable degree of self-government in the seventeenth and even in much of the eighteenth century. Their difficulties in governing themselves after independence came from the fact that they had become polarized by the same issues—only exacerbated by race-relations controversies—that divided Spain and plunged that country, experienced in self-government for centuries, into political turmoil. Conspicuously present among those issues were questions of religion and church-state relations.

RELIGION AND THE IMPLICATIONS OF INDEPENDENCE

Most liberals of early nineteenth century Andean America, it will be recalled, came to their ideology by way of the Spanish Enlightenment. Obsessed with progress and desiring reform from above, they fully expected the new society that they would shape to be every bit as much elite dominated as the previous one had been. But a complicating factor had appeared by the time of the independence movement in that a handful of articulate leaders had fallen under the influence of the more radical political and social ideologists of France, England, and the United States. These Andean liberals, discarding the social conservatism of the Spanish Enlightenment, hoped that progress would shatter the old order and prepare the way for democracy.

Whether socially conservative or revolutionary, liberals were hostile to the temporal influence the Catholic Church had traditionally exercised throughout the Hispanic world. Equally dedicated to progress, both groups saw the church as responsible for the pervasiveness of an other-worldly set of values that impeded development of the physical environment and its resources. Furthermore, both groups professed that governments should derive their legitimacy from their efficiency and effectiveness in introducing progress, not from the claim of a linkage to supernatural power. For liberals of either stripe, in fact, customary ties between the polity and the church had to be sacrificed in the quest of secularization—a process that involved the expansion of the state, at the expense of religion, into all major areas of social life.

For their part, Andean clergymen were wont to insist that the church was the one institution capable of conferring legitimacy on governments. In their eyes, the right of statesmen to rule depended upon their being invested with a sacredness that transcended the human realm. Theorists and theologians of this persuasion contended that within the body politic obedience was not just the servitude of man to man, but also submission to the will of God, exercising His sovereignty through the medium of men. Accordingly, church spokesmen by and large rejected the doctrine of popular sovereignty on the ground that all power has its origins in God. If God alone was the fount of political power, it followed in the logic of the churchmen that only the men of God, that is the clergy, had the right to bestow sovereignty on a particular regime, once satisfied that it would govern in accordance with divine laws.

Defining the church's position on sovereignty, Federico González Suárez, perhaps the greatest Ecuadoran churchman of the late nineteenth and early twentieth centuries and a man generally noted for his restraint and moderation, had this to say: "Ecclesiastical history ... can only be the action of the supernatural in the temporal realm by means of men, who have received from the sublime being the charge of directing their fellow beings by the path of goodness to the attainment of their eternal destinies."[11] Applying this interpretation to matters of political legitimacy, González Suárez maintained: "Politics is inseparable from morality. The only true morality is Christian morality, and this morality has to determine politics, if politics is to be good. The priest has to teach and has to direct, and therefore to take part in politics, considering each political point from the viewpoint of Christian morality." Elaborating slightly on this conclusion, the Ecuadoran wrote: "in those temporal matters related to the spiritual, the state should work always in accord with the Church, and submit to it, without ever having the right to take part in those matters which are purely spiritual."[12]

If churchmen alone could confer legitimacy on a government, it followed that they could withdraw it should that government deviate from the norms of Christian conduct as defined by the clergy. At the very least, churchmen could rescind laws judged to be morally offensive. Acting in line with this belief, Peruvian churchmen in the 1850s demanded the right to prohibit compliance with new laws, under pain of excommunication, "until the Church has had time to examine them."[13]

Convinced that state and church were "consubstantially united," that politics was permeated by religion, and that therefore the church must be present "in all the different branches of human activity,"[14] the clergy in Andean America developed a distinctive definition of the atheistic state. According to them, the atheistic state was one which did not accept the interpenetration of politics and religion and which questioned the right of the church to assume a role in all phases of human activity. Thus any body politic in which state and church were separated automatically became, in the eyes of this clergy, an atheistic state. Moreover, through their presence in temporal society, many clergymen hoped to maintain the body politic as an institutional replica of what was considered the providentially ordained hierarchical, authoritarian structure of the church.[15]

The issue of religious toleration provided an additional source of ideological and political divisiveness in nineteenth-century Andean

America. Liberals, such as Ecuador's statesman Vicente Rocafuerte and Peru's defrocked priest Francisco de Paula González Vigil, were convinced that political liberalism, based on individualism, could come to their lands only after the establishment of religious liberalism, based upon toleration and the free choice of the individual conscience. Believing that political order inevitably reflected the religious life of a country, they sought to alter the religious climate so as to be able to transform the temporal environment. The clergymen, who condemned religious toleration as the fruit of the Protestant heresy which placed undue importance on private judgment in religious matters, tended to agree at least with the liberal assessment that the political order necessarily reflected a country's religious life. But, guided by altogether different objectives than those of the liberals, they assailed toleration on the grounds it would encourage, as the temporal reflection of religious individualism, an individualistic social order in which the traditional ties of domination and subordination could not endure.

A dispute involving administrative control over the church led to further controversy. The clergy, insisting upon their right to dominate the state, took it by and large as a foregone conclusion that the church should be an autonomous institution within the political structure, free from the intrusion of civil government. The Peruvian priest Juan de la Cruz García, for example, denied that the state had any power whatsoever to limit ecclesiastical rights of self-government or to curtail traditional privileges and immunities enjoyed by the priesthood.[16] Liberals, on the other hand, insisted that as part of the attributes of sovereignty the new republican governments had inherited the powers to control the church, especially through patronage or appointment to ecclesiastical benefices previously exercised by the Spanish crown. The dispute between clergymen and their adversaries over the question of church control, as so many other aspects of the conservative-liberal confrontation, can only be understood in terms of the colonial background; for it was during the colonial period that the two sides had begun "to take up positions for a struggle that would have to be mortal."[17]

From the earliest days of conquest, churchmen and civilians had entered into bitter rivalry. Missionaries in particular regarded many of the conquerors as ruthless exploiters whose cruel instincts had to be curbed, while the civilians resented the attempts of churchmen to interfere with the control they had established over Indian laborers. Through the years, the two groups continued their struggle as the priesthood persisted in denouncing the licentious ways and unholy lives of the civilians while the latter responded by pointing to the wholesale violations by the religious of their vows of poverty, chastity, and obedience.

Tensions between churchmen and civilians could always be resolved in the colonial period, as both adversaries accepted the crown as a final arbiter. Although recognizing their duties of obedience to the crown, churchmen were extremely loathe to abide by policies formulated by the crown's bureaucracy that adversely affected their interests. Even in the seventeenth century the confrontation between officials of church and state could be bitter and in the eighteenth century the chronic rivalry was stimulated by new issues. In the name of regalism, Bourbon regimes curtailed church prerogatives and also (in 1767) expelled the Jesuits, an order that had been regarded with suspiciousness by Spanish kings since the time of Philip II because of its tendency to look to Rome rather than to Madrid for direction. While most of the Spanish American clergy, both secular and regular, were happy to see the Jesuits go, they grew increasingly uneasy over regalistic limitations and over various challenges to the church's economic independence that came at the end of the eighteenth and the beginning of the nineteenth century. To such a degree was this so that many of the priests who supported the independence movement in Andean America did so in the hopes that they would be able to give a "theocratic" orientation to liberty,[18] thereby escaping the infringements of regalism and, beyond this, establishing theocracy as the form of government in the new republics. On the other hand, anticlerical civilians hailed independence as providing at last the opportunity to humble, once and for all, the haughty ecclesiastical aristocracy at whose hands they believed that they, and their ancestors dating back to the establishment of Spanish rule, had suffered.

The issue, then, was this: both churchmen and liberal anticlericals hoped, with independence achieved, to gain the total, definitive victory over their adversaries that had been denied them by the compromises devised through the years by the Spanish crown in the exercise of its moderating power. To the churchmen, victory meant theocracy, in line with which they would be the dominant rather than, as in the colonial past, the subordinate power in the church-state relationship. To the liberals, victory meant the removal of religious influence from politics and unfettered state control over the church.

As the independence movement began in Andean America—and here a new and complicating factor must be introduced into the narrative—the church was a bitterly divided institution. Many of its priests were themselves advanced regalists and secularists: they advocated not only state control over the church[19] but also the separation of church and state and religious toleration. Many priests were, moreover, decidedly anticlerical, in that they wished to banish the priestly influence from temporal society. As the first step toward depriving the church of a power base from which it could intervene in politics, the anticlerical clergymen urged that the ecclesiastical institution be stripped of its capital holdings and that its lands be confiscated and put to more productive use in the hands of a new capitalist bourgeoisie. Francisco Javier de Luna Pizarro is perhaps the most conspicuous example of such a churchman in Peru during the 1820s;[20] but he had a great deal of company in the ranks of the Peruvian clergy and also a large number of counterparts both in Ecuador and Bolivia. Gradually, however, the Andean clergy, in part because they were dismayed by the chaos and virtual anarchy into which the young republics plunged immediately after independence, began to unite behind a conservative position that stressed order and looked to the moral authority of the church as the sole source of political and social stability.

The clergy's unity in conservative clericalism resulted not only from internal circumstances; it was also the product of outside influences. Contributing to establishing a common front of conservatism among the clergy was the influx of Spanish priests, many of them forced to leave Spain because of their connection with the ultraconservative Carlist position. The Andean clergy's unity in conservative clericalism was also inspired by, as one approving writer has put it, "the admirable Catholic reaction of the Old World."[21] The stiffening line of the Vatican under Piux IX, as well as the writings of Juan Donoso Cortés in Spain and Louis de Bonald and Joseph de Maistre in France all contributed to the doctrinal base around which the clergy rallied. The result was a "brand of Catholicism less amenable to modernity,"[22] which affirmed the authority of Rome and looked for support in the struggle to prevent the liberally inspired *embourgeoisement* of society to the rural masses—among whom the churchmen, in contrast to their mainly urban-based liberal opponents, maintained a presence extending back to early colonial times.

Increasingly unified in their own ranks, the clergy were able to reach out and establish civilian alliances not only with rural masses but also with landowners and other accommodated interests who, alarmed by the appearance of new commercial and banking groups often allied with foreign capital, feared a decline in their own status. In the church—traditionally the foe of a bourgeois society, traditionally the defender of a hierarchical order determined by ascription rather than achievement, and now united in defense of order, stability, and the old customs—the threatened elites found their source of political ideology.

As the battle lines hardened between the opposing forces, Andean conservatives and liberals increasingly drew from the United States examples and illustrations with which to bolster their arguments. Even during the course of the independence struggle certain Andean Americans, among them the Peruvian Manuel Lorenzo de Vidaurre and the Ecuadoran Vicente Rocafuerte, had lived in the United States and developed enthusiasm for its political culture.[23] Both men praised the republic for its practice of complete religious toleration; both attributed the decline of Spain to the political influence of the clergy and the progress of the United States to the political nonintervention of the clergy.[24] They agreed further that Protestant countries were generally richer than Catholic countries because the former were more inclined to accept the separation of church and state.[25] For Rocafuerte, moreover, religious competition encouraged competition in the economic order which in turn led to progress—a conclusion, incidentally, in which John Adams concurred, as a result of which he sought to pressure Latin American governments, as the price for obtaining commercial treaties with the United States, into establishing religious toleration.[26]

If liberals found in the United States a living, ongoing demonstration of the validity of their political ideology and a justification of their faith in progress, Andean conservatives regarded the far-off land in an altogether different light. They rejected out of hand the assumption, common in some liberal circles, that the Andean independence movement had been inspired by the same quest of individual liberty that gave birth to the rebellion of the English colonies against their motherland.[27] What is more, conservatives looked upon the introduction of what they regarded as the atheistic doctrines of the eighteenth century and also upon the establishment of Masonic lodges by emissaries of the United States in the period immediately following independence as responsible for many of the subsequent ills of Andean America. Thus the United States, whether its citizens were aware of the fact or not, was drawn into Andean America's nineteenth-century identity debate.

The controversy between conservatives and liberals, often waged in terms of religion and focusing on church-state relations, involved a struggle between two distinct life styles. Thus it was inevitable that the clash would have as one of its key features a debate concerning the respective merits of the corporative, compartmentalized, particularistic society in which status was ascribed and the individualistic, universal, achievement-oriented society. This struggle, even as the one that centered on religious issues, had its origins in the colonial period and had already assumed well-defined proportions by the end of the eighteenth century.

When Bourbon reformers had moved against corporative privileges and immunities in the name of efficiency and universal application of progressive laws, aggrieved colonial interests sought to defend themselves by an appeal to the decentralized, democratic traditions and institutions of medieval Spain.[28] To conservatives—then and later—democracy meant the autonomy of corporations, even though in each corporation patron segments dominated clients. In contrast, for many liberals democracy meant equal rights for all, extending throughout society, an interpretation that necessitated the breakdown of compartments and particularisms.

Apologists of conservatism, at least as this position came to be defined by clergymen once they had achieved a consensus on their political ideology, championed a compartmentalized society in which priests were universally present, acting in each corporation as conciliators between patrons and clients and attaching, through religious ritual, a sacred nature to the relationships of domination and subordination. Beyond this, conservatives proclaimed the need for a supreme national government at the apex of the political structure, charged with the exercise of a moderating power by means of which the activities of the multiple corporative entities might be synthesized. The supreme government, receiving its legitimacy through the church, would employ its moderating power in advice and consultation with the clergy. One of the leading proponents of this type of corporative organization to appear in nineteenth century Andean America was the Peruvian prelate, Bartolomé Herrera.[29]

For the liberals, independence from Spain was expected to bring with it freedom from the corporative restraints that had in the past curbed individual initiative and, allegedly, impeded progress. With the corporative compartments destroyed there would be no need for national government with a universal presence in society deriving from its exercise of a moderating power. Rather than being imposed from above, order would issue from the strife of individuals; for this was the way in which the laws of the universe were seen to function.

The initial assault against Andean corporativism began in totally unplanned and uncontrolled fashion during the course of the independence struggle. The protracted military operations severed the official linkage between corporations and a central government with its moderating power. Once freed from control imposed from above, those corporative bodies that continued to exist sought merely to maximize their own advantages while ignoring considerations of the common good. Edward C. Banfield describes a situation he found in twentieth-century southern Italy as one of "amoral familism." The southern Italians, he contends, acted as if they were following this rule: "Maximize the material short run advantage of the nuclear family; assume that all others will do likewise."[30] The conditions that arose in the course of the independence movement in Andean America contributed to what can be described as amoral corporativism.

As centralized order collapsed, more and more Andean Americans found themselves unable to protect their basic interests; so they sought out a man of power and placed their destinies in his hands. The result was the creation of myriad new patronalist-clientelist relationships, while all the time the corporative superstructure that had previously rationalized asymmetrical relationships was undergoing further weakening—in part because of the assaults against it inspired by the liberal ideology. *Caciquismo*, or rule by local and regional strong men with armies of clients, had become the most notable feature of the political culture.[31]

Ideologically inspired reluctance to accept corporativism and to move toward the reestablishment of an effective moderating power tended to tie the hands of liberals as they faced, whenever in power, the problems of creating the order and stability necessary for progress. Soon this situation had fostered a basic ambivalence in the attitude of liberals toward power. While committed to the theory that harmony would result, in accordance with laws of nature, from free competition, they could clearly perceive that Andean Americans were not acting in line with the laws of nature that governed the actions of people in the progressive countries. Hence the liberals were tempted to undertake the task of changing the nature of their fellow citizens. This endeavor, of course, could only be approached through the exercise of authoritarian controls. The dilemma of the Andean liberals was similar to that confronting European liberals in the previous century: "[They] wanted . . . to limit power; but confronted with the heritage of ancient corporative society, they were forever devising sharp and sovereign instruments that might be used to put it down."[32]

In spite of ideological protestations, liberal leaders all the while continued to accept old, and even to seek new, master-vassal relationships with less powerful persons. Nowhere was the calm acceptance of iron laws of dependency more clearly demonstrated than in the prevailing attitude of liberals toward women. Typically, Pedro Carbo, one of the most prominent products of nineteenth-century Eucadoran liberalism, maintained that even when constitutions did not specifically address the matter, women "found themselves excluded from all political rights" because of the weakness to which their natures condemned them. It was against the laws of nature, Carbo argued, for women to seek escape from the moral subordination established by custom and education, a subordination imposed first by the family into which the female was born and later by her husband. Carbo further observed that some males must also live in situations of dependency—the clearest example being afforded by soldiers—and therefore could never develop the degree of individual judgment necessary for the proper exercise of suffrage rights.[33]

The great Peruvian iconoclast Manuel González Prada shrewdly observed that the assumption of women's natural dependency led many liberals and freethinkers to the conclusion that although religion could be discarded by men, it should be retained among women.[34] Many Andean liberals advanced beyond this to the conclusion that while religion should be eliminated among the upper classes of reasoning, male society, it should be tolerated among the semirational masses, male and female.

Undoubtedly the all-pervading racism among Andean upper classes contributed to liberalism's acceptance of the ties of command and obedience. The whitish members of society simply could not bring themselves to accept the darker-skinned elements as equals. As a result, true liberalism, requiring insofar as possible the elimination of asymetrical relationships, never had a chance to establish itself.

Under the liberal impulse there occurred only the elimination of the corporative control mechanisms which had in the past synthesized patron-client relationships into a cohesion whole. Liberalism was confined to the surface, to the top level of political culture; the surface never reflected the inner substance, and thus liberalism remained a sham. In order to forge a political culture that was not in its very essence hypocritical, Andean Americans would have had either to destroy the unequal relationships which continued to be the foundation of the social order, or else to have unabashedly accepted these relationships while seeking to rationalize them through some type of corporative structure. Through the years, the constant cultural pressures and influences emanating from the United States would make it difficult for Andeans to opt for the second alternative.

Economic Collapse and the Blow to Liberalism

In the long term, Andean liberalism was weakened by inherent contradictions in attitudes and values that rendered it impossible for the ideology to penetrate beneath the surface of the sociopolitical organization. In the short term, it was undermined by the economic collapse and depression that endured for some twenty years following independence in Peru and for most of the nineteenth century in Ecuador and Bolivia.

Much of the thrust in favor of Andean liberalism had come from a business- and commerce-minded group of creoles who hoped to fill the position once occupied by *peninsulares* and, by establishing connections with foreign capital, gain dominance over the export-import trade. In the case of Peru and Ecuador the ambitious creoles were concentrated mainly on the coast; and they hoped to expand their commercial operations so as to encompass the interior. Thus there reappeared in the postindependence era the rivalry spawned by Bourbon reform measures between the artisans and small-scale manufacturers of the highlands and the commercial magnates of the coast. Now, however, the coastal business groups were headed by creoles rather than *peninsulares*. The issue, therefore, that had once pitted the monied interests of the interior against the motherland in an imperial struggle now pitted them against their fellow citizens in what had become a domestic rivalry.

Fulfillment of the ambitions of the business-minded sectors depended upon export surpluses which could finance importation of the foreign goods with which it was hoped to capture control of internal markets. However, in the early postindependence era Andean America lacked export surpluses. The decline of Upper Peru's silver production that had alarmed Bourbon rulers continued throughout much of the nineteenth century. Moreover, operation of many of the coastal plantations had been disrupted by the independence struggle and the capital necessary to bring them once more into effective production was hard to come by. In many ways, the independence wars had delivered the coup de grâce to an economy that had been in decline in much of Andean America, both coastal and interior, since mid-to-late eighteenth century.

In the course of the wars urban elites—bureaucratic, commercial, and ecclesiastical—lost power to rural patricians. In some ways the process resulted from a population shift. The number of residents in major cities, such as Lima, declined as people fled to the countryside to seek security on landed estates.[35] As late as 1842 a perceptive visitor to Lima commented upon the many uninhabited houses, noting that the owners had moved to rural areas, emigrated, or died during the independence campaigns and the ensuing epidemics, earthquakes, and civil strife.[36] "In Europe," it has been observed, "the rise of capitalism was accompanied by a determined struggle to weaken the authority of the manor and to transfer its power to the centralized state."[37] In early postindependence Andean America, the manor was strengthening its authority at the expense of commercial, capitalist interests. Thereby traditionalism gained force in its encounter with modernity.

The hopes for a revival of bourgeois, urban, commercial activity depended, in the view of most Andean liberals, on a massive infusion of foreign capital. For a time it seemed that these hopes might be rapidly fulfilled. Thus the British consul in Lima wrote in 1826 that because of the famous silver mines, the new republic of Bolivia enjoyed a highly favorable financial situation. He predicted that the country's rulers would have adequate authority and resources to promote projects of economic and social development, "such as roads, port facilities, river navigation and public schools." On this basis, he urged extensive British investment.[38]

British capital, however, was not forthcoming. Except in Brazil, British merchants found Latin American markets much poorer than they had supposed, and in all of the Andean region trade with Great Britain remained virtually dormant.[39] In the period immediately following independence, a British consul in Peru estimated that commercial capital in all of Lima amounted to only about one million dollars, down from an estimated fifteen million in the years between 1790 and 1800.[40] In part, the dearth of commercial capital, and capital of any sort, was the consequence of the drainage of funds to Spain occurring during the revolutionary struggle. Shortage of capital resulted also from the drainage of funds to England as debts contracted to finance military operations against Spain were repaid. Under these circumstances, power remained in the hands of a conservative aristocracy dedicated to autarky; and the idea of progress, based on a flourishing export-import trade, seemed more and more absurd.

According to Marxian analysis (which in this instance is quite compelling), the triumph of liberalism depended, above all else, on economic development of the type needed to serve the interests of "the bourgeois exporters of agricultural products."[41] In the Marxian interpretation, then, liberalism could not gain the upper hand in its encounter with conservatism until there had occurred a conspicuous increase in the production and exportation of raw materials. The age of guano in Peru, beginning in the 1840s, lent impetus to the liberal cause and helped the commercially oriented Lima-Callao complex establish clear primacy over the rest of the country in the following decade. Not until the end of the nineteenth century, however, did Ecuador and Bolivia develop the large export surpluses which facilitated the triumph of liberalism and at the same time established the dependency of newly emerging political elites first on British and then, more notably still, on U.S. capital.

ANDEAN KRAUSISTS AS EARLY CRITICS OF LIBERAL MODERNIZATION

The nineteenth century affords the first examples of the attempt by Andean Americans to forge a compromise between the demands of modernity and traditionalism. The turning of many Andeans to the ideology of Krausism, which flourished early in the second half of the nineteenth century, represents just such an attempt. In Krausism, a concern for progress joined with a respect for hierarchical social organization, for corporativism, and for certain values that transcend material development. Through the next one hundred years and more, Krausism's attempted synthesis of modernity and traditionalism provided an ideological point of departure for most Andean thinkers anxious to forge patrias that could absorb some of the trends discernible in advanced nations without having to sacrifice authentic traditions.

Krausism found its inspiration in a German philosopher named Karl Christian Friedrich Krause (1781–1832), who was little-known outside the Spanish-speaking world. His works were revealed to Andean Americans through the translations of the Spaniards Julián Sanz del Río and Francisco Giner de los Ríos, and also through the Spanish translations of the works of Krause's principal European popularizer, Heinrich Ahrens. In the form in which it was disseminated in the Andean republics, Krausism was primarily associated with a comprehensive view of natural law and with the philosophy of law in general. In addition, Krausism embodied a social philosophy which, very much in the approach of Saint-Simon, sought the means to achieve material progress while at the same time preventing the diffusion of individualism throughout society. While Andean intellectuals under the influence of Bonald and Maistre urged the destruction of individualism in the name of preserving the traditional, other-worldly society, Krausists saw the possibility of establishing a society that was both progressive and free from the individualistic challenge to time-honored social restraints.

Krausists urged the need for scientific, empirical investigation in order to spark materal progress, but they also stressed the transcendent values of the mind and soul. No matter how lowly their social estate, persons could be taught, according to Krause and his disciplines, to respond in some degree to the higher callings of human nature. Beyond vocational training, the lower classes should be taught to appreciate the beauty of their physical surroundings and given a liberal education that included instruction in art, literature, and music so as to awaken in them regard for the world of aesthetic pleasure. By learning to perceive, however dimly, and to appreciate, however imperfectly, the higher truths and beauties of life, human beings would be liberated from an obsession with material desires, from base passions and appetites, from selfish inclinations, and from resentment and rancor against others. Once freed from baser instincts by their ability to appreciate a hierarchy of values, pleasures, and rewards, lower-class persons would tolerate and even welcome a social hierarchy. To Krausist *pensadores*, the intellectual inferiority of the lower classes was so obvious that its members must themselves recognize it as, awestruck, they entered, through the rudiments of a liberal education, into the periphery at least of the exalted world in which only an elite could be fully at home. Lower classes shaped by the social engineers of Krausism would take for granted their dependence upon their cultural betters. While Horace Mann naively professed that "Education . . . is a great equalizer of the conditions of men,"[42] Krausists maintained that education could be utilized to preserve the inequality of human beings.

As humanists concerned with the hierarchy of values on which social hierarchies were seen to depend, Krausists stressed that legitimacy demanded more than the effectiveness of rulers in attaining progress. Legitimacy also required that a government be "ideologically true,"[43] so that it could safeguard truth and beauty against the assaults of crass materialists. Finally, as intellectuals concerned perhaps more with order than with progress, Krausists recognized the value of corporativism.

In a passage that appealed enormously to his many admirers in the Spanish-speaking world, Krause observed that the saddest phenomenon in contemporary society, and the one that militated most against realization of the ideals of humanity, was class struggle and competition. As the solution to this saddest of all social phenomena he envisioned not only mass education, as he defined it, but also the organization of men into subsovereign and semiautonomous municipal and professional associations. The municipality and each association could then impart to those participating within them a sound understanding of their proper function in society as a whole. Once the citizens of each municipality and the members of each association were afforded the satisfaction of helping to shape the policies that affected them most directly within their group and were at the same time trained to see the function served by their subsidiary entity in the overall social scheme, they would accept the need for divisions and stratification; and "thus the prevailing competition of classes and professions would disappear."[44]

In establishing associations, Krause maintained, it would be absurd not to distinguish between the various professions on a hierarchical basis as "obviously the man who works with his mind is above the one who works just with his hands; the more fully a man employs all his human gifts, the higher is his status in life." In his view of society, then, Krause saw a stratified structure at the base of which were the manual laborers "who rented their arms to others." Above them were the free artisans and businessmen who worked for themselves; and at the very top stood the "profound scientists" and the men of "poetic genius."[45]

In order to understand Krausism's impact it must be remembered that it appeared in Peru during the prosperity ushered in by the guano age, and also in Ecuador and Bolivia at a time when there were at least a few transitory signs of economic development, often the consequence of the entry of a trickle of foreign immigrants and capital. Krausism was the first humanistic reaction to the alleged crudeness and vulgarity of the *nouveau riches* who had begun to appear on the scene. Understandably, then, it was often associated with a hostility to the business culture of the United States.

Peru

Andean Regionalism

Louis Hartz has attributed the quick success of the United States in attaining political stability to the absence of value struggles. He notes the Constitution did not fare well when a value struggle did emerge at the time of the slavery controversy. "Thus," he writes, "a hidden and happy accident has lain at the bottom of the American constitutional experience."[46]

Much of the political instability in Andean America can be explained in terms of a value struggle involving fundamental disagreement over national identity; but it is easy to exaggerate the importance of deeply felt ideological convictions and values in contributing to tensions, civil strife, and political instability in nineteenth-century Andean America. Joining with ideology in contributing to the nearly chronic state of civil discord were various factors, among them unalloyed self-interest and group interest, and also a lack of geographic integration that helped generate and perpetuate regional animosities.

Overwhelmed by its geography, as are all who have known it at first hand, an English author has written of Peru (the third largest republic in South America, behind Brazil and Argentina, with a total area of about 1.3 million square kilometers):

> A space traveller in search of a pleasant place to land on earth might be excused if he turned away hastily at his first sight of Peru. For, if viewed from the stratosphere, the country would appear to consist of nothing but three equally uninviting kinds of wilderness—a pitiless desert running down the whole length of the Pacific coast; a few miles inland, one of the most formidable mountain systems in the world; and to the east of the Andes, perhaps the most forbidding wilderness of all, a green carpet of Amazonian jungle extending without a break to the horizon.[47]

The green carpet to which the English author refers is the *selva*. Through the years depicted as the Peru of the future, the *selva* remains sparsely populated to the present time, connected by only the flimsiest of transportation ties to the rest of the country. In between the *selva* and the Andean highland lies the *montaña*, at altitudes ranging from six to ten thousand feet. Until the advent of the airplane, towns of the *montaña* were isolated from each other and from the rest of Peru. During the early 1960s more air cargo was handled at the *montaña* town of Tarapoto than at Lima; but residents of the community were handicapped by a road system that did not extend more than forty miles in any direction from their town.

The Andes, whether in Peru, Ecuador, or Bolivia defy adequate description. "One way to visualize its [the Andes'] effect is to consider the mountain range as a ladder super-imposed on the country with the rungs corresponding to the intermountain ranges connecting the two lateral mountains." The author of these lines also notes that peaks of the Andes range up to well over 20,000 feet.[48] The series of plateau basins delimited by the rungs and laterals of the ladderlike Andes make up the area known as the *altiplano*.

Actually, Andean geography is even more complex than this description suggests, for throughout much of the Peruvian area at least there are three, not just two, principal cordilleras that run approximately from northwest to southeast and parallel to the coast. Only the western range runs in a relatively unbroken chain down the whole length of the country. The central and eastern cordilleras, "while well defined in the north and ... in some parts of the south" lose themselves in between in "great knots of tranverse mountain ranges which at intervals block north-south communications. These knots have the effect of dividing the sierra into a number of separate basins," each hemmed in by mountains "except where the rivers escape through deep gorges, either to the Pacific or to the Amazon."[49]

The 1,400-mile narrow Peruvian coast is for the most part relatively flat desert land, interspersed by some fifty rivers flowing down from the Andes and providing means of irrigation. The coast presents far fewer transportation obstacles than the sierra or Andean highland, the *montaña*, or the *selva*. Still, as late as the 1930s Lima did not enjoy land communications with many nearby cities either to the north or south, and coastal traffic was almost exclusively by sea. Since then the situation has improved dramatically. Even in the 1960s, however, travelers were impressed and often exhausted by the difficulties of transportation when they made the fourteen-to-seventeen-hour automobile trip of just under five hundred miles between Lima and Arequipa, Peru's second largest city situated on the western slopes of the southern sierra and dominated by volcanic peaks rising nearly 20,000 feet. They could readily understand why in 1880 during the War of the Pacific geographic obstacles prevented some 8,000 troops in the Arequipa region from getting to Lima to help defend the capital against attacking Chilean forces.

Historically, little love has been lost between the two most populous areas of Peru, the coast and the sierra. Particularly keen has been

Ecuador

the rivalry between Lima and Arequipa. Arequipeños, priding themselves on their Catholic devoutness, have looked down in disdain upon the allegedly materialistic *limeños*. For their part, *limeños* have tended to be contemptuous of the purported backwardness and lethargy of Arequipa. Coastal elites, moreover, refer constantly to the racial inferiority of the *serranos*, among whom Indians have always constituted the largest ethnic group. In turn, *serrano* elites, made up of whites and mestizos, refer disparagingly to the admixture of African blood found in many *costeños* (coastal residents). With considerable reason, moreover, *serranos* are constantly resentful over the exploitation to which they are subjected by the coastal power centers. The conviction that coastal elites are manipulating the affairs of the sierra while draining it of its resources has contributed to a widespread *serrano* persecution complex.[50]

For Peruvians, the issue of centralism versus federalism has represented far more than an academic discussion between political philosophers. The basis of the issue is this: Lima, at the heart of a highly centralized political and economic system controlled by people who know little of and often care no more about the rest of Peru and whose main economic and cultural ties are with foreigners, has been able to syphon off wealth from the country as a whole and to use it for the exclusive benefit of coastal interests. It is little wonder that every reforming movement that has appeared since independence has made decentralization a plank of its platform. Often decentralization has been defined in terms of a corporative structure based on functional and regional representation. Since independence the problem has defied solution, and regional rivalries and the bitterly contested issue of centralism versus federalism have exerted powerful influences in preventing Peru from achieving the ties of broadly shared goals and values.

About the size of Colorado, Ecuador (with its approximately 270,670 square kilometers) is the second smallest Latin republic in South America—only Uruguay is smaller.[51] While technically speaking there are at least six distinct regions in Ecuador, people most generally speak just of the coast, the sierra, and the *selva* or *Oriente* (eastern region). Owing to loss of territory suffered at the hands of neighbor republics, Ecuador's *Oriente* has shrunk to a relatively small area.

Unlike Peru with its coastal power center, the capital of Ecuador since colonial times has been the highland city of Quito. In Ecuador, then, the centralism versus federalism issue has generally involved the attempt of the coast to escape the domination of a *serrano* bureaucracy.

Repelled by the unhealthy living conditions of the coast (a humid area, in contrast to coastal Peru, owing to different ocean currents) and frequency of yellow fever and other epidemics, and lured by the employment opportunities afforded by the civil and ecclesiastical institutions that had their headquarters in the capital city, the greater number of Spanish immigrants in the colonial period made their way into the highland region. The sierra also attracted Spaniards because of the large Indian population. In the highlands, the Spaniards established a replica of the cultural environment they had left behind in Spain. Describing this region, an Ecuadoran writes that here, in such cities as Quito, Cuenca, Ibarra, Riobamba, and Loja, "there still vibrates the colonial spirit... In the inner recesses of the inter-Andean people tradition is still intact, with all its beauty and pomp, with all its prejudices and beliefs, its fears and enthusiasms."[52]

In the Ecuadoran sierra, the Catholic Church established an influence that has remained, except for a period of rabid anticlericalism presided over by liberal governments in the late nineteenth and early twentieth centuries, "more coherent and systematic than in somewhat analogous situations in other Latin American countries with large Indian populations." Participating intimately in the life of the Indian communities of highland Ecuador, "the rural clergy is not an absentee class, as in Guatemala and Mexico."[53]

For many highland Ecuadorans, even those of the upper classes, the *patria* does not extend beyond the narrow confines of their native town. They are willing to sacrifice, if at all, only for this local *patria chica* (little fatherland) where they can see the fruits of their efforts; and they eye suspiciously projects concerned with national development.[54] Typical of the *altiplano's* urban centers, Cuenca has whenever possible taken advantage of its geographic isolation to pursue an independent course. The same is true of Loja, Ecuador's southernmost city. In its solitude, "far from governmental authority, Loja has clung to its autonomy."[55]

However separated by geographic barriers and local loyalties, *serranos* have found a common ground in their prevailing traditionalism and their suspiciousness of the more open, business-minded, and purportedly money-grubbing and untrustworthy *costeños*. Exalting the sierra as the cradle of romantic poets, idealistic politicians, and ingenuous intellectuals, the people of highland Ecuador dismiss as unworthy of their association the "bankers, merchants, politicians of action and men of practical understanding" produced on the coast.[56]

Colonial chroniclers, generalizing on the population of coastal Esmeraldas, which had been settled by Highland Indians fleeing from persecution and by runaway slaves, tended to refer to all *costeños* as wild mulattoes and *sambos* (a cross between Africans and Indians) who acknowledged no law and waged war at the slightest provocation.[57] In the intervening centuries, *serrano* perceptions of a coastal populace that is volatile and possessed of only the rudiments of civilization have not altered markedly.

Ecuador's major coastal city, Guayaquil, has throughout its history waged an unrelenting struggle against domination by the *quiteños*. Guayaquil began to make significant headway against the claims of Quito only in the early twentieth century when commercial prosperity created a new-rich aristocracy whose members were often far wealthier than the elites of the capital city. The colonial and aristocratic aura of many *altiplano* towns is conspicuously absent in Guayaquil, and so is the influence of the church. In this, Guayaquil is typical of the coast in general. One of Ecuador's major intellectual figures of the twentieth century has observed that since colonial times the priests neglected the coast. He finds various reasons for this neglect, including the lack of population density which made evangelical work less rewarding, the bad climate, and the "insolent character of the people" —the writer is obviously a *serrano*.[58] The result has been a popular indifference to religion, and an anticlerical intelligentsia that have easily been able to spread their prejudices among the masses.[59]

The coastal lower classes are made up largely of the *montuvios* who, according to one formula, are 60 percent Indian, 30 percent Negro, and 10 percent white. Until recent times, the *montuvios* participated in Ecuadoran politics primarily as guerrilla fighters. The presence of this large working class, whose members are less tied by feudal obligations to the land than the Indian serfs of the sierra, explains why most of Ecuador's revolutions have been launched from the coast.[60]

Of the coast, the prominent Ecuadoran man of letters Alfredo Pérez Guerrero has written: "Tradition is not the marrow and soul as in the sierra. The coast is open to the outside, to what is new, to what is foreign and in vogue. The function of the coast is economic because of its very location. A perennial restlessness agitates it, a perennial change of ideals and enthusiasms." Pérez Guerrero notes that Ecuadoran liberalism came from the coast and contends that also from the coast "will come, if someday per chance it does come, socialism."[61] Certainly during the first half of the twentieth century, Ecuador's various varieties of socialist ideologues and political organizers have found their most enthusiastic followers among the *montuvios* who steadily gained importance as voters even as the frequency of their guerrilla activities began somewhat to wane.[62]

To the contemptuous view in which they are held by *serranos*, the *costeños* reciprocate in full, dismissing the sierra as an area occupied by people who because of their Indian blood and long years of isolation are hopelessly indifferent to progress if not indeed refractory to civilization. The bitterness of feeling is all the more intense because not until recent years has there been a significant degree of cultural interpenetration between the two regions. When Friedrich Hassaurek arrived at the beginning of the 1860s as the U.S. minister to Ecuador, he was dismayed to find that there was not even a road joining Guayaquil to Quito.[63] Because of the lack of mining resources and exportable surpluses in the sierra, there had seemed no need to provide transportation routes between it and the coast.

Better means of communication established during colonial times in Peru to facilitate trade between the coast and rich highland mining communities permitted more extensive cultural interpenetration and brought about in Lima the frequent mingling of sierra landowners and coastal merchants. Moreover, from the early days of conquest, the church established a strong presence both in the Peruvian sierra and on the coast. Its presence along the Pacific littoral was encouraged by a climate that was infinitely dryer and far healthier than that of the Ecuadoran coast. These are among the circumstances helping to explain why the clash between liberalism and conservatism was less intense in Peru than in Ecuador, and less clearly identifiable with regional sentiments.

Although it has lost since independence roughly one-half of its national territory, including its coast, the republic of Bolivia comprises still an area (roughly 1.1 million square kilometers) about the size of Texas and California combined. The largest part of Bolivia consists of the area extending eastward from the slopes of the eastern arm of the Andes, the Cordillera Real. Here are found the *yungas*, or deep valleys that line the mountainside, the *selvas* or forest lands, and finally an extensive area of prairie land bordering on Brazil and Paraguay. Sparsely inhabited, this is the area that optimists often refer to as the Bolivia of the future.

The Bolivia of the present, and of the past, where most of the population resides, is the *altiplano*, nestled between the Andean ranges. At about the fourteenth degree of south latitude, the Andes divide into two great branches which cross the Bolivian territory from north to south. The western or coastal range obstructed travel between the *altiplano* and the coast. After independence, it was always easier for Peruvians and Chileans to make their way by sea to the Bolivian coast; and it was far easier for them once there to maintain communications between Lima to the north and Valparaíso and Santiago to the south than it was for Bolivians to establish east-west links between the highland and the coast. This is one reason why Bolivia proved unable to retain the coast as part of its national domain.

Unlike the Ecuadoran highland, the Bolivian *altiplano* has been

Bolivia

richly endowed with mineral deposits, and mining has generally been the mainstay of the economy. The somber, imposing landscape of the mineral-rich *altiplano*, ranging in width from sixty to ninety miles, forms the setting for such cities as La Paz, a major trade center from colonial times on the route between coastal Peru and Upper Peru's fabled mining region, Potosí, the principal silver producer of the colonial era, and Oruro, which yielded the bulk of its mineral wealth only in the postindependence period. Both La Paz and Oruro are situated at altitudes of above 12,000 feet, while Potosí is 14,350 feet above sea level.[64] Much of the Bolivian highland is utterly unfit for cultivation or for human habitation, and this has resulted in the crowding of the populace into certain narrowly confined areas where soil conditions permit the raising of crops and the grazing of livestock.[65]

Far to the south, and tucked into a pleasant and fertile valley at an altitude of about 9,500 feet, lies the city which served as administrative headquarters for Upper Peru in colonial times and also as the seat of one of the most renowned universities in Spanish South America. Known variously as Chuquisaca, Charcas, and La Plata, the city was eventually renamed Sucre after the Venezuelan military leader Antonio José de Sucre, who played the leading role in establishing Bolivia as an independent republic. The people of Sucre have been referred to as the Castilians of Bolivia. Proud of their colonial background and inclined to boast of their relatively pure Spanish lineage, they consider themselves the country's true aristocracy and have continued to regard their city as the cultural capital of the land, even after it ceased to be the political capital at the end of the nineteenth century.

On the rugged slopes of the Andes about 250 miles southeast of La Paz lies the Cochabamba valley. One of the country's richest agricultural regions, the valley is populated largely by Indians who are more apt to speak their native Quechua than Spanish, and by mestizos who are at home in both tongues. Possessing a strong regional loyalty, people of all social ranks in this area are proud of being *cochabambinos*.[66] Simón Bolívar is said to have regarded Cochabamba as the city most ideally suited to be the Bolivian capital, and to the present day *cochabambinos* tend to share this view.[67]

Far to the east lies another distinctive town, Santa Cruz. Settled largely from Argentina and Brazil, the Santa Cruz populace (*cruceños*) has only the smallest Indian base, as the few Guaraní Indians who once lived in the area have been absorbed through miscegenation. Proud of their modern, capitalist spirit, the *cruceños* often feel closer cultural ties to progress-oriented Argentines and Brazilians than to the far-off allegedly unenlightened power wielders in La Paz. With good reason, Bolivian central governments have fretted over Santa Cruz's separatist tendencies.

As elsewhere in Andean America, racial factors have contributed to Bolivian regionalism. From Lake Titicaca southward to the salty swamps of Uyuni, the Aymara Indians provide the main racial base of the *altiplano* population. In other parts of Bolivia, principally the Cochabamba valley, Quechuas have constituted the main population stock. Most Bolivians are convinced that these two Indian groups exhibit strongly contrasting traits. It is a commonplace that the Aymara are dull, stolid, unimaginative,[68] coarse of mind but hardy of nerve,[69] while the Quechuas are said to be happier, sweeter, more tractable in character. Alcides Arguedas, one of Bolivia's best-known writers, maintains that the people of La Paz (paceños), because of their Aymara blood, are grave, serious, inclined to be meditative, sad, proud, fierce, and disposed to lie. "They are," he adds, "battlers, warriors, as no other people of Bolivia." Arguedas, whose views are important not for their scientific accuracy but instead for the degree to which they reflect widespread prejudices, describes cochabambinos as dreamers, given to impulsiveness, and the most "feminine of all Bolivian people"—also a bit lazy because of the richness of their valley's soil. *Cochabambinos*, he concludes, have been shaped mainly by their Quechua origins.[70]

Considerable rivalry exists between La Paz and Cochabamba. Writing in the 1920s, Margaret Marsh observed that the cochabambino looked upon the paceño with the intense jealousy that only well-matched rivals can feel.[71] Far greater has been the rivalry between La Paz and Sucre, similar in many ways to that existing between Guayaquil and Quito, Lima and Arequipa. La Paz, its origins linked to trade and commerce, has nurtured a people who look down upon the purportedly impractical, obscurantist inhabitants of Sucre, thought to be more concerned with geneology, poetry, and oratory than with progress. At the convention that declared Bolivian independence, the paceño delegates counterproposed union with Lower Peru on the ground that otherwise their region would be denied access to its natural port of Arica, which was certain to remain in Peruvian hands. Such practical considerations made no impact on the delegation from Chuquisaca (the name had not yet been changed to Sucre), made up of self-centered creoles "who were more attracted by the idea than by the practicalities of independence."[72]

The Trotskyist Bolivian intellectual Guillermo Lora describes the nineteenth century enmity between the two cities in these terms: "If the city of Sucre symbolized the spirit and ambitions of the Conservative Party, so tightly tied to clericalism . . . , La Paz was the capital of the young liberals of daring ideas and bellicose anticlericalism, above all anxious to project their economic power into political power. It was a case of the north, filled with initiative and vitality and rude men, against the south, which languished with the memories of the colony."[73]

In the light of bitterly divisive regionalism, it is understandable that a prominent Bolivian writer could declare in the early 1940s: "Bolivia is the culmination of South American confusion. It is the land that least knows itself . . . Bolivia, a tragic country, is sustained by the opposition of the elements that comprise it."[74]

THE RACIAL ISSUE AND THE IMPLICATION OF INDEPENDENCE

Throughout the Peruvian and Bolivian sierra, but to a much lesser degree in the Ecuadoran highland, whites and mestizos have lived in intermittent terror occasioned by "the lurking dread of an Indian uprising."[75] Terror was especially in evidence during the period immediately preceding and accompanying the wars of independence. It was awakened by the Indian uprisings, led initially by Túpac Amaru II, that erupted throughout the *altiplano* in 1780 and continued sporadically until 1821. In the course of these uprisings, Cuzco very nearly fell to besieging Quechua Indians in 1781 and La Paz was barely able to withstand a 109-day siege led against it by Aymara forces. At this time, whole regions of the Bolivian highland were virtually depopulated as whites were slaughtered and towns burned to the ground. Three years later in 1784 came a new uprising highlighted by an Indian siege of Puno, on the Peruvian edge of Lake Titicaca. Another insurrection of major proportions exploded in 1814. During its course Indians captured La Paz, massacred its Spanish garrison, "mercilessly attacked Europeans, pillaged their property and sacked their houses."[76]

Fearful of the Indians, with the memory of native uprisings very much alive as they embarked upon independence, and also dubious about the mestizos, the *altiplano* elites who prided themselves on their white ancestry entertained little immediate hope for the future betterment of their countries. Eventually, when the Indians had disappeared, the victims of the exhaustion, indolence, and unhygienic ways thought to be characteristic of their race, and when the mestizo population had been purified and uplifted through a lengthy process of miscegenation with waves of white European immigrants somehow to be lured to the area, it might be possible to think about progress. Meantime, progress was the dangerous chimera pursued by a heedless people, especially the *costeños* of Peru and Ecuador, who were not aware of the extent of the Indian problem.

When development-minded elites captured control of Andean America as the nineteenth century ended and established the close links with foreign capital that their liberal predecessors had sought in vain, they were themselves quickly submerged beneath the traditional racial attitudes of the *altiplano*—even as the victorious North in the U.S. Civil War soon adopted and even added new refinements to the racist views of its defeated adversary. By the early twentieth century the close ties forged with foreign capitalists were looked upon as the means by which Andean Americans might perpetuate their domination over supposedly racially inferior masses and achieve a superficial degree of development that was not based on attempts to arouse the slumbering giant at the base of the social pyramid.

Before this point was reached, Andean America had suffered through an agonizing period of chaos and confusion, the complexity of which has dismayed its students.

4

The Nineteenth-Century Quest for Stability and Progress

Independence and the Age of Caudillos Peruvians, it is often charged, did little on their own to achieve independence from Spain, but instead awaited liberation by patriot armies raised elsewhere in Spanish America. The charge is not warranted. Given the strength of the Spanish forces in the viceroyalty[1] and given also the prevailing fear by the white classes of starting any move that might lead to mobilization of the much feared Indians, Peruvian creoles and mestizos actually made remarkable efforts on their own account to end the colonial status.[2] The final drive for independence, however, did await the 1820 arrival on Peruvian soil of Argentine-born José de San Martín at the head of an army raised largely in Chile and La Plata. Balked both by Spanish resistance which continued in the highlands even after he occupied Lima in 1821, and also plagued by the opposition of liberals led by the priest Francisco Javier de Luna Pizarro, who opposed his monarchical ideas and generally conservative tendencies, San Martín withdrew from Peru in 1822. Spain's royalist armies still controlled a vast part of Peru's territory and threatened at any moment to obliterate its factious patriots.

This was the situation when Simón Bolívar, the successful liberator by now of Colombia, Venezuela, and Ecuador, arrived in September of 1823 at the head of forces made up mainly of recruits from the already independent northern republics—and also from England and Ireland. Final success came to the patriots on December 9, 1824, when forces directed by the Venezuelan Antonio José de Sucre, Bolívar's

81

most trusted and ablest subordinate, defeated the Spanish armies high in the Andes at Ayacucho.

Even as the final fighting against the Spaniards was in progress, Peru's liberal and conservative factions struggled with each other to gain the upper hand; and they continued the struggle with still greater militancy once independence was achieved. These circumstances doomed Bolívar's hopes to remain as president of Peru and ultimately to bring that country into a loose confederation with Bolivia and with the three republics of Ecuador, Colombia, and Venezuela, joined together between 1823 and 1830 in the political dominion known as Gran Colombia. Bolívar soon discovered he could satisfy neither liberals nor conservatives, and less than two years after the triumph at Ayacucho had secured Peru's independence Bolívar departed from the country.

During the short period he remained at the head of the Peruvian state, Bolívar addressed himself to some of its fundamental problems. It is not remarkable that the colorful and magnetic creole from Caracas failed to find solutions; for solutions still eluded Peru's national leaders more than a century later.

Bolívar backed the attempt of José Larrea y Laredo, minister of finance in 1826, to find a compromise between the free trade and autarky factions in Peru. Devising a far-sighted policy, Larrea had sought to encourage some degree of free trade while at the same time giving tariff protection to locally manufactured goods such as soap, candles, hats, aguardiente, and furniture.[3] As it turned out, the attempted compromise satisfied neither faction. Failure to find policies that would unite Peruvians was even more glaring in Bolívar's approach to the Indian problem.

The Liberator from Venezuela was not without his racial prejudices. Probably no white Spanish American aristocrat of this age could have been. Yet, for his period, Bolívar was remarkably open in his racial attitudes. His mind was not yet made up on such questions as the nature of the Indians and the consequences of *mestizaje* or race mixture. And therefore Bolívar hoped to carry out social experiments through which he might discover the potential of peoples of diverse ethnic origins. Despite some doubts and misgivings, he inclined toward the belief that through firm-handed direction from above the nonwhite lower classes of Spanish America could be led into habits and virtues that were bringing progress and development to the more advanced countries of the world.

Through decrees of April and July of 1824 issued in Peru and one of August 1825 proclaimed in La Paz, Bolívar sought to end the system of Indian communal property, to halt the collection of tribute, and also to abolish feudalistic, personal service exactions on Indians. His hope—even as that of San Martín who at an earlier time had issued similar decrees—was to make Indians productive, and happy, by enabling them to become private property owners or, if not this, then at least free, wage-earning laborers.[4] Aspiring to economic development, Bolívar dreamed of bringing income and capitalist incentives, as well as private security and self-reliance, to the lower classes of Spanish America—which, in Peru, Bolivia, and Ecuador meant basically the Indians. Through his projected reforms the Liberator sought to create a mass of purchasers whose existence would facilitate not only growth of the export-import trade but also a vast expansion of local industrial production. For Bolívar, development required more than just the input of foreign capital; it required internal transformations based ultimately on changing the culture of the people.

Nothing came of Bolívar's projects. His reforms, conceived in terms of the cultural tampering and engineering that is now abhorred by most anthropologists, were at once sabotaged by the upper classes "who regarded a free and landed peasantry as a threat to their dependent labour supply."[5] To the upper classes, especially to those who owned land in the sierra, the Liberator was just another outsider who, like the Bourbon reformers and the *costeno* merchants, did not understand the inferiority of Indian nature. Bolívar's Indian policies proved the last straw for many Peruvians, adding decisively to the pressures that forced his withdrawal.

Following Bolívar's departure, Peru remained in a deep depression that rendered political stability elusive. Power was usurped by ambitious generals, some of whom demonstrated considerable political astuteness, whose armies as often as not were made up of the *montoneros*, persons who by one offense or another had run afoul of authorities and turned to a life beyond the pale of the law. Centralized power virtually disappeared, and the country split into largely autonomous regions, focusing around Cuzco, Arequipa, Trujillo, and Lima.

Finally, beginning in 1845 Ramón Castilla, the greatest of Peru's military *caudillos*, brought his country a longed-for interlude of political stability. Castilla's success was owing not only to his astuteness but also to luck. In the 1840s the prolonged depression finally ended and nitrate-rich bird droppings, called guano, projected Peru into an era of prosperity. Guano had become one of the most sought-after fertilizers in many parts of the world and Peru had what appeared, for a time, to be an inexhaustible supply. Although an essential element in Inca agriculture, guano had been relatively ignored by the Spaniards and had been accumulating for centuries along the arid coast and offshore islands.

The Age of Castilla and of Guano In 1840 an external trade in guano did not exist, yet in 1860 Peruvian guano was one of the principal Latin American exports. In that year alone 400,000 tons, worth over $24 million, were exported to the farmers of Europe, Asia, and America.[6] Initially, guano transactions had been handled by British firms, such as Antony Gibbs & Sons which gained the dominant position in the trade in 1849. The British houses served essentially as commission agents, conducting most of their business with goods taken on consignment and always paying in advance to the Peruvian government a certain percentage of anticipated profits.

In spite of the charges of economic imperialism leveled for many years against the foreign firms, the British historian W. M. Mathew is persuasive in his refutation. According to him, in the relationship between the foreign firms and the Peruvian government it was always the government which was the stronger and more secure party and which derived the greater advantage. The government became the undisputed owner of the guano reserves; it performed no entrepreneurial functions in the trade; it secured for itself the major share of profits; and it acquired loans amounting to hundreds of thousands of pesos in advance of sales. Thus the government, he insists, consistently got the better of the contractors.[7]

As the supply of internal capital increased in Peru, a group of wealthy citizens appeared, their fortunes enhanced in many instances by fraudulent deals arranged during the government of José Rufino Echenique (1851–1854) in connection with the consolidation of the internal debt—a consolidation made possible by the state's guano income. The unprecedented revenue also enabled the government to achieve the peaceful abolition of slavery in 1854—an accomplishment which merited Castilla (who had just overthrown Echenique) the title of Liberator—by bestowing generous compensation on the slave owners. Thereafter some of the new wealth in Peru found its way into the importation of laborers who were scarcely better off than slaves: Chinese coolies. Between 1850 and 1875 it is estimated that some 90,000 Chinese males were imported to meet Peru's labor needs for agriculture and railroad construction.[8] The new source of cheap labor facilitated the rise of a cotton exporting economy dominated by large coastal estates.

The swelling fortunes of a new bourgeoisie brought a challenge to the consignment system worked out with British establishments. Beginning in the 1850s Peruvian capitalists wrested valuable trade concessions from the government. In 1862 Peruvians took over the British consignment contract, and the same year saw the founding of the first commercial bank in Lima. For the next six years the percentage of the guano trade controlled by Peruvians rose steadily, and all the while the ranks of the new millionaires and near-millionaires continued to grow. Lima, the center of the new financial elite, began now to forge links of domination, both economic and political, over the rest of the country.

Against the background of prosperity, Ramón Castilla ruled two times as president of Peru, the first term extending from 1845 to 1851 and the second from 1854 to 1862. Exhibiting breathtaking political sagacity and combining the qualities of the lion and the fox, Castilla reached an understanding with the more powerful provincial families and military chieftains.[9] Above all, however, it was the unprecedented government income that enabled Castilla to maintain political order. Guano gave him the means to maintain a standing army as a disciplined arm of the state. Guano income further enabled Castilla to gain a host of civilian followers as he vastly expanded the bureaucracy and produced thousands of additional jobs through public works projects. All the while the Peruvian Liberator consolidated his position among the new commercial and banking bourgeoisie and the cotton-producing plantation owners by assiduously refraining from interference in their economic transactions and by granting them virtual immunity from taxation. At the same time that government expenditures soared to unprecedented levels, because of the burgeoning army, bureaucracy, and pension lists and because of war with Ecuador (1859) and Spain (1865–1866), the internal tax system was "all but wiped out."[10] For the 1861 budget of 21,400,000 pesos, only 3,400,000 came from internal taxes (almost exclusively customs duties) while 16,300,000 came from guano. It was now, as never before, that Peruvian upper classes began to be indulged in their grave infirmity, "the horror of taxes."[11]

Peru, so it seemed in the age of Castilla, had been saved by guano. A new group of modern capitalists had come into being, and signs of prosperity were everywhere (including the latest steam machinery on the sugar estates), provided one did not venture into the highland interior. To achieve this remarkable evidence of progress it had not been necessary, as Bolívar had supposed, to change the nature of the Indians, or of anyone. It had been necessary, however, for native capitalists to accept a dependence on foreign markets for their exports and upon foreign industries for their necessary consumer and conspicuous-display goods.

Castilla, the provincial mestizo from the south who presided over the coming of good times, has, in retrospect, been widely criticized for financial shortsightedness. Looking on his age in hindsight, it is easy to conclude that he should have financed government expenditures by taxes while channeling the proceeds of the rapidly dwindling guano reserves into long-term development projects. Yet had Castilla sought to impose taxes on Peru's new capitalist class he probably could not have survived in office. Moreover, the astute ruler was following the development formula most widely subscribed to at the time by the more rapidly developing nations of the world, the formula of laissez faire. Given the widespread assurances of those who prided themselves on the mastery of economic theory, and given the nearly uninterrupted prosperity that lasted until his death in 1867 at the age of sixty-eight, Castilla could scarcely have been expected to question the effectiveness of laissez-faire development prescriptions, or to foresee that Peruvian capitalists would not respond to complete freedom in the same way as their U.S. and English counterparts.

Following upon the years of dismaying political instability, moreover, Castilla was bound to have been blinded to economic problems that lurked beneath the surface by his very real accomplishments in providing order. Conservative and liberal *pensadores* continued, it is true, to carry on a bitter polemic, but in the age of prosperity in which business sectors came increasingly to control government, no one paid much attention to intellectuals. The eclipse of the intellectuals helped Castilla in his quest of stability, and so did the accord that some traditional elites established with the nouveau riches. While a few interior landowners remained hostile to the new coastal bourgeoisie, many members of the old-line landed aristocracy invested in the commercial-banking capitalism that was rising on the coast; and frequently families of the "ancient geneological nobility" married into families of the commercial-financial complex. Thus the new plutocracy was blending with the old aristocracy to form what Peru's great historian Jorge Basadre has called a plutocratic-aristocratic class.[12]

Because Peruvian ideologues had become irrelevant in the prosperous guano age, and because old aristocrats were finding a basis of accord with new plutocrats, Castilla was able by 1860 to do what Ecuadoran political leaders, as will be seen, were unable to accomplish until nearly a century later: effect a workable compromise between the conservative and liberal camps.

Herrera versus Vigil On January 4, 1842 in a sermon preached from the pulpit of Lima's cathedral, Bartolomé Herrera delivered a sweeping indictment against the theological and political implications of Peruvian liberalism. The occasion for Herrera's remarkable sermon, which helped establish the thirty-six-year-old *limeño* priest as a leading spokesman of conservatism, was the funeral of President Agustín Gamarra who had been killed during a disastrous invasion of Bolivia. Herrera attributed Peruvian political instability and Gamarra's defeat by the "weak and puny arm of Bolivia" to the loss among citizens of a sense of obedience. He asserted that authority came to rulers through God and that once political sovereignty was duly established, all citizens were obliged, by divine law, to respect and obey the ruler. The lantern-jawed young priest ended his sermon by exhorting God to grant to all Peruvians "unalterable respect for legitimate authority."[13]

In numerous other sermons and political writings, Herrera justified authoritarian political organization, provided such organization conformed to the law of God, and maintained that only a tiny minority could legitimately exercise political power. According to him, the Creator endowed only a few men with genuine intelligence. An "aristocracy of intelligence," which alone "possesses the divine gift of sovereignty," must, Herrera maintained, hold all political power.[14]

Peru's conservative laymen found much of Herrera's political thought to their liking, for they had always maintained that stability depended upon authoritarian rule by an elite and the corresponding subordination of the masses. They welcomed his argument that just as bishops and laymen must not question popes, so also it was contrary to right reason and the design of providence "to allow electors to give instructions to deputies or to set limits upon them, for electors do not delegate authority, they merely recognize superior capacity and prerogatives and submit to them."[15] Now that a majority of the clergy subscribed to Herrera's thinking and had abandoned the liberal ideas that many of them had espoused after independence, the church came increasingly to be recognized by civilian conservatives as an invaluable ally in the quest of authoritarianism.

Meantime the former priest Francisco de Paula González Vigil, defrocked and excommunicated for his attacks against the authoritarian control exercised over the church by popes and the Roman curia and for other allegedly heretical views, had become the leading spokesman of Peruvian liberalism.[16] Born in the southern town of Tacna in 1792 (which made him Herrera's senior by thirteen years), Virgil had studied at the San Jerónimo Seminary in Arequipa and had been ordained to the priesthood in 1819. Beginning a political career as a deputy to a national congress in 1827, Vigil turned his initial attention to the defense of political liberalism, federalism, and parliamentary supremacy. Already by the 1830s, however, he had become convinced that the church must organize along more democratic lines and throw off the alleged tyranny of popes and the curia. Otherwise it could not be an acceptable institution within a liberally structured republic of the type Vigil hoped to see established.

The more Peruvian liberals, following Vigil's lead, attacked the church's traditional internal organization, the more the clergy sought to intervene in the temporal order, hoping to make it reflect the church's highly ordered and hierarchical structure. And, the more the liberals sought to introduce democratic political rule, the more conservative civilians encouraged the clergy's intervention in the political order.

In the late 1850s President Castilla sought to arrange an accommodation between the forces of conservatism and liberalism. When neither side proved conciliatory, the president in 1860 played the key role in imposing upon the country a new constitution that embodied an ingenious compromise. The charter pleased conservatives by keeping intact a centralized and somewhat authoritarian structure, by perpetuating religious exclusivism and church-state union, by safeguarding the church's wealth and property, by guaranteeing the church relative autonomy in its internal organization, and finally by preserving the rights of its leaders to speak out on and even to participate directly in politics. On the other hand, to gratify liberals the 1860 charter suppressed separate law courts for clergymen, ended state collection of tithes, and provided for a system of public education that would end monopolistic ecclesiastical control over instruction.

Herrera was not satisfied with the new charter, in part because it ignored his proposal for the corporative organization of Peru and for the intimate collaboration of church and state in the exercise of a moderating power. But the Archbishop of Lima, José Sebastián Goyeneche y Barreda, was willing to go along. Herrera was appointed

Bishop of Arequipa in 1859, probably in the expectation that this office would reduce the time available to him for political activities. Disillusioned by the drift of events and plagued by deteriorating health, Herrera died in 1864.

Vigil had also been displeased with the 1860 constitution, for it meant the defeat of his efforts to separate church and state, to substitute national control over the church for that exercised by Rome, and to achieve religious toleration. Despite grumblings from both sides, though, the constitution provided a middle way that a solid core of both conservatives and liberals found endurable. Thus it helped in the long run to reduce the passion with which the two sides had waged the struggle between traditionalism and modernity.

In the late 1850s the writings of Vigil began to reveal the degree to which he had fallen under the influence of Krausism—one common ground he shared with Herrera who had been the principal Peruvian populizer of a censored form of Krausism that made it compatible with Catholicism.[17] In an essay published originally in 1858, Vigil parted company with many of his fellow liberals who, still under Rousseau's sway, believed that removal of restraints upon individual action would result in social, economic, and political improvement. Instead, Vigil—looking ahead in some ways to Emile Durkheim whose corporativist views are indicated in the first chapter—urged that excessive individualism be curbed by encouraging the formation of autonomous associations, on an intermediate level between citizens and government. Such associations, he argued, would limit selfishness and "play a complementary role with civil institutions in leading to the common good."[18]

Both Vigil (who died in 1875) and Herrera had adhered to a corporativist political ideology in the light of which unchecked individualism was seen as morally disastrous for the individual and socially catastrophic for the nation. Perhaps this is why the influence of both men has remained alive in Peru to the present day. The differences that separated the two thinkers in the nineteenth century no longer seem important, while the similarities that bound them together, regarded in the past century as flimsy at best, have been perceived as increasingly important with the passing of time.

Economic and Political Disintegration, 1868–1879 Even though the two headstrong men often quarreled and shouted at each other and once came very close to blows, the key figure in José Balta's administration (1868–1872) was Nicolás de Piérola. Born in 1839 in

89

Arequipa, Piérola, ebullient and dynamic, small in stature but erect and aristocratic in bearing, became President Balta's minister of finance. Almost at once he issued a challenge to the banking-commercial elite that had become accustomed to having things their own way. The government, by 1868, had come up against hard times, and it was this fact that precipitated the confrontation between Balta's most powerful minister and the capitalists. Nothing now remained in the national treasury of the huge guano earnings accumulated in the past twenty-five years; and Peru's government faced a projected two-year (1869–1870) budget deficit of over 16 million soles.[19]

Convinced that laissez-faire policies had not resulted after all in progress, Piérola decided on a larger measure of government planning. Thus he ended the guano concession to native capitalists and contracted directly with the French firm of Dreyfus and Company for the sale of this commodity.[20] In exchange, Dreyfus and Company agreed upon large advances to the Peruvian government. Piérola believed that by directly controlling guano sales the government could derive greater revenue. Then, through careful centralized planning, government could employ its augmented funds to accomplish national development.

With the Dreyfus contract a fait accompli and the treasury saved from bankruptcy, Piérola grew indifferent toward other reforms originally encompassed by his economic program. He failed to implement plans to curtail government expenditures and he failed also to institute a balanced tax program about which he had talked. Satisfied that in the Dreyfus firm he had struck an inexhaustible well of capital, Piérola contracted for huge new loans with the French company and also with British lenders. While the original contract was defensible, the new loan agreements were not, for they resulted in an unrealistically large debt for Peru at ruinous interest and commission rates.

A main cause of fiscal madness was the railroad fever that had gripped Piérola, Balta, and a host of other Peruvians. The contagion had been introduced into Peru by Henry Meiggs, a U.S. entrepreneur whose vision, daring, and ambitions were matched by his lack of scruples. Fresh from railroad building triumphs in Chile, Meiggs convinced the Peruvian president and his minister of finance that the country could surmount all its economic problems and plunge boldly ahead into a glittering future if only enough miles of track were laid. Railroads, it was promised, would bring the same kind of prosperity and progress achieved by the United States and by making all Peruvians wealthy, banish once and for all the specter of revolutions.[21] Enticed by these visions, the Balta regime began to pour borrowed funds into hastily improvised railroad construction schemes.

By the beginning of the 1880s the Central Trans-Andean Railway had advanced only as far as Chilca, far away from the projected Andean terminus of La Oroya. In all, though, some 700 miles of track had been laid; and already it was apparent that the Peruvian railroads, many of which seemed to go nowhere, were overcapitalized and underutilized. Not until the late 1880s and the 1890s, when extended into the mining heartland of the Andes by British capitalists who had foreclosed on the enterprises because of defaulted debts, would the railroads produce their most important effect of connecting the sierra to international markets and stimulating output of ore.

Dismayed by the circumstances that would see Peru's total foreign debt soar to nearly 35 million pounds by the mid-1870s,[22] Manuel Pardo formed in 1871 the first true political party in Peru,[23] to which he gave the name Civilist (*Civilista*), a word with a decided anti-military connotation. The new party brought together diverse elements. Many members of the Peruvian intelligentsia, smarting because of their eclipse by purportedly uncultured military officers and businessmen, flocked to the party. Its central core of strength, however, came from the banking, commercial, landowning elites created by the age of guano and expanded in the 1860s to include the exploiters of nitrate deposits along the southern coast. The plutocracy, as its enemies soon dubbed this capitalist core, were furious with Piérola for having introduced some semblance of government planning into the guano industry and hoped to recapture control from Dreyfus and Company and to reestablish a government whose relations with businessmen would be limited to conferring favors and concessions. The plutocracy was bound to clash with the intelligentsia within the Civilist party. What is more, many of the businessmen were at odds with the economic theories of the party's founder, Manuel Pardo.

The son of one of Peru's most distinguished families, Pardo—born in Lima in 1834—had completed his education in Barcelona and Paris. In the second city he had been impressed by theories of state intervention in the economy. Although the matter is far from clear, Pardo apparently saw Peru's development not exclusively in terms of an export-import economy basically dependent on foreign market-places and capital.[24] While by no means hostile to the interests of

91

commerce, Pardo hoped to create an industrial base in Peru.[25] For accomplishing this he recognized the importance of government economic controls, for Peruvian capitalists in general seemed uninterested in industrialization. Beyond this, he saw the need for a massive expansion of public education through which practical skills and incentives could be imported to the populace. Reviving, it would seem, some of Bolívar's dreams, Pardo hoped that Indians might be transformed into small-scale, self-reliant private capitalists. For this reason he looked optimistically on the ultimate consequences that railroads might produce by integrating Indians into a marketplace economy. Differing from Castilla and from the young Piérola, Pardo saw prosperity not in terms of bonanzas and physical resources. In his view, formed in response to the economic adversity of the early 1870s, prosperity would come only through developing the economic potential of the people of Peru.

With the Civilists sweeping the election, Pardo assumed the presidential office in 1872. The economic situation remained bleak in the first years of his four-year term. In 1875, facing a desperate need of funds, the government decreed the nationalization of a large part of the nitrate industry. The move did not produce the hoped-for revenue, for nitrate prices continued at unusually low levels because of the nearly worldwide depression. The only important consequence of nationalization was to antagonize the Peruvian, Chilean, and French capitalists who had previously controlled the nitrate industry. In 1876, his last year in office, Pardo had to suspend payments on the foreign debt. One year later death brought an end to Henry Meiggs's frantic attempts to stave off the bankruptcy of his numerous Peruvian ventures.

With the depression of the 1870s came a return to political instability. Early in 1874, Piérola had led an uprising against Pardo, the suppression of which had placed further burdens on the treasury. Then in 1878, two years after he had surrendered the presidential office to Mariano Ignacio Prado, the candidate backed in the 1876 elections by the Civilists in spite of the fact he was a general, Manuel Pardo was assassinated in Lima. Civilists blamed Piérola for having masterminded the plot and although no evidence was ever found to support their suspicions they briefly jailed Piérola's wife—he was out of the country—in a senseless act of spite. It was years before Piérolists found it possible to forgive this outrage that demanded vengeance; and meantime Civilists kept passions at fever pitch as they continued to attach the assassin label to Piérola and his followers.

Peru was not only prostrate economically but hopelessly divided politically when suddenly it found itself in 1879 dragged into war, as an ally of Bolivia, with Chile.

BOLIVIA

The Attainment of Independence   Bolivian independence, in the analysis of one school of thought, resulted not from any deep longing among the people of Upper (Alto) Peru to exist as a separate political entity, or from any awakening sense of national self-awareness. Instead, independence was imposed by foreign generals at the head of foreign troops, simply because no other way was seen to avoid chronic military rivalry between La Plata and Peru over ownership of the once-rich silver mining area. According to many historians, moreover, the people of Upper Peru who favored the creation of a self-governing republic, once the Spanish forces had been defeated by the patriot armies comprised largely of Colombians and Venezuelans, were animated mainly by an unfounded optimism about the wealth of the area and an obsessive desire to keep this wealth to themselves. Some historians proceed beyond these assumptions to the conclusion that there was no logical justification for the creation of Bolivia as an independent state and that the actions which produced this result were tragically misguided.

Many Bolivians are, of course, outraged by these interpretations.[26] They point to the Universidad de San Francisco Xavier of Chuquisaca, founded in 1624, and to the Academia Carolina, founded in 1780 in the same city, as having prepared the intellectual climate for independence; and they point with pride to the sporadic but chronic insurrections against Spanish rule that began in 1809 and involved La Paz, Potosí, Cochabamba, and Charcas or Chuquisaca and also to protracted guerrilla campaigns.[27] Beyond this, national writers such as Jaime Mendoza (1874–1939) have insisted that Bolivia is a natural geographic entity whose unique telluric influences have through the centuries shaped a people who are altogether distinct from those of the surrounding areas.[28] Bolivia, and Mendoza is insistent on this point, was not created by the intervention of foreign armies. Instead, it was the Upper Peruvians themselves who called the country into being. Franz Tamayo (1879–1956), even more influential during his lifetime than Mendoza, concurs completely. For him, a race is in a certain sense the product of an environment. And Bolivia, with its unique environment, created a race of beings perfectly adapted to the

93

geographic setting. "This land, therefore, is a patria in the historic sense."[29]

Whether or not the basis of a distinct culture and nationality did exist in Upper Peru prior to 1825, there are certainly more than enough reasons of a more practical and tangible nature to account for Bolivia's emergence as an independent republic. After being joined to the newly created viceroyalty of La Plata in 1776, Upper Peru was financially drained by the contributions it was forced to make to the viceregal government in Buenos Aires. Thus, "it is understandable that when Spanish hegemony was finally removed, Alto Peru felt compelled to break away from its costly and unequal relationship with the Río de la Plata region."[30] Relations between the two areas had been further strained when the *porteños* (as the residents of Buenos Aires are called) who had toppled the Spanish viceroy and assumed rights of self-government in 1810, dispatched troops to liberate Upper Peru. It soon became apparent that the *porteño* forces were interested not only in liberating Upper Peru from Spain but in attaching it, in an underling status, to Buenos Aires. Thus, Upper Peruvians were by-and-large relieved when troops loyal to the Spanish crown defeated the patriot invaders in 1815.

The prospects of permanent union with Peru were scarcely more attractive than those of rule from Buenos Aires. Once again, Upper Peru would have been cast in a subordinate position, unable to protect its own interests. Furthermore, during the long period when Upper Peru had been ruled from Lima, deep-seated tensions had developed. As a result, the highland populace was little disposed to accept the reimposition of control from the old viceregal capital. Little wonder, then, that the Upper Peruvians cherished the isolation of their "rugged and hidden land" and hoped to close the door altogether against outsiders who, armed with promises of progress, sought to penetrate that isolation.[31]

The triumphant patriot armies that subdued the remaining royalist forces of Upper Peru in 1825 were led by Marshal Antonio José de Sucre, and by a host of lesser-ranked Venezuelan and Colombian officers. The northerners sympathized neither with the La Plata nor the Peruvian claims on Upper Peru and were inclined to turn a sympathetic ear to the natives of the region who for a variety of reasons, ranging from personal greed to the pangs of incipient nationalism, desired independence. This inclination was particularly evident in Sucre himself; for he did not want the northern powers of South America, where his true interests lay, to be faced by a unified and formidable southern bloc. Soon after arriving in La Paz in February of 1825, Sucre came out in support of Upper Peru's independence. Before long he managed to persuade a highly dubious Bolívar to go along. With Sucre's approval, and perhaps even his subtle urging, an Upper Peruvian assembly meeting in Chuquisaca declared independence in July of 1825 and christened the new republic Bolivia, hoping thereby to melt whatever doubts the Liberator might still have entertained.

If the independence of Bolivia was in some ways an accident, it was a happy accident. Independence spared Bolivia rule from Buenos Aires, where even by 1825 the contempt of the *porteños* for Upper Peru's Indians and mixed bloods was notorious—and where this contempt was only further nourished during the course of ensuing generations. Through its independence, Bolivia also escaped the sort of domination from Lima that has, through the years, evoked frustration and even rebellion among the highland communities of Peru itself. Moreover, if a true basis of nationalism and self-awareness did not already exist in Bolivia as of 1825, it soon developed as that country sought to defend itself against the designs of its not very friendly or trustworthy neighbors.

The Rule of Sucre, Santa Cruz, and Ballivián, 1826–1847   In 1826 Sucre was installed as president of Bolivia, a position he was to hold for life, according to the provisions of a constitution written by Simón Bolívar himself. Sucre's tenure proved of somewhat shorter duration. April of 1828 witnessed an uprising against the Marshal, accompanied by cries of "down with mulattoes," for the Venezuelan officer and most of the Colombian-Venezuelan troops remaining in Bolivia under his command had been dubbed mulattoes by the local inhabitants. Sucre survived the uprising, as well as a severe wound in the right arm—the first wound he had suffered in his brilliant military career—but withdrew from Bolivia a short time later in the face of rising opposition, an invasion from Peru, and deteriorating economic conditions. In many ways, the Venezuelan Marshal was the victim of his own idealistically motivated but ill-conceived reform attempts.

In the short time he was in Bolivia, Sucre sought to enforce a far more sweeping series of liberal reforms than Bolívar had attempted in Peru. In the first place, the Liberator's ill-fated Peruvian experiment with ending Indian tribute and personal service and distributing land to the natives in fee-simple ownership was attempted by Sucre in Bolivia.[32] Beyond this, in the endeavor to train the masses to become economically free so that they might become politically free and thus "contribute to the creation of a true social democracy,"[33] Sucre supported the establishment of a Model School in the country's capital (the colonial capital with its three names of Charcas, Chuquisaca, and La Plata was rechristened Sucre in 1839). Within five months, however, opposition of the upper classes, who rightly considered the educational program a threat to the established class structure, had ended the experiment. Contributing to the failure of the school was the opposition of the clergy, resentful of the challenge to their traditional monopolistic control over education and also outraged by the attempt to stamp all Bolivian education in a utilitarian, rationalist mold prescinding altogether from the religious influence.[34]

If the secularist-minded Sucre incurred defeat in seeking to wrest control of schools away from the church, and also in trying to end ecclesiastical control over charity, he scored a notable triumph in his move to strip the church of much of its wealth and land. In no part of Spanish America, in fact, "was confiscation carried out with as much rigor as in Bolivia."[35] Bolivian confiscation of church capital and land as well as the suppression of monasteries stands in striking contrast to the situation both in Peru and Ecuador, where anti-clericalism was kept in check until the end of the nineteenth century. "Because the power of the secular and regular clergy was effectively undermined during the first years of the republic, the Bolivian Church never represented a serious political challenge to state authority."[36]

The purchase from the government of land taken from the church undoubtedly diverted capital from more productive investments and contributed to the economic problems faced by Sucre. Moreover, the president's endeavors to attract British capital to revitalize the silver mines, many of which had been abandoned during the independence struggle, failed completely. And his tariff reductions, enacted in accordance with liberalism's free-trade credo, resulted in an inundation of English and French goods that brought ruin to local artisans.

Facing disaster on all sides, and his unpopularity rising steadily because of his overt partiality toward foreigners in filling top positions, Sucre had decided, even before the April coup and the Peruvian invasion, to withdraw from office before the end of 1828. At least the presence of one of Spanish America's ablest and most honorable military commanders at the Bolivian helm during the initial and highly critical period of the republic's life helped guarantee its independence and thus provided Bolivians with the opportunity to make their own attempts at shaping the national destiny.

Following several months of chaos, Andrés Santa Cruz in 1829 began what was to prove a fruitful ten-year presidency. Born in a tiny Bolivian village not far from La Paz in 1792, his father of pure Spanish extraction and his mother of Indian origins and said to be descended from Inca nobility, Santa Cruz had already gained distinction as a military commander and as a political administrator, having served briefly as Peru's chief executive following Bolívar's withdrawal. One of the ablest men of his generation in all Spanish America, despite his vast amour-propre and extreme sensitivity to slights, Santa Cruz has not always received from national writers the credit due his accomplishments. A common charge brought against him is that he was more Peruvian than Bolivian at heart, an allegation often supported by pointing to the fact that in the confederation he established with Peru (the confederation is discussed in the following chapter) Santa Cruz provided for two regional Peruvian congresses while allotting only one to Bolivia.

Put off by his authoritarian leanings and his replacing the utilitarian-rationalist influences in education with those of traditional Catholicism, Bolivian liberals have generally been negative in their assessments of Santa Cruz.[37] Conservatives, on the other hand, have not forgiven Santa Cruz his "Masonic sympathies."[38] In addition, those of aristocratic origins tended to resent his success in currying the favor of the Indian masses. What is more, they never tired of pointing to the copper hue of his skin, and one of Bolivia's primary exponents of white supremacy wrote: "Everybody knows that Marshal Andrés Santa Cruz is the ugliest mixed-blood of his time."[39]

Despite opposition and lack of funds in the treasury, Santa Cruz governed Bolivia wisely and, on the whole, successfully. During the decade of his rule, Bolivia may have been the best organized and most stable republic in Spanish America. Ultimately, what brought about his downfall was not the inadequacy of his internal policies but rather the foreign opposition evoked by the Peru–Bolivia confederation that he established. Defeated by invading Chilean armies, Santa Cruz went into exile in 1839.

Following two years of intense rivalry among various *caudillos*, José Ballivián came to the presidency in 1841. A man of humble origins and scanty education who had risen by dint of a successful military career, Ballivián did all in his power to make up for his cultural shortcomings. He read assiduously and even turned his hand to writing, producing a treatise on firearms and leaving behind at his death an unfinished novel.[40] He also showed excellent ability to judge character and surrounded himself with the ablest and best-educated men the republic afforded. Gaining acceptance by the creole landowning gentry of the south, Ballivián became their most resolute defender.

One of the president's most controversial actions was his encouragement of free trade as he reversed Santa Cruz's protectionist policies. Many artisans were driven out of business and some of them were reported in 1847 to be, together with their families, on the verge of starvation.[41] Numerous newspapers now launched a spirited campaign against the free trade that had encouraged "the invasion of capitalism from abroad."[42]

The drama and clash of personalities contributed even more than unpopular economic policies to Ballivián's downfall. The notorious schemer Casimiro Olañeta, as with previous presidents who had trusted him, played a role in Ballivián's undoing. Olañeta, who delighted in advancing the false claim that he had fathered the idea of Bolivian independence,[43] described himself in these terms: "Always frank and always noble, I never wound in the back."[44] As Ballivián had occasion to find out, though, Olañeta richly deserved the titles conferred upon him by some of his fellow citizens: "doctor in treasons" and "specialist in disloyalty." Thanks to this brilliant but unstable person, there has come into use in Bolivia the word *olañetismo*, designating duplicity and deceit.

In some ways Ballivián was his own worst enemy, because of his all-consuming passion for the fair sex. He was accused, in fact, of "having placed in danger the honor of all the married women of Bolivia."[45] One of his most notorious amours was conducted with the intelligent, vivacious, and attractive Argentine-born Juana Manuela Gorriti de Belzu, the wife of Manuel Isidoro Belzu. Enraged by these circumstances, Belzu lived only for vengeance. He sought to kill Ballivián in the national palace and, having failed in this attempt, led an insurrection that forced the president to flee over the roof tops for his life.

Having survived Belzu's two plots against him but apprehensive about more to come, Ballivián decided in 1847 that Bolivia was ungovernable and hastily undertook a diplomatic mission to Chile. Although he declared at the time "My most ardent desire is never to return again to Bolivia,"[46] he soon changed his mind and began plotting from abroad to oust Belzu, who had meanwhile seized the presidency. The ex-president continued to scheme until struck down by yellow fever shortly after arriving in Rio de Janeiro in 1852.

Tata Belzu, the Precursor of Andean Populism, 1848–1855 Belzu, who had joined Upper Peru's patriot armies in 1823 at the age of fifteen, came to the Bolivian presidency in 1848 after defeating his rivals for the office at the battle of Yamparáez that followed closely upon Ballivián's departure. His more than seven years in the presidency are most notable because of his unprecedented wooing of the masses, an approach in which he anticipated twentieth-century populism. Critics maintain he was forced to adopt this policy because his friendly overtures were rejected by the aristocrats who regarded the new president as a mestizo upstart and could never forgive him for his obscure background of poverty. It is also possible that Belzu, recognizing the precariousness of basing his rule on the support of the miniscule upper classes among whom *olañetismo* seemed all pervasive, had decided even before coming to his high office to seek a base of power among the lower classes.[47] Whatever the truth, the volatile leader quickly initiated a campaign against the aristocratic landowners, exiled many and seized their wealth, and occasionally incited the masses to burn and loot their homes.

In Bolivia's pre-Inca Kolla confederation the patriarchal, paternalistic head of each *ayllu* was called *Tata*. It is significant that soon the masses were hailing the unorthodox president as Tata Belzu. In him they saw the symbol of the father on whom they were happy to be dependent, confident that he, in his superior wisdom and charity, would attend to their needs. Occasionally the lower classes would even greet Belzu with cries of Viva nuestra dios Long live our god. Not even death seemed to rob the masses of their confidence in the power of their Tata to protect them. The burial service of Belzu culminated, amidst the delirium of the masses, when a fanatic grasped the cadaver's hand and with it blessed the multitude.[48]

Bolivia's 1846 population was estimated at 1.37 million, somewhat more than 700,000 of which was assumed to be Indian. Artisans engaged in the making of consumer goods were thought to number some 20,000,[49] thus constituting a significant percentage of the non-Indian populace. This group, made up overwhelming of mestizos, was won to Belzu—the Lion of the North as he was called by the admiring populace of his native La Paz—by a program of tariff protection.[50] Belzu further delighted the artisans by his xenophobic antagonism to foreign business interests in line with which he stipulated that all internal trade was to be conducted exclusively by Bolivian nationals and that "foreign wholesale commercial houses were to be severely restricted."[51]

At the same time, Belzu took steps to strengthen the syndicalist organization of the artisans along the strictly vertical, nondemocratic lines that had characterized the *gremios* (guilds) of the colonial past.[52] In his endeavor to firm up Bolivia's old corporativist structure, Belzu stands out as one of the earliest Andean political leaders who sought to mobilize the masses, from above; for the president insisted that each guild be placed under strict state control. A critic of these policies has aptly observed that Belzu's revival of the guilds was "based on a colonial mentality."[53] It was remarkable, though, to find a nine-teenth-century leader, priding himself on advanced ideas and widely denounced as a dangerous innovator, who was willing to be guided by colonial traditions.

Toward the end of Belzu's term in office, leading Bolivian intellectuals had begun to forge what could well have served as a rationale for the entire approach to sociopolitical organization that the president was following. In 1852, under the leadership of teachers such as Manuel Ignacio Salvatierra in Sucre, Krausism was introduced into Bolivia and soon established itself as one of the most important influences in intellectual circles. Even as in Peru, so also in Bolivia Krausism was interpreted in such manner as to render it ideologically compatible with the Catholic faith; and it served as the main bond between those many liberals and even more numerous conservatives intent upon preserving the patronalist-clientelist society against the perceived threat of society-wide individualism.[54]

The popular support enjoyed by Tata Belzu and the fact that Krausist intellectuals, whether of liberal or conservative persuasions, could justify his policies, even though they might object to his crudeness in keeping the masses entertained in a circuslike environment, served only to strengthen the hostility of most well-born and affluent Bolivians. One leading representative of the tightly knit aristocracy that remained inflexible in its opposition was José María Linares, born in Potosí of a Spanish father and a creole mother. Linares is said to have masterminded no fewer than thirty-three insurrections against Belzu.[55] The harassed president's problems were compounded by the economic crisis in which Bolivia continued to live. Nevertheless, Belzu succeeded in serving out his constitutional term in 1855, thus becoming the first Bolivian president not to be driven from office by rebellion. In his speech to the national congress at the conclusion of his term, Belzu made some very revealing statements that help establish him as a precursor of Andean populism:

> The popular masses ... have made their voices heard ... The appearance of this formidable power is a social fact of eminent transcendency ... Gentlemen, make the necessary reforms yourselves, if you do not want the people to make revolutions in their own way ... Give them [the popular masses] participation, ... guarantees, work, and subsistence; and then you will have nothing to fear from them. It is not with violence that we can moderate and contain the masses. Protect them in order that they will respect you. Establish the communism of justice in order to avoid political communism.[56]

Belzu's program was self-serving, intended above all else to provide him with the support necessary to remain in power. His appeal to the masses, his attempt to awaken them so as to dominate them better (which is always the fundamental objective of the populist leader in the Andean context), had not been prompted by any threat of upheaval from below. When, in the twentieth century, the social problem had assumed gravely menacing proportions, a number of political leaders and intellectuals devised programs bearing remarkable similarity to Belzu's. By then it had become necessary to take up Belzu's populist approach not just to serve individual political interests but also to safeguard a beleaguered class structure.[57]

Civilian and Military Rule, 1857–1879 José María Linares had been Belzu's major nemesis. Perhaps it was only just that this stern patrician, who prided himself—with considerable justification—on his own moral rectitude and was determined to force his norms of conduct upon others, for their own good of course, succeeded to the presidency two years after Belzu had completed his term. Linares was Bolivia's first civilian chief executive.

Convinced that Belzu had undermined the moral fiber of the masses by encouraging their dependence, Linares hoped to reform the nature of the Bolivians by instilling in them the traits of self-reliance.[58] Turning the national palace into a bleak monastery and punishing vice with an iron hand, Linares "undertook the greatest and most ill-fated crusade of moral regeneration that has been produced in Bolivia ... The grave *potosino* wished to impose a new

101

rhythm on political and private customs, a rhythm of austerity, discipline, and labor, very different from the character of the previous government."[59]

Persuaded that development would come to Bolivia not only as the result of implanting puritanical, capitalist motivation among its people but also as a consequence of an unfettered export-import economy, Linares brusquely abolished Belzu's protectionist policies and did all in his power to encourage the coming of foreign capital.[60] By enraging the artisans, Linares created a climate propitious to the plotters of *golpes de estado* (the Spanish term for coups d'état). Soon the plotters included two of the president's closest and most trusted associates. They struck in 1861 when Linares was in the midst of a serious illness and sent the ailing executive into an exile of poverty and stoic suffering, culminating in death. In other times, in different countries, it has been written, Linares might have been a great leader.[61] However, he could not abide the Bolivian people as he found them and was utterly unrealistic in his belief that he could transform them, by force, within a short time.

Bored by reform and outraged by heavy-handed methods bordering on terrorism to remake them, Bolivians found the man who seemed right for their mood in Mariano Melgarejo, who seized the presidential office by force in 1864. Noted for his excesses of nearly every conceivable type, Melgarejo was singularly uninterested in reforming himself or others. Born in 1820, the illegitimate son of an alcoholic father, Melgarejo, who early in life entered upon a military career in which he gained quick recognition because of his ferocity and personal bravery, became an alcoholic himself. Before entering the service Melgarejo, a tall and well-formed mestizo, had been apprenticed to a notary, under whom he learned to write with a "perfect hand," a skill of which he was enormously proud. One of the most revealing of the countless anecdotes told about Melgarejo has to do with his skill.

It seems that a particular decree had to be prepared one day, so Melgarejo told his young secretary, Isaac Tamayo, to write down the words as he, the president, dictated them. "Considering ...," Melgarejo began, and then lapsed into a long silence as he furiously paced the floor. "Considering ...," he began again, followed by another long silence and agitated pacing. Finally, despairing of finding the words, Melgarejo peered over his secretary's shoulder and when he saw the one word on the paper exploded: "What a terrible hand, no one could read that." Taking the secretary's chair Melgarejo announced that he would do the writing and then commanded his secretary, "Now, you dictate this decree." And thus it was done.[62]

In his despotic rule Melgarejo inflicted grave injustices on many of the well-to-do. The injustices suffered by the Indians, however, were far more serious; for Melgarejo unleashed an all-out assault against the communal holdings of countless communidades. If Belzu had sought legitimacy by gaining the support of the masses, Melgarejo sought it by making landowners of as many as possible of Bolivia's more successful urban middle sectors. And this necessitated taking land from the Indians.[63] The plundering of these lands brought into being a new class of landowners, including in its ranks the family of Juana Sánchez, Melgarejo's favorite mistress.[64]

The assault against church properties beginning just after independence had, by making rural property available to urban sectors, broadened the ranks of and strengthened the power of a landowning aristocracy. Under Melgarejo, the same process was repeated. The victims this time were not only the Indians, but also, indirectly, the artisans. Already buffeted by free trade policies, these local producers lost all hope of protecting their interests as political power shifted increasingly to landowners with a mania for importing foreign-made goods. Similar results had accompanied an 1852 Civil Code that facilitated establishment of new latifundia in Peru's sierra.

Widespread uprisings in 1871 brought the fall of Melgarejo and his flight to Lima, where later in the same year he was assassinated by José Sánchez, a brother of his long-time mistress. Like Casimiro Olañeta, Melgarejo, unwittingly, contributed a new word to the Bolivian vocabulary: *melgarejismo*, signifying amoral, debauched militarism. Perhaps the kindest appraisal of the founder of *melgarejismo* has been written by José Vázquez Machicado: "Melgarejo, when he was not dominated by the terrible demon of alcohol, had gentlemanly attitudes and was inclined toward noble gestures ... But, unfortunately, his lucid moments were very rare."[65]

It seemed that Bolivia would not receive better rule from the man mainly responsible for overthrowing Melgarejo and who replaced him in office: Agustín Morales. A coarse drunkard who some years before had tried, unsuccessfully, to assassinate Belzu—who, incidentally, under the most dramatic circumstances had been shot to death by Melgarejo during the latter's dictatorship—Morales seemed interested in little save private gain. Announcing a program of "more liberty, less government," Morales was soon removed from the scene by assassination, shot down in the national palace in late 1872 by a nephew. Two high-minded men—both of whom espoused the principles of civilian rule triumphant at the time in Peru under Manuel Pardo—followed in rapid succession in the presidency: Adolfo Ballivián, son of José Ballivián, whose promising term ended with death from illness in 1874; and Tomás Frías, one of the towering figures of intellect and integrity produced in nineteenth-century Andean America whose candor had earned him frequent exile. The aging Frías, though, was overthrown in May of 1876, just three days before scheduled elections which probably would have been won by a reputable civilian candidate. Leading the move that ousted Frías was Hilarión Daza, a military *caudillo* cast in a mold similar in many ways to Melgarejo's—though Daza lacked some of Melgarejo's excesses and also, it would seem, some of his bravery. Barely established in office, Daza was at once threatened by the usual series of insurrections and also by a massive demonstration staged in July of 1876 by the artisans of Sucre. They were protesting the continuing free-trade policies.

A railroad fever, spread largely by an adventurous U.S. Civil War colonel from Massachusetts named George Earl Church had gripped Bolivia toward the end of Melgarejo's rule. Ultimately, nothing save disappointment, recriminations, and lawsuits came from Church's scheme to link Bolivia to Brazil via a railroad around the Madeira-Mamoré falls of the Amazon river system. Thanks, however, to the ventures initiated in Peru by Henry Meiggs, the port of Mollendo was by 1874 joined to Puno on Lake Titicaca; and two steamers were now in service on that lake, connecting Puno with the Bolivian shore, which in turn was linked by a forty-mile wagon road to La Paz. The new transportation route helped turn Bolivian attention to the long-neglected coast, where guano and nitrate reserves up until this time had been worked mainly by Chileans.

Suffering the consequences of Melgarejo's mismanagement and currency debasement and further afflicted by the world depression that handicapped Pardo in Peru, the Bolivian economy was in worse shambles than ever when Daza took office. Desperately needing funds to prop up his government, the *caudillo* focused his hopes on the coastal resources, thus paving the way for armed conflict with Chile—since 1831 Spanish America's most stable republic. For this conflict Bolivia was, if possible, in even worse shape, politically and economically, than Peru.

ECUADOR

Independence from Spain and Gran Colombia   The people of the area soon to be named Ecuador are said to have proved their national self-awareness by the uprisings against Spanish domination that began in Quito in 1809, soon spread to other locales, and resulted in creation of the State of Quito, for which a constitution was promulgated in 1812.[66] Royalist troops brought a quick end to this venture, and the area had to await liberation until the arrival of forces from Venezuela and Colombia, and also from Peru. In May of 1882 Sucre, at the head of these forces, defeated the Spaniards at the battle of Pichincha (close to Quito). Bolívar arrived upon the scene shortly thereafter and the area of the future Ecuador was incorporated into the Confederation of Gran Colombia as the District of the South.[67]

This political arrangement could not endure, according to Ecuadoran writers, because of the national consciousness that had already developed in the District of the South. They may be right, but there are other reasons that account more directly for Ecuador's emergence as an independent republic. While *guayaquileno* upper classes were pleased that the arrangements imposed by Bolívar and Sucre spared them rule from Lima, a situation in which they would have been subordinate to the vested interests of the Lima-Callao business class, they were disturbed by certain features of the union with Gran Colombia. For one thing, the liberating armies, which stayed on after defeating the royalists, were made up largely of mulattoes and mestizos. Purportedly, the presence of the foreign dark-skinned soldiers gave a dangerous sense of power to the local mulattoes and blacks and threatened the coastal region with social upheaval. For the conservative upper-class *serranos*, the presence of the dark-skinned liberators, whose numbers included many officers with liberal, anticlerical convictions, was equally onerous.

Perceiving that separation from Gran Colombia was inevitable, Juan José Flores, the Venezuelan officer who had been the general prefect of the District of the South, wisely decided not to resist the local pressures. In May of 1830 an assembly of notables, meeting at the University of St. Thomas Aquinas in Quito, dissolved the union with the Confederation. Shortly a constituent assembly conferred the name Ecuador on the new republic and chose Flores, who had married a *quiteña* of the aristocratic Jijón family and gained acceptance in upper-class circles, as the first president.

The Age of Flores, Rocafuerte, and Urbina, 1830–1860   The Venezuelan president of Ecuador, a man of humble origins and little formal education but nonetheless endowed with far more than the ordinary measure of astuteness while happily undersupplied with vindictiveness,[68] faced enormous problems. To begin with, the mysterious assassination of Sucre which occurred just after Ecuador separated from Gran Colombia was attributed by certain hostile elements to Flores, who thus began his rule under a cloud—a cloud that has never entirely lifted even though no persuasive evidence linking him to the crime has ever appeared. Further, although Flores was accepted by many of the upper classes, his enemies continued to dwell upon his dark skin color, claiming his mother had been a Negress. Increasingly, moreover, the Venezuelan-Columbian troops on whose backing Flores' political power depended to some extent grew ever more unpopular, and the expense of supporting them placed an almost impossible burden on the treasury. Soon cries of "out with the Ethopians" reverberated in all corners.

Opposition to Flores intensified when he failed totally in his 1832 attempt to wrest a good portion of the Cauca valley away from Colombia to make it a part of Ecuador. The following year a group of liberal intellectuals, chafing under what they considered the authoritarianism of Flores' allegedly priest-ridden regime, began publication of *El Quiteño Libre*, a paper in which they denounced the pillaging of the national treasury by foreigners and raised demands for individual freedoms.[69] Officials left in command by Flores when he was temporarily out of Quito launched a violent suppression of the liberal critics in the course of which several of the latter were killed and their naked bodies strung up in a public plaza. Among those killed was Francis Hall, an English disciple of Jeremy Bentham who had fought in the battles of Pichincha and Ayacucho.

Accusing Flores, unfairly, of responsibility for the 1833 bloodletting, liberals found further cause for complaint the following year when Flores—quite wisely—called off the attempt to sell at public auction some of the communal property of Indian comunidades.[70] Meanwhile, Flores had failed to please a good many clergymen and was accused by them of leaning toward Freemasonry and of "ideological frivolity."[71]

In 1833 liberalism's ablest Ecuadoran spokesman, Vicente Rocafuerte, had returned to his native Guayaquil after fourteen years spent traveling in various parts of the world, including Mexico, Cuba, the

United States, Spain, and numerous other European countries.[72] The year after his return Rocafuerte became involved in a Guayaquil uprising against Flores. The insurrection failed and Rocafuerte, through the treachery of comrades, was turned over to Flores. The wily Venezuelan, whose term was about to end, recognized his inability to turn back the rising tide of opposition and therefore arranged matters so that presidential power would pass to Rocafuerte. By no means all Ecuadorans accepted the transaction, and only by defeating a sizeable army in the bloody battle of Miñarica was Flores able to implement his plan. Thus the liberal Rocafuerte came to power under the aegis of Flores, who remained in Ecuador with the hope of returning to the presidency upon the completion of Rocafuerte's term in 1839.[73]

During his years of foreign travel, Rocafuerte had if anything become more firmly set in the ideology of the radical, non-Spanish Enlightenment that had captured his youthful fancy. In one of the statements that best reveals his bent of mind, Rocafuerte, while in Mexico in 1831, wrote: "Religious monopoly is just as prejudicial to the spread of morality and development of the human intelligence as mercantile monopoly is to the expansion of commerce and the prosperity of the national industry, and thus the triple unity of political, religious, and mercantile liberty is the dogma of modern societies."[74] For Rocafuerte, economic progress and development, assumed to be the fruit of individual liberty and initiative, could not come about unless liberty and individualism were guaranteed and nourished by a democratic political order; but, the political culture could not assume a democratic character unless the religious culture guaranteed the free conscience of the private individual against all outside pressure and coercion. Understandably, the *guayaquileño* was particularly impressed by the manner in which the United States, through religious tolerance, "had skilfully connected Christianity to the political and economic systems of independence and liberty."[75]

Very quickly upon his return to Ecuador, however, Rocafuerte had concluded that the quest for progress through unfettered individual liberty could not begin until people had acquired the values that established a connection between private productivity and virtue. If too much freedom was introduced into a society not properly prepared, it would result only in chaos and the undermining of order, without bringing progress.[76] Persuaded that anarchy was a more immediate danger than despotism,[77] Rocafuerte set himself to the establishment of an authoritarian regime, and thus it was that while a liberal in theory he became a conservative in practice.[78] He was not long in office before writing to Flores that the backwardness of Ecuador "makes enlightened despotism necessary."[79]

Rocafuerte's authoritarian efficiency, the product of his intelligence, immense integrity, and administrative skills, brought order to Ecuador, an expansion of education, a program of road building, and fiscal regularity. All of this was achieved despite the need for the president to accept 21.5 percent of the debt incurred by Gran Colombia in waging the independence struggle, thereby saddling the country with a huge financial burden. Not until 1974 was Ecuador at last able to pay off its obligation on this debt.

Returning to the presidency in 1839 as planned, Flores named Rocafuerte governor of the Province of Guayaquil and settled into a rather unproductive four-year rule. When 1843 arrived and his official term ended, Flores decided to extend his tenture. A constituent assembly that he summoned framed a new constitution, "the Charter of Slavery" as it was called by the opposition, and elected Flores to a new eight-year term. The clergy was outraged because the constitution excluded priests from certain high political offices and did not invoke the name of God. On the other hand the anticlericals—the designations conservative and liberal had not yet come into wide use in Ecuador—were infuriated by the constitutional provision establishing Catholicism as the state religion and excluding the public practice of all other faiths. What most angered Ecuadorans, however, regardless of ideological preferences, was the prospect of eight more years of rule by foreigners. To the young Gabriel García Moreno the prospect was so abhorrent that he organized a plot, unsuccessful as it turned out, to assassinate Flores.

From Lima, where he had gone into exile, Rocafuerte smuggled into his native land various pamphlets denouncing Flores. In one of them, printed in 1844, he wrote: "Alas, the white oppressors of the peninsula were less oppressive than the Negro vandals who have replaced them."[80] The following year Ecuador was shaken by one of its bloodiest convulsions, touched off by an insurrection in Guayaquil against the foreign president and his foreign retainers. The rebellion triumphed in March of 1845 and Flores was forced to leave the country.

Because their uprising had occurred in March (*marzo*), the now successful anti-Flores groups called themselves the *Marcistas*. A heterogeneous coalition, the *Marcistas* included liberal ideologues such as the renowned poet José Joaquín Olmedo, justly famed for his ode to Bolívar, who was reputed to be a deist. The coalition also included some of the most staunchly conservative clergymen, as well as successful merchants and businessmen, among them Vicente Ramón Roca who served as the first *Marcista* president, 1845–1849.

Divided among themselves, beset by financial problems, and having to face the constant threat of invasions from abroad organized by Flores who hoped either to return to power himself or to impose a European prince on an Ecuadoran throne,[81] the *Marcistas* lost in 1847 the man who may well have been Ecuador's greatest nineteenth-century asset. Vicente Rocafuerte died at the age of sixty-four in Lima while on a diplomatic mission aimed at enlisting support against an anticipated Flores invasion. Before expiring he confessed to one of Andean America's noblest figures, the about-to-be excommunicated Peruvian priest and apostle of liberalism, Francisco de Paula González Vigil.[82]

Unlike the usual situation, Rocafuerte, it has been remarked, was more esteemed by his contemporaries than by subsequent generations.[83] One reason for this is that during his lifetime the battle lines between conservatism and liberalism had not hardened. Shortly they would, and once this occurred conservatives would find it impossible to forgive Rocafuerte for his liberal theories, while liberals proved incapable of pardoning his conservative practices.

The no-holds-barred confrontation between conservatism and liberalism, destined to reap havoc for a century, began to shape up during the rule of José María Urbina. Coming to power through a *golpe* in 1851, Urbina subsequently arranged his constitutional "election" to the presidency and remained in office until 1856. He then dominated the political scene from behind the throne until 1860 when his fortunes abruptly declined. The next fifteen years of his life, spent almost entirely in exile, he devoted to plotting to regain power.

His country's most audacious general of the period, Urbina frankly asserted that the armed forces must form the base of public power in young republics. Anticlerical, in the colonial mold of the countless laymen who had resented having to compete for influence and power with the clergy, Urbina was obsessed with the desire to remove priests altogether from politics, and to do so at once. In 1852 he exiled a group of Spanish Jesuits—most of them arch-conservative Carlists— who had been admitted into Ecuador following their ouster from Colombia by a liberal regime. For his action, prompted by the conviction that the Jesuits could not refrain from political intervention,[84] Urbina was denounced from some quarters as a Mason and as an

109

enemy of the church and society. Leading the attack against him was García Moreno, the man who had plotted unsuccessfully to assassinate Flores. A defender of the clergy and an ardent antimilitarist, famous for his statement that the black coat must prevail over the red coat,[85] García Moreno was doubly unacceptable to Urbina. The military president exiled his antagonist in 1853, branding him a "traitor and enemy of order."[86]

The major ingredient of Ecuador's emergent liberalism, as shaped by Urbina, was anticlericalism. Other ingredients, however, were also present. Urbina freed the country's slaves in 1851—three years before Castilla took this step in Peru. Thereafter, Urbina sought and to a considerable degree gained the support of the dark-skinned *costeño* lower classes. This situation was denounced by many whites, who objected in particular to Urbina's shock troops, made up largely of blacks, many of whom were liberated slaves. On the whole, Urbina favored the interests of the coastal business classes as opposed to those of the *altiplano* landowners. Under him, therefore, regional as well as ideological divisiveness became more pronounced.

Regional, ideological, and racial tensions, as well as personality clashes, brought Ecuador in 1859—the Terrible Year as it is called by national historians—to the worst state of anarchy it has experienced since independence. Cuenca and Loja both declared their autonomy, various *caudillos* fought for power in Quito and Guayaquil, a Peruvian army under Castilla invaded the country, Colombians came to the brink of an invasion, and the division of the country among its neighbors seemed a real possibility. For a moment García Moreno, who had returned to the country in 1856, schemed to place Ecuador under a French protectorate. It was not necessary to follow through on this scheme, for by 1861 García Moreno, thanks to his shrewd bargaining skills and the military prowess of Flores, now back in Ecuador and allied with the antimilitarist who had once sought to kill him, had established himself as president and was rapidly restoring order.

The Age of García Moreno and the Aftermath, 1861–1883   Born in Guayaquil in 1821, García Moreno had, following the death of his father which left the family in straightened circumstances, studied in Quito, where he entered the university and received a scholarship from the Rocafuerte administration. In 1847 he married an older woman from a distinguished Quito family. His detractors have always been ready to accuse him of marrying for self-interest rather than love and some go so far as to accuse him of poisoning his wife in order to

110

marry (in 1866) her attractive young niece. The fact that not the slightest proof has ever emerged to substantiate this charge does not bother García Moreno's critics; for they, even as his champions, have been guided almost exclusively by passion and prejudice in assessing this controversial figure.

As a young man, García Moreno had been known for his liberal ideas, his libertine ways, and especially his Don Juan escapades. Travel in Europe in 1849, however, seems to have produced a profound effect, causing the *guayaquileño* to become more serious and more disciplined, and also more devout in his religious practices. The transformation was completed in 1855 and 1856 when García Moreno studied chemistry and the writings of eminent Catholic theologians and political philosophers in France. His personal experiences seem to have influenced his attitudes toward governing his country. In his own case, liberalism and religious indifference had gone hand-in-hand with personal debauchery and lack of self-control, while religious fervor had been intertwined with a life of rigorous self-control and spartan discipline. After coming to the presidency, García Moreno set out to rekindle religious fervor among Ecuadorans in the expectation that the entire country could be made to undergo a transformation paralleling his own. There was little doubt in the president's mind that he could succeed in remaking Ecuador because, as he stressed again and again in his letters, God was on his side.

An enormously complex man, García Moreno was not without his contradictions. Reactionary in some aspects, he was in other ways a modernist who could be boldly innovative. Cruel and bloodthirsty in the eyes of his enemies—one of them has described him as the Saint of the Gallows[87]—he could also be gentle and loving with his family and show enormous compassion toward his fellow citizens, as when between his first and second terms he headed an operation to bring relief to earthquake victims. Reviled by secularists for purportedly surrendering control of Ecuador to priests, he was disliked and opposed by the bishop and much of the clergy of Cuenca who felt that the president was tyrannizing the church.

García Moreno was convinced that "modern civilization, created by Catholicism, degenerates and becomes hybrid in proportion to the distance by which it separates itself from Catholic principles."[88] Further, he regarded the church, with its hierarchical organization and its rigidly institutionalized structure, as the only backbone that could prevent a society from becoming invertebrate. The trouble was that in the Ecuador of the 1850s, the church had itself become weak and even degenerate. Therefore García Moreno considered his first task to be the reform of the church. This, he believed, could not be accomplished unless the Vatican came to exercise a greater degree of control over the church in Ecuador than in the colonial period or in the republic up to that time. The desire for reform of the clergy under Vatican supervision led García Moreno to undertake the negotiations with Rome that resulted in a concordat, signed in 1862 and promulgated the following year.[89] This instrument, which led to the arrival of an apostolic delegate with full powers to institute reforms, bestowed vast temporal powers upon the church, particularly in the field of education. With the church accorded the major influence in shaping the nation's cultural environment, the state, on the other hand, was assured a measure of administrative control over the ecclesiastical institution. The concordat, for example, gave to the president the right, to be exercised with the advice of the episcopacy and always subject to Vatican approval, to select archbishops and bishops and also to appoint to lesser benefices. With the promulgation of the concordat, the president seemed to be well on the way toward achieving his primary purpose of strengthening the civil power by uniting it to a revitalized religious power.[90]

The enemies of García Moreno have never tired of charging him with introducing theocracy into Ecuador.[91] This is not true if one accepts the common definition of theocracy, according to which it is rule of a state by God and hence government by priests claiming to rule with divine authority. García Moreno "never recognized a power superior to his own,"[92] and he brooked neither opposition nor interference from priests in exercising his sovereignty. Had fate not placed in the Vatican a man, Pius IX, who happened to be a kindred soul, García Moreno could very well have clashed with the papacy.

Ecuador's liberals, however, had their own definition of theocracy, just as conservatives had theirs of the atheistic state. For conservatives, it will be recalled from the preceding chapter, the atheistic state was one in which religion and politics were not mutually interfused. For liberals, the theocratic state was one which accepted, even to a minimal degree, the interpenetration of religion and politics. As liberals defined the term, therefore, García Moreno did encourage theocracy. And they have never forgiven him for what they regard as an endeavor to turn back the tide of secularism and to "keep his people isolated from the dynamic currents of their century."[93]

Angered by the administration's ultramontanism which had given to the Vatican an influence in Ecuador's intertwined ecclesiastical and civil affairs more extensive than it had ever wielded up to that time, liberals were sent into a blind rage by the large influx of foreign priests that García Moreno encouraged. Prior to this, liberals had been confident that time was on their side; for vocations among the Ecuadorans had declined dramatically and the church had been falling into slack and dissolute ways, with an accompanying diminution of influence. Now the situation was changed; scores of foreign religious were arriving to take charge of the educational structure that García Moreno was energetically enlarging, and at the same time the native clergy were taking on a new discipline and vitality. When García came to power, the total number of priests in Ecuador, secular and regular, was probably under 350; in 1871, owing mainly to the influx of foreigners, the number stood at 759—one priest for about every 1,000 Ecuadorans.[94]

García Moreno liked to contend that Catholicism was the most vital element of national identity and the only cohesive element that could maintain the patria intact. Yet he had had to turn to foreigners to provide Ecuador with what was said to be the true source of its national essence, a situation that left him vulnerable to the barbs of liberals and that also provoked numerous uprisings against him.

In 1864, the stern autocrat's regime was saved by the military talents of the old general and former president, Juan José Flores, who defeated an invading army organized by Urbina. The ailing Flores died shortly after this victory. With the liberal threat apparently contained, García Moreno turned power over to a carefully selected successor in 1865, but two years later, finding the puppet wanting, removed him from power. Deciding in 1869 that the country once again required his firm-handed rule in order to save it from a new liberal threat, García Moreno seized the presidency and wrote a new constitution. One of its clauses provided that in order to be a citizen a person had to be a Catholic.

What was especially galling to liberal intellectuals about the citizenship provision of the new charter was the fact that García Moreno, the foreign clergy, and Pius IX with his *Syllabus of Errors* (1864) and shortly with the definition of papal infallibility (1870) were insisting on ever-narrower definitions of what it meant to be a Catholic. In the past, upper-class men had been left very much alone by the clergy and had often approached their faith in a highly individualistic manner. Now, in a way totally at odds with religious traditions of the colonial period and early republic, they were being told they must conform to narrow and inflexible norms established largely by for-

113

eigners but enforced by a martinet in the national presidency. If they demurred, the penalty was excommunication which brought with it, after the 1869 constitution, loss of all civil rights.

Typical of the Ecuadoran liberals who were outraged by the new constitution was García Moreno's long-time bête noire, the brilliant man of letters from Ambato, Juan Montalvo. A liberal, who nonetheless had a vast regard for tradition (perhaps even more than García Moreno whose policies were often thoroughly antitraditional), Montalvo found his model for the religious toleration that he desired not so much in the United States as in medieval Spain. An elitist, in the humanist-Krausist tradition, who believed that hierarchical social organization could be maintained without supernatural sanctions and appeals to divine law,[95] Montalvo was at the same time a Catholic in the customary sense in which upper-class Spanish American intellectuals were Catholics—in their own way, that is, defining for themselves their relationships to God and not accepting clerical intrusion in the matter. Montalvo condemned the tyrant for the manner in which he invaded the sanctuary of upper-class intellectuals and sought to suppress their rights to think freely and to develop, thereby, their full human potential. No person who tolerated such an invasion, Montalvo believed, could retain the independence of judgment required if one was to play a responsible role in the governing of states. For him, persons who were Catholics, as defined by García Moreno, could not be good citizens.

Despite the bitter opposition he evoked, García Moreno brought greater progress to Ecuador than any president before him—or since him, for that matter. The divisiveness that he was spawning would plague the country after his death, but while he was alive his autocratic ways kept it in check. Esmeraldas was at last connected by road with Quito, great progress was made toward completing a Guayaquil-Quito road, and the first kilometers of the Transandean Railway were laid. Unlike Peru's Balta and Piérola, the Ecuadoran leader was cautious and responsible in his approach to economic modernization and refused to assume huge foreign debts in order to advance more hastily toward his goals.[96] While encouraging cacao and quinine exports, García Moreno was ahead of many liberals in realizing that development could not come solely from an expanding export-import trade. Consequently he established incentives for importation of machinery from the United States with which to establish native industry and also devised a protectionist policy.[97]

All the while the vigorous president concerned himself with the massive expansion of education. "Schools, schools above all," he wrote, "and our lovely patria will take advantage of the roads, of the scientific instruction, . . . because it will have morality and the means of deriving advantages from these goods." An another time, as he urged the creation of new schools, the president wrote: "We are sowing for the future [and] the diffusion of teaching, with a basis in Catholicism, will make our country the most advanced and happy in the world."[98] Even liberals were impressed by the Polytechnic School opened in 1870, by the large number of scholarships for impoverished university students, and by the fact that primary school enrollment rose from 13,000 to over 32,000 between 1865 and 1875.[99] But they objected, it goes without saying, to the religious focus of education.

Through the strengthening of corporative organizations, including Indian comunidades whose communal landholdings he took pains to protect[100]—much to the disgust of liberal intellectuals—García Moreno sought, with the help of the foreign clergy, to establish a connection between piety and productive enterprise. However, such enterprise was to be undertaken not for the advantage of the private citizen so much as for the interests of the group of which he was a member, and to which he was subordinate, and also for the advance of the nation as a whole. Predictably, some liberal pensadores grumbled at the manner in which this corporativist approach stifled individualism.

For García Moreno, who was seeking a way toward development that did not require the society-wide individualism associated with liberalism, progress depended not only upon efficient, skilled, and productive functionally organized groups but also upon state planning and economic intervention as well. In the Ecuador that he foresaw, the national elite would consist basically of technocrats in high bureaucratic posts. Obviously this did not appeal to businessmen who embraced the liberal credo. To them, getting ahead meant private success as a capitalist entrepreneur; and success was to be achieved through freedom from government control.

Surely a major reason for the enduring liberal outrage against the Messianic president derives from the fact that he achieved the country's greatest progress in history through formulas that were totally opposed to liberalism's tenets. Thereby he provided refutation to the claims of liberals that they alone understood how to achieve progress and to their assertions, voiced so eloquently by Rocafuerte, that the influence of Catholicism in the temporal order was incompatible with progress. By changing the customary temporal impact of the time-honored Hispanic-Andean religious beliefs through encouraging the immigration of progressive Catholic thinkers from advanced countries, García Moreno—who anticipated R. H. Tawney in the conviction that Catholicism could be as conducive to capitalist development as Protestantism—established his own distinctive approach to the issue of traditionalism versus modernity. Frustrated because the Catholic disciplinarian was actually achieving progress through means that allegedly could not produce it, liberals were forced to ignore the advances of the Garcian period and to assert the illegitimacy of the president's rule on the grounds of his despotism and purported personal depravity.[101]

García Moreno provided new grounds for the charges of despotism when he arranged his reelection to yet another presidential term. As a result of the reelection, he noted in a July 17, 1875 letter to Pius IX, "the [Masonic] lodges of neighboring countries will vomit forth against me all kinds of atrocious insults and horrible calumnies." He concluded: "I need more than ever the Divine protection to live and die in defense of our Holy religion, and of this small republic which God has wished me to continue governing."[102]

When he wrote this, García Moreno had only a few more weeks to live in defense of his religion and republic. On August 6 he was struck down by a group of assassins organized by the Colombian Faustino Lemo Rayo. The assassins included several youthful, idealistic Ecuadoran liberals, their passions inflamed by the diatribes against the dictator that Juan Montalvo had been writing in exile.

By the great emphasis that he always placed on religious issues, García Moreno obscured every other aspect of his administration. Understandably, then, it is on the religious issue that he has most commonly been judged by his own generation and subsequent ones.[103] García Moreno's responsibility for allowing theological disputations to obscure every other facet of national existence, at a time when the tide of secularism was advancing inexorably throughout the world, is a heavy one. Furthermore, by dealing total defeat to the liberals in their desire to reduce the interpenetration of religion and politics, he made it inevitable that the liberals would settle for nothing less than total victory of their own in the quest for vengeance.

Upon the assassination of García Moreno, it appeared likely that the country would be convulsed by a struggle between the conservative and liberal camps. In 1877 the archbishop of Quito was killed by poison drunk from the chalice as he presided over Good Friday services, a sensational incident which seriously intensified the bitter-

ness of the conservative-liberal contention. The following year a leading liberal statesman was assassinated in Guayaquil. By now, "conservatives, in the eyes of liberals, even as liberals in the eyes of
conservatives, were infamous rogues and vile assassins."[104]

Ignacio de Veintemilla managed to postpone the all-out battle
between conservatives and liberals. This military *caudillo,* idolized by
his troops, seized power in 1876 and ruled until 1883. Despite his
heavy drinking habits and passion for gambling, Veintemilla proved a
crafty ruler. In the early days of his rule he toyed with liberal ideas,
but much to the relief of conservatives soon abandoned them, welcomed the Jesuits back into the country, and in 1882 signed a new
concordat with the Vatican not unlike the 1862 instrument.

In a style reminiscent of Belzu's in Bolivia, Veintemilla successfully wooed the masses. His ability to please them by festivals and
lavish public dances and by employment on public works projects
rested upon the prosperity that Ecuador enjoyed during most of his
rule. The country's relatively good times resulted from the export of
cacao, coffee, hides, and timber and from its capture of a larger than
usual share of Pacific coast trade when Chile, Peru, and Bolivia were
locked in the War of the Pacific (1879–1883).[105]

A widespread series of rebellions toppled the caudillo in 1883—
despite the heroic endeavors of his attractive niece Marietta de Veintemilla who fought the insurgents in Quito while her uncle sought
to suppress an uprising in Guayaquil.[106] For a time after Veintemilla's
downfall, it seemed that moderate conservatives and liberals might
be able to join together in common political programs. But divisiveness was still too deep and extremists on both sides doomed the
conciliation attempts. As of the mid-1880s Ecuador was more deeply
ravaged by internal cleavages than Peru and Bolivia had been by the
conquering armies of Chile. And for Ecuador, recovery from the self-
inflicted wounds would be longer in coming than Peruvian-Bolivian
rehabilitation following the War of the Pacific.

5

Rivalry, Diplomacy, War, and Reconstruction in the Nineteenth Century

The internal history of the Andean republics has frequently revolved about the attempt of elites to maintain domination over clients and to prevent the widespread establishment of interdependent, pluralistic relationships among parties of more or less equal power. Foreign affair involving these republics have been carried out in the same spirit. Relationships of genuine interdependence have consistently been spurned as one republic, regarding itself as the stronger, has sought to establish domination over a neighbor country. Thus internal patronalism has found its external counterpart in imperialism, however small the sphere in which that imperialism is exercised. This analogy, however, cannot be pushed too far, because the harmony that has often characterized asymmetrical social relationships within countries has been little evident in the foreign relations among the Andean republics.

An Ecuadoran has commented that his country finds itself crushed between two robbers, "the one to the north [Colombia], the other to the south (Peru)."[1] Fortunately for Ecuador, it has been possible to play off the robbers against each other, for each in its own quest of domination is resolved not to allow the other one to gain clear-cut supremacy over the victim in the middle. Ecuador, then, is both blessed and cursed by its position as a buffer zone between two more powerful neighbors.

The situation is rendered more complex by various games of leapfrog diplomacy. Thus Colombia in order to gain a freer hand in its dealings with Ecuador may encourage Chile to keep Peru off balance through territorial and displomatic disputes. Peru, on the other hand, has often encouraged Brazil to press ahead with its various claims against Colombia. And, in order to relieve Chilean pressures, applied often with the blessings of Colombia, Peru may encourage Argentina to heat up its traditional enmity with Chile; whereupon Chile may urge Brazil to intensify its rivalry with Argentina.

In some ways Bolivia's situation as a buffer republic is even more complex than Ecuador's. Bordering directly on Brazil, Argentina, Chile, and Peru (as well as Paraguay), Bolivia has had four major aggressors to contend against. According to an understandably sensitive Bolivian writer, the country's powerful neighbors consistently "have worked against the sovereign life of our nation."[2] Bolivia has survived by playing its not very friendly neighbors off against each other, but frequently its national interests have suffered grievously in the vicious balance-of-power game.[3] Like Ecuador, Bolivia by mid-twentieth century found itself with approximately one-half the territory claimed at independence.[4]

Peru has also had to seek protection of its vital interests by resorting to balance-of-power diplomacy. Seen as a menace, as a would-be imperialist *patrón*, by its two weakest neighbors, Ecuador and Bolivia, Peru recognizes contiguous Colombia as a more-or-less equal rival. With its two other neighbors, Chile and Brazil, Peru has generally been at a distinct power disadvantage. In order to protect itself against their often unfriendly designs, Peru has had to enter into complex intrigues especially with Argentina, casting itself thereby in a position of clientelism vis-à-vis the statesmen of Buenos Aires.[5]

In the colonial period, the Spanish crown maintained an uneasy calm among the rival components of its American empire. Independence from Spain was viewed by the former colonies as providing the opportunity to press ahead in settling regional grudges and grievances in line with uninhibited self-interest. However, through balance-of-power diplomacy the weaker republics thwarted the more grandiose designs of the mightier and managed to cling to part of their national domain and to some semblance of sovereignty.

With the entry of the United States upon the scene, a new dimension was added to South American balance-of-power politics. From the late nineteenth century on, whenever Andean republics felt unable to protect their interests adequately through power manipulations as traditionally carried out through sister republics, they could turn to the United States for support. Or, they could simultaneously curry U.S. backing while dealing through customary channels in Latin America, all the while playing off one process against the other. Complicating procedures still further, the Andean republics could upon occasion seek to draw England and European powers into the diplomatic cockpit. Sometimes their overtures to European countries were extended in all sincerity. Just as often, the overtures were intended to pressure the United States to move so as to block the possibility of intervention from outside the hemisphere, thereby defending the principles associated with the Monroe Doctrine. This Doctrine the Andeans alternately extolled and condemned, as it suited their purposes.

With the southward flow of its diplomatic influence, the United States became the pretender to the role of arbiter once played by Spain in the regionalist labyrinth of South America. It is virtually impossible to know if Washington's expanding diplomatic presence brought any improvement to the process of resolving inter-Andean disputes within a self-contained Latin American power structure. What is certain is that the attempt to act as mediator, often at the behest of Andean statesmen, earned for the United States a share in the bitterness that the Andean—and other South American—republics felt toward each other.

INTERVENTION AND BALANCE-OF-POWER POLITICS TO THE 1870s

Close upon Bolívar's departure from Peru, a liberal faction gained control over that country in 1827. The following year the Peruvian liberals framed a new constitution and prepared for war against Gran Colombia, aided and abetted in their schemes by their ideological counterparts in Colombia. It was hoped that a Peruvian victory over Bolívar's forces would discredit the increasingly conservative Liberator and allow the liberals to gain power in Colombia and at the same time strengthen their position in Peru as well as in Ecuador. Thus throughout Andean America the way would be prepared for a new age of progress under liberal aegis.

The liberal grand strategy came to naught when in the major northern campaign the invading Peruvians were defeated by the armies of Gran Colombia at the battle of Portete de Tarqui in Ecuador, fought at the beginning of 1829. The outcome of this engagement strengthened the hand of Gran Colombia's conservatives while simultaneously weakening the liberal rulers of Peru. Taking advantage of this situation Peruvian General Agustín Gamarra, with the support of his country's conservatives, staged a *golpe* and seized the presidency.

By this time Gamarra was already obsessed with the idea of ending the existence of Bolivia as an independent republic. His dream was to reestablish the union of Peru and Upper Peru (now rechristened Bolivia) that had prevailed in colonial times until the jurisdictional changes accompanying the creation of the La Plata viceroyalty in 1776. By 1831 Gamarra's armies were poised on the Bolivian border, ready for an invasion. The Peruvian president was all the more eager for the fray because of personal enmity toward Santa Cruz who was now the president of Bolivia. At the final minute, Chilean diplomacy averted the invasion and Bolivia and Peru signed a short-lived treaty of peace and amity.

It was now Santa Cruz's turn to try his hand at restoring union. Born in the environs of La Paz, Santa Cruz was a mestizo from the Andean heartland of the old Inca Empire of Tahuantinsuyo. His Peruvian rival Gamarra, also a mestizo, came from Cuzco. Both men respected the wisdom of their Inca forebears who had forged the original bonds between Peru and Upper Peru. To both men it seemed only logical that these bonds, strengthened during almost the entirety of the Spanish colonial period, should be reestablished. The dream of union was so logical that if Santa Cruz and Gamarra had not attempted to realize it other *caudillos* surely would have done so.

Strengthening his grasp on power in Bolivia through his efficient authoritarian administration, Santa Cruz turned his attention increasingly to politics in neighboring Peru, hoping to gain support for his schemes among Peruvians who were discontent with the central government in Lima. Particularly in Arequipa and the southern highlands the Bolivian president found Peruvians who were attracted by the sort of decentralized Peru-Bolivia confederation he had in mind. As Santa Cruz envisioned it, the confederation would be divided into three semiautonomous political jurisdictions, each with its own congress: North Peru, with its capital in Lima; South Peru, its capital to be either Arequipa or Cuzco; and Bolivia, with La Paz as its capital.

In his own country, Santa Cruz received the greatest support for confederation from La Paz. Through confederation the commercially-minded *paceños* would have derived the advantage of unencumbered access to the Peruvian port of Arica. Communities farther to the south and to the east in Bolivia, however, could anticipate little direct advantage from a revival of the colonial Arica-La Paz trade route. In fact, the increase in foreign commerce that would result might well threaten artisans in Cochabamba, Chuquisaca (Sucre), and elsewhere. What is more, Bolivians from most of the important cities, other than La Paz, objected strenuously to the provisions for two political subdivisions within the confederation for Peru while there was to be only one for Bolivia. This, they insisted, would render Bolivia forever subordinate to Peru. All the while Bolivians in the Tarija and Santa Cruz regions objected to the confederation on the grounds it would impede trade with Argentina and Brazil by focusing commercial interest exclusively on Pacific ports.[6]

Despite the opposition, Santa Cruz played his cards shrewdly and selected military leaders who proved efficient in carrying out an invasion of Peru. As a result, the confederation came into being in 1836. But Santa Cruz's moment of triumph led only to new difficulties.

To Juan Manuel de Rosas, the dictator who from Buenos Aires had established his power over the republic that would later bear the name Argentina, the confederation portended a shift in the South American balance of power that could only be disadvantageous to his country. The fact is that many of the Buenos Aires ruling classes had never abandoned the hope of annexing Bolivia—a hope that had led to invasion of Upper Peru by *porteño* armies during the independence struggle. Obviously, the Peru-Bolivia confederation thwarted this aspiration. More important, the confederation meant that Bolivia's foreign trade would be conducted through Pacific coast outlets; and, if the silver industry should ever revive, this could entail serious economic losses for Argentina. Logically, then, from the viewpoint of Argentine interests, Rosas sent an army into Bolivia, its purpose being to end the confederation and to annex the town of Tarija along with its surrounding territory.[7] Bolivian troops under General Felipe Braun defeated the Argentines in three bloody battles and thereby significantly altered the future course of Andean history. Had the Argentines triumphed, a strong Argentina-Bolivia axis might have been established and Bolivia would then have been less vitally absorbed in Pacific coast balance-of-power politics.

General Braun's victory granted only a short reprieve to the confederation; for the main threat to Santa Cruz came not from Argentina but from Chile, and the reasons were largely economic. At the outset of the independence period the Chilean port of Valparaíso was well on the way to commercial dominance in the South American Pacific.[8] Now, in the 1830s, Chile was ruled by elites among whom the coastal banking and commercial interests were becoming increasingly important. These interests, led by the country's most powerful political figure Diego Portales, were intent upon retaining and expanding Valparaíso's commercial preeminence. Understandably, they feared that the confederation might shift the economic scales in favor of their northern neighbors, causing the Lima–Callao complex to eclipse Valparaíso.

The first military expedition sent by Chile against the confederation was roundly defeated. A second expedition, far more formidable and reenforced by Peruvians who opposed the confederation, including Gamarra and Ramón Castilla, defeated the Santa Cruz forces at Yungay, nestled in the Andes north of Lima. The battle took place in January of 1839, and Santa Cruz was fortunate to escape the field with his life. Immediately following this battle the confederation was abolished and Peru and Bolivia went their separate ways once more as independent republics.[9]

The end of the confederation, greeted with wild rejoicing in Chuquisaca (secure once again as the capital) where the paceño Santa Cruz had never been trusted,[10] marked Bolivia's second winning of independence. As was true on the first occasion, independence resulted not only from the desire of Bolivians, motivated both by selfish and patriotic considerations, independence resulted also from the fact that Bolivia was indispensable as a buffer state in South America's balance-of-power diplomacy and thus could not be allowed to pass out of existence as a separate state.

Agustín Gamarra, once again the president of Peru following the battle of Yungay, failed to learn this lesson. So far as he was concerned, the time had at last arrived for him to attempt the deed that had always inflamed his imagination: the establishment of a centralized Peru–Bolivia confederation under his authoritarian rule. Gamarra refused to be deterred by Chilean diplomacy, as he had allowed himself to be in 1831, and his armies swept into Bolivia. The main battle took place at Ingavi on November 18, 1841. There, owing mainly to the fact that Peruvian General Miguel San Román followed his usual custom of withdrawing while the battle was still in progress, the Bolivians under José Ballivián defeated the invaders. Gamarra met his death at Ingavi and with him there perished serious thought of confederation. For several years after Ingavi, the action in Andean diplomatic intrigues shifted away from the Bolivian to the Ecuadoran scene.

In 1840 Colombia (whose official denomination at the time was still New Granada) was convulsed by a civil struggle known as the War of the Supremes. Ecuador's president Juan José Flores intervened in this struggle, hoping that if he chose and aided the eventual winner he might be rewarded with the Pasto region of southern Colombia that he had tried unsuccessfully to seize by force of arms in 1832. Nothing came of Flores' schemes to turn Colombia's civil war to Ecuador's territorial advantage and by 1841 he transferred his attention to the south. Ecuador, probably with considerable justification,[11] claimed the territories of Jaén and Mainas which had been incorporated as provinces into the northern domain of Peru at the time of independence. Flores now hoped to take advantage of Gamarra's involvement in war with Bolivia to seize the disputed provinces. Under pressure from Chile, Ecuador and Peru signed a treaty in June of 1842 which averted all-out war and provided a momentary quietus in the boundary dispute. However, relations between the two countries remained strained and by the end of the year war again seemed imminent.

Prospects of a struggle between Ecuador and Peru alarmed Colombia. Bound by a treaty of alliance and friendship to Ecuador, Colombia had no desire to become involved in a war with Peru. Such involvement might have weakened the ruling conservative regime and encouraged the liberals, defeated in the War of the Supremes, to renew their bid for power, this time with Peru's backing. A war between Ecuador and Peru, moreover, was viewed as a distinct menace in Bogotá, even if Colombia ignored its treaty and remained aloof. If Peru won the war, it would increase its influence over Ecuador and weaken Colombia's; but if an unaided Ecuador triumphed it might be so emboldened as to seek once more to wrest Pasto from Colombia. At this point Colombia enlisted Chile's support in bringing pressure on Ecuador and Peru to avoid hostilities and, for the time being, the war clouds dissipated.[12]

By 1845 new complications were at hand. In March of that year Flores, it will be recalled, was overthrown in Ecuador. The deposed president proceeded to Spain where he plotted to establish a Spanish prince on an Ecuadoran throne, hoping to serve himself as regent until the prince attained his majority.[13] The plot was thwarted when England seized the ships that Flores had outfitted for the expedition. Meantime, though, the Pacific coast powers of South America had become alarmed by the rumors of an impending attempt to establish a European monarchy in Ecuador. Clearly, such a development would have totally disrupted the delicate balance of Pacific coast power politics. Apprehension over the Flores conspiracy led Peru's president Ramón Castilla to summon the first Congress of Lima. Delegates from Bolivia, Chile, Ecuador, New Granada, and Peru convened in 1847 and signed a treaty pledging a defensive alliance among the five republics should an invasion or overt foreign intervention materialize. The treaty was directed not only against the Flores venture but also against the United States which had alarmed South American states by its war against Mexico.[14]

Fear of the Flores schemes and of U.S. expansionism had produced a rare display of unity among the Andean republics. Unity was of brief endurance, however. Shortly Peru's conservative president José Rufino Echenique (1851–1854), an interim executive between Castilla's two terms, grew alarmed over the liberal policies of Ecuador's president José María Urbina, who had seized power in 1851 with the backing of Colombia's newly installed liberal government.[15] Echenique therefore supported an invasion that the indefatigable plotter Flores was preparing to launch, from Peruvian territory, against Urbina's Ecuadoran administration. It may well be that Echenique hoped that Flores, if successful in Ecuador, would proceed on to Colombia and oust the liberals, who at the time were widely regarded among Spanish American conservatives as posing a socialist menace to the entire continent.[16] These plans backfired when Flores was defeated in 1852, and the Ecuadoran liberals strengthened their grip on power. Then in 1854 liberals in Peru, aided by Bolivia's Tata Belzu, who desired the fall of Lima's conservative regime with which he had severed relations over economic issues, staged a successful revolution under Castilla and drove Echenique from office.

The dreary spectacle of Andean intrigues and interventions continued unabated during the next ten years. In 1857 Ecuador celebrated an accord with British creditors, ceding to them in satisfaction of its debt an extension of territory that happened to be claimed by Peru. This led in 1859 to a Peruvian invasion, headed by President Castilla. Ecuador was in the throes of its Terrible Year (circumstances that inspired García Moreno to seek the establishment of a French protectorate) and Castilla, unable to find among the several claimants any Ecuadoran with clear title to the presidency, withdrew from the troubled land without demanding additional territory. For this act of magnanimity, Castilla has ever since been condemned by Peruvian expansionists.

The focus of trouble next shifted to Bolivian-Peruvian relations. Opponents of Bolivian president José María Linares (1857–1861) organized, on Peruvian soil, the so-called "crusade of Peru." With the blessings of Belzu extended from Europe where he was now in exile, the "crusaders," backed by considerable Peruvian money and recruits, swept into Bolivia, where they were soundly defeated. Linares, of course, lodged sharp protests with the Lima government, which in turn complained about the haven that Bolivia was affording the deposed Echenique. The two countries prepared for war, but it failed to materialize mainly because Linares required the full services of his country's armed forces in suppressing internal insurrections.

As the 1860s began the liberals of Colombia exchanged suspicious glances—and also invasions—with the conservatives of Ecuador, now entrenched in power under García Moreno. One of the consequences of this uneasy situation was an invasion of Colombia carried out by Flores, loyally attached now to García Moreno. Decisively defeated by the Colombians, Flores died in 1865, disdained by García Moreno because of his failure to realize the abiding Ecuadoran dream of adding part of Colombia's Cauca valley to its national domain.

And now there came another brief moment of Andean unity, inspired this time by a dispute between Spain and Peru that brought the two powers into war in 1865. The war produced a quadruple alliance that joined Peru, Chile, Ecuador, and Bolivia in the struggle against the former motherland—which had never recognized Peru's independence and hoped initially to reconquer at least a part of the old viceroyalty. The war gave rise to an Andean appeal for U.S. intervention on the grounds that Spain's objectives were in violation of the Monroe Doctrine. Secretary of State William Seward rejected the plea for direct intervention in defense of the Monroe Doctrine, for it became clear, soon after the eruption of hostilities, that Spain had abandoned hopes of territorial conquest.[17] Nevertheless, Seward followed developments with close attention, anxious to arrange for peace through U.S. mediation. He was especially apprehensive that if not settled under U.S. auspices, the war could produce European mediation; and this, in his view, would constitute a threat to U.S. influence in the New World. The secretary of state also feared that, "if too excited, all of Latin America might combine into one super alliance against the Spanish which might be used against the United States at some future date."[18] Seward need not have worried. Inter–Latin American rivalries, in various forms and guises, prevented additional countries from adhering to the quadruple alliance. Both sides to the contest became increasingly anxious for an end to hostilities, and an armistice was finally signed in Washington in April of 1871.[19]

The war between the alliance and Spain marks a significant development in U.S.-Andean relations. It produced one of the first explicit invitations for direct U.S. intervention in Andean affairs. It also gave rise to resentment when the United States refused to intervene in the ways specifically desired by the Andean republics. Finally, it brought one of the first indications that the United States might be preparing to assume the tasks of peacemaker and even peacekeeper in South America in order to contain the influence of Europe in the New World.

The winds of dissention swept once more through the Andean republics in the 1870s, ending the tenuous unity produced by the war with Spain. Dissension steadily escalated and before the end of the decade produced what up until this time had been avoided through balance-of-power diplomacy: a protracted, all-out war.

THE WAR OF THE PACIFIC

In the mid-1860s Bolivia and Chile had come to the brink of war because of disagreement over coastal boundaries. Chile claimed 23 degrees latitude as the boundary while Bolivia insisted on the 26th parallel. When Spain and Peru went to war (1865) Chile assumed a more conciliatory attitude and Bolivian president Melgarejo revealed a "romantic desire for fraternity."[20] As a result the two countries signed a treaty in 1866. It stipulated that, pending final resolution, Chile would limit her effective sovereignty to 24 degrees. Between 23 and 25 degrees, however, both countries could exploit mineral resources. This was an important provision as the area in question was rich in nitrate deposits. The provision was mainly beneficial to Chile which, with its superior financial resources and easy access by sea, was in a much better position than Bolivia to tap the coastal subsoil wealth.

Interpower rivalry in this period was by no means confined to the Pacific coast countries of South America. In 1865, in fact, there had erupted the War of the Triple Alliance, pitting the three allies (Argentina, Brazil, and Uruguay) against Paraguay. At the outset of this struggle which lasted five years Melgarejo had been sorely tempted to intervene on the side of Paraguay; and he gave encouragement to the many Bolivians who enlisted privately in that country's armed forces. Dissuaded by his advisers from formal entry into the war, Melgarejo signed a treaty in 1867 with a mission from Rio de Janeiro, thereby resolving a long-standing boundary dispute that had nearly led Bolivian president Ballivián to invade Brazil in the 1840s. Through the 1867 treaty Melgarejo ceded in all some 150,000 square kilometers to Brazil. With this territory went Bolivia's most likely means of access to the Atlantic by way of river transportation. In exchange, Brazil decorated Melgarejo with the Great Cross of the Order of the Cruzeiro.[21]

The treaty with Brazil, and also the collapse of George Earl Church's Madeira-Mamoré railway-building enterprise caused Bolivia to turn its attention away from the Atlantic and to concentrate its interest more exclusively on the Pacific coast. This, in turn, led inevitably to mounting friction with Chile. Difficulties were compounded when Chileans in 1870 discovered the rich Caracoles silver vein in territory which, lying just south of 23 degrees, was claimed by Bolivia. Intent upon gaining fuller control over its coastal mineral deposits and blocking the increasing penetration by Chilean capitalists, Bolivia now sought to renegotiate the 1866 treaty. After complex diplomatic maneuvering accompanied by bitter recrimination on both sides, a new treaty emerged in 1874. According to its terms, Chile recognized the 24th parallel as its definitive boundary with Bolivia. For its part, Bolivia committed itself for twenty-five years not to raise imposts on Chilean enterprises already established on the Bolivian coast between the 24th and 23rd parallels.

Coming to power in 1876, Bolivia's military *caudillo* Hilarión Daza found himself chronically beset by shortage of funds. His pecuniary needs rendering him insensitive to treaty obligations, Daza in 1878 imposed a slight increase on the export taxes which a Chilean nitrate firm, operating between the 24th and 23rd parallels at Antofagasta, was required to pay the Bolivian government. The Chilean company objected and was backed fully by its home government in Santiago. When Daza refused to revoke the tax increases, Chile broke off diplomatic relations and on February 14, 1879, landed troops that took possession of Antofagasta, thus triggering the War of the Pacific.[22]

The fundamental cause for the eruption of hostilities was the mounting power and prestige and the economic and political stability of Chile, on one hand, and the weakness and the political and economic deterioration of Bolivia, on the other. Bolivia had valuable nitrate and silver lands which because of geographic barriers and conditions of internal instability the national populace seemed unable to utilize effectively. The war—and its outcome—was as inevitable as the 1846–1848 conflict between the United States and Mexico. In both instances, a relatively well-governed, energetic, and economically expanding nation had been irresistibly tempted by neighboring territories that were underdeveloped, malgoverned, and sparsely occupied. If the pretexts to which they resorted at the time had not proved adequate to produce war, both Chile and the United States would soon have found—or fabricated—other provocations demanding a martial response.[23]

The War of the Pacific having begun, the combatants at once focused their attention on Peru. If that country chose to honor its 1873 "secret" treaty of alliance (Chile's government) was actually aware of the treaty) that the Civilist regime of Manuel Pardo had negotiated with Bolivia, then automatically it would become involved in the war. The Peruvian populace, given the long-standing and deep-seated "feeling of antipathy" toward Chileans,[24] tended to favor war. In official circles, however, pacifist sentiment was evident, with prominent statesmen advocating that Peru ignore the treaty and avoid war at all costs because of the lack of preparedness.

Personally siding with the pacifists, perhaps because of his Chilean investments, Mariano Ignacio Prado, elected to the Peruvian presidency by the Civilist party in 1876, dispatched a mission to Santiago to seek a formula for preserving peace. These efforts failed, in part because the Peruvian negotiators feared that without their country's military commitment Bolivia's unpredictable and unreliable administration might come to terms with Chile and actually join with it in despoiling Peru of its Tarapacá nitrate lands. The truth is that Chile did indeed approach Bolivia's government with just such a scheme in mind. The plan hatched in Santiago called for Bolivia to cede its coast to Chile in exchange for compensation in the form of coastal territory to be wrested from Peru.[25]

Aware of the need to stiffen the resolve of its ally, the Peruvian mission in Santiago refused at the last minute to disavow the treaty with Bolivia. In consequence, Chile declared war on Peru on April 3, 1879.[26] President Prado at once sent a mission to Buenos Aires in the hope of persuading Argentina to join the war against Chile. By the time the Peruvians arrived, however, Argentina and Chile were well on the way toward resolving the most serious of their boundary issues, and in a manner that appeared favorable to Argentina. The Buenos Aires government therefore refused to become involved, and Peru and Bolivia were left to face Chile on their own.

The War of the Pacific was fought along the stretches of an inhospitable desert where armies had to be supplied from the sea. Thus, sea power was all-important in determining the outcome. In this respect the allies were at a decided disadvantage, for Peru's Civilist president Pardo in an economy move had canceled the order on two warships under construction in England. For a time, though, some remarkable feats of seamanship performed by Peru's Miguel Grau provided the allies with a glimmer of hope. Between May and October Grau became the scourge of the Chilean navy, preventing the enemy from obtaining the effective control of the sea that its superior naval power should have guaranteed from the outset. Finally on the morning of October 8, 1879, the Chilean fleet caught up with Grau off the point of Angamos, some forty miles north of Antofagasta. It was one ship against five and the battle lasted less than two hours. Grau and many of his crew members were killed and his ship, the *Huáscar*, sank just as the Chileans were boarding it.

On the land, events now turned decisively against the allies. A badly managed campaign around Tacna, featuring a "countermarch" (a euphemism for retreat) of the Bolivian troops commanded by Daza, resulted in a Chilean victory. Daza shortly departed for Europe, in possession of a large sum of money. His detractors maintained that the money came from a Chilean bribe, but their accusations have never been substantiated.[27] Internal bickering and the gathering strength of a group that favored peace with Chile regardless of consequences combined virtually to eliminate Bolivia from the war before the end of 1880.[28]

In Lima, President Prado faced an almost impossible situation. Congress refused to vote taxes to support the war effort, determining instead to rely on new issues of paper money. Furthermore, Nicolás de Piérola, the implacable rival of the Civilist president, was now back in Lima and he and his supporters refused to cooperate with the administration. Prado sailed for Europe in December of 1879, ostensibly to seek foreign loans and ships through which Peru might yet snatch victory from defeat. Suspicious that their president had fled the country in cowardice, the majority of *limeños* welcomed an uprising proclaiming Piérola president of Peru. Duly installed in the national palace, Piérola declared Prado a traitor to his country. By the time he arrived in Europe, then, Prado had been stripped of the prestige of the presidency and banking circles were unwilling to deal with him. In truth, Prado did not try very hard to obtain aid for his country. Furious at Piérola, he decided to do nothing in Europe that might benefit even indirectly his hated rival. Hampered by the dissension among politicians and also by the inefficient management of civilian administrations behind the lines, the Peruvian troops, fighting heroically all the way, were forced into steady retreat and finally in January of 1881 Chilean forces occupied Lima.

From the very outset of the struggle the allies had turned for protection to the far-off United States. In Bolivia, Manuel Vicente Ballivián appealed to U.S. minister S. Newton Pettis for North American intervention aimed at blocking Chile's expansionist ambitions. Both

Pettis and his successor Charles Adams sympathized with the Bolivian position and favored U.S. arbitration to end the war and safeguard Bolivia against transfer of territory. In Washington Bolivian minister Ladislao Cabrera held out to Secretary of State William M. Evarts the prospect of lucrative guano and nitrate concessions to U.S. investors in return for official protection of Bolivia's territorial integrity. "There is need of a new element," he wrote Evarts in February of 1881, "capable of giving renewed vigor and a different form to the industry and commerce of those republics [Bolivia and Peru]." A few weeks later he wrote to James G. Blaine, who had replaced Evarts as secretary of state, stressing that his objective was to establish peace and "to strengthen and develop the wonderful productivity of North America by opening new and profitable markets to its commercial activity; [and] to secure to your Excellency's government that influence in South America which rightfully belongs to it by reasons of its proximity, its civilization, and the similarity of its institutions."[29]

Peruvians turned also to the United States and for a time received encouraging signals. Immediately after coming to power, Piérola had sounded out U.S. minister Isaac P. Christiancy on the possibility of Washington's mediation on behalf of Peru. Christiancy's reaction, as revealed in dispatches to Washington, proved more enthusiastic than Piérola could have hoped. On the grounds that English capital was gaining predominance in Chilean nitrate enterprises and would only expand its South American presence if Chile despoiled its northern neighbor of nitrate territory, Christiancy urged establishment of a U.S. protectorate over Peru. Beyond this, he advised that the United States should annex Peru and, after a period of ten years in which Peruvians would be educated so as to become "wholly North American" in their ideas, admit it as a state into the Union. With Peru in tow, the United States could control all the other countries of South America, assuring that "large markets would be opened to our productions and manufactures and a wide field opened for the enterprise of our people."[30]

Christiancy was succeeded by Stephen J. Hurlbut as U.S. minister in Lima, occupied at the time (1881) by Chilean forces. As a leader of the Grange in Illinois, Hurlbut had been among the foremost advocates of U.S. commercial expansion into South American markets.[31] Like Christiancy, Hurlbut hoped the United States would take a strong stand to protect Peru against territorial despoilment and thereby gain important commercial concessions and an opportunity to check the expansion of British economic influence along the Pacific coast of South America. Hurlbut, however, was far more circumspect than his predecessor as well as more attuned to opinions in Washington, and apparently the thought of a U.S. protectorate over Peru never entered his mind. But, he did hold out to beleaguered Peruvians the hope that the United States might indeed intervene diplomatically in order to prevent the loss of national territory.

Blaine fully appreciated the possibilities of checking British economic penetration and providing an opening for U.S. capitalists by protecting the territorial integrity of both Peru and Bolivia. Moreover he was interested in the claims that certain U.S. promoters now produced, ostensibly establishing their ownership of Peruvian and Bolivian nitrate and guano concessions. Apparently, however, principles of American hemisphere diplomatic hegemony were more important to Blaine than economic considerations as he shaped his country's policies toward the War of the Pacific. Basically, what appealed to the secretary of state was the opportunity to take up anew the attempt initiated by Seward, when the Andean republics had been waging war against Spain, to make the United States the guardian of order and peace in the American hemisphere, to the exclusion of European influences.

In dealing with issues concerning the War of the Pacific, Blaine resolutely opposed various European plans of mediation and good offices. The South American republics, he argued, "are younger sisters of this government" and in the course of time they have been removed ever farther from the "European system." Contending that the interests, "commercial and political, of the United States, on this continent, transcend in extent and importance those of any other power," Blaine would not tolerate European intervention in the political affairs of South America.[32] It followed in his mind that the United States must itself intervene so as to reestablish international order and decency when the "younger sisters" proved incapable of managing their own affairs. Therefore toward the end of 1881 Blaine dispatched William Trescott, accompanied by his son Walker Blaine, on a mission to Chile to convey to that country the U.S. insistence that in the American hemisphere transfer of territory must not result from armed conflict.

Nothing came of Blaine's strategy. With the assassination of James A. Garfield and the accession of Chester A. Arthur to the presidency, Blaine was replaced by Frederick T. Frelinghuysen as secretary of state. Relatively indifferent to American hemisphere political and economic issues, the new secretary recalled the Trescott mission and calmly stood by as Chile in 1883 exacted from Peru the Treaty of Ancón.[33] By its terms, Chile would obtain outright the southern desert region of Tarapacá with its important nitrate center of Iquique. Chile would also occupy and administer Tacna and Arica for ten years, after which a plebiscite would be held to determine the final disposition of the two areas. The following year Bolivia signed a truce with the victor, recognizing Chile's right to occupy the coast. Subsequently, in 1904, a new treaty was signed in which Bolivia formally recognized the transfer of its entire coastal territory to Chile.

Disputes over the ultimate dispositon of Tacna and Arica—for it proved impossible ever to hold the plebiscite stipulated by the Treaty of Ancón[34]—and unremitting Bolivian efforts to reacquire a coastal territory, either from Peru or Chile, produced discord and rancor for years to come among the South American republics. Chile's seizure of territory also contributed indirectly to the later and bloody Chaco War (1932–1935) between Bolivia and Paraguay; for, having been denied access to the Pacific coast, Bolivia fixed its hopes on an Atlantic outlet, thereby precipitating eventually a clash with Paraguay. Thus Blaine was proved all too correct in his belief that the transfer of territory at the conclusion of the War of the Pacific would give rise to other wars and political disturbances.[35] The frustration of Blaine's diplomacy also bore an immediate consequence: the deep-seated enmity of Peru and Bolivia toward the United States. Neither country could forgive North American statesmen for having failed to produce an effective counterpoise to traditional South American balance-of-power politics. Chile, on the other hand, could not forgive the North Americans for their aborted attempt to establish Washington's diplomatic hegemony.[36]

Peruvian and Bolivian resentment against the United States only intensified in the years ahead when the Washington-dominated Pan-American movement, launched in 1888 under the aegis of Blaine who was serving once more as secretary of state, failed to respond to importunings to pressure Chile for at least a partial return of territories. Resentment was all the while combined with a predisposing tendency toward abject subservience whenever such demeanor was perceived as likely to win Washington's support for renegotiation of the territorial settlement. Undoubtedly Peruvians and Bolivians have at times despised themselves for their vacillation between haughty resentment and subservience in their approach to the United States. Undoubtedly, too, they have tended to blame the United States for having placed them in this unenviable position of psychological ambivalence, conveniently forgetting that to some extent this situation is of their own making.

RECONSTRUCTION IN BOLIVIA AND PERU

The silver mining entrepreneurs of Bolivia who played a large part in that country's economic rehabilitation following the War of the Pacific[37] had come close to averting that war in the first place. By the late 1870s, largely because of his success in attracting Chilean and British capital, Aniceto Arce had turned his Huanchaco mines, a short distance southwest of Potosí, into Bolivia's major silver producer. When the war clouds had begun to gather Arce, in Santiago at the time, returned quickly to Bolivia in an attempt to persuade the president of the foolhardiness of war. Daza had listened attentively but, remaining unconvinced, had persevered in the policies that afforded Chile the pretext for war.

Following the defeat of Bolivian forces in the Tacna region and the departure of Daza for Europe, Arce and other mining interests who were economically dependent upon Chilean and British capital had done all in their power to terminate the alliance with Peru and enter into immediate peace negotiations with Chile. These men, derisively dubbed pacifists by their foes, formed the nuclei of two new parties about to appear on the scene. Most of them found a political base in the Conservative party, but a few joined with the mining tycoon Gregorio Pacheco in organizing the ephemeral Democratic party.

Their pacifist sentiments brought charges of treason and also resulted in the temporary exile of Arce and some of his companions. In the period between 1880 and 1884 Bolivia was ruled by Narciso Campero and a group of partisans who in 1883 founded the Liberal party. Favoring all-out opposition to Chile, the Liberals looked to the United States for support and also for the capital investment that would facilitate postwar recovery.[38] The signing of the truce with Chile in 1884 represented a triumph for the pacifists; and it prepared the way for the additional penetration of Chilean and British capital into Bolivia, signifying a setback for those who had hoped to serve their own interests, and perhaps also those of national recovery, by attracting U.S. capital.

The 1884 elections brought to the presidency Gregorio Pacheco, proprietor of the Guadalupe silver mines whose proceeds he spent lavishly in smoothing his way to the high office. Called the "new man," Pacheco, who was born in humble circumstances, may well have been the wealthiest man in Bolivia at the time he became president. His Democratic party, however, little more than the vehicle of his personal ambitions, soon fell apart, leaving the political arena to the Conservative and Liberal parties. The Conservatives elected Arce (whose Huanchaco mines now produced over 40 percent of Bolivia's silver output) in 1888, Mariano Baptista (the only Conservative president who was not a wealthy man) in 1892, and Severo Fernández Alonso (another mining entrepreneur) in 1896. Not until 1899 were the Conservatives driven from power, and then not by elections but rather by a Liberal revolution.

Between 1884 and 1899, especially at the beginning of the period, Bolivia enjoyed relative political calm. After the disastrous military struggle a lull had developed in foreign intrigues and intervention, and the leaders of the two major political parties were close enough in their social and economic views to permit a considerable degree of collaboration. Perhaps the sense of shock evoked by the military calamities contributed to the new spirit of accord. The highly perceptive national writer Ignacio Prudencio Bustillo is convinced that it did. The defeat, he argues, "strengthened the spiritual ties uniting individuals . From 1880 it was possible with reason to begin to speak of a national soul."[39]

On social and economic issues there was at first little to separate the opposition Liberal party from the ruling Conservatives. Following the example of their leader Aniceto Arce, most Conservatives were obsessed with practical, material progress, with industrial and commercial development, and with the construction of means of communication, especially railroads.[40] Frequently, in fact, in economic policy Conservatives were more progressive than Liberals. They incorporated the country into the orbit of the world economy.[41] And, to facilitate this, they removed obstacles to foreign capital, and encouraged railroad construction that resulted in completion of the Antofagasta-Oruro line in 1892. In accord with their pursuit of progress, "they tied the banking structure to those English interests which had already established their base of operations in Chile."[42]

Similar in their approach to the economy, Conservatives and Liberals showed little difference even on doctrinal-ideological questions. Although Liberals employed a certain amount of anticlerical rhetoric in advocating secularism, most of them conceded the folly of breaking brusquely with tradition and denigrating religious influences. It was necessary, according to one of their principal leaders, to avoid the excesses of the French Revolution and the "repugnant extremes of European socialism."[43] For their part some Conservatives, most especially Mariano Baptista and Monsignor Miguel de los Santos Taborga who became archbishop of La Plata (Sucre) in 1898, could at times be adamant and strident in condemning Masonry, positivism, and religious toleration, in railing against secularism, and in insisting that any sound political and social order had to be based exclusively on Catholic doctrines.[44] The majority of Conservatives, however, were rather indifferent to doctrinal issues, and many had a strong attachment to French anticlericalism, "if for no other reason than their enchantment with Paris."[45]

It is reported that an associate once remarked to Arce: "The Liberals have gained the advantage over us in choosing that name for their party. We are the ones who should have baptized ourselves with that title of liberals." To this Arce is said to have replied, "It is true: we are the true liberals."[46] Certainly Mamerto Oyola Cuellar of Santa Cruz, one of Bolivia's leading late nineteenth-century philosophers, saw little to separate the two political camps. Sounding like a mid-nineteenth-century Krausist, he condemned them equally for their unattenuated materialism which he feared was threatening Bolivia's moral foundations.[47]

As the 1890s advanced Bolivia faced an increasingly adverse trade balance owing to the fall of silver prices on the international market. The hard-pressed silver elites, closely intermarried in many instances into the more prominent landowning families of the south, began to see the advantage of encouraging small-scale industrial production so as to reduce dependence on imports. The formation of government capital with which to stimulate manufacturing was one of the objectives President Arce had in mind when in 1892 he raised the export tax on tin. Meanwhile tin production, abetted by the growth in railroad transportation that occurred during Arce's administration, was assuming a new importance. Tin entrepreneurs, comprising a group of nouveau riche capitalists based in Oruro and other northern regions, now joined with older, more established tin producers of the south, headed by Félix Avelino Aramayo, to oppose the entrenched silver mining, landowning oligarchy.[48] The newly rising elites made the Liberal party their political instrument, and at last some real issues began to divide the Liberals from the Conservatives.

With ever-mounting vehemence Liberals were, by the mid-1890s, equating progress with laissez-faire policies that would suppress such nonproductive uses of the past as the social paternalism which still found convinced advocates among the Conservatives. At the same time Liberals eschewed government intervention aimed at encouraging manufacturing. Development, in the eyes of the would-be rulers of Bolivia, depended upon attracting foreign capital with which to stimulate tin output, and then relying upon sales of that commodity to finance imports. Here was a formula for progress that did not necessitate restrictions on the profits of tin miners for the advantage of a national artisan and manufacturing class.

If the Liberals had come to power in, let us say, 1888, few policy changes would have been discernible. As it turned out, however, they achieved political control in 1899, following a revolution that claimed many casualties. Representing by that time a distinct challenge to the status quo, they began at once to set the country on a new course.

Meantime Peru had been achieving a postwar reconstruction even more dramatic than Bolivia's. To a considerable degree Peru's recovery, like Bolivia's, was based on British capital.[49] In Peru, however, military officers rather than civilian politicians presided over rehabilitation. The heroism with which Peru's officers, the "heroes of defeat," had conducted themselves during the War of the Pacific contrasted dramatically with the self-seeking and incompetence displayed by the civilian politicians behind the lines. With this contrast in mind, the officers decided that only they were morally competent to preside over the destinies of the fatherland. At the outset of the recovery period, a majority of the populace probably agreed with this assessment. The main beneficiary of the popular support for militarism was Andrés Cáceres, one of the few Peruvian generals who had actually won more engagements than he had lost to the Chileans. Backed by his Constitutionalist party, Cáceres was the dominant figure in Peruvian politics from 1884 to 1895.

A group of bondholders, with headquarters in London, posed the most immediate problem facing Cáceres. The bondholders demanded resumption of service on Peru's foreign debt. The securities which they held, issued during the late 1860s and in the 1870s, had a face value of between forty and fifty million pounds, an indebtedness which Peru was totally unable to amortize.

Late in 1886 Michael A. Grace came to Peru as the representative of the London bondholders and began a protracted series of conferences with Cáceres and his treasury officials. The negotiations proved difficult and not until the end of 1889 was the "Grace Contract" ratified, under pressure from the president, by a reluctant Peruvian congress. Following approval of the contract, the bondholders in London formed the Peruvian Corporation, Ltd. In line with contract terms, the government of Peru turned over to the corporation all 769 miles of the state railroad system for a term of sixty-six years (later extended another seventeen and finally granted in perpetuity). To the corporation the government also extended the exclusive right to export two million tons of guano annually from the offshore islands. The government further "granted the former bondholders an annuity of 80,000 pounds—later reduced to 60,000 pounds—for thirty years, [as well as] 500,000 hectares of land in the Perene Valley."[50]

While the Grace Contract cannot be regarded as an act of charity toward Peru on the part of foreign capitalists, and while it has been attacked through the years by many of Peru's leading intellectual and political figures, it may well have been the best settlement that Cáceres could have obtained under the circumstances. Critics of the Peruvian Corporation often fail to note that the London firm in its early years generally fulfilled its obligations and began at once to extend Peru's railroad lines to important mining centers, thereby fulfilling at last some of the expectations of José Balta and Henry Meiggs. By 1893 the Central Railroad, beginning at Callao, had been pushed on to La Oroya, the heartland of an area fantastically rich in a broad variety of ores. Had it not been for expanding railroad services, Peru's "silver era" would have been considerably delayed and recovery from military defeat would have been far less striking. Moreover, since Peruvian administrations ultimately decided that almost all of the guano reserves was required for domestic agriculture, the bondholders received relatively little of the valuable fertilizer. Instead, guano contributed to an enormous expansion of sugar and cotton production on the plantations of coastal Peru.

Thanks to silver production and the growth of coastal agriculture, a new Peruvian power elite took shape. By the mid-1890s it was beginning to match in affluence and aggressiveness the earlier bourgeoisie of the guano age. Also influential in the emerging elite were the owners of large sierra estates or *latifundistas* (often referred to in Peru as *gamonales*). Although the Indian serfs of the *latifundistas* were denied the right to vote—disfranchisement having been accomplished by legislation of 1890—the apportionment of congressional representatives still took into account the Indian populace. As a result, the *latifundistas* gained more power than ever in congress.[51]

The reemergence of a Civilist oligarchy, connected now more closely than ever to British capital,[52] evoked nothing but disgust from Peru's great man of letters, Manuel González Prada (1848–1918). Born into an aristocratic Lima family and afforded the best education available in his country, González Prada had appeared as an important figure among the group of intellectuals who after the War of the Pacific sought to regenerate the national spirit. Taking the rampant materialism that accompanied Peru's remarkable economic recovery as a symbol of moral, spiritual, and intellectual decay, González Prada, in manner far more radical than Bolivia's Oyola Cuellar and the early Krausists, railed against the individualistic greed that underlay capitalism and called for a system of production calculated to supply the needs of all rather than the profits of a few. An atheistic humanist who feared that excessive concern with material gain must inevitably undermine the higher capacities of human nature and produce an alienation in which the mind and spirit were prostituted to the senses, González Prada discovered his formulas for a better society first in socialism and later in anarchism. Actually, however, despite the manner in which he reviled Catholicism and the entire colonial past, González Prada reflected a great deal of the anticapitalist, humanist sentiments of Hispanic traditionalism, nourished ever since medieval times by hosts of thinkers throughout the Spanish-speaking world. This helps explain his lingering influence in Peru, and sheds light on the appeal he has exercised over those opposed, for one reason or another, to the culture and values associated with the United States. Also accounting for González Prada's enduring attraction is his attention to the Indians of his native land. Despairing of reinculcating virtue and a proper sense of values among the prospering capitalist of coastal Peru, the nineteenth-century atheist—much like some sixteenth-century Catholic missionary priests—found in the nonindividualistic, nonmaterialistic Indians the hope for regeneration.[53]

Few people heeded González Prada during his lifetime. Not until Peruvians had had a chance to become disillusioned by the failure of laissez-faire, liberal capitalism to provide the panacea promised by the newly forming oligarchy would they begin to take seriously the great iconoclast's admonitions. When this disillusionment set in, beginning most discernibly in the 1920s, González Prada came to be recognized as one of the most high-minded and prescient idealists that Peru has produced. In the 1890s, though, the revolution that enticed the civilian intelligentsia of Peru was not of the type preached by González Prada; instead, it was a revolution intended to give greater impetus and encouragement to the new class of capitalists, many of whom flocked to the Civilist party and revitalized the antimilitarist doctrines popularized by its founder Manuel Pardo at the beginning of the 1870s.

The 1872 elections, described in the preceding chapter, had accomplished a significant political turnabout. The Civilists had at that time replaced in power the economic interventionists, associated with the military president Balta and his minister of finance Piérola, who had sought to place limits and restraints on the native guano capitalists. The new Civilist elites surfacing by 1895 felt that their own financial interests, and ostensibly those of the nation as well, were being blocked by the unsympathetic rule of a military government that did not adequately understand the laws of progress. As the catalyst in producing the new turnabout perceived to be necessary, the Civilists turned to their old bête noire, Nicolás de Piérola.

Having reconsidered many of his original economic doctrines, Piérola as of 1895 was no longer at odds with Civilist concepts. He had now found a basis of rapport with Civilists, resting upon a common approach to economic policy that stressed the importance of exports by an unfettered private sector and also upon mutual dissatisfaction with the heavy-handed, arbitrary rule of Cáceres, who was increasingly isolating himself from all civilian sources of support. Accordingly, Civilists joined with Piérola's Democrats in staging, with the support of the *montoneros* or rural brigands and guerrillas, an insurrection that toppled Cáceres. Shortly after the insurrection, Piérola was elected president.

In many ways, the Peruvian revolution of 1895 resembled the 1899 insurrection that placed the Liberals in control of Bolivia. At the turn of the century, both countries were in the hands of new elements convinced that they knew how to preside over faster national development, and altogether persuaded that progress resulted from the creation of private fortunes which in turn could best be made through collaboration with foreign capital in stimulating export economies.

Through remarkably parallel circumstances, Ecuador in 1895 had also experienced a liberal revolution that brought to power a regime whose leaders saw eye to eye with the new rulers in Peru and Bolivia.

ECUADOR. 1883–1895

The 1883 overthrow of military *caudillo* Ignacio de Veintemilla had brought in its wake the restoration of Conservative party rule under President José María Plácido Caamaño (1884–1888). While liberally inclined in his youth, Caamaño had by now been transformed into the man whom most Ecuadorans consider to be second only to García Moreno as the embodiment of conservative ideology.

The conservative restoration provoked a mounting tide of liberal

140

verbal attacks and armed uprisings against the government. Although some political leaders, most notably Antonio Flores Jijón (the son of Juan José Flores who served as president from 1882 to 1892), sought to compromise the conservative-liberal doctrinal issues through a movement that bore the name of Progressivism (*Progresismo*), it proved impossible to heal the old wounds.[54] Many Conservatives remained intransigently set against any deviation from the principles of García Moreno, and many Liberals—among them the "old battler" (*el viejo luchador*) Eloy Alfaro who constantly plotted uprisings from abroad—could think only of completely undoing the Garcian policies.

Seriously handicapped in his presidential term by opposition both from Conservatives and Liberals, Flores nonetheless presided over a period of impressive economic gain. Cacao production on the coast flourished, forming the basis of a promising export economy, and Ecuador acquired its first sugar refining plants. Government revenues increased and on the whole Flores invested them wisely, building roads and schools.[55]

For a brief moment in 1890, when war with Peru over the usual boundary disputes seemed imminent, Ecuadorans rallied behind their president; but the support was short-lived. Various men of new wealth, who saw in the Liberal party the means to political power and who found in its program an economic ideology to their liking, complained that Flores was too closely associated with the financial capitalists of the Conservative party. Furthermore, the out-of-power Liberals were concerned by the passion of Flores for attracting foreign capital, an outgrowth of his faith that the country's economic redemption lay in credit and investment from abroad. Liberals were just as desirous as Flores of luring foreign capital, but they feared that if it entered Ecuador under the aegis of his government it would strengthen the entrenched Conservatives and render them virtually invulnerable to attack.

In spite of Flores' failure to make Progressivism a genuinely popular movement, the 1892 elections brought a close victory to its standard-bearer, Luis Cordero Crespo. Increasingly harassed by both uncompromising Conservatives and Liberals, Cordero earned the outraged condemnation of the latter when he declared that in the event of a conflict between state and church he would have to support the church.[56] It was not just doctrinal points, however, that continued to nurture political divisiveness. Economics was also involved. The high command of the Conservative party represented the interior aristocracy and showed little of the enthusiasm for economic progress that had distinguished García Moreno. For many Conservatives in the 1890s, the economic desideratum was a limited-growth, self-sufficient structure based on agriculture and local handicrafts industries. To most Liberals, however, with their expectations aroused by the rise of coastal cacao and sugar production, the future lay in encouraging the export sector and increasing the importation of manufactured goods which could then be distributed in the country's highland interior by means of railroads to be financed through foreign capital.

The contest was resolved by a civil war fought in 1895 in which the Liberals, under Eloy Alfaro, triumphed. Power shifted abruptly from the landowners of the isolated highlands to a group of outward-looking capitalists whose base of operations was the coast, particularly the city of Guayaquil.[57] Thirsting for vengeance ever since the Conservatives led by García Moreno had gained a total victory, the Liberals now prepared to savor the fruits of their own total victory.

By the end of the nineteenth century Bolivia, Peru, and Ecuador, as a result in every instance of revolution, had fallen under the control of new ruling classes which demonstrated striking accord in their economic attitudes and views on progress. The liberal, free-trade, export-import ideology that had helped spark the move for independence from Spain, but then had been generally suppressed except for about twenty-five years in Peru during the guano age, had finally triumphed. Similarities, of course, were not all-inclusive. While still very much a factor in Ecuador, the old doctrinal debates involving issues of church and state, of "theocracy" and "atheism," had been largely laid to rest in Bolivia and Peru. In those two republics the rampant anticlericalism associated with earlier nineteenth-century liberalism had undergone attenuation, and the liberal cause would triumph mainly on its social and economic policies.

Liberalism's triumph in Andean America coincided with the increasing entry of U.S. capital. Liberalism's ascendancy also brought with it a social problem of sufficient magnitude to cause concern among the directing classes about upheaval from below. The connection between (1) Yankee economic penetration and (2) internal social problems may very well have been fortuitous rather than causal. But, the image of the United States and of its form of liberal capitalism has suffered for some seventy years from the simplistic assumption prevailing among Andean—and also some U.S.—analysts that the relationship was causal, the first giving rise to the second.

6

The Apogee of Liberalism and the Rise of U.S. Influence, 1900–1920

The Civil War in the United States has been described as the last capitalist revolution.[1] But, to judge from their rhetoric, the triumphant Andean liberals who came to power some thirty years after the end of the U.S. Civil War had in mind nothing short of creating their own capitalist revolution. The new political leaders incessantly gave voice to their obsession with national material progress and their conviction that progress depended upon making universal in society the values of competitive, individualistic capitalism.

Consumed by the desire to transform the masses by instilling in them new values of hard work and self-reliance, some Andean liberals were willing to grant the state, at least for the time being, a far larger social interventionist role than was in keeping with the dictates of liberalism—as defined by the thinker most in vogue in turn-of-the-century Andean America, Herbert Spencer. Thus the Bolivian sociologist Daniel Sánchez Bustamante, a man who exerted enormous influence over upper-class youth at this time, saw the need for government-directed educational projects aimed at eradicating dependency inclinations among the masses and infusing them with the "economic energies of the self-reliant individual."[2] Similarly, Juan Benigno Vela, in some ways the most inflexible and incorruptible of Ecuador's Liberals, saw the need for forceful government intervention in order to educate the masses: "I will make a confession that until now I have not dared to make," he wrote in 1900. "We require still the tutelage of the wise man, . . . the sword in one hand, the torch of civilization in the other."[3]

143

In all the Andean region, no one was more dedicated to the task of inculcating among the masses the ethic of individual labor and self-reliance than the Peruvian Manuel Vicente Villarán. For him the 1895 insurrection that brought Nicolás de Piérola to power afforded the opportunity to make a capitalist revolution from above. It afforded, that is, the opportunity to initiate intensive state programs of education to spread among the masses the values of individualistic capitalism. "Only if given education," Villarán insisted, "will the lower classes be able to protect themselves and to contribute to, because they are sharing in, the increase of national wealth."[4] A practicing lawyer, an influential San Marcos professor, and a powerful figure within the Civilist party, Villarán had the opportunity to take some initial steps toward implementing his ideas while serving as minister of justice and instruction during the first term of the Civilist maverick Augusto B. Leguía (1908–1912). At that time he brought the first mission of U.S. educators to Peru, hopeful that they could introduce into his country the same universal spirit of progress that had, purportedly, banished backwardness in the country of Horace Mann.[5]

However much he admired the United States and wanted to follow the same paths that had led it to success, Villarán was determined to avoid Yankee hegemony in Peru. To him, and to a number of others who thought along similar lines, the fostering of capitalist expertise among Peruvians was the means whereby they could safeguard themselves against economic dependence on the United States which, once established, could only lead to political dependence.

Together with massive state-supported primary and secondary education, Villarán and many other Andean liberals saw the need for widespread industrialization. In this era before manufacturing industry had become capital and technology intensive, industrialization would, it was assumed, provide massive employment opportunities for those who through the public school system had acquired capitalist values and the incentive to become self-reliant. Like Villarán, the Bolivians M. Rigoberto Paredes and Carlos Romero, as well as the Ecuadoran José Peralta, stressed that once the majority of citizens acquired economic independence, they could then advance to political independence; for always the necessary prerequisite for political power was economic power.[6]

The advice of thinkers such as Villarán, Paredes, Romero, and Peralta was not applied, and herein lies the major reason why turn-of-the-century liberalism remained—even as it had been in the early nineteenth century—a theory divorced from practice. For all of their

144

obeisance to individual liberty and freedom, the fact remained that those in power did not, by and large, wish to undermine the clientelist system which perforce reduced the great majority of citizens to dependence.

Rather than seeking national wealth as generated by the society-wide quest of economic self-reliance through industrial employment, the directing classes opted for a new form of mercantilism. National wealth, in the purview of the new mercantilism, arose from export trade balances. And, as of 1900, Peru, Bolivia, and Ecuador seemed at last to have at hand the exports that could guarantee favorable trade balances. This being the case, there was no need to seek progress through methods that might prove dangerous to the established social structure. This is why the capitalist revolutions apparently heralded by the liberal insurrections of the 1890s remained narrowly circumscribed: they applied only to the upper classes and lent encouragement to commercial and financial but not to industrial capitalism.

LIBERALISM AND THE INDIANS

The overwhelming majority of Spencerian liberals were out-and-out racists, convinced that Indians were racially inferior and hopeful that they would gradually be eliminated and replaced by European immigrant labor, somehow to be attracted through inducements devised by the national government. A few, however, like the Ecuadoran Pío Jaramillo and the Peruvians Joaquín Capelo and Manuel Vicente Villarán, believed that Indian nature, weakened through the centuries by the communal setting in which the natives had lived since preconquest times, could be revitalized by converting the descendents of the Tahuantinsuyo Empire into private landowners. Once given his own plot of land the Indian would in time acquire habits of hard work, thrift, and self-reliance and become a positive element in the population; he would, in short, be transformed into a person exhibiting the character traits prized by advanced western societies.[7] Similar approaches to the "Indian problem" were in evidence in the United States at the turn of the century.[8]

Bolivia also produced men who believed in the potential of Indian nature, among them Octavio Salamanca who in 1914 published a book depicting land distribution in fee-simple ownership as a sure means of transforming the natives into a positive economic force.[9] By far the best-known Bolivian to extol the capacity of the Indian and to affirm his ability to contribute to national advancement was the paceño Franz Tamayo (1879–1956). The illegitimate son of Isaac

Tamayo, an important man of letters who had held high government posts (including the position of secretary to Melgarejo), and his Indian mistress, Franz Tamayo was an introverted individual who surrounded himself with mystery. He seems, in fact, to have "withdrawn in disdain from the society with which he carried on a dramatic struggle for half a century."[10] In 1910 Tamayo published his major work, *Creación de la pedagogía nacional*. It caused a sensation at the time and has had an enduring influence on Bolivian *pensadores*.

Basing his views on his observations of the Aymaras rather than the Quechuas, the aloof *paceño* praised his country's Indians as the one source of progress available to it. Bolivian whites, especially those in the Liberal party, might pride themselves on their advanced ideas, competitive drive, and wealth-producing potential. Basically, however, the whites were hopelessly inclined toward parasitism, perennially predisposed to live off the labor of others; they were, Tamayo said, incapable by nature of acquiring the spirit of enterprise needed to propel the country ahead. In contrast the Indians were autonomous and self-sufficient, individualistic and strong: they were the repository of 90 percent of national energy.[11]

According to Tamayo, who was much under the influence of Nietzsche, energy, vitality, the will to conquer, persistence, and the capacity for sustained effort were vital to civilization, while altruism, humanism, science, and even intelligence counted for little.[12] Alone among Bolivians, the Indians were superbly endowed with energy and will[13] and all other qualities regarded by Tamayo as important in forging national strength. If allotted private plots of land together with advanced farming tools and instruction in modern methods of agriculture, if granted opportunities for employment in industry and in mining and equipped for these opportunities through vocational training, the Indians would perform prodigies in transforming Bolivia into a modern country. Only the Indian, because he had the highest potential for Westernization and possessed all the qualities associated with the inner drives of the capitalist ethic, had the capacity to turn Bolivia into a replica of the United States.[14] True, the Indian lacked intelligence and he could not, at least not until "much, much later" developed into a statesman;[15] but intelligence and leadership could be provided by mestizos who, Tamayo believed, were capable of absorbing the good qualities of the Indians and combining these qualities with their own superior intelligence.

Tamayo was one of the few thinkers in early twentieth-century Andean America who sincerely wanted to give the Indian the opportunity to develop self-reliance and to acquire economic and even some degree of political power—just as Villarán was one of the few sincerely concerned with transforming the urban laborers into self-reliant capitalists through education and industrialization. The overwhelming majority of the accommodated sectors, because they doubted Tamayo's appraisal of Indian capacity, or perhaps because of a gnawing fear that this appraisal might be accurate, did not intend, despite all their protestations to the contrary, to permit the Indian to develop as a competitive individual responsive to capitalist motivations. Their notion of Westernizing the Indian—and Westernization was almost universally hailed at the time as the solution to the Indian problem—consisted of despoiling him of his communal property, then leaving him adrift without the means of survival in an alien world.

In dealing with the Indians, upper-sector Bolivians acted not only out of racist convictions but out of fear. José Manuel Pando, the leader of the successful Liberal insurrection of 1899 and subsequently the president of the republic (1899–1904), had enlisted the support of Indians by promising them redress of various grievances. Thousands of Indians had flocked to the cause of Tata Pando, only to be frustrated when the Liberals, having won their struggle, chose to ignore their promises. The result was a series of Indian uprisings, the most threatening one led by the remarkable Pablo Zárate Willka, that constituted "one of the largest-scale social upheavals ever promoted and carried out by the native population in Bolivia."[16] Not since the Túpac Amaru uprisings of 1780 had the whites and mestizos of the highlands been so terrorized by Indians, or so determined, once the menace had been overcome, upon the permanent repression of the natives.

The Indian violence of 1899 transformed Mariano Baptista, a pillar of the Conservative party and a former president who had previously praised the Indian as the great hope of Bolivia, into a thoroughgoing disparager of the natives, whom he dismissed as beasts.[17] When a terrible famine around Lake Titicaca led to massive starvation among the Aymaras beginning in 1903, not a few Bolivians hailed the development as the punishment of God against intractable beings.[18] With these attitudes providing the justification, many of those in the new Liberal power elite resumed the assault against the Indian comunidades that had been a major feature of the Melgarejo administration in the 1860s.[19]

The creation of new and the expansion of old estates in the sierra, always at the expense of Indian comunidades, was even more striking

147

in Peru. The process got underway during the presidency of Piérola (1895–1899),[20] a fact that would imply the Indians had known what they were doing when, on the whole, they supported Andrés Cáceres in his unsuccessful resistance against the liberal revolution of 1895. Under Piérola, the landowners moved quickly to seize Indian properties, and frequently the president dispatched the country's armed forces to attack the natives.[21] Piérola also used the army to suppress Indian insurrections precipitated by the plunder of the land.

The rise of the large estate, the consolidation of power by the landowning elites of the sierra (termed *latifundistas* or *gamonales*, the latter word deriving from the name of a parasitical plant), and the extension of serfdom among the Indian populace were all the results of the response by the well-to-do sectors to new economic conditions.[22] As the coast began to develop scientifically farmed plantations for export crops and as the number of urban dwellers increased steadily in the early part of the twentieth century, demand for the food crops and cattle of the sierra soared. This in turn tempted the *gamonales* "to increase productivity by seizing Indian communal property."[23] Foreign demand for wool, the sierra's principal export, also contributed to the plight of the Indian, inciting land grabs not only by Peruvians but also by English textile firms which began to expand their operations from Chile into the areas around Cuzco and Puno.

A social and economic revolution was underway in Bolivia, the Peruvian sierra, and even in highland Ecuador where in general the pace of change was slower. As a result Indians were removed from the security of their semiautonomous communities and reduced to vassalage on the estates of whites and mestizos. Even as in colonial times, expansion of the frontier continued to mean the extension of feudalistic ties and the strengthening of patronalist-clientelist patterns. Indian serfs in exchange for their labor received the use of small plots of land—sometimes no more than a furrow or two—and also certain paternalistic benefits that custom and enlightened self-interest induced landowners to extend. Thus while political leaders and intellectuals in the capital cities reached their most eloquent pitch in extolling the virtues of capitalist self-reliance, abject dependency became the life style for more and more of the rural populace.

At the time the Liberals came to power in Ecuador a good deal of the labor on privately owned highland estates was performed by Indian debt peons, tied to the landowner-creditor through a system known as *concertaje*. Indians who did not work off their monetary obligations to the satisfaction of the landowner could be jailed as debtors. During his first presidential term (1895–1901), Eloy Alfaro moved to establish certain restrictions on the *concertaje* contract by, among other stipulations, requiring that it be entered into before two witnesses.[24] These and some additional measures were enforced sporadically, if at all, during most of the period of Liberal ascendancy. Then, in 1918, under President Alfredo Baquerizo Moreno (1916–1920) a more meaningful blow was struck aganst *concertaje* when legislation was enacted prohibiting imprisonment for debts.

Motivation for this legislation was by no means purely altruistic. The traditional *concertaje* system included certain paternalistic features. For example, the Indian retained his *huasipungo* (plot of land) even if unable to work because of sickness, accident, or old age; further, his widow inherited the plot and also received assistance from the estate owner until one of her children was old enough to begin to work the plot. Along with debt imprisonment, the 1918 law struck down these provisions of the *concertaje* system. The legislation has, in fact, been viewed as simply an attempt on the part of the new-rich landowners who had come into possession of estates since the Liberal takeover to free themselves from the economic burdens of paternalism.[25] Moreover, the 1918 law was designed to help the owners of the coastal cacao plantations who in the past had relied upon *concertaje* contracts in securing at least a part of their labor force. Convinced by now that a wage-earning, free labor force was in the long run cheaper than one held in bondage through paternalistic practices, the coastal plantation owners welcomed the 1918 reform.

Whatever its motivation, the 1918 legislation remained a dead letter in some of the more remote highland regions of Ecuador.[26] And where *concertaje* was abolished in the sierra, it was replaced by a new type of vassalage labor that left the Indian serfs no better off then before. In the new system, called *huasipungaje*, the landowner advanced no loans but did confer upon the laborer the use of a plot of land. In exchange the laborer (*huasipunguero*) assumed the obligations to work from three to five days a week for the estate owner.[27]

The era of Liberal rule produced no important new laws on Indian relations in Bolivia. In Peru, though, it witnessed congressional enactment in 1916 of what has been called "one of the most important pieces of Indian legislation in the twentieth century." The Peruvian law placed restrictions on debt peonage and "provided that each worker was to receive a minimum daily wage of twenty centavos apart from any concessions of land for crops and grazing."[28]

The 1916 law did nothing to slow the ongoing assaults against independent Indian comunidades. It did, however, take the first significant step to provide the Indians who had been reduced to vassal status on the large estates owned by whites and mestizos with a minimal amount of purchasing power. To understand this departure from custom, it is necessary to take into account the timing of the law. As a result of the trade dislocations produced by World War I, Peru's source of foreign manufactures had largely dried up. As in many other Latin American countries of the period, the Peruvian leaders had begun to experiment with import-substitution industrialization, a move which suggested the expediency of spreading some purchasing power among those who made up the internal market, even if they happened to be Indians. The section of the 1916 legislation dealing with monetary wages for Indians was lifted "almost verbatim" from Simón Bolívar's decree of July 4, 1825.[29] Bolívar's decree, however, had been intended to foster creation of a free and independent rural labor force and was just one facet of a program aimed at ultimately making most Indians owners of their own small farms. In the Peru of 1916 there was little sympathy for the Liberator's overall design. The Indian laborers of the sierra estates had by that time been placed securely within the confines of a system of vassalage. It was safe, therefore, to provide them with a certain minimum of purchasing power, for it would not facilitate their emergence as an independent labor force motivated by capitalist incentives. Here is a classic example of how in Andean America "capitalism has been linked with feudalism."[30]

LIBERALISM AND THE CHURCH

The traditional hostility of Andean Catholicism toward laissez-faire capitalism was strengthened by the publication in 1891 of Pope Leo XIII's landmark social encyclical *Rerum novarum*. In this remarkable document the pope attacked the spirit of liberal capitalism for the manner in which it had contributed to a type of exploitation that created a grave social problem with the risk of mass upheavals that could only strengthen the hand of atheistic socialists. At the same time the pontiff urged the corporative restructuring of society as the means for restoring social justice and harmony.

In Andean America where the proponents of liberal capitalism had at last gained control after a struggle that stretched back over several generations and where social upheaval was considered not even a remote possibility, the Catholic Church, insofar as its clergy rallied behind the encyclical, suffered a decline in influence. Peru's Civilist oligarchy regarded it as a largely irrelevant institution. In Bolivia it endured a mild anticlerical attack which did not, however, extend to the point of ending its role in maintaining hospitals, various charitable establishments, and schools. Nor did the anticlerical program threaten the church's role as a large landowner.[31]

If Peru's and Bolivia's governing elites viewed the church as somewhat beside the point in modern societies, they never challenged the influence which clergymen continued to exercise over the masses. In Ecuador it was altogether different. Here the Liberals had been thirsting for vengeance against entrenched clericalism ever since the age of García Moreno. And, unlike the situation in Bolivia where the church had never enjoyed a strong economic position or a major temporal influence, the clergy possessed the means to wage a spirited struggle against their adversaries. Predictably, national writers are in complete disagreement over which side bears responsibility for initiating the bitter, and often bloody, struggle between the anticlerical Liberals and the defenders of the clergy's interests. This struggle got underway almost at once after Alfaro came to power in 1895,[32] and from then until August of 1896 Ecuador was ravaged by a civil war during the course of which clergymen wherever they could incited the masses to rise and were themselves subjected to harsh repression —not necessarily in that sequence.

With order temporarily restored as Alfaro, taking personal command over many of the campaigns, triumphed over the partisans of the clergy, a Liberal-dominated National Assembly met in 1897 and framed a new constitution providing for religious toleration (although Catholicism remained the official religion of the state), barring the entry of new religious communities from abroad, and prohibiting foreigners from serving as bishops.[33] The new constitution provoked intensified efforts on the part of the Conservatives to organize an invasion from Colombia, where a proclerical government was in power and where clergymen exiled by the Alfaro regime were doing all in their power to make sure the invasion occurred. As rumors of an invasion from Colombia persisted in 1900, Federico González Suárez, named the Bishop of Ibarra in 1895, won the plaudits of many Liberals and the denunciations of quite a few Conservatives when he declared: "We, the priests, should never sacrifice the patria in order to save Religion."[34] The invasion schemes came at least temporarily to a halt when Colombia and Ecuador signed a protocol of peace in June of 1900.

151

The Liberals now continued their anticlerical onslaught. A new patronage law left the church largely at the mercies of the anticlerical administration. The 1900 Law of Public Beneficence sequestered the property of religious communities, while a 1904 law prohibited the establishment of new novitiates.[35] In 1906 the government unilaterally rescinded the concordat with the Holy See, and from that time on the church in Ecuador remained in an insecure position.[36] A new constitution, enacted by a National Assembly meeting in 1906 and 1907, incorporated into its text many of the earlier anticlerical provisions and added to them some new ones of its own devising. Called by its detractors the Atheistic Constitution, the new charter was enacted with the enthusiastic backing of Alfaro who had returned to power in 1906 by overthrowing a constitutionally elected president. Serious dissension had by now appeared within the Liberal ranks and Alfaro had apparently grown convinced that only he and his closest friends understood how to govern Ecuador.[37]

Contributing to Liberal divisiveness was an intraparty debate over the anticlerical issue. Grouped behind the high-minded and moderate Luis Felipe Borja, a number of Liberal party senators spoke out against what they considered the excesses of the anticlerical legislation. According to them, this legislation constituted a betrayal of liberal principles, for it denied liberty to the church to control its own affairs.[38] For Borja and his supporters, extreme anticlericalism was only one instance of betrayal of liberalism's norms by Alfaro and his henchmen. Increasingly, disillusioned Liberals complained that governmental highhandedness and the violent repression of dissent had destroyed the ideals that underlay the 1895 revolution. The liberalism of Alfaro, they charged, was the liberalism of the machete.[39]

The church-state controversy subsided slightly for a time after 1906 as the Conservatives reconciled themselves, in view of the strength of their adversaries, to biding their time in seeking to turn the tables. Contributing to the uneasy calm were the moderation and superb statesmanship displayed by González Suárez who became Archbishop of Quito in 1906. In an abrupt departure from the Garcian position, González Suárez (who was his country's finest historian in addition to being its ablest church leader) sought to depoliticize the clergy. He thereby won the grudging admiration of many Liberal political figures and as a result was able to maneuver with them so as to block actual implementation of certain anticlerical decrees.[40]

Despite the abilities of Gonzáles Suárez as a peacemaker, the bitterness with which Conservatives and Liberals divided over the church issue had only begun to abate ever so slightly by the time of his death in 1917. As of that date, many Conservatives remained as intent upon vengeance as the Liberals had been during the rule of García Moreno.

Helping to maintain hatred at fever pitch was the lynching of Alfaro by a mob of *quiteños* in 1912. Some Liberals were as happy as the Conservatives to see the end of the "old battler" who at the time of his death had just completed his second term and was plotting to seize power once more by overthrowing his duly-elected Liberal successor. But the anti-Alfaro Liberals disguised their true feelings and sought to arouse passions against the Conservatives by picturing the fallen *caudillo* as the victim of the Ecuadoran clergy who "from a hundred pulpits" had instigated the bloody deed.[41]

While directing the battle of anticlericalism, Alfaro had also produced some tangible evidences of economic progress. However, owing largely to the continuing bitterness of the doctrinal issue and his own disregard of constitutional procedures, Alfaro had not been able to legitimatize his two administrations on the basis of material accomplishments. Both in Peru and Bolivia, where the old church-state ideological issues remained muted and where governments during the period of liberal ascendancy were outwardly a bit more respectful of electoral formulas and constitutional niceties, governments gained a certain degree of legitimacy, at least until the outbreak of World War I, by means of the material advances they brought about.

PROGRESS AND THE RISE OF A NEW PLUTOCRACY

The contrast between the presidential terms of the two Pardos, father and son, bears eloquent testimony to Peru's economic transformation. Manuel Pardo had served (1872–1876) at a time of adversity and was constantly faced with the specter of national bankruptcy. José Pardo's two terms (1904–1908, 1915–1919) came during an era of unprecedented expansion that overshadowed the fabled guano age. The continuing expansion of the railroad system lent further impetus to mining, with the value of its output rising to 8.5 million pounds sterling by 1916—compared to 423,000 pounds in 1886. Railroads played a part also in facilitating the shipment of food products from the sierra to the coast and, together with the expanding road system, helped bring into existence a new class of *serrano* middlemen who bought the products of the highland estates and then shipped them to coastal urban centers.

As important as mining was, the main stimulus to economic growth came from the startling increase of cotton and sugar production along the country's coast. Foreign and local capital combined in bringing about the creation of this technically advanced agricultural export economy.[42] Mining and agricultural wealth in turn led to the rise of new export-import firms, some of them in the hands of the steadily rising number of Italian and Spanish immigrants,[43] to the founding of textile mills, and to the birth of a modern system of financial capitalism. Between 1897 and 1908 the number of banks in Lima rose from four to ten, and their paid-in capital more than quintupled.[44] Peru's directing classes, provided they refrained carefully from probing beneath the surface signs of development, could congratulate themselves on the success of the new mercantilism, content in the fact that between 1900 and 1913 the country enjoyed an uninterrupted favorable balance of trade.[45]

Far more so than in Peru, economic growth in Bolivia was associated with the production of one item: tin.[46] Helping to account for the dizzying rise in tin production, even as for mining's increased productivity in Peru, was the building of a national railway system. Already by 1892, Oruro had been linked by rail to Arica. Bolivia acquired a second means of access to the coast in 1908 with completion of the railroad line that joined La Paz to Guaqui on Lake Titicaca. As a result the Bolivian capital was connected, by means of the steamers that crossed Lake Titicaca, with the Southern Railway of Peru running between the coastal port of Mollendo and Puno, located on the Peruvian side of the lake. By this time yet a third link between the landlocked republic and the coast was well underway. In 1904 the administration in La Paz had celebrated a treaty with Chile recognizing that country's definitive ownership of the entire area that had once constituted the Bolivian coast.[47] The terms of the treaty included a provision that the Chilean government would undertake the building of an Arica-La Paz railway, and this line was completed in 1913.[48] Moreover, the 300,000 pounds sterling which the treaty called upon Chile to pay Bolivia contributed toward financing the construction of a La Paz-Oruro railroad. And, the year 1917 brought completion of the Oruro-Cochabamba railway, thus connecting Bolivia's granary to the heartland of the mountainous mining region.[49]

Thanks in large part to the building of railroads, Bolivia's exports doubled between 1898 and 1906, the tin age got off to a promising start, and "the economy of the country was saved."[50] In the five-year period 1892–1896, Bolivia exported a total of 31,583 tons of tin, while for the 1917–1921 period the figure stood at 245,364 tons.[51] Its share of the world tin market rose from 12 percent in 1900 to 22 percent in 1925,[52] while the percentage of the total value of Bolivian exports accounted for by tin jumped from 41 percent in 1900 to 62 percent in 1905, declined to 49 percent in 1910 and held steady at this figure in 1915, and then surged to 72 percent in 1920.[53]

The dominant political figure presiding over Bolivia's era of progress was Ismael Montes. Twice the president of his country (1904–1909, 1913–1917), Montes, a stocky man with a powerful chest "whose face was hidden behind his thick Prussian whiskers,"[54] gave his whole-hearted commitment to the principles of classical economic liberalism. "A country in itself," he wrote, "has nothing. Its wealth is nothing more than the sum of private wealth. Therefore it is scientifically necessary to stimulate the growth of the latter so that it will contribute with the greatest effectiveness to the national prosperity."[55] During the age of Montes, a number of Bolivians proved remarkably successful in accumulating private wealth; but whether in the process they contributed to overall national development has always been heatedly debated by the country's writers.

The giants of Bolivia's new tin export economy were Félix Avelino Aramayo, born in Paris and the son of one of the country's richest and most influential citizens, Mauricio Hochschild, a German of Jewish extraction who upon arrival in South America had initially become a naturalized citizen of Argentina, and, towering above all others, Simón Patiño, a mestizo of humble origins from the Cochabamba valley.[56] All three came eventually to head companies that were incorporated abroad, that depended to a considerable extent on foreign capital, and that were involved in the processing of the tin ore exported from Bolivia—which had no tin smelters of its own until the second half of the twentieth century.

For Bolivia's new tin tycoons, the primary objective was to obtain ore at the cheapest possible price because their major profits derived from the sale of the refined product. The lower the value of the ore they shipped abroad, the less they paid their national government in export taxes. All the while the profits earned by their companies went in considerable portion to the foreign stockholders. Bolivia's gains from its mushrooming tin industry included the niggardly wages paid the mine laborers and the export taxes collected by the government, which fluctuated between 4 and 16 percent of total government revenue during the first two decades of the twentieth century.[57] Beyond this, a host of lawyers, accountants, managers, white-collar functionaries, and—most important of all—politicians on the make benefited from Bolivia's tin enterprises. These were the persons who comprised the notorious *Rosca* (literally, the screw).

The circumstances that gave rise to the *Rosca* are described well by Herbert Klein:

> To these new [tin] miners, with their... complex relations with the industrial and financial capital of the outside world, direct involvement in national politics became an impossible and even distasteful goal... Rather than participate themselves, these new capitalists left the defence of their interests to the developing pressure groups of native lawyers, economists, and advisors with whom they surrounded themselves and whom the Bolivian public soon gave the label *Rosca*.[58]

Progress in Bolivia under the management of the *Rosca* was associated with impressive export statistics which actually did not result in capital inflow into the country, given the foreign participation in ownership of the tin industry. With ample reason, Augusto Guzmán has commented upon the irony of a situation in which an underdeveloped country became a major exporter of capital.[59] All the while the government failed to develop an adequate tax structure, for it was not powerful enough to impose significant taxes on the tin magnates. Consistently, government expenditures exceeded income; and of the approximately $80 million which the government invested in building railroads, $58 million was borrowed, principally from U.S. capitalists.[60]

Like Peru and Bolivia, Ecuador had its fling at railroad building, and the result was the Guayaquil-Quito railway, completed in 1908. Construction of the railway, the project dearest to Elroy Alfaro's heart, did not unlock national treasures as in the two sister republics, for Ecuador's highland interior lacked mineral resources. As a result, Ecuador remained without many of the signs of progress apparent in Peru and Bolivia. A critic of Alfaro made this fair assessment of the situation in 1913: "General Alfaro has left us, then, the railroad, but in exchange for a situation of ruin in almost all the territory. The progress of the cities has been slight and owing entirely to local efforts. Funds collected to provide special services . . . have been siphoned off into immorality."[61]

If Ecuador lacked Peru's copper, silver, cotton, and intensive sugar production as well as Bolivia's tin, it did at least possess on its coast an important export crop: cacao. And this proved sufficient to bring into being Ecuador's equivalent of the *Rosca*, the *Argolla* or ring.

156

Much of the money made through cacao exports found its way into the Commercial and Agricultural Bank of Guayaquil, founded just after the Liberals came to power. The bank controlled foreign exchange operations and gained a virtual monopoly over extending credit to the national government. In fact, the government acquired most of its capital not through taxes, but by turning for credit to the bank. The process assumed its most dramatic proportions in 1914 with enactment of a moratorium law providing that banks no longer need redeem the money they issued in gold. This legislation allowed the bank sharply to increase its lending operations to the central government, thereby assuring increased profits, guaranteed by government interest payments, to the coterie of capitalists who ran the bank.[62] With considerable justification, an Ecuadoran writer has charged the Commercial and Agricultural Bank of Guayaquil with primary responsibility for demoralizing Ecuadoran liberalism and transforming its adherents from a patriotic party into "an infamous ring."[63]

Other figures of prominence in the *Argolla* were the members of the Association of Agriculturists of Ecuador, founded in 1912 and made up principally of the owners of the coastal cacao plantations. In order that the association might carry on a worldwide advertising campaign and investigate the possibility of forming an international cartel of cacao producers, the government assigned to it a major share of the export taxes assessed on the commodity. These funds were diverted from the intended purpose by the association and used primarily to line the pockets of its members, and to enable some of them to buy more shares in the Commercial and Agricultural Bank. When the association managed to spend more money than it took in, the deficit was covered by a loan from this bank.[64] Needless to say, the bank's unrestrained issuing of paper money to cover loans both to government and private parties brought on inflation which was ruinous to the laboring classes and to the lower middle sectors.

In all three of the Andean republics under consideration, a new plutocracy had, to a considerable extent, joined forces with the old-line aristocracy. Cleavages and tensions still existed, but a basis of fundamental rapport had been found. The merging elites were well satisfied with the type of economic development that depended on exports. For them, the new mercantilism had proved extremely advantageous. Most of them would have agreed with a Bolivian public figure who insisted that forces of nature had determined that his country must depend economically on the export of its mineral wealth to foreign markets. Therefore, it was necessary to concentrate on the few enclaves within the country where the export economy was based and to some degree forget the rest of the national domain.[65]

Already by 1895, Peru's influential and monied classes had coalesced, and it was the joint efforts of a new plutocracy and an older aristocracy that brought about the end of military rule in that year.[66] The revolution of 1895, according to Jorge Bravo Bresani, was made by an alliance of the "bourgeois urban rich that began to emerge in the guano age" and the "old landowning aristocracy."[67] In Ecuador and Bolivia, the beginning of the twentieth century found the upper classes far more divided. The revolutions bringing the Liberals to power had pitted urban bourgeois against rural agrarian interests, as well as upward-bound mestizos against a long-established, whiter aristocracy.[68] In both countries the urban, bourgeois, predominately mestizo elements, concentrated in Guayaquil and La Paz, had formed the backbone of the successful Liberal movement. Within a surprisingly short time, however, the victors and vanquished had begun to form alliances; like Peruvians, they were proceeding toward the consolidation of a ruling class.[69] This development requires a word of explanation.

If the Ecuadoran and Bolivian Liberals had been intent upon establishing manufacturing industry, they would necessarily have sought to destroy the whole feudalistic labor structure of the countryside that kept the vast majority of the populace out of a money economy. Thanks to the profits to be made through exports, however, it was possible to achieve prosperity merely by developing a few beachheads of capitalist modernity while leaving all of the remaining national domain untouched by the winds of change. This being the case, it was not in the interest of the Liberal rulers to interfere with the manner in which a traditional aristocracy managed its affairs. As a result, it shortly proved possible for the new and the old elites of Ecuador and Bolivia, despite ever so many individual cases of animosity, to collaborate almost as smoothly as in Peru. Because the new men who had seized power in the 1890s were willing and even anxious to maintain the traditional social system in which the lower classes were subservient clients without either economic or political power, the economic-social clash between liberalism and conservatism that seemed to be shaping up in the nineteenth century never took place.

Had it not been for the flourishing of capitalism abroad, and for the resulting availability of markets and capital, Andean America could not have acquired a façade of modernity while leaving intact the traditional social structure. In this regard the analysis that José Fellman Velarde makes for Bolivia is equally applicable to Ecuador and Peru. He asks how it was that values of modernity reigned in the urban centers while traditionalists remained supreme in the countryside. And he answers: "The reason was that the bourgeoisie that operated then in Bolivia was principally dedicated to producing prime materials, and did not need to expand the internal market of consumption, now that its market of consumption was the United States, England, or Germany."[70]

At the turn of the century the U.S. capitalist system expanded to the extent of beginning to encompass Peru, Bolivia, and Ecuador within its sphere of operations. From this moment, U.S. capitalism began to have an ancillary role in shaping the internal social and economic structures of the three republics. The role was no less important because of the fact that most North American capitalists did not realize they were playing it.

THE PENETRATION OF U.S. CAPITAL

The period 1897–1914 witnessed the first massive outpouring of U.S. capital into fields afar. By 1914 U.S. direct foreign investment, estimated at $2.65 billion, was equal to 7 percent of the GNP—exactly the same percentage, incidentally, as in 1966.[71] South America's share in U.S. direct private investment, although remaining insignificant in comparison to the figures for Mexico, Canada, and Europe, amounted to an estimated $38 million in 1897 and to $323 million in 1914.[72] As Americans invested in the lands to the south, trade increased. Between 1900 and 1913 U.S. imports from South America more than doubled, rising from a value of $94 million to $218 million. The rise in the value of U.S. exports was more impressive: from $38 million to $146 million. In Peru, Bolivia, and Ecuador, as in the rest of South America, U.S. investment in "supply-oriented activities," such as mining, and also in trading houses helped account for the growth.[73]

Facilitating the southward thrust of U.S. capitalism at the turn of the century was an approximation in hearts and minds between the influential classes of North America and Andean America. The United States as perceived by admiring Andean elites was a country dominated by successful businessmen who operated according to the principles of the divine right of wealth and assumed that low economic status was the result of personal inferiority and moral depravity. Members of this North American plutocracy, in a manner that appealed enormously to many Andean elites, criticized democracy on the grounds of its alleged inefficiency while maintaining that only business leaders could provide efficient national direction.[74]

Hannah Arendt contends there has always been an ambivalence within the United States as to whether the real goal to be pursued is freedom within an egalitarian setting or prosperity.[75] The choice, beginning in the gilded age, seemed to have tipped toward the second,[76] and nothing could have delighted the Andean ruling classes more than to have the Great Republic of the North abandon the quest for equality that had so impressed Tocqueville and other early nineteenth-century observers. Little wonder that Franz Tamayo returned from a brief visit in 1905 singing the praises of the United States. Here he found not altruism, but the ambitions of those who ran the "devouring trusts." The spirit of the United States, he wrote in admiration, is "make yourself strong," not "make yourself wise."[77] Another Bolivian, Alberto Gutiérrez, who visited the United States at about the same time, noted there was no longer evident a "sincerely equalitarian spirit, or a real attempt to approximate the ideals of democracy and justice"; politics was so tied in with big business and the trusts that "one cannot really talk about democracy."[78]

The approximation in hearts and minds between U.S. and Andean upper classes took place precisely at the moment in history when it was bound to be the most disadvantageous to Andean America. At an earlier time, U.S. culture and education had reenforced the notion that the "enlightened citizen should surrender himself to the nation, contemplating only the universal good and disregarding petty personal, or local interests. From the beginning, therefore, the citizen's role, according to predominate American doctrine, was one of sublimation." At an earlier time, moreover, the American doctrine had cautioned that lust for material gain was cause for anxiety, for it "threatened to distract men's thought from the elevating ideas about the American purposes." At the turn of the century, however, "the inroads of mammon, passion, and partisanship seemed about to overwhelm the Republic,"[79] and there was nothing of the sublimated man in the new class of business leaders.

The United States had emerged as a nation only because during the formative period there had been an American doctrine that stressed subordination of private material gain to loftier national ideals. Enough of this principle remained to contain to some degree the later inroads of mammon; and much of the spirit of early twentieth-century progressivism was concerned with strengthening the old

American doctrine. But Andean Americans, who had not yet begun even remotely to transform their republics into true nations, took with undisguised delight to the new American exaltation of the unsublimated being while choosing to ignore the progressive reform currents. The particular aspect of U.S. culture that they chose to emulate contributed not to the making but to the unmaking of their nations.

In yet another way the approximation in hearts and minds between the North American and Andean upper classes took place at a time that was particularly unfortunate, for it brought together men of increasingly blatant racist attitudes and served mutually to reenforce their prejudices. The 1890s was a period when Jim Crow gained supremacy in the United States, and when the "attempt at a decent tone and some semblance of rationality gave way to an unvarnished, crass racism."[80] Their views buttressed by the latest "scientific" theories, "most middle-class Americans of the 1890s agreed in attaching great importance to the concept of race, and it was that agreement which gave the intellectual life of the period its peculiar tone."[81] Thus in viewing the United States of this period, the leaders of Andean America could find an example to confirm their conviction that the dark skinned must not be governed by the same laws that pertained to the light skinned. The United States also seemed to provide proof that the effects of progress could be confined to the better elements of society and need not benefit the unfit. Even the most advanced country in the world could maintain, at no apparent risk to its snowballing progress, what in effect was a two-culture society.

Because Andean America's liberal leaders admired so much of U.S. culture as they perceived it, they were ready to afford an enthusiastic reception to North American capitalists, welcoming them as frontiersmen with whom they could fruitfully collaborate in reclaiming for civilization what had long remained a vast wilderness. This, then, was the background against which U.S. capital began its rapid penetration into Peru, Bolivia and Ecuador. That penetration brought with it not only certain economic transformations but also some new diplomatic twists. This will be revealed by the three brief case studies that follow.

Peru In 1871 a thirty-nine-year-old Irishman named William R. Grace, who had been active in Peruvian commerce ever since 1854 and had married the daughter of an American sea captain, organized with Michael P. Grace in Lima the firm of Grace Brothers. By the 1880s Grace Brothers had branches in Valparaíso, San Francisco, New York, and London, and had assumed an American-Anglo-Peruvian character. W. R. Grace had become an American citizen, making New York his headquarters and serving two terms as mayor of that city; but Michael Grace maintained his closest ties, personal and financial, with England. In 1884 Grace House (*Casa Grace*), as the firm had become known, acquired through the settlement of a private debt the huge Cartavio sugar plantation in northern Peru. Subsequently the firm took an important role in financing Peru's railroads and in handling the country's foreign debt; it also undertook the operation of nine Bolivian railroads and helped build two new ones. In 1894 it consolidated its various enterprises in the American corporation, W. R. Grace and Company. The new corporation, however, remained closely linked with British interests, and not until World War I "did W. R. Grace and Company take on a character that was clearly North American."[82] Even by 1900, however, the company had gained control over most of the commerce between the United States and Peru.

By 1902 North American capital had become active in Peruvian mining. There had been formed in that year the Cerro de Pasco Mining Company, staking out for its field of operations the rich copper, silver, lead, and gold deposits that lay at a height of some 14,000 feet in the Andean ranges to the northeast of Lima. After gaining the upper hand in a dispute with a Peruvian firm, the North American controlled Cerro de Pasco Company acquired nearly six thousand acres of land, laid some eighty-three miles of railroad track to link its plant to the national line, and established a refining plant eight miles south of the town of Cerro de Pasco. The smelter at first functioned improperly, owing in part to the low-grade fuel, and huge additional outlays of capital were required to put the operation on a sound basis.[83] By 1912 the North American owners had already invested some $25 million in their Cerro de Pasco holdings. They had also begun to alienate certain Peruvians. According to one critic, the company had created a vast latifundium, where before there had been a thousand small proprietors, and it had ruined the vegetation and the fauna of the whole region with the smoke of its ovens. Its estates allegedly had become like a "new California," where gambling, drunken fights, assassinations, and assaults on Indians abounded.[84] Whatever the drawbacks, North American capital had helped initiate the age of copper. On the eve of World War I, Cerro de Pasco was

Peru's largest producer of the commodity, and a firm recently formed by the North Americans J. H. Johnston and Jacob Backus (a nephew of Henry Meiggs) was in second place.

By 1915 U.S. investments in Peru were estimated at $50 million,[85] well below the British total of approximately $120 million[86] but climbing much more rapidly. Thanks to British and American investments in mining, sugar production, railroads, commerce, and also utilities Peru had been integrated into the world economy, with the whole process accelerated by the opening of the Panama Canal in 1914. Already far advanced was the process that would result in the "integration of the Peruvian economy into the internal market of the United States."[87]

Bolivia　As early as 1898, Guggenheim funds had begun to flow into Bolivian mining enterprises,[88] and the Liberal administration that came to power the following year was desperately anxious to attract more North American capital. A boundary dispute with Brazil served only to heighten the desire to attract Yankee capital and at the same time demonstrated the predisposition that Bolivia had acquired since the War of the Pacific to accept dependence on the United States in the interest of protecting its national domain against greedy neighbors.

A rubber boom had by the beginning of the century caused Bolivia to focus its interests and hopes for the future on its eastern territory of Acre, bordering on Brazil.[89] The rubber boom had also stimulated Brazilian interest in the territory, thus injecting new life into a long-standing boundary dispute. At this point the Bolivian administration of José Manuel Pando (1899–1904) entered into an arrangement assigning rights for rubber exploitation in much of the contended region to certain North American capitalists who in 1901 had helped found the Bolivian Syndicate. Pando and his advisers hoped that the U.S. government would now intervene to protect its investors by preventing Brazil from despoiling Bolivia of the territories which had been assigned, on a thirty-three-year concession, to the Bolivian Syndicate.

Nothing came of the Bolivian hopes, owing to skillful Brazilian diplomacy and to the fact that at this time the United States had established as a fundamental principle of its Latin American policy the maintenance of a special relationship with Brazil. Thus Bolivia did not obtain the desired U.S. intervention and had to face Brazil unaided in a short war that ended with the 1903 Treaty of Petropolis.[90] By its terms, Bolivia ceded to Brazil an area of 73,726 square miles. "The territorial loss of the Acre rubber country," J. Valerie Fifer writes, "was the largest single land cession by Bolivia in the whole troubled history of its boundary changes with five neighbor nations."[91] In exchange, Brazil committed itself to the payment of three million pounds sterling and the construction of a railway to join certain sections of the two republics. As it turned out, though, Brazil "failed to make payment and no further arrangements concerning the projected railroad or the promised payment were made until 1928."[92]

While it had not proved possible to use U.S. private capital as leverage for gaining official protection of national territory, Bolivia was soon employing North American funds to achieve the better integration of its remaining territory through the building of railroads. With the enthusiastic backing and insistent encouragement of President Montes, there came into being in 1906 the Bolivia Railway Company. The company resulted from an agreement between the republic of Bolivia, the National City Bank of New York and Speyer and Company to build a number of railroads within a period of ten years. This arrangement, known in Bolivia as the Speyer Contract, was denounced at the time by opponents of Montes, and has been criticized ever since as an unsound scheme that was excessively generous to U.S. bankers.[93] Of the 1,000 miles of track envisaged in the Speyer Contract, only 416 were laid, and this at a cost of some $22 million to the Bolivian government. Moreover, the government's subsequent financial difficulties permitted a British firm, the Antofagasta and Bolivia Railway Company, to gain control over the lines constructed by means of the Speyer Contract, and most of the country's other railway facilities as well. The Speyer Contract has been accurately described as a "transaction which cost the National City Bank and Speyer and Company practically nothing, netted them several millions of dollars on the sale of their share of the Bolivia Railway Company's stock, and won for . . . [a] British company the key to the control of Bolivia's entire railway system."[94]

Montes, of course, had his defenders, Bolivians who were convinced that the price being paid for their railway system was not excessive and who regarded the influx of foreign capital, whether invested in mining, railways, or any other enterprise, as a panacea for national problems. Among the many considerations accounting for the receptivity to U.S. capital was the expectation that as economic ties grew stronger Bolivia would be more likely to gain Washington's backing in the effort to reacquire a coastal territory. Bolivians took heart when in his January 22, 1917 message to congress President Woodrow Wilson included the statement that every country has the right of a direct outlet to the sea, "either by the cession of territory ... or by the neutralization of direct rights of way under the general guarantee which will assure peace." Wilson's statement was a decisive factor in Bolivia's severing of diplomatic relations with Germany later that year. "Deference to the wishes of the U.S.A. had become of paramount importance."[95] Although the United States did not necessarily want Bolivia as a client, Bolivia was eager to become the client of Washington.

Ecuador   Eloy Alfaro had the very highest regard for North Americans, originating perhaps in 1884 when an Irish American had saved him from drowning,[96] and a passionate conviction that railroads would bring Ecuador into "the modern life of economic abundance."[97] It is not surprising, then, that he set as his goal of highest priority the signing of a contract with North American capitalists for the building of a Guayaquil Quito railway. The negotiations that Ecuador's minister in Washington, Luis Felipe Carbo, carried out with "honorable and rich" persons, principal among them being Archer Harman, resulted in the signing of a contract in 1897 calling for the formation of a company that would raise $17.5 million for the building of the line.[98]

Alert for any additional pretext to justify their unremitting attacks against Alfaro, Ecuadoran Conservatives began at once to accuse the president of delivering the republic to the Yankees, thereby facilitating the eradication of the sacred Catholic religion.[99] As Alfaro increasingly alienated former associates within his own Liberal party, they joined with Conservatives in condemning the railroad contract, picturing it as the darkest crime in the annals of Ecuadoran politics. Through his ties with U.S. capital Alfaro had vastly strengthened his power base, and this is what so enraged his foes who now recognized the added difficulties they would have in topping the president. In the ceaseless propaganda war they waged, the enemies of Alfaro found it de rigeur to blacken the reputation of all Yankee capitalists who operated in Ecuador at the same time they assailed the "old battler"; for a relationhip of such intimacy now existed between the capitalists, especially Harman, and Alfaro that to besmirch one was to sully the other.

Harman arrived personally on the Ecuadoran scene in 1897, and soon Alfaro came to regard him as a great benefactor of the nation who deserved to have his statue erected on one of the peaks of the Andes.[100] But most Ecuadorans with whom he had contact regarded Harman in a different light, resenting his arrogance and his flaunting of "the immorality of his private life."[101] In a 1902 letter to Alfaro, Harman confessed that Ecuadoran public opinion was manifested against him "to a degree the equal of which I've never seen."[102] In spite of rising public opposition and the assurance of advisers that Harman was a crook,[103] Alfaro rammed through congress whatever legislation was deemed suitable to the interests of the Guayaquil and Quito Railway Company which Harman had founded and through which he gathered funds in the United States and in England. By the time the railway was completed in 1908 Harman, according to one highly critical observer, "was the owner of the Republic."[104]

Part of the Ecuadoran customs revenue had been pledged to meet interest payments on the securities floated by the Guayaquil and Quito Railway Company. By 1910, however, the government required all available funds as it prepared for what seemed a certain war with Peru over the chronic boundary dispute.[105] As a result, Ecuador had fallen into default on its railroad obligations and was being pressured both by the State Department from Washington and by the English Council of Bondholders from London to resume payments on the debt. Ostensibly to facilitate resumption the government of Alfaro, now in his second term (1907–1911), arranged a $2.5 million loan from Speyer and Company. Much of this money, however, went into armament purchases and the bondholders remained without satisfaction.

Through the mediation of the United States, Brazil, and Argentina, war between Ecuador and Peru was averted. At this point, though, the entire situation in Ecuador became still more involved. Interested in the Galapagos Islands (an archipelago owned by Ecuador lying about 600 miles off its coast) as a possible outer base for protecting the approaches to the about-to-be-completed Panama Canal, and above all desiring to prevent this strategic area from falling into the hands of any other major power, the United States began to negotiate with Alfaro for a ninety-nine-year lease. The terms suggested by Washington called for the payment of $15 million to Ecuador, the money to be spent for sanitation work in Guayaquil, for adjusting defaults on foreign loans and bonds, and for payment of the internal debt. Secretary of State Philander C. Knox, however, complicated matters by insisting that the lease invest the United States with full and complete sovereignty over each and every one of the islands during its ninety-nine-year duration, and at this Alfaro balked. Moreover, Washington rejected Alfaro's condition that in return for the lease the United States should agree to guarantee Ecuador's territorial integrity.[106]

The Ecuadoran public learned of the negotiations in late 1910 and responded with outrage against Alfaro who was accused of willingness to alienate national territory in return for private gain. Contributing to indignation was the fact that the portion of the proposed $15 million payment assigned to railroad building would go to an Archer Harman company. Yielding to the pressures of the public mood, Alfaro called off negotiations on the lease.

Attention next shifted to a $30-to-$40 million loan that the Alfaro administration was seeking from Speyer and Company. The State Department was willing to sanction the loan, which would allow Ecuador to put its economic house in order, provided the customs revenue to be pledged for servicing the debt would be honestly collected and administered by an agency that was 51 percent American owned. Alfaro rejected this stipulation and nothing came of the project.[107] As a result, the whole issue of satisfying the bondholders dragged on. In 1916 the State Department, now directed by Robert Lansing, was still trying to pressure the Ecuadoran government into resumption of payments. These efforts prompted an Ecuadoran statesman to declare that in spite of its public abjurations of imperialism, the United States persisted in treating Latin American republics as minors.[108]

A reliable study on U.S. relations with Ecuador during this period concludes that "concern over Panama, the desire to push and protect American business and obtain a field for new American investment" are all in evidence.[109] Also evident, however, were the tremendous obstacles faced by Washington in trying to conduct relations with a country perennially on the brink of war with one of its neighbors and a country where out-of-power politicians had already learned how to derive advantage from charging incumbents with complicity with nefarious Yankee capitalists.

If in the early twentieth century some Andean leaders had done all in their power to facilitate an expanding inflow of U.S. funds, others—including even those of liberal persuasions—registered alarm at the threat of Yankee hegemony posed by the abundance of the new source of investment and loan capital.[110] And, in future years many

167

Andean intellectuals would look back on this period as the time when national character had begun to be undermined by the flow of funds from abroad. One of the most commonly made allegations is that availability of foreign funds prevented the national citizenry from learning how to develop their own capital and stymied within them the spirit of enterprise, circumstances which in turn caused the Andeans to become dependent on foreigners.[111] It is impossible, though, to know if the coming of foreign capital brought about dependence, or if the Andeans purposely resorted to clientelist demeanor in the hopes of attracting capital from abroad so that they would not themselves have to develop the enterprising spirit—a spirit that despite the ephemeral cult of Spencerian liberalism continued to be regarded with widespread suspicion.

Until World War I the debate over the desirability and the consequences of foreign capital was waged by the tiny minority of educated, accommodated, and politically active citizens of Peru, Bolivia, and Ecuador. The war, however, brought with it huge economic dislocations that dealt staggering blows to the swelling ranks of urban laborers, causing them to turn to political action in seeking amelioration of their conditions. Out-of-power politicians who felt their own interests had not been served by the entry of foreign capital now turned for support to the awakening masses, assuring them that economic adversity was the consequence of the alliance that had been forged between the native oligarchy and a foreign plutocracy. In order to escape the onus placed upon them, the incumbent power-wielders themselves sometimes resorted to describing and exaggerating the dependence of the national economies on foreign capitalists. Thereby they might pass the blame for the ills which afflicted the masses along to outsiders. Thus the social problem that had surfaced in Andean America involved not just the local citizens but foreign, especially U.S., capitalists as well.

The Social Problem Surfaces

According to an analysis that prevailed among turn-of-the-century intellectuals in Peru, Bolivia, and Ecuador, the republics of South America would remain exempt for years to come, perhaps for as long as a century in the view of a Bolivian writer, from the sicknesses that beset the Old World and threatened it with social disruption.[112] European countries had a "worker question," an Ecuadoran explained, because "there you find an abundance of laborers and a scarcity of work; but in Latin America there is an abundance of work and a scarcity of laborers."[113] It followed, in his mind, that Latin America would be spared a social problem. Great was the consternation among Andean upper classes when this confidence was shattered as a worker question of serious magnitude appeared at the time of World War I.

Between 1914 and 1918 Peru suffered through ten major strikes, most of them accompanied by bloodshed. All of these were minor in comparison to the strike of 1919 waged in demand of the eight-hour day. Paralyzing Lima and Callao, the strike was eventually broken by the Pardo government, but only after the army was called out to restore order.[114] The strike bore far-reaching consequences, for the charge that Pardo was unable to deal with a worsening labor situation served as one of the justifications employed by Augusto B. Leguía in seizing power through a *golpe* before the end of the year—and initiating a new socioeconomic program that is described in the following chapter.

Bolivia's First National Congress of Worker assembled in La Paz in 1912, addressing itself to the task of labor organization. The following year witnessed the country's first mining strike when workers left their posts at the Huanchaco enterprises, and beginning in 1914 the pace of syndical organization accelerated. Widespread strikes occurred in the mining industry in 1918, and in October of the following year the workers of Huanuni after arduous negotiations won their demand for an eight-hour day, the first such concession in the country's history.[115] During roughly the same period labor unrest spread among the *montuvios* (the Negro-Indian-white mixed bloods) who worked the coastal plantations of Ecuador, producing the warning from the country's foremost sociological essayist that the social problem could lead to a race war.[116]

Of fundamental importance in explaining the appearance of a social problem was a demographic shift that had been underway since the late nineteenth century. In part because of the assault on Indian estates, abetted by the operations in the sierra of labor recruiters from the coast, more and more rural dwellers were immigrating to urban centers in Peru and Ecuador, and especially in Bolivia to mushrooming mining towns. As a result a proletariat labor force was coming into being. Lima provides a striking example of the population shift. A city of 114,788 in 1890, Lima experienced a growth of 11,748 in the course of the ensuing ten years. For the next decade. 1900–1910, the population grew by 19,390, and between 1910 and 1920 it rose by 27,081.[117]

In their migration the rural masses passed directly from either a semifeudal or a communal situation—in which they had been provided for paternalistically or had lived in their own self-sufficient, nonindividualistic comunidades—into the modern, competitive conditions of urban and mining camp life. Lacking education and initially without organizational aptitudes or the aggressive instincts of self-protection, they formed a readily exploitable mass. The rising urban and mining capitalist classes would have been more than human had they done other than exploit the new proletariat. By doing otherwise, moreover, they would have betrayed their liberal, laissez-faire ideology and their Spencerian concept of nation-building by eliminating the unfit.

Conditions for the urban lower classes worsened during the World War I years. With the soaring international demand for sugar and cotton, a good deal of land in Peru was pressed into growing these commodities and withdrawn from food production. In Lima, the price index for food products rose from 100 in 1913 to 208 in 1920; during the same period working-class wages remained almost stationary. Meanwhile in Ecuador workers suffered from runaway inflation brought about by the wholesale issuing of paper money by Guayaquil's banking plutocracy. As prices jumped, wages clung to the same low level. Largely in response to their deteriorating economic status the workers of Peru and Ecuador, and also of Bolivia, began of necessity to learn how to organize. Sometimes they had as their mentors anarcho-syndicalists from Spain and Argentina. What is more, they began to receive verbal support from the lower middle classes whose situation had also deteriorated.

Andean America's artisans had long since ceased to enjoy the tariff protection for which they had clamored, with some success, in the nineteenth century. Still, lack of transportation facilities had accorded them de facto protection. The building of the railroads and finally the opening of the Panama Canal, however, brought an end to that protection and posed a new threat to the artisans at just about the time the international war began. In Peru and Ecuador the artisans and other members of the lower middle sectors, including small-scale retail merchants, white-collar employees in new import-substitution industries and lower level government functionaries, suffered just as much as the laboring masses from the effects of rising food costs and general inflation. The situation of many middle-sector employees in Bolivia was even worse. Government had traditionally depended on import taxes for the major part of its revenue; but imports plummeted during the war as the usual sources of foreign manufactures dried up.

Bolivia's government responded not by raising taxes on tin exports, which would have offended the tin magnates, but by reducing the salaries of the public sector bureaucracy by 30 percent.[118]

Their security in jeopardy, middle sectors throughout Andean America began to cast about for new leadership that would prove more sympathetic to their needs and wants than the oligarchies that had been in command since the end of the nineteenth century. Unquestionably it was the alienation of the middle sectors, more than the discontent of the masses below, that brought an end to the experiment with liberalism.

DISILLUSIONMENT WITH LIBERALISM

Peru's beleaguered old guard responded to the new challenges with some timid social legislation, including an eight-hour day for many workers. In Bolivia also a few concessions were made. In both countries, however, the responses were generally viewed as inadequate to meet the dangers of massive social disruption posed by the discontent both of laborers and middle-sector employees. As a result Leguía enjoyed widespread support among Peruvians when he came to power in 1919 promising sweeping reforms. The following year, Bolivia's recently established Republican party ended the twenty-year Liberal party ascendancy by overthrowing the banker president José Gutiérrez Guerra. Departing the country to take a banking position in the United States, Gutiérrez Guerra vowed he would never return to Bolivia, "a land where only exotic plants abound and few noble souls are to be found."[119]

Commenting on the change of government in Bolivia, one writer observed: "Twenty years of privilege for one group ends, and ten years of privilege for another begins."[120] If the numbers, twenty and ten, were changed slightly, the same statement could be made for Peru. The statement, though, whether applied to Bolivia or Peru, is only partially true. The groups newly installed in office did at least recognize, far more than their predecessors, the need to expand somewhat the political power base so as to include more of the middle sectors. The new governments also recognized that the spread of liberty, independence, and self-reliance among the lower classes could be better prevented by a restoration of certain paternalistic devices than by repression and the type of heartless exploitation justified by many liberals.[121] Both in Bolivia and Peru the new government elites accepted the need to depart from the classical liberal ideology and to seek fresh formulas for protecting minorities against majorities.

171

The same necessity was accepted by the reform-minded military officers who seized power in Ecuador in 1925 and brought an end in that country, some five years after it had ended in Bolivia and Peru, to the apogee of liberalism.

Andean liberals had perceived a certain identity in the United States and they had tried to assimilate it, at least in their urban life, as their own identity. This endeavor had resulted in some profound socioeconomic changes. And these changes had in turn, or at least so it seemed to many observers by 1920, threatened society with the collapse of order. Responding to this situation, Andean Americans began to abandon the attempt to change identities and turned to the task of strengthening and adapting to modern times their traditional social control mechanisms. These developments would have a profound bearing on U.S.-Andean relations in the years ahead, a bearing that can best be explained in terms of an analogy between the sixteenth-century Spanish conquest of the Indians and the partial conquest of Andean America by U.S. capitalists that had begun at the turn of the century.

At the time of the Spanish conquest, some Indian leaders (caciques) had assumed that the invaders were godlike beings in possession of a new truth that must be spread among all the subjects of the old Empire of Tahuantinsuyo. Genuine "sell-outs" to the Spaniards, they collaborated with them in every conceivable way in the attempt to remake and uplift themselves and their fellow natives. Then they began to discover that the Spaniards were not demigods after all, that they had moral and all other types of weaknesses, and that many of their "superior" ways produced calamitous consequences. The caciques began further to see that by spreading Spanish culture among their old subjects they would lose control over them; for this control depended upon the survival among their subjects of the old faith and the old social, economic, and political usages. The caciques next discovered that by acting as intermediaries between the conquerors and their old subjects they could have the best of two worlds: they could participate in the new life of Spanish culture and from their ties with the conquerors derive greater economic resources and prestige that would facilitate the maintenance of their customary role as paternalistic, patriarchal patrons who protected their dependent wards. The Spaniards accepted this situation and, except for a few zealots, desisted from their initial attempts to Hispanicize all of the natives.

At the turn of the century the Andean elites can be depicted as the new caciques and the U.S. capitalists as the new conquerors. At first some of the new caciques believed the intruders from the north possessed a truth that when spread among the entire populace would result in a temporal Utopia. But the more they dealt with the strangers, the more they discovered that the new conquerors were human after all. They bribed and they accepted bribes, and they were unreliable friends. Often they cheated on their commitments and some of their engineering prodigies, such as the railroads they built, betrayed shoddy construction. Moreover, the individualistic life styles they exemplified would, if spread throughout the populace, have deprived the local elites of the power they had traditionally wielded over the masses. And then, beginning in the 1920s, the new caciques would discover that they could act as intermediaries between the new conquerors and the local masses. Thereby they could themselves participate in the fruits of the capitalist life and accumulate in the process some of the wherewithal required to administer paternalistically to the dependent masses who were to remain isolated from the competitive thrust of the capitalist system. For many years thereafter the new conquerors proved willing to go along with this arrangement and did not push very insistently toward the goal, never abandoned by a few fanatics, of North-Americanizing all the natives.

It is difficult for the historian to know whether Spaniards were using Indian caciques, or the caciques the conquerors. And it is well nigh impossible for the sociologist, the economist, and the political scientist to be certain whether the Yankees who seemed intent upon and occasionally may even have managed to wield economic and political hegemony were using the local oligarchies or being used by them.

7

Andean Political Establishments and Transition, the 1920s

By the 1920s Spencerian liberalism had ceased to be the preferred socioeconomic philosophy of those who directed the political establishments in Andean America. The principal reason for this is not hard to find. Frightened by the mounting rebelliousness of the masses during the World War I era, the upper classes were ready to take to heart, at least partially, the warnings that intellectuals had for many years been raising about the consequences of laissez-faire capitalism.

Andean *pensadores*—beginning with the mid-nineteenth-century Krausists—had ample reason for voicing protests when the auguries of the liberal, business society had appeared in their midst. Traditionally in the Andean culture, the intellectuals were humanists, trained in philosophy, theology, law, and literature; and as the initial fruits of modernity came to their lands they saw themselves being pushed aside by a new breed of thinkers who boasted of scientific certitude in such practical disciplines as economics and sociology. This new breed of specialists served as the prophets and pundits for the age of liberalism; and it was to them that business and political leaders during the apogee of liberalism were most likely to turn for advice and on whom they were most likely to confer their favors and rewards. So far as the humanists were concerned, the new self-proclaimed masters of scientific thought and the plutocracy they served were initiating an era of crass vulgarity that threatened true culture. Beyond this they were, however unwittingly, creating the danger of a leveling social movement by reducing all values to material, quantifiable considerations. Social hierarchy, the humanists insisted, demanded for its maintenance a hierarchy of values. Unless society recognized this hierarchy in which spiritual and aesthetic took precedence over material concerns, unless society accorded special recognition to the elites who were capable of safeguarding, nourishing, and contributing to the higher values, then nothing could prevent the barbarians below from rising to power.

During the guano age, Peruvian intellectuals resentful of the new power of the allegedly vulgar new rich had embraced the social philosophy of Krausism. Under the leadership of Bartolomé Herrera they "sought to introduce into the democracy of guano . . . the sovereignty of intelligence."[1] Although not the autocratic elitist that Herrera was, the defrocked priest Francisco de Paula González Vigil had also challenged the prevailing materialism of the guano era. In their day, Herrera, Vigil, and the Andean Krausists in general had made a considerable impact, but not nearly so great a one as that of their spiritual heirs in the early twentieth century. By then the relative prosperity of the Andean republics had created a new plutocracy from which intellectuals felt ever more alienated; what is more, the circumstances under which capitalism was developing in the three countries had produced the sort of rumblings from below that nineteenth-century Krausists and also Catholic traditionalists had, prematurely, warned against.

The twentieth-century spiritual heirs of the Krausists bore the name Arielists, derived from the book *Ariel*. Written by the Uruguayan intellectual José Enrique Rodó and published in 1900, *Ariel* became vastly influential in Andean America and throughout the Spanish-speaking world. In the work Rodó depicted Ariel (one of the protagonists in Shakespeare's *The Tempest*) as the creature of intellectual and cultural pursuits, concerned with art, beauty, and moral development as ends in themselves, rather than with material progress. Ariel was used to symbolize what, for Rodó, was most authentic in Hispanic culture. Through the words he gave to Ariel, the author chided Spanish Americans, sometimes directly, sometimes by implication, for having abandoned the culture and values natural to them and having embraced the materialistc, utilitarian, mechanistic life styles associated with alien cultures, most specifically with Anglo-Saxon civilization.

Ideologically, Arielism was closely allied to Hispanism, another movement that enjoyed considerable vogue in turn-of-the-century Andean America. Hispanism originated in Spain in the early nineteenth century[2] but began to flourish there only in the 1890s. Its proponents, known as Hispanists (*Hispanistas*), taught that the Hispanic *raza* (meaning race, but defined more in a cultural than a biological sense), which was made up of the citizens of all the Spanish-speaking countries throughout the world, had its own unique *ser* or essence that set it apart from all other peoples and cultures. Distinguishing those who shared in the Hispanic *ser* was an indifference to material considerations, a paramount concern with cultural, spiritual, and intellectual values, and a devotion to the hierarchically, corporatively structured stratified society. Any attempt to alter the vital elements of Spanishness, said the Hispanists, would lead to the gradual disappearance of the Hispanic *raza*.

Especially after the defeat of Spain by the United States in 1898, Hispanists feared that the survival of the Hispanic *raza* was in dire jeopardy. The danger was thought to be greatest in Spanish America, where the republics were most exposed to and most apt to be seduced by the leveling U.S. life style. The basic flaw in that life style, said the Hispanists, was its exclusive concern with material development and progress. In a society characterized by a mania for material aggrandizement and a lack of appreciation for higher values, the masses allegedly would acquire an insatiable appetite for enhancing their physical comfort and multiplying their wealth and possessions. Incapable of experiencing satisfaction and fulfillment regardless of how much in the way of things they received from society, they would eventually in their frustration rise against that society.

In this view of life, then, capitalism, democracy, and materialism were inseparably linked handmaidens serving, often unwittingly, the cause of social revolution. Only if all members of the Hispanic *raza*, the Hispanists warned, turned inward and discovered and nourished their true cultural identity as it had originally been forged in Castile, could they avoid the destruction of their unique way of being. Only, moreover, if they reasserted their own cultural being and banded together to resist alien life styles could the countries within the fold of the Hispanic *raza* avoid social revolution.[3]

As U.S. imperialism became a mounting source of concern in Andean America, Hispanism provided the ideological vehicle from which a growing number of intellectuals hurled their shouts of defiance at the Colossus. However, U.S. imperialism was not the major stimulus to Andean Hispanism and Arielism. The main reason underlying the acceptance of these ideological schools was the dissatisfaction of alienated intellectuals and of a broad spectrum of out-of-power elites with the groups that had been in power since the late nineteenth century.

What most distinguished the oligarchy that had been governing in Peru, Ecuador, and Bolivia since the revolutions of the mid-to-late 1890s was the attempt to establish Spencerian liberalism as the public philosophy. The oligarchy therefore was attacked by its opponents on the grounds of its commitment to liberal capitalism. And, to establish the baseness of liberal capitalism it became immensely useful to point to its evils, real and imagined, in the country most dedicated to its practice: the United States. Whether it was imperialist or not, whether it pursued generous and enlightened or selfish and sordid policies with Andean America, the United States would have suffered denunciation because of the manner in which it was, often without even knowing it, dragged into purely domestic squabbles. Hispanists and Arielists and all others concerned with preserving "authentic" Hispanic identity lumped their domestic opponents together with U.S. capitalists as embodying the negative identity.

Meantime as Andean America's established power-wielders began in the 1920s to experiment with social interventionist policies, in pursuit of domestic tranquility, they became associated in the United States with that country's negative identity. Apprehension over the Russian Revolution had heightened dislike among North Americans of statism and socialism in any form. More than ever, statism and socialism had become the great national heresies, assumed to lie at the heart of all that was un-American. Thus North American power-wielders were predisposed to react unfavorably to their Andean counterparts as the latter increasingly voiced misgivings about Spencerian liberalism.

Andean Political Establishments Respond to New Challenges

The men in the ruling groups that came to office in Andean America through Leguía's 1919 *golpe* in Peru and the Republican party's 1920 revolution in Bolivia and through a 1925 military takeover in Ecuador had, prior to coming to power, criticized the selfish materialism of the elites they hoped to replace. Thereby, they had sought to enlist the support of Hispanist and Arielist intellectuals. Once in power, however, they threw themselves as much into the capitalist pursuit of gain for themselves and their associates as had the ousted oligarchies. In this pursuit, the new ruling sectors sought fresh inputs of U.S. investment and loan capital, hoping thereby to speed the process of capitalist development. Their actions suggest that their objections to foreign capital in the period before they came to power lay not with its presence but with the fact that they were not in a position to derive for themselves the greatest benefits from it.

In some ways, though, Andean leaders of the 1920s acted in accordance with the criticisms of liberal capitalism they had formulated while still aspiring to power. They flirted with ideas of technocracy according to which socioeconomic policy should be guided in the interest of the public good by an elite of government experts ostensibly immune to the pressure of self-seeking private groups. Regimes of the 1920s also accepted the expediency of introducing state-supported programs of paternalism intended to ameliorate the conditions of urban and mining town laborers. The goal was to transfer to an urban setting, under state control, the paternalistic devices which, as administered by private landowners, had traditonally kept the mass of rural laborers subservient wards of *hacendados*. In this way government would become a new superpatron in the urban, modernizing sections of the country, thus updating the patronalist-clientelist sociopolitical control mechanisms associated with the past.

The political establishments in the 1920s ignored the advice of Hispanist-Arielist intellectuals to meet the challenge to the social order by instilling in the masses an interest in the sort of nonmaterial rewards that could be conferred by cultural elites. Instead, the governing regimes embarked upon programs of "economism," hoping to placate the urban laborers exclusively through material security and bread-and-butter rewards. It is true that especially in Peru and Bolivia, where the issue of Catholicism versus modernity had left fewer scars than in Ecuador, governments turned to the church, encouraging it to expand efforts to calm the masses by heightening their preoccupation with spiritual rewards. Governments themselves, though, largely ignored nationalism and secular mythology in the quest of social solidarity and harmony.

Reliance on economism added, of course, to the expenses of governments, forcing them to raise not only development but also social overhead capital. These circumstances increased dependence on foreign direct investment, which it was hoped would tackle the tasks of development. At the same time these circumstances increased dependence on foreign loan capital as the source of seed money for new experiments in social spending.

In seeking social tranquility, Andean leaders began to see the theoretical advantages of abandoning the endeavor to Westernize the Indians by converting them into self-reliant capitalist types. In many cases, the Andeans were influenced by Joaquín Costa (1846–1911), perhaps Spain's most prescient intellectual of the late nineteenth century. Costa, whose influence grew throughout the Spanish-speaking world after his death, was concerned with devising the means for adding a superstructure of modernity onto a foundation of traditionalism. In particular, he had urged the restoration of the communal properties that most rural towns had held prior to the onslaught of liberal reforms that got underway in Spain in 1836. Costa believed that the rural masses, if provided with security in collectivized property ownership, would not intrude into the process of development over which an urban, capitalist, and individualistic bourgeoisie would preside.[4]

The Costa prescription for guaranteeing social tranquility and economic development by juxtaposing rural collectivism with urban capitalism appealed immensely to many Andean elites in the 1920s. Here was a prescription for maintaining the Indians as agrarian laborers who were culturally isolated from the modernizing sectors of society. In the Spencerian formula as most commonly interpreted, good Indians had been dead Indians, even though lip service had been paid to Westernizing them. Now it appeared that good Indians, the ones most likely to stay out of the way and not interfere with development as pursued by more enlightened urban elements, were collectivized Indians.

In the cities, therefore, there should be one way of life for the enlightened bourgeoisie, and another way of life, that of dependence upon the government, for the labor force. For some rural Indians, there should be still another way of life, that of dependence upon their own, collectivized communities. Thereby the Indian problem could be solved with a minimum of expense to the government.

Andean political establishments took the first timid steps in the 1920s toward carrying out the social, economic, and political transition that new elites were beginning to envision. That regimes in the 1970s were still concerned with the same type of transition through which the past might be retained in the future only points to the significance of the 1920s as a watershed in Andean history.

Leguía and the Political Establishmen in Peru "I have come not only to liquidate the old state of affairs," the newly inaugurated Leguía is reported to have said in 1919, "but also to detain the advance of communism."[5] Throughout his eleven-year rule (the *oncenio*) Leguía did seem to seek, if not the liquidation, at least the vast modification of the old state of affairs. Yet in many respects the so-called old state of affairs was one that had been introduced only since 1895 under the aegis of Spencerian liberalism. In moving against the established order that he inherited as he sought to forge what he called a new fatherland (*patria nueva*), Leguía turned back toward some of the country's older traditions.[6]

In none of his policies was Leguía's traditionalism more evident than in his favoring of an expanded temporal influence for the church. He collaborated closely with Catholic Action programs, the aims of which were two-fold: to stimulate the well-to-do to take up anew their obligations of Christian charity to the lower classes; and to provide the clergy with broadened access to the masses in the attempt to persuade them of the priority that spiritual rewards took over material gratifications. When Juan Benlloch y Vivó, a distinguished Spanish church leader and cardinal, reached Peru in 1923 in the course of a short South American tour, Leguía provided a lavish welcome. In Spain, Benlloch's mission was viewed as an endeavor to spread among the New World members of the Hispanic *raza* the understanding that without Catholicism as a buttressing force, the hierarchical social order would always be in danger.[7] Leguía, apparently, required little additional persuason in this regard.

The president's announced policy of encouraging government paternalism vis-à-vis the working classes struck many as being in line with new socialist theories. Actually, the approach owed far more to the traditions of the past, especially to the concept of the patronalist-clientelist society in which the lower classes were not allowed to develop power of their own. A new constitution, promulgated in January of 1920, committed the state to improving the working conditions of the laboring classes and to constructing hospitals, asylums, clinics, and primary schools for all of the coustry's needy.[8] At the beginning of the *oncenio* a new labor section was created in the Ministry of Development, and it became the basis of a future independent ministry. Through these and related measures, such as the founding of a government labor arbitration commission, the state moved to end the isolation of labor that had resulted from the Spencerian approach and to forge a relationship in which workers would come to depend upon government for protection and security. Independent labor organizations, of course, were not to be tolerated. Whenever labor associations showed signs of unacceptable aggressiveness, Leguía moved energetically to crush them.[9]

Migrants streamed into Lima as never before during the *oncenio*, coming mainly from the southern and central regions of the sierra and finding the rigors of their journey eased by the new road system in which Leguía took inordinate pride. During the 1920s some 65,000 provincials came to live in the capital, helping to swell its population to 376,097 by 1930—up from 223,807 in 1920.[10] Most of the new arrivals found employment at wages far exceeding what had been available in the countryside. The number of manual labor jobs in Lima rose from 66,132 in 1920 to 110,406 by 1930. If jobs were not available in private industry, then they were to be found readily enough in the huge number of public works projects that Leguía undertook not only in Lima but also in the country's other urban centers. Money was readily available in the *oncenio*, in part because of borrowing processes that saw the foreign debt rise from approximately $10 million to $100 million. Largely thanks to loans from abroad and deficit financing, the Peruvian budget by 1929 called for an expenditure of approximately $80 million, a figure which exceeded income by a considerable margin and represented nearly a fourfold increase over government outlays in 1920. As a result of what seemed an endless supply of money, government was in a position to become the employer of an ever-increasing percentage of the urban labor force.

Government also used its supply of capital to build more than eight hundred new primary schools. As a result the number of primary students increased from 176,680 to 318,735 between 1921 and 1929. In addition, new efforts were undertaken to protect the health of the young through the launching of campaigns against various childhood diseases and through the expansion of clinical facilities and the building of a modern children's hospital in Lima.

Expanding school and health facilities benefited not only the manual laboring classes but also many segments of the middle sectors, helping to secure for the government a wide base of support among people who came increasingly to rely upon it for protection and for services previously available mainly to those with large private resources. Middle sectors benefited further from the leveling off in the cost of living and from the fact that under Leguía the demand for bureaucrats, commercial employees, technicans, and teachers grew at perhaps the fastest rate in the country's history.[11] Further, the country's first important social security legislation was designed more for the benefit of middle sectors than for the lower classes. Formed in 1922 under government encouragement, a Society of Employees of Commerce grouped together not only employees in commercial enterprise but those in the professions and public services as well.[12] The

Employees' Statute, written largely by the president of the new society and promulgated in 1924, provided members of the society with protection against arbitrary dismissal, retirement benefits, and life insurance.

Through the Employees' Statute Leguía's regime moved toward re-erecting, under careful state control, the *gremios* or guilds that had been largely destroyed through the liberal, laissez-faire programs that got underway in the nineteenth century. Thus at the precise time that the collective bargaining process was being strengthened in the United States in line with the principles of interest-group pluralism, Peru was taking a most important step to establish the dependence of white-collar workers on an all-powerful government.

In dealing, then, with labor and lower-middle-class sectors, Leguía proved himself a traditionalist, oriented toward the status quo ante Spencerianism and hoping to blunt competitive, capitalist, individualistic drives. But, in his approach to the upper middle class, to the haut bourgeoisie, Leguía was thoroughly responsive to the capitalist ethic. For many years he had been intimately associated with mercantile and insurance firms, and also with the commercial agriculture that predominated in the economy of the northern region around his native Lambayeque.[13] The shrewd and aggressive figures of export, commercial, and financial capitalism, especially the self-made nouveau riches who had begun to prosper only during the previous ten years or so, he viewed as the persons with the vision and dynamism required to move Peru ahead on the road to progress. The old guard Civilist oligarchy, it seemed to Leguía, had lost its drive and, interested only in enjoying fortunes already accumulated, was blocking the country's potential for development. Therefore control must be wrested from this oligarchy, while government did all in its power to encourage and facilitate the operation of the new type of capitalist. These were the objectives to which Leguía set himself and which he largely accomplished as he presided over the *patria nueva*.[14]

Banks and insurance companies multiplied, commercial agriculture received a tremendous impetus through the soil reclamation projects on the coast and the creation of new estates in the sierra, and manufacturing industry was encouraged through tariff protection.[15] In the wake of these developments, "new names appeared on boards of directors and a new monied class arose which, through its exercise of bureaucratic functions, began to gain economic and political power."[16] In this process Leguía, a *caudillo* of enormous cunning, managed to avoid a complete break with the old Civilist elites. His purpose was to discipline them into becoming collaborators with the new and purportedly more dynamic sectors, not to eliminate them altogether from the power structure. At first the Civilists grumbled indignantly, but toward the end of the *oncenio* a growing number had been persuaded as to the advantages of collaborating with the upstarts.[17] A considerable change in their attitudes can be detected between 1924 and 1929. Widespread complaint from the displaced oligarchy greeted Leguía's 1924 manipulations to amend the constitution so as to permit two successive presidential terms. Far less criticim arose from the old guard when Leguía again had the constitution amended, this time to permit indefinite reelection, and after running unopposed began his third term in 1929.

For Leguía the constitution was a malleable instrument to be used, ignored, or altered as he saw fit. This was much in evidence in the dictator's Indian policy. Article 58 of the *patria nueva*'s 1920 constitution stipulated that Indians would be protected in the ownership of their *comunidades*. In accepting the principle of communal landownership for the natives, the lawmakers made a startling departure from earlier attempts to Westernize the perplexing Indians. Apparently Leguía both respected and ignored the constitutional provision. The leading student of the subject suggests that at the beginning of his rule, as he began the process of disciplining the Civilists, Leguía protected *comunidades* against land-grabbing by old guard, Civilist *gamonales*. Anxious, however, to establish a more productive and commercially minded group of landowners in the sierra, the dictator encouraged the formation of estates by more progressive members of the new bourgeoisie. In the process, he turned a blind eye as new *hacendados* despoiled *comunidades*.[18]

In dealing with the Indians, Leguía found himself involved in a difficult dilemma. Undoubtedly he appreciated the social tranquilization to be obtained by protecting them in their traditional collectivized life style. On the other hand, he was obsessed with developing Peru through modern, capitalist methods. This meant encouraging greater production of such sierra commercial products as wool, leather, and cattle; and here was an objective that could only be achieved by permitting seizure of relatively nonproductive Indian properties. Furthermore, seizure of *comunidades* would result in making more laborers available for the expanding economic sectors both of the coast and sierra. "It must be said," a perceptive study of this subject concludes, "that the injuries inflicted upon the Indian were, in great part, a consequence of the brutal penetration of a modern economy into

183

the rural world of the highland. Who really could have found a remedy in such a short time?"[19]

Saavedra and Siles and the Political Establishment in Bolivia   The Republicans who came to power in 1920 included many fallen-away Liberals, men whose ambitions had been thwarted by the heavy-handed, personalist policies of Ismael Montes. Included also in the ranks of the new party were a good number of Conservatives whose political fortunes had been in decline since 1899. To the heterogeneous Republicans, the middle sectors and the mining and urban manual labor forces looked for relief from the economic adversity that had accompanied World War I. By and large the tin mining plutocracy also looked hopefully toward the Republicans in 1920, confident that Daniel Salamanca, the principal founder of the party and one of the strongest exponents of liberal capitalism in all Bolivia, would become president.

Salamanca also expected to become president. But, in the bitter infighting that followed the Republican takeover he and his henchmen were outmaneuvered by Bautista Saavedra. In 1921 Saavedra was duly installed as chief executive for a term that would end in 1925. The personal hatred that had by now come into being between him and Salamanca, and between the successful and bested factions of the Republican party, persisted for years to come, weakening not only that party but Bolivia's entire political fabric as well.[20]

A distinguished intellectual and also an imperious autocrat who brooked no questioning of his actions by subordinates, Saavedra has been described as a combination of a European thinker and an Aymara chief.[21] Ignoring constitutions and political programs (in his inaugural address he announced "My program will be my acts"), Saavedra ruled generally under a state of siege in which constitutional guarantees were suspended. At least there was a refreshing candor about the man, for he never paid the lip service to democracy that was typical of so many Andean autocrats.[22] "It is the honor and glory of mediocre men," he wrote, "to follow the paths indicated by superior men; it is not only their glory and honor, it is a duty and a fatal law which cannot be altered."[23]

Once in the presidency, Saavedra had difficulty finding followers. The tin plutocracy was suspicious of the president's economic interventionist ideas which led him to recommend moderate reforms so as to avoid the unpleasant consequences to which unregulated capitalism might lead.[24] Many of the landowning conservatives, loyal to the defeated Republican leader Salamanca, remained ill-disposed toward the "caudillo of the North," as Saavedra was called. Not even Saavedra's enthusiastic backing of Catholic Action and his dedication of the republic to the Sacred Heart of Jesus in 1925—two years after Leguía had presided over similar ceremonies in Lima—earned him widespread Conservative support.[25] Failing to enlist the traditional wielders of power among his followers, Saavedra—much like Tata Belzu in the late 1840s—turned to social sectors that had been largely ignored by the political establishment.

Even as in the Peru of the *oncenio*, the social laws pushed through congress by Saavedra were intended primarily to benefit the lower middle sectors, particularly the Bolivian artisans and white-collar salary earners, rather than the "truly exploited laboring masses."[26] However, Saavedra by no means ignored the emerging urban proletariat, "many of whom were literate and fully absorbed into the national system." This new type of industrial wage worker had appeared on the scene in the 1900–1920 period with "the rise of light industry and heavy mining, the growth of government services and, most important, with the development of the communications and transportation network."[27] With the appearance of the urban proletariat, there had come into being an organized labor movement, and Saavedra made a bid to establish state control over it, in part through a 1921 law setting up government councils of conciliation to resolve questions between management and labor. Demonstrating further similarities to Leguía's approach, Saavedra provided more and more jobs for urban laborers through public works projects, intended to modernize La Paz and other cities in time for the celebration of the first centennial of the attainment of independence.

Saavedra's hopes to mobilize the mine laborers in his support suffered a rude setback on June 4, 1923. On that date government troops near Oruro perpetrated a massacre of labor protesters who were affiliated with the Central Federation of the Miners of Uncía.[28] Realizing his administration was now held responsible for the bloodletting, Saavedra moved to placate miners by having his subservient congress enact new social legislation that called for safety measures in mines, provided insurance coverage for worker accidents, and established a Workers' Savings Bank.

In need of funds to support the country's first timid social provisions, Saavedra raised slightly the export taxes on tin ore and for the first time assessed a graduated levy on profits of the tin enterprises. The rise in export taxes produced little additional revenue,[29] and although the impost on profits came to 5.97 million *bolivianos* (the *boliviano* was worth 34¢) in 1925 its yield was down to 2.06 million in 1929.[30] The low yield from the new taxes resulted in part from a decline in silver prices in the late 1920s. Above all else, however, it indicated the strength of the Bolivian mining tycoons who, in order to block the government's new fiscal policy and also to thwart its endeavors to protect mining labor, organized in December of 1924 the Association of Mining Industralists of Bolivia. The association effectively obstructed government endeavors to collect taxes and to gain a following among the more than 27,000 mine laborers, who made up about one-tenth of the active population, by dispensing economic favors. Labor relations remained a matter between the owners and their hands, and as a result a new law requiring paid vacations and compensation for accidents and such work-related diseases as tuberculosis and silicosis remained a dead letter.

Facing a more powerful opposition by entrenched interests than Leguía had encountered in Peru (in part because the Bolivian oligarchy was concentrated around one industry whereas in Peru its economic base was far more diverse, contributing to lack of internal cohesion), Saavedra left office in 1925 with his hopes for tapping new sources of political support largely unrealized. The man who shortly succeeded him in power proved even less willing than Saavedra to challenge the mining establishment, which by now seemed clearly stronger than the government.[31] Hernando Siles, Bolivia's president between 1925 and 1930, early in his regime accepted Simón Patiño's offer of a generous loan to the government, with one of the conditions apparently being a pledge not to raise imposts on the mining industry.[32]

Engaging in personality and displaying a considerable degree of magnetism, Siles, who has been called a "sensuous Machiavellian,"[33] was thoroughly unfocused in his long-term political objectives, a man who drifted in whatever direction seemed at the moment best suited to enhance his own interests. Upon coming to power he apparently was pledged to serve merely as an interim president who would arrange matters for the reelection of Saavedra in 1930. Soon, however, he broke with Saavedra who departed for Europe in 1928 in a state of high dudgeon. All the while Daniel Salamanca waited in the wings, more convinced than ever that he was Bolivia's man of destiny and determined to do all in his power to prevent Siles from becoming a formidable political figure.

Unable to attract the consistent backing of traditional political elites, Siles formed the Nationalist party[34] and through it sought to mobilize the support of youth, particularly university students[35] and young military officers. Speaking vaguely about the need for state socialism, and thereby luring into his orbit some of the socialist groups recently organized in Bolivia, Siles began to advocate forced loans from the rich as one of the several steps needed to bring about sweeping transformations. He began also to speak in glowing terms of Mussolini and of Spanish dictator Miguel Primo de Rivera.[36]

Lacking a definite program and also without the organizational skill to mold youthful elites into an effective political movement, Siles provided Bolivia with four years of inconsistent rule. At first hoping to capitalize on Indianist sentiment that had appeared among intellectuals in the mid-1920s, he organized a National Crusade in Favor of the Indian. Behind the crusade were many of the same ideological considerations that had led to the stipulation for protection of comunidades in the 1920 Peruvian constitution. In Bolivia, however, the Indianist ideology was even less productive than in the neighboring republic, one reason being that several Indian uprisings in 1927 spread terror among whites and mestizos. Indian violence also appeared in Peru's sierra during the 1920s. Unlike Bolivia, however, only a small percentage of the white and mestizo population was concentrated in the Indian highland regions. The violence of the Peruvian Indians therefore did not stifle the Indianist sentiments which from the outset had been largely confined to coastal intellectuals.

Civilians, the Military, and the Political Establishment in Ecuador When José Luis Tamayo was elected to the presidency in 1920 it appeared that Ecuador might have weathered the storm produced by the economic imbalances of the World War I period. Tamayo was optimistic that with a modicum of restraint on the part of the Guayaquil banking plutocracy and its various allies in the *Argolla*, the country's problems could be resolved. Conferring with the leaders of the banking community in Guayaquil he cautioned: "Gentlemen, content yourselves with less profit."[37] The bankers chose to ignore the advice and the president did nothing to back it up, perhaps because he had previously earned his livelihood as a lawyer for the banking interests.

Early in the Tamayo administration a monopolistic control over the production, sale, and transportation of sugar, tobacco, alcohol, and the alcoholic beverage aguardiente—cheap, potent, and popular among the masses—was granted the Commercial and Agricultural

Bank of Guayaquil. At once the monopolists reduced production of these commodities so as to force prices up. Moreover, they drove many of the small tobacco producers out of business by cutting the prices they paid for the product. Charged with collecting taxes on the products they controlled, the banking-trust monopolists advanced a small part of the anticipated yields to the president who in turn "delivered the country to them."[38] Government deficits mounted steadily, reaching the highest level yet recorded in 1922 and then soaring still higher the following year. By 1923 the old methods of covering deficits by borrowing additional revenue from the Commercial and Agricultural Bank was no longer sufficient to stave off fiscal disaster, for the Ecuadoran export economy was in the throes of an almost total collapse.

Cacao had been virtually the sole commercial export crop for Ecuador. Its production hit at all-time high in 1916, and then began to decline as a result of blights that attacked the unmatured chocolate pods. The worst blight, known as the witchbroom disease, struck with savage intensity in 1922, and the age of chocolate came to an abrupt end. The situation was all the more desperate because of the declining international price for cacao,[39] resulting from increased production in Africa, especially in Ghana which by 1926 was supplying half of the world's total exports.[40] Large plantations on the coast were abandoned altogether, fortunes were wiped out overnight, and the *montuvio* labor force faced a bitter struggle for survival.[41]

All along the coast but especially in Guayaquil labor agitation became the order of the day. Laborers of the cacao estates were joined by railroad shop and electricity plant workers, by transportation laborers, and by employees of various services in demanding wage increases that would bring them abreast of the inflation that had reached runaway proportions. Late in 1922 a coastal labor confederation began a strike that brought the commercial and industrial life of Guayaquil almost to a standstill. The government ordered the paramilitary Civic Guard into action against the strikers, some of whom had begun looting Guayaquil stores that stocked firearms. The number of persons killed in the resultant massacre that occurred on the 15th of November has been estimated at close to one thousand.[42] Disorder now spread even into the highland interior around Ambato, where a group of peasant owners of small plots were driven from their property by a newly formed commercial and agricultural enterprise. The peasants (*campesinos*), many of them of Spanish extraction whose land parcels had been in their families since colonial times, resisted the ouster, whereupon the government summoned the armed forces into action. There ensued in September of 1923 "one of the most frightful massacres of *campesinos* in Ecuador's history."[43]

In the same month as the *campesino* massacre the Liberal party held an assembly in Quito to choose a candidate for the next presidential election and to revise its platform. Given the background of social unrest, most of the delegates inclined to agree with Pío Jaramillo Alvarado that if a revolution was not made by a strong government from above, the masses would make one from below.[44] The assembly soon developed a consensus view that individual liberty had to be curtailed in the interest of harmony and fraternity and that Ecuador must abandon "humiliating equality" in the quest of "inequality in justice."[45]

In abandoning Spencerianism to embrace what they described, with considerable hyperbole, as socialism, the Ecuadoran Liberals were responding not only to the discontent of the laboring masses but also to the discomfiture of the lower middle sectors. There was, for example, a sizeable and relatively independent force of mestizo artisans, most of whom operated shops in their homes, and small merchants, many of whom peddled goods from hand-pushed carts. These sectors had been joined in recent years by a burgeoning group of white-collar service employees, and both the old and the new members of the lower middle classes had been equally threatened by the spiraling inflation. If their plight was not eased, they might consider at least a temporary alliance with the violence prone proletariat in order to challenge the established order. The danger seemed all the more imminent in view of the spread among some of the country's intellectuals of what polite society described as Bolshevik ideas.

In 1914 the Peruvian Arielist Víctor Andrés Belaúnde had warned that immediate social upheaval was more likely to be produced by the insecurity of an inchoate middle class than by the poverty of the proletariat. Accordingly he had urged the seeking of a basis of rapport between the entrenched oligarchy and the swelling middle sectors.[46] Essentially the same thesis had been developed by the Ecuadoran sociologist Carlos Manuel Tobar y Borgoño in 1913.[47] Now, in 1923, the Ecuadoran Liberals had in the majority come around to the Belaúnde-Tobar views. Accordingly, they approved a new program which was largely the work of Agustín Cueva who had founded the chair of sociology in Quito's Central University in 1914.[48]

The 1923 document called for state intervention to regulate prices and curb inflation, for the formation of worker and professional syndi-

189

cates, and for the introduction of functional representation in the senate as a means of giving the "living organisms of the state" a direct participation in policy making. Here were measures calculated to appeal primarily to insecure middle sectors. For the laboring classes, the Liberals promised medical facilities and accident insurance, adequate housing, profit sharing, and also government tribunals of conciliation and arbitration to resolve management-labor disputes.[49] The social provisions of the new Liberal party platform are strikingly similar to those included in a policy statement ratified by the Conservative party two years later. Perhaps the major difference is that whereas the Liberals envisioned a system of state-controlled social security, the Conservatives demanded "respect for the initiatives of the private institutions of social welfare and protection,"[50] hoping thereby to strengthen the church's secular influence.

If the Liberals were ready to talk a bold game of social intervention, they stopped short of nominating a standard-bearer who could be counted on to act in accordance with the party's announced principles. Gonzalo S. Córdoba, although a man of integrity, was cautious in his social attitudes. He was also associated with the banking plutocracy. A group of dissident Liberals now advanced the candidacy of Colonel Juan Manuel Lasso who quickly gained a large and enthusiastic following among the coastal laboring classes and also among those who were lodged precariously on the periphery of the bourgeoisie. Lasso won further backing from the lower-rank army officers who were overwhelmingly of mestizo background and sympathetic to the hard-pressed artisan and employee sectors. Moreover, many Conservatives deserted their party's official candidate, Jacinto Jijón y Caamaño, in order to cast their ballots for Lasso. Had there been honest elections, Lasso undoubtedly would have been the victor. But the outgoing Tamayo administration, labeling Lasso a Communist, resorted to massive repression during the 1924 campaign and to fraudulent tabulation of votes. Consequently, Córdova was declared the winner. In what ranks among the classic statements in the annals of Andean politics, J. Gonzalo Orellana writes: "Lasso lost the elections because of his excessive popularity."[51]

Once installed in office, Córdova managed to put down a revolution organized on Colombian soil by Conservative leader Jijón y Caamaño. Suffering from bad health, however, Córdova had to delegate more and more authority. The result was an irresolute government that proved utterly incapable of dealing with the continuing economic crisis. Against this background the League of Young Military Officers of Ecuador staged a bloodless coup, informing Córdova on July 9, 1925 that his functions as president had ceased.

The lower-grade military officers who had brought off the *golpe* with clockwork precision ruled through two successive juntas and then in 1926 turned the presidency over to Isidro Ayora. Married into one of the wealthiest coastal families, Ayora possessed a social conscience and was concerned with the problems of laborers and employees— and with how these problems could ultimately endanger the upper classes. With the backing of the military, Ayora remained in power until 1931 and helped put into effect a good part of the reform program that had been espoused and to some degree devised by the officers. The creation of a Central Bank in 1927, structured along the lines suggested by a U.S. advisory mission headed by Princeton professor Edwin W. Kemmerer,[52] brought an end to the Guayaquil banking *Argolla* that had manipulated the national economy for its own private gain ever since 1914. The tobacco, sugar, alcohol, and aguardiente monopolies were ended, and the prices of these goods began to decline. Instead of farming out the taxes to the banking ring, government now began itself to collect the national imposts and as a result found itself with more disposable funds than it had ever enjoyed up to that time. Much of the revenue windfall went into enlarging the bureaucracy, thereby solving the problems of many members of the lower middle sectors by providing dignified employment. A good deal of federal revenue also went into financing a new social security program which included a pension plan for teachers and public employees and a retirement savings bank for certain urban laborers.[53] A Ministry of Social Security and Labor was established to oversee the innovative programs and the new Office of General Supervision of Labor was charged with studying and resolving labor-management problems.

The fresh social provisions, as well as many additional measures addressed to enhancing the security of laborers, artisans, and employees, were incorporated into a constitution, the thirteenth in the country's history, promulgated in 1929. The new charter also provided for a senate of mixed composition with some of its members elected by provinces and others by functional associations representing the press, primary and normal school teachers, secondary teachers, university professors, various academies and industries, agriculture, and manual workers. In the move to restructure Ecuador along corporativ-

191

ist lines, in such a way as to bring especially the associations of middle sectors into the political arena, some observers have seen the influence of Italian experiments conducted under Mussolini. Actually, the move was in line with colonial traditions and the main overseas influence came from Spain's re-emergent corporativist ideology.[54]

Ecuador's leadership during the 1925–1931 periodic reveals considerable programmatic confusion. Overtones of socialism accompanied the notes of traditional corporativism sounded by some of the country's major political figures. And Luis Napoleón Dillon, the minister of the treasury during part of the period and the person largely responsible for implementing banking reforms, exhibited a good deal of the Wilsonian New Freedom approach: he wished to break up monopolies so as to provide a setting conducive to genuine individual competition. This is why he insisted on crushing the "Jews," as he called them, who had controlled Ecuador's financial capitalism.[55]

Despite the confusion as to ultimate goals, the leadership brought to power by the July military *golpe* managed to thwart the endeavors of the Guayaquil plutocracy to strike back through a civil war; thereby they ended the power of the *Argolla*. Thus Ecuador's new rulers were far more successful than Saavedra and Siles in their faint-hearted endeavor to curb the Bolivian counterpart, the *Rosca*. The Ecuadorans, though, had required the help of nature in disciplining the plutocracy, whose power had rested on the cacao export economy. Nature did not intervene so forcibly against the tin-based *Rosca*.

In all three of the countries under study, even though the process was decidedly less discernible in Bolivia than in Peru and Ecuador, the oligarchy in the 1920s underwent a change in composition as its base was somewhat enlarged. The enlarging of the ruling sectors both increased their strength and added to their problems by introducing new sources of internal divisiveness. Meantime, laboring masses and lower middle sectors, unable to claim real input into political decision making, had at least been made to feel somewhat more secure and also more dependent upon the privileged sectors who comprised the effective state. This was a development that could never be reversed and it meant for all practical purposes the end of liberalism. U.S. capital facilitated the end of liberalism by helping Andean governments to finance the institutionalization of dependency, in line with which the states vastly increased the numbers of their clients.

Intensification of U.S. Economic Penetration

World War I left the United States a legacy of expanded economic activity together with a large disposable surplus of capital resources. As of July 1914, America was still a debtor country, to the extent of $3.7 billion; by the end of 1919, however, that situation had "more than reversed itself."[56] Having paid off its debts and extended wartime credits to the Allies, the United States was now in a position to become a massive lender of capital throughout the world. At the same time the consequences of the war had forced Great Britain to begin to retrench in its role as the world's principal international financier. The Bolivian minister of the treasury caught the significance of these developments when in 1921 he noted it would be desirable if his country could attract both British and North American capital and play the two financial powers off against each other. As it was, though, he observed, England "is completely depressed in its finances as an immediate consequence of the war," and therefore Bolivia could turn only to the United States for capital infusions.[57]

So far as planners in Washington were concerned, it seemed the time was at last at hand to begin to implement a Latin American policy first set forth by Thomas Jefferson in 1808: "We consider their interests and ours as the same, and that the object of both must be to exclude all European influence from this hemisphere."[58] Always until now the presence of British capital had made impossible the exclusion of non-American influence from the hemisphere; and early in the twentieth century the problem had been compounded by the rise in German investments in Latin America. But, as of 1920 most German assets had been seized and the United States stood ready to submerge the British economic presence, and the diplomatic influence it had given rise to, with a massive outpouring of its own capital.

Between 1919 and 1929 U.S. investment in Latin America, direct and portfolio, rose from approximately $2 billion to $5.24 billion, representing in that latter year about one-third of total foreign investment.[59] Even in Peru, which among the three countries under consideration had always claimed the major concentration of British capital, the dollar gained supremacy over the pound in the 1920s. As of 1925, British capital in that country stood at its high water mark of some $125 million; in 1930, however, U.S. direct investment had reached the $200 million mark, more than a thirtyfold increase over the modest $6 million figure for 1897.[60]

The wartime experience still very much in mind, policy makers in Washington entered the 1920s with security considerations claiming priority. In their view, investment capital must be harnessed to national security interests, and this was particularly vital in the strategically important Latin American region. Before the war, national interest had dictated the maintenance of peace in the Caribbean Danger Zone. Now, it had become essential to the national interest "to extend—to all parts of the hemisphere—American cable facilities, the influence of American bankers, and American control over petroleum reserves."[61] Hoping to exercise some degree of control over the flow of funds into South America, so as to make sure at all times that U.S. capitalists did not act in a manner inimical to security considerations, the State Department recognized the need for the sympathetic support of congress. To gain this support, and to protect itself against possible complaints by the business-minded Department of Commerce, the State Department had to prove itself eager and aggressive in defending the rights of American investors in Latin America. "The more sensitive the department's position in Congress, the more aggressive the diplomats would be."[62]

Undoubtedly, considerations beyond national security influenced policy makers. The 1920s witnessed a re-emergence of the "older, idealistic view that American businessmen, by their enterprise, would serve the . . . purposes of stabilization," thereby making it unnecessary to extend into South America the Caribbean policy of relying on Marines.[63] Acting as economic missionaries the U.S. businessmen would, by their zeal in preaching and practicing the capitalist ethic, bring into being throughout South America a successful and virtuous middle class which would in turn introduce democratic practices and banish forever the specter of instability that had in the past produced the troubled waters in which international powers from outside the hemisphere liked to fish. Businessmen, of course, would not have the opportunity to accomplish this mission unless safeguarded in their South American operations.

Intent upon burnishing its image as the implacable defender of the rights of U.S. investors, the State Department turned its attention immediately after the war to Ecuador. That country remained in default to the bondholders in possession of the securities of the Guayaquil and Quito Railway Company. Despite a heavy-handed and threatening approach, the department was unable to induce the Ecuadorans to resume payments. To make matters worse, a new problem had appeared by 1925, occasioned by the failure of the Cacao Growers' Association to make payments on an earlier loan made through a U.S. bank. Secretary of State Frank Kellogg sought to persuade the Ecuadoran government to force the association to resume services on the loan, noting in a letter to the U.S. minister in Quito: "the government of the United States will always assert the right to interpose diplomatically on behalf of its citizens whenever in its judgment there is occasion for such action."[64] The secretary went so far as to threaten the rupture of diplomatic relations.

Kellogg's efforts were unavailing, and so Ecuador remained on the department's black list. This situation, combined with the depressed Ecuadoran economy, held new U.S. investments to a minimum in the 1920s. At the end of 1928, North American investments in Ecuador aggregated about $25 million, an increase of only $5 million over the 1920 figure. As late as 1951, U.S. investments remained smaller in Ecuador than in any other South American state.[65] In Ecuador, therefore, discussion over the effects of U.S. economic penetration did not become an important feature of domestic politics.

Altogether different was the situation in Peru where from the very first days of the *oncenio* Leguía did everything possible to demonstrate his readiness to protect U.S. investors. In one of his first acts in office, he responded to State Department suggestions by having congress annul a law that Washington considered potentially menacing to the interests of Yankee investors.[66] Thereafter he sought to demonstrate his good intentions by such gestures as proclaiming the fourth of July a Peruvian national holiday and hanging a picture of President Monroe in the National Palace.[67] Perhaps Leguía reasoned that if the old Civilist oligarchy which he hoped to supplant had depended for some of its strength on close ties with British capital, then the new ruling class he was intent upon shaping must establish an intimate relationship with U.S. capital—a consideration that also entered into play as Bolivia's Republicans sought to maintain the upper hand over the Montes-affiliated Liberals who had been closely tied to British capital.

For the funds required to initiate new social security measures and to finance lavish public works programs, Leguía turned to North American bankers who, in the years between 1920 and 1930, would dispose of Peruvian securities with a face value of nearly $90 million to the U.S. bond-buying public.[68] "Loan proceeds were riotously squandered"[69] and there developed what Adalberto J. Pinelo calls "a sort of carnival for foreign capital," run by the dictator and his son Juan Leguía. The latter "would travel to New York and arrange loans of up to $50 million; the bankers would charge exorbitant commissions and then sell the bonds to the American public. Juan Leguía usually got a percentage of the proceeds and everyone benefited except the Peruvian nation and the Americans who bought the . . . bond securities."[70] The carnival flourished all the more after 1924 when the State Department largely abandoned efforts to control capital investments in Latin America in line with overall U.S. security goals. For one thing, huge domestic petroleum resources had recently been discovered and it was no longer urgent to direct foreign policy toward the acquisition of South American reserves.

Freed from the supervision that the State Department up to 1924 had sought to exercise over their actions, American businessmen found themselves in a situation in which, so far as their government was concerned, anything went in Latin America. Policy control was surrendered to business interests precisely at a time when businessmen, even in their domestic operations, were providing dramatic indications of shortcomings of every conceivable type.

Along with Peru, Bolivia benefited, or at least initially appeared to, from the new El Dorado that had been found on Wall Street. As of 1908, Bolivia had the distinction of being a country without a foreign debt. By the beginning of 1927, its foreign debt stood at well over $40 million, the major part of it accounted for by the 1922 Nicolaus loan obtained by the Saavedra administration.

Sorely in need of funds with which to launch his social programs and to underwrite extensive public works and railroad extension, Saavedra sent to negotiate with the New York bankers a man who "was honest but incompetent."[71] The result was a loan with a face value of $33 million (91.7 percent of which was actually delivered to Bolivia) arranged for primarily through the banking house of Stifel-Nicolaus, with the Equitable Trust Company and Spencer, Trask and Company playing a subsidiary role. The terms stipulated that customs receipts, the source of 45 percent of the country's total national revenue, would be pledged to service the debt and that a three-man Permanent Fiscal Commission, two of its members appointed by the U.S. bankers, would be placed in charge of collection of national imposts during the quarter-century life of the loan.[72] One of the few Bolivian defenders of the transactions offers this appraisal: "With these funds, railroads were built, cities were modernized, and, what is of ultimate importance, we did not repay them . . . The international loan was the only recourse of the liberal economy in South America, a necessary evil of its time."[73]

Predictably, the main criticisms of the loan were leveled by Daniel Salamanca and the other political foes of Saavedra. They fumed over the manner in which the infusion of money from abroad strengthened the regime and permitted Saavedra to organize the Republican Guard with which to carry out political repression. The president did not turn the country over to rule by Yankee capitalists, as his enemies charged, but through the Nicolaus loan he did weaken the revolution-making potential of his foes.

To strengthen his political base President Siles also found it essential to turn to the bankers, and in 1928 he arranged a $23 million loan with Dillon, Read and Company. Needless to say, the loan was roundly denounced by foes of the regime, including Saavedra who had recently come to a parting of the ways with Siles. Meantime in 1927 the Siles administration, partly in order to smooth its negotiations with Dillon, Read and Company, had accepted the recommendations of fiscal and banking reorganization made by the Edwin Kemmerer mission.[74] Making shrewd propaganda use of the mission findings, Siles was able to create the impression that the North American economists had been shocked by the fiscal mismanagement and irresponsibility of preceding Bolivian administrations, particularly the one headed by Saavedra. Ecuadorans made similar political use of the Kemmerer mission, for the Ayora administration cited its findings in condemning earlier regimes said to have been controlled by the unsavory clique of Guayaquil bankers. It was becoming ever more obvious that U.S. loans and investments and even U.S. economic advice could never be judged on their own merits or faults. Instead, they were assessed within the context of ongoing domestic political struggles.

An especially striking example of the way in which internal politics determined the reaction to U.S. capital is provided by the entry of Standard Oil into Bolivia and Peru. In Bolivia the Saavedra administration conducted the extremely complex negotiations that resulted in the concession of more than 3 million hectares to Standard Oil of New Jersey.[75] The 1921 concession was bitterly contested in the senate and denounced as a virtual invitation to Standard Oil to wield the same sort of hegemony over Bolivia that it had purportedly become accustomed to exercising over Mexico. Senator Abel Iturralde compared Standard Oil to an ever-expanding, all-absorbing octopus and charged it with responsibility for the operation of Tammany Hall in New York and for the assassination of President Venustiano Carranza in Mexico (1920). Already, Iturralde charged, the

United States had taken over Panama, Nicaragua, Costa Rica, Puerto Rico, Santo Domingo, Haiti, and Cuba, while intervening ever more scandalously in Mexico. The motivation for Yankee imperialism he attributed exclusively to the desire to protect U.S. investors. All of South America, he declared, Bolivia most definitely included, was in danger, and Standard Oil was the advance column of the Yankee peril. "Not even the government of the United States has been adequate to curb the domestic practices of Standard Oil, so what can Bolivia expect?"[76]

A stalwart in the Conservative party with a vast personal dislike for Saavedra and strong ties with Salamanca, Iturralde took full cognizance of the degree to which the entry of Standard Oil would strengthen his political adversaries. The senator was also an ardent Hispanist and a defender of traditional Catholic social values. According to him U.S. capital could only serve in Bolivia to spread the bourgeois ethic, to weaken hierarchical order, and to increase the likelihood of social upheaval. To advance the domestic interests, both political and cultural, dearest to his heart, it was incumbent upon Iturralde to depict Standard Oil in the most lurid terms possible, borrowing all the while from North American muckraker literature.

Joining with Iturralde in spearheading the attack against the Standard Oil concession was Daniel Salamanca. Had he been president, as he felt he deserved to be, undoubtedly he would have jumped at the chance of luring Standard Oil into the country. As it was, he feared that oil production would go only to strengthen the hand of his hated rival, making it possible for him to gain new adherents by spreading patronage and social services. As it turned out, Iturralde and Salamanca need not have worried. Although the Standard concession did gain congressional approval, it resulted in little benefit to Saavedra or those who succeeded him in power. With more promising fields to tap elsewhere in the world, Standard largely ignored its Bolivian grant. Apparently, moreover, it falsified records so as to reduce tax payments on the miniscule amounts of oil it did pump.[77]

Standard Oil also entered Peru under circumstances of internal political dissension. Early in the *oncenio* the International Petroleum Company (IPC), a Canadian-based subsidiary of Standard Oil of New Jersey, came into possession of the oil rich fields of La Brea and Pariñas on the northern coast around Talara. Facilitating the IPC acquisition was a 1921 arbitration award, handed down by an ad hoc tribunal established in Paris, confirming the controversial claims of the London and Pacific Petroleum Company on the vast territory it had begun to exploit late in the nineteenth century. Once its rights were confirmed, London and Pacific disposed of its concession to IPC.

With IPC in possession of the concession by 1922, the enemies of Leguía accused him of a shameful surrender of national resources. Further, they denied the legality of the 1921 arbitration award and maintained that, lacking ratification by congress, it had never become binding. Beyond this opponents of the transaction insisted that IPC had obtained rights over the use of far more property than was legitimately included in the London and Pacific claims. Here the matter becomes frighteningly complex, for in Spanish law *pertinencias* (the unit of measure involved in the dispute) can be defined both as regular plots of land of 40,000 square meters and also as irregular demarcations that may be much larger. The issue remained unresolved through the years, initiating "a long and for the most part acrimonious tripartite relationship between Standard Oil (New Jersey), the United States government and the Peruvian government."[78]

The intensification of U.S. direct investment in other sectors of Bolivia's and Peru's economy during the 1920s provoked somewhat less controversy and also produced more important immediate consequences. Guggenheim interests acquired a strong foothold in Bolivian tin and wolfram mining,[79] while the Patiño Mines and Enterprises, Consolidated, was incorporated in Delaware in 1924. The following year two hundred shares of the firm's stock were floated on the New York market, "the first offering to the American public of Bolivian tin securities of any consequence."[80] In all, American investments in Bolivia had grown by 1928 to about $100 million, 40 percent in government bonds and the rest in mining, petroleum, and communications.[81]

The flow of U.S. direct investments into Peru was even more striking during the 1920s, raising, as has been mentioned, the total amount by the end of the decade to some $200 million. Cerro de Pasco's stake was recorded as $40 million in 1929, making up a large share of the total of nearly $80 million invested in mining and smelting.[82] Investments in petroleum stood at $68.5 million, and meantime W. R. Grace and Company was expanding its sugar production and marketing, financial, and manufacturing operations to such a degree that soon there would be scarcely "a Peruvian participating in the money economy of the country who does not eat, wear, or use something processed, manufactured, or imported by Casa Grace."[83]

Most U.S. capitalists and political leaders could see nothing but good in the increasing takeover of the Andean economies by capital from the north. After all, in its formative years the United States had depended upon a huge input of foreign investment and loan capital. Those in the United States who devoted any thought to the long-term implications of what was transpiring tended to conclude that North American investment in South America would bring about economic development, and with it political virtue, to parallel that achieved by their own country. The scholarly community in the emerging field of Latin American studies was by now offering assurances as to the increasing congruence of economic, social, and political culture in North and South America.[84] It did not occur to the ethnocentric business and political leaders to question this appraisal of the ethnocentric scholars. All three groups seemed incapable of foreseeing that capital poured into a basically patronalist-clientelist setting would go to strengthen the traditional social structure, rather than causing the massive spread of the self-reliant, capitalist dynamic that had accompanied the infusion of foreign capital into the individualistic, nonfeudal ambience of the young United States.

If the long-term consequence of capital penetration into the Andean region could scarcely have been foreseen, at least some U.S. leaders might have been better prepared for the anti-Yankee reaction that North American capital provoked. There were ample experiences in the U.S. past to suggest that such a reaction was inescapable. Any number of patriotic groups dedicated to the highest callings of Americanism, including the Grangers, the Mugwumps, and the followers of Bryan in 1896, had spoken out against the presence of foreign, especially British, capital in U.S. railroads, banking, mining, and manufacturing establishments, attributing to that presence many of the ills suffered by the national economy, especially by those who had only a marginal stake in it.

The inevitable Andean reaction to economic penetration could only have been hastened by the increasing diplomatic influence that the United States came to wield during the 1920s on issues of inter-South American diplomacy. In view of this situation, the Andean republics tended to depend more and more upon the support of the United States in protecting their interests in boundary and other types of disputes with neighbor republics. When incumbent administrations sustained diplomatic setbacks, sometimes because of their own incompetence and the inflated nature of their claims and demands, the United States was readily available as a scapegoat.

A Peruvian writer charged in 1930 that his country was directed, governed, and supervised by the U.S. secretary of state.[85] The charge was patently false, yet it was one that Leguía's detractors had for some time delighted in hurling against him. Moreover, the myth of U.S. domination was one that Leguía himself had found increasingly useful in explaining away his failures to satisfy nationalistic aspirations in the field of diplomacy. All the while the increasing visibility of U.S. capital served to inspire widespread credence in the myth of Washington's diplomatic hegemony.

THE RISE OF U.S. DIPLOMATIC INFLUENCE

Disappointed in its hopes that President Wilson might back its claims to an outlet on the Pacific, Bolivia turned for assistance to the League of Nations. In that forum it presented the revindicationist claims of the Republican party. The Revindicationists (*Reivindicacionistas*) demanded revision of the 1904 treaty with Chile so as to restore to Bolivia all or most of the coastal territory it had held prior to the War of the Pacific.

In 1921 the League refused to take action on the Bolivian request to revise the 1904 treaty, fearful that had it considered the matter Chile would have followed the earlier Argentine example of withdrawing from membership.[86] The decision in Geneva brought relief to the United States which, intent upon expanding diplomatic influence in the hemisphere, was resolutely set against the intervention of a European-based international assembly.

Aware of Washington's attitudes and having given up on League intervention after 1921, Bolivians recognized that their only hope for regaining a Pacific outlet lay in enlisting U.S. support.[87] Daniel Sánchez Bustamante saw a connection between the penetration of U.S. capital and Washington's diplomatic protection. He put it this way: "The day on which North American capital and enterprise have seriously penetrated Bolivia, the government of the United States will interest itself in this country and then there will have sounded the hour of our security."[88] For Sánchez Bustamante, there was no question that national security required the reacquisition of coastal territory.

By 1921 the United States had become active with Bolivia's neighbors Peru and Chile in seeking final resolution of the Tacna-Arica issue. According to the 1883 Treaty of Ancón, a plebiscite was to have been held in 1893 to determine whether these territories would be returned to Peru or retained by Chile as the spoils of war. The plebiscite had never been held, and the on-going debate over how to determine the final disposition involved not only Peru and Chile but virtually all the republics of South America. When the United States took up the troublesome issue by initiating arbitration sessions in Washington to which the Lima and Santiago governments sent delegations, Bolivian President Saavedra wrote President Warren G. Harding to the effect that Bolivia, because of its right in international justice to a port, should be a party to any negotiations aimed at finding a solution to the "question of the Pacific." Harding rejected this contention, maintaining that Bolivia would have to resolve the matter through direct negotiations with Peru and Chile.[89]

In 1925 President Calvin Coolidge announced the U.S. decision on the arbitration between Peru and Chile: The Tacna-Arica matter was to be settled by a plebiscite to be held under U.S. supervision.[90] Commissions sent by Washington to assure the honesty of the balloting were soon overwhelmed by the difficulties of the situation. As despair grew in the State Department, Secretary of State Kellogg, casting about desperately for some means out of the impasse, suggested in 1926 that most of the disputed territory be given to Bolivia, with that country then pledging indemnity payments to Peru and Chile. Bolivia, of course, was delighted,[91] but Peru and Chile were dismayed and managed to see to it that nothing came of Kellogg's suggestion.

The State Department's quandary continued, but out of it at least came some results beneficial to the U.S. delegation at the 1928 Pan American Conference held in Havana. At the conference, the Argentine delegation led a strong move to pressure the United States into renouncing intervention in Latin American affairs. Heading the U.S. delegation, former secretary of state Charles Evans Hughes encountered widespread hostility as he intransigently defended the right of his country to intervene under certain circumstances. He was immensely relieved, therefore, when the Peruvian delegation came to his assistance with an eloquent defense of interventionist principles in hemisphere relations.[92] Understandably under the circumstances Bolivia also refused to back the Argentine position. Given the hopes that both Peru and Bolivia placed in the United States, neither could have afforded to offend that country.

As of the mid-1920s, the diligent efforts of the State Department, and especially of Secretary Kellogg, had brought Peru and Chile into intense negotiations over the Tacna-Arica matter but had not succeeded in producing final accord. That was attained at last in 1929 when the two countries, acting largely on their own, agreed that Chile would retain Arica while Tacna would be restored to Peru.[93] The

warm welcome that Bolivia had provided U.S. capital and the syco-
phancy it had demonstrated toward the Washington government in
diplomatic relations had proved unavailing; the country was still without a Pacific port or free and independent access to one.

For Leguía, the diplomatic intervention of the United States had
proved more productive. It had led to a reopening of negotiations
with Chile and contributed ultimately toward a partially satisfactory
compromise solution. What is more, Leguía was able to reply to the
zealous nationalists who denounced him for having agreed to the
definitive surrender of Arica by insisting that Washington had forced
this surrender upon him. While this was not true, it was a very useful
fiction for the dictator to maintain. Once more, then, the United
States had discovered the pitfalls of trying to act as a peacemaker in
the exercise of American hemisphere diplomatic hegemony. Little
wonder that the U.S. minister to Bolivia would write in 1928: "but
efforts . . . as third parties to controversies [produce] dissatisfaction,
suspicion, and disadvantage."[94]

Even Leguía, who apparently had emerged as a beneficiary of U.S.
diplomacy, was by the end of the 1920s growing apprehensive over
Washington's rising influence in the hemisphere. He may also have
been growing tired of the circumstances that he felt forced him, in
the national interest, to utter statements of servile flattery, as when
in December of 1928 he eulogized the Monroe Doctrine and assured
President-elect Herbert Hoover, then on a South American good will
tour, that Pan Americanism was "the religion of the future." [95] A
certain souring on the United States contributed, in fact, to Leguía's
eagerness to compromise the long-standing dispute with Chile. While
the debates over Tacna and Arica were underway, Leguía had been
subjected to pressure by the State Department to accept a Colombian
boundary settlement that most Peruvians regarded as highly prejudicial to national rights. So long as Chile remained a hostile southern
neighbor, Leguía realized that Peru would find it difficult to resist
U.S. pressures to be generous in dealing with its northern neighbor.
Beyond this, Peru's president may have thought that reconciliation
with Chile would permit the two countries henceforth to present a
united front in disputes that were bound to arise with Washington
in the aftermath of penetration by U.S. capital.[96]

The northern boundary issue had assumed prominence in Peru in
1922, and for the next six years had disturbed diplomatic relations
between Lima and Washington. The Peruvian minister of foreign
relations Alberto Salomón and the Colombian minister to Lima Fabio

Lozano signed in 1922 a treaty providing Colombia with access to the Amazon at Leticia. In exchange, Peru's ownership over a strip of territory south of the Putumayo river was recognized. There is no question that the United States was anxious to see the boundaries in this region, disputed for decades, clearly delineated. A renewed interest in the area's rubber-producing capacity had developed because of the high prices demanded by the British-controlled international rubber cartel that dominated production in Asia. Obviously, no U.S. firm would be inclined to invest in rubber exploitation in an area where sovereignty was in doubt.

However great its interest in seeing the boundaries established, Washington probably did not pressure Peru into negotiating the Salomón-Lozano Treaty. But, once it had been entered into, the State Department applied considerable pressure on the Leguía administration to obtain congressional ratification. This is what caused the dictator's difficulties, for as soon as the terms of the treaty, negotiated in secret, were made public they were denounced by influential politicians, especially by Civilists in league with the Peruvian rubber lord Julio César Arana whose domain had been largely ceded to Colombia by the treaty, as an abject surrender of national territory.[97] In view of public opposition, Leguía hesitated to push for treaty ratification. Pressure from Washington, however, did finally help secure ratification in 1928 under circumstances in which other Leguía and his opponents joined in denouncing Washington's intervention.

Educador's interests were also affected, adversely, by the Salomón-Lozano Treaty, and as a result the government in Quito joined in denouncing the State Department's arm-twisting tactics. By the terms of the treaty, Ecuadorans found themselves "brusquely confronted by a three hundred mile boundary with their enemy, Peru, instead of the same line with Colombia, a country they had formerly regarded as a friend." While the treaty was disadvantageous to Peru in its boundary with Colombia, it was decidedly advantageous to the Lima government in respect to Ecuador. Whatever the irritation of the Peruvian government over the loss of Leticia, it had secured "a geopolitical position from which it could deal with Ecuador on its own terms and at leisure."[98]

An intensification of ill will was the price the United States had to pay for its diplomatic intrusion during the 1920s. Against this background there was emerging a new breed of Andean ideologues and aspiring elites. They ran the gamut from Marxism to fascism, but their basic importance arises from a large centrist core whose quarrel with the prevailing order derived from historical backgrounds and national traditions far more than from alien influences. Convinced that liberal, democratic and capitalist regimes were doomed throughout the world, the Andean prophets of a new order dismissed as totally inadequate the transitions presided over by their countries' political establishments during the 1920s. And with a virulence never approached by the Arielists and Hispanists, they denounced all that was associated with the social, economic, and political culture of the United States. A new era in U.S.-Andean relations was at hand.

8

Aspiring Elites and Transition

For the United States, the 1920s was a decade of smug satisfaction with the prevailing order and of resolute determination to protect that order against change and innovation. The contrast with Andean America is enormous. Andean thinkers or intellectuals (*pensadores*), who far more often than in the United States were also active political figures, were convinced that "their America" was, as the Peruvian philosopher Antenor Orrego put it, at a "terrible crossroads."[1] This mood helps explain the tremendous popularity of José Ortega y Gasset. In no small part, the Spanish thinker was lionized because of his "prophetism," his foretelling, that is, of the passing of the present order.[2] "The ground of the modern age which begins beneath the feet of Galileo," wrote Ortega, "is coming to an end beneath our own. Our feet have already moved away from it ... we are surely moving out of one age in order to enter another."[3] Helping further to explain Ortega's cult is his prediction of the downfall of capitalism and of the utilitarian man who had ruled in the past two centuries, and the rise of a new social hierarchy.[4]

Like many of their contemporaries in Europe, the Andean intellectuals had little doubt that they were "the future saviors of society."[5] To their mind, nation building was primarily a spiritual undertaking, and the first task of the intellectuals who were to lead their people into a new era was to discover what their people really were: to discover, that is, the national identity. Overwhelmingly, the intellectuals agreed with the appraisal of an Ecuadoran man of letters: "The United States has contributed nothing to our singular spiritual character."[6]

Pensadores in the 1920s tended also to agree with the Bolivian Ignacio Prudencio Bustillo who wrote that the individualism sweeping the Western world from the time of the French Revolution had never really taken root in Andean America. Instead, Andeans had clung to their faith in a corporative division of labor that "creates the dependency of men among themselves" and calls on the individual to yield his interests before those of the collectivity.[7] Andean thinkers tended further to share the Bolivian's belief that the historical past, often ignored or disparaged following the attainment of independence from Spain, contained invaluable clues as to the destiny that awaited their countries. The past was coming to be appreciated if for no other reason than for its purported absence of utilitarian, individualistic materialism.

Many foreign intellectual currents, including Marxism, fascism, and Hispanism, gave courage to the Andeans in their endeavors to find themselves by closing the door against cultural penetration from North America. In this regard, Freud was extremely useful. His actual works may not have been widely read by Andean thinkers in the 1920s, but a popularized version of them was very much in vogue. What appealed particularly to the would-be molders of Andean transition was the message that although some basic drives in persons are physiologically conditioned and therefore constant, others are psychologically socially determined, and therefore subject to modification. In the view of many *pensadores*, this Freudian insight proved that capitalist drives and incentives were not basic to human nature and that the United States had not developed a culture that must triumph throughout the world because it was in harmony with that nature. Bolstered by Freudian analysis, Andean thinkers could argue that the capitalist ethic had been instilled in people only as the result of a culture that was deeply flawed and, happily, subject to change.

As it was widely interpreted in Andean America, Freudian thought also called into question the rationality of positing society-wide freedom and independence as a goal of political culture. If the vast majority of persons were only apparently free, while in reality controlled by various forces that lurked in their own subconsciousness and in the idiosyncratic behavior of family and society, then concern with universal freedom should be discarded as totally misconceived. Andean thinkers, however, tended to temper this conclusion by reading into it certain elitist implications. By achieving a superior degree of awareness (consciousness) of the various social and psychological forces that were operative on them, an elite could, it was believed, attain a high degree of mastery over those forces which would lead to a correspondingly high degree of independence. Elites thus liberated could proceed then to manipulate the social-psychological environment so as to steer the masses, held to be incapable of attaining to a high degree of consciousness and independence, into conforming to the norms selected as rational by the elites. In short, Freudianism could now be interpreted, or twisted, so as to repudiate the old liberal goal of society-wide independence while at the same time opening virtually unlimited fields to the social engineer.

Any number of foreign prophets, in addition to Ortega and Freud, helped build in Andean intellectuals the belief that destiny had imposed upon them the task of leading their countries away from the post-Enlightenment, post-French Revolution Western world. The new racists, among them Houston Stewart Chamberlain, Madison Grant, and Lothrop Stoddard, called into question the logic of striving for democracy in countries inhabited by sizeable segments of inferior people. Furthermore, Thomas Carlyle, immensely popular in Andean circles during the 1920s, denied that the masses wanted independence; instead, he contended, they wanted sympathetic leadership and security, and this implied the need for great men, for heroes, who would overturn the established structure in which the masses were either ignored or foolishly exhorted to seek an independence which they could not fruitfully use.[8]

Even more popular than Carlyle among Andean America's self-perceived leaders of transition were a trio of German thinkers, Spengler, Keyserling, and Nietzsche. Persuaded as to the failure of democracy, Spengler hoped for the emergence of a new age that would be dominated by great men. "There are men whose nature is to command and men whose nature is to obey," he wrote, "subjects and objects of the political or economic process in question." To be fit to command, according to Spengler, man must be free "from the filthy craving for profits." Keyserling's message was similar. A sound social order required the passivity of the masses, and the rise of elites whose legitimacy would be assured by their ability to convince the common man of his own inferiority—a key tenet, incidentally, in the Krausist social philosophy. Like Spengler, Keyserling stressed the need for true elites to disdain private material gain.[9]

A number of facets of Nietzsche's thought delighted Andean *pensadores*, among them the conviction that "the democratic movement is . . . a form of decay, namely the diminution of man, making him mediocre and lowering his value."[10] Also appealing was the Nietzschian belief that elites should act upon the basis of an ethic entirely different from that of nonelites. Here was a perfect justification for a society perpetually divided into two cultures, one for the independent leaders, the other for the dependent masses. The Andean prophets of transition further concurred with Nietzsche in his disdain of the businessman. But, like many Germans, they rejected Nietzsche's contention that the great men should ignore the masses and refrain from paternalistic efforts to promote their welfare.

In their conclusion that parliamentarianism, democracy, and individualistic capitalism were inevitably doomed and that a new order was emerging, the Andeans showed little of the pessimism that often underlay the analysis of Europe's prophets of transition, or of the handful of like-minded observers in the United States—with Brooks and Henry Adams in the forefront. The European powers and the United States had, after all, amounted to something in the age of liberalism, and belief in the passing of that age was bound to inspire a certain uneasiness. For the Andean Americans, however, backwardness, as measured by all the liberal criteria, suddenly became a great source of pride in the past and hope for the future. This backwardness meant that Andean America had remained uncontaminated by the now moribund liberal order and that it was in a position of special advantage to lead the way into a future, postliberal world. Even as the Spanish pensador José Antonio Primo de Rivera, Peruvian, Bolivian, and Ecuadoran thinkers could point to their countries and exclaim: "blessed by your backwardness."[11]

To some Andeans even the ethnic composition of the national populaces, once regarded as constituting a terrible obstacle to progress, now came to be viewed in a hopeful light. Perhaps the Indians and mestizos were refractory to the civilization of liberalism; perhaps the telluric influences (influences of the soil, of the physical environment) to which Andean writers paid so much attention in the 1920s had fashioned people who could not operate effectively and advantageously in a liberal, individualistic culture. In the new, postliberal order about to dawn, however, mestizos and even Indians, as the products of Andean telluric determinants, enjoyed an advantage: they already possessed the nature that the masses of the once dominant liberal powers must now begin, painfully, to acquire. Understandably, the *pensadores* of Peru, Bolivia, and Ecuador responded enthusiastically to the message of Mexican intellectual and statesman José Vasconcelos that Latin Americans constituted a "cosmic race" that was best suited of all races to attain greatness in the new stage into which the world was evolving.[12]

Had they attended at all to the situation, business, political, religious, and academic leaders in the United States might have been able to brace themselves for shocks ahead by observing that the most influential guides for young Andean intellectuals in the 1920s included such antidemocratic, antiliberal figures as Ortega y Gasset, Carlyle, Spengler, Keyserling, and Nietzsche, and especially Marx and Lenin. U.S. observers might also have profited by taking note of the gathering strength of Catholicism, both as a religious faith and a social philosophy. Although Catholicism made adaptations to the new times, particularly by borrowing from the models of Christian Democracy being developed in Italy and Spain, it retained its traditional hostility to liberal capitalism and to the whole life style that, rightly or wrongly, was associated in the minds of most Andeans with the United States.

CATHOLICISM AND TRANSITION

Much like the Arielists and Hispanists, intellectuals of the 1920s raised the banner against positivism, with its emphasis on empirical observation, measurement, and quantification, and rejected the notion that "science constitutes man's sole possible significant cognitive relation to external reality."[13] This is one reason why they turned for inspiration, in matters of epistemology, to France's Henri Bergson.[14] Stressing the "radical incompatibility between the method of natural science and the method of intuitive sympathy or inner understanding," Bergson insisted there were many truths which science knew not of.[15] Among intellectuals of the transition period, especially those who did not claim to have been influenced by Marxism, it ceased to be fashionable to deny religious beliefs simply because they were not subject to scientific verification. Even if they did not choose themselves to profess the faith, intellectuals were not about to deny the masses the right to cling to their old religious beliefs.

Influenced also by such nineteenth-century French thinkers as Ernest Renan, Fustel de Coulanges, and Durkheim,[16] many Andean *pensadores* came in the 1920s to appreciate the useful function that religion could play in preserving social tranquility. Now that a social problem had indeed appeared in their midst, they were also inclined to take to heart the assertions voiced by the clergy since the beginning of the nineteenth century: economic remedies would not suffice to keep the multitudes quiescent; and only Catholicism could prevent social revolution by providing moral curbs to the material appetites of the masses and inducing them to direct their expectations toward the next world. The clergy, of course, had always insisted that Catholicism could not make its vital contribution to social tranquility unless the church was allowed to play a major role in temporal society. In the post-World War I setting, Andean intellectuals perhaps as never before since independence were willing to consider these priestly assertions with respect.

Arielism had been launched by and was at first popularized largely by lapsed Catholics who were satisfied that humanism provided an adequate foundation upon which to base the higher values they extolled. But a new pattern became discernible roughly between 1910 and 1930. More and more of the leaders of the spiritual reaction against utilitarian and mechanistic criteria began to return to the church, persuaded that higher human values, if they were to prevail, required a theological foundation.

At the beginning of the 1930s the Peruvian medical doctor and philosopher Honorio Delgado declared the need for a return to Catholicism, which is the only "true principle of hierarchy and dignity."[17] At approximately the same time José María Velasco Ibarra, a young Ecuadoran writer about to embark upon a long and spectacular political career, averred that humanism of itself would not suffice to keep the masses in line: "only religion is capable of educating the generality of the people in the principles of sacrifice and fraternity ... Catholicism is a doctrine eminently conducive to ... a sense of sacrifice ... and discipline."[18] In a way the passage from humanism to Catholicism in Andean America parallels the experience of T. S. Eliot. Beginning as a humanist in the school of Irving Babbit and Paul Elmore More in the United States, Eliot moved on to Catholic absolutes, affirming it is necessary "to have not merely high ideals, but absolute ideals, Catholic ideals." Otherwise, Eliot contended, it would be impossible to induce men to want the right things.[19]

In a number of ways the church was permitted, even encouraged, to expand its temporal influence. In Lima, a Catholic University was established in 1917, with the Spanish professor Emilio Huidoboro playing an influential role in its early years and helping initiate a revival of Thomism among young intellectuals. The Catholic University was concerned primarily with forming an elite that could appreciate, guard, and nourish the most exalted of human values.[20] Practical studies were largely eschewed as beneath the dignity of a privileged intellectual class. By the 1930s, the new university in Lima could claim greater social prestige than the venerable national San Marcos University which, under the pressure of the university reform movement that came at the end of World War I, was beginning to open its doors to students of humble origins. In contrast, the Catholic University reserved its instruction for members of the aristocracy.

The appearance of Christian Democratic precepts, introduced mainly by the missionary clergy from Spain where the movement had appeared at the beginning of the twentieth century,[21] added a significant new dimension to the church's social philosophy. Especially in Ecuador where it gained a decisive influence in the old Conservative party, Christian Democracy directed an appeal not so much to the aristocracy as to the marginal middle sectors whose revolutionary potential was coming more and more to be feared. Ecuador's advocates of Christian Democracy argued in favor of the largest possible middle class "in between the lowest workers and the wealthy."[22] Toward this end they urged restrictions against the continued growth of the large estates and advocated government encouragement to the creation of numerous family-sized farms. In addition they recommended tariff protection and other state measures designed to enlarge the ranks of the artisans and small manufacturers. Moreover, displaying the animus against large-scale financial capitalism that was a significant feature of Spain's Christian Democracy, Ecuador's revitalized Conservative party called for the creation of credit cooperatives among the employee classes, and also for the establishment of consumer cooperatives so as to eliminate gouging middlemen.[23]

As mentioned, many of the one-time Liberals who in the 1920s made an opening toward what they described as socialism were convinced that the way to deal with the discontent of the marginal middle sectors was to make them increasingly dependent on state paternalism and bureaucratic patronage. The Christian Democrats, however, believed that the lower middle sectors aspired to some minimal degree at least of economic independence, in part as the means of separating and distinguishing themselves from the proletariat for whom abject dependence on the state seemed inevitable—and, in the middle-sector view, desirable. Christian Democrats feared that if the middle sectors lost their desire for economic independence, and for ownership of their own property and capital goods, then society would be deprived of one of the most effective barriers against the sort of state socialism that would lead ultimately to atheistic communism.

Formulators of the church's social philosophy in postwar Andean America also urged the reestablishment of the corporative social struc-

212

ture. Thus they tempered the defense of individual self-reliance with the admonition that persons must organize into functional and municipal associations upon which they were to some degree dependent for their material security and to which they were willing to sacrifice their private interests. Andean Catholic corporativists found the roots of what they considered the proper social organization in the Spanish middle ages and in their own colonial background. And they hailed Leo XIII's 1891 encyclical *Rerum novarum*—and Pius XI's follow-up encyclical of 1931, *Quadragcsimo anno*—as a vital new exposition of corporativist principles. Outside of small clerical circles *Rerum novarum* had been dismissed, before the social problem appeared, as applicable only to Europe. But with the signs of the class struggle at hand, more and more Andeans discovered the encyclical's relevence. It is important to note, however, that the relevence they found in Leo XIII's social doctrine differed considerably from that discovered by most churchmen in the United States. The North American clergy, in stressing during the 1920s the anti-Communist content of *Rerum novarum*, tended to picture it as an apology for capitalism. Andean Americans came closer to the real essence of the encyclical when they used it to condemn the abuses of capitalism and to stress the need not only for private property but also for corporative collectivism in the quest for social justice.[24] When liberalism had been ascendant, this condemnation had placed the clergy beyond the pale of the dominant socioeconomic philosophy. By the 1920s, however, circumstances had so changed as to place them once more within the intellectual main stream.

The Catholic corporativist movement produced a few Andean apologists of fascism, a word that must be used with extreme caution as it means different things to different persons and is impossible to define with pinpoint precision. Peru's José de la Riva Agüero, the founder in 1915 of an Arielist political party, ceremoniously returned to the practice of the Catholic faith in 1932 and began thereafter to proclaim that only Catholicism and fascism could contain the Communist menace. "Up with Catholicism," he wrote, "up with the corporative state and fascism, with order, hierarchy and authoritarianism."[25] However, the vast majority of Andean corporativists in the 1920s and 1930s drew their ideological inspiration from sources far older than fascism, sources reaching back to medieval Spain and including in times closer to hand the writings of the nineteenth-century Peruvian bishop of Arequipa Bartolomé Herrera and of a broad array of Krausists.

In the United States, the position of most Catholic corporativists was not understood. Fascists after all did advocate the corporative state (their own version of it, in which an all-absorbing state exercised such a degree of control over corporative entities as to leave them without any vestige of autonomy); and because Fascists were corporativists, North Americans tended to conclude that corporativists must be Fascists. It followed that if Catholics and other groups customarily associated with the political right in Andean America directed criticism against the political culture and liberal capitalism of the United States, it was owing to the spread there of the fascist conspiracy.

Italian and, later, German fascism were accidental to the revival of Catholic corporativism and to the whole questioning of the liberal economic and political order in Andean America. The revival and the questioning would have occurred even had fascism never appeared on the scene, albeit perhaps in a somewhat less bold and assertive manner. The situation was similar in regard to Marxism-Leninism, an ideology seized upon as a new and stylish means of justifying aspirations, attitudes, values, and prejudices that were deeply rooted in Andean culture. And, if relatively few corporativists were Fascists, even fewer Andean Marxists-Leninists were Communists.

One reason why few Marxists-Leninists became bona fide Communists,[26] which entailed accepting discipline from the International, was their insistence upon interpreting the ideology in line with their own predilections and self-interest and in keeping with the historical traditions of their own cultures. By and large, Andean leftists agreed with a Peruvian Marxist who proclaimed: "The true disciples of Marx are not those pedantic professors who can only repeat his words, those incapable of adding to the doctrine but rather limited by it; the real disciples of Marx have been the revolutionaries stained with heresy."[27]

Marxism-Leninism and Transition

Marxism-Leninism began to make its major impact in Andean America precisely at a time (the 1920s) when the traditional political parties were ideologically bankrupt and in the throes of organizational disintegration. Thus it was not politically risky, it was in fact politically expedient, to ignore the old parties and to take up with new organizations whose claims to being au courant depended upon their Marxist orientation. An Ecuadoran writer observes that in his country it had suddenly become good business to be a Marxist. Since 1925, he notes, the intellectuals of the left "have waxed rich and held high office in various administrations. To proclaim oneself a leftist has opened all kinds of doors."[28] In Bolivia and Peru it was largely the same, in part because the more menacing the aspiring elites made themselves by taking up the Marxist-Leninist cloak, the more intent the entrenched political interests became upon co-opting their critics.

Beyond considerations of political expediency, Marxism-Leninism's vogue emerged out of the ideological appeal that it exercised on many Latin Americans. Its attraction has been explained in these terms: "it has been faithful to the deep-rooted cultural bias favoring collectivism and centralized control by the state. In this sense, Marxist ideas have spread through the urban middle classes as well as the intelligentsia."[29] Even more important in explaining the popularity of the foreign ideology was the way in which Marxism-Leninism could be used to exonerate Latin Americans from blame for their lack of development. Up until this time some of the more widely voiced theories utilized to explain the area's underdevelopment and material backwardness placed the principal blame on the character of the people. But, Marxism-Leninism shifted culpability for underdevelopment to the workings of a capitalist system controlled and manipulated by foreigners, by outsiders. Thus it helped Andean Americans to shed debilitating inferiority complexes.

For its partisans, Marxism served to reenforce the traditional humanism that had been manifested earlier in Andean America by such philosophical movements as Krausism and Arielism. Both Krausists and Arielists—as well as defenders of Hispanic Catholicism—had maintained that competitive, acquisitive capitalism did not correspond to the inevitable laws of human nature but was instead contrary to those laws and antithetical to the full development of human capacity. Marx's writings tended to confirm this view and undoubtedly contributed to the type of interpretation *pensadores* gave to Freud: for Marx maintained that competitiveness and acquisitiveness were not matters of private motivation determined by the nature of individuals, but rather the "inexorable conditions of the situation in which individuals are placed."[30] According to Marx, the felt need for private material wealth is a peculiarity of certain cultures, created by those cultures and therefore subject to elimination by the transformation of the cultures.[31] In Marx, therefore, Andean humanists found vindication for their conviction that rule over society need not be left to the businessmen but could, and indeed must, be wrested from them and entrusted to people concerned with the cultural, spiritual, intellectual callings to which human nature, once liberated from suffocating materialism, could respond.

Although the writings of the young Marx in which he most fully revealed his humanism were not then available—they came to light only in 1932—Andean *pensadores*, even as Europeans such as Georg Lukács,[32] intuited the original, humanistic approach of the father of communism. And this humanism is above all else what endeared Marx to many of his Andean followers.

As interpreted by the humanists, Marxism taught that obsession with private material gain led to alienation in which the higher endowments of human nature were subjected to its baser components. Thus, development of the life of the spirit required the gaining of freedom from the whole syndrome of rising material expectations that capitalism had imposed upon humanity. This interpretation of Marx led the Peruvian philosopher Mariano Iberico to write in 1926 that the essence of socialism

> is the sentiment that man needs to be redeemed from secular inequity which, consecrated in a new form of slavery, has subjected him to the laws of an inhuman economy and converted him into simply the means, the mere instrument of production. Thus socialism is a liberation, a force to redeem humanity . . . a desire to resuscitate the man inside of himself and to return to him full sovereignty over his spirit.[33]

A similar interpretation runs through the writings of most Andean socialists of the 1920s and 1930s. Typically, Bolivia's José Antonio Arze writes:

> Only communism, never before realized in any part of America, will permit men to develop their full human capacity . . . A socialist regime, emancipating man economically, thereby emancipates him for full enjoyment of the other aspects of human life . . . Art will flourish in proportions never before seen and delights of beauty will not be monopolized by minoritics any longer, but instead extended to all.[34]

For Iberico, Arze, and Andean humanists in general, economism (reliance on bread-and-butter rewards and incentives) would not suffice to content the masses. It would lead to the atrophying of the spiritual-intellectual potential among the masses, which was to be deplored on idealistic, humanitarian grounds. Beyond that, it would lead in the long run to massive discontent and pressures from below, which in their own self-interest the gifted elements of society had to take steps to direct toward acceptable outlets.

The Peruvian socialist Hildebrando Castro Pozo in a 1936 publication complained that many of his countrymen took into account only the economic content of socialism, and thus deformed the doctrine so as to make it unrecognizable. "This is because they approach it from a bourgeois mentality and are thus not equipped to appreciate the importance of the integral wholeness of the message of Marx and Engels, which takes into account the economic-political, moral and intellectual realms of the human personality."[35] Castro Pozo's words are also applicable to the view of Marxism that has prevailed in the United States, and this is why it has been so difficult for North Americans to understand that ideology's impact in Andean America.

High-minded idealism and humanism, of course, have been only partially responsible for Andean America's infatuation with Marxism-Leninism. Marxism, as thinkers of that region interpreted it, appealed to the humanists, but Leninism attracted hosts of men with a lust for power and the faith that they were superior beings, destined in the proper order of things to dominate lesser mortals. Lenin affirmed the efficacy of purposeful, conscious minorities in bringing about change in the world. For him, the socialist revolution was not the product of an inexorable historical process so much as the conscious creation of human activity. The sensitive intellectual, Lenin believed, would come, far sooner than the exploited proletariat, to full comprehension (consciousness) of the alienation, the assault on human dignity, and the drying up of human potential that resulted from capitalism. The unaided proletariat could not achieve this consciousness; it "had to be brought by intellectuals from without."[36]

Convinced they were living in an age of transition and angered that the present regimes did not accord them adequate recognition, Andean thinkers delighted over Lenin's call to the intellectual to lead society into the next stage and then to rule, at least initially, in the new era through a dictatorship of the vanguard of the proletariat. The vanguard would, of course, be those who had attained to high stages of consciousness.

In Andean America, Leninism updated Krausism, Arielism, and Hispanism. These latter three intellectual movements, it will be recalled, advocated rule by cultural elites. The legitimacy of these elites was to depend upon recognition by the masses of their own cultural inferiority. Leninism was greeted by a new generation of Andean intellectuals as providing the formula for legitimizing the rule they longed to exercise. Legitimacy would depend upon convincing the masses that the leaders had somehow gained a higher degree of intuitive insight into what was best for the overall well-being of the masses and were proceeding in the best way possible toward attainment of that well-being.[37]

Lenin, to be fair, expressed the hope that eventually the gulf between the intellectual leaders and the proletariat would disappear, as the latter gained a higher level of consciousness that would permit them to absorb the leaders on whom they had once depended. In Russia this process would require forty or fifty years, he explained to a Spanish visitor in Moscow toward the end of 1919.[38] But many Andean *pensadores* in the 1920s seemed to be acting out of behavior patterns described by the Polish revolutionary Waclaw Machajski in his 1904 work *The Intellectual Worker*. According to him socialism was being grasped at by intellectuals as the means of attaining permanent domination over the proletariat.[39] Regardless of whether they had short-term or permanent consequences in mind, Andean intellectuals found in Leninism the same sort of justification for their ambitions that businessmen in a preceding generation had found in Spencerianism. Undoubtedly, the use of Marxism-Leninism "as the ideology of the aspiring elites of pre-industrial societies . . . was never anticipated by Marx and Engels."[40]

The vogue that Marxism-Leninism came to enjoy in Andean America in the generation arising after World War I[41] contributed to the posthumous veneration of Manuel González Prada. This aristocratic Peruvian intellectual, already mentioned in connection with his criticism of the new-rich Civilists who rose to prominence in the period of recovery following the War of the Pacific, was one of the major iconoclasts produced in the American hemisphere.[42] Above all else he urged transformation, thoroughgoing, radical transformation, of virtually every aspect of the prevailing order. Only after his death in 1918 had Andean intellectuals developed a consensus on the need for transition. Thus his message came to be appreciated in the 1920s, especially by intellectuals who embraced the Marxist-Leninist ideology.

A sincere humanist who wanted to liberate persons from the pressure of economic wants so that they could become fully human, González Prada after flirting with socialism found in anarchism the antidote to laissez-faire capitalism and the corrective to the attempt of the ruling oligarchy to bring about the *embourgeoisement* of society.[43] At the moment, however, as it awaited the antidote and corrective, Peru was sick, so sick that, according to González Prada, everywhere you pressed it pus came out.[44] Recovery, he believed, depended upon a type of radical surgery that could be performed only by a select elite that had liberated itself from the capitalist ethic and the desire for private ownership of property. The working classes, he asserted, needed the revolutionary impulse of the intellectuals, for otherwise they would remain as brutes.[45] "We hope," he stated, "that the necessary man will arise in the opportune hour." When the superior figure does appear in our midst, he exhorted, "let us embrace him at once, follow him on the road, making the sacrifice of our pride and personal ambitions: if there is merit in preaching an idea, there is greater merit in ceding the place to the man capable of realizing it."[46]

Many an Andean intellectual in the 1920s harbored the suspicion that he must be the man of destiny foreseen by González Prada. In most instances, though, the men who saw themselves in this light ignored González Prada's obsession with the ultimate attainment of liberty, spiritual independence, and self-reliance for all human beings, male and female. They ignored also his insistence that although the great leader was necessary to shake the masses out of their lethargy, he must quickly disappear into the ranks of the masses below who carried out the revolution.

While most men of the era following the War of the Pacific affirmed the need to Westernize the natives, González Prada proclaimed that Indians in the nonmaterialistic collectivism of their comunidades lived in a higher state of virtue than the citizens of the purportedly advanced Western countries. What was necessary, therefore, not only in Peru but elsewhere in Latin America as well, was for the Indians to play a major role in a sweeping social revolution that would result in the imposition of their way of life upon all citizens. Already by the 1890s González Prada had seen the Indians as they would come more and more to be seen by Marxists-Leninists in the 1920s: as the persons who because of their lack of capitalist instincts were the ones most likely to respond to the call for radical transition that some prophet of genius would sound against the liberal order.

In developing this position González Prada, and even more notably the Marxist Indianists who in the 1920s would begin to hail him as their mentor and precursor, helped lend credence to two myths that have proved particularly hardy in Andean America: (1) the myth of the eternal Indian who remains forever closed in his preconquest way of life and whose nature is insulated against all forces of change; and (2) the myth of the Indian as a natural revolutionary, predisposed toward violence and requiring only the slightest provocation to perpetrate a blood bath that will destroy the white man's world in its entirety. Both myths, together with other González Prada influences, are apparent in the Marxian Indianist programs of Andean America in the 1920s and 1930s.

MARXIAN INDIANISM AND REVOLUTIONARY TRANSITION

Because the urban proletariat was weak and inchoate in Andean America, Marxists who hoped for revolution in the not-too-distant future turned to the rural proletariat, which meant they turned to the Indian.[47] In the communalism of the Inca past they found the first successful implementation of the socialist ideology. Indians, they professed, by their very nature always had been and always would be socialists, and thus they were predisposed at the present moment to take part in a great revolution that would introduce—or restore—socialism to Andean America.

By extolling the nonacquisitive Indian way of life, Indianists were in effect criticizing capitalism per se, but most especially its present group of practitioners in Andean America. This attack delighted humanist intellectuals, resentful over the manner in which they were shunned by the present order; and, it delighted no less the struggling middle sectors who saw their hopes for security, let alone upward mobility, doomed by the greedy monopolists who controlled the economic and political apparatus. For intellectuals and marginal middle sectors the Indian, even though he might be regarded as a racial antagonist, became the symbol of defiance to the capitalism and political control of the entrenched oligarchy.

Because the issue of capitalism had been interjected into a new power struggle beginning to take form, the United States, as always the symbol of capitalism, had again become implicated, unwittingly, in the domestic political life of Andean America. The Indian became a symbol that was useful for challenging not only the local directing classes but also the international power of U.S. capitalism that allegedly lay behind those classes. The Indian issue, moreover, could be seized upon to arouse the animosity not just of intellectuals and middle sectors, but of urban laborers as well, against the oligarchy and their Yankee collaborators.

The continuing seizure of Indian lands in the 1920s contributed to the swelling of the urban populace, as the dispossessed made their way into the cities. Thus, the source of cheap urban labor was constantly replenished under circumstances that delighted employers but dismayed the longer established urban laborers.[48] These laborers—many of them "former Indians" who had acquired the rudiments of an education and in habits of dress and speech and perhaps even thinking had come to identify with Western urban life—enthusiastically backed Indianist demands that the comunidades be scrupulously protected against further plundering. Once the comunidades gained security, it appeared likely that migration into the cities would be slowed.

Indianists fixed responsibilty for the confiscation of comunidad lands not only upon local *gamonales* or *hacendados* but also upon U.S. enterprises—which either seized land directly or by buying the products of local landowners encouraged them to expand production by absorbing more land.[49] Although they might not understand the full complexities of the argument, the Andean urban proletariat could grasp the notion that their plight was somehow associated with the operation of international capitalism. Probably the mestizo lower middle sectors responded with even greater alarm to the processes that the Marxian Indianists depicted as being linked to the workings of local and international capitalism; for these mestizo sectors were faced with the prospect of having to compete for respectable white-collar employment with a steadily rising number of "former Indians" from the countryside.

In Ecuador, in contrast to Peru and Bolivia, Marxian Indianism created relatively little intellectual or political stir during the 1920s. Some of the reasons for this are readily apparent. With its economy in collapse throughout the 1920s, Ecuador did not experience the pressures of economic expansion and modernization that contributed to the plundering of Indian lands elsewhere in Andean America. As a result, there was no substantial exodus from the countryside to threaten marginal urban sectors. Moreover, the most visible component of the oligarchy, the Guayaquil bankers, fell from power with the military takeover in 1925; and U.S. capital, failing to increase its stake appreciably in the course of the decade, remained inconspicuous. Thus many of the factors that contributed to the impact of Indianism in Bolivia and Peru were missing in Ecuador.

In Bolivia as well as Peru, Marxian-inspired Indianists in the 1920s harped upon the telluric influences that had shaped the collectivist attitudes of Indian life. According to them, people formed by the awesome geography of the Andes could never develop individualistic traits; for they lived in constant awareness of the need for collective, group effort in order to survive in their challenging environment. All attempts to introduce liberal, capitalist culture were bound ultimately to fail in Andean America because of the telluric factor.

In their stress on telluric factors, the Indianists were influenced more by spokesmen of Spanish traditionalism than by Marxists. Angel Ganivet, Miguel de Unamuno, and other Spaniards associated with the "Generation of '98" had insisted that Spain's telluric determinants rendered it forever unsuitable to the modernity of European culture. The Spaniards found in their peninsula's telluric influences a guarantee that it would retain its own distinct character and avoid Europeanization. On their part, Andean Indianists found in their countries' telluric forces that assurance that their lands would never be North Americanized.

Bolivia's most important Indianist in the 1920s and 1930s was Gustavo Adolfo Navarro, a fervent admirer in his youth of the father of Arielism, José Enrique Rodó. An outspoken foe of the Liberal party, he was rewarded by the Republicans, when they came to power in 1920, with the post of consul in Le Havre. His exposure to European intellectual influences, begun when he was in his early twenties, caused him "to abandon his earlier enthusiasms and to adopt a revolutionary stance, a common change among intellectuals . . . of this period." Navarro took to his new revolutionary calling with passionate intensity and in order to display his "Russophile tendencies" adopted the pseudonym of Tristán Marof.[50]

In 1926 Navarro published in Brussels a short book with the title La justicia del Inca. It was destined to become a widely influential work. In it, he asserted the need to reject the "individualistic, capitalist bourgeois way of life . . . because it animalizes men."[51] Rhapsodizing over preconquest Indian civilization, he declared that the Incas had forged a people who were innocent of all individualistic inclinations. Free from greed and without any concept of money, the Incas organized a domain in which privation and hunger were not known. "Furthermore, the wealth of the soul was not neglected. The empire was impregnated with poetry and art." Inca excellence in poetry, art, and astronomy, he argued, came about because the state encouraged artistic inclinations and relieved persons from economic preoccupations.[52] The communist idea, Navarro asserted, was nothing new in America. "Centuries ago the Incas practiced it with the greatest success and produced a happy people who swam in abundance. All was planned and economically controlled."[53]

The gravest error of politicians since Bolivia's attainment of independence had been to attempt to impose European ways upon the wise and virtuous descendants of the Incas.[54] By returning to Inca socialism, and combining with its old modes the use of modern advances, especially the machines that economize time, it would be possible to bring into being a new form of existence in which persons allotted only a short amount of time to labor, being free the rest of the day to devote themselves to the "speculations of the spirit."[55] For this utopian existence to the ushered in, Navarro explained, it was necessary that a "wave of renovation and mysticism . . . take possession of the working classes," by which he meant both the intellectual and manual workers of the cities. Once renovated, the select urban spirits would then liberate the Indians from the exploitation imposed on them since colonial times and thereafter treat the natives with tenderness and love.[56] Obviously, a great deal of elitism and paternalism underlay the fraternalism and social harmony that Navarro proclaimed.

Growing more skeptical about human nature as he advanced in age, Navarro had by the 1950s withdrawn from political struggles. He felt, he said, like Don Quijote who, when close to death, was cured of his madness and admonished his heirs to spurn books of chivalry. Nevertheless, the Indianist writings of Navarro continued to exert an influence, and many Bolivians remain proud that a countryman urged a socialist revolution, extending throughout Latin America and based on the social forms of Inca life, before the better-known and internationally recognized Indianist from Peru, José Carlos Mariátegui, took up the cause.[57]

Born in 1895 in Lima (a few authorities hold out for the year 1894 and the southern coastal town of Moquegua) Mariátegui was already a cripple and in precarious health when, early in the *oncenio*, the government financed a study tour for him in Europe. Perhaps Leguía was anxious to be rid for the time being of a talented journalist who had demonstrated a highly independent and unconventional mind.

In Europe Mariátegui came into contact with a number of prominent intellectuals, among them Georges Sorel, Benedetto Croce, and Piero Gobetti.[58] Undoubtedly they helped form Mariátegui's spiritualized version of Marxism. The spiritualization of Marxism, deriving from the belief that liberation from obsession with private material gain would allow persons to attain development of their full human potential, was, after all, in the European intellectual air of the 1920s.[59] Influenced by his European associates, Mariátegui apparently came to the conclusion, one that would later be explicitly articulated by Erich Fromm, that Marx's socialism "is the realization of the deepest religious impulses common to the great humanistic religions of the past."[60]

While in Europe Mariátegui also met and was deeply influenced by that quintessential genius of the Spanish-speaking world, Unamuno. As a result the frail Peruvian, according to a perceptive biographer, built his own personal philosophy around Unamuno's concept of the "agonic soul."[61] Those who were animated by the agonic soul realized that the purpose of life lay in the struggle with pain and adversity and that only through this struggle could one achieve a sense of identity and the full realization of the human potential for good, while at the same time preparing wisely for the emancipation of death.

In Mariátegui's view, the superiority of preconquest Inca civilization over modern, technological, Western capitalism lay in the ability of its subjects to accept the inevitability of death, to liberate themselves from materialistic attachments to this world, and to begin, while still alive, to prepare for separation from this earth by living in the realm of the spiritual. Mariátegui soon decided, and here perhaps the influence of Sorel was uppermost, that myths constituted the highest form of liberating spiritualism. Christianity had in the past provided the most important myth by which persons liberated themselves. However, the myth of Christianity might now be spent and ready to be replaced with a new myth, that of the socialist revolution —which in its turn would in the remote future give way to yet another myth or great ideal.

"A proletariat," Mariátegui wrote after his return to Peru, "without a larger ideal than the reduction of working hours and wage increases of a few pennies will never be capable of a great, historic achievement."[62] The Peruvian Indians, though, were seen as singularly indifferent to the inducements of economism. Because they were the spiritual heirs of the socialist empire of Tahuantinsuyo, they were ready to respond to the new myth, "the mystique, the idea of the socialist revolution," that would uplift mankind.[63] "There is a mysticism in Marxism," Mariátegui enthused, "and those who adhere to it come very close to the spirit of the Christianity of the catacombs."[64] For him, the Andean Indians were, perhaps in all the world, the proletariat most likely to be consumed by this mysticism.

But, before the Indians could be awakened by the great Marxian mystique that recalled the splendors of their past,[65] Mariátegui insisted that socialist city dwellers had to play the role that the Andean bourgeoisie had failed to play: the socialist urbanites who understood the laws of history, and here the intellectual workers were looked to as the key element, must establish full-blown capitalism. This would bring about the alienation of the urban proletariat and thereby prepare the way for a socialist revolution which would then reach out to and envelop the Indian rural proletariat which was ripe for revolution.[66] Establishment of mature capitalism would, moreover, bring into being modern means of production. Then after the socialist revolution had occurred, these means, directed toward satisfying the needs of all rather than providing profits for a few, could free workers from long hours of toil and facilitate their development as full human beings.

Critics of Mariátegui and of Andean Indianists in general have charged them with seeking to turn the Indians loose in a war against whites in which the culture of the coast would be submerged beneath that of the sierra.[67] In the case of Mariátegui at least, this charge is unfounded. Even as in Gustavo Adolfo Navarro, there was a great deal of elitism in Mariátegui, as is surely attested to by the name he gave to the review he founded and in which he published some of his most important writings: *Amauta*. In the Inca empire, *amautas* had been the wise men entrusted with guarding and passing on religious, scientific, and historical truth. Undoubtedly, Mariátegui hoped that men of this type, white and mestizo urban intellectuals, would serve as the new *amautas* once the socialist revolution took place. Like González Prada he was careful to give a social connotation to the term race. That is, race was seen as determined by social-cultural rather than ethnic-biological factors. This being so, white men could become Indians and provide leadership in the new Indian utopia.

Probably it is not fair to explain Mariátegui's revolutionary Indianism purely in terms of the hostility of an intellectual to a materialistic society that gave short shrift to persons occupied with "higher things." The humanism and idealism of the gaunt cripple, who died in stoic resignation in 1930 after suffering an acute illness and the amputation of a leg, emerge from his writings with an exalted sincerity that could leave only the most hardened cynic unmoved. But the lust for power on the part of aspiring elites undoubtedly has contributed through the years to the cult of Mariátegui. In addition, his writings are complex, perhaps even contradictory, and a vast variety of types can find in them what they are looking for—including the millionaire communist types who justify their financial success on the grounds that by contributing to the full maturation of capitalism they are preparing the way for the ultimate socialist revolution.

Throughout Andean America, Hispanists, especially those of the conservative, Catholic stripe, were outraged by the Marxian Indianists' glorification of the native and by their contemptuous dismissal of all that Spain had contributed to Andean culture. For years, Hispanists and Indianists engaged in a vitriolic dispute over the relative merits of Spaniards and Indians, and their polemic served to hide the rather ample common ground that both schools shared. The Hispanist as well as the Indianist was apt to be a humanist, put off by the materialism of the ruling bourgeoisie, and an elitist, groping for ways to control the masses through the allocation of nonmaterial rewards. What is more, Mariátegui himself reveals a certain indebtedness to Spanish traditions and political theory in his advocacy of what in many ways was a corporativist political structure.[68]

In spite of the ferocity of the Hispanism-Indianism debate, Andean America's Spanish and Indian traditions, as interpreted by the intellectuals of the 1920s, continued to a remarkable extent to be mutually reenforcing. The overlapping of the two traditions is readily apparent in the most consequential—and also controversial—political vehicle of middle-sector and intelligentsia discontent that appeared in Andean America: the American Popular Revolutionary Alliance or APRA (*Alianza Popular Revolucionaria Americana*), founded and directed, both with opportunistic cunning and idealistic zeal, by Peru's Víctor Raúl Haya de la Torre. The movement launched by the APRA is designated Aprismo, and its members are styled Apristas.

THE APRA AND ITS FORMULAS FOR TRANSITION

The president of the Peruvian Federation of University Students, Haya de la Torre was one of the many intellectuals harried out of the country as Leguía in the first term of the *oncenio* moved to stifle criticism. Throughout the 1920s Haya traveled widely in the American hemisphere and in Europe, and he was in Mexico in 1924 when, at the age of twenty-nine, he founded the APRA. Beyond doubt, he was influenced by the various intellectual ingredients that had gone into the 1910 Mexican Revolution and that country's 1917 constitution with its stress on social intervention by the state. Never an especially original thinker, despite his contrary claims, Haya possessed a certain genius in weaving together the thought of others so as to form a synthesis that could attract a broad and disparate array of thinkers and activists. Thus while some of the thought of the Mexican Revolution found its way into the APRA program, a good deal of Marxism-Leninism, a certain dose of fascism, and above all a generous portion of traditional Andean political, social, and economic thought gained a place in the Aprista synthesis.

A brilliant conversationalist whose presence in small gatherings could be overwhelming, Haya was also a superb mass orator, able to moralize and to wax didactic without diminishing the attention of his listeners. The stocky Peruvian was well aware of his exceptional gifts and totally unabashed in calling attention to them. This was the age in which such proponents of the hero as Carlyle, Keyserling, Nietzsche, and González Prada[69] were in vogue in Andean America, and it was common practice for ambitious politicians and intellectuals to play the role of the hero.

It never occurred to Haya de la Torre to confess a shortcoming or admit a mistake, for this would have destroyed the whole mystique he was trying to create as the leader set apart from the rest of mortals and endowed with charisma. He agreed with Ferdinand Lasalle that "the rank and file must follow their leader blindly, and the whole organization must be like a hammer in his hand."[70] Antenor Orrego, an important figure in early Aprismo, provides a clear demonstration of the sort of adulation Haya demanded and received from his followers. Mentioning Aprismo's maximum leader by name, Orrego enthused: "Only the superior man, the man of impelling emotion, of faith, of passion to accomplish, the man with internal discipline and creative impulse, can lead Indo-Americans toward their destiny ... [Aprismo] can succeed only through the genius of a great-man leader, just as communism would not have taken over Russia without Lenin."[71]

Desiring to bestow on himself a virtually sacred aura of leadership, Haya was fully sensitive to the function that religion and religious imagery could play. Only by means of the APRA cross, he assured the faithful, could Peru be redeemed. He explained, moreover, that "he bore a 'never healing wound' from which he drew the inspiration for his life's work." This was the wound of the sorrow of the people, "sorrow which would one day be victory."[72]

A penetrating and original study explains the use that the APRA made of religion:

> By seeking to legitimize their movement through reference to religious images and beliefs held in reverence by their Catholic followers, the Apristas infused these images and beliefs with a new, revolutionary sense. In particular, the image of the suffering Christ, which has a strong appeal in Peru, especially among the

227

lower class mestizos and Indians, was appropriated by the Apristas as a symbol of the Apra's trials as well as of its steadfast refusal to surrender to its enemies . . . the Apra's assimilation of religious symbolism . . . facilitated the active participation of Peruvian Catholics in the party, without many of the agonizing problems of conscience which they would have had if the Apra had been a typical representative of liberal or leftist anti-clericalism characteristic of other parts of Latin America.[73]

In order to assure its domination over the mob and mediocre men, a ruling clique must in the final instance base its legitimacy on its claims to moral superiority.[74] Again and again in their publications and in their oratory, Haya and other Aprista spokesmen asserted the moral superiority of their movement and its leaders. Most of the Andean Marxists up to this time, Mariátegui included, had based the pretense to moral purity and the subsequent right to leadership upon their higher consciousness of the socialist revolutionary mystique. Haya and his lieutenants, avowed apostles themselves of an unorthodox Marxism-Leninism, combined their claims of socialist revolutionary consciousness with assertions of their embodiment of traditional Catholic morality in justifying their rights to command. Thus the bonds of the patronalist-clientelist relationship that they sought to establish with the Peruvian masses were to be sanctified both by the new and the old faiths.

Apristas, who saw their party in terms of the Leninist concept of the vanguard of the proletariat, hoped to establish a legitimacy that was based on recognition by the masses not only of their moral but also of their intellectual superiority. Priding themselves on their role as teachers, Apristas took up the task of introducing the masses to the joys of the mind. They agreed with Keyserling that the masses, once they had been adequately schooled, would discard the foolish belief in the equality of all. Through the instruction provided them by superior spirits, they would come to recognize their own cultural inferiority and to welcome a society in which all persons had their appropriate stations.[75]

In a famous passage, the Chinese sage Mancius declared: "Great men have their proper business, and little men have their proper business . . . Some labor with their minds, and some labor with their strength. Those who labor with their minds govern others; those who labor with their strength are governed by others."[76] The Chinese sage's appraisal had since time immemorial been a part of the con-

ventional wisdom of Andean America—a fact that may help explain
the frequency with which prophets of Andean transition in the 1920s
compared their own civilization to those of the East. In the mid-
nineteenth century this conventional wisdom had found reaffirmation
in Bartolomé Herrera's advocacy of the sovereignty of intelligence and
also in the teachings of Krausism. To Krause and his disciples it was
obvious that "the man who works with his mind is above the one
who works just with his hands; the more fully a man employs all his
human gifts, the higher is his status in life."[77] In the post-World
War I era, Aprismo simply gave new expression to an ingrained faith
that had characterized both Spanish and Indian civilization (the latter
with its *amautas*), bolstering it by turning to the Leninist concept of
the importance of the intellectual worker in leading the manual
worker.

To provide cultural elites the occasion to approach manual workers, Haya de la Torre was instrumental in organizing in 1921, two
years prior to the exile imposed by the Leguía government, the González Prada Popular Universities.[78] Naming the universities after
González Prada seemed logical in view of his celebrated 1905 discourse, "The Intellectual and the Laborer." It was also a masterful
ploy for winning Anarchist support.[79] Organized along the lines of the
extension programs initiated at the beginning of the century by
Krausist-inspired professors of the University of Oviedo in northern
Spain, Popular University classes met three nights weekly in Lima and
twice weekly in the nearby textile manufacturing zone of Vitarte.

In his 1973 path-breaking study of the APRA, Stephen Jay Stein
writes that the story of the origins and growth of the movement is
largely the story of the careful building of bonds of friendship and
personal loyalty between Haya de la Torre and the urban labor groups
that later came to constitute the mass base of his populist movement.[80] The building of the bonds began in 1919 at the time of the
Lima-Callao strike for the eight-hour day when Haya first arranged
for contact between university students and the working classes. But
the most important work in preparing the way for the emergence of
a coalition of intellectual and manual workers was carried out between
1921 and 1923 in the Popular University classes.[81]

Another major study of the rise of Aprismo argues that APRA
leadership came mainly from intellectuals and middle-sector economic
groups resentful of the diminution of their social status and political
power resulting from the rise of a new superwealthy bourgeoisie.[82]
Along the northern coast, stretching out in both directions from Haya

de la Torre's native city of Trujillo, the status and power decline of the one-time leading classes was especially noticeable; and it was here, in the north, that Aprismo found its principal leaders and enjoyed for many years its greatest strength.

In the period following the War of the Pacific, competition had already developed along the northern coast between the "old-fashioned" planters and the more competitive, modern newcomers, many of them foreigners. In the first two decades of the twentieth century, the old planters lost out increasingly. By the time of World War I, three of the largest commercial agricultural firms operating along the northern coast had absorbed no fewer than thirty-nine of the older haciendas.[83] The one-time owners of the absorbed estates as well as their retainers, relatives, and heirs were deeply resentful of these developments, and the remaining smaller landowners faced the future with fear and misgivings. Moreover, the laboring forces of the old haciendas, protected in line with traditional dictates of rural paternalism, found themselves now as a vulnerable rural proletariat on the huge new commercial estates, their position rendered all the more precarious by the constant influx of cheap Indian labor from the sierra.[84]

As the twentieth century advanced, the development of new pockets of economic modernization with the tendency to create economic and social relationships, as well as to disrupt and destroy old patterns of life, served to broaden APRA's political appeal. "Buffeted by dislocative winds of rapid economic change, many would turn to APRA in an effort to protest against what seemed to them to be a suddenly topsy-turby world ... The movement further extended its political focus by ... addressing itself to all those Peruvians of the middle and lower classes who harbored resentment against the existing system."[85]

Dislocations and disruptions were also underway in Bolivian cities and helped account for the rise of movements that in many ways paralleled the APRA. Bolivia's urban artisans fell progressively under the domination of a reduced number of merchants who controlled their operations and brought about "a growing proletarianization of salaried workers and eliminated the mutual assistance devices which until then the *gremios* had maintained."[86] This contributed to the fact that, as Augusto Guzmán observes, much of Bolivia's early socialism was simply "the ideology of the urban middle classes, resentful of a dominant mining bourgeoisie."[87] And in Ecuador a similar set of circumstances was discernible in the 1920s.

Regardless of which republic they lived in, numerous Andean middle sectors faced a status decline that threatened to drive them into the ranks of the proletariat. They were bound to respond to the message, whether it was voiced by Haya de la Torre or the Ecuadoran socialist Jorge Hugo Rengel,[88] that the small bourgeoisie was actually suffering more than the proletariat from the new landowner-haut bourgeoisie coalition that presided over and derived all of the advantages from modernization. Beyond this they were likely to agree with Haya de la Torre and also with Luis Maldonado Estrada, another Ecuadoran socialist, that the lesser bourgeoisie must lead the proletariat in a struggle to restore balance, justice, and harmony.[89]

Italian fascism, it has been suggested, was the movement of those who had lost out to industrialization.[90] In Andean America, Aprismo and various kindred socialist movements were led by those who had lost out in the process of unbalanced modernization produced by agricultural, commercial, and financial capitalism that linked together local and foreign plutocracies. Predictably, the middle-sector victims of modernization turned for support to the masses.

In their approach to the masses, Apristas and most of the non-Aprista socialists of Andean America were populists. For the Andean populists, of whom Bolivia's Tata Belzu was an important precursor, the support of the masses was to be obtained in such a manner as to prevent their acquisition of autonomous power.[91] The desire of the populist leader was to inform the masses of what they wanted, but were scarcely conscious of desiring. Unlike their counterparts in the United States,[92] Andean populists came to their position by way of St. Thomas, Machiavelli, and Bourbon enlightened despotism. While they wished something for the people, they did not want anything by the people. Like many German elitists of the 1920s, they sought "a final mobilization of the masses that would lead speedily to their permanent demobilization."[93] Above all, the Andean populists sought ties with the masses that constituted an "authority-dependency relationship."[94]

In the political structure envisaged by Aprista ideology,[95] the masses would be kept subordinate not only through their recognition of the moral and intellectual superiority of their paternalistic patrons, but also through their organization into corporative functional associations. Within their corporations they would derive the nonmaterial rewards of participation. Their political appetites sated by their involvement in decision making within the functional group, they would contentedly entrust national level control to technocratic specialists, a new breed of aristocrats distinct from the common people.

231

Those who exercised the moderating power that synthesized the activities of the various corporations into a national program directed toward attainment of the common good must be, Haya asserted, specialists, men of science and solid culture. "To speak of a Peruvian transformation based on suffrage is laughable."[96]

The functional state desired by Apristas would stifle the individualism of the masses by accustoming them to dependence upon their economic guild, thereby inculcating in them the habits and mental attitudes predisposing them to accept and welcome ultimate dependence on an all-knowing, paternalistic government. At the same time the organic state would provide a place for the function of the businessman-entrepreneur who sought self-realization through the practice of capitalism. Given its Marxist-Leninist orientation, almost unavoidable at the time of its inception, Aprismo attacked capitalism and proclaimed the need for the nationalization of "all the industry it is possible to nationalize."[97] But Aprismo made it clear that some industry would be left in private hands for years, perhaps generations, to come. The private bourgeois capitalists would not be eliminated but simply disciplined and effectively integrated into the pursuit of rational, overall national development by the technocratic elites of superior culture who exercised the moderating power.[98] This position made the APRA acceptable to many Andean middle sectors with capitalist instincts.

While they directed their appeal mainly toward the urban middle sectors and manual laborers, Haya and the rest of the Aprista leadership paid lip service to Indianism.[99] Indians were depicted as good by nature because, as Mariátegui and so many other Marxian Indianists insisted, they were nonmaterialistic by nature, inclining more toward Oriental mysticism than the values of Western capitalism.[100] Obviously under the influence of Spain's Joaquín Costa, who had seen rural collectivism as the best means for maintaining tranquility in the countryside while urban elements attended to the tasks of national development, Haya spoke out strongly in defense of the Indian comunidad. He and other party ideologues, among them Antenor Orrego, also denounced attempts to Westernize the Indians and defended their traditional way of life.

For the Apristas, who were closer to reality in their assessment of the Inca past than many Marxian Indianists, the traditional Indian way was a corporativist and also a two culture way of life, in which the compartmentalized masses accepted their collectivized dependence on elites who themselves not only controlled private resources of wealth but responded to certain individualistic incentives.[101] Because of the ingrained tradition of Indian culture that they perceived, Apristas were confident that, once they got around to dealing with the Indian problem, they could readily establish their patronalist sway over the natives and keep them in line just as much as had the aboriginal lords in preconquest times.

PROPHETS OF TRANSITION AND U.S. RELATIONS

Those who shared the Aprista faith—and throughout Andean America a great many accepted the fundamentals of APRA analysis without being in any way affiliated with Haya de la Torre's political movement—saw themselves as the Davids who must challenge the Goliath, symbolized by local and U.S. capitalists locked in a symbiotic relationship. Thus they thrilled when Sandino in Nicaragua during the 1920s took on his own country's rulers and also the defenders of investors from the north, the U.S. marines. They identified with disgruntled U.S. intellectuals, among them Waldo Frank, Theodore Dreiser, Sinclair Lewis, and Upton Sinclair, whom they saw as challenging the North American bourgeois political establishment; and they applauded works by North American authors, such as Scott Nearing and Joseph Freeman, denouncing U.S. dollar diplomacy.[102] They even cheered Al Capone, as Aprista intellectual Luis Alberto Sánchez explains: "The gangster acquired heroic stature. He was our avenger. The really bad guys were the corrupt judges, the voracious bankers and financiers. To a certain extent, Capone was the idealist, fighting against the venal, bureaucratic prohibitionism."[103]

Many Andean proponents of thoroughgoing transition, with Bolivia's Gustavo Adolfo Navarro providing one of the most conspicuous examples, urged nationalization of the export enterprises that had fallen increasingly under foreign control. With the income derived from nationalized tin mines Bolivian governments, Navarro asserted, could bring into being an ideal order of social justice in which the needs of the masses were attended to by a solicitous state.[104] Throughout Andean America hard-pressed middle sectors saw in the revenue obtainable through state control of the export economies the means to keep the masses permanently quiescent, thereby eliminating the perceived threat of the proletariat.

The bulk of Apristas apparently felt the desired objectives could be achieved short of total nationalization of foreign-controlled enterprise. Haya himself was often less blatantly anti-imperialist than some Marxists would have liked, and he attempted to counter their criticism by a series of essays he wrote in 1928.[105] Even in these writings aimed at refuting the charges he was soft on imperialism Haya urged the creation of a state that would not eliminate foreign capital, but rather establish greater control over it so as to capture a larger share of its earnings. Once the proper type of anti-imperialist state was established, Haya evidently believed it would be advantageous to national interests to permit an economic role to foreign capital. He also believed it would be easier for a united Latin America to insist, in dealing with U.S. capital, on a larger share of profits. Undoubtedly this was one of the reasons that prompted him to stress in APRA's Maximum Program the political and economic unification of Latin America, or Indo-America as Apristas preferred to call it. Like many of the Aprista ideals enunciated in the 1920s, this one retained a hardy vitality in the decades ahead.

In his 1928 essays on anti-imperialism, Haya wrote that he knew the Latin American middle classes. They were, he said, lashing out against their feudal lords with their imperialist allies in order to be able to gain fuller power themselves, whereupon they would form their own self-serving alliances with the imperialists.[106] The APRA, he stated, must prevent this by fashioning a strong state that would make the middle sectors the instruments of state capitalism. One wonders, though, how much Aprista leaders had by 1928 already succumbed to the sort of middle-class weakness that Haya warned against. It is revealing that with Leguía's fall in 1930, which seemed to provide Apristas with the chance to come to power and establish their own ties with foreign capital, much of the anti-imperialist rhetoric was hastily dropped.[107]

In the decades after the 1920s the aspiring elites of Andean America would, upon becoming the governing elites, often turn, even as Haya had warned, to seeking personal advantage through ties with foreign capital, ignoring national interests in the process. But men formed intellectually in the post-World War I generation would, when they became power wielders, find it more difficult than the turn-of-the-century ruling classes to view North American capital as the means of transforming their republics, culturally, socially, and politically, into replicas of the United States; for out of the experiences of the 1920s had come a burgeoning sense of national identity.

The disaster (*el desastre*, as it was called by national writers) that Spain sustained in its 1898 war with the United States turned the country's intellectuals to the task of rediscovering and reasserting their own national identity, thereby helping to bring into being the

234

celebrated Generation of '98. This Spanish generation bears striking similarity to the Andean generation of the 1920s, for the disaster that many Peruvian, Bolivian, and Ecuadoran middle sectors sustained at the hands of the liberal modernizers in league with U.S. capital turned them toward a reaffirmation of their own national heritage. In this process Andean *pensadores*, whether Arielists or Marxists, Hispanists or Indianists, Christian Democrats or Apristas, Fascists or Communists, gave life to the whole corpus of values, criteria, preferences, and prejudices that has dominated intellectual life ever since. The enduring strength of the intellectual attitudes forged in the 1920s is owing to the fact that the *pensadores* who proclaimed them did not so much invent them as rediscover them. They had hit upon what the great Spanish conservative ideologue Marcelino Menéndez Pelayo had always insisted was the key to originality: the willingness to be oneself.[108]

In being themselves, the Andean Americans served notice they were rejecting the goal of the noncompartmentalized society based on universal economic self-reliance and competitive interest-group pluralism under the control of the unseen hand; they were opting instead for the corporative society in which the vast majority, regardless of function, would be dependent upon a few and in which elites, set apart by their claims to a higher truth, would direct the various choruses that comprised the body politic and orchestrate their voices into harmonious unison.

This view of what it meant to be themselves was shared by virtually all of the persons who shaped the intellectual environment of the 1920s; and the bitter ideological polemics and political skirmishing in which they engaged, often to the point of violence, should not be allowed to hide the fact. The Andean intellectuals shared in the failings of intellectuals throughout the world: they were unable to examine with sufficient serenity their respective ideologies in order to discover the coincidences, which often were fundamental. Instead, goaded by personal and interest-group ambitions and by vanity, they stressed the differences, which frequently were accidental and secondary.

9

Experiments with Reformism: The Depression and Wartime Years

So long as prosperity had endured, Leguía in Peru was taken "as a magician endowed with mysterious powers, and the public was willing to judge his administration by the tangible signs of progress."[1] The climate of opinion changed abruptly in early 1930 when the impact of the world depression began to be felt and the magician was no longer able to perform his tricks. The *oncenio* had lost its raison d'être and, in August of 1930, Luis M. Sánchez Cerro, newly promoted to lieutenant colonel, led a military uprising in Arequipa against its faltering director. By the end of the month Sánchez Cerro was the presiding officer in a military junta that briefly governed Peru. Leguía, unsuccessful in his attempt to flee the country aboard a warship, was living out his last days in excruciating pain in the national penitentiary, about to succumb to an improperly treated prostate condition.

Even before Leguía, Bolivian President Siles had fallen victim to the discontent triggered by the depression. He was ousted from power at the end of January 1930 by a military coup. The price for a ton of tin on the international market, standing at $794 in 1927, was down to $385 in 1932,[2] and prospects for the regimes that succeeded Siles were not bright. In Ecuador, Isidro Ayora managed to weather the economic storm a bit longer. He was not overthrown by the military until August of 1931. Thereafter, however, the country's economic woes contributed to even greater political instability than that afflicting Peru and Bolivia. In the four years following Ayora's fall, seven different men served as Ecuador's chief executive.

In their trials, the Andean republics for once found a sympathetic

North American audience. With the collapse of the business prosperity in which they customarily took inordinate pride, U.S. leaders were suddenly consumed by doubts as to national purpose and the viability of the whole system of liberal capitalism. The complacency of the 1920s was rudely shattered and after Franklin D. Roosevelt came to power at the beginning of 1933 political leaders were willing to experiment with expedients, including massive government intervention and even corporativism,[3] previously anathematized as un-American. A group of prominent U.S. intellectuals affixed their signatures to a document announcing the demise of free enterprise capitalism, and in the early 1930s many observers detected signs of imminent revolution. Against this background, it became possible for U.S. officials and even for the general public to look tolerantly upon the methods of state planning through which Andean administrations hoped to stave off social upheavals.

Intent upon enlarging their markets in Latin America for the sale of manufactured goods, and hoping also to increase the flow of cheap raw materials from that area,[4] policy makers in the United States stood ready to abandon many practices which had in the past given offense to the southern republics. Washington was now prepared to be more circumspect in entering boundary dispute diplomacy and even to welcome, although this meant a complete reversal of the policy of the 1920s, League of Nations involvement. Hopefully, some of the onus previously reserved to the United States in its thankless task of hemisphere peace maker could be shifted to the international tribunal.

In a mood to refrain from unilateral intervention in American hemisphere diplomatic disputes, U.S. administrations were also less inclined to assume truculent stances in defense of private capitalists embroiled in controversies with Latin American governments. Businessmen suffered a tarnished image during the depression years, and the national government found it politically useful to be less overtly sympathetic toward them, in both their domestic and their international operations. Furthermore, even prior to the official inception of Roosevelt's Good Neighbor policy, Republican Secretary of State Henry L. Stimson had noted that interventions in behalf of private capitalists had "been used by the enemies and critics of the United States as proof positive that we are an imperialistic people ... And these accusations, however unjustified, have damaged our good name, our credit and our trade far beyond the apprehension of our own people."[5] With hope for economic recovery resting to some degree on increased trade, administrations in the 1930s became increasingly sensitive to the inexpediency of intervention.

At the sixth Pan-American Conference held in Havana in 1928, the Latin American delegates had by no means presented a solid front in urging the United States to desist, once and for all, from intervention in the affairs of its sister republics in the hemisphere. In fact, the Peruvian representative had spoken eloquently in defense of the principle of intervention. It was a different story, however, at the seventh Pan-American Conference, held at the end of 1933 in Montevideo. There the Latin American delegates lined up unanimously to press Secretary of State Cordell Hull, personally representing the Roosevelt administration, to subscribe to absolute nonintervention.

It is rare indeed that the Latin American republics achieve a united front on any issue. What was responsible for the unanimity with which they supported the nonintervention doctrine in 1933 (and again in 1936 at a Buenos Aires Conference of American States), thereby wresting from the United States pledges to refrain henceforth from intervention? The answer lies in the economic adversity resulting from the great depression.

The depression rendered vulnerable, as never before, the position of the ruling elites. With foreign loans no longer available, with foreign investment having virtually ceased, and with revenue from export taxes declining precipitously because of plummeting world prices for raw materials, the governing classes no longer had available to them the funds to finance such modest social programs as had been introduced in Peru, Bolivia, and Ecuador, among other countries, and on which their continuing ability to remain in control seemed to depend. They still might retain their power, however, if the U.S. government did not prod them too insistently to resume payment on defaulted foreign debt obligations and if it permitted them to renegotiate contracts with North American firms so as to increase their tax rates.

Up to a point, Washington officials went along, because of their recognition of the need to create a friendly climate of relations in order to facilitate the hoped-for expansion of trade with South America.[6] Thus the Roosevelt administration refrained from directly assisting the Foreign Bondholders' Protective Council in its efforts to force Latin American governments to resume payments on foreign debts. Moreover, in the case of Ecuador in 1936, the State Department accepted the advice of its legation in Quito not to pressure the government to remove recently imposed exchange controls and import restrictions. Even though the controls and restrictions clashed with U.S. policy guidelines, they were prompted, the North American diplomats advised, by the magnitude of Ecuador's financial crisis, and Washington should show understanding.[7]

The new Latin American policy was prompted partially by Washington's recognition that the increase of U.S. economic presence in South America, accomplished during the 1920s, had for the time being at least decreased the possibility of diplomatic leverage. In effect, past U.S. investment had become a hostage that permitted South America to assume a freer hand in dealing with Washington by making periodic threats against the life of the hostage. Bolivia went so far as to execute one of its hostages, Standard Oil, by expropriating its holdings. The Roosevelt administration, in the acid test of its Good Neighbor policy vis-à-vis the Andean republics, allowed the act to go virtually unpunished. This was owing to the crisis created by World War II and the need for solid South American backing in the military endeavor against the Axis forces.[8] The war forced the United States to become a better neighbor than it had originally intended to be, thereby allowing the South Americans to bargain for a more generous share of North American capital, both private and public.

Peruvian administrations were not slow in putting this tactic to work. Complaints in 1939 by the Peruvian president concerning shabby treatment from Washington, accompanied by the observation that perhaps his country should seek a closer understanding with Germany, led to State Department support, the following year, for an Export-Import Bank loan to the Lima government.[9] Then in 1941, in order to block an impending economic transaction between Peru and Japan, the State Department helped fashion an agreement whereby the Peruvians would sell all surplus metals to the Metal Reserve Company in the United States.[10] With the war once underway, agreements not only with Peru but also with Bolivia and Ecuador for the purchase of their resources, for technical training of advanced students in the United States, and for health and sanitation missions as well as military assistance programs all served to strengthen the hand of established regimes—although out-of-power critics constantly complained their countries were being shortchanged by the prices the United States paid for Andean exports.

In their policies of the depression and wartime years, incumbent Andean leaders moved consciously and of their own volition, in line with what they perceived to be their own self-interest, to increase their

239

economic dependence upon the United States. It is wrong, therefore, to picture the mounting dependence of Andean America, and the rest of Latin America for that matter, that came about during the Good Neighbor era as the consequence just of U.S. pursuit of national economic interests.[11] Factors produced by the internal Andean situation were every bit as important as policies formulated in Washington in causing a situation in which, by 1945, Peru, Bolivia, and Ecuador were more then ever dependent upon the North American giant.

Aspiring elites predictably denounced the manner in which incumbents had safeguarded their position by strengthening ties with the United States. Beyond this, those who were out of office cast about for means to come to power by enlisting the support of the Washington government in their own behalf. In their approach, therefore, they were just as colonial, just as much predisposed toward dependence, as were the established regimes they hoped to oust. A classic case in point is provided by Haya de la Torre and the Aprista leadership. These men, some of whom visited the United States in the early 1940s and received redcarpet treatment from Washington officialdom, began to issue lavish statements in praise of the Good Neighbor policy. Prompting their statements was the expectation that after its crusade against fascism in Europe came to a successful conclusion, the United States would undertake intervention in Latin America aimed at toppling all of that area's allegedly fascistically inclined administrations. Needless to say the Apristas pictured the regimes, whether in Peru or elsewhere in South America, that opposed their interests and ambitions as fascistic.[12] The success of Apristas—beginning in the 1940s, in persuading North American officials of the degree to which they would be favorable, once in power, to U.S. economic interests and of the fascistic inclinations of all their foes (conveniently switched to communist leanings once the cold war began)—led to a pro-APRA orientation in Washington's Peruvian diplomacy that endured into the 1960s.

Having to contend with rival Andean factions, most of which were interventionist when it came to furthering their own interests but adamantly anti-interventionist in regard to any action that could conceivably, directly or indirectly, enhance the cause of their opponents, the United States was in a hopeless bind on the intervention issue. Regardless of how it acted, it could not have won solid, widespread approbation among Andean Americans. Moreover, although the fact was not recognized at the time, the intervention issue was a latent obstacle to the development plans in which Good Neighbor policy architects began to take an interest as they responded to Latin American pleas to make public funds available for loans.

The year 1938 was a historic one in U.S.-Latin American relations, for it witnessed the granting of a development loan to Haiti by the Export-Import Bank (established in 1934). The United States had now embarked upon a policy of committing public funds to Latin American development. Ever-present security considerations accounted in part for the new approach, which was shortly expanded with development loans to Mexico, Brazil, Ecuador, and Bolivia, among other republics. Behind the approach there also lay the conviction that the more economically developed Latin America was, the more economically beneficial it would become to the United States. The rationale for entering into a new type of relationship with the republics to the south was set forth by Assistant Secretary of State A. A. Berle, Jr., in 1941:

> we are both morally and economically better off as the American nations strengthen their economic position. Any rise in their standards of living we consider a direct benefit to our economy and to our hemispheric security. Second, the steady and continued development of other American countries is in the economic interest of the United States as well as those countries.[13]

To Berle and other planners of the Good Neighbor policy, as well as to Nelson Rockefeller who as the coordinator of Inter-American Affairs backed the fresh approach, development necessarily implied the use of U.S. models. It entailed contributing to the economic self-reliance of the masses by turning them into capitalists with their own purchasing power so that they could acquire U.S. manufactured goods and obtain the happiness that supposedly accompanied the satisfaction of consumer wants. Thus the use of public money would result in better long-term opportunities for private U.S. business and contribute to political stability in Latin America. The initiation of the new tactic was accompanied by a mounting faith in the viability of private capitalism in the United States, and by the belief that the worst of the depression had been weathered and that the future economic success of the hemisphere depended upon spreading the capitalist ethic throughout its confines.

Conceived in the spirit of nonintervention, the Good Neighbor policy by 1938 had, as a conscious decision of its planners, taken on an interventionist aspect that bore some parallel to the sort of moral crusade that Woodrow Wilson had sought to wage in the Caribbean. Between 1938 and 1942 the men who directed the policy clearly hoped to regenerate Latin America by uplifting the masses to the values and purchasing-power levels that were deemed indispensable for the proper functioning of business and the attainment of human dignity, to say nothing of the growth of U.S. capitalism.

Recipient Andean republics welcomed the loans from Washington, but their rulers in general had in mind dramatically different concepts as to what development entailed. Above all they did not want to see the masses converted into self-reliant capitalists in possession of significant amounts of private capital resources. To governing classes in Andean America, and to aspiring elites as well, development was most likely to mean two things: (1) enhancing economic opportunities for the tiny minority of the population permitted by the traditional system to function as self-reliant, independent citizens; and (2) increasing government revenue in order to make possible social justice programs designed to maintain the dependence of the masses on the state and prevent them from acquiring the individualistic incentives of capitalism.

The confrontation between the United States and the southern republics that seemed inevitable because of profoundly differing concepts of development did not take place in the era of the Good Neighbor policy. The reason for this is that the demands of World War II forced the United States to abandon the commitment of significant amounts of public funds to development projects south of the border. Confrontation, therefore, was delayed. It did not really begin to shape up until the end of the 1950s, and it assumed major significance only in the 1960s when the Alliance for Progress resurrected the development policies of Berle and his Good Neighbor policy associates.

POPULISM IN PERU AND ECUADOR, 1930–1934

Hailed upon his arrival in Lima as Peru's liberator from the tyranny of the *oncenio*, the forty-year-old Sánchez Cerro from the very outset displayed an ability, rarely matched by national political figures, to evoke the adulation of the masses. In the course of his political campaigning in 1930 and 1931 he visited not only the populous urban centers but also many of the most remote regions. Almost wherever he went he gained the enthusiastic approval of the multitudes, presented for the first time with the spectacle of a politician who seemed to take them seriously, who personally carried his message to them and explained his programs in down-to-earth language.[14]

Presiding over a military junta in 1930, Sánchez Cerro hoped to gain election to the presidency. He realized, however, that fulfilling his ambition rested not only upon his winning broad-based mass support but also upon enlisting the cooperation of the Civilist upper classes who had suffered an eclipse of power during the *oncenio*. At first, these upper classes simply could not take seriously the frail, dark-skinned mestizo officer from Piura who seldom weighed as much as 120 pounds. He seemed too outspoken, too lacking in tact and concern for protocol, too moody, emotional, volatile, and even, upon occasion, vulgar. Moreover, many aristocrats found it difficult to accept his dark skin which, they assured each other, attested not only to Indian but also to some Negro blood.

Upper-class suspicions, plus friction with his fellow officers, led to Sánchez Cerro's resignation in March of 1931 from the military junta. He still hoped, though, for victory in the elections scheduled for later that year. And this brought him onto a collision course with another presidential aspirant, Víctor Raúl Haya de la Torre of the APRA.

Trying to broaden his electoral base in 1931 to include more than the masses, the intellectuals, and the disgruntled, marginal middle sectors to whom he had principally addressed his appeals during his exile in the 1920s, Haya de la Torre sought the support of Leguiistas—the partisans of the ousted Leguía. This involved him in the attempt to attract the members of a nonradical bourgeoisie whose former preeminence had depended upon close ties with U.S. capital and who saw their future well-being in terms of an increase, rather than a diminution, of North America's economic presence. Haya found himself now in an ideological bind as he sought a middle ground that would combine "the best elements of both capitalist and socialist systems."[15] This middle ground was difficult to find. If Haya stressed the capitalist ingredient, he risked alienating the intellectuals and those middle sectors whose chronic economic vulnerability had led them to radicalism; but if he stressed the socialist factor, he was likely to put off the new elements he hoped to recruit, the *Leguiistas*.

Haya's greatest success in bringing ideological consistency to his campaign came in his August 23, 1931 speech delivered in the Plaza de Acho bull ring. In it he stressed the corporative features of the state that the APRA hoped to establish. While the state would be run as a technocracy by recognized experts in each field of public endeavor, there was to remain ample room for the private capitalist. Further, Haya explained, Apristas did not propose to oust existing foreign enterprises. Rather, they urged the revision of contracts so as

243

to provide a basis for collaboration between foreign firms and the government that would result in a more just share of advantages for the latter.[16]

More than anything else, fortuitous circumstances accounted for APRA's failure in the 1931 election. Its leaders had introduced populist theories into Peruvian politics, and in the campaign Haya proved himself a populist leader of enormous talent. He happened, though, to face a rival who was still more successful in practicing the new political role, a man whose dark skin color and humble origins contributed to a closer rapport with the masses and enabled him, better than the light-skinned, more aristocratic Haya de la Torre, to gain credence as a father figure in whom the humble could place their trust. Even the Civilist upper classes that had at first spurned Sánchez Cerro came to recognize his great gifts. Unable to produce a leader more to their taste, they swung into line behind him. In the October 1931 election, probably the freest and most honest Peru had known, the mixed-blood officer defeated the APRA leader by a tally of 152,062 votes to 106,007.[17]

Apristas immediately branded the election results fraudulent and in December Haya de la Torre called for revolution. His main justification was that only the APRA was morally qualified to govern Peru. Throughout the campaign Apristas had pictured Sánchez Cerro as a dupe of the oligarchy, and had denounced him as lacking culture, as vain, small, dirty, and illiterate, as a "latent homosexual,"[18] and "as the type of advanced paranoic who can only be studied with the books of Freud and Adler in hand."[19]

The 1931 presidential election touched off virtual civil war in Peru, the result not so much of ideological cleavages as of the rival ambitions of two headstrong and talented leaders, each of whom enjoyed fairly widespread support among various upper-class interest groups and among the masses. The most dramatic incident in the struggle occurred on July 7, 1932 when Apristas attempted a massive uprising in Trujillo.[20] In the course of the insurrection some sixty military officers of the local garrison, taken prisoner as the uprising got under way, were assassinated and their bodies mutilated. When government troops crushed the attempted revolution and recaptured Trujillo they retaliated by executing about a thousand residents of the city, with some Aprista accounts placing the number of victims at close to six thousand.

In the midst of the civil discord, as the armed forces carried out a widespread campaign against Apristas and their sympathizers, Sánchez Cerro had few opportunities to demonstrate whatever talents for constructive rule he may have possessed. Soon, moreover, he had not only the internal Aprista enemies to contend with but a foreign foe as well, Colombia. The situation arose out of lingering Peruvian discontent with the Salomón-Lozano treaty, ratified under U.S. pressure in 1928, and resulting in Peru's ceding to Colombia the small Amazonian port of Leticia. Most Peruvians were ready to cheer when on the last day of August 1932 a group of heavily armed countrymen occupied Leticia. Proclaiming they had come to protect their persecuted fellow Peruvians and to reclaim the land that had been unjustifiably relinquished, the invaders proceeded to expel all Colombian officials.

At first, Sánchez Cerro condemned this highhanded action as a patent violation of Peru's treaty obligations. But, when Apristas gave enthusiastic support to the invasion, the president quickly reversed himself; for he feared that if he did not take position against Colombia, his bitter political rivals, who were demanding war if necessary in order to retain Leticia, might gain sufficient popular support to tilt the ongoing civil struggle in their favor. The beleaguered president found his position worsening when it became apparent that Ecuador would side with Colombia in the event that the Leticia dispute produced a Peru-Colombia war.[21]

The well-aimed bullets that an Aprista assassin fired at Sánchez Cerro on April 30, 1933 released the president from his dilemma. His successor, chosen by congress to serve out the unexpired portion of the fallen president's term, was General Oscar R. Benavides, the most powerful figure in the Peruvian armed forces. Not inclined to base his legitimacy on the support of the masses, Benavides, who was more the old-fashioned autocrat, was ready to incur public wrath in resolving the dispute with Colombia.

The Benavides stance came as an immense relief to the United States which had sought to avoid an overt role as peace maker, given the fact that it had interests both in Colombia and Peru and did not wish to offend either power. Secretary of State Stimson had declared: "We have no responsibility of keeping peace in Latin America, nor do we have the desire to assume such responsibilities."[22] He had, in fact, welcomed the mediation of the League of Nations in the controversy, and it was through that tribunal that Peru made arrangements to return Leticia to Colombia.[23]

The duel between Peru's two titans of populism had led to the electoral and then to the military defeat of one and to the assassination of the other. Meantime in Ecuador a new populist demagogue had appeared on the scene, one who would be a dominating figure in that country's politics for much of the next forty years. The background that brought José María Velasco Ibarra to the presidency for the first time in 1934 was one of almost indescribable political chaos and the nearly complete ideological bankruptcy of the two traditional parties, Conservative and Liberal. By the 1930s Ecuadorans were simply no longer interested in the old doctrinal debate. Especially in the midst of the depression, the issues that had divided the champions and disciples of García Moreno from the partisans of Alfaro no longer seemed relevent. Furthermore, the country was disillusioned by the shortcomings of military reformism and by the inability of Isidro Ayora, installed in power in 1926 by the military, to cope with the problems of a worsening economy. On the whole, Ecuadorans had rejoiced when Ayora was toppled in August of 1931.

The Ecuadoran Socialist party, organized in 1926, attracted many adherents to the Marxist doctrines it propounded, quickly establishing itself as a major rival to the debilitated Liberal party for the backing of the coastal masses and employee classes. Because of internal dissension, however, the star of Ecuadoran socialism enjoyed only a brief ascent. The party's difficulties reflected the divisiveness from which the socialist left suffered throughout Andean America. Major issues of ideological dispute, leading to fragmentation, included: whether there could be a socialist revolution before capitalism had matured; whether a social revolution could best be made by a single-class or by a pluriclass movement; whether a liberal, bourgeois revolution against the prevailing semifeudal order should be encouraged in the expectation that it would "grow over" into a genuine revolution of the proletariat.[24]

Velasco Ibarra was the politician who derived the maximum benefits from the collapse of the traditional parties and the fissures within the Socialist party. As early as the beginning of the 1930s it was becoming evident that there had never been an Ecuadoran who possessed such a knack for talking elbow-to-elbow with the people, or for haranguing them from a balcony.

Trained as a lawyer in Quito and briefly a student of philosophy at the Sorbonne, Velasco Ibarra (born in 1893) had embarked on a political career that reached a new high in 1933 upon his gaining the post of president of the Chamber of Deputies. When Peruvian forces seized Leticia, Velasco Ibarra won a great deal of support by his call for a joint Ecuadoran–Colombian war against Peru. By this early date he had hit upon what would be a political stock in trade throughout his career: warmongering directed against Peru. Before the end of 1933 he had helped depose the president then in office, while professing his total lack of personal presidential ambitions. Shortly later, as the head of a coalition of almost all the Conservatives and many Liberals, who expected moral rectitude and fiscal responsibility from him,[25] Velasco Ibarra was overwhelmingly elected president of Ecuador, garnering 50,000 of the approximately 60,000 ballots that were cast. Much of his support had come from "ex-Indians" living in small rural communities, from lesser merchants and struggling artisans, from low-level government employees, and from the country's primary school teachers.[26]

To at least a few ideas Velasco Ibarra seemed honestly committed. He blamed Alfaro and the Liberals for having sought to destroy one source of morality, the Catholic religion, without having any ethical principles or lofty ideals with which to replace it. The time had come, he believed, to end sterile anticlericalism and to accept the church in the hope that it might rekindle moral values among the populace.[27] Beyond this, the new Ecuadoran president believed sincerely that democracy was useful only insofar as it helped create "aristocratic organizations."[28] Socialism appealed to him, but only as he defined it: as the intervention of the state in economic matters in order to save the weak from the selfish.[29] This type of socialism was seen as useful in inducing the masses to follow their natural leaders, thereby restoring social solidarity and ending class conflict. Also useful in attaining solidarity would be the corporative reorganization of society. In his corporativism, Velasco Ibarra was profoundly influenced by Ramiro de Macztu, the Spaniard who in the late 1920s had become perhaps the major spokesman of his country's Catholic, conservative position.[30]

The important feature of Velasquism, however, was not ideology, but rather the uncanny ability of José María Velasco Ibarra to articulate the dissatisfactions of a broad social cross section of Ecuadorans. "The great tragedy," he once wrote, "is that in recent times the country has lacked a single personality who can understand the profound and distinctive desire of the masses and orient it, define it, with efficiency, amidst all the dangerous and threatening innovations that lurk in shadows along the edge of an abyss."[31] Once Velasco Ibarra appeared on the scene, Ecuador no longer lacked a man who could at least persuade the masses that he understood and could direct their profound desires.[32]

Part of Velasco Ibarra's success lay in his ability to project the image of a man who was enjoying himself and having fun, and to convince his listeners at any rally that they, too, could have fun. He did not call upon them to sacrifice or to embrace a great ideal. His brand of populism was far more pernicious than the one purveyed by Haya de la Torre and Sánchez Cerro. The two Peruvians exhorted the masses to lofty achievements requiring abnegation and discipline. Velasco Ibarra, however, was simply "Mr. Promises Unlimited."[33] He capitalized on the moral and ideological bankruptcy of the established order and was himself a symbol of that bankruptcy.

Coming to power in 1934, Velasco Ibarra tried to rule, as he would in each of his five presidential tenures, by relying on his skill in manipulating men so as to forge constantly changing coalitions of supporters bound together by the opportunism of the moment. This is an expensive way to govern, requiring ample resources in the national treasury and vast sources of patronage and employment with which to attract and reward supporters. But the grip of the depression had not yet abated, the till was empty,[34] and so Velasco Ibarra's days in office were numbered. On August 20, 1935, shortly after arrogating to himself dictatorial powers, the mercurial politico was ousted by a military *golpe*. He had been in office just under fifty-one weeks.

In Benavides, Peru had found the strong hand required to steer it toward economic recovery. Ecuador was still adrift in 1935. But its plight was far less grave than Bolivia's. While Ecuadorans had been finding distractions in the antics of their unique political showman, Bolivians had been waging a disastrous war with Paraguay, the consequences of which exacerbated the social and economic problems occasioned by the great depression. Before carrying the story of Peru and Ecuador through the comparatively calm 1935–1945 decade, we turn to sixteen of the most troubled years in Bolivia's entire history.

THE CHACO WAR AND THE AFTERMATH IN BOLIVIA, 1930–1946

When the Tacna-Arica accord of 1929 dashed their hopes of reacquiring a port on the Pacific, Bolivians turned their renewed interest toward the east. Before long, statesmen were picturing the building of an oil pipeline to the Paraguay River as a panacea for national problems. It seemed not to occur to them that La Paz would lack the resources to develop a port there or that the administration in Asunción (Paraguay's capital) would never be able to overcome the navigational hazards of the Paraguay River to the degree necessary to accommodate oil tankers.[35] Led on by the myth that an oil port on that river would at last guarantee it a position of international respectability, Bolivia prepared to incorporate the territory of the Chaco, governed at the time from Asunción, that would extend its national boundaries all the way to the coveted river-bank site. Paraguay, of course, was unwilling to allow Bolivia to seek a better future at its expense. Nor could either republic have been impervious to the ideology then sweeping Europe that equated national grandeur and dignity with eschewing all save military solutions to vexing problems.

Issues less fundamental than national honor were also involved in precipitating the armed struggle. Following the overthrow of Her nando Siles and the rule of a provisional military junta, Daniel Salamanca had triumphed in presidential elections held in 1931. Highly intelligent but vain and inflexible, introverted and isolated, irascible and autocratic, this sway-backed, hollow-chested little man who dressed always in black had been convinced ever since 1920 that only he was morally qualified to rule Bolivia. Brooding for eleven years over the circumstances that denied him the office properly his, he had at last fulfilled his ambitions in 1931. But he could scarcely have done so at a worse time, for the national economy was in shambles. Perhaps the economic conditions accounted for the fact that Ismael Montes, twice the president of Bolivia in the apogee of liberalism period, supported the Salamanca candidacy. Asked why he backed the man whose implacable foe he had always been and with whom he was not even on speaking terms, Montes is reported to have replied: "This is my revenge."[36]

Economic adversity gave rise to social unrest and to demonstrations by laboring masses and middle-class, white-collar employees throughout much of Bolivia. As criticism of the administration mounted, the man who had so long aspired to the presidency found himself wondering if he could survive in that office. The enemies of Salamanca have always maintained that he deliberately led Bolivia into war in order to salvage his own position. The case against him—and it is not altogether convincing—is summed up in these words: "Completely defeated in internal politics, . . . unable to stop the economic crisis which was destroying his government's stability day by day, Salamanca turned toward the international scene where he believed that all his personal glory and promise of future greatness could at last find unfettered expression."[37]

Salamanca's hopes that the war, which began in 1932, would mobilize the country behind him were soon shattered. Faced with impossibly long supply lines, and having to fight on terrain totally unfamiliar to them, and also in a sea-level environment to which *alti-*

plano recruits could not readily adjust, the Bolivian forces sustained one defeat after another. Dissatisfaction with the Salamanca administration grew by the day and the president responded by hurling the label of Communist against all critics. Internal dissension hampered the war effort, and when a friend asked the president why he did not try to reconcile his differences with Montes—who was president of the Central Bank that bore heavy responsibility in financing the war —by inviting him for a cup of coffee, Salamanca curtly replied, "I do not drink coffee."[38] Blaming inefficiency behind the lines for their failures on the field of battle, disgruntled officers overthrew Salamanca, who was conducting a tour of the front lines, in November of 1934. The deposed president is reported to have said of his dissident generals: "I have given them all they have asked for; it's only brains that I have not been able to give them."[39]

From the end of 1934 until May of 1936, José Luis Tejada Sorzano served as president of Bolivia and accomplished a minor miracle in keeping the country together, even though at one point a civil war seemed imminent. Under him, the Bolivian armed forces managed to pull themselves together and to stop the Paraguayans short of the Chaco oil fields and the cities of Santa Cruz and Tarija. By early 1935 a military stalemate had developed.[40] Meantime, the League of Nations and two rival groups of American hemisphere neutral powers, one headed by the United States and the other by Argentina, had been trying their hands at arranging a cease fire. Not until June of 1935 did these efforts lead to a temporary truce.

There next ensued a prolonged period of diplomatic bickering and maneuvering, in which the rivalry between the United States and Argentina—and also between Brazil and Argentina—was almost as intense as that between Bolivia and Paraguay. A definitive settlement was finally reached in 1938. The concessions made by each side were disguised under the form of a so-called arbitral award agreed to in advance by the Bolivian and Paraguayan negotiators.[41] Bolivians, although they had sustained casualties of over 65,000 (the total population was just under three million), could take heart because they retained the oil districts in the Villa Montes area to the east of Tarija. Although Paraguay acquired some 50,000 square kilometers of territory beyond the boundary lines tentatively agreed to in 1907, its gains did not touch "the extreme claims described by Paraguay's own definition of the Chaco Boreal."[42] The major fruit of victory for the Asunción government was the relinquishing by Bolivia of all claims on the Paraguay River littoral.

250

The pessimism that gripped Bolivia's traditional ruling classes after the Chaco War was reflected in the preface that Alcides Arguedas wrote in 1936 to the third edition of his famous book *Pueblo enfermo* (*A Sick People*). Arguedas noted that when he had first published the book in 1909 he had been widely condemned for the disparaging views he expressed of his fellow Bolivians and his low assessment of their potential. The Chaco disaster, Arguedas contended, had proved his pessimism well founded while establishing once and for all the naïveté of those who had found hopeful signs in the Bolivian "race."

A younger generation of Bolivians, and a large group of middle sectors who had never gotten closer to the power structure than the extreme periphery, shared Arguedas' belief that something was terribly wrong with Bolivia. They were disillusioned, however, not in the Bolivian "race," but only in the old ruling class; and they were pessimistic only about the ability of that particular class to lead Bolivia toward a happier future. The dissatisfaction with the established order that had produced Gustavo Adolfo Navarro and like-minded intellectuals in the 1920s and had occasioned the complaints of marginal middle sectors took on a new urgency and gained a new justification because of the manner in which the old regime had disgraced itself in initiating and conducting the Chaco War.

The blows of the mid-1920s to the Ecuadoran economy had given rise to experiments in military socialism. A decade later, the blows to national pride, combined with the moderate inflation and other economic dislocations accompanying the Chaco War and compounding the effects of the depression, eroded the last bastions of the old guard's legitimacy and ushered in three years of Bolivian experimentation with what is often described as military socialism,[43] although it might better be termed military corporativism.

Bolivia's experiments got underway in May of 1936 when a group of young officers ousted Tejada Sorzano and installed Colonel David Toro in the presidential office. However confused he and his advisers may have been about the basic orientation of his regime, Toro was resolved as to its corporativist nature. He stressed the values of functional democracy and pointed to the advantages of encouraging the formation of syndicates for lawyers, doctors, engineers, agriculturalists, shoemakers, industrialists, merchants, and workers. Out of this would come a resolution of the capitalist-proletariat conflict, for in the functional associations persons would be grouped together not as capitalists and laborers. Instead, society would be divided according to technical and professional aspects.[44]

Toro, it goes without saying, confronted enormous problems. Government income was inadequate to meet war-associated obligations and finance the internal development promised by the nationalistic regime, which in order to bolster its legitimacy was trying to spread optimism about future prospects. At the same time, many urban supporters of the military experiment fretted over the large number of Indian veterans from the Chaco armies who refused to return to the soil. The Bolivian regime, therefore, faced two problems of paramount importance: (1) how to obtain revenue with which to finance development and also social services programs; and (2) how to keep the Indians, many of whom had been made aware of the world beyond the villages where they had been born and raised as a result of wartime experiences, in the countryside.

The urgency of these two problems explains the impact of Navarro's 1935 book, *La tragedia del altiplano*. In it the author, who preferred to be known by his adopted name of Tristán Marof, raised the famous slogan that was hailed by virtually all radicals and also by many moderates: "Land to the Indians, mines to the state." In giving land to the Indians, Bolivians saw the means to keep the natives in their traditional role as agrarian laborers. And through nationalizing the mines they saw the possibility of obtaining virtually unlimited funds for the state with which to finance development projects and provide any number of free social services.

Toro deferred the Indian question and took up first the matter of nationalization. State expropriation of the mines was out of the question, for in the early days of the military administration Bolivia's major private tin magnates established a strong influence over the inexperienced Toro.[45] Rather than the mines, therefore, Toro turned to Standard Oil as the El Dorado that would provide a solution to the country's economic and social problems. Wildly optimistic about the extent of Bolivian oil resources and the revenue that could be obtained by exploiting them through a state enterprise, Toro in March of 1937 proclaimed the expropriation of Standard Oil holdings.

Additional considerations beyond an anticipated economic bonanza dictated the nationalization. Already by 1937 many Bolivians had been seized by the delusion that Standard Oil had goaded the Salamanca regime into the war with Paraguay, hopeful of obtaining thereby the huge new oil reserves thought to lie beneath the Chaco's desert soil. This delusion has grown through the years and has been incorporated into the writings that serve as national history.[46] In defending expropriation, the Toro administration was on far firmer ground when it accused Standard Oil of falsifying its records and shortchanging the Bolivian government on tax payments, and also of price gouging in its sale of petroleum products during the Chaco War.[47] These considerations may well have justified the government's refusal to pay compensation to the U.S. firm.[48]

Toro's hopes to save his foundering administration by the popular expropriation vanished in July of 1937 when one of his Chaco war companions in arms, Germán Busch, staged a successful *golpe*. Duly installed as president, Busch, a man of humble origins raised in the remote Beni region who had emerged from the Chaco War as one of the best-known and most admired officers, was ready to proceed more rapidly and to go farther than Toro. But the direction in which he was moving never became clear, for elements of Marxism-Leninism, fascism, corporativism, and Indianism coalesced in his regime.

Persuaded that the political stability necessary for development must rest upon a corporative structure and upon "equilibrium between capital and labor and gratuitous social services,"[49] Busch summoned a constituent assembly to frame a new charter that would reflect reformist aspirations. In a decided departure from political traditions, the assembly included a strong middle-sector, and even some labor, representation. The constitution it prepared, promulgated in October of 1938, stressed the social obligations of property, conferred vast interventionist powers upon the government in social and economic relations, and incorporated a new labor code devised by the military administration.[50] The 1938 assembly also followed the pattern established by the framers of Peru's 1920 constitution by providing legal recognition of Indian comunidades.

On June 7, 1939 Busch issued the most popular decree of his administration; in fact, the response evoked by this decree was probably more enthusiastic than that which had greeted Toro's nationalization of Standard Oil.[51] The June decree called for delivery to the state of all foreign exchange earned by tin exports. By the terms of the law, tin magnates from that time on would have to approach the government and negotiate for the foreign currency required in connection with running their enterprises.[52] The measure was in no way intended to jeopardize the continued private ownership and operation of the mines. It did, however, provide the government with effective means to capture some of the earnings of the tin industry—an objective that had eluded Saavedra in the 1920s—so that they could henceforth be used for national development and social programs. Above all, it asserted the right of the state to intervene in economic processes so as "to avoid the flight of capital and the impoverishment of the nation."[53]

Although Busch's newly announced policy evoked enthusiasm on the streets of La Paz, the president continued to be assailed by various Marxists for settling for halfway measures. On the right side of the political spectrum, the *Rosca* swung into action to denounce the June enactment, enlisting the support of the older, conservative military officers, resentful over having lost power to the junior ranks. Two-and-a-half months after issuance of the decree, Busch was dead, and with him there died not only the attempt to regulate the mining enterprise but also the entire reformist thrust of military corporativism.

At the time, many Bolivians assumed that Busch had been murdered at the behest of the mining interests. This explanation for the president's death continues to find its proponents. No proof, however, has ever come to light, and it is far more likely that the harassed president committed suicide. Eduardo Diez de Medina's explanation of the events of August 1939 is convincing:

> Busch, in the noble desire to improve the economic conditions of the country and provide for a more rational solution to its social problems, dictated measures which would have forcefully affected the vested interests. The consortium of the large mine owners and the handful of banking magnates who saw in the attitude of the president a threat to the predominance of privileged groups, unleashed a violent opposition to his measures. Busch received anonymous threats from all points of the country. Exhausted by the work, by the responsibilities which he had assumed, not finding the aid he had expected to receive and at the same time deeply disillusioned by the attacks to which he was subjected, Busch decided, perhaps in the moment of a terrible depression, to put an end to his days by his own hand.[54]

With the death of Busch the time seemed ripe for the traditional parties to make their bid for a return to power. Outrage over the Chaco War had now abated somewhat, the worst effects of the depression had been weathered, tin prices were on the rise as the European powers prepared for war, and to many Bolivians the need for sweeping innovation was not so apparent as it had been in 1936. Further, the military reformers and their civilian advisers had not been able to accomplish the miracles that their oratory had led the populace to anticipate and this contributed to a discernible feeling that a return to the old order might not be altogether undesirable.

Actually, the number of those demanding radical reform had not diminished, but their efforts were hampered by the same sort of splintering and proliferation of groups that debilitated the socialist left in Ecuador. Meantime the components of the political old guard, the Liberal party and the two main offshoots of the Republican party, had managed to hammer out a unification agreement in March of 1939 that gave birth to the Concordance (*Concordancia*). Following the provisional regime of Carlos Quintanilla, the Concordance presented as its candidate in the 1940 presidential election General Enrique Peñaranda, the nearest approximation to a military hero produced by the Bolivian side in the Chaco War. The general won all but 10,000 of the 58,000 votes cast, the opposing ballots going to José Antonio Arze, a Marxist professor of law and sociology from Cochabamba who had only a few weeks in which to organize his campaign. Virtually devoid of his own political ideas, Peñaranda was an ideal puppet to be manipulated by the defenders of a political and social order that had been under assault since 1920 and that had been threatened with oblivion between 1936 and 1939.

The restoration accomplished by the Concordance was opposed on many fronts. Opponents included the members of the Bolivian Socialist Falange or FSB (*Falange Socialista Boliviana*), an organization that a national historian refers to as "the most romantic and the most bloodied in our history."[55] Founded in 1937 by Oscar Unzaga de la Vega, a young Cochabamba teacher who had studied agronomy in Chile, the FSB stressed the need for discipline and hierarchy, and for the transformation of liberal individualism into social collectivism. The individual, according to FSB ideology, must be subordinated to the service of the collectivity, and allowed to "participate in the organic unity of the state through a corporative regime in which each person fulfills his function in accordance with his quality and the specialization of his work."[56] At the same time, the FSB stressed the need to combat communism and made clear its concern with protecting small-scale capitalism as practiced by a lesser bourgeoisie. "Our economic reforms," Unzaga stated in 1941, "will not be directed against those Bolivians who contribute to national production with their small capital and enterprise, for such Bolivians fulfill a fecund social function. But, we shall be audacious in destroying the *Rosca*, and the financial circles which create within the state a still more powerful state." Although repudiating democracy, because of its alleged responsibility for social injustices, and advocating a totalitarian state that would regulate the economy and education in addition to the political structure, the FSB denied any ideological connection to fascism. With considerable credibility, FSB spokesmen claimed their inspiration came from Bolivian traditions, not from Germany or Italy.[57]

Its power base confined essentially to Cochabamba, the FSB did not begin to play an important role in Bolivian politics until 1947. It remained, then, for the National Revolutionary Movement or MNR (*Movimiento Nacionalista Revolucionario*)—the first mass party in Bolivian history that brought together intellectuals, professionals, and both white-collar and blue-collar organized labor groups— to provide the Concordance with its principal opposition. Founded in 1941 by a group of intellectuals and labor leaders, prominent among whom was the economist Víctor Paz Estenssoro, the MNR was the first major political organization in Andean America explicitly to promulgate the idea of a third position, one that was neither purely capitalist nor purely communist but instead the sort of combination of the two approaches said to have been devised initially by the Incas.

Capitalism, according to the MNR, was inevitably associated with Yankee imperialism while Marxism in its Stalinist form posed no less grave a danger of imperialism. Attempts to practice liberal democracy had only opened Bolivia to domination by U.S. capitalism, and therefore Bolivia had to set its sights on a different type of political structure. Marxist theories could not provide the model, for they called for the abolition of all private property. In respect to private property, the MNR showed a strong parallel to the FSB: both groups of aspiring elites, concerned with the interests of the lesser bourgeoisie, urged the breakup of the huge enclaves of economic privilege so as to create greater opportunity for small capitalists. At the same time, MNRistas hoped to placate the laboring masses through a plethora of social services. Understandably, Gustavo Adolfo Navarro's message of land to the Indians, mines to the state appealed tremendously to MNR leaders who wished to keep the natives safely out of the way in the countryside and were on the lookout for means whereby social overhead could be financed.[58]

Hoping to play down the Marxist concept of class conflict, MNRistas proclaimed the need for Bolivians of all classes to unite against the local and foreign financial tycoons who controlled Bolivia. Much of their rhetoric, therefore, was directed against North American investors and against Jews,[59] who for some time now in much of the Spanish-speaking world had been linked together as the symbol of exploitative capitalism.

While it borrowed from fascism some of its condemnation of liberalism, and while it made decided use of the Marxist-Leninist analysis of imperialistic capitalism, the MNR followed very much in the tradition established by Tata Belzu in the mid-nineteenth century. It will be recalled that Belzu recognized the need to strengthen the lower middle sectors through *gremio* organizations and that, in a populist style, he appealed to the lower classes. "The popular masses ... have made their voices heard," Belzu had declared to the national congress in 1855. "Gentlemen, make the necessary reforms yourselves, if you do not want the people to make revolutions in their own way ... Protect them in order that they will respect you."[60]

When Belzu had made these observations, no social problem had yet appeared, and the accommodated sectors had no reason to take them seriously. In the early 1940s a social problem was very much at hand, and the indifference of the ruling elites to it dismayed the lower middle sectors. Already in a precarious position, they feared they might be totally submerged if the policies of the ruling classes continued much longer to goad the masses toward revolution.

Peñaranda and the members of the Concordance meantime hoped to ease some of the country's social pressures by obtaining a large development loan, perhaps as much as $80 million, from the Export-Import Bank. However, the continuing failure of the government to provide compensation to Standard Oil for its expropriated holdings led the State Department to block the loan negotiations.[61] Then in July of 1941 the U.S. minister in La Paz delivered to Minister of Foreign Relations Alberto Ostria Gutiérrez an ostensibly intercepted letter from the Bolivian military attaché in Berlin to the German minister accredited to Bolivia, Ernest Wendler. The letter called for a revolution by Nazi sympathizers against the Peñaranda administration. At a much later time the document was shown to be a clever forgery prepared by British intelligence agents, but for the moment its authenticity was accepted by the State Department.[62] Acting now to thwart the "Nazi Putsch," Peñaranda expelled minister Wendler and had alleged German sympathizers detained throughout the country. Among those sent into jail, hiding, or exile by the government crackdown were the leaders of the MNR, accused of being Nazi collaborators. Washington officials were predisposed to accept the allegations of Nazism,[63] for the MNR had raised the most vociferous objections to granting compensation to Standard Oil, had made anti-semitic pronouncements, and had condemned both U.S. capitalist imperialism and Soviet communist imperialism. No additional proof of its Nazi affiliations was required.

U.S. officials hailed the anti-Nazi crusade undertaken by Peñaranda. Loan negotiations began to proceed with alacrity and fewer references were made in Washington to the matter of compensation for Standard Oil. Delighted on its part by the manner in which its strong response to the alleged Nazi menace was being rewarded with a more friendly attitude on the part of the Good Neighbor, the Bolivian administration made a goodwill gesture in January of 1942, the month after the Japanese attack at Pearl Harbor had brought the United States into World War II, by awarding $1.7 million to Standard Oil.[64]

When the La Paz government made the Standard Oil settlement, a U.S. mission headed by Mervin Bohan was already in Bolivia investigating the ways in which loan capital from the Export-Import Bank could best be utilized.[65] His recommendations led in 1942 to a $15.5 million loan which was used to help establish a Bolivian Development Corporation intended to undertake road and railroad building and increase agricultural and mining production. By the following year another U.S. mission, headed by Judge Calvert Magruder and charged with studying living and labor conditions, especially among mine workers, had completed its report.[66] In an approach to development that paralleled A. A. Berle's and anticipated that of the Alliance for Progress in the 1960s, Magruder recommended that Bolivian education be restructured so as to produce among the masses self-reliant individuals with capitalist skills and incentives. With the right kind of education even the Indians, the judge was confident, could be Westernized and assimilated as full-fledged participants in a capitalist, democratic society. This, of course, was not the type of development that appealed either to the members of the governing Concordance or to the MNR and FSB opposition.

The Concordance was by now experiencing problems with increasingly aggressive mine laborers, and a strike at the Catavi tin mines in December of 1942 led to one of the bloodiest labor massacres in Bolivian history. The political opposition took full advantage of resulting public indignation and Peñaranda began to lose his grip on power. Not even the loans and military assistance from the United States or a much publicized trip to that country, where he was effusively greeted in Washington, could revive his sagging fortunes.

In December of 1943 leaders of the MNR, who had been forced underground by the Concordance's repression, managed to do what Peruvian Apristas tried in vain through the years to accomplish: they reached an understanding with junior grade military officers that produced a successful assault against the government. Peñaranda and many of his associates were forced to flee into exile. The new president, Major Gaulberto Villarroel, had served with distinction in the Chaco War. In choosing his cabinet members and other high officials he turned not only to the civilian leaders of the MNR but also to his fellow officers, some of whom had come to regard fascist methods as essential to Bolivian rehabilitation.[67]

The MNR members of the new administration were decidedly less profascist than many of the highly placed military officers. Nevertheless, State Department official, including Secretary of State Hull, still clung to the delusion that the MNR was a Nazi front.[68] Not until the Villarroel regime responded to department pressures by cleansing itself of MNR associates did Washington extend recognition, in May of 1944. With recognition achieved, Villarroel began readmitting MNRistas into his official family and in 1945 Paz Estenssoro, serving as minister of the treasury, was the most important political figure next to the president himself.

A social-economic turning point in Bolivian history came in 1945, when Paz Estenssoro designed a budget that shifted government expenditures from economic development to social services. According to James W. Wilkie, this budget allotted 26.7 percent of federal expenditures to social spending and 15 percent to economic outlays. In 1942 under Peñaranda, who was responding to the advice of U.S. missions and also to guidelines established by his country's liberals then enjoying a resurgence of influence, the figures had been 20.3 percent for social and 27.9 percent for economic spending.[69] Many students question the pinpoint accuracy of the Wilkie figures, but his statistics do provide an indication at least of an important shift in policy.

The innovative social spending policies, plus the fact that the increase in cost of living declined from 32 percent in 1942 to 8 percent in 1944 and 1945 (the result of brisk export sales rather than effective economic management) won the president and his MNR financial policy maker considerable support among a broad segment of lower and middle classes. Villarroel's was the first government in Bolivia's twentieth-century history that excluded altogether from high office "members of the dominant classes" and of the Rosca.[70] The result, in the opinion of many Bolivians, was a decided improvement over the past. Also praiseworthy, in the eyes of many urban sectors, was the 1945 legislation that abolished the *pongueaje* system that required Indians on private estates to render services without pay to the *hacendados*. Had the law actually been enforced—it was not—life for the Indians, who constituted 56 percent of the population,[71] would have improved and they might have felt less compulsion to migrate to the cities.

Despite the positive features of his regime, Villarroel made many enemies, and the list of them was by no means confined to the old elites of the Concordance and the *Rosca*. A repressive and even cruel dictator, Villarroel turned many former supporters against him by his arbitrary use of power. In particular, intellectuals of communist leanings felt the lash of the dictator's whip, and they responded by branding him a Fascist. Catholic elements, moreover, were disturbed by the secular orientation of Villarroel's MNR collaborators and by their reliance almost exclusively on economism to ease social tensions.

Perhaps Villarroel's greatest weakness lay in his tendency to fancy himself a Bolivian Mussolini. With the outcome of World War II, Mussolini types had gone out of fashion. So also, for the time being, in Bolivia and elsewhere in Latin America, had condemnations of liberal capitalism and democracy. The liberal countries had, with the aid of Russia, won the war, the depression had been surmounted, a new era of prosperity seemed at hand, and many in Andean America began to wonder if liberalism might not be the political-economic system best in accord with the laws of nature.

All the while Bolivians looked hopefully to the United States to provide a painless solution to national problems. If only the great republic would vastly increase the input of public and private capital, a reward Bolivians felt entitled to because of cooperation in the war effort, then it would not be necessary to experiment with radical programs of mobilization and sacrifice and state controls that reformers both of the left and right had been urging since the end of World War I. With a sufficient influx of U.S. capital it would be possible to keep the lower classes in line through social devices hit upon by Saavedra and Siles and improved by Paz Estenssoro, while the directing classes resumed their old heedless life styles of muddling through.

As of 1946, however, Villarroel's administration was on Washington's black list, with many of its members accused of fascist leanings. Given this situation, it seemed unlikely that North American assistance would be forthcoming until Villarroel was toppled. Furthermore, the commodity purchase agreement had lapsed and apparently could be advantageously renegotiated only by an administration more to Washington's liking. This belief, at least, helped provide the catalyst that united the various elements of opposition to Villarroel so as to produce a successful revolution. In July of 1946 the dictator was not only ousted from office, he was lynched and his body strung from a lamppost. It was the most spectacular act of political violence in the Andes since the 1912 lynching of Alfaro in Quito.

Like his Ecuadoran counterpart, Villarroel would salvage his reputation, posthumously, emerging before long as a national martyr-hero —at least to many of his countrymen. Meantime, though, the old-guard oligarchy, the *Rosca* and all its friends, proclaiming themselves now the true believers in liberal democracy, would enjoy their final fling at governing Bolivia. Shortly before this, traditional ruling classes had staged a comeback in Peru and Ecuador, and under more promising circumstances than in Bolivia.

Weathering the Storm in Peru and Ecuador, 1934–1945

Their will to wage violent revolution sapped by the military suppression to which Sánchez Cerro had subjected them, Apristas nursed their wounds and remained relatively quiet during the six years that Oscar Benavides ruled Peru. As the economy staged a strong recovery and the established order gained strength under this military officer's skillful administration, Apristas grew conciliatory and gradualist reformism began to replace their cry for radical revolution. The party remained officially banned, but in its underground existence it was less and less harried by the authorities. However, when an Aprista-backed candidate defeated the administration supported standard-bearer in the 1936 elections held at the end of the unexpired portion of the Sánchez Cerro term, it proved too much for Benavides. Canceling the election result, the general announced he would serve a full six-year term, to end in late 1939.

While not seeking to play the role of a populist leader, Benavides nevertheless put into operation many of the devices of state paternalism recommended by such leaders as Haya de la Torre. Impressive workers' housing projects were undertaken, approximately 900 new primary schools were opened, low-cost popular restaurants were constructed in Lima's slum areas, and the serving of free breakfasts to thousands of public school children was initiated.

Government's most notable accomplishment in welfare legislation came in 1936 with enactment of a social security law,[72] its provisions to be enforced by the Ministry of Public Health, Labor and Social Security, created in October of the previous year. The new legislation provided for retirement at age sixty with pensions of between 40 and 60 percent of income while working, as well as for sickness, disability, maternity, and death benefits. While the law was initially quite limited in coverage, applying mainly to labor elites, it was steadily expanded in the years ahead. Opposed, in the Spanish-American tradition, to independent worker organizations with power to gain concessions through collective bargaining, Benavides did not devise the social security or other labor laws in response to union pressures. The laws were imposed from above, as a means of co-opting labor leaders and persuading them that the surest way to gain benefits for their constituency lay in becoming the cooperative clients of the charitably inclined government.[73]

As part of his public works projects, Benavides launched one of the most extensive road-building programs in the country's history; and he devoted attention to the Indians. The year 1937 witnessed the creation of an Office of Indian Affairs, charged with studying Indian problems, formulating new protective legislation and enforcing old laws, resolving land claims that involved comunidades, stimulating the establishment of comunidad cooperatives, and devising education programs for the natives. These functions were to be carried out through six brigades of Indian Culturalization. Achievements of these brigades were not spectacular, but they pioneered an approach that later administrations would follow more energetically. Under Benavides, the brigades accomplished the official registration of some 470 of the estimated 5,000 comunidades.[74]

For the 1939 elections Benavides chose Manuel Prado, a socially prominent banking and business leader, as the official candidate. In balloting that was by no means a model of the proper functioning of democratic processes, Prado triumphed handily. In spite of consistent APRA denials, there were indications that before the election Prado had reached a secret understanding with the Apristas: in exchange for their promise to support him or at least not oppose him at the polls, Prado agreed to legalize their party after coming to power.[75]

Prices for Peruvian exports continued at the high levels reached in the late 1930s during Prado's six-year term (1939–1945), which coincided with World War II, and the president took full advantage of the situation through his administrative cunning. This tiny man with an aristocratic bearing and suave manners, who so delighted in wearing his medals and in other ways indulging his considerable vanity, proved to be one of the most adept jugglers of men, factions, and groups that Peru has produced. As a result the country remained on the surface calm, tranquil, and orderly as programs initiated by Benavides were continued and in many instances expanded.

Through tax incentives and customs concessions Prado helped call into being a whole new class of small-scale manufacturers, concentrated in Lima and Callao.[76] The "factories" of the new producers were often confined to a garage or a shed. Thus under government stimulus there emerged an economic sector bearing many resemblances to the old artisan groups that had been largely eliminated by the liberal free-trade policies initiated in the nineteenth century. This development would assume enormous future significance in influencing relations with the United States. As the new artisan class came to feel threatened in the postwar period by manufactured goods imported from the United States or produced by large-scale subsidiaries, they would form a militant vanguard of anti-Yankee economic nationalists, often aligned with the few local mass producers who were similarly threatened by North American competition.

Ecuadoran administrations of the mid-to-late 1930s tried many of the same expedients that Benavides found useful in safeguarding Peru's social tranquility. Federico Páez, who ruled as a dictator between September of 1935 and October of 1937 took the lead in introducing new social legislation. An engineer who had previously used his political connections to gain lucrative contracts for his firm, Páez has been described by an Ecuadoran writer as possessing only one political principle: "to achieve the greatest comfort possible in life without having to rouse himself from his idleness, already proverbial."[77] Nevertheless, Páez possessed some grasp of what the times required and was not without the instincts of a populist leader. The workers, he insisted, had to understand that they could not trust unions; instead, they should come directly to him if they had a grievance or a problem. "I am always ready to receive and attend to the workers; I do not want to deal with their intermediaries, but personally with them." In his personalist approach to labor problems, Páez forced management to make many concessions to workers and with some justification he could observe: "The workers felt my desire to serve them, and they showed their gratitude in the clearest manner."[78]

At first, Páez surrounded himself with socialist advisers, not because he felt any ideological kinship but because he believed they possessed the skills and inclinations to frame the sort of labor and social laws that would ease tensions. With the collaboration of Socialists, the engineer-president promulgated laws to protect not only urban laborers but also Indians. The 1937 Law of Communes conferred juridic personality upon the comunidades—one year before the Bolivian constituent assembly enacted a similar decree, seventeen years after Peruvians had taken the step—and in several instances small amounts of land were actually returned to the Indian settlements. Besides recognizing existing Indian comunidades, the 1937 legislation encouraged the formation of new communal villages, both by Indians and mestizos, holding out to them the promise of certain limited rights of self-management. Páez and his consultants obviously recognized the advantages that the established order could derive from blunting the spirit of individualistic competitiveness among the lower-class rural populace.

In theory, the Ministry of Social Security was to exercise control over the communal organizations, thereby in effect mobilizing the peasants in support of the government. However, the administration lacked the financial and personnel resources to accomplish this objective. To a large extent, then, the Law of Communes remained a dead letter; but it did point to future developments not only in Ecuador but the rest of Andean America.[79] Shortage of funds also hampered Páez's attempts to provide protection for urban laborers. Lacking the export commodities that had contributed to Peru's recovery, Ecuador remained mired in economic stagnation and the president was forced to turn to deficit financing to underwrite his social programs. The resulting inflation spawned resentment among all save the small minority of marginal sectors who were directly benefited by government largesse.

His standing among leftists slipping as he refused to introduce more radical measures of reform and constantly indicated his faith that increased foreign investment would solve the country's problems, Páez turned to the right for support. In a bid for Catholic backing, he arranged a modus vivendi between the government and the Holy See as a result of which the church reacquired autonomy in its own internal affairs.[80] Páez's political maneuvering, however, was to no avail and toward the end of 1937 he was overthrown by his supposed friend, General Alberto Enríquez Gallo. Similar in many ways to Bolivia's ill-fated practitioner of military populist corporativism, Germán Busch, Enríquez saw the need for an opening toward the left. But, even as Busch, he lacked a clear-cut social program of his own, and the leftists on whom he sought to rely for advice were themselves confused and hopelessly divided by their "juvenile quarrels over orthodoxy."[81]

Enríquez deserves credit for the promulgation of a 1938 labor code, coordinating the scattered social provisions enacted up to that time. But the most significant feature of his brief administration was his confrontation with U.S. capital as represented by the gold and silver producing firm that operated in Portovelo (in the southern coastal province aptly named El Oro, or gold), the South American Development Company. Its operations dating back to the turn of the century, the company in the 1930s employed between 2,000 and 3,000 workers. In 1934 this labor force had begun to organize to seek higher wages and in the same year Ecuador's government had wrested from the company a new concession contract calling for annual dollar payments of an amount equal to 4 percent of the gross production of the mines. Hard-pressed for funds, Enríquez in 1938 began negotiations to raise the 4 percent figure to 12 percent and to force the company to increase wages and benefits for workers. When the company assumed an intransigent attitude, the military president deployed troops around its holdings and threatened a government takeover. Duly impressed, the company resumed bargaining, but at too slow a pace to suit the chief execuitve who in February unilaterally announced establishment of the 12 percent figure as the base for tax payments. Meantime the company had enlisted the support of the State Department, assuring it of Enríquez's fascist leanings. While its officials may not have been fooled by this ploy, the State Department had grown increasingly apprehensive over the rampant economic nationalism previously manifested by the Bolivian oil expropriation and by the demands of the Mexican government on the foreign oil firms which would lead to their expropriation in March of 1938.

At the inception of the Good Neighbor policy the State Department had hoped that in exchange for the renunciation of North American political intervention the Latin American governments would provide a climate that was propitious to the operation of U.S. firms. So far as Washington officials were concerned, first Bolivia and now Ecuador—among the Andean republics—had failed to reciprocate in the manner expected of them. In both instances, therefore, the State Department took a hard line, clearly bordering on if not passing overtly into intervention, in support of North American capitalists.

Enríquez refused to back down, and so did the administration that followed upon his overthrow in August of 1938. Even as in the case of Bolivia, it was the State Department that softened its stand when the entry of the United States into World War II seemed imminent. Ecuadoran cooperation was essential if the United States was to benefit from that country's balsa wood and rubber resources and to establish military bases on the Galapagos Islands. As a result, the South American Development Company had to learn to live with the new financial arrangement.[82]

Owing to the circumstances of impending war, Ecuadorans had scored a victory in the endeavor to utilize more effectively the earnings of U.S. capital in preserving the country's social harmony. But the administration of Carlos Alberto Arroyo del Río, installed in power at the end of 1939, failed in its hope to win U.S. backing in the defense of national territory. Another flare-up in the boundary controversy that had soured relations between the neighboring republics since the earliest years of independence led Peru, whose armed forces had been revitalized under Benavides, to launch a series of armed strikes against an unprepared Ecuador in July of 1941.[83] Vastly outnumbered and unable to stand up against the aggressor on the field of battle, Ecuadorans looked to the United States for rescue. Hoping to avoid some of the onus that was bound to be incurred regardless of the stance it assumed, the United States turned to Brazil and allowed that country to bear the brunt of peace restoration activities.

The conflict was still unresolved when the Japanese attack at Pearl Harbor brought the United States into World War II. The following month, January of 1942, there assembled in Rio de Janeiro the third Conference of American Foreign Ministers, its purpose being to resolve hemisphere problems so that a united front might be established in waging the war. The issue between Peru and Ecuador was one of the major points of contention the ministers had to settle.

Obviously the stronger of the two rivals, Peru enjoyed all the advantages and its armed forces had actually occupied the territory under dispute. In view of this situation, Brazil and the United States called upon Ecuador to accept the inevitable sacrifice of territory, while all the while exerting more subtle pressures on Peru to curb, at least ever so slightly, its demands. The result was a protocol signed in Rio, to be guaranteed by the United States, Brazil, Argentina, and Chile, according to which Ecuador relinquished claims on about 80,000 square miles of unoccupied territory in the Amazonian *Oriente* and 5,000 square miles of land actually occupied by nationals.[84] Peru, like Chile after the War of the Pacific, regarded the new boundary arrangements as binding for all time. But Ecuador continues to pro-

claim that it was, is, and shall be an Amazonian nation, just as Bolivia continues to announce the eventual reacquisition of a port on
the Pacific.

Although Arroyo del Río ruled with considerable talent and fiscal
responsibility, slowing inflation, avoiding deficit financing, and gathering taxes effectively so that the treasury accumulated surpluses, he was
unremittingly criticized as a president who had not been able to defend national honor. The Ecuadoran Democratic Alliance now
emerged, bringing together politicians of nearly all varieties, from
Conservatives to Communists, and dedicated to just one objective,
overthrowing Arroyo del Río.[85] Enlisting the support of the armed
forces, the alliance attained its objective in May of 1944. The ousted
president was replaced by that consummate master of populist demagoguery, José María Velasco Ibarra.

The following year, under far happier circumstances, Peru's President Prado, still basking in the glow of popular enthusiasm over the
vanquishing of Ecuador, allowed relatively free and honest elections
that resulted in the victory of José Luis Bustamante. An *arequipeño*
of middle-sector background whose personal integrity was unassailable, Bustamante was helped to victory by the APRA, now called the
Party of the People or PAP (*Partido del Pueblo*), which had been
legalized on the eve of the balloting. By this time the APRA had shed
its revolutionary image altogether, the reason being quite apparent.
As of the end of World War II, capitalism seemed to be functioning
even more successfully than during the *oncenio*. Middle groups along
the coast, including those that were relatively marginal, had become
optimistic about their prospects within the capitalist system. If Haya
de la Torre hoped to retain their support, he had to change his movement's ideology, something that was easily accomplished given the
total control that he continued to exercise. Moreover, discouraged by
the failures of the 1930s to seize power through revolution, Apristas
had now resolved to become rulers of Peru through elections. In order
for them to gain recognition of the PAP as a legal party, and also in
order to dispose Washington favorably toward them, it was necessary
to discard the rhetoric of radicalism and to disavow the old methods
of violence.

As the post-World War II era began, the situation in the three
Andean republics presented some notable similarities as well as contrasts. In Peru, the major party of radical socialism formed in the
1920s had joined the establishment. Meantime, the Civilist oligarchy,
restored to power by the Sánchez Cerro *golpe*, had proved extremely

porous, absorbing more and more middle sectors including the one-time supporters of Leguía and also the Christian Democrats for whom Bustamante was a spokesman. The social tensions that had contributed to virtual civil war in the early 1930s had all but disappeared, eased out of existence by the return of prosperity.

While Ecuador lacked Peru's promising economic foundation, its politicians had at least showed considerable flexibility, which can be attributed either to a commendable spirit of compromise or to a total lack of principles. The major group of political innovators, the Ecuadoran Socialist party, had grown progressively weaker during the 1930s, the victim of internal divisiveness and of the populist appeal of Velasco Ibarra. While many established political leaders might dislike and distrust this man, they could hardly regard him as posing a revolutionary threat to the prevailing order, and this was an important factor helping to account for the absence of intransigence.

In stark contrast both to Peru and Ecuador, political lines in Bolivia had hardened during the 1930s and 1940. A decided break with the old order had been made by Toro and Busch, whereupon the old guard had successfully struck back through the Concordance, only to be totally dispossessed by Villarroel and the MNR in 1943. Within two-and-a-half years the Rosca was back in power but facing difficulties because of the declining productivity of the tin mines and the reluctance to impose direct taxes in financing the social services which even its members had come to recognize as essential. Against this background the MNR, lusting for vengeance and gathering popular support even though operating underground, was plotting to destroy the oligarchy.

One highly significant element the three republics shared in common. In each of them a new phenomenon had briefly appeared and then, for the moment, passed from the scene: populist, corporativist, socialist militarism, as exemplified by Sánchez Cerro, Toro and Busch, and Enríquez Gallo. This new phenomenon would reemerge in the three republics in the 1960s as new dislocations and crises made their appearance. Meantime, the old order muddled through in Peru and Ecuador, while Bolivia underwent a civilian-directed social revolution.

10

Revolution in Bolivia, Muddling Through in Peru and Ecuador, 1945–1960

With World War II about to end, Haya de la Torre expressed an attitude widely held by Andean statesmen. Collaboration in the war effort, he wrote, had earned the southern republics the right to demand more from the United States once peace was restored.[1] At about the same time a perceptive U.S. ambassador to Bolivia warned about the effects if his country cut back on the volume of goods purchased from Latin America or reduced the prices it had paid during the period of military crisis. Such action would result in confirmation of "the suspicion that a large part of our good neighbor policy, at least in its economic aspect, is simply a matter of expediency . . . limited to the duration of war pressures."[2]

As the cold war emerged hard on the heels of the fighting against the Axis, the United States was in no position to meet the hopes of Haya de la Torre or to avoid the consequences that its ambassador in La Paz had warned against. By 1945 and 1946 statesmen in Washington had come to see the emerging confrontation with Russia as involving the very survival of democracy and free enterprise capitalism. With the effects of the great depression still clearly in mind, political and business leaders feared that another economic tailspin could result in the destruction of the Western system and the worldwide triumph of communism. Economic crisis could best be averted, it seemed, through the discovery and creation of vast new opportunities for the growth of capitalism. In this respect, attention was focused primarily on Europe. Not only were economic opportunities the most promising there, but the threat of communist takeovers loomed with greatest immediacy. Andean America, and indeed all Latin America, would have to content itself with a low priority status. But the southern republics were expected all the while to give a free reign to North American investors so as to facilitate the expansion of capitalism on which the survival of Western civilization was said to depend.[3] Thus the relative tolerance that the State Department of Good Neighbor days had shown toward Andean republics in their treatment of North American capital would have to end. So would the concept of employing public funds to facilitate Latin American development. All available public funds were now required for the rehabilitation of Europe and whatever economic input the United States might provide the republics to the south would have to come from private investment alone.

Andean leaders and their sister republic counterparts had their eyes opened to emerging U.S. attitudes at the Chapultepec Conference of American States that assembled in Mexico early in 1945. At the conference sessions the Latin Americans tried to impress upon the U.S. delegates the enormous danger of communist insurrections faced by incumbent regimes.[4] They warned that only direct government assistance from the United States, based upon the use of public funds, would enable hard-pressed regimes to withstand the Marxist menace. At the time, however, U.S. officials were not impressed with such arguments. Their message was that only the proper functioning of free enterprise could eliminate the communist threat. Therefore it behooved Latin American administrations to think in terms of according inducements and guarantees likely to attract private North American investment.

Throughout the 1950s, Latin Americans continued to urge the United States to commit public funds to economic and social development loans. To these pleas Washington administrations consistently turned a deaf ear. The Republicans' John Foster Dulles, who as secretary of state set foreign policy during much of the Dwight Eisenhower administration (1953–1961), was particularly insistent in depicting liberal capitalism as the only solution to Latin American problems. Furthermore, even as many Democratic shapers of cold war policy during the Harry Truman years (1945–1953), Dulles saw a connection between liberal capitalism and liberal, individualistic democracy. In addition, Dulles looked to the nourishing of individual liberty, both economic and political, as the best means for combating the communist menace. In June of 1946 he stated that Soviet leaders were intent upon spreading their system throughout the world because of "their honest belief that individual freedom is a basic cause of human unrest and that if it is taken away, it will promote world-wide peace and security."[5] Dulles found it well-nigh impossible to understand the ruling classes of Andean and the rest of Latin America; for in their attitude toward the masses of their countrymen they were in accord with Soviet thinking. Both the ruling classes and the aspiring elites were convinced that, so far as the masses were concerned, individual freedom was indeed a basic cause of human unrest and that denying it would promote the peace, security, and stability of the established, traditional order. This is why they turned to methods of statism to preserve the masses in their accustomed dependence, hoping all the time that the United States would help to finance these methods.

Until the mid-1950s, the divergence between the United States and the republics to the south over hemisphere policy did not assume crucial dimensions. Prices for exports, stimulated by the Korean War that was fought in the later years of the Truman administration, had remained high and this enabled many regimes to obtain the funds required for survival in office. All the while private foreign investment grew dramatically. Between 1946 and 1958, in fact, the book value of direct foreign investment in Latin America rose from approximately $6 billion to $13 billion (about 60 percent of which represented U.S. investment), the most dramatic increase in the hemisphere's history.[6] In spite of the increase in private investment from abroad, most Latin American countries found themselves in a severe recession as 1958 began. This was most definitely true of the three Andean republics under consideration, each of which was suffering from a serious decline in the prices of exports.[7] More than ever convinced of the meaninglessness of U.S. assurances that private investment would solve all problems, the Andean and their sister republics began to push aggressively for a change in Washington's policy. In their sharpening dispute with the United States, the Andean republics turned for justification to the economic analysis of the United Nations Economic Commission for Latin America (ECLA) whose most persuasive spokesman was its Argentine secretary, Raúl Prebisch.

According to ECLA analysis, Latin America through the years had been drained economically by foreign investment. This investment had gone mainly into extractive industries, thereby facilitating exports. The drain occurred because the underdeveloped Latin American republics (referred to as the periphery) suffered from deteriorating terms of trade in their relationship to the developed countries (the center). Prices for the primary goods exported by the periphery had steadily declined, it was said, while the prices paid for finished goods had consistently risen. As the way out of the economic bind, Prebisch recommended import-substitution manufacturing, to be financed initially in part by U.S. loans and assistance. In this aspect of his program Prebisch had come to the conclusion reached by Alexander Hamilton in the early 1790s when he wrote: "Not only the wealth but the indcpcndcncc and security of a country appear to be materially connected with the prosperity of manufactures."[8]

Since the first major presentation of the ECLA-Prebisch analysis in 1949,[9] its long-term validity has been challenged by many economists. They contend that Latin America and the countries producing raw materials in general have not suffered from a long-term disadvantage in terms of trade. Looked at just from the perspective of the 1950s, however, the ECLA analysis is not easily assailable. During that period the exports of Peru, Bolivia, and Ecuador, and most of the other Latin American countries as well, were declining in value while the prices of manufactured goods imported from the United States and the nations of the industrialized center in general remained steady or rose.[10]

Since the first impact created by Marxism, no economic analysis matched the popularity that ECLA theories enjoyed for about fifteen years in Latin America.[11] Like Marxism, ECLA analysis exonerated Latin Americans from blame for their economic underdevelopment and shifted responsibility to outside forces controlled by the center. Although rejecting Marxist conclusions in favor of Keynesian objectives concerned with the strengthening of capitalism, ECLA assessments in one instance did bolster those of Marxism. Both schools concurred in the judgment that up to that time the development of one kind of country involved and was indeed paid for by the underdevelopment of other kinds of countries. However, ECLA economists believed that this situation could be altered without the destruction of world capitalism, provided that the center countries could be persuaded to mend their ways and aid the development of balanced capitalism in the periphery.

In late 1954 the first Economic Conference of the Organization of American States convened in Petropolis, near Rio de Janeiro. With Raúl Prebisch himself in the forefront, the Latin American delegates urged government-to-government aid upon the United States, insisting that private foreign investment was, in its long-term consequences, weakening their national economies. Their arguments produced no effect. What is more, at a subsequent economic conference held in

1957 in Buenos Aires, U.S. spokesmen still stood firmly by their customary position.[12]

Although it was not apparent at Buenos Aires, U.S. policy was under reassessment by 1957. The reason could be traced in large part to the serious recession that gripped most of the hemisphere's republics. As economic conditions worsened, it became necessary to question the assumption that private investment constituted an adequate stimulus to progress. Also contributing to a willingness to consider new economic policy was the fact that the U.S. share of trade (exports and imports) in the Latin American market, standing at 60 percent in 1948, was steadily declining—it would drop to 44 percent by 1962.[13] Under these circumstances, economic policy makers had come to see that by assuming a more direct role in hemisphere development, in such manner as to oblige aid and loan recipients to spend the funds in North America, the United States could increase its share of Latin American trade.

A reassessment of the communist menace and how best to combat it was also in order by the mid-1950s. Private investment had not resulted in the economic prosperity for Latin America that Washington officials had hoped for as the cold war began. Economic and social problems were on the rise, and this suggested the need for direct commitment of North American public funds. In 1955 former Ecuadoran president Galo Plaza Lasso, directing his words toward the U.S. audience, had written: "Action should be taken to improve the standard of living of the great masses, for poverty is a breeding ground of communism, [and] to strengthen the middle class, which is the stabilizing element of democracy."[14] Within two years, the United States was beginning to act on this advice, pushed in this direction by recent experience with Bolivia.

In responding to the social revolution successfully launched by Bolivia's MNR in 1952, the United States had initiated a massive infusion of public funds, persuaded that if the revolutionary regime foundered the country would fall under communist control. So far as Washington was concerned, the policy had proved its effectiveness by 1957. The MNR had disavowed much of its early radicalism and it appeared to be firmly in control of the country. The likelihood of a communist takeover had all but disappeared. By 1957, however, new communist threats had surfaced elsewhere in Latin America, their immediacy often exaggerated by the ruling sectors who, profiting from the example of the Bolivians, had learned how best to appeal to

Washington for funds. By now, Washington officials were in a mood to consider applying the Bolivian experiment to other countries.

Influential in making policy for Bolivia, Milton Eisenhower, the president's brother, had by 1957 come to accept the need for the United States to begin to employ public funds in alleviating social problems in much of Latn America, lest these problems lead to communist takeovers. He explains his position in these words:

> I was stimulated to reach certain convictions by Pedro Beltrán of Peru, who made an eloquent plea for U.S. help in social development . . . What we were doing in Latin America, he said, was well and good, but it was not enough and it was doing too little for the people who needed housing, better diets, education, health services. He urged that we finance such projects in Latin America.[15]

A staunch defender of the interests of Peru's wealthiest capitalist sectors who had previously shown little social conscience, Beltrán had by now acquired the foresight to understand that the established order was threatened unless a vast amount of additional spending was channeled into social projects. Above all, he wished to spare the native oligarchies the burden of contributing their own funds to social spending. Therefore he directed his "eloquent plea" to the United States, pointing constantly to the rising communist menace so as to bolster his arguments—and often fabricating communist threats through the irresponsible journalism of his influential Lima daily, *La Prensa*.

Milton Eisenhower harbored certain reservations, for he perceived that Latin America's directing classes remained hesitant to commit their own funds to essential reforms: "They were concerned only about more money from abroad for social projects."[16] Nevertheless, a crisis seemed at hand. Guatemala had barely been saved, so it appeared to U.S. observers, from a communist takeover in 1954 through the covert intervention of the CIA. Then in September of 1958 Salvador Allende, backed by Marxian Socialists and Communists, missed winning the Chilean presidential election by less than 40,000 votes. In May of the same year the hostile reception accorded Vice President Richard Nixon in Peru and Venezuela had shocked many U.S. officials into awareness of the need for a revised Latin American policy. At the very end of the critical year Fidel Castro came to power in Cuba, and soon Eisenhower would write: "There can be no doubt that Castro's wicked influence in the Hemisphere was spurring us onward."[17]

In September of 1960 the third Economic Conference of the Organization of American States convened in Bogotá—the city that had hosted the founding meeting of the OAS in 1948. By now the United States was ready to accept the position urged on it by Latin Americans since the end of World War II. Subscribing to the Act of Bogotá produced by the Economic Conference, the Eisenhower administration agreed in principle to commit public funds to social reform projects in Latin America.

Andean elites welcomed Washington's commitment, at the same time rejecting altogether the reasoning that lay behind it. While U.S. policy makers believed that only the free, democratic, and capitalistic masses could be happy and therefore ready to resist communism, the Andean elites were persuaded that only dependent masses, satisfied that their needs were being attended to by wise and generous patrons, could be happy and disposed to block the advance of radicalism. In no sphere of social thought were ruling sector assumptions more clearly revealed than in the new and respectable Indianism that was taking shape. Had the nature of this Indianism been appreciated in Washington, the planners of the new approach to hemisphere relations would have understood the hopelessness of the attempt to combat communism by spreading, along with dollars, the social values and political goals associated in the United States with the American way of life.

RESPECTABLE INDIANISM IN ANDEAN AMERICA

A central issue in the 1964 novel *Todas las sangres* (*All Bloods*) by the internationally recognized Peruvian novelist José María Arguedas revolved about the clash between two brothers, Fermín and Bruno. Fermín exemplified the approach to Indian relations pursued by the vast majority of Andean capitalist classes at the turn of the century: his goal was to Westernize the Indians, to convert them into workers "with individuality and ambition." Bruno, on the other-hand, wanted to retain the Indians in their traditional way of life and under the direction of "charitable masters."[18]

Midway in the twentieth century, the Brunos were gaining the upper hand. One indication of this was the Act of Arequipa, signed by the ministers of education of Peru and Bolivia in 1945. It proclaimed that Indian culture of the Andes was altogether distinct from Western culture, that people have the right to their own culture, and that

Indians must be protected and allowed to develop as autochtonous beings, even to the point of being educated in their native tongue rather than in Spanish. Indian culture, according to the act, was essentially agrarian in nature, and therefore education of the natives should be directed mainly toward teaching them to become better farmers.[19]

So long as Westernization had been the solution to the Indian problem held out by well-to-do spokesmen of the bourgeoisie, most politically aware members of urban society had tended to turn their backs on the whole matter; for Westernization of the natives posed the threat of multiplying the competitors of all save those most affluent and most secure in their urban existence. But, when the notion of preserving the Indian as an Indian, in his customary way of life and in his customary rural habitat, became the rallying cry of the Indianists they found a huge and receptive audience. This explains the upsurge of respectable or nonrevolutionary Indianism.

The school of respectable Indianism pictured the Indian past in terms of a two-culture society.[20] The elites at the top were individualistic to a considerable degree and owned private property and goods, while the masses were thoroughly collectivized, totally dependent upon their communes and benevolent masters for security, and enjoyed only the use but never the private ownership of property.[21] A Bolivian writer succinctly set forth the views of this school when he wrote that in the Inca empire one found the economic collectivism prescribed by Marx combined with the political order based on the rule of superior persons that Lenin had found indispensable.[22] The coexistence of collectivized masses and self-reliant, independent rulers is described by Peru's Luis E. Valcárcel, perhaps the most influential Indianist his country has produced, as "a synthesis of the two principles, communist and monarchical."[23]

In the analysis that the respectable Indianists began to popularize, the Indian masses were not revolutionary by nature; rather, when allowed to be themselves, when afforded collectivist security guaranteed by the paternalism of a master class, they were inclined toward meekness, docility, and passivity.[24] This was the viewpoint of Pío Jaramillo Alvarado, one of Ecuador's best-known Indianists. Writing in 1954 he celebrated the death of the old "romantic" school of Indianism (closely associated with González Prada) according to which the natives were predisposed toward violent revolution. Recent and serious studies of Indian culture, he maintained, established that the aborigines were, "in their Franciscan sobriety," among the least revolutionary of all persons.[25]

In the appraisal of respectable Indianism, the Indian masses were "ideal masses," in the meaning Ortega y Gasset gave to these words: they were predisposed, that is, to accept the rule of elites. Bolivia's Gustavo Adolfo Otero observed that the Inca masses had sought direction from men whom they recognized as superior;[26] and Peru's Rafael Larco noted that the Indians had always relied upon a leadership class that understood the nature of the people and how to draw them forth and render them useful.[27] Finally, Hildebrando Castro Pozo, one of Peru's most celebrated champions of Indian reform from the 1920s through the 1950s, contended that Inca political organization did not permit the masses to develop initiative or a spirit of enterprise. Nevertheless, the leadership knew how "to take advantage of all the vital energy of its subjects" who were "incapable of taking a step by themselves."[28]

By the 1930s and 1940s many Andean upper-class figures were caught with the vision of reestablishing the sort of command over the Indians once exercised by native elites, hoping thereby to take advantage once more of the vital energy of the aboriginal masses. One of the most influential books in which men of this hope found their inspiration was *El nuevo indio* (*The New Indian*) by the Peruvian José Uriel García, published first in 1930 and then in a more widely read revised edition in 1937. According to García, Andean whites and mestizos who had acquired command over the advanced technology of Western civilization were at the same time Indians, provided they had been subjected to the telluric influences of the *altiplano* which had constituted the crucible of Indian nature through the centuries. Men who were the product of advanced Western education and also of the telluric determinants operative in the Andes were, according to the Cuzco-born writer who taught at the university in his native city, "new Indians." Able to penetrate into the psyche of the Indians, to whom they were united by a telluric bond, they formed an elite with the mission to animate the native masses, whose natural mode of existence was to remain in hibernation until awakened by the leadership of superior men.[29]

Properly conceived and executed reforms, respectable Indianists contended, could lead the natives to assume more economically useful roles within the nation, without stimulating them to seek what was really beyond their nature: the dynamic of individualistic aggressiveness. The proper approach to reform consisted in leaving the Indians unchanged in their traditional collectivism, while an elite class inspired them to make the comunidades more efficient and more productive. Only on the basis of preserving the old comunidad, with its collectivist spirit, should the attempt be made to convert the Indian "into an element of progress for the nation."[30]

Allegedly not inclined by nature toward the capitalist ethic, Indians would expect little in the way of private material aggrandizement as a result of the increased efficiency of their comunidades. Instead, provided they were guaranteed security by paternalistic patrons as well as unassailable domain over their comunidades, they would happily accept a situation in which they gave to the state according to their abilities while receiving from the state in accordance with their needs.[31] Once again, then, Indian masses would begin to work for the common good, as they had done, under the tutelage of native elites, before the Spanish conquest.[32] Once again, they would live under the discipline of the communal bonds of collective labor which "unite the will of all in the same task" and symbolize "compliance with and performance of the obligations which each owes to the community . . . as the user of a parcel of land which he cultivates.'[33]'

Although rejecting the González Prada view of the Indian as a natural revolutionary, a view that was later taken up by many Marxists, the proponents of respectable Indianism followed the Peruvian iconoclast's example in placing their faith in the myth of the eternal Indian: the Indian who, determined by his nature, always was and always would be a collectivist being. In reality, many Indians had by the 1940s, and even before then, discarded the collectivist approach to life and taken to the values of individualism.[34] A few respectable Indianists, among them Castro Pozo, accepted this fact but attributed it to the pressures that society had exerted upon Indians to depart from their traditional way of life and accommodate to Western standards. Castro Pozo remained convinced, however, that Indians still retained a natural predisposition toward a collectivist existence. National governments, he insisted, should take advantage of this by organizing Indians into cooperatives, always under the careful control and scrutiny of a Bureau of Indian Affairs within the Ministry of Labor and Social Security.[35] All the while it was assumed that the few exceptional, atypical Indians who developed individualistic achievement traits and desires of upward social mobility could be absorbed by white society and safely co-opted by the leaders of that society.

Believing what it suited their purposes to believe, respectable Indianists also placed credence in another facet of the eternal Indian myth: Indians, by and large, were and must remain, unless they were to do violence to their very nature, agricultural laborers. As early as 1903 Bolivia's future president Bautista Saavedra had sounded this theme in a book dealing with the *ayllu* in preconquest Andean America. In order to fulfill their ethnic mission, Saavedra argued, Indians must be rural workers. Years later a Bolivian authority on education averred: "The Indian must be educated in the countryside, so as not to fall under the attraction of the city; he must, above all else, remain an agricultural laborer."[36] In the 1930s Peru's Castro Pozo added his voice to the chorus that demanded education for Indians, but only an education that prepared them to be better agriculturalists.[37] This was the type of education that the Oscar Benavides administration (1933–1939) inaugurated with an agricultural school in Puno, one of its principal purposes being to reduce internal migration of Indians.[38]

Believing, because they wanted desperately to believe, that there "exists a . . . spiritual fusion between the Indian and the land,"[39] Indianists soon perceived that education alone would not suffice to maintain that fusion. Increasingly they came to agree with the Mexican Moisés Sáenz, who visited Peru and Ecuador in the early 1930s[40] and whose views on Indian reforms gained wide currency, that only land reform, carried out in such manner as to benefit the comunidades, even if that meant depriving *hacendados* of their estates, could maintain the Indians in the way of life that purportedly corresponded to their nature.

In the 1930s, the notion of land reform still struck most politically aware members of society as radical. But as the years went by, it came increasingly to be viewed as the best means to reduce internal migration and thereby protect the interests of urban laborers and middle sectors. By the late 1950s, Indians constituted an estimated 46 percent of Peru's population of about 10 million, 62 percent of Bolivia's population of just over 3 million, and 38 percent of Ecuador's population of slightly more than 4 million.[41] The possibility of a massive demographic shift from the countryside was perceived as an ever greater threat to urbanites. Indeed, many had already been disadvantaged by the first stages of the realization of the threat, in the course of which several Andean cities between 1935 and 1945 doubled in population as rural regions underwent depopulation.[42]

As a consequence of actual and projected demographic transformations, land reform became a cause that appealed to a broad cross section of urban interests. This was a development that caused

Indianism to lose its revolutionary image and to be taken up by accommodated sectors intent upon saving their way of life by protecting Indians in what was assumed to be their natural way of life.[43] Here are circumtances that help explain the alacrity with which Bolivia's 1952 social revolution turned attention to land reform. Not only in Bolivia but elsewhere in Andean America land reform of the 1950s, 1960s, and 1970s demonstrates anew how often it is that innovations at first associated with extremist groups are ultimately introduced after their expediency is recognized by those who hope to conserve as much as possible of the traditional order.

The Bolivian Social Revolution

Though actually somewhat less than six years, the period between the overthrow of Villarroel in December of 1946 and the successful MNR revolution of April 1952 is referred to as the *sexenio*. Political power during these years was exercised first by a provisional junta (1946–1947), then by Enrique Hertzog (1947–1949) and Mamerto Urriolagoitia (1949–1951), and finally by a military junta (1951–1952). With prominent MNR members in exile or hiding and Falange (FSB) leaders ignored and disdained, the party base of power rested on a coalition between the major factions of the old Republican party, united in the Party of the Socialist Republican Union or PURS (*Partido de la Unión Socialista Republicana*), and the Marxist-Leninist-inspired Party of the Revolutionary Left or PIR (*Partido de la Izquierda Revolucionaria*). Founded in 1940, the PIR advocated a proletarian revolution led by intellectual elites.[44] The coalition was strictly a marriage of convenience, brought about by the fact that members of the PURS, many of whom came from the ranks of the *Rosca* and the Concordance, recognized the need for labor support. To achieve it, they continued the social spending policies begun during the Villarroel administration by Minister of the Treasury Paz Estenssoro; and they relied upon the PIR to mobilize labor support.

Although a new constitution promulgated in 1947 included provisions for expanded social security coverage, the PURS—which was the dominant element within the coalition—inclined to be niggardly in the economic rewards conferred on labor. This was inevitable in view of the reluctance to increase direct taxes on mine owners and other privileged sectors. Widely accused of having sold out lower-class interests because of their collaboration with the PURS, leaders of the PIR proved totally ineffective in the Bolivian labor movement. Organized labor, especially the powerful Syndicalist Federation of

Mine Workers of Bolivia or FSTMB (*Federación Sindical de Traba-jadores Mineros de Bolivia*), headed by the dynamic Juan Lechín, tended more and more to subscribe to the 1946 Thesis of Pulcayo. According to its highly inflammatory language, the workers must reject the leadership of bourgeois elites, arm themselves, and with the collaboration of the peasants and the few untainted middle-sector revolutionaries spark a movement of the proletariat which would basically alter the social structure.[45] Largely responsible for the Thesis of Pulcayo was the Revolutionary Labor Party or POR (*Partido Obrero Revolucionario*), inspired by Trotskyist ideology.

By the late 1940s MNRistas, plotting clandestinely to return to power, had begun to infiltrate the labor movement and had established ties with Lechín and the POR. In consequence, the MNR, originally a party of intellectuals and nonrevolutionary middle sectors, acquired a labor base and also an influential Marxist wing. At this point also the old-line MNR leadership began for the first time to show a real interest in the Indian problem and in land reform. Fearful of their ability to control the new labor and Marxist elements being added to the party, they were thinking in terms of balancing them through a peasant or Indian constituency. Profoundly influenced by the tenets of respectable Indianism, the original MNR high command trusted in the nonrevolutionary nature of the Indians and the ability of elites to dominate and manipulate them.

The problems of the PURS-PIR coalition mounted steadily. Unable to establish control over increasingly radicalized labor, the administrations of Hertzog and Urriolagoitia resorted more and more to repression. Out of this policy came a second massacre of mine workers at Catavi. It occurred in 1949, some seven years after similar bloodletting had weakened President Peñaranda and his Concordance supporters. Even more important than labor disaffection in undermining PURS-PIR power was the alienation of middle sectors, produced in large part by an inflationary spiral that seemed to have gotten totally out of hand. With the year 1938 providing the base of 100, the cost-of-living index had soared to 1,170.3 by early 1952.[46] Various factors contributed to inflation, among them the stagnation of agriculture which necessitated the importation of food. The basic impetus to inflation, however, came from fiscal policy. Reluctant to impose direct taxes but compelled to maintain social services so as to avoid further loss of labor and employee acceptance, government found its only way out in deficit financing and in new issues of debased currency.

For once, even the tin magnates confronted an adverse situation. The tin content of Bolivian ore produced by the major mines had declined from 12–15 percent at the beginning of the century to 1.3–3.9 percent by 1950.[47] Moreover, the country's tin mines faced increasing competition from those of Indonesia. These were among the factors accounting for the fall in the value of major Bolivian exports from $78 million in 1950 to $59.3 million in 1951. The situation worsened as the price of tin sold in the United States declined from $1.27 the pound in 1950 to 95.8 cents by the beginning of 1953.[48] This decline produced a tremendous outpouring of anti-U.S. oratory, for that country was blamed for forcing an unfair price on Bolivian producers. For domestic politics the important fact was that the new difficulties of the tin industry contributed to overall economic deterioration that made it ever more difficult for the old order to keep labor in line and placate the growing middle sectors through employment, patronage, and avenues of upward mobility.

By the beginning of 1952 the MNR was plotting with disgruntled military officer Antonio Seleme to duplicate the *golpe* of 1943 that had brought Villarroel and the MNRistas to power. Recognizing the seriousness of its own internal divisions and the conflicting aspirations of its constituencies, the MNR would have welcomed a period of close collaboration with the military once the oligarchy was overthrown. But it was not to be this way. With the revolution already having begun and with the incumbent military junta showing unexpected strength, Seleme lost his nerve and withdrew his support from the rebels. At this stage the MNR had to call the laboring masses, especially the mine workers of Lechín's FSTMB into the fray, and it was only their support that tipped the scales in favor of the revolution. As a result, the MNR came to power under circumstances that found its leaders beholden to the newly acquired labor and Marxist elements within the party. Moreover the military, having disgraced itself in the revolution, entered a period of relative impotence that endured for over five years.

With the military no longer a power broker, the disparate civilian elements within the MNR embarked upon a struggle to gain the upper land. The social revolution over which the MNR presided was therefore destined to be marked by extreme internal tensions, for the three major groupings within the party had little basis for agreement. These principal contenders for power were: (1) the rightist reformers who repudiated liberal democracy and free enterprise capitalism and wished to establish a corporativist society; (2) the leftist Marxian socialists who found their program in the Thesis of Pulcayo and who at the very least expected a bourgeois-democratic revolution that would eventually grow over into a revolution of the proletariat;[49] and (3) the centrist-pragmatic middle sectors who simply hoped to become a new oligarchy, who were relatively indifferent to forms of government, and who hoped, in spite of their nationalistic, anti-Yankee propaganda, to obtain from the United States the means to establish the financial security of the administration.[50]

The Revolution and the Indian or Campesino When the MNR came to power in 1952, 4.5 percent of the rural population owned an estimated 70 percent of all agricultural property.[51] The figures would have been even more striking had it not been for the large number of small property owners in the Department of Cochabamba who comprised about one-half of all the owners of private rural property.[52] Of the total rural population of some 2.5 million, about one million were Indian *colonos*: laborers, that is, who lived on the approximately 109,000 haciendas or *fincas* and in return for the use of a tiny plot of land worked the fields of the estate owner. Despite the laws of the Busch regime ending *pongueaje*, a high percentage of *colonos* were also *pongos*, obliged to perform not only agricultural labor but all sorts of gratuitous personal services for the *hacendado*. The rest of the Indian population, estimated at about one million and therefore roughly equal to the number of *colonos*, lived on native-owned *comunidades*, the number of which is generally placed at 3,779.[53]

The MNR theoreticians who framed the land reform decree of August 2, 1953 represented the party's centrist-pragmatist faction. They favored giving special attention to the *comunidades* while at the same time abolishing the *colonato-pongueaje* system by confiscating latifundia estates and turning them over to the cooperative ownership of their former laborers. They hoped also to preserve intact the private ownership of medium-sized farms. Their plans therefore contemplated the coexistence of agrarian collectivism and capitalism. Little came of these intentions for by the time the reform law was issued cadres of the left-wing Marxist branch of the MNR had already swept into the countryside and incited many *colonos* to seize the land plots, seldom more than an acre or two, they had previously held in usufruct.

To avoid being outmaneuvered among the peasants by the leftists, MNR centrists had to abandon their original plans and join in encouraging the *colonos* to establish outright ownership over their miniscule plots. The result was the emergence of widespread minifundia as thousands of Indians came into private ownership of parcels often too small to support a family. In a few instances the process was helped along by the initiative of the Indians themselves who, through the instrumentality of the syndicates that they had formed in the days following the Chaco War in order to bargain more effectively with *hacendados*, simply seized haciendas and distributed the land among themselves, always in private rather than collective ownership.[54]

The chaotic manner in which land reform was carried out stemmed from the internal divisions within the MNR. By catering to the desires of *colonos* for private ownership of parcels rather than a share in collectivized estates the leftist elements hoped to gain a backing among the Indians that would give them the power to launch an eventual attack against free enterprise urban capitalism. The centrists, led by Paz Estenssoro who served as president from 1952 to 1956, had to outdo the leftists in catering to the *colonos* because of their ambitions to mobilize the Indians in defense of urban, bourgeois capitalism.

In the maneuvering between leftists and centrists, comunidad Indians were almost totally ignored. The reason for this is readily apparent. The *colonos-pongos* on the latifundia had attained a higher degree of awareness than the *comuneros* residing in comunidades; they exhibited more intense discontent over their pre-1952 status, and generally inhabited more accessible regions. Their mobilization therefore promised more immediate political advantages. However, because each faction sought to prevent its rival from gaining credit for land distribution, reform of the haciendas initially proceeded at an extremely slow pace. Only 1.5 percent of the cultivable land that was given out between 1952 and 1969 was distributed during the first four years.[55]

One of the few generalizations that can safely be made on the early stages of Bolivian land reform is that the disappearance of personal service and forced labor constituted a positive gain, bringing a new sense of dignity to thousands of Indians. This development, in fact, is one of the few features of MNR rule that justifies use of the terms social revolution in describing 1952–1960 events. Beyond this, generalization is hazardous because land reform was carried out differently in the various regions of Bolivia and produced widely divergent results.[56] To begin with, the Bolivian *Oriente* became the setting for important agricultural projects that did not involve the native populace.

In this area lying to the east of Cochabamba, large-scale settlement of Okinawan and Japanese immigrants took place under government auspices. Benefited by completion in 1954 of the Cochabamba-Santa Cruz highway, the colonists made spectacular gains in the commercial production of rice. But for their efforts, Bolivia might have faced a serious shortage of food in the early years of land reform.

In the northeastern area of the *yungas* (along the eastern slopes of the Andes where the terrain is distinguished by deep ravines) land reform came about through internal colonization ventures that retarded the influx of Indians into urban centers and encouraged the commercialization of agriculture.[57] In the region around Lake Titicaca and also in certain parts of the *yungas*, where the Aymara Indians were concentrated, the syndicates formed among the former *colonos* of the expropriated haciendas gained a considerable degree of autonomy. However, power was generally concentrated in the hands of a syndicate secretary general and his small coterie of henchmen. In the old days, the *hacendado*, acting as a broker and patron, had mediated all contact between the Indians and the outside world. Now, the secretary general performed the task. In many ways he was similar to the *kurakas* who with the assistance of important men or *principales* mediated contact between the Indian and Spanish republics during the colonial period. Thus in spite of the ending of Spain's colonial system in 1825 and in spite of the 1953 land reform, a system of patronage-clientage remained in operation.[58]

In southern Bolivia, around Sucre, land reform took on characteristics quite distinct from those most visible in the Lake Titicaca region and the *yungas*. In one respect, though, the results have been similar; for the old hacienda patterns of social hierarchy in which the many are dependent upon the few have remained constant, even though now manifested in new ways. The new hierarchical structure in parts of the south is confined largely to peasants, with marginal landless laborers dependent upon the few Indians who became landowners through the workings of agrarian reform.[59]

Respectable Indianism laid down formulas which purportedly would enable urban elites to establish control over Indian collectives. In the early years, Bolivian land reform policies failed dismally to accomplish this goal. Where powerful syndicates appeared, the secretaries general operated as laws unto themselves, emerging as a new breed of caciques beyond the control of the government in La Paz. In many cases their independence was the result of their ability to play off the rival factions of MNR leadership. Independence was further abetted by the virtual destruction of the country's military institutions that followed upon the heels of the MNR triumph in 1952. In the absence of a centralizing power there came into being in some areas the sort of undisciplined sociopolitical relationships described in chapter 3 as amoral corporativism. In these areas the syndicates, dominated by local leaders, constituted corporative entities that were not subjected to the control devices of a moderating power. In other regions where strong syndicates did not appear the national government sought to establish control over the fee simple owners of minifundia plots by banding them together into cooperatives subject to bureaucratic manipulation from La Paz. The endeavor enjoyed little success, as the peasants proved extremely "resistant to any attempts to organize them into collective farm organizations and they jealously defended all the inequities in the size of their meager farm plots."[60] The result was a type of amoral agrarian individualism that coexisted with amoral corporativism.

Helping to account for the slow progress in cooperative organization was the indecisiveness of Paz Estenssoro, who was torn between the collectivist approach of respectable Indianism and the old concept of Westernizing the Indian. Although he recognized the undesirable consequences of tolerating unorganized, minifundista ex-*colonos* and spoke about the need to form cooperatives, he also stressed his desire not to embark upon forced collectivization of the farmers, "because we believe that the private interest of the peasant is a stimulus to productivity."[61]

All the while, shortages of personnel and funds impeded the establishment of agrarian control mechanisms. But, the most formidable obstacle resulted from the intensifying power struggle waged among the MNR factions. Rightist reformers, who remained the weakest of the MNR cliques between 1952 and 1960, urged an all-out effort to fit the agrarian sector, and urban sectors as well, into a carefully structured corporative apparatus under the control of a powerful moderating power. Leftists naturally objected to the rightist prescriptions and hoped that continuing chaos in the countryside would play into their hands. The centrist pragmatists in general favored neoliberal policies at odds with the rigid socioeconomic controls and interventionism associated with corporativism; but many of them, as the case of Paz Estenssoro illustrates, were themselves unresolved about the proper course of action.

Land reform as carried out between 1952 and 1960 at least served to ease peasant discontent, while at the same time slowing the influx of natives into urban centers. Thus, for the moment, the reform contributed to preserving the "eternal Indian" as an agrarian laborer. That this was a paramount purpose of the whole reform endeavor can be deduced from the fact that shortly after the MNR came to power the word Indian was officially eliminated from the Bolivian vocabulary. Henceforth the natives were to be called *campesinos*, the word which denotes peasants or agrarian laborers. This indicates the proper place of the Indian in the outlook of those who shaped Bolivia's social revolution.[62]

The Revolution and the Urban and Mining Sectors With land finally beginning to go to the Indians, the time seemed at hand for the MNR to have recourse to the second of the two panaceas suggested by Gustavo Adolfo Navarro in 1935: mines to the state. One of the early, and undoubtedly one of the most popular, acts of the MNR administration was the nationalization of the three major tin corporations controlled by the families that for years had been reviled by intellectuals as constituting the very core of the *Rosca*: the Patiños, the Aramayos, and the Hochschilds. In justifying nationalization, President Paz Estenssoro in late 1952 declared it would result in millions of dollars remaining each year in the hands of the government, and this would mean roads, schools, medical services for the poor, houses for workers, expansion of social security benefits, better vacations, and salary increases. Finally, nationalization would provide the funds required to implement land reform.[63]

Commenting upon the blow delivered against the *Rosca*, one of the MNR's most eminent intellectuals noted that so long as the great mines had remained in private hands they had constituted the most important means by which the masses were kept dependent upon the tin magnates.[64] While he did not explicitly make the point, it soon became apparent that through nationalization of the mines government hoped to render the workers grateful to it, beholden to it, and altogether dependent upon it. The Paz Estenssoro regime proceeded toward this objective by allowing featherbedding to reach prodigious proportions in the state-controlled Bolivian Mining Corporation or COMIBOL (*Corporación Minera de Bolivia*) and by conferring generous wages and lavish fringe benefits upon the workers. Through these expedients and by permitting the most important national labor union, the Bolivian Labor Confederation or COB (*Confederación*

Obrera Boliviana), to hold an influential position in governing circles Paz won support of union leadership and widespread approval among the rank and file.[65]

Revolution, it has been written, involves moral renewal; and economic success "is immaterial to revolution, while economic deprivations may well be essential to its success."[66] But the Bolivian revolution, as shaped by Paz Estenssoro, scrupulously avoided exhorting Bolivians to moral renewal (certainly the leaders never set an example of moral awakening), and economic success became the one means through which the administration wooed the masses. Understandably, a one-time enthusiast of the MNR could observe at the beginning of the 1960s: "We need an affirmative mysticism."[67]

In defense of his reliance on the bread-and-butter rewards of economism, Paz Estenssoro could present a rationale that, in theory, sounded persuasive. Bolivia, he averred, needed industrialization in order to overcome its problems of underdevelopment.[68] If Bolivia was to industrialize, the urban laborers must be given purchasing power; and this conviction accounts for the fact that to Paz, a trained economist of the Keynesian school, the generous salaries granted to workers made sense. Industrialization also required a rural populace with purchasing power, and this is one reason why the president was anxious to end the *colonato-pongueaje* system which had left agrarian laborers without wages.

Well aware of what was transpiring in Spain as that country entered upon its "economic miracle" in the 1950s, and influenced also by Peronism because of his extended stay in Argentina during his 1946–1952 exile, Paz perceived that the modern way to render the masses dependent was not to keep them totally without purchasing power. At the turn of the century, most elites throughout the Spanish-speaking world had believed that the spread of individual purchasing power among the proletariat would bring economic power and in its wake political influence, thereby setting loose forces of social leveling. In the 1950s, however, Spaniards and Argentine Peronists, and with them Paz Estenssoro, had come to see that money in the hands of the lower classes would not result in power, provided the masses were steered, by all the means of social engineering becoming available through expanding communications media, toward the habits of compulsive consumerism. If all their wages went into consumption, the masses would remain bereft of economic power and dependent upon a benevolent government for medical services, housing, education, retirement pensions, sickness and unemployment insurance, and a plethora of other fringe benefits coming to be equated with the good life.

To encourage the manufacturing without which the masses could never be kept dependent through consumerism, Paz Estenssoro's regime devised an incredible array of tax incentives and flexible exchange rates that facilitated importation of capital goods and impeded importation of manufactured products. As a result, industrial production by 1955 soared to a value of $57.7 million, far and away the highest peak in the country's history up to that time. The new industries, however, were colossally inefficient and their products monumentally expensive, in part because social security taxes collected from employers amounted by 1956 to 67.5 percent of wages paid. Owing to the scarcity and high cost of national manufactures, the urban and mining-sector lower classes, who were the major beneficiaries of a fairly extensive 1952–1956 income redistribution, found their newly awakened consumer appetites unappeased. These circumstances contributed to the worst inflationary spiral in the country's history. With a base of 100 calculated for 1951, the cost-of-living index had climbed by June of 1956 to 2,034.[69]

The attempt to increase the consuming potential of workers, especially of miners, had come at the worst possible time. Low world prices for Bolivian tin[70] combined with a decline in COMIBOL output resulted in a veritable collapse of the tin industry. Declining production was owing not just to COMIBOL's mismanagement and labor-pampering policies but also to depleted resources. The deterioration of the tin industry was a major factor accounting for a decline in the gross value of mining products from $137.8 million in 1952 to $60.2 million in 1960.[71] Far from providing a panacea, nationalization of the major tin mines had simply aroused false hopes that led the government to undertake economic programs doomed to failure.

By 1954 the FSB (*Falange Socialista Boliviana*), which had once criticized the MNR on the grounds of its alleged communist leanings, had begun to castigate the party for its adherence to the ruinous policies of individualistic capitalism.[72] During the mid-1950s, taking more and more to a Spanish-American, corporativist form of Christian Democracy that was beginning to attract followers in Chile, Ecuador, and elsewhere in the continent, the FSB grew as hostile to free enterprise capitalism as to Marxian communism. The rising crescendo of FSB criticism, and also its revolutionary plottings, led to increased repression at the hands of the MNR, culminating in the 1959 assassination of Falange leader Óscar Unzaga de Vega.[73] Repression failed to accomplish the desired results, and the strength of the opposition grew. Meantime, various Marxist intellectuals, still hopeful that the bourgeois-capitalist revolution spearheaded by the MNR might evolve into a dictatorship of the proletariat, directed mounting criticism against the government's economic bungling and corruption.[74] The Marxist wanted, after all, to inherit a viable economic structure, not one that was in shambles.

By 1956, however, the greatest difficulties for the MNR still came from within the party rather than from its political foes. In implementing its early policies, the MNR had conferred the major share of rewards on its laboring-class constituency, while bringing on an inflationary spiral that was ruinous to the majority of the middle sectors. For them, the price of winning the lower classes through economism had proved altogether too high. So far as they were concerned, populism—at least in so far as it rested on material rewards for the laboring masses—had to be curtailed or abandoned.[75]

Demanding that their interests be taken into account, the middle-sector constituency of the MNR found their leader in Hernán Siles Zuazo, elected to the presidency in 1956. The son of ex-president Hernando Siles (1926–1930), Siles Zuazo had played the leading role in the April 1952 revolution that installed the MNR in power. With the goading of the United States, which made continuation of aid dependent upon economic rationalization, Siles introduced a fairly tough anti-inflation program. Although he proved unable to reduce social security fringe benefits—perhaps he did not dare go that far— he did move to curtail featherbedding, to hold down salary increases, and to dismantle the program of flexible exchange controls and other inducements to local manufacturing. Part of the burden of the change fell on the small group of privileged industrialists, but its main brunt had to be borne by the urban and mining labor classes. The situation led to several serious confrontations between government and organized labor, and because of this Siles began, in 1957, to rebuild the country's regular army.[76]

The most important sociopolitical feature of the four-year tenure of Siles, who revealed a moral stature somewhat above that of his predecessor, was the emergence of a new Bolivian elite: the upper-echelon bureaucratic managers. Some Bolivians, in fact, began to complain that a new Rosca had replaced the old one. The complainers exaggerated, for in its heyday the old Rosca had exercised fairly effective control over the small number of politically aware and active Bolivians. The so-called new Rosca could claim little genuine control over the vastly expanded sectors of politicized Bolivians. By 1960 it had gained only the most tenuous authority over organized labor, and in some parts of the countryside its power was virtually nonexistent. The re-election in 1960 of Paz Estenssoro, with FSTMB leader Juan Lechín as his vice president, caused the bureaucratic elites to wonder if they could protect their interests and prevent a return to leftist populism. As of 1960 the Bolivian revolution remained uncompleted.[77] Government had not been able to establish control over the new forces set in motion since 1952; and considerable question remained as to just which of the MNR factions exercised the major influence over the government.

Bolivia's middle sectors on the whole hailed the policies of Siles Zuazo. Like the president, however, they recognized the lower-class discontent caused by the stabilization program and resorted to blaming its enactment solely on the insistence of the United States. This was largely a subterfuge, intended to disguise the extent to which middle-sector MNR leadership welcomed the switch in economic policy. Nevertheless, the ability of MNR centrists to blame an unpopular policy on the United States manifested the degree to which their revolution had actually become dependent upon North America for the capital input needed to stave off financial catastrophe and to pay the all-important social overhead bills.

Because of the close collaboration with the United States that Paz Estenssoro established from the early days of his first administration, and that Siles continued, the MNR deprived itself of the possibility to create a revolutionary mystique, of the type so useful in the formative years of the Mexican Revolution, that was based on anti-Yankeeism. In the cause of escaping dependence on the northern Colossus, workers—as the Mexican example proved—could be exhorted to assume burdens and sacrifices. But, as already pointed out, Paz Estenssoro was not interested in a revolutionary mystique that could be used to excite the workers with prospects of nonmaterial rewards. He was interested only in the material rewards of economism, and thus a large capital input from North America was essential to his purposes, and continued to be so for the purpose of Siles.

Many Bolivians and some North American leftist intellectuals criticize the United States for having diverted MNR leaders from their revolutionary ideals through the massive infusion of money. The truth is that men like Paz Estenssoro and most of the original founders of the party never entertained the sort of revolutionary ideas attributed by numerous observers to the MNR because of its highly vocal, late acquired, far left faction. For the type of revolution that Paz and his close collaborators had in mind, intimate ties with the United States were, from the very outset, imperative. To Navarro's two panaceas (land to the Indians, mines to the state) they added a third: dependency on the United States. Their initial success was assured because they found the U.S. government in a responsive mood.

The Revolution and the United States   When Milton Eisenhower arrived in La Paz in July of 1953 it was apparent that the revolutionary regime newly installed in power faced immediate problems of staggering proportions. Upon returning to Washington, Eisenhower urged, successfully, that massive economic aid be extended to bolster the modest program of technical assistance to Bolivia that had been in operation since 1942.[78] Thus was launched a program which by 1964 would result in the channeling of between $350 million and $400 million of U.S. assistance and loans into a country with a population that barely exceeded three million.[79]

By the time of Eisenhower's visit the State Department aversion of the early 1940s to the MNR because of its alleged fascist leanings had been forgotten. As a matter of fact, by the mid-1950s a bit of fascism in the MNR closet could be viewed in Washington as not an altogether bad thing, for it might guarantee that the party was sincerely resolved to combat communism. In any event, the president's brother and other U.S. officials accepted at face value Paz Estenssoro's assurances of his determination to crush communism. Already by the end of 1952, moreover, Paz had abandoned the anti-imperialist rhetoric formerly associated with the MNR as he stressed the importance of foreign investment in achieving development.[80]

In 1955 and 1956, U.S. taxpayers "were contributing nearly three times as much to Bolivian government revenues as the Bolivian taxpayers," and without this aid Paz Estenssoro conceded the revolutionary government could not have survived.[81] But, owing to Bolivia's rampant inflation and fiscal mismanagement, it appeared to the U.S. under secretary of the treasury by 1956 that aid was going "down the drain."[82] This appraisal, widespread in Washington, led to pressure on the La Paz government, as already mentioned, to initiate a stabilization program. Once the measures recommended to combat inflation had been accepted by the Siles regime, the flow of U.S. aid and assistance rose to new levels. Moreover, the purpose of aid was no longer just to save the MNR from the emergencies that had threatened to do it in during the first years of rule. By 1957 Washington planners

292

had glimpsed the usefulness of financing social services as a tactic in waging the cold war. Bolivia, it was hoped, might become a showplace to demonstrate the effectiveness of U.S. assistance in easing social problems, thereby eliminating the material privation that purportedly contributed to communist takeovers. The small republic seemed ideally suited to become such a showplace because MNR leaders were just as convinced as U.S. officials that economism was the key to turning the lower classes away from communism.

Of the total assistance channeled into Bolivia by 1961, perhaps no more than one-third went into capital investment of the type that "could conceivably have been helpful to economic development."[83] The balance went into social projects (health and sanitation, education, labor affairs, and the like) and into budgetary support that enabled the government to cover its public sector deficit. In 1957, the high-water mark, "32.0% of Bolivian treasury revenue came from USAID."[84] A good part of the budgetary deficit covered by U.S. funds resulted from the featherbedding-fringe benefits policies relied upon by the La Paz administration to win labor approval. When the program of extensive U.S. aid to the MNR first got underway, a party stalwart hailed the arrangement because it meant the government could avoid the political risk of "obliging the workers to produce intensively."[85] He was not disappointed in his expectations.

Many valid criticisms have been brought against U.S. assistance to Bolivia—among them the charges that this assistance rendered Bolivians complacent and unwilling to take heroic measures on their own and that it was used to provide leverage in persuading the La Paz government to denationalize petroleum holdings on terms excessively favorable to private North American firms.[86] Nevertheless, the infusion of U.S. funds helped ease Bolivia's transition from control by one oligarchy, the tin producers, whose days were numbered even without the 1952 revolution due to declining resources, to control by a new oligarchy. Social suffering, including starvation, as well as violence and bloodletting, might have been far greater had it not been for U.S. economic assistance—even admitting that such humanitarian considerations were not primarily responsible for that assistance. Whether greater suffering and violence might in the long run have had a purifying effect, resulting in the emergence of an administration more selflessly devoted to the common good, is anybody's guess.

The new rulers of Bolivia understood the need to use more modern methods in establishing their legitimacy. On the whole, however, they proved to be no more honest, no more sincerely concerned with problems of the masses, no more willing to sacrifice personal gains in the interest of overall development than the old oligarchy. Thus U.S. aid never achieved optimum efficiency in contributing either to social justice or national development. The fault herein lies less in the aid program, and the incompetence with which North Americans often administered it, than in Bolivia's internal situation—and perhaps, ultimately, in the weakness of human nature.

THE OLD ORDER IN PERU

Having weathered the storms of the *oncenio* when Leguía favored the interests of a new bourgeoisie and having survived the scare of APRA's early radicalism, Peru's traditional upper classes emerged from the World War II period with their power intact. In the ensuing fifteen years they seemed, if anything, to enhance that power. Their ability to do so depended in no small part on the continuing diversification and high earning power of the export economy. In 1950 the total value of the ten major exports stood at $146.6 million, and the six leading export commodities, in order of their importance, were cotton, sugar, petroleum, lead, zinc, and copper. Ten years later the combined value of the ten major exports registered $376.9 million, and the six leading commodities, again in order of importance, were copper, cotton, fishery products, sugar, iron ore, and lead.[87] Unlike many Latin American countries, Peru's economy did not depend on one or two products, and when production or international prices for one commodity slipped, part of the economic slack was generally taken up by others. Beginning in the mid-1950s the economic situation worsened, but the consequences were less severe than in many South American countries.

Postwar prosperity enabled the Peruvian oligarchy, representing banking, landownershp, mining, and commerce that rested on the export of a wide variety of goods, to provide opportunities to middle sectors that were adequate to secure their support of the established order. The oligarchy's political shrewdness in understanding the importance of middle-sector co-optation was demonstrated in 1945 when many of its leading figures arranged and supported the presidential candidacy of José Luis Bustamante y Rivero. A man of middle-class background, Bustamante was a spokesman for Catholic social justice, in line with which he demanded curtailment of economic privileges enjoyed by the wealthiest classes and greater attentiveness to the social obligations of propriety. A few well-to-do Peruvians, frightened by the oratory of the new president and by his sincerity and integrity, began to deposit their capital in foreign banks. The majority of affluent citizens, however, believed that Bustamante's political ineffectiveness combined with the control exercised in congress by Apristas, whose old-line leaders now included some of the most uncompromising defenders of liberal capitalism in all Peru, guaranteed their security. This appraisal proved correct. If the oligarchy had little to fear in the social or economic sphere, political tensions did become an unanticipated source of concern.

Altogether confident that they would elect Haya de la Torre in the next presidential election, Apristas acted as if they were already in power. When it became clear that Bustamante would pursue an independent policy, they embarked upon programs of harassment and uncompromising opposition.[88] The political climate became tense and as angry congressional debates over whether to grant a new exploratory concession to the International Petroleum Company (IPC) ran their course, Francisco Graña Garland, an important newspaper figure who opposed the concession, was assassinated by a member of the APRA, which had now become the IPC's voluble defender. This was in January of 1947, and from that time on the political situation only worsened. Finally in October of 1948 a group of young Aprista leftists, disgruntled by the rightward drift of Haya de la Torre and the party's high command, gained the support of junior military officers and staged an uprising against Bustamante's government.[89] The rebellion, which may have taken Haya and his close associates by surprise, was suppressed by the armed forces which, on the whole, followed the directives of the senior officers. Enraged by the manner in which Apristas had sowed divisiveness within the military and eroded discipline, and justifying their move on the grounds that Bustamante was not prepared to take the harsh measures needed to repress the APRA, Peru's senior officers staged their own *golpe* and, with the blessings of the oligarchy whose members avidly desired a return to political stability, installed Brigadier General Manuel A. Odría in power. Thus began an eight-year military dictatorship known as the *ochenio*.

Forced to spend more than half of the *ochenio* within the Colombian embassy in Lima, because the military petulantly refused to grant a safe conduct, Haya de la Torre smuggled out reports to friends in the United States alleging that Odría was permitting widespread communist infiltration.[90] While Odría did replace some Aprista labor leaders with Communists, who at this time were pursing a cautious, nonrevolutionary policy throughout Latin America, Haya's charges were wildly exaggerated. Obviously he hoped that in the cold war setting he could encourage U.S. intervention in his behalf by branding the incumbent regime as soft on communism. The tactic did not work, for by his friendly attitudes toward U.S. capital Odría won the enthusiastic approval not only of the North American business community but of many State Department officials as well.[91]

Although he moved systematically to crush any semblance of independence in organized labor, the military president also sought energetically, and fairly effectively, to woo labor. While in power he decreed seven blanket wage increases and was even more generous in augmenting fringe benefits.[92] Odría's labor policy has been described as "in an elephantine manner, paternalistic." Using government power "to make employers deliver his presents to the workers," he managed to leave power "with many people convinced that he had done more for the worker than anyone in the history of Peru."[93] Aiding the general in his attempt to become labor's father figure was his able wife María Delgado de Odría, who headed a charitable foundation that cared for the poor. When Latin American women enter politics, it has been observed, they tend to do so as a projection of their home function as mothers. Rather than becoming active competitors, they assume roles of "supermadres," ministering to the needs of poor, heedless men.[94] In this they are acting in accordance with the values of the cult of the Virgin or Marianism, in line with which moral superiority is ascribed to women.

With the financial demands of the social services sector soaring because of a vast expansion of social security coverage, and with education expenses mounting because of the 1,500 new public primary schools constructed during the *ochenio*, Odría found himself in a bind when international prices for primary goods began to decline in 1955 and 1956. He hoped to save himself through a huge new concession to IPC and other foreign oil firms. But the Sechura desert on the northern coast where the firms conducted exploratory drilling "proved to be a barren wasteland for oil."[95] Awareness of the increasing difficulties he would face in paying the bills of economism probably influenced Odría's decision not to extend the *ochenio*. The elections which he permitted in 1956 resulted in the re-election of Manuel Prado. Although it could hardly have been apparent at the time he left office, Odría was the last practitioner—at least for the next twenty years, which is as far as coverage of this book extends—of the old-style militarism in which the officers used their power to protect the interests of the political establishment.

Prado's second term is customarily described as the period of Convivencia: living together in harmony. It was marked by collaboration between the relegalized APRA or PAP and the upper classes. Chastened by their repression at the hands of Odría and willing to bide their time until the next elections, Apristas did not harass Prado as they had Bustamante. The president reciprocated by allowing Apristas to return to high labor positions. If political problems appeared to be easing, the economic situation grew less stable and became the principle source of concern to Prado.

From Odría, Prado inherited a badly mismanaged economy, a virtually empty treasury, and an unrealistic commitment to the continuation of vast public works projects and to the expansion of the bureaucracy and the increase of their salaries. Also, Peru's terms of trade had worsened appreciably in the years preceding the Convivencia. While export tonnage had tripled between 1950 and 1955, the value of exports had risen by less than 70 percent. Meantime, the volume of imports had doubled, but the value increased at an even greater rate, rising from $186 million to over $400 million.[96]

When the Eisenhower administration in 1958 proposed quotas that would reduce Peru's exports of lead and zinc to the United States by 20 percent, Prado talked about selling the commodities to the Soviet Union. Washington promptly agreed not to curtail purchases. But Prado continued to be wary of the United States and explored with French President Charles de Gaulle, much to the latter's delight, the possibility of establishing closer economic and cultural ties between Latin America and a united Europe.[97]

Perhaps because the economy was tighter than it had been in the early postwar period, the oligarchy became somewhat less generous in sharing power and opportunities with the middle sectors. An indication of this is provided by the fact that during the twentieth century the proportion of high political offices held by members of Lima's exclusive and aristocratic Club Nacional progressively declined, "except during the Prado administration when this trend was temporarily reversed."[98] Not finding a secure haven during the years of the Convivencia, some middle sectors began to form new political parties, the most important being Popular Action or AP (Acción Popular) headed by Fernando Belaúnde Terry.

Despite economic problems and signs of middle-sector discontent, the traditional ruling classes perceived no immediate challenge to their status as Prado approached the end of his term in 1962. In fact, an upswing in the U.S. economy and the prospects of the newly launched Alliance for Progress led them to hope for improving commodity prices and for a massive inpouring of U.S. public funds through which they might strengthen their position.

In Ecuador, where bananas had by the early 1950s provided a new national resource, it also seemed likely that the old order could continue to muddle through, a process in which—as we are about to see —politicians had proved reasonably adept since the end of World War II. While there was no basic threat to the established order, political predictability remained lower than in Peru between 1945 and 1960, for Velasco Ibarra hovered constantly over the scene. The shadow he cast seemed often to grow when he was out of the presidential office and even out of the country altogether in the course of his several protracted exiles. In the postwar era whenever conditions deteriorated beyond a tolerable point it was safe to assume that Velasco Iabarra would be either overthrown or called back to office, depending on whether he happened to be in or out of power when the crisis broke. Such was the extent of his political dominance that Ecuadorans contented themselves with alternately calling upon him as a savior or banishing him as a diabolical spirit, all the while neglecting to turn their attention to the basic problems that underlay personalistic politics.

THE ESTABLISHED ORDER AND THE POLITICAL KALEIDOSCOPE IN ECUADOR

For 1950 the combined total value of Ecuador's major exports registered $55.2 million, with coffee in first place followed by cacao and bananas. The following year bananas had edged into first place, maintaining that position into the early 1970s. By 1960 the aggregate value of leading exports stood at $136.5 million, with bananas accounting for about two-thirds of this total, followed by coffee and cacao. Since 1953 Ecuador had been the leading exporter of bananas in all Latin America, and by 1960 it produced over one-quarter of the world's banana exports—the figure rose to its all-time peak of 31 percent in 1964 before beginning gradually to drop back.[99] Prior to the beginning of the banana boom, however, Ecuador struggled through difficult days.

In 1944, it will be recalled, the followers of Velasco Ibarra toppled the unpopular Arroyo del Río, blamed for the loss of national territory to Peru, and installed their leader in power for the second time. The coalition responsible for the *golpe* included both rightists and leftists. At first Velasco Ibarra turned for support to Liberals, Socialists, and even Communists as he meted out vengeance to Arroyo partisans, baited bankers and businessmen, and courted labor and students. Then, once the right understood who was master, the president turned against the left, having discovered, so he said, a Bolshevist menace. The discovery may have been inspired, to some degree, by the desire to assume a cold war stance pleasing to Washington in anticipation of generous rewards. Basically, though, it came about because of his need for an excuse to justify assumption of dictatorial powers. A 1945 leftist-oriented constitution was replaced one year later with a conservative instrument, and from late 1945 until his overthrow in mid-1947, Velasco Ibarra persecuted labor and students and the political factions he had previously favored. As he veered rightward, the president sought the support of Conservatives by facilitating the establishment of the Catholic Pontifical University of Quito and encouraging the general expansion of church influence in primary and secondary education.[100] From this time on some clergymen began to say that the church owed more to Velasco Ibarra than to García Moreno.[101]

The president's shifting and juggling did not bring stability. His three years of rule witnessed three attempted insurrections and were marked by "permanent public convulsion, political instability, and systematic destruction of the institutions and ethics of government."[102] These pre-banana-boom years also produced a sustained assault on the national treasury so that associates might be rewarded, as well as a proliferation of the bureaucracy, accompanied by forced loans levied on political foes so that the emoluments of partisans might be increased.

A military *golpe* toppled Velasco Ibarra in August of 1947, and in the ensuing fifty-three weeks three different men exercised presidential powers[103] before Galo Plaza Lasso, who narrowly defeated a Conservative candidate in the 1948 election, was installed in the chief executive's office. The son of former Liberal president Leonidas Plaza Gutiérrez (1901–1905, 1912–1916), Galo Plaza was born in New York (1907), eventually studied at the Universities of California and Maryland as well as Georgetown University, and served as his country's ambassador to the United States, 1944–1946 (some twenty years after becoming Ecuador's president he was elected secretary general of the Organization of American States, completing his term in 1975). His close ties with North America rendered him vulnerable to charges by Velasco Ibarra and other demogogic opponents of being the lackey of U.S. imperialism.[104]

In 1949, the year after Galo Plaza came to power, Ecuador suffered one of the worst series of earthquakes and landslides in its modern history. The following year brought the affliction of massive floods. Over 6,000 persons died and 100,000 were left homeless by the disasters that buffeted the *altiplano*, especially in the regions to the south of Quito, wreaking devastation in an area of some 4,000 square kilometers. The president's exalted leadership in the tasks of reconstruction evoked widespread popular support and helped enable him to become the first executive since José Luis Tamayo (1920–1924) to serve out his term and turn office over to his constitutionally elected successor. This accomplishment was facilitated, as Galo Plaza is the first to admit, by the economic boost that banana exports began to provide.[105] It was also facilitated by his political conduct. Throughout his term Galo Plaza remained calm and serene in the face of the bitter attacks unleashed against him, especially by the Concentration of Popular Forces or CFP (*Concentración de Fuerzas Populares*), a leftist group that preached war against the oligarchy and their imperialist masters. Founded by Carlos Guevara Moreno in 1947, the CFP gained considerable following among the coastal laboring classes and in its formative period generally supported Velasquism.

Triumphant in the 1952 election, Velasco Ibarra in his inaugural address delivered a scathing denunciation of virtually every aspect of his predecessor's administration. Yet his own performance in office made Galo Plaza's loom increasingly as a kind of high plateau in Ecuador's recent political history. Throughout his 1952–1956 term—which he managed to complete, aided by banana income—Velasco Ibarra continued to resort to his customary inflamatory, indeed vulgar and sometimes indecent and profane, denunciations of his enemies, the list of which was likely to change on a monthly basis. Furthermore, he ruled with his usual political zig-zagging and indifference to fiscal responsibility. Nevertheless in his third presidential tenure Velasco also enlarged upon two positive contributions he had already made to his country. By strengthening his following among the coastal populace, the *quiteño* president demonstrated that regional differences were not irreconcilable. With ample justification, an authority writes: "Velasco has come closer than any other leader in bridging the gap between the two regions [coast and *altiplano*]."[106] Moreover, the president continued to reiterate his message, and actually to act in accordance with it, that the old doctrinal, church-state, Conservative-Liberal issues must be forever laid to rest.[107] His position on these issued helped to calm tensions, to the point of allowing Camilo Ponce Enríquez, a Conservative although the political organization he founded in 1951 bore the name Social Christian Movement, to attract some Liberal support and to gain election to the presidency, by a bare 3,000 votes, in 1956. Velasco Ibarra's contributions to bringing the two traditionally warrying regions of Ecuador somewhat closer together and to rendering irrelevent the old disputes between the disciples of García Moreno and Alfaro may just possibly outweigh the negative aspects of his long-lingering influence on Ecuadoran politics.

Appointing Liberals as well as Conservatives to his cabinet, Ponce Enríquez governed with moderation and statesmanship and with far more probity in the handling of national funds than his immediate predecessor. But he was never able to kindle any real enthusiasm among the populace or to move toward realization of the Christian social reforms about which he spoke vaguely. During his presidency the country's economy suffered from the fall of banana, coffee, and cacao export prices. To lead them out of their difficulties the people turned once more in 1960 to Velasco Ibarra, electing him "this time with the greatest popular mandate of the century."[108]

In the 1950s the Ecuadoran Nationalist Revolutionary Action or ARNE (*Acción Revolucionaria Nacionalista Ecuatoriana*), founded in 1942, had virtually no political following and was split for a time between two rival leaders, Jorge Luna Yepes and Jorge Crespo Toral. Still, it was the ARNE that proclaimed the sort of political-social ideology destined to exercise the major impact throughout Andean America in the late 1960s as social and economic conditions deteriorated to such a point that muddling through ceased to be a tenable approach.

In line with a traditional Catholic position, and reflecting also the stance of the early APRA and MNR (and also of Argentina's Peronism in the 1940s as well as of Spain's Falange in the 1930s and 1940s), ARNE condemned both communism and capitalism.[109] It urged the corporative structuring of society, so that all persons could acquire a sense of participation in their appropriate functional associations, whose activities were in turn to be coordinated by a technocratic elite that exercised a moderating power.[110] According to ARNE, the state must assume an expanding paternalistic role in resolving social problems, and this required massive capital formation that could only be accomplished through rapid economic growth. This growth was to be achieved by a national bourgeoisie, but a bourgeoisie that was disciplined and directed by the central government. While certain middle sectors, located between the masses and the technocratic elite, would be permitted to practice capitalism, the laboring classes would be protected against the purportedly wasteful, disruptive effects of individualistic competition by means of the security guaranteed by the state. In some instances, moreover, workers were to be allowed to share in the ownership of private industry.[111] In resolving disputes between management and labor, and also in exhorting workers to appreciate the values of nonmaterial rewards, church and state were to function in harmony.[112]

In the 1960s, the neoliberal U.S. approach to the hemisphere's socioeconomic problems failed to deliver on the lavish promises held forth by the Alliance for Progress. Increasingly, intellectuals in Andean America decided they liked neither of the two ways of life pitted against each other in the cold war. All the while the mounting problems of the old order in Peru and Ecuador—and of the new but in many ways still quite old order in Bolivia—portended the collapse of political control mechanisms. Under these circumstances, ARNE and ARNE-like ideologies—including those of the MNR's corporativist-rightist faction and of the Bolivian FSB—found an increasingly propitious climate. As Andean Americans moved away from the liberalism that had enjoyed a new vogue after World War II they resumed the search, seriously begun in the 1920s and 1930s when many of the ideas propounded by the ARNE had first begun to circulate widely, for their own political identity.

11

The Alliance for Progress and Andean Transitions, 1961–1968

Periodically, the United States passes through alternating cycles of trying to make the world safe for its type of democracy and of endeavoring to make its type of democracy safe from the world. It alternates, that is, between periods of defending its liberal institutions and political culture by trying to propagate them in foreign lands and of rejecting crusades for liberalism in order to remain liberal at home. Which cycle prevails at any given time is determined not only by the ebb and surge of North American faith in liberalism but also by the way in which the outside world impinges upon the United States.

As the 1960s began North American confidence in liberalism ran at flood tide. The economy had met the threat of recession and renewed growth seemed at hand; the paranoid domestic fears about the spread of alien beliefs that had contributed to McCarthyism had been largely laid to rest, and communism had been contained in Europe. Fear of communist expansion remained, but it was coming to be focused on Latin America.

In 1960 the Corporation for Economic and Industrial Research warned that the Soviet Union was trying to neutralize Latin America in the worldwide power struggle. It was time, the Corporation asserted, for the United States to shift its foreign policy so as to place major emphasis on Latin America.[1] This advice took on urgency as Communists strengthened their beachhead in Cuba and as the United States failed to dislodge them in the 1961 Bay of Pigs invasion. John F. Kennedy, the vigorous young president who took office at the beginning of 1961, had much of the public behind him in his conviction that the decisive stages of a world struggle were at hand and

303

that Armageddon spread all the way from Southeast Asia and Africa to the Cuban beaches and the Andean mountains.

To mobilize free-world forces for the encounter in Latin America, the Alliance for Progress was unveiled in March of 1961 and defined in greater detail through the Charter of Punta del Este (Uruguay), signed the following August, that built upon the principles contained in the 1960 Act of Bogotá. The charter called for a vast cooperative program in the Americas to raise standards of health, housing, and education (goals that appealed particularly to Latin Americans, as they were to be pursued in part through the use of U.S. funds) and to improve tax collection processes and achieve better income and land distribution (goals that appealed especially to U.S. officials, even though they seemed unable or unwilling to achieve better domestic income distribution). To help meet Alliance objectives, the United States pledged $11 billion over the course of ten years, two-thirds to be provided by public funds, one-third by private investment. The bulk of loan and assistance funds received under the auspices of the Washington government was to be spent in the United States for the purchase of goods and services.[2]

In the early 1960s, U.S. leadership seemed more convinced than ever before that the lack of self-reliance, individual freedom, and the spirit of competition was the basic cause of poverty, that happiness was the fruit of prosperity, and that only relatively happy people could resist communism. Leaders were ready to apply within the United States a few finishing touches to the prevailing system so that the poorest sectors might gain somewhat more money at least in absolute terms—even if they did not necessarily gain a larger share of overall national wealth. Toward this end intellectuals, often recruited from the universities, formulated plans, to be implemented largely by youthful cadres engaged in overhauling bureaucracies, in community development and voter registration projects, to raise the consciousness of the poor, especially of blacks and other minority groups, so that they might attain to the degree of individualistic competitiveness that would allow them to wax more prosperous and therefore more content. The domestic approach was speedily projected into the shaping of hemisphere policy and consciousness raising among the underprivileged masses of Latin America became an Alliance for Progress goal. Toward this end community development programs, to be launched through USAID (United States Agency for International Development) personnel and through the Peace Corps, were devised. Toward this goal, moreover, the efforts of the AFL-CIO were enlisted. North American labor leaders were to teach their Latin American counterparts how to abandon clientelist dependence on paternalistic governments and to acquire the competitive aggressivenes on which the collective bargaining system, and indeed liberalism's whole theory of interest-group pluralism, rested.[3]

If the Latin American masses were transformed into individualistic capitalists they would not only become good democrats and reliable anticommunists; they would also become purchasers of U.S. goods. Beyond doubt, this was an important consideration that entered into Alliance planning. The desire to increase the number of local purchasers for goods manufactured in the southern republics by the growing number of U.S. subsidiary firms contributed to Washington's encouragement of Latin American economic integration so as to reduce tariff and other barriers that had previously limited the market for goods to the one country in which they were produced. Beyond this the desire to spread purchasing power led to the assault unleashed by the Alliance for Progress against the planter aristocracy, an assault that was particularly evident in Andean America where it contributed to pronounced anti-U.S. sentiments among Peruvian and Ecuadoran *hacendados* and their urban, upper-class allies.

Barrington Moore has brilliantly described the endeavors of Thaddeus Stevens and other northern Radicals in the post-Civil War Reconstruction period to bring "40 acres and a mule" to the South's previously dispossessed agrarian labor force. He depicts the Radicals' efforts as intended to destroy the planter classes so as to serve the interests of certain sectors of northern industrial capitalism.[4] The same motivation helps explain the enthusiasm with which the Alliance for Progress took up the cause of land reform in Andean America, and in the case of Bolivia prodded the national government to proceed far more rapidly in that direction than it had ventured up until that time. The objective was to end a semifeudal agricultural system that had through the decades and centuries left the vast majority of the agrarian labor force without purchasing power or capitalist incentives.

While confidently awaiting the long-term effects of sowing capitalism in order to guarantee an enduring triumph over communism, the U.S. government in the 1960s took all possible short-term and immediate steps to suppress the enemy and those assumed to be the dupes of the enemy. In Ecuador, for example, the CIA spent lavishly on political contests and on propaganda programs calculated to lead the country to sever relations with Cuba.[5] Its efforts, in which as elsewhere in Latin America it sometimes used the AFL-CIO American Institute for Free Labor Development as a front, extended even to assisting the election of anti-Castro candidates to student government positions. Thus U.S. money and attention channeled through the CIA became a significant factor in the politics of Ecuador[6] and of Peru and Bolivia as well.

In Bolivia, U.S. diplomacy successfully directed its efforts toward persuading the government to strengthen the armed forces, and then moved energetically to facilitate increased Pentagon influence over those forces. The policy seemed to pay off handsomely when U.S.-trained forces managed in 1967 to wipe out the guerrilla movement through which Ché Guevara had hoped to turn Bolivia into another Vietnam.

In still another way the United States resorted to direct and immediate measures to serve its interests during the Alliance for Progress era. Under Kennedy, and possibly even more so under Lyndon B. Johnson who succeeded the assassinated president in November of 1963, the government insisted on a friendly climate for U.S. investors. To at least some degree this insistence grew out of the conviction that only if their short-term interests and profit-making possibilities were protected could U.S. businessmen accomplish the long-term task of fostering the creation of a robust free enterprise system which would in turn lead to democracy and seal the doom of communism.

It should be clear, then, that the Alliance's probusiness policy—at least in the pre-Johnson days—is not attributable solely to an interest in augmenting the profit-making potential of U.S. capitalists. Even as Theodore Roosevelt, so also John Kennedy showed a certain disdain for the business community and a desire to use, and whenever necessary to discipline, that community so as to serve what were perceived as loftier national goals, involving in the case of Kennedy the defeat of international communism. Business had a role to play in inflicting that defeat, but the ultimate design for victory had to be shaped by intellectuals and implemented by youthful elites who supposedly could be counted on to serve a higher cause than mammon's.

Andean Americans could sympathize with a program to be devised by intellectuals and carried out by youthful elites. This seemed more in keeping with their tradition than that of the United States, a fact that may help account for the initial popularity of President Kennedy and the high hopes generated by the Alliance for Progress. But the admiration and hopes were short lived, at least in most quarters. Soon the Andeans, and Latin Americans in general, were alienated by the underlying Alliance assumption that only the U.S. system could contain communism and lead to attainment of the good life.

When it came to containing communism and attaining the good life, there was no significant distinction between the approach of the Democratic officials who planned and implemented the Alliance for Progress and that of John Foster Dulles. As mentioned, Dulles had noted that the Communists believed individual freedom was a basic cause of human unrest; therefore, by taking it away they hoped to promote peace and security. It followed in the Dulles view, and in that of the Kennedy administration as well, that the way to combat communism was to maximize individual liberty and freedom throughout the world. This conclusion emerged from the belief that the United States, precisely because of its widespread enjoyment of individual freedom, presented the most hostile climate possible for communism. Other areas of the world could likewise be immunized against the communist infection if their leaders could be persuaded to emulate U.S. political, social, and economic models.

Increasingly, Andean Americans found insulting this assumption that only U.S. leaders understood how to combat communism by creating the sort of society that satisfied basic human needs and aspirations. Increasingly, they rejected the simplistic assessments emanating from Washington that pictured the fate of their countries in terms of either liberal democracy resting on free enterprise capitalism or dictatorial, totalitarian communism. Andean America's ruling classes and its aspiring elites hoped, by and large, to minimize the risk of communism and other movements of radical change by keeping the masses without individual freedom and by perpetuating their dependence upon a benevolent state.

The conflict between two differing concepts of development that had dimly appeared in 1938, when Good Neighbor policy planners first glimpsed the possibilities of stimulating development in the southern republics through commitment of public funds, had by the early 1960s assumed center stage prominence. If Washington continued to make a nuisance of itself by insisting on its approach to development and containment of communism, then the traditional economic relationship, in which the ruling classes had accepted dependence on the United States in order to help them preserve the internal dependence of the masses, would have to be reconsidered.

Many other factors, in addition to basic disagreement between North and South America over development goals, contributed to the failure of the Alliance for Progress. Among Alliance planners and their constituent bureaucracies tensions were generated by disagreement over the priority and even the nature of objectives.[7] Transcending these and all other difficulties was the fact that failure was virtually preordained because of an underlying assumption on which the Alliance was founded. This assumption was that the United States possessed sufficient economic resources and also adequate expertise to solve social problems and to build nations in Latin America according to the blueprints of U.S. society.

By 1966, in the light of Vietnam commitments, international trade difficulties, and internal problems, including urban riots, it was becoming clear that the United States did not have adequate funds either to make substantial improvements in Latin America's social conditions or to carry out nation-building projects. Visiting La Paz in 1966, Senator Allen Ellender explained that the United States would have to limit economic assistance to Bolivia, and other underdeveloped countries as well, because of its own balance-of-payments problems. Bolivia's president responded to this news by a pronouncement, published on the front page of the leading La Paz daily: "We have to stop believing that we can live forever from foreign aid . . . The approach [has] . . . passed which accustomed us to throw stones at the American Embassy and say, 'There is communism here and if you do not help, Bolivia will go under.' "[8]

By 1968, moreover, U.S. officials were coming to see that an outlay of $11 billion in ten years would scarcely make a dent on the problems of two or three of their own major cities. And the confidence that experts possessed the know-how required to solve these problems, even assuming they were given virtually unlimited funds, had been shattered. All the while the end of innocence was hastened by the fact that intellectuals and youthful, ostensibly idealistic elites, who had been counted on to solve Latin American problems by applying U.S. formulas, were coming to question the acceptability of those formulas even within the national boundaries.

As of 1968 the North Americanization of Latin America had been abandoned as an unattainable objective. What is more, members of the New Left, audible and visible beyond all proportions to their small numbers, sounded more and more like Andean ideologues as they stressed the values of humanism and denounced capitalism and the oligarchy, as they developed programs calling for new elites to lead the transition to Utopia, and as they deemphasized science and rationality as the source of knowledge and wisdom. The Latin Americanization of the United States suddenly became a possibility that terrified establishment figures—all the more so when the cult of Ché Guevara swelled to astonishing proportions after his death in Bolivia. This possibility counseled a shift in the focus of surveillance from Bolivia and Ecuador and their sister republics to the home front. As Johnson completed his last year in the office, his hopes for another term shattered by rising opposition to the Vietnam conflict, and as Richard Nixon began his first term in January of 1969, the question was no longer one of spreading liberalism abroad but of finding the means to protect the ostensibly liberal establishment at home. The country that witnessed the transfer of power to Nixon was scarcely the same one that had responded just eight years earlier to President Kennedy's inaugural address with its mixture of naiveté and arrogance, idealism and hard-nosed concern for realpolitic, and above all with its confidence that America was about to get on with its mission of growth and development.

Change was also taking place within the three Andean republics under consideration. While this change was basically the result of internal circumstances, its pace and intensity were seriously affected by the transformation underway in the United States. Bolivia, which had already passed through its timid and uncompleted version of a social revolution, muddled through within the parameters established by that revolution and few basic departures from 1952–1960 patterns were discernible as 1968 came to an end. However, for Ecuador and even more so for Peru, where pressures for revolutionary change had heretofore been contained, the disintegration of the old order seemed to reach such desperate proportions between 1961 and 1968 that muddling through would no longer suffice. In 1968 perturbed Ecuadorans turned for the last time to Velasco Ibarra to lead them to salvation—even though his 1960–1961 presidential tenure had only added to the country's problems and confusion. But Peruvians under the command of the military took more substantial and imaginative measures as they sought to forge a viable social order out of the one that was collapsing.

BOLIVIA AND THE ATTEMPT TO IMPOSE ORDER, 1960–1968

Installed in power for a second term in 1960, Paz Estenssoro followed with avid interest events that led to the birth of the Alliance for Progress the following year. Anticipated windfalls from the Alliance, in fact, soon produced a mood of euphoria among Bolivian officials.[9] On its part, the Kennedy administration hoped that the careful planning and supervision of expenditures on which allotment of Alliance funds was theoretically to depend would at last bring order out of Bolivia's economic turmoil and cause that country to emerge as a showcase of what U.S. aid might accomplish.

The two governments approached each other cautiously as they bargained over the amount of loans and aid. Washington wanted the amount to be determined not just by responsible planning but also by the degree of Bolivia's resolve to combat communism—as manifested by its support for ousting Cuba from the Organization of American States and severing diplomatic and commercial relations with the Castro government. On the other hand, Paz Estenssoro insisted the communist menace to his government was so enormous that he could not join in the U.S.-inspired boycott of Cuba until his administration had been strengthened and the country's more pressing social and economic problems had been mitigated through a new infusion of North American funds.[10] On the whole, Bolivia gained the edge in the economic haggling. Largely because of Paz Estenssoro's mastery in brandishing the communist menace, U.S. commitments for aid stood by 1962 at double the figure for 1960; and foreign funds financed 75 percent of Bolivia's capital formation in 1963, up from 35.4 percent in 1960.[11]

When Bolivia lined up in support of Kennedy in the September 1963 Cuban missile confrontation with Khrushchev—under threat that otherwise the State Department would support Chile in a boundary dispute that had recently flared—Paz Estenssoro was rewarded with an invitation to visit Washington. In the agreements signed in that city in October, the Kennedy administration promised to take steps to prevent a serious decline in prices of Bolivian exports, while Paz Estenssoro was pressured into acknowledging that the shortage of U.S. funds would force Bolivia to rely more on internal capital formation and on attracting private funds from abroad. Here was an ominous sign of trouble ahead, for until this time Paz's ability to remain in office had depended to a very great extent on Washington's supply of public funds.

By this time opponents both within and outside of the MNR were stepping up their criticism of the regime. Their favorite charge was that Paz Estenssoro because of his dependence on Washington had sold out the national interests. Leftists railed against the fact that North American private investment in Bolivia's petroleum had risen to $117.7 million by the end of 1963[12] and accused the Paz government of forgetting Bolivians "in order better to serve the interests of Yankee imperialism."[13] But the most persuasive criticism came from the moderate Augusto Céspedes, at one time an enthusiastic backer of Paz Estenssoro. According to this eminent man of letters, the type of development that his country had undergone since 1952, and especially during the second Paz term, benefitted primarily the U.S. bourgeoisie which was increasing its share of control over manufacturing in Bolivia. Therefore foreigners were deriving a large share of the profits created by the notable rise in manufacturing output in the early 1960s. This development, Céspedes argued, tended to confine the activities of the national bourgeoisie to trade and commerce.[14]

Even if charges of selling out to U.S. interests had never been raised against him, Paz Estenssoro faced more than enough internal problems to weaken his hold on power. More than fifty public entities, including the national development corporation and the state petroleum enterprise and tin corporation as well as several insurance banks, enjoyed varying degrees of autonomy, and the national government was virtually powerless to control their uses of funds.[15] Contributing further to a breakdown in central control was the continuing power of labor syndicates. Fernando Diez de Medina, a one-time MNR stalwart, complained in 1962 that "present-day government is two-headed. The MNR commands, and the syndicates command. They are in perpetual combat." In consequence, improvisation, violence and disorder had become the rule of the day. Every successful revolution, he concluded, witnessed a "forced transition from initial anarchy to a new ordering." But Bolivia had not yet entered upon that transition.[16]

Against this background, the Bolivian military, in part because of U.S. insistence, was being strengthened. Between 1956 and 1963 the percentage of government expenditures devoted to the military rose from about 7 to 13 percent.[17] The result was to bring into existence "a new social force with the capacity for independent action."[18] As their power gradually surged, the armed forces devoted increasing attention to civic action projects, often financed by U.S. aid. Through these projects the military built roads, installed drinking water and sewage systems in remote areas, and organized *campesinos* to collaborate with the soldiers in improving conditions in rural communities.[19] In addition to providing a popular following for the military and helping them shed their old reputation as reactionaries uninterested in public welfare, civic action led many officers to speculate on how much more efficient they could be than civilian politicians in directing development, not just at the grassroots but at the national level of government.

One of the ambitious officers indulging in such speculation was the colorful *cochabambino* head of the air force, René Barrientos, a general who was fluent in Quechua and who by 1964 had acquired a large following among the *campesinos* of his native district. Although Paz Estenssoro did not trust the armed forces—he was relying increasingly on peasant militias recruited in the *altiplano* rather than the army to maintain control over miners and other sectors of organized labor—and although he was particularly suspicious of Barrientos, he nonetheless grasped at the possibility of winning the support of this imposing officer by accepting him as his running mate for the 1964 presidential election.[20] Paz's decision to stand for re-election—which produced an automatic victory and a third term that began in August of 1964—led to further splintering in the MNR, student riots, and protest demonstrations. Openly breaking with Paz, Vice President Barrientos encouraged the opposition and soon the president found his situation hopeless. Picking up support from the FSB and many MNR dissidents, the vice president was joined by General Alfredo Ovando, commander in chief of the armed forces and a person who matched Barrientos in political ambition but lacked his personal magnetism, in proclaiming against Paz Estenssoro on November 3, 1964. Powerless to resist the *golpe*, Paz was soon in exile as Barrientos occupied the presidential palace.

Barrientos insisted it was not his purpose to undo the reforms introduced by the MNR. The spirit of reform, he maintained, had originated with the armed forces on the fields of the Chaco, and had briefly flowered under the military officers Toro and Busch in the 1930s and Villarroel in the 1940s. The MNR had taken up this reform spirit, but after coming to power in 1952 had proved incapable of giving direction to innovative processes. Together with Bolivia's other political parties, it had lapsed into ideological and moral stagnation. It was up to the armed forces, therefore, to provide control mechanisms for the social renovation that had originated with them. In restoring a sense of direction to the revolution the armed forces would, Barrientos announced, establish discipline, unite citizens through the "mystique of work and sacrifice for the patria," organize the *campesinos* into effective cooperatives, and preside over a moral renovation based on the teachings of Christian Democracy.[21]

Barrientos was the Bolivian president—elected by 700,000 out of 1,100,000 votes to a four-year term in 1966 after having first served as president of a military junta of government—to whom Senator Ellender explained the inability of the United States to continue the massive infusion of public funds.[22] The warning was not an empty one, for U.S. "subventions to Bolivia diminished from $18.4 million in 1964 to $3.5 million in 1968."[23] This was one reason why Barrientos did all in his power to encourage an inflow of private investment. His efforts proved remarkably successful, and by 1968 the private mining sector, vastly bolstered by U.S. investment especially in medium-sized enterprises, produced more tin than COMIBOL, the state-controlled corporation. Led by Gulf Oil, which incidentally delivered a total of $464,000 to Barrientos in what was euphemistically labeled "political contributions,"[24] foreign capital also poured into petroleum development. Between 1958 and 1968 the value of oil exports rose from $5 million to $15 million and during the last five years of this decade petroleum's contribution to the gross domestic product grew from 3 to 7 percent.[25]

Accompanying the inflow of foreign funds was a substantial growth during the second half of the 1960s in domestic investment and savings that reflected the confidence of local capitalists in Barrientos. Under his rule it became immediately apparent that populist tactics of relying on labor as a main pillar of support had been abandoned.[26] The turn from labor to middle sector capitalists as the principal source of backing, begun by Siles Zuazo, was, in fact, completed by Barrientos. With him as president, the urban middle groups prospered as seldom before in the country's history and a new class of entrepreneurs, speculators, administrators, and technocrats emerged.

With the power of labor and its Marxist leadership crushed and with urban leftists further weakened by a Peking-Moscow ideological struggle, Barrientos could point not only to the widespread backing of middle sectors but also to the enthusiastic support of the Quechua-speaking Indians, extending from the Cochabamba valley down to the area lying to the southeast of Sucre. On his frequent forays into the hinterland, Barrientos had visited many of the remote native communities, addressing the inhabitants in their native tongue. With Barrientos' popularity and power approaching their zenith in 1967 and with his opposition cowed and splintered, the Argentine-born revolutionary Ché Guevara, who had gained his renown in the Cuban Revolution, began his guerrilla campaign in Bolivia. He could scarcely have chosen a less auspicious moment.

For his field of operations Guevara selected the area to the south of Santa Cruz and to the west of Sucre. The Indian peasants either ignored the stranger who could not speak their language or fled in fright from him. Virtually no help was forthcoming from the cities, in.part because xenophobic prejudices overcame Marxism's internationalist sentiments, causing Bolivian leftists to look askance at the Argentine guerrilla leader. The Bolivian armed forces made short work of the insurgents. Guevara was captured and summarily executed, and Barrientos had achieved his most spectacular triumph.[27] In Washington, officials found vindication for the whole program of assistance to Bolivia, and especially for the military aid and for the extensive CIA activity which had contributed to Guevara's failure.

While Barrientos, with U.S. assistance, had proved more than a match for the foreign guerrillas, he was unable to establish a reliable basis of internal order. Shunning institutionalization, he settled into a highly personalistic approach to politics, meeting crises through compromises of the moment manipulated by his own brand of arm-twisting. By early 1969 this approach was losing much of its effectiveness, but the agrarian scene at least remained calm.

Immediately upon assuming power, Barrientos had removed pro-MNR directors from most of the country's approximately 7,500 *campesino* syndicates, replacing them with men personally loyal to him. This heavy-handed approach provoked little protest because of Barrientos' vast popularity among the Indians who recognized him as a protector "who would solve their problems."[28] During the Barrientos years, moreover, syndicate members began to pay less attention to national affair and to concern themselves almost exclusively with the immediate issues of their association. As national consciousness ebbed from the syndicates, they lost much of their "revolutionary force and transforming impulse."[29] In this one respect Barrientos achieved the classic corporativist objective of distracting the masses from national affairs by providing at least the illusion of participation in local associations, while at the same time persuading them that a leader, removed by his charisma from the ranks of ordinary persons, could be trusted to direct matters at the national level.

If the rural sectors were generally tranquil as the year 1969 began, urban order was disintegrating. Barrientos faced rising political opposition, economic problems, and an ominous falling out with General Ovando. His personalistic approach had lost its magic and many Bolivians anticipated a military *golpe* at any moment. The president's enemies did not have to strike, for the fifty-year-old General—who had survived several assassination attempts in his career—died in a helicopter crash in April. At his death Bolivia seemed still not to have entered upon the transition to a "new ordering" that Diez de Medina had urged in 1962.

THE POLITICAL SCENE IN ECUADOR

Installed for a third term that began in September of 1960, Velasco Ibarra found it more difficult than ever to forge a coalition that would provide for some degree of political stability. The Socialists had just undergone one of their more serious splits, both the ARNE and the CFP were weakened by leadership rivalries, and Conservatives were divided between supporters of a social justice ideology that demanded basic structural changes in society and those who hoped the most timid of palliatives would suffice to maintain order. In this confused situation, Velasco Ibarra turned for a time to the Communists and even made friendly gestures toward Fidel Castro, moves which perhaps were intended to persuade the United States to increase the price it was willing to pay for his friendship. Certain military officers, however, were sincerely worried by Velasco's "softness on communism," and also by rising popular discontent. Out of these circumstances came a *golpe* led by the air force in November 1961 that ousted Velasco Ibarra and installed Vice President Carlos Julio Arosemena as chief executive. This prominent Guayaquil banker was the son of a man who had served for just under thirteen months as president in the 1940s.

It soon became apparent that Arosemena had a serious drinking problem that surfaced even on the most important state occasions, as during his 1962 visit with President Kennedy in Washington. As president, furthermore, Arosemena continued to make the favorable comments on the Cuban Revolution he had first begun to utter upon completing a visit to the island while serving as Velasco Ibarra's vice president. Thus military officers had new grounds to distrust the stance of a chief executive on the communist issue. Beyond this the military feared that Arosemena's incompetence and inability to institute reforms would result in a worsening of the social problem and perhaps facilitate the re-election in 1964 of Velasco Ibarra, with whom the president remained on warm terms, and thus saddle the country with an indefinite continuation of the political stagnation and total ineffectiveness that Latin Americans refer to as *desgobierno*. Such circumstances might, the officers feared, provoke an insurrection from below that could result in the destruction of the regular military institution, as had occurred in the wake of both the Bolivian and Cuban revolutions.

The military struck in July of 1964, after an intoxicated Arosemena had made a particularly unhappy spectacle of himself at a banquet honoring the president of the Grace Line Shipping Company.[30] Masterminding the coup was Colonel (soon General) Marcos Gandara Enríquez, a devout Catholic and staunch anticommunist. He became one of the four members of a military junta of government presided over by Captain (soon Admiral) Ramón Castro Jijón. Announcing full adherence to the reformist principles of the Alliance for Progress and stressing that economic development and social justice were necessary to prevent a violent revolution which could be exploited by Communists,[31] the junta gained speedy recognition from Washington as the Kennedy administration reversed its early policy of frowning on military takeovers. During the nearly three years that it was in power, the junta received some $84.5 million in aid and assistance from the United States.[32]

Pointing with pride to the social reforms introduced under military auspices in the second half of the 1920s and also in 1938, the junta officers announced their intention to take up anew the cause of renovation. Like most of the high-ranking armed forces officers throughout Andean America, the members of the junta came from the middle class and the lower middle class; and they reflected growing middle-sector resentment over the manner in which a plutocracy, headed by the commercial and banking community, had ruled Ecuador in their own exclusive interests ever since the recovery from the depression.

Adopting a ten-year development plan completed just before the July *golpe* by the National Junta of Planning and Coordination, the military administration announced its intention to establish firmer controls over the country's privileged capitalists, so as to assure that their activities were directed toward national development goals. At the same time it moved to aid middle sectors by extending social security coverage to artisans and by establishing a program to encourage the organization of professional groups.[33] To aid the lower classes, the junta introduced a veritable revolution in education[34] aimed at sharply reducing the nearly 50 percent illiteracy rate by making primary education available, and eventually compulsory, for all children. The officers vastly increased the scope of civic action and turned their attention to benefiting the *campesinos*, who made up the overwhelming majority of the 64 percent of the Ecuadoran population that lived in rural areas.[35] Under military supervision, however, agrarian reform got off to an unspectacular start—and ground almost to a complete standstill when the civilians returned to power.[36]

Income from banana exports began to decline in 1965, owing largely to difficulties in controlling diseases attacking the trees on the marginal land pressed into service to take advantage of the boom of the late 1950s. By 1966 the junta faced a serious budgetary problem and the highly demogogic opposition of an opportunistic coalition of the extreme left and the extreme right. Justly proud of the moderation that had characterized their rule, the officers refused to prolong their power through unrestrained force and so permitted the restoration of civilian government.[37]

Two interim presidents followed upon the April 1966 fall of the junta before the 1968 election brought Velasco Ibarra to the presidential office for a fifth time. His margin of victory was 15,000 votes, the narrowest in his career. Ecuador's 5.6 million population was now divided almost equally between the coast and sierra (in contrast to the 1870s when 75 percent of the 1.3 million Ecuadorans had resided in the sierra),[38] and Velasco Ibarra garnered roughly 27 percent of the coastal and 42 percent of the sierra vote.

In the three years preceding Velasco Ibarra's fifth term U.S. grants had declined by roughly 35 percent as a result of cuts in congressional appropriations.[39] A ray of hope, however, was provided by the upturn in private foreign investment. The annual average of this source of capital rose to around $16 million in 1966 and 1967, and by the end of 1968 total private investment in Ecuador was estimated at $148.8 million. U.S. funds, placed preponderantly in petroleum exploration and extraction, made up about 70 percent of this amount. As Velasco began his new term, discovery of reserves in the Oriente brought about a substantial increase in U.S. oil investments, most of the money coming from the Texaco-Gulf consortium with which the military junta had signed a contract in 1964.

A prominent national writer declared in 1970 that oil provided Ecuador with the means to emerge from poverty. Earnings from it, he wrote, would construct schools, houses, hospitals, pave streets, install universities, create employment, and raise salaries for the needy: all of this provided the government could learn to contract shrewdly with the foreign firms and then administer its income wisely.[40] On the basis of past performance, Velasco Ibarra could not be expected to measure up to these two provisos. Thus the oil prosperity which Velasco believed would ease the problems of rule actually would have the effect of shortening his fifth presidential tenure. Ecuadorans had suddenly glimpsed a rendezvous with destiny and were becoming ill-disposed to accept the sort of desgobierno they had tolerated when the country seemed totally lacking in prospects for a brighter future.

The Political Scene in Peru

The 1962 election to choose a successor to Manuel Prado pitted three candidates against each other, two of them familiar figures in the political arena and the third a relative newcomer: Víctor Raúl Haya de la Torre, Manuel Odría, and Fernando Belaúnde Terry. Newcomer Belaúnde, the handsome and magnetic fifty-year-old scion of an aristocratic family, had been trained as an architect at the University of Texas. Possessing the instincts of a populist leader, he realized that the traditional upper classes would have to introduce reforms in order to contain the pressures of revolutionary change. Thus he disagreed profoundly with Haya de la Torre who in 1962 maintained that Peru's social and economic problems were not terribly pressing and counseled against innovations that might rock the boat.

A good ideal of the support for Belaúnde's Popular Action or AP came from struggling middle sectors who either fretted over a declining social status or, having recently struggled upward into bourgeois respectability, were concerned about their ability and that of their children to remain at this level. Insecure middle sectors were attracted by Belaúnde's promises to achieve rapid economic development and to provide an expanding array of social services.

While promising to accelerate the development of the private capitalist sector, Belaúnde advocated an approach to the Indian problem that came directly out of respectable Indianism. The Indian, he proclaimed, must be allowed to develop in his own way, as a collectivist being. Thus the 5,000 or so comunidades must be protected, even if this meant expropriating land from some of the larger sierra estates. Beyond this, surplus Indian population in the Andes must be drained off: not toward the coastal cities, where problems of unemployment and underemployment already were out of hand, but rather toward the selva, the eastern region of the Andean foothills and the river valleys formed by Amazonian tributaries. To facilitate this, Belaúnde spoke of colonization projects and above all of a giant north-south selva highway (the Carretera Marginal de la Selva) which would provide the communications and transportation infrastructure needed to support new colonies.[41]

In the 1962 election none of the candidates received the third of the 1,689,618 votes cast which would have assured election. As a result congress, in line with constitutional provisions, was called upon to choose between Haya, with his approximately 557,000 votes, Belaúnde with his slightly more than 544,000, and Odría with some 520,000. When an accord was reached between Odriistas and Apristas that would have given the presidency to Odría but guaranteed the actual seating of the large bloc of APRA senators and deputies elected to congress by the 1962 balloting, the military intervened. Overthrowing Prado six weeks before completion of his term, the officers established a military junta. Just as the Ecuadoran military feared that continued inattention to socioeconomic problems by Arosemena and Velasco Ibarra would bring an insurrection from below, so the Peruvian military feared that *desgobierno* by Odriistas and Apristas, the two political camps most willing to rely on muddling through in protecting the interests of the oligarchy, would bring about a revolutionary situation.

From the outset, the military junta promised to rule for only one year and to hold free elections in June of 1963. Belaúnde managed now to expand his support and this fact contributed to the military's willingness to abide by its commitment; for the officers felt he was the presidential aspirant most likely to introduce the type of reforms needed to render the political structure viable. In the 1963 election Belaúnde received more than the required one-third of the ballots cast, thereby triumphing over the same two candidates he had faced the previous year, and was duly installed in office in July.

His reform programs consistently blocked by an obstructionist Aprista-Odriista majority in congress, Belaúnde was at least able to gain approval of an agrarian reform bill, considerably watered down from the one he had presented.[42] Designed to take some property away from the owners of large sierra estates for redistribution among the Indian *comunidades*, the legislation also provided for ending the *yanacona* system (similar to Bolivia's pre-1952 *pongueaje*), by replacing vassalage with a wage labor structure. At the same time, Indians were encouraged to become active participants in cooperative associations intended to increase efficiency in the utilization of land collectively owned by *comunidades*. They were exhorted also to find pride in the communal institutions of the Inca past. If successfully carried out, Belaúnde's agrarian reform would have protected the Indians in an existence relatively free from the intrusion of individualistic and capitalist incentives and provided them with a sense of political participation by allowing them a voice in managing reinvigorated *comunidades*. In return, of course, Indians were expected not to intrude into the individualist-capitalist world that the president hoped to strengthen in urban Peru.[43]

Agrarian reform failed to function in the hoped-for manner, in part because Belaúnde seemed primarily interested in encouraging industrialization and the extractive industries and as a result had insufficient funds to devote to the agricultural sector. Moreover, AP found itself locked in competition with the APRA in the attempt to mobilize peasants benefited by the reform. Consequently, AP was reluctant to push ahead with reform, lest it redound to the advantage of its major political rival. Owing to these circumstances, the number of people benefited by land redistribution failed to keep pace even with rural population growth.

A plethora of economic ills soon beset the Peruvian economy.[44] The fishmeal industry, which at the beginning of the 1960s had soared into the number one place in world production, replacing Japan in that category, entered into serious decline in 1965 as a result of a partial disappearance of the anchovy schools. During most of his time in office, moreover, Belaúnde was denied the Alliance for Progress funds to which his reform programs certainly entitled him. The main reason for the cutoff was the president's insistence on working out a new contractual arrangement with IPC and his threat, failing that, to nationalize the firm.[45]

Basically responsible for Belaúnde's downfall was his insistence upon being both a developmentalist and a populist president. Thus he spent money on economic development projects, including the *Carretera Marginal* so dear to his heart, at the same time that he increased the social spending intended to safeguard the masses and struggling middle sectors in a secure clientelist status. He did not want to impose steep taxes on the wealthy—nor could he have done so in view of the congressional control exercised by the Aprista-Odriista watchdogs of oligarchy interests—for he placed a basic faith in the ability of private capitalism, with only a modicum of government stimulus, to solve urban-sector problems. His access to foreign funds severely curtailed and unable to stimulate adequate domestic capital formation because some of his reformist rhetoric frightened the oligarchy into increasing their deposits abroad, he watched helplessly as mounting inflation estranged the insecure middle sectors who had so recently placed their trust in him.[46]

In 1963 Belaúnde, together with the military, had hoped that the old order could be patched and wired and somehow held together. Circumstances, however, had prevented the well-intentioned president from performing cosmetic surgery. And five years after his accession to the presidency, an Aprista victory seemed a distinct possibility in the next election, scheduled for 1969. This prospect goaded the military into action once more, and in October of 1968 they ousted Belaúnde and assumed power on their own. Their immediation justi- fication, and the grounds on which they initially appealed to the citizenry for support, was that Belaúnde had betrayed national inter- ests by a new contract signed with IPC in August, one of the pages of which was allegedly missing when the president made the docu- ment public. Capitalizing on this issue the officers promptly national- ized IPC holdings.[47]

Underlying the military decision to make its political move was the conviction that in view of the breakdown of the old order, in both the agrarian and urban sectors, a revolution from above was necessary to prevent one from below. Civilians had proved incapable of per- forming cosmetic surgery, and now the officers must try their hands at iron surgery.

It would not be long before a somewhat parallel set of circum- stances would lead the Ecuadoran military into renewed political activity. The agrarian situation, it is true, was far less menacing in Ecuador than in Peru; but in both countries, as will be seen, the urgency of the urban-centered threat to the established order was enough to persuade the military that their time had come.

Breakdown of the Old Order: The Agrarian Sector

The year 1963 witnessed a veritable explosion in various parts of the Peruvian sierra. Syndicates formed by *colonos* on haciendas dur- ing the preceding ten to fifteen years became more aggressive as they demanded higher salaries and, above all, elimination of personal and gratuitous obligations associated with *yanaconaje*.[48] At the same time *comuneros*, the residents of indigenous *comunidades*, gave vent to frustrations by conducting invasions, often spearheaded by Indian women, to reoccupy land which they maintained had, through the decades, been plundered by white and mestizo *gamonales*. The peak of a *colono* aggressiveness and the largest number of *comunero* in- vasions "coincided with the first 'hundred days' of the Belaúnde government, a period when strong expectations of land reform pro- vided a great stimulus."[49]

Only to a limited degree did Ecuador share in Peru's highland ferment. Because mining had not been a factor in the Kingdom of Quito's colonial economy, Spaniards had been less concerned than in Peru with congregating Indians into comunidades to facilitate periodic allocation of labor for the mines. Instead, the Indian populace had been widely dispersed on the many agricultural estates that Spaniards established in the highlands. These circumstances permitted a more thoroughgoing absorption of the natives than in either Peru or Bolivia. Through the years, moreover, many relatively small estates remained in existence. As late as 1964, 55 percent of the total farm land in Ecuador consisted of estates not large enough to employ as many as twelve persons.[50] In comparison to Peru, Indians were less concentrated and therefore less able to act on grievances. And, there were fewer comunidades in Ecuador to serve as focal points of discontent. These are among the factors explaining why the Indians remained relatively complacent in Ecuador.[51] In neighboring Peru, though, Indian violence was assuming an intensity, as well as a geographical extension, that seemed to set it apart from earlier protest movements experienced since independence. A wide variety of circumstances contributed to this situation.[52]

In the course of the twentieth century, many Indian *comuneros* and *colonos* had the opportunity, depending on the region where they lived, to establish contact with town life. *Comuneros*, taking advantage of expanding road and rail facilities, might sell products to nearby towns and might find employment in a textile firm in an Andean town such as Sicuani located to the south of Cuzco;[53] *colonos* might work in the house the *hacendado* maintained in a provincial capital and even attend school there.[54] In a variety of ways, Indians were exposed to urban customs and ideas, and when they returned to their comunidades or haciendas they often applied their new knowledge and values to improving their conditions. In many instances they established schools and clinics in comunidades, or pressured an *hacendado* into establishing them on his estate. As a result, there came into being "structural binds:" Indians acquired new capacities, but the rigid structures which controlled their lives did not provide adequate opportunity to utilize those capacities.[55] The situation could only give rise to discontent.

Even when Indians did not go to the cities, sometimes the cities came to them, contributing thereby to the urbanization of rural life. The city might come to the countryside by means of the famous radio school of Puno.[56] Or, it might come through *forasteros* or outsiders, ranging from political organizers to merchants with an eye for profit.[57] By the mid-1960s, *forastero* political organizers, including Marxists and Trotskyists, Apristas, members of Belaúnde's AP, and priests and laymen involved in church-sponsored programs, were competing with each other in the attempt to mobilize support,[58] and all the time creating new cases of structural bind.[59]

Meantime community development projects carried out under the auspices of the Peace Corps[60] and various aid programs were duplicating an experiment initiated by Cornell University anthropologists in the 1950s at Vicos, located in the inter-Andean valley of Callejón de Huaylas, about 250 miles northeast of Lima.[61] Awakened by the Cornell group to the economic potential of their community, the *vicosinos* had forged ahead rapidly in modernizing their methods of production. Regarded for some time as unique, Vicos by the 1960s provided only one among dozens, even hundreds, of examples of peasant communities that were "digging their own way out of their Andean isolation, punching through their own farm-market and access roads, bridging the gullies that cut them off from the national economy, providing school rooms for their children, quarters for their local officials, and starting on the task of providing basic modern public utilities."[62]

Slowly in the 1950s and 1960s awareness began to spread among non-Indian Peruvians most in touch with the situation that the "eternal Indian" of the *comunidades* was ceasing to be a collectivist being. More and more the *comuneros* were developing traits of individualism, claiming what amounted to virtually fee-simple ownership over the plots of land assigned each family within the *comunidad*, seeking more and more to augment individual income through part-time work in a town or seasonal labor on a private estate, and paying less and less attention to the old obligations of collective labor. White and mestizo elites were alarmed by the rise of individualistic traits among the Indians, which portended enormous future difficulties in maintaining the natives under control. But many of society's dominant sectors remained convinced that enough of the old collectivist mentality still survived among the natives to make possible, under suitable conditions, its resurgence. Among the factors that would contribute to suitable conditions, the pre-eminent importance of land reform came to be recognized. Enough property would have to be returned to the *comunidades* to make them once more viable as collective enterprises.

Especially ominous to Peruvian elites aware of what was transpiring in the sierra was the fact that *campesinos* were assuming leadership themselves in their quest of progress. In the vanguard of peasant seekers of a better life was a group of assertive and aggressive *cholos*, whose number was constantly growing. *Cholo*, as the word is used in Peru,

323

designates a person who is Indian by birth but has begun to move toward the Westernized, mestizo way of life.[63] *Cholos* took the leading part among *comuneros* in pressing for a return of plundered land and in leading invasions. Among *colonos*, *cholos* dominated the syndicates that demanded higher wages and the end of *yanaconaje*.

In the old days, mestizo culture had absorbed and co-opted the *cholos*. But by the 1950s and 1960s the Indians passing into *cholo* status were far too numerous for mestizos to absorb.[64] Increasingly mestizos revealed fear and hatred of the burgeoning *cholo* populace. In turn, some *cholos* began overtly to manifest hatred of mestizos, to find pride in their Indian background, and to envisage future roles as leaders of Indians rather than as hangers-on in the mestizo world. *Cholification*, in short, was bringing about the collapse of the old control devices and making apparent to all who followed the situation the need to create new devices so as to avoid rural chaos. One ray of hope was discernible in these circumstances. The vast masses of Indians still retained a mentality of dependence; they had simply transferred their dependence to *cholos*. If the central government could devise methods for co-opting the *cholos*, they might become as useful in maintaining the dependence of Indians as labor leaders had historically been in perpetuating the clientelist behavior of rank-and-file urban laborers vis-à-vis the central government.

Heretofore, the power of the *gamonales* had rested in large part on society's recognition of their effectiveness in keeping the Indians pacified and out of the way. By the 1960s, however, the *gamonales* had become a dangerous anachronism. They were powerless to stem Andean unrest and in many instances contributed to it. If the government hoped to establish direct contact with Indians or *cholos* in the hopes of bringing them into the orbit of the central state, the *gamonales*, who had kept the peasants isolated from contact with the state, would have to be eliminated. Furthermore, the means whereby government might make *campesinos* beholden to it lay not in conferring the fringe benefits of social security, for adequate funds were not available, but rather in bestowing upon them the land held in private estates and abolishing, with one flourish of the pen, the gratuitous services that many *colonos* were obliged to render *hacendados*. Once this was accomplished, through obliteration of the *hacendado* class, it might be possible for the government to proceed to organize grateful *comuneros* under some semblance of centralized control through the linkage provided by *cholos*.

The immediate usefulness of distributing land to *comuneros* and ending *yanaconaje* among *colonos* had been demonstrated in the mid-1960s. Principally through these expedients the Belaúnde regime had been able to restore calm to the most troubled sections of Andean Peru and to remove at least for the time being the revolutionary potential. Conservatively inclined observers of these events were as delighted as the revolutionary Marxists were dismayed. The latter saw their hopes for mobilizing Indians in support of immediate and total social revolution rudely shattered. Outside of a few trouble spots of most immediate urgency, however, Belaúnde's agrarian reforms were mired in inertia by 1968. This contributed a serious barrier to fulfillment of long-term hopes to end a revolutionary threat throughout rural Peru. Awareness of this helped prod the military into taking power.

The sierra by no means encompassed all of the problems of agrarian Peru that attested to the breakdown of the old order. In many southern coastal towns such as Ica small farmers were beginning to organize into cooperative associations through which they rented tractors and other equipment and purchased water rights.[65] By means of their cooperatives they were becoming increasingly assertive and powerful; and government held virtually no direct check on them. On the northern coastal sugar plantations, laborers were in the fold of APRA-dominated unions. Economic and social conditions on the plantations were determined by collective bargaining between unions and owners, with government little more than a powerless observer.[66]

Along the coast as well as in the sierra, agrarian Peru was developing all sorts of relatively independent power foci. The making of a system of uncoordinated interest-group pluralism seemed well underway. Here was a development totally at odds with the traditional political culture. According to its norms, all activities must be regulated by a group set apart from common citizens. If the traditional political culture was to be preserved, then a strong government must assert itself and put an end to incipient interest-group pluralism. This, at least, was the reasoning of the Peruvian military. And the urgency of their task was made all the greater by the decentralization and breakdown of control mechanisms within the urban sector—a breakdown that was also becoming discernible in Ecuador.

Breakdown of the Old Order: The Urban Sector

By the late 1960s the bitter opposition in Ecuador between the industrialists and the commercial interests, especially of Guayaquil, virtually eliminated any possibility of "common action for the good of the country."[67] The absence of a national policy-making apparatus, however, reflected a far more serious breakdown of centralized authority than that occasioned by the competition of just two functional groups. For years, government institutions had been established as "autonomous agencies with their own special funding sources from various excise, import and export taxes, and with bureaucracies independent of executive or legislative control." These institutions guarded their prerogatives jealously, for each autonomous agency constituted a "secure fief." By the time of the military takeover in 1963, over nine hundred of these independent agencies existed and the national treasury "was the destination of only some 43 percent of the total amount of taxes collected."[68] The remainder of national revenue was collected and controlled by the agencies.

Since the 1950s Peru had witnessed the mushrooming of functional associations formed by new and old elites in order to protect their interests. Even nonelite groups were learning how to acquire a political input through organizing. Competition among the groups was fierce and uncompromising, for each exhibited a limited good mentality leading its members to assume that gains by a rival organization would automatically result in a loss for them. Among the spoils that the various association competed for were those of social security. Coverage provided by this system was determined not by any rational allocation of funds, but by the influence that a particular group happened at the moment to enjoy in government circles.[69]

Many of the functional interest groups comprised both an upper or patrón (managerial-ownership) sector and an employee-labor sector as well. The patronés mediated outside contact with their clientelist employees and laborers. Government was not only incapable of exercising effective and consistent control over these mediators but also increasingly blocked by them in any endeavor to assert a direct influence over the country's compartmentalized lower classes.[70]

The burgeoning of elite-dominated groups came about largely because of a dramatic expansion in educational facilities. No matter what their other faults, Andean governments in the post-World War II era were considered acceptable by a majority of voters provided they expanded educational opportunities, assumed by more and more people to hold the key to upward mobility. In order to maintain their grip on power, governments responded with notable energy to the educational demands of voters. In the process, though, they undermined the traditional basis of social stability.

Ever since the colonial period, upper classes, by remaining open and permitting the incorporation of newly risen sectors into their ranks, had managed to enlist the support of middle groups. The system's success depended, of course, on limiting the size of middle sectors and this was accomplished by maintaining a highly limited educational structure.[71] However, between 1950 and 1961, enrollment in Peru's secondary schools trebled, and by the early 1960s in Ecuador it was increasing at an annual rate of about 10 percent.[72] Almost overnight, countless cases of urban structural bind had appeared.[73]

Since the end of World War II Andean middle sectors, their hopes for a better life buoyed by the unrealistic promises that politicians and also members of the Catholic clergy held out to them, had become wildly optimistic about the opportunities for rapid advance that a secondary education would open to them. Even domestic servants in Lima as well as slum dwellers dreamed of professional careers for their children.[74] Yet the truth was that in Peru and also in Ecuador the gulf between certain middle sectors and the masses seemed actually to be diminishing. One indication of this was the tendency of manual labor (*obrero*) income to catch up with and even to surpass the earnings of white-collar employees (*empleados*). Faced with this fact, mestizo middle sectors increasingly sought a better quality education for their children by enrolling them, often at great financial sacrifice, in private secondary schools, in consequence of which the public schools were left mainly to the *cholo* and lower middle groups.

Middle sectors might still hope for dignified employment opportunities, through which they could remain aloof from the masses, in the government bureaucracy and in private service. But openings on a sufficient scale did not exist. A study conducted in Ecuador in the mid-1960s found that only 31 percent of those whose secondary education was intended to prepare them for this type of employment would be able to find jobs in public administration and private services.[75] There remained the possibility of a university education which might provide a key to more prestigious sources of livelihood. University population in Peru grew between 1960 and 1970 from 30,983 to 111,078. Yet in the last year the National Inter-University Planning Office warned that "only 40,000 of 110,000 university applicants would be able to secure admissions in any one year."[76] In Ecuador, the percentage of successful applicants for university matriculation was even lower. Nor was there any certainty that winning a place in the university would necessarily result in hoped-for types of employment. Both in Peru and Ecuador the expansion of education was raising self-ascribed status among large population sections, but the socioeconomic structures denied positions commensurate either with that status or the level of training that had been acquired.

Exacerbating the problems faced by Peru and Ecuador was an annual population increase that hovered around 3 percent, and that rose to between 4 and 5 percent in the cities that continued to attract migration from the countryside.[77] When population remains relatively stable, a demographer explains, a structure of authority in the form of customs, rules, and laws grows up to justify the distribution of social advantages and income.[78] But the Andean populations were no longer stable and increasingly they were made up of young persons with aroused ambitions who no longer accepted the traditional justifications of the distribution of advantages.

For most of the 1960s the situation had remained manageable only because of relatively high economic growth rates, particularly in Peru. But then, toward the end of 1967, economic decline set in and in 1969 the GNP grew only by 1.7 percent.[79] At this point the attainment of growth rates that would equal or surpass the best previous levels loomed as the only alternative to political disintegration.

As early as the 1950s and even more so in the early 1960s, an increasing number of secondary students had indicated a desire to become engineers or technical specialists or even to enter the previously shunned profession of business management. They were concerned, in short, with acquiring the skills that would facilitate rapid development and nation-building and they were convinced that the skills of the old elites had become irrelevant. "Technically minded utopians," originating mainly in Andean middle groups and operating within the "traditional framework of an authoritarian ideology that finds little place for effective power sharing" were preparing to assert themselves.[80]

Beginning to understand that a part of their difficulties sprang from the fact that their countries had been "tertiarized" (owing to the high percentage of the active labor force employed in services) before they had been modernized through development of the primary (agricultural) and secondary (manufacturing) sectors, a new generation of Andeans turned attention to righting the order of development. Above all, their interest lay in industrialization. No matter that previous results had demonstrated that formation of new capital-intensive manufacturing enterprises did not create enough blue-collar jobs to keep up with increasing population and that after every spurt of growth in industrial output more *obreros* were unemployed or underemployed than before.[81] What mattered was that industrializa-

328

tion would provide dignified and self-realizing positions for hundreds and thousands of aspiring management and technically skilled elites. The thrust for industrialization came primarily from aspiring elites and was not motivated principally by solicitude for the urban masses.

The immediate cause of concern to the "technically minded utopians" during the 1960s was less the lower classes than the oligarchy, that 5 percent or so of the economically active population in Peru and Ecuador that "somehow gets hold of 45 percent of the gross national income."[82] Many of its most influential members seemed either indifferent to rapid development spearheaded by industrial growth, or else anxious to bring this growth about in such manner as to monopolize all its advantages for themselves, their families, and their heirs. Conjuring up the vision of a monolithic oligarchy that actually did not exist,[83] dissatisfied middle groups were ready to welcome a revolution, even if they lacked the temerity to launch it themselves, that would displace the oligarchy from its power pinnacle. Into this situation, in which traditional intraelite conflicts had been replaced with interclass confrontations,[84] the Peruvian military stepped in 1968, to be followed by their Ecuadoran counterparts four years later.

THE UNITED STATES AND THE BREAKDOWN OF THE OLD ORDER

Beginning in the 1940s, IPC had served as a trail blazer for other U.S. firms operating in America as it moved to become a model employer by showing solicitous concern for its workers. As a result, the company won worker loyalty to such an extent that its labor force backed IPC rather than the Peruvian government at the time of nationalization. By the mid-1960s workers of many U.S.-owned firms, even if not inclined to back their employers in case of a conflict with the national government, had become accustomed to turning to company managers, rather than the state, in seeking higher wages and better conditions. Welfare corporatism as practiced by North American companies was thus beginning to spread the practice of collective bargaining, breaking down the old patterns of political bargaining in which workers had accepted dependence on government rather than employers, and in general threatening to destroy the direct control apparatus through which the state had customarily maintained patronalist-clientelist relations with the labor force.

The role played by U.S. labor, with the backing of the Alliance for Progress, speeded up this process. Carried out with particular energy in Peru where a close collaboration with APRA-controlled unions was established, AFL-CIO programs taught local labor leaders how to develop nonpolitical unions that relied on collective bargaining. To the degree that North American efforts were successful, not only labor but also management would achieve freedom from state intervention in labor-capital disputes.[85] Recognition that national control over foreign capital and labor was being eroded by North American involvement in the local labor scene helped spur both the Peruvian officers (whose feelings were all the stronger because U.S. programs were strengthening the detested Apristas) and the Ecuadoran military into action.

Not only the Peruvian and Ecuadoran military but also vast elements of middle-sector leadership agreed with the Bolivian intellectual Augusto Céspedes who as early as 1963 had appealed for government to re-establish control over organized labor. Otherwise, he predicted, U.S. agents would succeed in molding Andean labor in the North American image.[86] By the late 1960s this prediction seemed on the way to fulfillment in all three of the Andean republics. Organized labor that had been most in contact with North American union leaders and with North American firms had become the most aggressive in demanding the material rewards of economism. As Andean elites assessed the situation, economism might indeed work to maintain social peace in the richly endowed and thoroughly developed United States; but their own underendowed and late-modernizing countries lacked the resources to employ this approach and had to concoct a blend of material and nonmaterial rewards. The difficulty was that among those labor groups most under North American influence Andean governments were least able to exhort workers to accept some of their compensation in the form of nonmaterial rewards derived from sacrificing for national interests. To a frightening degree, U.S. influence was denationalizing the urban labor sector. Out of this situation arose ever more militant demands for cultural independence from the United Sttaes.

U.S. educational assistance programs, conducted with the missionary zeal of spreading egalitarian, pragmatic, and materialistic values, made their own contribution to the denationalization of Andean America. The major impact of education missions, however, lay not so much in spreading these values among Andean masses as in disseminating new skills and leadership ambitions among middle-sector youths who were granted scholarships to pursue technical studies in North America[87] or were provided with opportunities to study agronomy, science, engineering, and business management in their own countries as a result of educational programs and reforms supported by U.S. funds, both public and private. To an enormous extent, the expansion of elites in Andean America, as well as the conviction among new elites that they had acquired the expertise needed to propel their countries toward development and that the skills of the old ruling class were meaningless, resulted from U.S. educational assistance. Thus part of the pressure directed againt the old order originated in the United States.

Contributing also to the breakdown of the old order, although this was not widely perceived until after that order had in fact collapsed, was the shift in U.S. investment patterns that saw private capital going increasingly into manufacturing, rather than into utilities and extractive industries as in the past. This shift in hemisphere investment preferences[88] reflected one that was worldwide in its reach.[89] More and more, U.S. businesses were going abroad "to sell and to make profits through sales in the countries in which they made investments;"[90] more and more, Yankee manufacturing was capturing markets "from within."[91]

The increase of U.S. investment in manufacturing was apparent in each of the three Andean republics under consideration, but most especially in Peru where by the late 1960s manufacturing produced 22 percent of the gross domestic product and employed 13.7 percent of the active labor force (for Bolivia the respective figures were 14 and 12.2 percent, and for Ecuador 17 and 13.5 percent).[92] By 1968 North American investment in Peruvian manufacturing, standing at an estimated $98 million and up from $13 million in 1950,[93] had become highly visible in the fishmeal, automobile assembly, chemical, textile, foodstuff, retailing, and sugar industries, among others. Many Peruvians were alarmed by estimates that 80 percent of industrial investment in the country was foreign. And they grew increasingly perturbed by the fact that a good deal of Peruvian capital was invested in U.S. controlled manufacturing firms, as a result of which some of the profits that it earned seemed certain to be expatriated.[94] Manufacturing was on the rise, as Raúl Prebisch and also many Andean economists had been urging since the end of the 1940s. But the manner in which this was accomplished had only added to the outflow of capital and to increased dependence on the United States.

Like Paz Estenssoro in the 1950s, many Peruvian and Ecuadoran leaders had come in the 1960s to appreciate the degree to which consumerism could be used to keep the masses, once they were induced to spend available capital on consumer goods, dependent upon the government for cradle-to-grave social services. Various U.S. aid programs combined with the operation of North American enterprises had opened their eyes to the development potential in their countries, to the possibility of increasing manufacturing output and spreading purchasing power. More than ever, manufacturing seemed the solution to economic and social problems, but only if it were so regulated as to leave its major yields within the Andean republics so that some of the earnings might find their way into social investment aimed at perpetuating the quiescence of the masses.

At the time the export economies were established, Andean Americans could afford a siphoning off of national capital, providing a large enough share of profits remained behind to serve the needs of the few politically aware and participating elites. By the 1960s, however, the number of elites had expanded dramatically. Even the masses had acquired rising wants; and through stepped-up political activity they turned to government for satisfaction of those wants. Under these conditions, a systematic drain on the national economies could no longer be tolerated. That such a drain did exist and that it was being increased as a result of "dependent industrialization"[95] became an article of faith, promulgated by a school of writers that included in its forefront Germany's André Gunder Frank, Chile's Osvaldo Sunkel, and Brazil's Theotonio Dos Santos. By the late 1960s the new school of economic analysis, prevailingly but by no means exclusively Marxist-inspired, had superceded among the Andean intelligentsia the essentially Keynesian influence of Prebisch.

External Dependency Theories

Dependency analysis receives one of its most succinct expositions from Dos Santos. "Dependency is a situation," he writes, "in which a certain group of countries have their economies conditioned by the development and expansion of another country's economy." The dominant countries, according to him, "impose a dominant technology, commerce, capital and socio-political values on the dependent countries ... and this permits them to impose conditions of exploitation and to extract part of the surplus produced by the dependent countries."[96] Patterns of dependency which would result in permanent underdevelopment could only be broken, in the opinion of Dos Santos and members of his school, if the less developed countries abandoned the liberal, capitalist models of the advanced states.

Marxists proclaimed the need to end for all time the pattern by which an oligarchy retained its ability to exercise internal control over the masses as a result of the economic crumbs it received from the table of foreign capitalists. But a large number of non-Marxist Andean aspiring elites, subscribing to the internal domination-external dependency theory, were anxious only to replace the incumbent oligarchy so that they might then begin to benefit from the domination over the national citizenry and from the profits that might derive from their own dependent relationship with foreign capital.

According to dependency theories, manufacturing industry, to the extent that it had developed, lay in the hands of one segment of the traditional oligarchy; but this segment was in turn in league with and dependent upon foreign capital. Both for Marxian and non-revolutionary would-be leaders this situation was intolerable, and they saw the need to strike before the alliance with outside capital gave to the manufacturing sector within the oligarchy the same strength that an earlier group of exporting tycoons had derived from their association with U.S. capital. Any number of factors had now coalesced to bring on the overthrow of the old order as well as a basic reassessment of economic relations with the United States. And some of the factors bore similarity to those that some two hundred years earlier had begun to weaken Spain's colonial hold over Andean America.

When Bourbon reformers of the eighteenth century tried to capture the American colonial market for goods manufactured by Spanish capitalists and their intermediaries in the colonies, the *peninsulares,* they sowed consternation among the domestic creole manufacturing classes who eventually came to see emancipation from the metropolis as their only salvation. When Alliance for Progress development projects seemed likely to bring into being new hordes of consumers in Andean America, but under circumstances causing their money to be channeled into manufacturing firms controlled by U.S. capitalists and a plutocracy of native intermediaries, middle-sector elites decided they had no recourse but to plunge into the struggle for greater economic independence from the United States. In both cases, competition over utilization of the economic potential of the masses was involved. In both cases, what is more, the military was at the heart of the struggle.

Independence from Spain had to be obtained on the field of battle, and obviously the military took center stage in that undertaking. Independence from the United States had to be sought through rearranging social and economic structures. And by the late 1960s Peruvian and to a lesser extent Ecuadoran military officers were convinced, with considerable justification, that they were the persons best equipped to take charge of socioeconomic engineering directed toward national development. To some degree the technological competence that U.S. programs had helped impart to the Andean military contributed to this conviction.

THE MILITARY AND ITS PERCEIVED ROLE OF NATION-BUILDING

In Bolivia, writers subscribing to dependency theories have denounced the military officers who assumed control in 1964, accusing them of having become the lackey of North American capitalist imperialists. In Peru, however, dependency analysis provided a rationale for a military *golpe* against the established oligarchy whose rule was viewed as destined to perpetuate underdevelopment. The Peruvian officers acquired much of their knowledge of dependency theories at the High Center of Military Studies or CAEM (*Centro Alto de Estudios Militares*).

Founded in 1950 on the outskirts of Lima, the CAEM trained officers of the army, navy, air force, and police, and also a few civilians, not only in concepts of external warfare but also in strategies of internal security, above all in employing economic development as a means of reducing social tensions. By the mid-1960s many Peruvians, including even those unsympathetic to the military, asserted that the best education on national social and economic problems was "not to be found in the universities, but in CAEM."[97] Out of CAEM came 80 percent of the army officers who would hold ministerial rank in the first four years after the military came to power through their October 1968 *golpe*.[98]

The new roles and missions assigned to the military by the internal security concepts developed at CAEM and at the similar Superior Schools of War established in Ecuador basically changed the nature of military professionalism. Traditional theory, Alfred Stepan notes, equated military professionalism with expertise in conducting external defense, and it placed a premium on apolitical attitudes. In contrast, the new professionalism was shaped by assumptions concerning the relationship between internal security and national developmenet. This tended "to mean that the content of military professionalism gradually encompassed all areas of the polity, thus contributing to a deep politicization of the military and often an *authoritarian military role-expansion*."[99]

During the early 1960s the Peruvian and Ecuadoran military came to see existing social and economic structures as security threats "because these structures were either so inefficient or so unjust that they created the conditions for and gave legitimacy to revolutionary protest."[100] In this situation, according to the head of Ecuador's military junta in 1965, officers had a duty to apply "their natural sense of discipline" to the constant improvement of their mastery over scientific, economic, and sociological matters, so that they might exercise their key function as teachers and leaders of the people.[101]

In Peru, consciousness of the new roles to be played was heightened by military operations undertaken to suppress Indian insurrections of the mid-1960s, organized in many instances by Marxian activists. These experiences made perfectly clear that "the mission of the armed forces no longer commences in the traditional battle fields, but on a variety of fronts before the internal enemy."[102] Consciousness of new roles was further heightened, both in Peru and Ecuador, by military participation in civic action programs. Through civic action, the military used their discipline and technical skills "in making war on unacceptable social conditions."[103] Undoubtedly, though, military perceptions of a new type of mission came primarily from grievances that officers felt within a society directed by people who seemed insensitive to the dislocations suffered by middle-sector elites.

Andean officers came overwhelmingly from middle-sector backgrounds. Like so many of the civilians who had responded to APRA and APRA-like programs in the 1920s and to AP exhortations in the early 1960s, the officers faced the project of becoming déclassé. Regardless of training and accomplishments, they were being eclipsed by new capitalist tycoons and relegated to a status of relative unimportance by those who directed society. Consistently in the past the guardians of the oligarchy, they were ready now to turn on the ruling sector because of the disdain it showed for the expanding middle sectors of which the officers were a microcosm. Boldness to strike against the group the officers had traditionally served was nourished by the rising mestizo self-confidence that was spreading throughout Andean America. At last mestizos were discarding, en masse, their inferiority attitudes in dealing with the whiter upper classes and finding in their mixed-blood origins a source of pride.

Resenting the treatment received from sectors enjoying a higher ascribed status, the officers at the same time worried, as typical Andean middle sectors, about the breakdown of old domination patterns. Paternalistic at best in their attitudes toward those below, they saw the need to overthrow an order that had lost the touch for keeping the masses pacified and that had unleashed any number of forces contributing to the mounting self-assertiveness of undisciplined underlings.

Condemning the impotence of the political system which threatened to have disastrous consequences for themselves and persuaded that they alone embodied national unity and continuity in countries that were in danger, the officers could point to promising accomplishments when, during the early and mid-1960s, they briefly exercised political power in Peru and Ecuador. Restoration of civilian rule had only quickened the tempo of social, political, and economic disintegration. Thus by the late 1960s Peruvian and Ecuadoran officers inclined to follow the example of their Bolivian counterparts, ensconced in power since 1964, and to take up the long-term direction of national destinies.

The development ideology to which the Andean military by and large subscribed called for a mixture of state and private capitalism. In the private sector, however, capitalists were to be disciplined by military and ancillary civilian technocrats who responded not so much to the instincts of private gain as to the heroic vision of national development. Willing to accept the business classes only in a subordinate position because of their alleged narrow materialism and nonheroic posture, the Andean military shared the belief expressed by Joseph A. Schumpeter in a classic study first published in 1942: "without protection by some nonbourgeois group, the bourgeoisie is politically helpless and unable not only to lead its nation but even to take care of its particular class interest. Which amounts to saying that it needs a master."[104] In line with this persuasion of the officers, and in consequence of their general development ideology, a manufacturing bourgeoisie would for the first time gain an equal footing in the decades-long struggle with an export-minded commercial bourgeoisie; but the manufacturers would achieve their gain only under the aegis of military masters.

To the military, the need for a master was demonstrated most clearly by the degree to which various business, professional, and functional associations, and even government entities, had become virtually autonomous. Military development strategy called for rationalizing this uncoordinated complex of power centers through establishment of a moderating power to be exercised by a group of technocratic elites clearly distinct from and above the particularisms of society. Thereby the amoral corporativism which had come into being, and which threatened to usher in wildly competive and chaotic interest-group pluralism, could be transformed into national corporativism directed in the interests of the common good.

The corporativist structure envisaged by military development ideology was to extend so as to encompass the laboring classes. Thereby individualistic instincts could be curbed by group concerns, while at the same time the lower classes were distracted from obsessive preoccupation with material appetites by the satisfactions deriving from a sense of identity with and participation within a particular functional compartment. Meantime intermediate organizations such as political parties and labor unions would be destroyed so that government might act directly upon the lower classes, collectivized within their appropriate associations.

The vision of a corporative society—which allowed some scope for the individualistic, capitalist instincts of those above but stressed collectivism for the masses, which eliminated intermediate power brokers so as to allow those who exercised the moderating power to establish immediate control over citizens, and which added to material compensation for the masses a sense of satisfaction in participating in the creation of a more perfect society—seems derived from the Aprista ideology of the 1920s. The similarity between the initial Aprista approach and that of the military over forty years later is not surprising; for both Aprista and military views were shaped by the Andean historical background, and especially by the predominance both in Indian and Spanish culture of patronalist-clientelist relationships. Beyond this, the Apristas and other prophets of transition in the 1920s as well as the military leaders of the 1960s were profoundly influenced by the traditional suspiciousness of the univeral bourgeois capitalist ethic and by the concern for humanism and spiritual development that had helped shape the character of colonial Catholicism and had influenced Krausists, Arielists, and Hispanists at the turn of the century, as well as such unorthodox Marxists as Mariátegui and Navarro in the twentieth century.

Thrown into doubt and confusion after World War II by neoliberalism, militantly proclaimed by Washington's cold war crusaders and then cultivated by U.S. technicians with massive dollar resources, Andeans had turned by the 1970s onto a homeward course that had been roughly charted following World War I. For North Americans, the situation was entirely different as they entered, after the Vietnam War, upon a period of diminishing faith in traditional political beliefs and social ties.[105] As the Andeans seemed to be finding their course, North Americans were losing theirs. Out of this situation of role reversal emerged a new stage in hemisphere relations.

12

A New Era Emerges, 1968–1976

In a two-year period between 1972 and 1974, as U.S. citizens pondered the lessons of the failure of the mission in Vietnam (lessons that seemed as ambiguous and contradictory as the motives that had inspired the mission), they moved several degrees toward isolationism. An isolationist policy appealed to 9 percent of the citizenry in 1972, and to 21 percent in 1974.[1] In the 1920s the United States had also turned inward as it assumed a relatively isolationist stance. The internalization, however, that occurred fifty years later was different; for accompanying it was the erosion of confidence that the United States possessed the answers to its own internal problems, let alone those of the world.

Old values were questioned as seldom before in the 1970s: the basic assumptions of capitalism were challenged by those who spoke of the need for limited growth or even for no growth, the idea of progress—so fundamental to the liberal value system—was abandoned by many,[2] and even the doctrines of democracy, after a century of steady celebration, appeared "to be losing their supremacy in the United States."[3] Gerald Ford, succeeding Richard Nixon in the presidency in August of 1974 as the denouement to the Watergate scandals, sought to revive the old values and beliefs in which Americans had found comfort in the 1920s. However, as of the beginning of 1976 (the cutoff date for this book) his endeavor had failed to evoke enthusiastic response. In all walks of life citizens were becoming vaguely but uneasily aware that America was in a stage of transition, passing from the industrial into some type of postindustrial society the nature of which could not yet be perceived. Thus the old-time beliefs no longer conferred the same degree of assurance that they had in the 1920s, when it was assumed that America was on the right track and that the rest of the world must either find its way onto that track or endure permanent retardation.

The neoisolationism of the post-Vietnam years gave a new cast to U.S.-Latin American relations. Business opportunities for North American capital still existed to the south—even though the relative stake of Latin America in total U.S. private investment declined between 1950 and 1970.[4] So, interest in the region remained alive; but, it flickered, sometimes almost to the point of extinction. One reason for this can be discerned by scanning the past. Historically, the United States has undergone its periods of most intense interest in foreign lands when security considerations and nation-building ambitions directed toward the uplifting of purportedly backward peoples have combined with profit-making aspirations. With the development of intercontinental missiles and missile-delivering submarines, Latin America's strategic importance had declined by the 1970s. And it no longer loomed as a promising missionary field for those intent upon spreading a better way of life; for at the same time that Latin Americans were becoming more assertive in defending their way of life, North Americans were wondering about the superiority of theirs. Under these conditions, Latin America evoked an interest that was motivated principally by economic concerns. This being so, many North Americans grew indifferent toward their southern neighbors.

The changing circumstances resulted in a dramatic switch in U.S. attitudes toward the presence of non-American foreign capital in Latin America. According to underlying assumptions of hemisphere policy that had remained fairly constant until the end of the 1960s, North America economic penetration into Latin America would help spread the values of the U.S. political culture. It followed, in the logic of traditional guidelines, that the U.S. government must be willing to protect the interests of its citizens who invested in the southern republics so as to guarantee them a favorable field of operations. It further followed that Washington must take steps to block economic penetration by the other advanced nations of the world, whose capitalists allegedly would not bestow nation-building virtue in the course of their business transactions. No one can say with any assurance how much humbug, how much economically self-serving rationalization, and how much sincere humanitarianism entered into these basic assessments of hemisphere policy.

Whatever their motivation, the assessment that guided the United

States from pre-Monroe Doctrine days to the Alliance for Progress era had been largely discarded by the 1970s. More and more, North American capitalists, with the support of their government, were enlisting investment partners from the other developed nations for their ventures in Latin America. Toward this purpose they helped found in the 1960s the Atlantic Community Development Group for Latin America (ADELA), bringing together some 235 of the largest banks and industrial firms of the United States, Europe, Japan, and Latin America. The internationalization of capitalist undertakings in Latin America is dramatically demonstrated by petroleum investment in Peru during the first half of the 1970s. To exploit reserves located about one hundred miles from Iquitos, U.S. firms made significant investments; but, the main pipeline was largely financed by Japanese capital, while the pipe itself came from Japan and Germany. Moreover, the Soviet Union supplied storage tanks, while the helicopters involved in the vast project came from Russian, French, and United States firms.[5]

In part, the new policy arose out of the lesson that advantageous economic relations could be carried out with countries as socially and politically divergent from North American norms as the Soviet Union and the Peoples' Republic of China. This being the case, it behooved the United States to collaborate in business ventures in Latin America with countries that had no interest in and were even hostile to the idea of reshaping the political culture of the southern hemisphere in line with the models once venerated by North Americans.

Underlying the new U.S. approach, then, was resignation to the reality of having to deal amicably with Latin American governments that chose "un American" political structures. Thereby North American statesmen faced up at last to the fallacy of the Jeffersonian conviction, enshrined in the Monroe Doctrine, that a unique American way of life set all of the New World apart from the Old World; and that even if the process was a slow one, all of Latin America was destined ultimately to evolve toward the sort of political culture that North Americans were perfecting. In a major 1974 address Secretary of State Henry Kissinger announced that the United States would abandon its old approach in favor of one of pluralism. And he conceded that a good deal of hemisphere friction had arisen in the past because "we are prone to set standards for the political, economic, and social structures of our sister republics."[6]

Acceptance of a pluralist approach helped bring into being what President Nixon described as a low-profile policy. Essentially, this policy committed the United States to curtailing the direct exercise of political and cultural influence and to refraining from overt, unilateral government actions to protect North American private investors. Helping make possible the low-profile policy was the fact that since the early 1960s a good deal of U.S. investment has been channeled into Latin America through multinational corporations. As a result, any number of advanced countries, whose citizens might be disadvantaged by the actions of a Latin American government in dealing with a multinational concern, can join together to exert subtle and clandestine pressures. Many of the multinational corporations, moreover, capitalize their operations in large part through funds invested by the local citizens of a particular Latin American country. In consequence, the multinational corporations have as their clientelist allies some of the most powerful citizens of the country in which they operate, and this has contributed to the ability of the firms to generate their own political capacity and to protect their interests without having recourse to home governments.[7] In terms of hemisphere relations, the internationalization of capitalism has made it possible for the U.S. government to refrain from some of the overt interventionist policies in behalf of its private investors that so often enraged Latin Americans in the past.

Basically, the reduction of economically motivated, overt U.S. government intervention has come about because in recent years the operations of foreign capital in Latin America have fallen under the protection of a virtually unseen hand. In fact, the low-profile policy might more accurately be dubbed that of the the unseen hand. In addition to the covert pressures that the multinationals can apply, the United States can appeal to one of its "most favored allies" in the hemisphere, such as Brazil, to exercise covert persuasion on problem-making republics.[8] This approach has been particularly useful in the case of Bolivia, in whose politics the conservative Brazilian military government—in power since 1964 and consistently cooperative with both the U.S. government and North American investors—intervened steadily in the early 1970s so as to undermine the position of leftists; undoubtedly, moreover, it was hoped that Chile after the September 1973 overthrow of Marxist president Salvador Allende and the establishment of a conservative military regime could be groomed as another most favored ally. Also, there is the possibility that the CIA can be resorted to in protecting enterprises thought to be endangered by leftist or excessively nationalistic administrations. Additional low visibility protection for North American capital invested abroad is provided through the U.S.-based Overseas Private Investment Corporation (OPIC), founded in 1969 and extended by act of congress for another three years in mid-1974. OPIC is empowered "to insure investment abroad against commercial risks (up to 75 percent) and political risks (up to 100 percent)."[9] These and other operations through which OPIC employs federal funds to aid private investors have helped eliminate the need for direct and highly publicized Washington confrontations with troublesome Latin American governments.

The radically altered circumstances of hemisphere relations have resulted in a veritable revolution in the conduct of diplomacy. For years, Latin Americans demanded that the United States take up the noninterventionist, pluralist approach that lies at the heart of the low-profile policy. The circumstances of the 1970s, however, that have made it possible and expedient for the United States to do—or appear to do—just this are not necessarily to the liking or advantage of Andean and sister republics; for the unseen hand can operate in just as ruthless a fashion as the gunboats and marines of a bygone era.

THE VIEW FROM ANDEAN AMERICA

Involved in the decision of the Peruvian military to seize power in 1968 was recognition that the old forms of dependency on the United States would no longer suffice to assure the viability of Andean regimes and that greater measures of self-help were necessary. Once in power, the officers—seeking to make a virtue out of necessity—joined the fashionable chorus of economic nationalism as they pronounced a death sentence on dependency. General Juan Velasco Alvarado, who emerged as Peru's chief executive following the 1968 military takeover, proclaimed: "To cancel the traditional dependency of our country is the fundamental objective of our nationalist revolution and the central goal of the full development of Peru."[10]

In Bolivia, condemnation of dependence on the United States and clarion calls for attainment of independence continued, as of 1976, to be favorite ploys of out-of-power elites. The country's MNR leadership had never developed an anti-U.S. orientation, and the military officers in power since 1964 have not, with only two brief exceptions provided by Generals Ovando and Torres (to be mentioned later in this chapter), sought to enhance legitimacy by assuming a stance in opposition to Yankee capital. In Peru and to a lesser degree in Ecuador the situation is different. There, the rhetoric of economic independence has been taken up as the preferred means by which incum-

bent military governments justify their assult against the old order while calling on the masses to contribute their sacrifices to the realization of lofty national goals.

In moving initially to match deeds to words, the Peruvian officers took full advantage of an unusual situation. They were able, on October 9, 1968, to nationalize the International Petroleum Company, a firm surrounded for decades by controversy but one whose importance to the national economy—and to its parent Standard Oil firm—had been steadily declining in recent years. In Ecuador, though, circumstances were quite distinct. There, foreign capital had appeared late on the scene and sizeable petroleum reserves had been discovered only toward the end of the 1960s. Thus when the military officers came to power in 1972 they found themselves dealing with recently established foreign oil firms that had built up no reservoir of national ill will. Expropriation would have been of only marginal usefulness as a symbolic act, and would have resulted in a virtual collapse of the petroluem production on which the military pinned their economic hopes. Therefore, in order to demonstrate their conviction that the national economy had become too important to be left to foreigners the Ecuadorans had to settle for the less dramatic expedient of seizing California tuna boats.

Ecuador's seizure of fishing boats was one manifestation of a serious diplomatic dispute with the United States that also involved Peru and, indeed, countries throughout the world with important offshore resources. In the American hemisphere the dispute pitted Ecuador, Peru, Chile, Panama, El Salvador, Nicaragua, Argentina, Uruguay, and even the most-favored ally Brazil, the republics most insistent on claiming jurisdiction over their waters for 200 miles off their coasts, against the United States which for many years had held out for a 12-mile limit. The complex issue, which has divided international law experts,[11] came into sharper focus within the hemisphere when the Latin American countries faced up to the fact that they could not count on aid and assistance from the United States to the degree once hoped for and must save themselves through their own efforts and by means of their own resources. If forced to share offshore sea-life wealth with the developed nations and their powerful fishing fleets, Latin Americans would be deprived of one of the most promising means of self-help potentially available to them. The issue became all the more important in view of the prospects for offshore oil drilling in various parts of the world.

One of many in a long series of Law of the Sea conferences was held in Caracas, Venezuela, beginning in June of 1974. By that time the United States had developed a compromise position: it backed recognition of a 200-mile offshore "economic zone" (having unilaterally asserted its own rights to such a zone) in which coastal states enjoyed exclusive ownership of resources, while at the same time urging control by an international agency over matters of ecology that involved cleanliness and preservation of species in the 200-mile zone and retention of the 12-mile limit for all other matters of international law. Peru, Ecuador and many other states represented at Caracas objected to the international ecological control suggestion. Disputes over this and a number of other points prevented agreement and left the control-of-the-sea issue pending as a source of international friction. Subsequently, in a Montreal speech in August of 1975, Secretary of State Kissinger warned that failure to reach agreements would lead to unrestrained military and commercial rivalry and mounting political tension. Against this background a United Nations Conference on the Law of the Sea convened in New York in mid-March 1976. Described as a now-or-never attempt to resolve the troublesome issues, the conference, which ran for six months, distinguished itself by a discouragingly slow rate of progress. New problems emerged and old ones intensified.

One of the new problems appeared when landlocked republics, Bolivia included, demanded access to the 200-mile "economic zones" of maritime countries. At the same time coastal republics among the developing countries, Peru and Ecuador included, raised new objections to permitting advanced nations to conduct worldwide scientific research within two hundred miles of the shore. The major powers, it was charged, would gather intelligence under the guise of carrying out scientific investigation.

The most heated controversy during the 1976 Conference revolved about the mining of minerals, such as cobalt, copper, and manganese, contained in nodules that carpet the ocean floor beyond the 200-mile offshore zones. Banding together in a so-called Group of Seventy-Seven, less-developed countries demanded that mining be conducted by an international agency, with profits to be divided so as to favor the poor republics. While some of the rich nations held out for the exclusive right of private companies to mine ocean-floor minerals, the United States introduced a compromise, calling for joint access by private firms and an international agency. The proposal evoked objections from both sides, and even if it should be accepted in principle, protracted bargaining will be in store over assignment of quotas and also over technological and monetary contributions to the international firm from the developed nations.

Various authorities concerned about relations of the rich nations with the poor have for many years concluded that significant international redistribution of existing wealth lies beyond the realm of the possible. Since the early 1970s, though, they have sometimes voiced the hope for a distribution of future wealth, as its potential is gradually realized by means of advancing technology, that will benefit primarily the poor nations. This they have urged not only in the interest of justice, virtually impossible to define, but in the interest of international stability. Difficulties besetting the attempt to arrange disposal of underseas resources show that problems of redistributing future wealth are no more readily resolvable than those involving redistribution of present wealth.

Meanwhile, as they sought to legitimize their regimes on the basis of seeking independence from the United States and as they turned their attention to economic self-help in urging "trade not aid" and in stressing the potential of their own agricultural, subsoil, and offshore resources, Andean leaders could not hide from themselves the reality of their continued dependence on foreign private investment. In Peru, for example, as of 1968 the book value of U.S. direct investment stood at $691 million;[12] and three huge North American firms dominated the mining industry and controlled between 40 and 50 percent of the foreign reserves that the country earned.[13] During the course of the ensuing six years of rule by the Revolutionary Government of the Armed Forces the amount of money invested by U.S. capitalists and those from other developed nations rose dramatically. In the February 2, 1975 *New York Times* Jonathan Kandell reported that the military government had been more successful than any of its predecessors in Peru's history in attracting foreign investment.

With the mining industry, the generals followed the precedent they had already established with petroleum: they nationalized the most visible firm, in this case the Cerro de Pasco Corporation which had been involved in controversies with various regimes for well over fifty years and had largely exhausted mineral resources in the north-central Andes locale, and then welcomed huge new inputs of foreign capital, including funds from Cerro de Pasco, to develop the giant Cuajone copper project on the western slopes of the Andes about 700 miles south of Lima. The arrangement was finalized only after Washington and Lima reached an accord in February of 1974 under which the

346

Peruvians agreed to pay $150 million in compensation to expropriated companies—which included W. R. Grace and Company interests.

Not only in Peru but also in Ecuador, following the 1972 military takeover, the generals talked about socialist reforms and the need for economic independence from the United States while seeking an unprecedented North American investment in pertoleum enterprises. A U.S. consortium made its first discovery of oil in the Ecuadoran *Oriente* in 1967, and by 1974 it was pumping oil at a rate of about 250,000 barrels a day over a 318-mile pipeline crossing the Andes, at altitudes sometimes exceeding 13,000 feet, to the Pacific coast at Balso, near Esmeraldas. The bubble soon burst under circumstances that are described later in this chapter. For the moment, though, Ecuador had become the second largest exporter of petroleum in Latin America, surpased only by Venezuela (its fellow Latin American member of the Organization of Petroleum Exporting countries or OPEC), and economic prospects seemed uniquely promising.

Critics have accused the Peruvian and Ecuadoran generals of hypocrisy and of creating, behind a diversionary barrage of nationalistic oratory, a new type of dependence on foreign capital. The military governments, however, defend themselves on the grounds that by permitting the operation of foreign capital they are making it possible to generate the funds required to bring about revolutionary reforms and transform the economy into socialist patterns. Above all they stress that the conditions they have laid down for the operation of foreign capital will not permit the outsiders to siphon off their earnings to the extent they did in an earlier era. As proof of their ability to enforce the more demanding terms to which foreign capital has been subjected, the military governments point to the added strength they have attained through Andean regional economic agreements that permit them to present a united front with sister republics in dealing with capitalists from abroad—until unity collapsed in 1976.

Realization that it was impossible to proceed rapidly toward transforming the masses of local citizens into purchasers contributed to Andean demands for access to the markets of the developed world for finished goods and lay behind their trade-not-aid pronouncements. Likewise, this realization inspired the push toward Andean economic integration. Through such steps as reduction of tariff barriers the republics involved could gain access to the wealthy purchasers of neighboring countries; and thus the success of manufacturing industry would not be solely dependent upon raising the purchasing power of economically marginal citizens, about which some of the new rulers—even as the old ones—had their doubts. Above all else, though, it was the desire to be able to curb the activities of the multinational corporations and to limit their capacity for independent political action that led the Andean republics to seek some measure of economic cooperation.

Preliminary moves toward the formulation of an economic accord got underway in 1968 with an agreement signed by Peru, Bolivia, Ecuador, Chile, Colombia, and Venezuela to create an Andean Development Corporation. Mid-way in the following year five of these countries, with Venezuela the exception, entered into the Cartagena Agreement. Providing for trade liberalization among the signatory powers by the creation of an Andean Common Market, the Cartagena Agreement also paved the way for adoption of a regional code for uniform treatment of foreign investments. Terms agreed to by the five republics at the end of 1970 distinguished between national firms (citizens of the nation concerned owning more than 80 percent of the capital of the enterprise), mixed enterprises (citizens of the nation concerned owning 50 to 80 percent of the capital), and foreign firms (citizens of the nation concerned owning less than 51 percent of the capital). The 1970 agreement stipulated that in many activities, especially in manufacturing, only those foreign concerns willing to transform into mixed or national operations would be allowed to export to other nations covered by the pact. Any new foreign investment had to obtain an initial local participation of 15 percent; and foreign investment in public utilities, financial institutions, transportation, or communications activites was prohibited. Existing foreign investment in those categories was required to disinvest by at least 80 percent within three years.[14] Beyond these provisions, Andean economic agreements have been aimed at establishing a regional policy regarding profit remittances, taxation and management policies[15] and at creating uniform "fadeout formulas" governing the short-term colloboration of foreign with national capital.[16]

Although many loopholes and exceptions to the provisions of the Andean economic agreements have been provided and although the Andean Common Market was soon beset by discord of a degree that renders its future uncertain, at least preliminary steps were taken to gain greater regional control over foreign capital. And this fact alarmed U.S. defenders of the privileges of investors in foreign lands. In Andean economic unification they saw a challenge to the situation of former years when "virtually all foreign investments return[ed] more income to the United States—and hence provide[d] financing for net import of goods, etc.—than they cost us capital at the outset."[17]

As the Andean countries grappled with problems of imposing adequate checks on foreign capital, they also cast about for effective means to establish control over domestic sectors. To attain this objective, without which there could be no possibility of national development, first the Peruvian officers and later the Ecuadorans turned to new forms of corporativism. In this they enjoyed some important advantages over their Bolivian fellow officers.

The Bolivian revolution had occurred before Andean leaders had gained the confidence and resolve required to proceed systematically with corporativist experiments. Many of its leaders remained under the spell of neoliberalism, while those who backed more sweeping innovation lacked the force that the presence of a strong military element within their regimes could have provided from the outset. Finally, because of the cold war setting which found Washington in a mood to undertake huge assistance programs in areas deemed vulnerable to communism, the revolution fell almost at once under U.S. mentorship. Perhaps Bolivia had its revolution at the wrong time. In any event, that country could not in the 1970s make more than a gesture at emulating the approach of Peruvian officers. Whether in the long run the Peruvians, and the Ecuadorans, will do any better than the Bolivians seems doubtful in light of 1976 developments.

PERU'S NEW CORPORATIVISM AND THE QUEST FOR CONTROLLED DEVELOPMENT

Sounding his own variation on a theme that had been heard with increasing frequency throughout Andean America ever since the 1920s, President Velasco Alvardo declared that the Revolutionary Government of the Armed Forces would build a new Peru that was neither capitalist nor communist. Capitalism, he averred, alienates men, destroys their control over their development, "and is contrary to humanistic ends." Communism he dismissed because, through its all-absorbing centralized bureaucratic structure that leaves no room for particularisms, it too "dehumanizes and alienates." Peruvians, he concluded, would do badly to copy either system. "Our greatest challenge in the revolution lies in showing ourselves capable of being ourselves, of being the forgers of our own historic destiny, the discoverers of our own solutions."[18] Carlos Delgado, a former Aprista who emerged as one of the leading civilian intellectuals collaborating with the military in shaping Peru's nationalist revolution from above, saw the country's challenge in a similar light. Peru, he affirmed, must develop its social system on the basis of the true and authentic character of its existence, being guided by the past as it approached the future: "To know who we will be or ought to be, it is necessary, beforehand, to know what we have been and what, in reality, we are today."[19]

In its traditional corporativist, two-culture society, Andean America had repudiated both capitalism and collectivism as universal sociopolitical cultures. Upper sectors, as has been suggested earlier, were expected to own private property and to incline to some degree toward the values of individualism and self-reliance, while the masses were expected to find realization in a collectivized way of life that blunted private material ambitions. The Bolivian historian-diplomat José Fellman Velarde gave voice to a time-honored view when he observed that collectivism was natural to those who are weak.[20]

Peru's revolution makers were resolved to reject both capitalism and Marxian socialism because of their desire to restore a patronalist-clientelist society that was structured and controlled from above. They rejected liberal capitalism because its objective was to universalize independence and self-reliance. And they turned their backs on socialism because it was seen, at least in the guise it had come to assume in the Soviet Union, as universalizing dependency or clientelism, with the sole exception of the tiny party elite that ran the state.

Endeavoring to establish points of contact with all Peruvians, whether they occupied a clientelist, collectivized status or one that was comparatively patronalist and individualistic, the revolutionary government moved to eliminate intermediaries, such as political parties, between the people and the state,[21] and to claim control over all citizens in the national interest. Thus, through nationalism the officers hoped to achieve the integration of Peruvians into a common political form, even though people would be exhorted to contribute to the nation in different ways, depending upon the particular status they occupied within the body politic. It would be the task of cultural elites "to legitimize the social revolutionary ideal by formulating a convincing national ideology that would bind all ... [citizens] together"[22] and persuade all to join, in the appropriate manner, in building a nation.

The cultural elites, whose role it was to exercise the moderating power in Peru's new corporativism, were to include technicians, engineers, and representative members of the intelligentsia, both military and civilian,[23] as well as a sprinkling of bishops and priests. Government's legitimacy was to rest upon recognition by the masses of the elite's cultural superiority and its mastery over the mysterious knowledge, unattainable by the rank and file, of how to forge a nation and achieve the security of its citizens. Including select beings who knew the proper approaches to spiritual development as well as those who knew how to bend the material world to their wishes, the new wielders of the moderating power were expected to devise a proper blend of nonmaterial and material rewards.

Rather than upon the use of force, the claims of the new leaders to the rights of sovereignty were to rest upon their ability to act as teachers (intellectual workers in raising the consciousness of nonintellectuals), who could persuade the citizenry to acknowledge their superiority. Especially during the early years of military rule, a fairly high percentage of Peruvians seemed willing to accept—even if somewhat glumly—Velasco Alvarado's typically populist contention that "our legitimacy has its origins in the incontrovertible fact that we are bringing about the transformation of this country in order to defend and interpret the interests of the people against those who would deceive them."[24] This being so, the military government between late 1968 and early 1976 could rule, most of the time, with only a moderate use of coersion, even while excluding national majorities from real participation in high-level decision making.

In the all-important quest of development, which would determine success or failure for the military, the governing elites could turn to many skilled university graduates, who had previously encountered difficulty in finding adequate employment in their specialties. This group of civilians became junior members in a coalition with the organizers of the military regime, "providing some of the technical and administrative skills which were lacking in earlier authoritarian stabilization and strong-man-type governments."[25] Aníbal Quijano caught the significance of this development when he wrote: "Since the Junta has come to power . . . a fairly substantial number of professional people and high-level technicians have been finding a place . . . in the numerous institutions created to carry out the reform measures. The broadening of urban-industrial activities . . . will operate for its part as a rather broad channel for extending the typical activities of the middle-level urban sectors."[26] In the new opportunities opening to them, many urban aspiring elites found the means to increase the gulf between them and the masses, thus relieving some of the anxieties that had contributed to the downfall of the old order.

New bureaucratic elites played a key role in government plans to establish a public sector of the economy that would include all "primary and essential" industries[27] and whose share of total investment within the country was projected to rise from its 20 percent level in 1968 to between 50 and 60 percent before the end of the 1970s.[28] While hoping to "restore to the State its principal and dynamic role,"[29] the military regime intended also to leave ample room, especially in manufacturing industry, for private ownership and management. Toward this end it held out to private entrepreneurs the lure of vastly increased markets, to be created through agrarian and other social reforms and through membership in the Andean Common Market. It sought also to inspire in the "national bourgeoisie"[30] a dedication to increased productivity. The Revolutionary Government of the Armed Forces sought, in fact, to eradicate *criollismo* from the set of bourgeois values. Described by David Chaplin as the "antithesis of the Protestant Ethic,"[31] *criollismo* was characterized by avoidance of hard and consistent effort and by a mania for getting ahead through connections, cunning and graft.[32]

The development design of the ruling officers included places not only for government and private industry, but also for the "industrial community" in which workers would participate, along with owners, in profits and management.[33] Under the terms of 1970 legislation pertaining to industry and commerce, various industrial concerns in fishing, mining, and commerce, but generally not in manufacturing or in public-sector industries, might set up workers' communities through which employees and laborers would share each year in profits, to be distributed partly in company stock, until they attained 50 percent control of the firm's capital, which would then entitle them to hold half of the seats on the board of directors.

In explaining the industrial community, President Velasco stated its primary purpose was to forge "a new personality" so that "workers will progress toward being not just salary earners, but the true creators of a human community which they feel is truly theirs. Under such circumstances the industrial workers of Peru will have . . . the responsibility and the creativity endowment of genuinely free men."[34] Clearly, the military concurred in the assessment of Carlos Delgado that in order to avoid the sort of alienation and anomie that spawn revolutionary pressures, it was necessary for persons to have participation in "economic processes that affect the totality of their organized groups. And this implies, too, increasing accessibility to the mechanisms of power."[35]

Access to power has been provided by government representatives who, under the military regime, assumed considerable importance within all worker groups organized into industrial communities. In this process unions have been eliminated. Thus, workers ceased to depend on organized labor officials as their intermediaries with government and became dependent instead directly on the government and its functionaries. Here was an important means by which the military enlarged its "patrón-like" control over the emerging masses[36] as it began to mobilize them for national purposes while at the same time impeding, through functional compartmentalization, the rise of concerted class consciousness.[37]

In the days preceding the breakdown of the old order, the highest degree of worker militancy was usually demonstrated by the best-paid labor elites. It is significant that industrial communities have been organized principally among the labor elites in Peru's new society. The objective is to combine the nonmaterial reward of full human development, a promised result of participation in the total process of economic production, with monetary remuneration in pacifying worker sectors. If workers can be induced to go along with this program, government will effect capital savings which can be channeled into development spending. It remains to be seen if the industrial communities will achieve the purpose of drawing from basic units of production some of the vigor and mystique that citizenship in general appears to lack.[38] By 1976 the experiment was in trouble.

The industrial community at first seemed an ingenious method of adapting the hacienda economy, with many of its values, to modern times. The hacienda "remained located on the border of two economies, and of two social sectors . . . capitalist business toward the outside," and collectivist on the inside. Thus the hacienda coordinated two apparently contradictory systems.[39] Were it to work as hoped, the industrial community would perform the same function. But, instead of the hacendado, government bureaucrats would serve as brokers between the two systems. The prospect of introducing updated forms of the hacienda economy was understandably enticing to the military corporativists, and attempts to accomplish this purpose have extended beyond the introduction of the industrial community.

In one of its earliest, and what appeared to be one of its most revolutionary, actions the armed forces government nationalized the huge sugar estates of the northern coast, those that were owned by Peruvians as well as by foreign firms that included "Casa Grace." Ownership of the estates was transferred to their workers, organized into cooperatives under careful government supervision. Through these measures government hoped to crush the mounting strength of the

Aprista-dominated unions that represented the sugar workers; and it wished to establish firm lines of control over this well-paid sector of the agrarian labor force that had been showing increasing independence, in a collective-bargaining setting, and demanding ever more in the way of economic rewards. Beyond the basic attempt to spread the pattern of a state controlled hacienda economy, nationalization fitted in with government attempts to encourage private capital investment in manufacturing. Peruvian citizens whose estates were seized received the major portion of their compensation in the form of government bonds that could only be invested in industrial enterprise. Thus the sugar aristocracy was offered the chance to join with the upper industrial class and thereby to conserve a considerable part of its wealth, "although not its traditional source of political power."[40] At the same time it was afforded the opportunty to earn future profits through the type of investment that would contribute most directly to the development needs of the nation as perceived by technocratic elites.

Difficulties in establishing control over worker cooperatives entrusted with ownership of the nationalized sugar estates resulted, for several months in 1970 and early 1971, in a serious challenge to the government's authority. The military rulers responded in June of 1971 by creating a new and complex corporativist mechanism that operated on a society-wide basis and bore the name National System of Aid to Social Mobilization, or SINAMOS (*Sistema Nacional de Apoyo a la Movilización Social*). SINAMOS' goal was to provide for participation, always under the state's bureaucratic control, not only within the sugar cooperatives and the industrial communities but also in virtually every sector of the economy and every nook and cranny of the social structure, with one notable exception: in contrast to the Cuban Revolution, SINAMOS plans largely ignored the mobilization of women.

The guidelines under which SINAMOS operates called for compartmentalizing Peru "into a series of parallel and in the main functionally defined communities."[41] Organized into work-based communities, the bulk of the population was expected to confine participatory activities to the work place. If SINAMOS achieves its objectives, it will perpetuate and rationalize dominance-dependence patterns on a nationwide scale, while demonstrating that "clientelism may mitigate the natural trend in modern politics toward alienation and egotistical individualism."[42]

The operation of SINAMOS extends into the *barriada* or squatter-settlement sectors of Lima and other urban centers. Residents of "squatments," many of them recently arrived immigrants from the countryside, had demonstrated a high degree of assertiveness and ability to protect their own interests, thus providing another indication of the collapse of the old order's control apparatus.[43] SINAMOS, taking up its paternalistic mission of teaching the people how to take part in the programs of the revolutionary government, imposed an institutionalized clientelistic relationship on slum dwellers. Further, SINAMOS acted as a broker or middleman, with its uniqueness lying "in the fact that this broker has been created, sponsored, supported, and imposed by the national government."[44]

SINAMOS also extends into the sierra and the Amazonian-basin jungles. In its rural operations it collaborates with the National Agrarian Confederation, established in May of 1972, in imposing state control over all of the cooperatives and comunidades of Indians—officially designated campesinos in 1969, in obvious emulation of Bolivia's abolition of the word Indian.[45] In its major agrarian reform law of 1969, the government proclaimed its intention to restore all lands alienated from comunidades since 1920. In addition, it would grant to comunidades all contiguous lands which the state declared abandoned, as well as property needed to provide irrigation facilities. Hoping to nourish a collectivist life style among the campesinos, government has moved to turn all comunidades (estimated to number about 5,600) into production cooperatives within which "social property," rather than fee-simple plots, is the norm. SINAMOS is expected to play its major rural role in coordinating cooperative activities, and in maintaining campesinos as a docile and "managed" labor force.[46]

Peruvian agrarian reform is not intended to end agricultural capitalism, for the government has established many cholos and mestizos as private proprietors of family-sized farms on land taken from gamonales. In the countryside, then, as in the cities, collectivism is to coexist with capitalism. Nor is agrarian reform concerned with the virtually impossible task of ending the migration of Indians into urban centers. Rather, its objective is to slow the rate of immigration to more manageable proportions. Most important of all, agrarian reformers seek to preserve many Indians as Indians, speaking their own language (about 40 percent of the Peruvian population is considered still to be Indian, and of this number approximately one-half speak little or no Spanish), and living within a cultural ambience assumed to be in harmony with their tradition and nature—but enjoying the opportunity, in exceptional cases, to pass into the non-Indian world.

A cursory glance at the situation in Peru might lead many to conclude that the endeavor to extend the corporativist, dominance-dependence, capitalist-collectivist model in a systematized way into the rural sector simply affords one more instance to corroborate the argument presented by Elias T. Tuma in his 1965 book *Twenty-Six Centuries of Agrarian Reform.* According to him, land redistribution is most likely to serve the political goals of those instigating and implementing the reform rather than the economic and social needs of the alleged beneficiaries.[47] In the case of Peru, however, this conclusion is simplistic. Through the military's approach to agrarian reform, Indians are being allowed to maintain a way of life that obviously appeals to many of them; they are being freed from the intrusions of those who would rob them of a sense of dignity by attempting to transform and "uplift" them, and they are being re-enforced in the attempt to find pride in their ethnic origins and historical traditions. Peruvian corporativism is thus encouraging an exciting experiment in biculturalism. It is as if the Peruvian corporativists in their approach to the Indian masses were acting in line with the advice given years ago by Unamuno in regard to treatment of Spain's rural masses: "Don't sacrifice them to progress—for God's sake don't sacrifice them to progress."[48]

For all its accomplishments, Peruvian corporativism under the generals was beset by many problems, some of them beyond the control of mortals. In 1970, for example, the country sustained a disastrous earthquake resulting in over 50,000 deaths and leaving some 300,000 homeless. In 1972 serious floods occurred, along with a drastic decline in the fishmeal industry owing to the disappearance of anchovies that was partially attributable to a change in the pattern of offshore ocean currents. The anchovy catch, reaching a record 12.4 million tons in 1970, was down to 2 million tons in 1973. Government responded in that year by nationalizing the fishing industry and placing it under a huge state monopoly called *Pescaperú.* By mid-1974 the anchovies had begun to reappear, but on a disappointing scale. As 1976 began, the cost to *Pescaperú* of producing a pound of fishmeal was higher than the world price, and the generals had discovered the pitfalls of nationalizing economically marginal enterprises—even as had Manuel Pardo in the 1870s with his nationalization of the nitrate industry.

In the vitally important coppor sector of its economy Peru suffered from the manner in which U.S. pressure—steadily applied until the 1974 agreement on compensation for expropriated firms—dried up sources of loans from the Export-Import Bank and other international lending agencies to finance development of new mines by multinational firms (in spite of which the foreign debt by 1976 stood at $3 billion). In addition, Peru was hit by a steep decline of world copper prices which contributed to heavy trade deficits in 1974 and 1975 (estimated at $1 billion for the last year). Although by 1975 Peru received more private North American investment per capita than any other South American country with the exception of Venezuela, local capitalists appeared still to be distrustful of national reform programs and were investing their own funds with extreme caution.

Meantime middle sectors and working classes found a source of complaint in the inflation of over 20 percent a year (some unofficial estimates placed it as high as 35–40 percent) that was led by increases in food prices, and in unemployment and underemployment that remained at just over 50 percent of the labor force. These circumstances sparked sporadic protest riots and strikes. A serious challenge to the administration came with a strike by Lima's 7,000-man police force. Suppression of this strike by the armed forces in February of 1975 resulted in over one hundred deaths and cost the administration dearly in prestige and popularity, making it all the harder for Velasco Alvarado to gain mass support. Respected by many for his sincerity, outspoken manner, and doughty toughness, Velasco just missed possessing the magnetism that can be so important to a populist leader. By 1974 more and more Peruvians were complaining about his inconsistency and irascibility, often attributing these traits to health problems that resulted in two serious operations, one of them for amputation of his right leg.

By mid-1975 the sixty-six-year-old Velasco Alvarado was in semi-retirement and the problem of succession, widely discussed in all circles, exacerbated rivalries within the military. Against this background, few Peruvians seemed greatly surprised or deeply perturbed when a bloodless military golpe brought about his ouster on August 20, 1975.

Succeeding Velasco in the presidency was General Francisco Morales Bermúdez, who had acted as the country's prime minister since the previous February. Earlier in the military regime Morales had served as minister of economy and finance (1969–1973), a post in which he had won the respect of many business sectors as a man who could curb his revolutionary ideology with a practical sense of what was economically feasible. Regarded even in the early 1970s as the man most likely to succeed Velasco in the presidency, Morales was expected to respond more sympathetically to importunings from the private sector—although by early 1976 there were rumblings of complaint from that quarter about the general's revolutionary ardor.

In his first six months in office Morales Bermúdez faced an intensification of many of the same problems that had helped bring about the fall of Velasco Alvarado. Private domestic capital, chafing under such restraints as those imposed by the industrial community, pursued a policy of disinvestment that forced government to take over an increasing number of marginal operations in order to avoid their liquidation, which would compound unemployment problems. Petroleum yelds from newly opened fields near Iquitos continued to disappoint, leading to withdrawal of foreign funds. Forced to commit almost the entirety of dwindling cash resources to urgent urban problems, government neglected the countryside, and this led to *campesino* discontent and to lethargic agricultural production which necessitated importation of basic food products. More discouraging still, contact of the military-civilian bureaucrats with the Indians seemed many times less dedicated to mobilizing *campesinos* for effective participation in national life than to providing bureaucrats with opportunities for private enrichment.

Something fundamental and abiding underlies the military government's difficulties with the agrarian sector. At least since the mid-nineteenth century, power groups have been accustomed to exploiting rural sectors for the advantage of urbanites. Land reform in the 1960s and 1970s afforded yet another instance of this phenomenon. By sacrificing the *hacendados*, new urban elites in quest of political legitimacy hoped to remove some of the rural bottlenecks that had resulted in high food prices and thereby sparked discontent among urban lower and middle classes. To some degree, the approach was influenced by the literature of city-based essayists and novelists who in simplistic terms had attributed the ills of the countryside—which were intolerable because they resulted in problems for city-dwellers— to villainous *hacendados*. But, once the revolutionary military officers effected a certain amount of land redistribution, they lacked sufficient funds to pursue integrated agrarian reform. Even as the MNR rulers of Bolivia before them, they were therefore tempted to extract cheap food, upon which the support of urban masses depended, from the hides of *campesinos*, thereby negating the humanitarian intentions that had motivated at least a few of the architects of reform. Thus the Peruvian situation affords a clear example of the ongoing struggle between rural and urban sectors—tinged in Andean America by racial prejudices—that Raymond Williams has placed in broad context in his penetrating 1973 study, *The Country and the City*.

Behind all of Peru's difficulties there lurked, in the mid-1970s, a constant reminder of continuing economic dependence on an international marketplace over which Peruvians have no control. Had the price of copper in early 1976 been the same $1.50 per pound it had been two years earlier, instead of 55¢ a pound, and had the recession in the developed countries not caused a sharp drop in the purchase of Peruvian commodities, many of the problems confronting the generals would have been less severe. Understandably, Peruvian analysts stressed international operations of capitalism as the cause of difficulties, while U.S. observers laid the cause to the folly of challenging capitalist guidelines in running the domestic economy.

Whatever the ideological merits of the case, economic conditions by mid-1976 forced the generals to act as if they subscribed to the U.S. explanation of Peru's difficulties. Responding to pressure exerted especially by the private U.S. banking firms that had extended vast loans and on whose continuing capital transfusions the Peruvian government pinned its hopes, President Morales Bermúdez announced in July a series of conservative changes. Subsidies on basic food items were ended, cuts in federal expenditures were pledged, and the fishing boats were returned to their former owners. At the same time hints leaked from the National Palace that labor legislation providing for worker ownership of 50 percent of certain enterprises would be altered so as to assure continuing control by private management. Moreover, the government suggested that distribution of agricultural lands would be terminated and that reform efforts henceforth would be concentrated on increasing production of crops. Against this background the beleaguered Morales Bermúdez, troubled all the while by increasing dissension among his fellow officers and rumors of plots to overthrow him, made a number of new cabinet appointments, clamped tighter censorship on the press, and imposed a state of emergency in the attempt to stifle various manifestations of protest. Commenting on these developments deposed President Fernando Belaúnde Terry declared, according to the August 4 New York Times, "The so-called Peruvian revolution has failed and every one of its banners has been destroyed."

In some ways, Peru's corporativists were the victims of what they took to be their early success. During the first years of the Revolutionary Government of the Armed Forces, with high export prices and the large-scale entry of foreign capital, Peru's experiment with a system that was neither capitalist nor socialist worked well enough to lull many of the less prescient directing classes into the belief that discipline could be eased and the country permitted to retain the relaxed style of criollismo. Thus the Peruvians failed almost as totally as the Bolivians had to generate a revolutionary mystique. This failure haunts those who preside over Peruvian corporativism in the bad economic times of the mid-1970s.

Ecuador's corporativist experiment began under circumstances different from Peru's. The Ecuadoran officers had the misfortune of introducing their version of corporativism just as the economy was on the brink of turning downward, and the policies of the new rulers contributed only to the severity of the turn. As a result, Ecuador's commitment to military corporativism, which had been immediately preceded by glowing optimism about the economic future, was not confirmed by an initial period of high satisfactions. In some respects, though, the overall consequences have been similar in the two countries. Facing an economy by 1974 that many viewed as likely to resist the most heroic endeavors to improve it, discouraged Ecuadorans were apt to decide that *criollismo* was an approach to life that was as logical as any other.

ECUADOR AND THE TRANSITION TO MILITARY CORPORATIVISM

Taking up for the fifth time the duties of the presidential office, José María Velasco Ibarra in 1968 unleashed a propaganda onslaught, bitter and inflamatory even by his standards, against Ecuador's capitalist elites. Although they knew enough to discount much of the rhetoric, bankers and commercial figures grew uneasy, as in fact did many members of the middle sectors who felt the verbal avalanche was directed against not just the oligarchy but, as Cyrano Tama Paz put it, against "all of us who are professionals, agriculturalists, and small entrepreneurs, those of us who as men of private initiative nourish with our money and efforts the weak and incipient economy of Ecuador."[49] One group at least was not made to feel uneasy: the large landowners of the interior highlands. Early in 1970 the regime placed the Ecuadoran Reform and Colonization Institute (created by the military junta in 1964) under strict government control and then proceeded to bring its efforts to a standstill.

Burdened by the obligations of servicing a government debt of $46.5 million and meeting the salaries of a huge bureaucracy,[50] Velasco Ibarra had few funds available for social overhead and almost none for development. Hoping to augment his popularity by baiting the United States, he stepped up seizure of North American tuna boats, and as a result Washington proclaimed an almost total suspension of aid. A further reason for suspending aid arose out of a dispute over terms of compensation for expropriated International Telephone and

Telegraph holdings. With banana revenues still in decline and with the Texaco-Gulf consortium reporting that significant petroleum production remained two or three years away, the economy continued its downward skid amidst mounting labor unrest and student riots. The president responded by assuming dictatorial powers in June of 1970, with the support of the armed forces. The officers, however, revealed dissension for one of their influential spokesmen, who happened to be the president's nephew, asserted the need to introduce Peruvian-style reforms into the troubled land.

New government controls over the Central Bank and a state monopoly on all foreign currency exchange resulted in fiscal chaos, "the bankruptcy of national banks, and the paralysis of commerce."[51] And rumors grew steadily about the plundering of the national treasury by the president's cohorts. Against this background the previously exiled Lebanese-born leftist Asaad Bucaram was allowed to return to the country and to launch his campaign for the 1972 presidential election. A former mayor of Guayaquil and leader of the Concentration of Popular Forces (CFP) which had long since abandoned its initial Velasquism, Bucaram was widely regarded in business and military circles as a dangerous Marxist.

Divided over how to deal with the worsening political and economic situation, some military officers approached the chief executive to suggest that he cancel the presidential election scheduled for June and remain in power, while others argued that the time had come to follow the example of Peru. The majority of officers, it appears, did not trust Velasco Ibarra to administer the oil revenue which would soon be flowing into national coffers and were relieved when the old político refused to prolong his stay in office beyond the constitutional limit. Acting now ostensibly to save the country from falling into the hands of leftists, the armed forces overthrew Velasco Ibarra in February of 1972 and placed Brigadier General Guillermo Rodríguez Lara at the head of the Nationalist Revolutionary Government. Engaging in personality, Rodríguez prided himself on his soccer skills, even though his rotund physique had earned him the nickname of "little balloon."

The example of the military governments of Brazil and Peru emboldened the Ecuadoran officers to regard their rule not as an interim expedient—in which light the armed forces had viewed their interlude of power in the 1960s—but rather as a long-term venture in the course of which a new sociopolitical structure would be introduced in the pursuit of oil-financed development. The officers promptly moved to curtail the power of key interest groups and the dozens of semiautonomous entities. And they took significant steps to bolster the educational infrastructure: in 1974, 55,000 students were enrolled in institutions of higher learning, compared to 10,000 in 1970.[52]

By late 1974, however, educational and various social reform programs began to grind to a halt owing to a shortage of revenue. The new economic difficulties confronting the regime resulted largely from serious miscalculations in regard to oil policy. The administration had waited until 1974 when a Texaco-Gulf consortium began to pump nearly 250,000 barrels a day from the *Oriente* before demanding a 25 percent government participation in the operation. The Ecuadorans had also raised the government take per barrel and resorted to other measures that combined to raise the price of oil approximately $2.50 a barrel above that of the Venezuelan product.[53] Texaco-Gulf responded to these measures, and to a government takeover of large parts of their concession lands, by reducing production to less than 100,000 barrels a day, claiming that Ecuadoran oil was too expensive for foreign buyers. A number of other oil concerns relinquished their concessions and left the country, and government failed in efforts to attract new foreign petroleum investors.

Clearly, the military had overplayed their hand with the foreign oil firms, and recognizing this they moved in mid-1975 to reduce their demands. Petroleum production, though, remained well below original expectations (helping to account for a 1975 trade deficit of between $300 million and $400 million) and the government was forced to limit spending and to introduce an unpopular austerity program aimed at curbing the 30 percent inflation resulting in 1974 from lavish spending based on unrealistic income estimates. Their legitimacy was seriously undermined when the officers had to inform the public that oil prosperity had been, for the time being at least, a chimera and that the country might have to revert to reliance on the less glamorous banana crops, foreign earnings for which rose by about 30 percent in 1975.

Overall effectiveness of the military rule suffered not only from economic setbacks but from the lack of a clear orientation. Some officers desired to forge a new national structure based on Peruvian models and also on the ideology of the ARNE. They desired, in short, a corporativism that involved popular participation, however carefully controlled from above, and that closely regulated private capitalists and permanently reduced their political power. Other officers, including it would seem President Rodríguez Lara, felt the collapse of the old order, occasioned by incipient modernization, had not proceeded nearly so far in the Ecuador of 1972 as it had in the Peru of 1968; therefore, less drastic measures would suffice. On the whole, officers of this second group were attracted by the Brazilian model of military corporativism in which little attention was paid to humanism and the nonmaterial rewards of participation, in which economism and heavy-handed repression were relied upon as control mechanisms over the masses, and in which private capitalists were dealt with through incentives and privileges rather than restraints.

Until the 1975 economic downturn, the Ecuadoran officers followed an inconsistent policy, alternating between the Peruvian and Brazilian approaches. Then, spurred by the August 1975 overthrow of Peru's Velasco Alvarado and his replacement by power wielders quickly perceived to be more moderate in their reformism, and by a bloody military *golpe* in Quito, triggered by economic frustrations, that came close to toppling Rodríguez Lara, the Ecuadorans swung more consistently toward the Brazilian policies. In the view of critics, however, they did not swing far enough. All the while, government was handicapped by a lack of the physical resources and the trained technocrats, both military and civilian, that the Brazilian military regimes have had at their disposal.

Economic problems of the same type besetting the Peruvians—disappointing petroleum yields, inefficient agriculture, inflation, and low export commodity prices—continued to plague the government, and the problems were compounded by inefficiency and graft. These circumstances contributed to another *golpe* against Rodríguez Lara, this time bloodless and successful, on January 11, 1976—confirming the old adage that *golpe* are most likely to occur on Sunday when bureaucrats and many military personnel are not at their posts. The three-man junta installed in office immediately announced that the military would remain in power until the end of 1977.

While it seemed clear that the January change of command was primarily the result of the dissatisfaction of the inflation-plagued middle classes and of the annoyance of capitalists over government restrictions, the junta justified the *golpe* on the grounds that up until this time the common people had not derived sufficient benefit from the revolution that began in 1972. This exercise in divisive demagoguery suggested that the Ecuadoran military was less intent upon experimenting with corporativism than with Velasquism without Velasco Ibarra.

At the same time, the Ecuadoran officers have retained a principal conciliatory feature of Velasquism. Even as their fellow officers in Peru, they have sought, and to some extent found, an accord with the Catholic Church, mainly on the issues of social justice. And, as of the mid-1970s, Bolivia's governing officers had also announced the association of their programs with the church's social teachings, as they sought to claim legitimacy not just because of alleged mastery over the techniques of improving this world but because of partnership with those professing command over the realm of the spirit. Certainly in all three republics the governing classes had ample reason to seek legitimacy in factors other than those of national material well-being.

BOLIVIA: SHIFTING PATTERNS OF MILITARY RULE

Six months after the April 1969 helicopter crash that claimed the life of the ebullient General René Barrientos, the austere General Alfredo Ovando Candia seized the Bolivian presidency. Almost as important as Barrientos had been in devising and executing the plot that toppled the MNR administration of Paz Estenssoro in 1964, Ovando had been quickly eclipsed by his more colorful colleague. Rumor had it he was planning to assuage his pride by overthrowing Barrientos at the time of the latter's death.

Decidedly under the influence of the internal security concepts as taught at the High Center of Military Studies in Peru, Ovando favored ideological solidarity with that country. Proclaiming the need to end the drain of wealth "fomented in the past by financial monopolies stronger than the state,"[54] he followed almost at once in the steps of his Peruvian counterparts by nationalizing Gulf Oil, the most visible foreign petroleum producer. Oil had begun to assume significance only in 1966 with Gulf's development of fields in the Santa Cruz region and with the completion the following year of a pipeline to the Chilean coast. Constituting only 0.6 percent of the value of exports in 1964, petroleum had risen to 17 percent by 1968.[55] Many Bolivians, Ovando among them, were impressed by the arguments of the leftist intellectual Sergio Almaráz that oil, becoming ever scarcer in the world economy, held the promise of a bright future for Bolivia if only that country retained possession over its reserves and did not sign them away to foreign firms.[56]

Oil nationalization brought a measure of quick popularity to Ovando, who proceeded then to consolidate his position through a reconciliation with organized labor. Elements within the armed forces, however, viewed his moves with distrust. Right-wingers wished a restoration of the Barrientos policies in which private capitalism had been relied upon as the principal motor of development, and they pointed with alarm to a decline in foreign investment. On the other hand, leftist officers preached the need to escape dependence on foreign capital altogether and called for basic structural reforms that would mobilize the masses in support of a socialist economy. A combination of luck and conspiratorial skill brought the leftists to power through an October 1970 *golpe* organized by General Juan José Torres.

Revolutionary rhetoric soared to new heights as Torres and his associates described the nature and purposes of their regime. The power of selfish capitalists, be they foreign or native, would be broken forever, and sovereignty would pass to popular assemblies representing the interests of the laboring classes within the various sectors of the economy. The Cuban Revolution was defended and diplomatic ties with the Communist powers were strengthened, while the United States came in for a barrage of vituperative propaganda and the Peace Corps was expelled on the grounds it was engaged in internal spying— a justification also resorted to by the Peruvian military when they banished the Peace Corps in 1974.

Plagued by an economic downturn resulting mainly from uncoordinated and inconsistent moves against private capital, the military officers proved unable to establish effective control over the "new, mass-dominated activities." Popular assemblies ratified worker takeovers of various enterprises, "but had no machinery to impose work discipline or a sense of responsibility to a common goal." To overcome similar difficulties, the Peruvian military would turn to SINA-MOS, but Torres lacked both the time and the solid military support necessary to fashion such control mechanisms. His ten months in power witnessed a collapse of management and a decline in production and services, a bleeding of businesses' financial resources "for immediate worker gratification, and a series of economically disastrous strikes in surviving privately owned mines and firms which could not satisfy the insatiable expectations of their employees."[57]

As the proportions of the debacle grew rightist military elements, who had contributed to the collapse of authority by their refusal to cooperate with Torres, laid their plans for a *golpe*. Santa Cruz was the focal point of discontent against the regime and it was here that the dissident officers concentrated their efforts. One of the most prosperous areas in all of Bolivia, Santa Cruz since the 1950s had witnessed the rise of an industrious middle class and the expansion of a broadly based free enterprise manufacturing and commercial agricultural econ-omy. The boom, which was also fed by expanding commerce with Brazil and Argentina, came to an end with the expropriation of Gulf Oil holdings and the Torres-decreed nationalization of locally owned sugar mills. *Cruceños* watched in growing apprehension as the plunge toward socialism gained momentum. Salvation for themselves, they were certain, lay in a return to free enterprise. They found their savior in Colonel Hugo Banzer who appeared in their midst toward the middle of 1971.[58]

A staunch proponent of conservative economics, Banzer, who had gone into exile in Argentina following a botched attempt to kidnap Torres, wisely chose Santa Cruz as the site from which to launch a new challenge to the regime. This time his move against Torres was "a well-planned campaign that reflected a thorough knowledge of military sentiment within the institution and an appreciation for broader political considerations." He fashioned an "unlikely political alliance" between members of the MNR and their sworn Falangist enemies of the FSB, which claimed its major support in Santa Cruz. Executing well-laid plans, his forces captured control of the Santa Cruz provincial government on August 19, 1971.[59] Within a few days after that Banzer took up the reins of government in La Paz, as Torres sought diplomatic asylum.[60]

Once installed in power, Banzer relied heavily on the backing of Brazil—which country, together with CIA agents,[61] had undoubtedly contributed to the success of the move against Torres. By the end of 1974 the Brasília regime had committed itself to an investment of $1 billion in a Bolivian industrial complex in return for a share of that country's natural gas. Much to the alarm of some of its own political leaders and those of several sister republics, Bolivia appeared to have fallen as much under Brazil's control as Central American and Caribbean republics had been under U.S. hegemony in the 1920s.

Although Banzer faced a problem of peasant revolts that continued to erupt over vast areas of the countryside, and although his regime was torn by political dissension that caused the withdrawal of the MNR from an uneasy governing alliance, the colonel managed to remain in office a good deal longer than most of his predecessors in the Bolivian presidency. By mid-1974, with the attempt to rule in col-laboration with the traditional parties having been abandoned in favor of an unalloyed military government, Banzer was confident enough of his position to announce that the armed forces would continue in power until 1980. Contributing to his confidence was the improved state of the economy. With Gulf Oil promised compensation of $78.5 million,[62] fresh foreign capital poured into petroleum extraction, just at the time that the world witnessed a phenomenal rise in prices as a result of policies adopted by the Organization of Petroleum Exporting Countries (Bolivia did not become an OPEC member, a status that was confined among the New World republics to Venezuela and Ecuador). In 1974 oil exports earned Bolivia $180 million, compared to $49 million the previous year. Export earnings for tin also rose, from $131 million in 1973 to $235 million in 1974. In that last year Bolivia enjoyed a favorable trade balance for one of the few times since the 1952 revolution, a situation that continued into 1975.

The taste of prosperity, altogether uncommon since the end of the tin industry's golden days in the 1920s, facilitated a rare outbreak of political stability and permitted the military government at least to tread water. Still, judged purely by economic criteria, Bolivian prospects were not bright. Per-capita income, estimated at $195 in 1975, was the lowest in South America—estimates for Peru and Ecuador were $335 and $350, respectively. Educational levels remained depressed and per-capita daily consumption of protein was the lowest in the American hemisphere. Per-capita caloric intake was also at the bottom in hemisphere statistics, estimated at 21 percent less than what was considered adequate—compared to about 7 percent less than adequate in Peru and 15 percent less than adequate in Ecuador. Although infant mortality rates remained high, the population continued to increase at a rate of about 2.7 percent a year—slightly lower than in Peru and Ecuador where the respective rates were 3.2 and 3.3 percent.[63] Above all other sectors, it was the poor, the uneducated, and the undernourished who were reproducing.

Under these circumstances it is not surprising that the Bolivian officers, even as the military rulers of Peru and Ecuador, should have decided to seek accord with the hierarchy of the Catholic Church. Clearly, the governing officers in all three republics have need for re-enforcement of their announced corporativist ideology—according to which nonmaterial are as important as material rewards—from the church's consistent denunciation of liberal capitalism and economism. Understandably, then, the Andean officers have sought to create the impression that the church participates with them in the exercise of a moderating power that establishes national policy. The fact that the officers have done so derives also from the degree to which both military and ecclesiastical corporations have come to concur, since the 1960s, on concepts of internal security.

Church-state relations could sour, of course, if the military, in the face of pressures from monied classes, should decide to permit a greater degree of free enterprise capitalism, customarily associated less with freedom than with special privileges for the bourgeois classes with which the church, throughout most of its history in Andean America, has seldom been on friendly terms. For the moment, though, the officers seem to be almost as successful as Apristas in the 1920s and 1930s in blending their development ideology with the teachings of the traditional faith.

THE CATHOLIC CHURCH AND THE NEW CORPORATIVISM

The Catholic Church in Andean America, as elsewhere in the Spanish-speaking world, has seldom functioned as a monolithic institution supporting only one clear set of policies;[64] and so, generalization is hazardous. Still, it is safe to say that by the 1960s a growing number of clergymen had come to believe that the old order of society was doomed and that in the interest of survival as a corporate entity the church must sever its ties with the traditional ruling classes and establish bonds with new, aspiring elites and with the masses. As many military officers, churchmen came to connect internal security not with suppressing communist insurgents but rather with mitigating the social problems that the alleged greed and blindness of an oligarchy had allowed to reach the explosion point.

In a number of pronouncements in the 1960s Peruvian bishops condemned the social injustices spawned by the existing order. And the newly formed and influential organization of so-called radical priests in Peru, the National Office of Social Information or ONIS (*Oficina Nacional de Información Social*), attributed the mounting social problem to an unsavory alliance between the local oligarchy and foreign capitalists, subscribing almost in toto to Marxist-inspired theories of dependency. Along with like-minded clergymen in Ecuador and Bolivia, ONIS members launched one of the most bombastic assaults against capitalist imperialism that Andean America had witnessed since the 1920s when the ideological offshoots of Marxism-Leninism had first begun to flourish.[65] By dissociating themselves from the native oligarchies, and from outside forces of liberal capitalism that allegedly shaped the domestic social and economic orders, the clergymen hoped to qualify for a leading role in the practice of "prophetic politics:" politics, that is, committed to criticism of the existing order in the light of prophetic standards, as understood by initiated elites, and to the mission of overcoming present evils so as to achieve a better way of life.[66]

Because they recognized the need for material development in order to satisfy the physical needs of the masses, the reform-minded clergy formed bonds with the new generation of specialists who had acquired training in agronomy, economics, sociology, business management, engineering, and all of the other skills considered essential to nation-building. And, they turned themselves to acquiring an education in these fields. Thereby they won greater self-esteem at the same time that they began to acquire greater prestige in the eyes of many others; for in the wake of spreading secularism, clergymen trained only in theology had acquired an image of uselessness. This helped account for the fact that among Peruvian high-school students in the 1960s the priestly vocation was viewed as among the least desirable of all professions.[67] Throughout Andean America, in fact, the image of the priesthood as irrelevant to modern society had contributed to a steady decline in vocations as a percentage of total population. The number of priests operating in the area would have been far lower had it not been for the huge influx of foreign clergy, especially from Spain, the United States, and West Germany, during the 1960s. By the end of that decade foreign priests accounted for about 60 percent of the clergy in Peru and Ecuador, and for over 75 percent in Bolivia.[68]

With ample justification a Peruvian statesman had observed in 1900: "Today there is no career less solicited than the career of arms."[69] Yet in the 1960s, a military career was the second most sought-after one among Peruvian high-school students, surpassed in popularity only by engineering. One reason for the change was that the military had suddenly come to be perceived as altogether relevant to the essential task of nation-building. Undoubtedly the Catholic Church hoped to increase the lure of the priestly life, and also to augment its influence throughout Andean America, by acquiring a new image of usefulness in leading the republics toward development.

In line with approaches developed by the lay religious order Opus Dei, founded in Spain in 1928 and active throughout most of the Spanish-speaking world by the 1960s, the revitalized and development-minded clergy of Andean America have sought to win the allegiance of professional elites by associating religious virtue with productive enterprise and expertise. The message is that persons can best sanctify themselves through remaining in the world and perfecting their professional skills so as to be able to contribute to the creation of new wealth, not so much for their private advantage as for the common good of the nation. To the degree that they succeed in identifying productive enterprise by skilled technocrats with a source of supernatural grace, churchmen may be able to impart a new meaningfulness to religion among development-minded civilian elites, and to win back to the church the largely alienated middle sectors of Andean America.

A young generation of Andean clergymen, often inspired by the example of foreign priests, has shown concern not only with establishing ties with aspiring elites, judged to be the power wielders of the future, but also with forging fresh bonds of leadership over the masses. In the latter regard they have been infatuated by the concept of *concientización*, literally, consciousness-raising. Much in the approach of the "intellectual workers" who in the view of Leninism were to raise the consciousness of the proletariat, the clergy has come to regard itself as an elite of "spiritual workers" who must increase awareness among the masses of their full human potential and of the obligations that society has to provide them with the material security required for spiritual developmnet. *Concientización* serves elitist purposes by casting the priests in the role of indispensable guides for the overall formation of complete human beings and as the one functional group capable of understanding the full spiritual needs of mankind. And, if it accomplishes what is expected of it, *concientización* can serve to dull the socially dangerous phenomenon of rising material expectations among the masses; for it promises liberation from materialism so as to make possible the savoring of the rewards of the life of the spirit.[70]

If the masses, under the spiritual leadership of a new type of clergy, could be induced to eschew concern with constant escalation of material gratifications, hard-pressed national governments would be saved some of the huge outlays required by economism and would have more money at their disposal to invest in development. This is one of the considerations that has attracted military corporativists to the fresh approaches of some Andean clergymen. There are, of course, additional considerations of some significance.

In their development strategy and elitist orientation, as well as in their recognition of the importance of technocrats and also of businessmen—provided the latter are disciplined by those possessing higher ideals—the progressive clergymen see eye-to-eye with many military corporativists. The two groups are further linked by the conviction that, as an important ONIS document expressed the matter, "energetic action by the state can be the most effective means for the transition of an alienated society into a society that is not alienated."[71] Under these conditions it is not surprising that, to employ the terms of Peter Berger, the "political cosmos" has begun to seek the support of a "religious cosmos" for the sake of the legitimacy which the latter can confer.[72]

Increasingly concerned with material development, Andean churchmen are acting in the conviction expressed by the internationally renowned Catholic theologian Pierre Teilhard de Chardin: "Our faith imposes on us the right and the duty to throw ourselves into the things of this earth."[73] Meantime many of the military corporativists have taken up the cause of spreading among the masses the spiritual rewards attendant upon sharing in a nationalistic mystique and ideal. As a result, religion and politics, the spiritual and the temporal, are fusing and once again acquiring the degree of interpenetration that characterized the empire of Tahuantinsuyo and the Spanish colonial structure. The liberals who began in the nineteenth century to rail against this interpenetration seem to have lost the fray. In another respect, though, the liberals have triumphed; for the clergy has been able to acquire mounting status and pretige only by becoming, as Ecuador's Vicente Rocafuerte and any number of other liberals vainly urged in the nineteenth century, concerned with the development of this world.

Collaboration between military governors and the clergy is likely eventually to be threatened by the clash between two headstrong and often arrogant power elites that has in the past so often soured relations between the state and the church. At least for the time being, however, collaboration has been strengthened by the traditional stance of the Catholic clergy in advocating the corporativist society and in rejecting both pure capitalism and unalloyed socialism. This, of course, is the same ideological position to which the Andean military has come. As the generals-turned-presidents return to their area's cultural traditions as the point of departure for the quest of modernization, it is not surprising that they would find a place for the institution that has been the most consistent defender of traditions.

The Uncertain Prospects of Andean Corporativism

The most consistently stressed international objective of Andean corporativism has been escape from economic dependence upon the United States, and toward this end the area's leaders have begun to concentrate upon industrial, especially manufacturing, development. In many ways, however, attainment of economic independence seems as unlikely of attainment as it has ever been. Even if Andean America does succeed in passing into an industrial age, it will be dealing with a United States that has passed into a postindustrial, "technetronic era."[74] The power disparity between postindustrial and industrializing societies, and the dependence of the latter on the former, is apt to be as great as that characterizing the relationship between the industrial and nonindustrialized countries from mid-nineteenth to mid-twentieth century. Perhaps, then, iron laws of domination and dependency are at work.[75]

In many ways the demands of the Andean republics for independence are no more than a rhetorical disguise for the fact that they would like the United States simply to become a more paternalistic *patrón*. As this fact becomes more widely recognized—it has already been perceived by leftist critics of the new corporativist order—it will grow increasingly difficult for Andean regimes to base their legitimacy, as they have been seeking to do, on the claim they are waging a struggle for economic independence.

Meantime, the multinational corporations have come along to pose a new threat to economic independence. The multinationals are moving toward the *privatization of dependence*—which will result when internationalized private capital, rather than a particular nation state, attains economic domination. In no area is the privatization of dependence more apparent than in the relationship that came into being in the course of the 1970s between Andean countries and the private banks of advanced countries, particularly of the United States. In this respect a new and perhaps massive problem in U.S.-Andean relations is building. The problem extends not only to the relations of the United States with Andean America but with much of the so-called Third World.

Developing countries during the 1970s, excluding the few such as Ecuador that were oil exporters, borrowed more money than in their entire previous history. According to an authoritative study by Emma Rothschild,[76] the fastest increase by far has been in their debt to private banks, for official aid is falling farther and farther behind the growth in the world economy. Among the Latin American countries Bolivia and more notably Peru, in addition to Mexico, Brazil, Argentina, and Chile, have been major borrowers from U.S. private banks.

The dramatic expansion in private lending has been facilitated by the control—sometimes accomplished through borrowing the funds in order to relend them—that U.S. banks have gained over Eurodollars: dollar holdings in Europe resulting from the outflow of U.S. dollars in consequence of negative trade balances and other factors.

The increasing availability of loan capital came just at the time—specifically, 1973 and 1974—when Andean and other developing countries began to have greater needs for capital infusion due to rising prices for imports of food and manufactured goods and the simultaneous reduction in the value of their exports.

A major question to be faced in the future concerns the degree of backing the U.S. government will afford its private bankers when some of their poor-country borrowers find it impossible to service obligations and demand a renegotiation of terms and threaten moratoriums on repayment, thereby raising the specter of the breakdown of the banking structure. In addition to causing international tensions, the situation may well increase the demands upon U.S. taxpayers as government turns to them to rescue bankers from the zeal with which they, even as their predecessors in the 1920s, urged borrowing upon South American republics as a panacea. Whatever the future may hold, it is already clear that Andean economic cooperation aimed at curbing the multinationals has been totally ineffective in preventing increased dependence upon multinational banking operations. And the effectiveness of economic cooperation in controlling other types of multinational operations remains very much in doubt as the Andean group faces mounting problems of internal divisiveness.

The same ideological controversies, and the same economically motivated clashes between stronger and weaker members that undermined the Latin American Free Trade Association and the Central American Common Market in the 1960s[77] are now exercising their disintegrating influences within the Andean group. The ideologically conservative stance assumed by the Chileans since the 1973 overthrow of Allende and their hopes to lure foreign funds sparked conflict with Peru over investment terms, and in late 1976 Chile withdrew from the 1968 Andean pact. Also, it has become increasingly difficult to reconcile the interests of relatively developed countries like Peru, and above all the far more developed Venezuela, with those of Ecuador and Bolivia. All the while traditional sources of dissension continue to afflict the Andean group. Although the beginnings of an Ecuador-Peru rapprochement have been discernible since the 1960s,[78] Ecuador's president Rodríguez Lara, citing his country's boundary dispute with Peru, refused to attend the Ayacucho Conference in December of 1974 through which the Andean republics were to celebrate the 150th anniversary of the victory over Spain that consummated the independence movement.

Additional obstacles to unity result from the attempt of powerful sister republics to use Andean republics as pawns in their games of power politics. Emboldened by the economic and political collapse of Argentina in the first half of the 1970s, Brazil in particular has been active in spreading its influence into the Andean region and has made Bolivia virtually a satellite republic. The situation is especially worrisome to Peru, where there is growing fear that Brazil will back Bolivia in seeking an outlet to the sea through Peruvian territory, a solution to the old international controversy that would be pleasing to Chile. Peruvians find further cause for concern in the re-establishment, following Allende's overthrow, of the traditional diplomatic rapport between Brazil and Chile. This looms as all the more ominous in view of talk since 1973 of the possibility of war between Peru and Chile, out of which has come an intensification of the arms race in which the two countries chronically engage,[79] with Peru turning increasingly to the Soviet Union for the purchase of tanks and also (by late 1976) supersonic fighter-bombers. In order to improve their country's standing with Brazil's rightist administration and reduce the likelihood of war with conservatively governed Chile,[80] some Peruvian members of the Revolutionary Government of the Armed Forces have urged an end to basic reforms and an opening toward the right that would go so far as to include an accord with the APRA.

Even had the countries remained united, many students of international economics feared that Andean integration would, in spite of contrary intentions, simply contribute to the penetration of foreign capital, particularly that of the multinational firms, and lead to new forms of imperial hegemony, an experience that befell the European Common Market according to Jean Jacques Servan-Schreiber.[81] The point, though, is that the Andean republics are not remaining united, and in the light of their intensifying rivalry they will find it ever more difficult to control the multinationals and to lessen dependence on the United States. Threatened by their neighbors, they will continue to turn, as they began to do in the 1880s, toward the United States for backing even though this means that in return they will have to curtail not only some of their economic but also some of their political independence.

Rivalries with sister republics sometimes mask even more severe domestic conflicts. In Peru, for example, the prospects of an accord with the APRA appeals primarily to the advocates of private capitalism among the armed forces governing class; and they may be exaggerating the threat from Chile and Brazil simply so as to provide a rationalization for the more conservative stance that, in self-interest, they would like to assume. A genuine ideological commitment to free enterprise as the best means to attain development accounts in part for the conservative inclination of some officers, but other considerations are involved. As they have grown accustomed to the perquisites of power, more than a few officers have been beguiled by the pleasures of the *dolce vita*, pleasures that could obviously be enhanced by an increasingly friendly relationship with the new civilian capitalist elites —and also with some of the old. Coming to appreciate the fruits of an intimate association with local capitalists, some officers—to the dismay of their more revolutionary comrades, who are often those farthest from the centers of power—have grown more tolerant toward the world of foreign capital with which the national bourgeoisie is linked. Factors that had earlier swung APRA leadership from left to right operated between 1968 and 1976 to induce a similar transition among certain military leaders.

Torn by doubts over the proper degree of collaboration with domestic and foreign capitalists, the Peruvian officers also show uncertainty about one of the revolution's keystones: popular participation. Leftist-leaning officers criticize participation that is little more than mobilization controlled from above. They fear that participation in name only will lead to political boredom and indifference on the part of the masses, facilitating control over them by government managers allied to the interests of big business. On the other hand, rightists fear that empty promises of participation will lead the workers to demand the substance of what is promised. In their view, government should abandon attempts at mass mobilization and rely on the authoritarianism thought to lie at the heart of Brazil's model of development.[82]

At the outset of their revolution the Peruvian officers, unlike their Brazilian counterparts, stressed humanism and the importance of nonmaterial rewards; and this helped bring them onto a common ground with the Catholic Church, which had never become integrated with bourgeois capitalism and its liberal values as have most formal religions in the United States. Similar approaches have been followed by Ecuadoran and Bolivian military rulers. Assuming the emphasis on nonmaterial rewards continues to any degree at all, it could facilitate for Andean America, despite its awesome problems, a relatively smooth cultural transition into the postmodern age—a smoother transition, in fact, than the United States seems likely to achieve.

13

Epilogue: On Life and Culture in Postmodern Times

In recent years a new school called "sociobiology" has been established by biologists who deal with human behavior in terms of patterns that are discernible in the animal kingdom. To psychological, sociological, and economic influences, the sociobiologists would add the importance of biological factors, governed by genes that are shaped in accordance with Darwinian evolutionary responses to the environment.[1] I do not pretend to be competent to judge the controversial claims of the sociobiologists, but I do find that some of their concepts provide insights into the comparative study of the United States and Andean America.[2]

In the opening chapter of this book I suggested that social and political stability in the United States had depended, since at least the middle of the nineteenth century, upon the ability of the established system to satisfy the rising material expectations of a high percentage of the population. Helping make this possible were abundant physical resources and the values of individualistic, competitive effort which arose out of an environment of plenty. What can the biologist tell us about this situation?

In biology, a high-energy environment (one characterized by bountiful resources) is often one in which there is a low degree of predictability in the actions of animal species. Where, for example, food sources are plentiful, individual, competitive foraging, which results in low predictability, serves as an adequate means to sustain life. Within the United States competitive individualism proved, it can be argued, a suitable human response to the environment of abundance.

Epilogue

In Andean America, beginning with preconquest Indian civilizations and continuing on through the Spanish colonial period and then into the nineteenth and twentieth centuries, a high degree of predictability has characterized social relationships—even when the political order fell into chaos after independence. Such predictability resulted in part from the fact that the masses accepted life styles in which subsistence was guaranteed not by individualistic self-reliance but rather by the protection of paternalistic patrons.

Harmony, and not the individualistic struggle, prevailed as the great social ideal in Andean America because of the widespread acceptance of "the image of the limited good." Within a society subscribing to this image there exists a broad consensus that the available amounts of wealth, goods, and resources are relatively fixed and that it is beyond the power of mortals vastly to expand the quotas consigned them by nature and nature's gods. This being so, persons acted not in response to the motivation of rising expectations. Instead, their actions were guided by the assumption that persons with power and those who were dependent upon them had always to interact in harmony, for stability could not endure in the face of competitive drives that threatened to result in any basic reallocation of the limited good.

Through the years, Andean cultural patterns have exhibited striking similarity to a biological system of mutualism, a system that prevails in environments where energy and resources are in low supply. The key feature of mutualism is symbiosis, which involves specific and mutually advantageous interdependencies between organisms—of the type that do not have time to develop in settings where abundance of raw materials gives rise to independent competition and therefore high unpredictability. Furthermore, within a low-resources environment, collectivism is likely to be found. Where, for example, food is scarce, adequate nourishment is more likely to result from group foraging and sharing than from individual foraging.

If biological patterns can throw some light on human endeavors to shape viable cultures, then it would be expected that Andean America, with its consistent shortage of resources, wealth, goods, and energy, would reveal a relatively high degree of predictability in social relationships; and it would further be expected that this high predictability would rest upon mutualist associations in which beings are dependent upon collectivist, group efforts and also involved in interdependent relationships with patrons.

As the reserves of essential goods and as sources of energy shrink

377

throughout the world in the 1970s, and as the population continues to grow, the limited-good image begins to make more and more sense in a worldwide context, while the image of unlimited material progress that underlay liberalism's rising expectations becomes untenable. As a result, sociopolitical structures based on individualism and classical liberal cconomics may cease to be viable in the postmodern era.

The United States, as it stands on the threshold of this era, finds itself undergoing a traumatic experience. This is especially true of the middle-sector populace, traditionally the most responsive to the motivations of rising expectations and the goals of upward mobility based on achievement.[3] Many of the values most cherished by the middle classes, including faith in the benevolence of growth, seem now only to contribute toward the making of a society that has ceased to be viable. It is ironic that the great North American dream of independence and self-reliance in the pursuit of happiness, confined in the past largely to white males, is beginning now to grip blacks, Chicanos, women, and various other groups precisely at the time this dream is becoming ever less realizable for anyone. The same irony is present in the mania of underdeveloped countries to become altogether self-determining.

In making the transition into the postmodern era, the United States appears called upon to discard the only identity it has ever known. Thus, having been born modern and without the ties of obedience and protection that bind persons begins to loom as a serious disadvantage. Andean America, on the other hand, having never become thoroughly steeped in the liberal set of values, seems better prepared psychologically to respond to the challenges of an energy-short world. In passing into the postmodern age, Andean America is reaffirming, in adapted form, its never altogether discarded premodern identity.

Analyses based upon physical resources and upon the perceptions of sociobiology can, I suspect, go only so far in explaining the human condition. Beyond this there are considerations of the mind and spirit. In this connection the observations of W. Warren Wagar are significant:

> From the middle of the eighteenth century down to the middle of the twentieth ... the central project of the Western spirit was to find a world-encompassing faith to replace the traditional Judaism and Christianity ... The great fact in the spiritual life of Western man in the years just after the second World War was the apparent suspension of the search for new systems of

secular faith. He suddenly found himself living in a post-ideological, . . . demythologized world in which the will to believe had withered and failed.[4]

Probably a major reason for the much discussed and debated "end of ideology" in the United States during the 1950s and 1960s was the fact that after the war this country entered a period in which more than ever it seemed that the satisfaction of rising material expectations could be relied upon exclusively as a sociopolitical control mechanism. Ideology and a great national ideal did not seem necessary. In Andean America, however, sociopolitical control continued to rest upon, to some degree, nonmaterial rewards of the type that can be supplied by myths, religions, and devotion to a great national ideal. And in many ways the old religious beliefs and myths have become more important in the 1960s and 1970s, coalescing and fusing with nationalism in a way that is traditional to Andean culture but alien to North America's. Thus Andean America appears more ready than the United States to enter a postmodern era in which people throughout the world may have to learn increasingly to settle for nonmaterial satisfactions.

If anything, Andean leaders are overconfident of their abilities to build upon lingering premodern values in turning the masses more toward spiritual-intellectual gratifications. Overconfidence that a society which "cannot produce enough wealth . . . can make a virtue of renunciation or create satisfaction in economy itself"[5] contributes to a reluctance to face up to the need to curtail population growth.[6] Whether basing their ideological position on Christianity, humanism, or variations of Marxism, Andean directing classes expect to be able through a type of social engineering—in which their faith is as vast as B. F. Skinner's—to curtail or eliminate rising expectations as a motivating force among the masses. They assume, in consequence, that the masses can be counted upon to continue to settle in their material aspirations for a no-frills kind of subsistence as guaranteed them by paternalistic governments and that population expansion will therefore not result in uncontainable social pressures. With its destabilizing potential minimized, population growth will, it is assumed, make possible the fulfillment of old aspirations of national grandeur and the occupation of sparsely inhabited national territory that otherwise might be seized by untrustworthy neighbor republics.

Yet social engineering of the magnitude required to encourage mass acceptance of nonmaterial rewards is, at best, extremely difficult to accomplish, especially in such countries as those of Andean America where no government in the twentieth century has been able to generate a true revolutionary mystique. Not even the Soviet Union was able to persevere in its early endeavors to replace material with nonmaterial incentives and, more recently, Yugoslavia and Cuba have faltered in the endeavor. The problems of countries with such goals in mind will remain formidable, perhaps insurmountable, unless the developed nations—which continue to exercise enormous cultural influence throughout the world—themselves abandon growth norms with a suddenness and thoroughness that do not seem possible.

Despite the obvious difficulties confronting them, many Andean corporativists bank on the possibility of shaping countries in which the masses will, to some degree at least, seek happiness through means other than private income and material possessions. If they are wrong, then life can only become increasingly unbearable for the burgeoning multitudes and naked force may emerge as the principal basis of political control.

This book has been based on the conviction that corporativism is the system most congenial to Andean cultural traditions and, beyond this, that it is a system suitable to late-developing nations in their struggle to retain political viability in the postmodern era. However, there are any number of different varieties of corporativism,[7] ranging from fascism (whatever that is) to anarchism with its autonomous communes. Each variety contains sources of serious internal tensions and weaknesses. For corporativism is, after all, a system—a political-social-economic system and sometimes a religiopolitical system. And no system really work, except during brief and rare moments in history when fortuitous circumstances operate in a particularly benign manner. Prevailing circumstances in Andean America's immediate future seem likely to be harsh, and thus corporativism cannot be viewed as a panacea. Among many other factors, the persistent though shifting patterns of a deeply ingrained elitism, combined with the lack of a homogeneous population base, strongly suggest a continuing story of strife.

It must be stressed that no system, even if not forced to contend against unfavorable circumstances in the general economic, ecological, and demographic environment, can of itself solve the problems of alienation and class tension resulting from the need for management in any kind of enterprise. In the economic sphere, even if workers to some degree own, share in the profits, and participate in the direction of firms, friction and frustration can still arise out of the relationships with their associates who in the final instance perform the function of management in the interests of efficiency. Thus in matters of alienation and class and division-of-labor conflicts, individual human equations, rather than overall systems, will remain the determinants of paramount importance.[8]

Nevertheless, Andean Americans, having at last turned a blind eye toward the fading enticements of liberalism, are on the right approach to finding a political system more likely to be congenial than counterproductive in the light of changing needs and challenges. In this regard, they may even be on a more promising approach than the United States. This possibility arises out of the fact that exceptionalism, equated with bringing into being some sort of millennialist existence perhaps reaching worldwide dimensions, has seldom been a major factor in the myth-fantasies that have helped shape Andean culture. Unlike North Americans, then, Andeans are not faced with having to adjust to the loss of a vital ingredient of their traditional culture. In postmodern times, as recognition of defeat and failure begins to curb the Western world's expectations of triumph and glory, Andean Americans may find it easier than their neighbors of the north to accept themselves for what they are and must be.

Abbreviations

AHR, *American Historical Review*
AI, *América Indígena*
CULASP, Cornell University Latin American Studies Program Dissertation Series
HAHR, *Hispanic American Historical Review*
I-AEA, *Inter-American Economic Affairs*
JIAS, *Journal of Inter-American Studies and World Affairs*
LARR, *Latin American Research Review*
RP, *Review of Politics*
TA, *The Americas*

Notes

1. The United States and Andean America: Perspectives of Cultural Contrasts

1. See Clyde Kluckhohn, "Have There Been Discernible Shifts in American Values During the Past Generation?" in Elting E. Morison, ed., *The American Style* (New York, 1958), p. 149, and Walter Gordon Merritt, *The Struggle for Industrial Liberty* (New York, 1922), p. 4. On the issue see also Alan F. Westin, ed., *Views of America* (New York, 1966).

2. Yehoshua Arieli, *Individualism and Nationalism in American Ideology* (Cambridge, Mass., 1964), pp. 345–346

3. Erikson, *Childhood and Society*, 2d ed. (New York, 1963), pp. 316–318.

4. See the classic study by David C. McClelland, *The Achieving Society* (New York, 1961).

5. See Gabriel Almond, *The American People and Foreign Policy*, rev. ed. (New York, 1960), p. 42, and Henry Steele Commager, ed., *America in Perspective* (New York, 1947), p. x.

6. See Robert Kelley, *The Transatlantic Persuasion: The Liberal-Democratic Mind in the Age of Gladstone* (New York, 1967), p. 67.

7. Steven Lukes, *Individualism* (New York, 1973), p. 27. In his excellent study *The Mind of America, 1820–1860* (New York, 1975), Rush Welter finds that one of the four basic attitudes among average, literate antebellum Americans was a view of society that reduced order to the self-interest of its individual members.

8. Talcott Parsons, *The Structure of Social Action*, 2 vols., 2d ed. (New York, 1968), I, 4.

9. Emile Durkheim, *The Division of Labor in Society*, trans. George Simpson (New York, 1964), p. 200. The English translation of this work, a classic refutation of Spencer, first published in France in 1893, appeared initially in 1933.

10. Philip Slater, *The Pursuit of Loneliness: American Culture at the Breaking Point* (Boston, 1970), p. 5.

11. Goodwin, *The American Condition* (Garden City, 1974), p. 75. Among the many writers in addition to Goodwin who in recent years have lamented the absence of a sense of community in America, Glenn Tinder figures prominently. See, for example, his book *Tolerance* (Amherst, Mass., 1976). In "Learning about Crime—the Japanese Experience," *The Public Interest*, no. 44 (1976), 55–68, David H. Bayley argues persuasively that the reason for Japan's declining crime rate during the past twenty-five years, in such dramatic contrast to the situation in the United States, lies in the preservation of intermediate groups which curb individualism and bolster respect for authority.

12. Paul Starr, "Who Are They Now?" *New York Times Magazine*, October 13, 1974, p. 110.

13. Editorial from an 1841 edition of the *Boston Globe*, quoted in Lukes, *Individualism*, p. 27.

14. See David Potter, *People of Plenty: Economic Abundance and the American Character* (Chicago, 1954), p. 92.

15. See ibid., p. 67 et passim. By 1840 the young republic had a gross national product per capita that was 40 to 65 percent larger than France's and was rapidly approaching Great Britain's. See Robert Gallman, "Gross National Product 1834–1909," in National Bureau of Economic Research, *Output, Employment and Productivity in the United States After 1800* (New York, 1969), pp. 5–7.

16. Bruchey, *The Roots of American Economic Growth 1707–1861: An Essay in Social Causation* (New York, 1965), p. 209. Making still more explicit the interconnection between American "character" and environment, Bruchey observes (p. 194): "While few if any men wished not to improve their circumstances, the latitude of their opportunities to do so necessarily influenced both the value and quality of economic effort."

17. Paul A. David, "New Light on a Statistical Dark Age: U.S. Real Product Growth Before 1840," *American Economic Review*, 57 (1967), 294–306.

18. See Ernest Lee Tuveson, *Redeemer Nation: The Idea of America's Millennial Role* (Chicago, 1968), p. 25 et passim.

19. Parsons, *Structure of Social Action*, II, 513.

20. In a review that appeared in the AHR, 74 (1973), 1130, Yale University historian Sydney E. Ahlstrom records his impression of "the remarkable degree to

which the changes in Protestant thinking seemed to intensify rather than weaken the ways in which the Protestant ethic encouraged the growth of an unregulated capitalist society" in the United States.

21. Enlightening on this matter is Thomas C. Cochran, "Cultural Factors in Economic Growth," *Journal of Economic History*, 20 (1960), 512–530.

22. See Margaret Mead, *And Keep Your Powder Dry* (New York, 1942), pp. 31, 40–41, 50–53.

23. Stephan Thernstrom in the concluding section of his *The Other Bostonians: Poverty and Progress in the American Metropolis, 1860–1970* (Cambridge, Mass., 1973) compares his findings with those of other recent urban studies. He concludes that a high degree of fluidity had indeed characterized U.S. urban life, even though various ethnic groups and most especially blacks stand as exceptions.

24. On this controversial matter see Herbert Gans, *More Equality* (New York, 1974), Richard Hamilton, *Restraining Myths: Critical Studies of U.S. Social Structures and Politics* (New York, 1975), Gabriel Kolko, *Wealth and Power in America* (New York, 1962), Robert Lampman, *The Share of the Top-Wealth-Holders in National Wealth, 1922–1956* (Princeton, 1962), Oscar Ornati, *Poverty Amid Affluence* (New York, 1966), and Richard Parker, *The Myth of the Middle Class* (New York, 1972).

25. Seymour Martin Lipset, *Revolution and Counter-revolution: Change and Persistence in Social Structures*, rev. ed (Garden City, 1970), p. 20.

26. See Richard N. Adams, "Brokers and Career Mobility Systems in the Structure of Complex Societies," in Dwight B. Heath, ed., *Contemporary Cultures and Societies of Latin America*, 2d ed. (New York, 1974), p. 84, and *The Second Sowing: Power and Secondary Development in Latin America* (San Francisco, 1967), esp. pp. 39, 257.

27. See George M. Foster, "Cofradía and Compadrazgo in Spain and Spanish America," *Southwestern Journal of Anthropology*, 9 (1953), 1–28, John M. Ingham, "The Asymmetrical Implications of Codparenthood in Tlayacapan, Morelos," *Man*, n.s., 5 (1970), 281–292, Sidney Mintz and Eric Wolf, "An Analysis of Ritual Co-Parenthood (Compadrazgo)," *Southwestern Journal of Anthropology*, 6 (1950), 341–368, and Arnold Strickon and Sidney M. Greenfield, eds., *Structure and Process in Latin America: Patronage, Clientage and Power Systems* (Albuquerque, 1972).

28. Ingham, "Asymmetrical Implications," p. 290.

29. See Gabriel Escobar, *Organización social y cultural del sur del Perú* (Mexico, 1967), esp. pp. 51–53, and John Gillin, *Moche: A Peruvian Coastal Community* (Washington, 1945), p. 27.

30. For thoughtful essays on the role of women in Latin America, essays which have been used as the principal point of departure for the treatment of Marianism, see Ann Pescatello, ed., *Female and Male in Latin America* (Pittsburgh, 1973), and Rosa Signorelli de Martí, "Spanish America," in Raphael Patai, ed., *Women in the Modern World* (New York, 1967). An exhaustive bibliographical study is Meri Knaster, "Women in Latin America: The State of Research, 1975," LARR, 11 (1976), 3–74.

31. Louis Hartz, *The Liberal Tradition in America* (New York, 1955), pp. 185–196, provides a brilliant description of the unsuccessful appeal of southern slaveowners to northern capitalists and employers.

32. See the introduction by Morse to the work which he edited, with Michael L. Conniff and John Wibel, *The Urban Development of Latin America, 1750–1920* (Stanford, 1971), p. 13. For other probing essays on Latin American culture and values as contrasted to those of the United States see Morse, "The Heritage of Latin America," in Louis Hartz, and others, *The Founding of New Societies* (New York, 1964), pp. 123–177, and "Toward a Theory of Spanish American Government," *Journal of the History of Ideas*, 25 (1954), 71–93. See also Robert Kern and Ronald Dolkhart, eds., *The Caciques: Oligarchical Politics and the System of Caciquismo in the Luso-Hispanic World* (Albuquerque, 1973), K. H. Silvert, "National Values, Development, and Leaders and Followers," *International Social Science Journal*, 15 (1963), 560–570, and Howard J. Wiarda, ed., *Politics and Social Change in Latin America: The Distinct Tradition* (Amherst, Mass., 1974).

33. See Magali Sarfatti, *Spanish Bureaucratic-Patrimonialism in America* (Berkeley, 1966). She describes society as divided into compartments among which virtually all lateral relationships were mediated through the imperial apparatus.

34. For pertinent observations on how the highly fragmented society of the corporativist model could safeguard hierarchical rule by preventing the "half-plus-one" type of decision making see David Apter, "Notes for a Theory of Nondemocratic Representation," in his *Some Conceptual Approaches to the Study of Modernization* (Englewood Cliffs, 1968).

35. Durkheim, *Division of Labor*, p. 28.

36. Ibid., p. 13.

37. Ibid., p. 26.

38. Foster applied the limited good image to peasant society. See especially his "Peasant Society and the Image of the Limited Good," *American Anthropologist*, 67 (1965), 293–315.

39. There is a strong connection between the type of heroes most widely venerated, especially by the masses, in Andean America and the Suffering Christ, one of the most important religious symbols to the area's Indian and mestizo mul-

titudes. See Miles Richardson, Marta Eugenia Pardo, and Barbara Bode, "The Image of Christ in Spanish America as a Model for Suffering," JIAS, 13 (1971), 246–257.

40. See Richard Slotkin, *Regeneration Through Violence: The Mythology of the American Frontier, 1600–1860* (Middletown, Conn., 1974), pp. 47, 264.

41. This description by Edward C. Banfield of a southern Italian village is equally applicable to Andean America. See his *The Moral Basis of a Backward Society* (New York, 1958), p. 109. Also helpful in providing perspective is Alexander Gerschenkron, *Economic Backwardness in Historical Perspective* (Cambridge, Mass., 1962).

42. See Harold Benjamin, *Higher Education in the American Republics* (New York, 1965), p. 16. For an excellent review of some of the literature pertaining to the contrasts in U.S. and Latin American perceptions of business and businessmen see Lipset, *Revolution and Counter-revolution*, pp. 77–140.

43. See Thomas C. Cochran, "The Business Revolution," AHR, 79 (1974), p. 1465.

44. Quoted in Lynn White, Jr., "Technology Assessments from the Stance of a Medieval Historian," AHR, 79 (1974), p. 2.

45. See Alvin W. Gouldner, *The Coming Crisis of Western Sociology* (New York, 1970), pp. 346, 348.

46. Edwin Corwin, *The "Higher Law" Background of American Constitutional Law* (Ithaca, 1959), p. 71.

47. Mark E. Neely, Jr., argues convincingly that pluralism scored its definitive triumph among U.S. intellectuals only in the 1920s. Prior to that, currents of elitism and organicism and of partiality to the powerful state had retained considerable appeal. Thus Neely challenges the Louis Hartz thesis on the uninterrupted devotion in the United States to Lockean principles of liberal individualism. See Neely, "The Organic Theory of the State in America, 1838–1918," Ph.D. diss., Yale University, 1973.

48. See Milton Derber, *The American Idea of Industrial Democracy, 1865–1965* (Urbana, 1970), p. 521.

49. Theodore J. Lowi, *The End of Liberalism* (New York, 1969), pp. 48–49.

50. See Paul S. Nagel, *This Sacred Trust: American Nationality 1798–1898* (New York, 1971), p. vii.

51. Among the writers who criticize the way in which pluralism has operated to impede democracy and who urge correctives aimed at achieving greater equality

are Peter Bachrach, Corine Lathrop Gilb, Michael Harrington, Christopher Jencks, Grant McConnell, Kenneth A. Megill, Carole Pateman, and John Rawls.

52. Sakari Sariola, *Power and Resistance: The Colonial Heritage in Latin America* (Ithaca, 1972), pp. 99–100.

53. Glen C. Dealy, "The Tradition of Monistic Democracy in Latin America," *Journal of the History of Ideas*, 35 (1974), 640.

54. José Fellman Velarde, *Historia de Bolivia*, 3 vols. (La Paz, Cochabamba, 1968–1970), I, 53.

55. See Donald E. Smith, *Religion and Political Development* (Boston, 1970), p. 115.

56. Quoted in Peggy K. Liss, "Jesuit Contributions to the Ideology of Spanish America in Mexico, Part I," TA, 29 (1973), 320.

57. This is Talcott Parson's description of Weber's concept of legitimacy, in *Structure of Social Action*, II, 669.

58. Robert Michels, *Political Parties: A Sociological Study of the Oligarchical Tendencies of Modern Democracy*, trans. Eden and Cedar Paul (Glencoe, 1915), p. 17.

59. Perry Miller, *The Life of the Mind in America from the Revolution to the Civil War* (New York, 1965), pp. 102, 110.

60. On the moderating power see Frank Jay Moreno, "The Spanish Colonial System: A Functional Approach," *The Western Political Quarterly*, 20 (1967), 308–320.

61. See James Payne, *Labor and Politics in Peru: The System of Political Bargaining* (New Haven, 1965), p. 3 et passim. On the clientelist mentality of organized labor see Henry A. Landsberger, "The Labor Elite: Is It Revolutionary?" in S. M. Lipset and Aldo Solari, eds., *Latin American Elites* (New York, 1967), pp. 256–300.

62. Hartz, *The Liberal Tradition*, p. 309.

63. See Robert A. Nisbet, *Social Change and History: Aspects of the Western Theory of Development* (New York, 1969), p. 191. In an important article that indirectly sheds much light on the identity quest of the Spanish-speaking world in the eighteenth and nineteenth centuries, Marc Raeff, "The Well-Ordered Police State and the Development of Modernity in Seventeenth- and Eighteenth-Century Europe: An Attempt at a Comparative Approach," AHR, 80 (1975), 1222, writes: "I would suggest the following as conveying the essence of what we call 'modern,' as opposed to earlier, 'traditional' . . . patterns of culture: . . . society's conscious desire to maximize all its resources and to use this new potential dy-

namically for the enlargement and improvement of its way of life." See also Joseph R. Gusfield, "Tradition and Modernity: Misplaced Polarities in the Study of Social Change," *American Journal of Sociology*, 72 (1967), 351–362.

64. For a good general discussion of the persistence of traditional political culture in spite of major socioeconomic innovations see Robert Levine, "Political Socialization and Culture Change," in Clifford Geertz, ed., *Old Societies and New States* (Glencoe, Ill., 1963), esp. p. 289.

65. Erik H. Erikson, *Dimensions of a New Identity* (New York, 1974), pp. 70–71.

66. Tuveson, *Redeemer Nation*, pp. 76–77.

67. See William Gribbin, "A Matter of Faith: North America's Religion and South America's Independence," TA, 31 (1975), 470–487. For valuable comparative insights see Nathan O. Hatch, "The Origins of Civil Millennialism in America: New England Clergymen, War with France, and the Revolution," *William and Mary Quarterly*, 31 (1974), 407–430. The study shows that at the time of the Seven Years' War, New England clergymen described the struggle against Frenchmen in terms of the confrontation of liberty and tyranny, of heaven and hell. They condemned the French enemy both on the grounds of their religious tyranny ("popishness") and their civil tyranny, and depicted the two forms of tyranny as inseparably intertwined. The same attitudes were evident in the initial appraisals formed by many U.S. leaders of the newly independent republics of Spanish America.

68. Grund, *The Americans* (New York, 1837), pp. 173–174.

69. Slater, *The Pursuit of Loneliness*, p. 2.

70. See John M. Baines, *Revolution in Peru: Mariátegui and the Myth* (Tuscaloosa, 1972), p. 95.

71. September 29, 1879 letter of S. Newton Pettis to Secretary of State William Evarts, in *Message from the President of the United States, ... Relating to the War in South America* (Washington, 1882), p. 19.

2. The Social Matrix of the Andean Past

1. It has long been assumed that the Incas lacked a system of writing and that therefore all their history had to be oral history. In the 1960s, however, the German ethnologist Thomas Berthel, working in collaboration with Victoria de la Jara of Peru, developed a theory that the Incas possessed a "partial writing system." See the *New York Times*, July 29, 1970.

2. Heming, *The Conquest of the Incas* (New York, 1970), pp. 599–600. On the controversial issue of preconquest native population numbers in America

see Sherburne F. Cook and Woodrow Borah, *Essays in Population History*, 2 vols. (Berkeley, Los Angeles, 1971, 1973), Ángel Rosenblat, *La población indígena y el mestizaje en América*, 2 vols. (Buenos Aires, 1954), and Nicolás Sánchez Albornoz, *The Population of Latin America: A History*, trans. W. A. R. Richardson (Berkeley, Los Angeles, 1974). Reliable, general accounts of Inca civilization are found in Burr Cartwright Brundage, *Empire of the Inca* (Norman, 1963) and Friedrich Katz, *The Ancient American Civilizations*, trans. K. M. Lois Simpson (New York, 1972). The outstanding archaeological survey of pre-Columbian Peru is Luis G. Lumbreras, *The Peoples and Cultures of Ancient Peru*, trans. Betty J. Meggars (Washington, 1974). On pre-Inca as well as Inca culture, see Henry F. Dobyns and Paul L. Doughty, *Peru: A Cultural History* (New York, 1976), esp. pp. 26–58. This highly original work offers a penetrating analysis of the entire span of Peru's history up to 1975 and is particularly valuable in dealing with the continuing importance of Indian culture in the Peruvian reality.

3. Acosta's principal work, the *Historia natural y moral de las Indias*, was published in Seville in 1590. An English translation appeared in London in 1604.

4. On this see Heming, *Conquest*, pp. 60, 171, and John H. Rowe, "Inca Culture," in Julian H. Steward, ed., *Handbook of South American Indians*, II, *The Andean Civilizations* (New York, 1963), p. 252.

5. Karen Spalding, "Kurakas and Commerce: A Chapter in the Evolution of Andean Society," HAHR, 53 (1973), 583.

6. John H. Rowe, "The Incas Under Spanish Colonial Institutions," HAHR, 37 (1957), 156–157, writes that a nucleus of Inca leadership survived in the form of a hereditary nobility, the caciques. In addition to *kurakas* who were more important lords with extensive jurisdictions, the cacique class included descendants of lesser Inca officials. Hereditary officials charged with civil and criminal jurisdiction over their subjects under the supervision of Spanish authorities, the caciques, who numbered 2,078 in 1754, were entitled to honors similar to those of hidalgos (the lesser nobility) in Spain. An excellent bibliographical article is Karen Spalding, "The Colonial Indian: Past and Future Research Perspectives," LARR, 7 (1972), 47–76. See also her "Indian Rural Society in Colonial Peru: The Example of Huarochirí," Ph.D. diss., University of California, Berkeley, 1967.

7. Spalding, "Kurakas," pp. 594–595.

8. See Marvin Harris, *Patterns of Race in the Americas* (New York, 1954), esp. pp. 25–34.

9. On the hacienda with its collectivism below, capitalism above patterns, and also on the external dependency-internal domination aspect, see Magnus Mörner, "The Spanish American Hacienda: A Survey of Recent Research and Debate," HAHR, 53 (1973), esp. pp. 191, 210–211.

10. Pablo Macera, "Feudalismo colonial americano: el caso de las haciendas peruanas," *Acta Histórica* (Szeged, Hungary), 35 (1971), 39.

11. Shane J. Hunt, "The Economics of the Haciendas and Plantations in Latin America," mimeo., Princeton University, Woodrow Wilson School Discussion Paper (1972), p. 6.

12. Frederick P. Bowser, *The African Slave in Colonial Peru, 1524–1650* (Stanford, 1973), p. 329.

13. Lipset, *Revolution and Counter-revolution*, rev. ed. (Garden City, 1970), p. 27.

14. See James Lockhart, *Spanish Peru 1532–1560: A Colonial Society* (Madison, 1968), esp. p. 228.

15. The term was coined by the Chilean Alejandro Lipschutz. See his *El indoamericanismo y el problema racial en las Américas*, 2d ed. (Santiago de Chile, 1944), p. 75.

16. Bowser, *The African Slave*, p. 321.

17. Ibid., p. 334.

18. Federico Páez, *Explico* (Quito, 1939), p. 105.

19. See the Brian R. Hamnett review of Philip Wayne Powell, *Tree of Hate: Propaganda and Prejudices Affecting United States Relations with the Hispanic World* (New York, 1971), in HAHR, 53 (1973), 672.

20. Montalvo, *Siete tratados*, 2 vols. (Besançon, 1882), I, 121–123.

21. Sánchez, *Un sudamericano en norteámerica: ellos y nosotros*, 2d ed. (Lima, 1968), p. 7. The work first appeared in 1943.

22. Ibid., pp. 160–161, 174.

23. Ibid., pp. 152–155.

24. Mariano Picón-Salas, *A Cultural History of Spanish America*, trans. Irving A. Leonard (Berkeley, Los Angeles, 1963), p. 99.

25. Ibid., p. 100.

26. See J. P. Cooper, "General Introduction," *New Cambridge Modern History*, IV, *The Decline of Spain and the Thirty Years War, 1609–48/59* (Cambridge, Eng., 1970), p. 22.

27. See Américo Castro, *The Spaniards: An Introduction to Their History,* trans. Willard F. King and Selma Margaretten (Berkeley, Los Angeles, 1971), p. 551.

28. Irving A. Leonard, *Baroque Times in Old Mexico* (Ann Arbor, 1966), pp. 25–26. For an excellent general treatment of the topic see John Tate Lanning, *Academic Culture in the Spanish Colonies* (New York, 1940).

29. See Rodolfo Kusch, "Pensamiento aymara y quechua," AI, 21 (1971), 389–396.

30. Barreda Laos, *Vida intelectual del virreinato del Perú,* rev. ed. (Buenos Aires, 1937), pp. 380, 382. The work was first published in 1909.

31. Porras, *Mito, tradición e historia del Perú* (Lima, 1951), p. 112.

32. James Lockhart, *The Men of Cajamarca: A Social and Biographical Study of the First Conquerors of Peru* (Austin, 1972), p. 296.

33. An excellent and quite original description of the situation is found in John Lynch, *Spain Under the Habsburgs, II, Spain and America 1598–1700* (New York, 1969).

34. Karl Mannheim, *Man and Society in an Age of Reconstruction,* trans. Edward Shils (London, 1940), p. 296.

35. On this see D. A. Brading, "Government and Elites in Late Colonial Mexico," HAHR, 53 (1973), esp. pp. 396–397. Brading's observations on the downward mobility of established creole families in contrast to the upward mobility of *peninsulares* is as applicable to Andean America as to Mexico.

36. By a date fairly early in the eighteenth century, creoles had come to dominate the *audiencias* (high law courts that also exercised administrative powers) of the Peruvian viceroyalty and thus to control one of the most important sources of power in the colonial system. Later Bourbon attempts to reestablish peninsular domination became an important contributing factor in an independence movement among Andean creoles. See Mark A. Burkholder, "From Creole to Peninsular: The Transformation of the Audiencia of Lima," HAHR, 52 (1972), 395–415, and Leon G. Campbell, "A Colonial Establishment: Creole Domination of the Audiencia of Lima during the Eighteenth Century," HAHR, 52 (1972), 1–25.

37. See Charles C. Griffin, "The Enlightenment and Latin American Independence," in Arthur P. Whitaker, ed., *Latin America and the Enlightenment,* 2d ed. (Ithaca, 1961), pp. 119–144. Additional material bearing on the matter is found in A. Owen Aldridge, ed., *The Ibero-American Enlightenment* (Urbana, 1971).

38. See O. Carlos Stoetzer, *El pensamiento político en la América española durante el período de la emancipación, 1789–1825: bases hispánicas y las corrientes*

europeas, 2 vols. (Madrid, 1966), and Rubén Vargas Ugarte, *Historia del Perú virreinato siglo XVIII* (Buenos Aires, 1957). A standard work on the Spanish Enlightenment is Richard Herr, *The Eighteenth Century Revolution in Spain* (Princeton, 1958).

39. On the degree of colonial self-government prevailing under the Habsburgs see John Phelan, *The Kingdom of Quito in the Seventeenth Century: Bureaucratic Politics in the Spanish Empire* (Madison, 1967), esp. p. 336.

40. See Arthur P. Whitaker, "Changing and Unchanging Interpretations of the Enlightenment in Spanish America," *Proceedings of the American Philosophical Society*, 114 (1970), 270. This is a superb study of revisionist literature on the Spanish American Enlightenment.

41. Prologue by Jorge Fernández Stoll to J. G. Leguía, *Manuel Lorenzo de Vidaurre: historia y biografía* (Santiago de Chile, 1936), p. v.

42. See Arthur P. Whitaker, *The Western Hemisphere Idea: Its Rise and Decline* (Ithaca, 1954), p. 2.

43. Bernard Bailyn, *The Ideological Origins of the American Revolution* (Cambridge, Mass., 1967), p. 319.

44. A large section of Baquíjano's address is reproduced in Barreda Laos, *Vida intelectual*, pp. 317–326.

45. See Arzáns de Orsúa y Vela, *Historia de la Villa Imperial de Potosí*, ed. Lewis Hanke and Gunnar Mendoza, 2 vols. (Providence, R.I., 1965).

3. Prelude to Chaos: The Implications of Independence

1. José Ortega y Gasset, *Man and Crisis*, trans. Mildred Adams (New York, 1962), p. 185.

2. See Richard Herr, *The Eighteenth-Century Revolution in Spain* (Princeton, 1958), p. 199.

3. See John Lynch, *The Spanish-American Revolutions, 1808–1826* (New York, 1973), esp. pp. 1–7.

4. See John R. Fisher, *Government and Society in Colonial Peru: The Intendant System, 1784–1814* (London, 1970), p. 130.

5. J. R. Fisher, "Silver Production in the Viceroyalty of Peru, 1776–1824," HAHR, 55 (1975), 25–43, offers a refinement on the treatment in his book cited above. While conceding a general decline in economic conditions, he shows that output of the silver mines increased after 1776 and remained relatively high

until after 1812, by which time creole opinion and arms had been mobilized in support of the Spanish crown's sovereignty.

6. Ernesto Niño, *El Ecuador ante las revoluciones proletarias* (Ambato, 1935), p. 109. See too Richard Graham, *Independence in Latin America* (New York, 1972), pp. 66–67, and Emilio Romero, "Peru," in Luis Roque Gondra and others, *El pensamiento económico latinoamericano* (Mexico, 1945), p. 294.

7. Fisher, *Government and Society in Colonial Peru*, p. 152.

8. Francisco Javier Eugenio Santa Cruz y Espejo, *Escritos del Doctor*, 3 vols. (Quito, 1912–1923), III, 177–180.

9. Richard Lindley, "Kinship and Credit in the Structure of Guadalajara's Oligarchy, 1800–1830," Ph.D. diss., University of Texas, 1976, esp. chap. 4, has shown the extent to which merchants in New Spain, some of them from Peru, Ecuador, and Panama, had established a reliance on British merchants and bankers even prior to the year 1800. Very probably a study of this aspect of the economic history of late viceregal Peru would reveal similar patterns.

10. Sergio Villalobos R., *El Comercio y la crisis colonial: un mito de la independencia* (Santiago de Chile, 1968), has documented the extent to which the Chilean market was saturated by foreign goods and the resultant desire of creole merchants to acquire control over trade rather than to obtain genuinely free trade. As yet, no adequately researched study of the situation in Peru has appeared.

11. González Suárez, *Obras*, ed. Carlos Manuel Larrea, in *Biblioteca Ecuatoriana Mínima: la colonia y la república* (Puebla, Mexico, 1970), p. 331.

12. González Suárez, *Nueva miscelánea o colección de opúsculos* (Quito, 1910), pp. 114, 140.

13. See *Exposición del capítulo metropolitano de Lima a la convención nacional sobre la exclusión de los falsos cultos y sobre los derechos de liberated y de propiedad de la Iglesia* (Lima, 1855), p. 21, and Daniel Gleason, "Ideological Cleavages in Early Republican Peru, 1821–1872," Ph.D. diss., University of Notre Dame, 1973, esp. pp. 213–214.

14. Julio Tobar Donoso, *La Iglesia, modeladora de la nacionalidid* (Quito, 1953), pp. 29–30.

15. On the desire of churchmen to have a body politic that reflected the institutional organization of the church and the opposing intention of many liberals to remodel the ecclesiastical institution according to democratic principles see F. B. Pike, "Heresy, Real and Alleged, in Peru: An Aspect of the Conservative-Liberal Struggle, 1830–1875," HAHR, 47 (1967), 50–74.

16. García, *La seudo-defensa que el Señor Vigil hace de los gobiernos refutada por si misma* (Lima, 1866), esp. pp. 204, 207–215, 249–251.

17. Alfredo Pérez Guerrero, *Ecuador* (Quito, 1948), p. 82.

18. Tobar Donoso, *La Iglesia*, pp. 283–284.

19. The regalism of some priests in the early independence period sprang from their animosity toward Rome, inspired partly by an encyclical of disputed authenticity in which Pope Leo XII counseled the rebellious colonists to accept once more the rule of Spain's King Ferdinand VII. For an authoritative treatment of the matter see J. Lloyd Mecham, *Church and State in Latin America: A Study of Politico-Ecclesiastical Relations*, rev. ed. (Chapel Hill, 1966), pp. 61–87.

20. On Luna Pizarro see F. B. Pike, *The Modern History of Peru* (London, 1967), esp. pp. 50–51, 62–63, 70–78.

21. Jacinto Jijón y Caamaño, *Política conservadora*, 2 vols. (Riobamba, Quito, 1929, 1934), II, 332–33.

22. Tulio Halperin-Donghi, *The Aftermath of Revolution in Latin America,* trans. Josephine de Bunsen (New York, 1973), p. 101.

23. See *Colección Rocafuerte*, ed by Neptalí Zúñiga, 16 vols. (Quito, 1947), introduction by Zúñiga to vol. V, pp. i–xxxi.

24. See esp. Rocafuerte, *Ensayo sobre tolerancia religiosa,* in *Biblioteca Ecuatoriana Mínima: escritores políticos* (Puebla, Mexico, 1960), p. 122.

25. *Ibid.*, pp. 126, 134–135. See too Rocafuerte's prologue to his *Ideas necesarias a todo pueblo americano que quiere ser libre* (originally published in 1821 either in Philadelphia or Havana), in *Colección Rocafuerte*, III, 12–14. On the ideas of Manuel Lorenzo de Vidaurre who had represented Peru at the Cádiz Cortes and subsequently found himself in the United States see his *Efectos de las facciones en los gobiernos* (Boston, 1828), and *Plan del Perú: defectos del gobierno antiguo, necesarias reformas, obra escrita a principios del año de 10 en Cádiz y hoy aumentada con interesantes notas* (Philadelphia, 1823).

26. Rocafuerte, *Ensayo sobre tolerancia religiosa,* p. 139, and Vidaurre, *Plan del Perú*, pp. 164ff. On John Adams' beliefs in this connection see Wilkins B. Winn, "The Efforts of the United States to Secure Religious Liberty in a Commercial Treaty with Mexico, 1825–1831," *TA*, 28 (1972), 311–332.

27. On this see Antenor Orrego, *Hacia un humanismo americano* (Lima, 1966), pp. 7–11. Orrego maintains that the persistence of this belief prevented Andean America, or as he prefers to call it Indo America, from going its own way and developing in accordance with its traditions.

28. Ramiro Borja y Borja, *Derecho constitucional ecuatoriano*, 3 vols. (Madrid, 1950), II, 551–552, writes that one very important element of colonial reaction to Bourbon reforms "was connected to the constitutional traditions, the decentralized and democratic traditions of medieval Spain, conserved in America with greater strength than in the peninsula."

29. See José Pareja Paz Soldán, *Las constituciones del Perú: exposición, crítica, y textos* (Madrid, 1954), esp. pp. 375, 848–880.

30. Banfield, *The Moral Basis of a Backward Society* (New York, 1958), p. 83.

31. See the introduction by Robert Kern and Ronald Dolkhart to their edited volume, *The Caciques: Oligarchical Politics and the System of Caciquismo in the Luso-Hispanic World* (Albuquerque, 1973), esp. pp. 1–2 and 34.

32. Louis Hartz, *The Liberal Tradition in America* (New York, 1955), p. 73.

33. Carbo, *Nociones de los derechos y deberes del ciudadano* (Guayaquil, 1883), p. 10. Undoubtedly J. J. Rousseau's attitudes on women influenced Spanish American liberals. In this connection see Victor G. Wexler, " 'Made for Man's Delight': Rousseau as Antifeminist," AHR, 81 (1976), 266–291. Wexler shows that Rousseau desired Emile to be a critical, self-reliant citizen and asserted his right to an elaborate education and full equality with his peers. In contrast, Sophie was to be trained only as a wife to Emile and as a mother to his children, in the belief that "Woman is made for man's delight."

34. González Prada, September 25, 1904 address, "Las esclavas de la Iglesia," in *Horas de lucha*, 2d ed. (Callao, 1924), pp. 83–84.

35. Carl F. Herbold, Jr., "Peru," in Richard M. Morse, ed., with Michael L. Conniff and John Wibel, *The Urban Development of Latin America, 1750–1920* (Stanford, 1971), p. 104.

36. Johan Jakob von Tschudi, *Travels in Peru, on the Coast, in the Sierra, across the Cordilleras and the Andes, into the Primeval Forest*, trans. Thomasina Ross (New York, 1854), p. 89.

37. Robert W. Fogel and Stanley L. Engerman, *Time on the Cross*, 2 vols. (Boston, 1974), I, 129.

38. R. A. Humphreys, *British Consular Reports on the Trade and Politics of Latin America* (London, 1940), p. 220.

39. For a thorough description of these developments see D. C. M. Platt, *Latin America and British Trade, 1806–1914* (New York, 1973).

40. Halperin-Donghi, *The Aftermath of Revolution*, p. 54.

41. André Gunder Frank, *Lumpenbourgeoisie: Lumpendevelopment. Dependence, Class, and Politics in Latin America*, trans. by Marion Davis Berdecio (New York, 1972), p. 15.

42. Quoted in Richard N. Goodwin, *The American Condition* (Garden City, 1974), p. 309.

43. On the concept of the "ideologically true" government see Donald E. Smith, *Religion and Political Development* (Boston, 1970), pp. 115–116.

44. Krause, *Ideal del humanidad para la vida*, trans. Julián Sanz del Río (Madrid, 1860), pp. 102–104. See also p. 34, where Krause develops the notion of social harmony based on the operation by each member of society within his own sphere, always subordinate to the overall demands of the common good.

45. On Krausism see Elías Díaz, *La filosofía social del Krausismo español* (Madrid, 1973), Juan José Gil Cremades, *El reformismo español: Krausismo, escuela histórica, neotomismo* (Barcelona, 1969), and F. B. Pike, *Hispanismo: Spanish Conservatives and Liberals and Their Relations with Spanish America, 1898–1936* (Notre Dame, 1971), esp. pp. 109–114, 146–147, 376–379, and "Making the Hispanic World Safe from Democracy: Spanish Liberals and Hispanismo," *RP*, 33 (1971), esp. pp. 309–313.

46. Hartz, *The Liberal Tradition*, p. 85.

47. Roger Marett, *Peru* (London, 1969), p. 21.

48. Peter H. Gore, *The Highland Campesino, Backward Peasant or Reluctant Pawn: A Study of the Social and Economic Factors Affecting Small Farm Modernization in Four Highland Ecuadorian Communities*, CULASP (Ithaca, 1971), p. 1.

49. Marett, *Peru*, p. 25.

50. See Edward Dew, *Politics in the Altiplano: The Dynamics of Change in Rural Peru* (Austin, 1969), p. 65.

51. See Charles R. Gibson, *Foreign Trade in the Economic Development of Small Nations: The Case of Ecuador* (New York, 1971), p. 35.

52. Pérez Guerrero, *Ecuador*, p. 62.

53. George I. Blanksten, *Ecuador: Constitutions and Caudillos* (Berkeley, 1951), p. 18.

54. Carbo, *Nociones de los derechos*, p. 53.

55. John D. Martz, *Ecuador: Conflicting Political Culture and Quest for Progress* (Boston, 1972), pp. 23–24.

56. Belisario Quevedo, *Sociología, política y moral*, excerpted in *Biblioteca Ecuatoriana Mínima: juristas y sociólogos* (Puebla, Mexico, 1960), p. 615. Quevedo (1883–1921) was a pioneering Ecuadoran sociologist.

57. John Murra, "The Historical Tribes of Ecuador," in Julian H. Steward, ed., *Handbook of South American Indians*, II, *The Andean Civilizations* (New York, 1963), p. 817.

58. Jijón y Caamaño, *Política conservadora*, II, 365.

59. Quevedo, *Sociología*, p. 609.

60. Blanksten, *Ecuador*, p. 23.

61. Pérez Guerrero, *Ecuador*, pp. 62–63.

62. See José de la Cuadra, *El montuvio ecuatoriano: Ensayo de presentación* (Buenos Aires, 1937), pp. 66–67.

63. Hassaurek, *Four Years Among Spanish Americans* (New York, 1867), pp. 102–103.

64. On Bolivian geography see J. Valerie Fifer, *Bolivia: Land, Location, and Politics since 1825* (Cambridge, Eng., 1972), and Harold Osborne, *Bolivia: A Land Divided* (London, 1955).

65. George M. McBride, *The Agrarian Indian Communities of Highland Bolivia* (New York, 1921), p. 2.

66. See William H. Brill, *Military Intervention in Bolivia: The Overthrow of Paz Estenssoro and the MNR* (Washington, 1967), pp. 4–5, for a fine, succinct depiction of Bolivia's geography and regionalism.

67. See Moisés Alcázar, "La revolución Federal," *Kollasuyo* (La Paz), 65 (1947), p. 13.

68. See Harry Tschopik, Jr., "The Aymara," in Steward, ed., *Handbook of South American Indians*, II, 501.

69. Waldo Frank, *America Hispana* (New York, 1931), pp. 34–35. See also José María Camacho, "La lengua aymara," *Kollasuyo*, 60 (1945), 412. Camacho maintains that Aymara language is dry, hard, energetic, concise, in contrast to Quechua which is sweet, sonorous, and sentimental. He argues that the differences in language reflect perfectly the differences in nature between the two Indian groups.

70. Arguedas, *Pueblo enfermo*, 3d ed. (Santiago de Chile, 1937), pp. 67, 70–72. This highly controversial book, attributing the "sickness" of the Bolivian people largely to racial factors, was first published in 1909.

71. Marsh, *The Bankers in Bolivia: A Study in American Foreign Investment* (New York, 1928), p. 67.

72. Fifer, *Bolivia*, p. 22. Further contributing to Andean regionalism was the tension between Charcas (Chuquisaca) and Lima. The origins of this tension are ably discussed by Josep M. Barnadas in the concluding chapter of his *Charcas: Orígenes históricos de una sociedad colonial, 1535–1565* (La Paz, 1973).

73. Lora, *Historia del movimiento obrero boliviano*, 3 vols. (La Paz, 1967–1970), I, 248–249.

74. Fernando Diez de Medina, *Franz Tamayo: hechicero del Ande, retrato al modo fantástico*, 2d ed. (La Paz, 1944), pp. 18, 23.

75. George Jackson, Eder, *Inflation and Development in Latin America: A Case History of Inflation and Stabilization in Bolivia* (Ann Arbor, 1968), p. 18.

76. Lynch, *Spanish-American Revolutions*, p. 164.

4. The Nineteenth Century Quest for Stability and Progress

1. For the conventional view that the strength of royalist armies in Peru delayed the development of a bona fide independence movement see Herbert Reffeld, "The Viceroyalty of Peru: Bulwark of Royalism, 1808–1821," Ph.D. diss., University of California, Berkeley, 1951. A persuasive revisionist interpretation, arguing that the royalist military establishment in Peru was a paper tiger and that other reasons must be sought to explain the late blooming of the independence movement, is Leon G. Campbell, *The Military and Society in Colonial Peru, 1750–1810* (Philadelphia, 1977). Fresh insights on the late stages of the independence movement are found in Timothy E. Anna, "The Last Viceroys of New Spain and Peru: An Appraisal," *AHR*, 81 (1976), 38–65.

2. By far the most comprehensive coverage of the Peruvian independence movement, dealing with the events from 1770 to the departure of San Martín in 1822, is the twenty-seven tome (with most of the tomes containing more than one volume) *Colección documental de la independencia del Perú* (Lima, 1971–1972). The massive *Colección* was published under the auspices of the Comisión Nacional del Sesquicentenario de la Independencia del Perú.

3. See Emilio Romero, "Perú," in Luis Roque Gondra and others, *El pensamiento económico latinoamericano* (Mexico, 1945), pp. 296–297.

4. See Thomas M. Davies, Jr., *Indian Integration in Peru: A Half Century of Experience, 1900–1948* (Lincoln, 1974), pp. 21–23, Thomas R. Ford, *Man and Land in Peru* (Gainesville, 1955), p. 43, and Arturo Urquidi, *Las comunidades indígenas en Bolivia* (Cochabamba, 1970), p. 58.

5. John Lynch, *The Spanish-American Revolutions, 1808–1826* (New York, 1973), p. 288.

6. Jonathan Levin, *The Export Economies* (Cambridge, Mass., 1960), p. 31.

7. W. M. Mathew, "Foreign Contractors and the Peruvian Government at the Outset of the Guano Trade," *HAHR*, 52 (1972), 598–620. See also Mathew, "Anglo-Peruvian Commercial and Financial Relations, 1820–1865, with Special Reference to Antony Gibbs and Sons and the Guano Trade," Ph.D. diss., London School of Economics and Political Science, and "Peru and the British Guano Market, 1840–1870," *Economic History Review*, 23 (1970), 112–128, and Juan Maiguashca, "A Reinterpretation of the Guano Age, 1840–1880," Ph.D. diss., Oxford University, 1967. A classic account of Peru in the third quarter of the nineteenth century is A. J. Duffield, *Peru in the Guano Age* (London, 1877). Interesting Marxian revisionism is found in Heraclio Bonilla, *Guano y burguesía en el Perú* (Lima, 1974).

8. See Watt Stewart, *Chinese Bondage in Peru: A History of the Chinese Coolie in Peru, 1849–1874* (Durham, 1951), esp. pp. 12–13, 74–75, 82.

9. See Carlos Wiesse, *Historia del Perú: la república* (Lima, 1934), p. 54.

10. Levin, *Export Economies*, p. 94.

11. November 14 and 15, 1878 address of Manuel Pardo before the Peruvian Senate, Perú: Congreso, *Diario de los debates de cámara de senadores, 1876–79* (Lima, 1879), III, 189.

12. Basadre, *Chile, Perú y Bolivia independiente* (Barcelona, 1948), p. 749. Basadre's treatment of Peru in this book is in some respects a succinct summation of a portion of his admirable *Historia de la República del Perú, 1822–1933*, 17 vols., 6th ed. (Lima, 1968), the standard account by which all other works must be judged and one of the finest histories of a single Latin American country ever written. Also valuable on the nineteenth century is Rubén Vargas Ugarte, S.J., *Historia general del Perú*, 10 vols. (Lima, 1960–1971), vols. VII and IX.

13. Sermon of Herrera in his *Escritos y discursos*, 2 vols. (Lima, 1929, 1939), I, 14–33. Writing the following year, Herrera pictured religion as "the only guarantee of property, of truth, and of subordination, the principles that safeguard society." And in 1846 he contended: "peace and harmony cannot be established without an authority that binds the citizen internally in his conscience, an authority to which he feels truly subject and on which he has a necessary dependence: and this authority is only God, sovereign of the universe." See ibid., I, 40, 83.

14. Ibid., I, 197–99.

15. Ibid., II, 69.

16. Treatment of Herrera and Vigil is based to some degree on F. B. Pike, "Church and State in Peru and Chile Since 1840: A Study in Contrasts," AHR, 73 (1967), 30–50, and "Heresy, Real and Alleged, in Peru: An Aspect of the Conservative-Liberal Struggle, 1830–1875," HAHR, 47 (1967), 50–75. See also John C. Broadhurst, Jr., *Francisco de Paula González Vigil: Peruvian Pensador*, Ph.D. diss., University of Virginia, 1974.

17. On the impact of Krausism in Peru see Estuardo Núñez, *La influencia alemana en el derecho peruano* (Lima, 1937), pp. 10–19, and Augusto Salazar Bondy, *La filosofía en el Perú: panorama histórica* (Lima, 1967), esp. pp. 65–75.

18. Vigil, *Importancia de las asociaciones; Importancia de la educación popular*, with notes by Alberto Tauro (Lima, 1948), pp. 26–27, 30–31. For other indications of Vigil's corporativist leanings see ibid., esp. pp. 49, 57–60. Vigil also argues (pp. 67, 77–78) that education must inculcate love for work directed not toward the private gain of the individual but rather toward the well-being of his association. Apparently some of Vigil's ideas on the importance of associations in blunting individualistic greed came not only from Krausism but from Freemasonry as well.

19. Basadre, *Chile, Perú, Bolivia*, p. 423; Levin, *Export Economies*, p. 96.

20. A comprehensive study is John Peter Olinger, "Dreyfus Freres, Guano and Peruvian Government Finance, 1869–1880: A Chapter in Economic Imperialism," Ph.D. diss., State University of New York, Binghampton, 1973.

21. See David Chaplin, *The Peruvian Industrial Labor Force* (Princeton, 1967), p. 25, and Watt Stewart, *Henry Meiggs, Yankee Pizarro* (Durham, 1946), pp. 75–76.

22. Robert G. Greenhill and Rory M. Miller, "The Peruvian Government and the Nitrate Trade, 1873–1879," *Journal of Latin American Studies*, 5 (1973), 108. By 1875, moreover, Peru's floating debt in London was the largest among all the Latin American countries. For a colorful treatment see William Clarke, *Peru and Its Creditors* (London, 1877).

23. See the Jorge Basadre introduction to Santiago Távera, *Historia de los partidos*, ed. Basadre and Félix Denegri Luna (Lima, 1951), p. xlviii.

24. Some of the best insights into the economic thought of Pardo are found in his extended essays "Estudios sobre Jauja," published in installments in the *Revista de Lima*, beginning with the first number of the journal that appeared in October 1859. A serviceable biography is Evaristo San Cristóval, *Manual Pardo y Lavalle* (Lima, 1945).

25. Jesús Chavarría, "La desaparición del Perú colonial (1870–1919)," *Aportes*, no. 23 (1972), 125–127, suggests that the group of Civilists who shared with Pardo the desire to attain development without dependence on foreign capital was quite small.

26. In his outstanding study *The Emergence of the Republic of Bolivia* (Gainesville, 1957), Charles Arnade casts a cynical eye on the role played by Upper Peruvians in bringing about Bolivia's independence. For a brief critique of the Arnade interpretation see Valentín Abecía Baldivieso, *Historiografía boliviana* (La Paz, 1965), p. 386. The controversial issue is explored in some depth in Charles H. Bowman, *Vicente Pazos Kanki: un Boliviano en la libertad de América* (La Paz, 1975).

27. See Federico Ávila, *La revisión de nuestro passado* (La Paz, 1936), p. 36, José Fellman Velarde, *Historia de Bolivia*, 3 vols. (La Paz, Cochabamba, 1968–1970), I, 213, and Enrique Finot, *Nueva historia de Bolivia* (Buenos Aires, 1946), pp. 175ff. For valuable material on the background to Bolivian independence see also Leone Ruth Auld, "Discontent with the Spanish System of Control in Upper Peru, 1730–1809," Ph.D. diss., University of California, Los Angeles, 1963.

28. See Mendoza, *El factor geográfico en la nacionalidad boliviana* (Sucre, 1925), esp. pp. 2–34. For an excellent analysis of the thought and writings of Mendoza see Guillermo Francovich, *El pensamiento boliviano en el siglo XX* (Mexico, 1956), pp. 72–77.

29. Tamayo, *Creación de la pedagogía nacional* (La Paz, 1944), p. 184. This influential work was first published in 1910. On this topic see also Charles Arnade, "The Historiography of Colonial and Modern Bolivia," HAHR, 42 (1962), esp. 339–40.

30. Herbert S. Klein, "Structure and Profitability of Royal Finance in the Viceroyalty of the Río de la Plata in 1790," HAHR, 53 (1973), 457.

31. See Gabriel René Moreno, *Últimos días coloniales en el Alto Perú*, 2 vols. (La Paz, 1940), II, 126.

32. See William Lee Lofstrom, "Attempted Economic Reform and Innovation in Bolivia under Antonio José de Sucre," HAHR, 50 (1970), esp. 279–285, and Luis Peñalosa, *Historia económica de Bolivia*, 2 vols., 2d ed. (La Paz, 1953), I, 270–271.

33. Guillermo Francovich, "Un precursor de las ideas socialistas en Bolivia, *Kollasuyo* (La Paz), no. 26 (1941), 110.

34. See Francovich, "La filosofía de Destutt de Tracy en Bolivia," ibid., no. 25 (1941), 3–8, and Rafael A. Reyeros, *Historia de la educación en Bolivia de la independencia a la revolución federal* (La Paz, 1952), pp. 22–36.

35. Rubén Vargas Ugarte, S.J., *El episcopado en los tiempos de la emancipación sudamericana, 1790–1830* (Buenos Aires, 1945), p. 60.

36. William Lee Lofstrom, *The Promise and Problem of Reform: Attempted Social and Economic Change in the First Years of Bolivian Independence*,

CULASP (Ithaca, 1972), p. 265. José María Dalence, *Bosquejo estadístico de Bolivia* (Sucre, 1851), p. 226, reports that the number of secular and regular clergy in Bolivia stood at 1,517 in 1847, about one-half the number at the beginning of the century.

37. See Faustino Suárez Arnez, *Historia de la educación en Bolivia* (La Paz, 1963), pp. 70–73.

38. See Alfredo Jáuregui Rosquellas, *Alrededor de la tragedia: un siglo de vida republicana* (Sucre, 1951), p. 23.

39. Gabriel René Moreno, *Nicomedes Antelo* (Santa Cruz de la Sierra, 1960), p. 26.

40. Ramón Sotomayor y Valdés, *Estudio histórico de Bolivia bajo la administración del jeneral D. José María de Achá* (Santiago de Chile, 1874), pp. 85–86. Sotomayor, a Chilean historian of considerable eminence, spent a lengthy period in Bolivia on a diplomatic mission. Even though showing a typically Chilean superiority attitude vis-à-vis Bolivians, he provides many valuable insights into the country's history from its independence to 1861.

41. Dalence, *Bosquejo*, p. 373.

42. Guillermo Lora, *Historia del movimiento obrero boliviano*, 3 vols. (La Paz, 1967–1970), I, 85.

43. Roberto Prudencio, "Escritores del pasado, Casimiro Olañeta," *Kollasuyo*, no. 60 (1945), esp. 125–126, shows that the person responsible for creating the myth that Olañeta won Sucre to the idea of independence was Olañeta himself.

44. See Gustavo Adolfo Otero, "Casimiro Olañeta," ibid., no. 11 (1939), 27.

45. Basadre, *Chile, Peru, Bolivia*, pp. 303–304.

46. Manuel Carrasco, *José Ballivián, 1805–1852* (Buenos Aires, 1660), p. 212.

47. Toward the end of his term, Belzu may have come to question the reliability of the masses and to have determined upon a more serious effort to enlist support of the country's aristocratic elements. There are even indications he came ultimately to favor a monarchy for Bolivia. See Augusto Guzmán, *Historia de Bolivia* (La Paz, 1973), pp. 144–145, and M. Rigoberto Paredes, "El General Mariano Melgarejo y su tiempo, conclusión," *Kollasuyo*, no. 59 (1945), 324.

48. Gonzalo Romero, *Reflexiones para una interpretación de la historia de Bolivia* (Buenos Aires, 1960), p. 107.

49. Fellman Velarde, *Historia*, II, 112–113.

50. Víctor Paz Estenssoro, "Bolivia," in Roque Gondra and others, *Pensamiento económico*, pp. 42–43, suggests that Belzu's protectionist policies may originally have been dictated simply by the fact that no major exports were available with which to finance the import of foreign manufactures. At the mid-point in Belzu's term, however, exports of quinine, guano, and silver ore began to increase and from this time on the president is alleged to have had second thoughts about protectionist policies. It is significant, though, that reversion to free trade came only after the fall of Belzu.

51. See J. Valerie Fifer, *Bolivia: Land, Location, and Politics since 1825* (Cambridge, Eng., 1972), pp. 238–239.

52. Jaime Ponce G., "El sindicalismo boliviano: Resumen histórico y perspectivas actuales," *Estudios Andinos*, I (1970), 31. In a move further aimed at strengthening the corporative structure of society, Belzu encouraged each of the guilds to maintain its own vocational schools and social insurance programs. See Reyeros, *Historia de la educación*, pp. 156–157.

53. Lora, *Historia*, I, 301.

54. See the very important treatment of Bolivian Krausism by Humberto Vásquez Machicado, *Facetas del intelecto boliviano* (Oruro, 1958), pp. 25, 197–208. Also useful are Manfredo Kempee Mercado, "La filosofía en Bolivia," *Kollasuyo*, no. 59 (1945), esp. 341, and Alipio Valencia Vega, *El pensamiento político en Bolivia* (La Paz, 1973).

55. Alfonso Crespo Rodas, "Historia de un caudillo," *Kollasuyo*, no. 25 (1941), 48. This is an extremely perceptive essay on Belzu.

56. Guillermo Lora, ed., *Documentos políticos de Bolivia* (La Paz, 1970), pp. 98–99.

57. Belzu has remained a controversial figure for historians. For unfavorable assessments see Manuel José Cortés, *Ensayo sobre la historia de Bolivia* (Sucre, 1861) and Lora, *Historia del movimiento obrero*, I, 361. On the other hand, Carlos Montenegro, instrumental in founding the twentieth-century National Revolutionary Movement which built its program to a large extent on the populist paternalism of Belzu's government, is altogether laudatory. See his *Nacionalismo y coloniaje: su expresión histórica en la prensa de Bolivia*, 3d ed. (La Paz, 1953), pp. 93ff.

58. Gustavo Adolfo Navarro, *Ensayos y crítica: revoluciones bolivianas, guerras internacionales, y escritores* (La Paz, 1961), p. 20.

59. Alfonso Crespo, "José María Linares: luz y sombra de una dictadura," *Kollasuyo*, no. 7 (1939), 52–54.

60. For an interesting justification of Linares' free-trade policies see José Vicente Dorado, *Indicaciones económico-políticos o sean cuestiones bolivianos* (Sucre, 1859).

61. Finot, *Nueva historia*, p. 243.

62. Roberto Prudencio, "Los escritores del pasado: Isaac Tamayo," *Kollasuyo*, no. 5 (1939), 68–69.

63. The congress, with a large representation of greedy lawyers and professionals, may have been more responsible than Melgarejo for the 1868 law that gave the government the power to dispose of Indian lands as it saw fit. On the culpability of this and succeeding congresses see Félix Avelino Aramayo, *Bolivia: apuntes sobre el congreso de 1870* (Sucre, 1871).

64. On the massive Indian uprisings provoked by the land seizures, contributing to Melgarejo's fall from power, see Ramiro Condarco Morales, *Zárate, el "Temible" Willka* (La Paz, 1965), pp. 41–46.

65. Vásquez Machicado, "La diplomacia boliviana y la tragedia de Maximiliano de México: una gestión generosa de Melgarejo ante Juárez," *Kollasuyo*, no. 26 (1941), 126. The classic study by Alberto Gutiérrez, *El melgarejismo, antes y después de Melgarejo* (La Paz, 1916), treats Melgarejo as symptomatic of the ills of Bolivia rather than responsible for them.

66. See Ramiro Borja y Borja, *Derecho constitucional ecuatoriano*, 3 vols. (Madrid, 1950), II, 552–53.

67. See Óscar Efrén Reyes, *Breve historia general del Ecuador, 1809–1940* (Quito, 1942), pp. 431–472.

68. See Carlos A. Rolando, *Biografía del General Juan José Flores* (Guayaquil, 1906). While not really satisfactory, this is probably the closest to an adequate account that has appeared. The study of Flores in which Mark van Aken has been engaged for many years should set a new standard when it appears.

69. On these events see Nick Dean Mills, Jr., "Liberal Opposition in Ecuadorean Politics, 1830–1845," Ph.D. diss., University of New Mexico, 1972.

70. See Pío Jaramillo Alvarado, *El indio ecuatoriano* (Quito, 1936), p. 114.

71. See Borja y Borja, *Derecho constitucional*, II, 596, 598.

72. See Jaime Rodríguez O., "Vicente Rocafuerte and Mexico, 1820–1832," Ph.D. diss., University of Texas, 1970, p. 23. A revised treatment of Rocafuerte's early public career is Rodríguez, *The Emergence of Spanish America: Vicente Rocafuerte and Spanish Americanism, 1808–1832* (Berkeley, Los Angeles, 1975). See also Kent Mecum, *El idealismo práctico de Vicente Rocafuerte, un verdadero americano independiente y libre* (Puebla, Mexico, 1975), J. J. Pino de Icaza, "Palabras preliminares," *Biblioteca Ecuatoriana Mínima: escritores políticos* (Quito, 1960), esp. pp. 29–38, and Joedd Price, "Images and Influences: The Legacy of the Founding Fathers and the Federal System in Ecuador," *LARR*, 10 (1975), 121–136.

73. See Pedro Carbo, "D. Vicente Rocafuerte," *Biblioteca Ecuatoriana Mínima: escritores políticos*, pp. 94–98, and Alfredo Pareja Diez Canseco, *Historia del Ecuador*, 2 vols. (Quito, 1958), II, 24–29.

74. See *Colección Rocafuerte*, ed. Neptalí Zúñiga, 16 vols. (Quito, 1947), VII, 17. See also V, 34–36.

75. State of the Union address, 1839, ibid., XIII, 213–214. On these ideas see also Zúñiga, preliminary notes, VI, i–xxvii, and V, 34–35.

76. Address of 1835, delivered in Ambato, ibid., XIII, 140.

77. Address of 1837, to the national congress, ibid., XIII, 168.

78. This is the accurate appraisal made by Jacinto Jijón y Caamaño, *Política conservadora*, 2 vols. (Riobamba, Quito, 1929, 1934), I, 283.

79. Roberto Andrade, *Historia del Ecuador*, 7 vols. (Guayaquil, 1936), VII, 2528–2529.

80. Rocafuerte manifesto, quoted by Reyes, *Breve historia*, p. 519.

81. On the various schemes and expeditions organized by Flores see Mark Van Aken, *Pan-Hispanism: Its Origin and Development to 1866* (Berkeley, Los Angeles, 1959).

82. J. J. Pino de Icaza, "Palabras preliminares," p. 67.

83. Roberto Andrade, quoted in *Colección Rocafuerte*, XIV, 291.

84. See Pío Jaramillo Alvarado, *La doctrine liberal: hombres e ideas en el Ecuador* (Quito, 1923), p. 11.

85. Gabriel Cevallos García, *Reflexiones sobre la historia del Ecuador*, 2 vols. (Cuenca, 1957, 1960), I, 89.

86. See the García Moreno pamphlet *La verdad a mis calumniadores*, in *Biblioteca Ecuatoriana Mínima: escritores políticos*, esp. pp. 303–304.

87. Benjamín Carrión, *García Moreno, el santo del patíbulo* (Mexico, 1959).

88. See Wilfrido Loor, *García Moreno y sus asesinos* (Quito, 1955), p. vi.

89. For the text of the concodat see J. Lloyd Mecham, *Church and State in Latin America*, 2d ed. (Chapel Hill, 1966), pp. 143–148. On the subject see also William M. King, S.J., "Ecuadorian Church and State Relations under García Moreno, 1859–1863," Ph.D. diss., University of Texas, Austin, 1974.

90. This is the cogent analysis of Belisario Quevedo, "Consideraciones sobre García Moreno," *Biblioteca Ecuatoriana Mínima: escritores políticos*, pp. 275–276.

91. See, for example, Alfonso Mora Bowen, *El liberalismo Radical en su trayectoria histórica* (Quito, 1940), p. 73.

92. José María Velasco Ibarra, *Conciencia o barbarie: exégesis de la política americana* (Buenos Aires, 1938), pp. 47–48.

93. Agustín Cueva, *Discurso del . . . , Presidente de la Asamblea Nacional del Ecuador, pronunciado en la Sesión Solemne del 17 de abril de 1929* (Quito, 1929), p. 9.

94. Richard Pattee, *Gabriel García Moreno y el Ecuador de su tiempo* (Quito, 1941), pp. 181, 381–382.

95. On Montalvo's humanist elitism see Roberto D. Agramonte, "La filosofía de Montalvo," *Revista Interamericana de Bibliografía*, 22 (1972), esp. 372, and Frank MacDonald Spindler, "Lamennais and Montalvo: A European Influence upon Latin American Political Thought," *Journal of the History of Ideas*, 37 (1976), 137–146. The best biography is Óscar Efrén Reyes, *Vida de Juan Montalvo*, 2d ed. (Quito, 1934).

96. See García Moreno, "Mensaje al Congreso Constitucional de 1875," *Biblioteca Ecuatoriana Mínima: escritores políticos*, p. 363.

97. See Loor, *García Moreno y sus asesinos*, p. xviii.

98. Letters of February 25, 1873 and January 19, 1875, in *Cartas de García Moreno*, ed. Wilfrido Loor, 4 vols. (Quito, 1953–1955), IV, 321–322, 501. On García Moreno's educational policies see Julio Tobar Donoso, *García Moreno y la instrucción pública*, 2d ed. (Quito, 1940). Among the Jesuits driven from Germany in the course of the Kulturkampf who aided in the expansion of Ecuadoran education was Theodor Wolf. Remaining many years in Ecuador Wolf, who withdrew from the Society of Jesus, published one of the classic descriptions of the country: *Geografía y geología del Ecuador* (Leipzig, 1892). The English translation by James W. Flanagan was published in Toronto in 1933.

99. J. Gonzalo Orellana, ed., *El Ecuador en cien años de independencia, 1830–1930*, 2 vols. (Quito, 1930), I, 79–80.

100. See Humberto García Ortiz, "Consideraciones acerca de una legislación indígena en el Ecuador," *AI*, 2 (1942), 26, Jaramillo Alvarado, *El Indio*, pp. 260–261, and Gonzalo Rubio Orbe, *Aspectos indígenas* (Quito, 1965), p. 183.

101. On the tendency of his critics to depict García Moreno as a personally evil man see Peter H. Smith, "The Image of a Dictator: Gabriel García Moreno," *HAHR*, 45 (1965), 1–24.

102. *Cartas*, IV, 537–538.

103. This is true even in the most recent detailed study, the massive *Vida de García Moreno*, 8 vols. (Quito, 1954–1968) by the Jesuit Severo Gómezjurado. The work is marred by its tone of hero worship, as was the much earlier work by the French Redemptorist Agustin Berthe, *Garcia Moreno: Président d l'Equaleur, venguer et martyr du droit Chréticn* (Paris, 1892). For a superb resumé of the literature on García Moreno see Adam Szászdi, "The Historiography of the Republic of Ecuador," HAHR, 44 (1964), 521–528. See also Mark Van Aken, "Ecuador," in Charles C. Griffin, ed., *Latin America: A Guide to the Historical Literature* (Austin, 1971), pp. 492–495.

104. Manuel J. Calle, *Figuras y siluetas: Liberales ecuatorianos* (Quito, 1899), p. ii.

· 105. See José María Le Gouhir y Rodas, *Historia de la República del Ecuador*, 3 vols. (Quito, 1920–1938), III, esp. 117–118.

106. A lively but not very reliable account of this period has been provided by Marietta de Veintemilla, *Páginas del Ecuador* (Lima, 1890). A refutation of this work was written by Antonio Flores, the son of Ecuador's first president: *Para la historia del Ecuador*, 2 vols. (Quito, 1891). For an unfavorable assessment of Veintemilla see, in addition to Flores, Luis Robalino Dávila, *Los orígenes del Ecuador de hoy*, 8 vols. (Quito and Puebla, Mexico, 1949–1969), V, part 1, pp. 339–341. This is the most detailed political history of Ecuador. Far friendlier to Veintemilla is José León Mera, *La dictadura y la restauración en la República del Ecuador: ensayo de historia crítica* (Quito, 1932).

5. Rivalry, Diplomacy, War, and Reconstruction in the Nineteenth Century

1. J. Gonzalo Orellana, ed., *El Ecuador en cien años de independencia, 1830–1930*, 2 vols. (Quito, 1930), II, 70. The basic work on Ecuadoran relations with Peru and Colombia, dealing especially with border disputes since 1810 in a manner favorable to Ecuador's claims, is Jorge Pérez Concha, *Ensayo histórico-crítico de las relaciones diplomáticas del Ecuador con los estados limitrofes*, 2 vols. (Quito, 1958). Subsequent editions of the work appeared in 1964 and 1968.

2. Alberto Mendoza López, *La soberanía de Bolivia estrangulada* (La Paz, 1942), p. 69. A highly useful listing of the more important literature on Bolivian boundary disputes since independence is found in Valentín Abecía Baldivieso, *Historiografía boliviana* (La Paz, 1965), pp. 341–355. See also Miguel Mercado Moreira, *Historia internacional de Bolivia*, 2d ed. (La Paz, 1930), covering background details and providing descriptions of major frontier treaties.

3. For an excellent study of South American balance-of-power politics, focusing on Chile, see Robert N. Burr, *By Reason or Force: Chile and the Balancing of Power in South America, 1830–1905* (Berkeley, Los Angeles, 1965).

Also important is Mario Travossos, *Projecão continental do Brasil: aspectos geograficos sul-americanos*, 3d ed. (São Paulo, 1938).

4. For general coverage see Gordon Ireland, *Boundaries, Possessions and Conflicts in South America* (Cambridge, Mass., 1938) and L. D. M. Nelson, "The Arbitration of International Disputes in Latin America," Ph.D. diss., University of London, 1970.

5. Useful diplomatic histories of Peru include Arturo García Salazar, *Historia diplomática del Perú* (Lima, 1928) and Pedro Ugarteche, *El Perú en la vida internacional americana* (Lima, 1927).

6. See Gustavo Navarro, "Ensayo sobre la conferencia Peru-Boliviana: El Crucismo," JIAS, 10 (1968), 53–73.

7. See Mercado Moreira, *Historia internacional de Bolivia*, pp. 335–347.

8. See Juan Maiguashca, "Breves apuntes sobre la situación de la historia económica en el Ecuador," in Comisión de Historia Económica del Consejo Latinoamericano de Ciencias Sociales, *La historia económica en América Latina*, 2 vols. (Mexico, 1972), I, 160.

9. Indispensable on the topic is *Confederación Peru-Boliviana, 1835–1839*, 2 vols. (Lima, 1972, 1974), published in the series *Archivo Diplomático Peruano*. See also Dante Herrera Alarcón, *Rebeliones que intentaron desmembrar el sur del Perú* (Lima, 1961), and F. B. Pike, *The Modern History of Peru* (London, 1967), pp. 79–83, with citations of some of the major Peruvian literature on the subject.

10. J. Valerie Fifer, *Bolivia: Land, Location, and Politics since 1825* (Cambridge, Eng., 1972), p. 46.

11. Óscar Efrén Reyes, *Breve historia general del Ecuador*, 6th ed. (Quito, 1960), pp. 817–825.

12. See John W. Kitchens, "General Mosquera's Mission to Chile and Peru: A Turning Point in New Granadan Diplomacy," TA, 29 (1972), 151–172, and also his "Colombian-Chilean Relations, 1817–1845: A Diplomatic Struggle for Pacific Coast Hegemony," Ph.D. diss., Vanderbilt University, 1969.

13. See Ralph W. Haskins, "Juan José Flores and the Proposed Expedition Against Ecuador, 1846–1847," HAHR, 27 (1947), 467–495.

14. See Óscar Barrenechea y Rayada, *Congresos y conferencias celebradas en Lima, 1847–1894* (Buenos Aires, 1947). Andean fear of U.S. expansion at the time of the William Walker incursions into Central America also prompted the Continental Treaties of 1856 signed in Santiago de Chile. See Gustave A. Nuremberger, "The Continental Treaties of 1856: An American Union 'Exclusive of the United States,'" HAHR, 20 (1940), 32–55.

15. See Julio Tobar Donoso, *Monografías históricos* (Quito, 1937), p. 182.

16. See Roberto Andrade, *Montalvo y García Moreno* (Lima, 1890), pp. 124–128, 173. The Andrade work, which must be used with extreme caution, seems reliable in this instance. On the widespread fear of Colombian "radicalism" at this time see Robert L. Gilmore, "Nueva Granada's Socialist Mirage," HAHR, 36 (1956), 190–210.

17. See Robert W. Frazer, "The Role of the Lima Congress, 1864–1865, in the Development of Pan Americanism," HAHR, 29 (1949), 319–348.

18. March 1, 1866 letter of Seward to U.S. minister in Madrid John P. Hale, quoted in James W. Cortada, "Conflict Diplomacy: United States–Spanish Relations, 1855–1868," Ph.D. diss., Florida State University, 1973, p. 409.

19. The best account of the subject is found in chap. 10 of Cortada's "Conflict Diplomacy." See also William C. Davis, *The Last Conquistadores: The Spanish Intervention in Peru and Chile 1863–1866* (Athens, Ga., 1950), Louis C. Nolan, "The Diplomatic and Commercial Relations of the United States and Peru, 1826–1875," Ph.D. diss., Duke University, 1951, and Mark Van Aken, *Pan-Hispanism: Its Origin and Development to 1866* (Berkeley, Los Angeles, 1959), pp. 111–114.

20. Enrique Finot, *Nueva historia de Bolivia: ensayo de interpretación sociológico* (Buenos Aires, 1946), pp. 274–275.

21. See ibid., p. 339, Jaime Mendoza, *El factor geográfico en la nacionalidad boliviana* (Sucre, 1925), p. 30, and also his *La tesis andinista, Bolivia y Paraguay* (Sucre, 1933), pp. 67–68, and Mariano Reyes Cardona, *Cuestión de límites en re Bolivia y el Brasil: defensa de Bolivia* (Sucre, 1868).

22. See William S. Coker, "The War of the Ten Centavos: The Geographic, Economic, and Political Causes of the War of the Pacific," *Southern Quarterly*, 7 (1969), 113–129.

23. Bolivian statesman Alberto Gutiérrez, *La guerra de 1879: nuevos esclarecimientos* (Paris, 1920) is altogether convincing in arguing that with or without the incident of the raising of the export tax by Daza war was bound to come, sooner or later. Gutiérrez's book was inspired by the desire to refute the standard Chilean account of the origins and conduct of the war: Gonzalo Bulnes, *Guerra del Pacífico*, 3 vols. (Santiago de Chile, 1911–1919).

24. February 19, 1879 dispatch of U.S. minister in Lima Richard Gibbs to Secretary of State Evarts, in *Message from the President of the United States, ...Relating to the War in South America* (Washington, 1882), p. 195. In his various communications, Gibbs was consistently penetrating in analysis.

25. On the Chilean plan which was presented to but rejected by Daza see Gabriel René Moreno, *Daza y las bases chilenos de 1879*, 2d ed. (La Paz, 1938).

René Moreno, Bolivia's leading nineteenth-century man of letters, spent most of his life in Chile. Accused of being a traitor for his alleged complicity in the Chilean plot, he defends himself in this work.

26. For the Peruvian version of the origins of the war see Pedro Irigoyen, *La alianza Peru-Boliviana-Argentina y la declaratoria de la guerra de Chile* (Lima, 1921). Sources on the war favorable to the Peruvian side include Andrés A. Cáceres, *La guerra entre el Perú y Chile, 1879–1883* (Buenos Aires, 1924), Carlos Dellepiane, *Historia militar del Perú*, 2 vols. (Lima, 1943), Clements Markham, *The War Between Peru and Chile, 1879–1882* (London, New York, 1883), Luis Felipe Paz Soldán, *Páginas históricas de la Cuerra del Pacífico* (Lima, 1942), and Mariano Felipe Paz Soldán, *Naración histórica de la guerra de Chile contra el Perú y Bolivia* (Buenos Aires, 1884).

27. See Adolfo Costa du Rels, *Félix Avelino Aramayo y su época, 1846–1929* (Buenos Aires, 1942), p. 112. Some years later when Daza received permission to return to Bolivia to defend himself against charges of treason he was assassinated almost immediately upon setting foot in his native country. The circumstances of the assassination have never been clarified.

28. See Richard Snyder Phillips, Jr., "Bolivia in the War of the Pacific, 1879–1880," Ph.D. diss., University of Virginia, 1973.

29. See February 18 and May 9 letters of Cabrera in *Message from the President*, pp. 64–66, 70–71.

30. March 24, 1880 letter of Christiancy to Evarts, and letters of March 21, 1881 and May 4, 1881 to Blaine, ibid., pp. 347–349, 468–469, 485–490.

31. See William Appleman Williams, *The Roots of the Modern American Empire: A Study of the Growth and Shaping of Social Consciousness in a Marketplace Society* (New York, 1969), p. 149.

32. See September 5, 1881 letter of Blaine to L. P. Morton, U.S. minister in Paris, in *Message from the President*, pp. 597–598. For an excellent brief summary of U.S. diplomacy during the War of the Pacific see Milton Plesur, *America's Outward Thrust: Approaches to Foreign Affairs 1865–1890* (DeKalb, 1971), pp. 157–164. For more detailed treatment see Kenneth Crosby, "The Diplomacy of the United States in Relation to the War of the Pacific, 1879–1884," Ph.D. diss., George Washington University, 1949, Stephen J. Hurlbut, *Meddling and Muddling: Mr. Blaine's Foreign Policy* (New York, 1884), and Herbert Millington, *American Diplomacy and the War of the Pacific* (New York, 1948). The involvement of other countries, especially Great Britain, is ably discussed by V. G. Kiernan, "Foreign Interests in the War of the Pacific," HAHR, 35 (1955), 14–36.

33. See R. H. Bastert, "Diplomatic Reversal: Frelinghuysen's Opposition to Blaine's Pan American Policy in 1882," *Mississippi Valley Historical Review*, 42 (1956), 653–671.

34. On the strains and tensions that the troublesome Tacna-Arica issue produced in inter-Andean American relations see William J. Dennis, Tacna and Arica (New Haven, 1931) and Alberto Wagner de Reyna, Historia diplomática del Perú, 1900–1945, 2 vols. (Lima, 1964).

35. On Blaine's view see Message from the President, pp. 177–178.

36. On Chile's keen and abiding resentment over Blaine's War of the Pacific diplomacy see F. B. Pike, Chile and the United States, 1880–1962 (Notre Dame, 1963), pp. 45–58.

37. For interesting material on the partial recovery of silver mining in the 1830–1870 period see Félix Avelino Aramayo, Apuntes sobre el estado industrial, económico y político de Bolivia (Sucre, 1871).

38. In a heavy-handed Marxian analysis, Isaac Sandoval Rodríguez, Nacionalismo en Bolivia: ensayo histórico-político (La Paz, 1970), pp. 57–61, charges the founders of the Conservative party with being entreguistas (deliverers of the national interests) to British capital, and with bearing heavy responsibility for Bolivia's defeat. The alleged pro-Chilean sentiments of Arce, attributed to his dependence on Chilean and also British investment capital, are described by Guillermo Lora, Historia del movimiento obrero boliviano, 3 vols. (La Paz, 1967–1970), I, 205–217, 231–233. Ignacio Prudencio Bustillo, in the excellent biography La vida y obra de Aniceto Arce, 2d ed. (La Paz, 1951), pp. 48–49, describes the manner in which Arce formed his early ties with Chilean capitalists.

39. Prudencio Bustillo, Páginas dispersas (Sucre, 1946), p. 94.

40. See Faustino Suárez Arnez, Historia de la educación en Bolivia (La Paz, 1963), p. 184.

41. See Herbert S. Klein, Parties and Political Change in Bolivia, 1880–1952 (Cambridge, Eng., 1969), p. 18.

42. Lora, Historia del movimiento obrero, I, 108–109.

43. Eliodoro Camacho quoted in Guillermo Francovich, El pensamiento boliviano en el siglo XX (Mexico, 1956), p. 12.

44. See Baptista, Obras completas, 7 vols. (La Paz, 1932–1935), esp. III, 7–11, 12–15, 21–22, 33–39, 45–46, 74–85, 101, 107, 265–267, 396–403. On the ideas of Miguel de los Santos Taborga, the leading clerical polemicist of the era, see his El positivismo, sus errores y falsas doctrinas (Sucre, 1905).

45. José Fellman Velarde, Historia de Bolivia, 3 vols. (La Paz, Cochabamba, 1968–1970), II, 357.

46. Quoted in Lora, Historia del movimiento obrero, I, 238.

47. See Francovich, *El pensamiento*, p. 18, and Manfredo Kempee Mercado, "La filosofía en Bolivia," *Kollasuyo*, no. 59 (1945), 338–343. Oyola Cuellar's best-known work is the rambling, prolix *La razón universal* (Barcelona, 1889), which levels a severe attack against the influence of positivist materialism that was widespread at the time.

48. See Fellman Velarde, *Historia de Bolivia*, II, 326, Lora, *Historia del movimiento obrero*, I, 235, and Víctor Paz Estenssoro, "Bolivia," in Luis Roque Gondra and others, *El pensamiento económico latinoamericano* (Mexico, 1945), p. 49. For a contemporary statesman's plea that government encourage establishment of manufacturing industries as a remedy to Bolivia's chronic trade deficit see Isaac Tamayo, *Memoria que presenta al Congreso Ordinario de 1889 el Ministro de Hacienda e Industria* (La Paz, 1889).

49. On the role of British capital both in the war of the Pacific and the reconstruction era see the review of Soviet literature on the matter by T. Stephen Cheston, *AHR*, 78 (1973), esp. 1149, and J. Fred Rippy, *British Investments in Latin America, 1822–1949* (Minneapolis, 1959).

50. Jonathan V. Levin, *The Export Economies* (Cambridge, Mass., 1960), p. 111. The corporation was nationalized in 1971.

51. See Thomas M. Davies, Jr., *Indian Integration in Peru: A Half Century of Experience, 1900–1948* (Lincoln, 1974), p. 35.

52. See Jesús Chavarría, "La desaparición del Perú colonial (1870–1919)," *Aportes*, no. 23 (1972), 131–132.

53. On González Prada see Eugenio Chang-Rodríguez, *La literatura política de González Prada, Mariátegui y Haya de la Torre* (Mexico, 1957), W. Rex Crawford, *A Century of Latin-American Thought*, rev. ed. (New York, 1961), pp. 173–182, Harold E. Davis, *Latin American Thought: A Historical Introduction* (Baton Rouge, 1972), Hugo García Salvatecci, *El pensamiento de González Prada* (Lima, 1972), and Miguel Jorrín and John D. Martz, *Latin American Political Thought and Ideology* (Chapel Hill, 1970), pp. 188–191. The author of the present work now regards his treatment of González Prada in *The Modern History of Peru*, pp. 175–180, as far too harsh.

54. On the failures of *Progresismo*, see Gustavo Alfredo Jácome, *Luis Felipe Borja* (Quito, 1947), pp. 172–178, and Jacinto Jijón y Caamaño, *Política conservadora*, 2 vols. (Riobamba, Quito, 1929, 1934), II, 363–364. An important incident that served to harden lines between Liberals and Conservatives, thereby dooming the prospects of *Progresismo*, was the excommunication of Felicísimo López in 1890. Elected in 1894 to the senate as the representative of Esmeraldas, López was denied his seat because of the strength of the clerical-Conservative outcry against him. See López, *Historia de una excomunión en el Ecuador* (New York, 1909).

413

55. On Ecuadoran progress during the rule of Flores see Luis Felipe Carbo, *El Ecuador en Chicago* (Quito, 1891), providing a good account of economic conditions on the eve of the Chicago World's Fair. For background see a work by Flores Jijón himself, *Conversión de la deuda inglesa* (Quito, 1888), considered by many to be the most impartial study of Ecuador's nineteenth-century fiscal history.

56. See Pío Jaramillo Alvarado, *La doctrina liberal: hombres e ideas en el Ecuador* (Quito, 1923), p. 47.

57. See Leopoldo Benites Vinueza, *Ecuador: drama y paradoja* (Mexico, 1950), p. 235.

6. The Apogee of Liberalism and the Rise of U.S. Influence, 1900–1920

1. See Barrington Moore, *Social Origins of Dictatorship and Democracy: Lord and Peasant in the Making of the Modern World* (Boston, 1966), pp. 111–155.

2. Sánchez Bustamante prologue to Carlos Romero, *Las taras de nuestra democracia* (La Paz, 1920), p. iv.

3. Quoted in Darío C. Guevara, *Juan Benigno Vela, titán del Liberalismo Radical ecuatoriano* (Ambato, 1949), p. 243.

4. Villarán, *Páginas escogidas* (Lima, 1962), pp. 337–338. This judiciously selected anthology of the works of Villarán includes a valuable prologue by Jorge Basadre.

5. See Villarán, "La educación nacional y la influencia extranjera," in *Estudios sobre la educación nacional* (Lima, 1922), pp. 58ff, and *Las profesiones liberales en el Perú, con especial referencia a abogados* (Lima, 1900), pp. 27–28.

6. See Paredes, *Política parlamentaria de Bolivia: ensayo de psicología colectiva*, 2d ed. (La Paz, 1908), p. 10, Romero, *Las taras*, pp. 233, 239–242, 244, and Peralta, "El problema obrero," in *Biblioteca Ecuatoriana Mínima: escritores políticos* (Quito, 1960), esp. pp. 688–694.

7. See Jaramillo, *El indio ecuatoriano*, 4th ed. (Quito, 1954), pp. 122, 149–150. On the Capelo and Villarán views see Thomas M. Davies, Jr., *Indian Integration in Peru: A Half Century of Experience, 1900–1948* (Lincoln, 1974), pp. 50–52, and Leopoldo Zea, *The Latin-American Mind*, trans. James H. Abbott and Lowell Dunham (Norham, 1963), pp. 194–195.

8. See Wilcomb E. Washburn, *The Indian in America* (New York, 1975), esp. pp. 233–249.

9. See Salamanca, *En defensa de Bolivia* (La Paz, 1914), esp. pp. 40–41.

10. Fernando Diez de Medina, *Franz Tamayo: hechicero del Ande, retrato al modo fantástico*, 2d ed. (La Paz, 1944), pp. 31–32.

11. *Creación de la pedagogía nacional: editoriales de "El Diario,"* 2d ed. (La Paz, 1944), pp. 69, 196–198.

12. *Ibid.*, pp. 50–53.

13. *Ibid.*, p. 151.

14. *Ibid.*, p. 172.

15. *Ibid.*, pp. 208–209. See also the analysis by Guillermo Francovich, *El pensamiento boliviano en el siglo XX* (Mexico, 1956), pp. 51–58.

16. See the splendid study by Ramiro Condarco Morales, *Zárate, el "Temible" Willka* (La Paz, 1965), p. 395.

17. See Rodolfo Salamanca Lafuente, "El Indio en la Revolución Federal," *Kollasuyo*, no. 63 (1946), 195–204.

18. Alcides Arguedas, *Pueblo enfermo*, 3d ed. (Santiago de Chile, 1937), p. 40.

19. See Edmundo Flores, "Taraco: monografía de un latifundio del altiplano boliviano," *El Trimestre Económico* (Mexico), 22 (1955), 209–230, and Jorge Ovando Sanz, *Sobre el problema nacional y colonial de Bolivia* (Cochabamba, 1961), pp. 197–198.

20. On the many positive accomplishments of the Piérola administration see Jorge Dulanto Pinillos, *Nicolás de Piérola* (Lima, 1947), Enrique Chirinos Soto, *Nicolás de Piérola* (Lima, 1962), and Alberto Ulloa Sotomayor, *Don Nicolás de Piérola* (Lima, 1949).

21. See Davies, *Indian Integration*, p. 36, and José Frisancho, *Del jesuitismo al indianismo* (Cuzco, 1921), pp. 35–38. See also the essay by Henri Favre in François Bourricaud and others, *La oligarquía en el Perú*, 2d ed. (Lima, 1971), pp. 92–95, and Mario C. Vázquez, "Immigration and Mestizaje in Nineteenth-Century Peru," in Magnus Mörner, ed., *Race and Class in Latin America* (New York, 1970), p. 76.

22. See Magnus Mörner, "The Spanish American Hacienda: A Survey of Recent Research and Debate," *HAHR*, 53 (1973), 211.

23. Jesús Chavarría, "La desaparición del Perú colonial (1870–1919)," *Aportes*, no. 23 (1972), 142. See too François Chevalier, "Témoignages littéraires et disparatés de croissance: L'expansion de la grande propriété dans le Haut-Perou au XXᵉ siècle," *Annales: Economies, Sociétes, Civilisations*, 21 (1966), 815–831,

and Henri Favre, Claude Collin-Delavaud, and José Matos Mar, *La hacienda en el Perú* (Lima, 1967).

24. On Alfaro's efforts in behalf of the Indians see Abelardo Moncayo, *El concertaje de indios* (Quito, 1896), useful despite the author's adulation of the "old battler."

25. Jacinto Jijón y Caamaño, *Política conservadora*, 2 vols. (Riobamba, Quito, 1929, 1934), II, 546.

26. Gonzalo Rubio Orbe, *Aspectos indígenas* (Quito, 1965), p. 185.

27. See Piedad Peñaherrera de Costales and Alfredo Costales, *Historia social del Ecuador*, 4 vols. (Quito, 1964–1971), IV, 8.

28. Davies, *Indian Integration*, pp. 63–64.

29. Ibid., p. 64.

30. Antenor Orrego, *Pueblo-continente*, 2d ed. (Buenos Aires, 1957), p. 118.

31. Vatican protests against Bolivia's anticlerical laws led the Montes administration to sever diplomatic relations in 1907. Excitement over the issue soon subsided and relations were reestablished. On the anticlerical program see Mariano Baptista, *Obras completas*, 7 vols. (La Paz, 1932–1935), III, 207–211, and Felipe López Menéndez, *Compendio de historia eclesiástica de Bolivia* (La Paz, 1965), pp. 207–211, both written from a proclerical viewpoint.

32. See J. M. Le Gouhir, *Historia de la República del Ecuador*, 3 vols. (Quito, 1920–1938), III, 509–510, and Luis Robalino Dávila, *Los orígenes del Ecuador de hoy*, 8 vols. (Quito and Puebla, Mexico, 1949–1969), VII, 23.

33. See Juan Ignacio Larrea Holguín, *La Iglesia y el estado en el Ecuador* (Sevilla, 1954), p. 39.

34. See Gustavo Alfredo Jácome, *Luis Felipe Borja* (Quito, 1947), p. 238.

35. See Pío Jaramillo, *El indio*, p. 261, and Larrea, *La Iglesia*, pp. 39–40.

36. Julio Tobar Donoso, *Las relaciones entre la Iglesia y el estado ecuatoriano* (Quito, 1938), p. 32.

37. See Óscar Efrén Reyes, *Breve historia general del Ecuador*, 6th ed. (Quito, 1960), pp. 693–698. For a defense of Alfaro's policies see José Peralta, *El régimen liberal y el régimen conservador juzgados por sus obras* (Quito, 1911).

38. Jácome, *Borja*, pp. 183–184, 190–195, 245–248. Important to an understanding of this period is Carlos de la Torre Reyes, *La espada sin mancha: biografía del General Julio Andrade* (Quito, 1962). Perhaps the best biography

produced by Ecuadoran scholarship, this work deals with the life of a moderate and independent general and member of the Liberal party.

39. Ecuadoran historians remain deeply divided in their appraisals of Alfaro. Works which suffer from the hero worship approach include Roberto Andrade, *Vida y muerte de Eloy Alfaro: memorias* (New York, 1916), Ángel T. Barrera, *Alfaro, el Garibaldi americano* (Guayaquil, 1916), and Alfonso Mora Bowen, *El Liberalismo Radical en su trayectoria histórica* (Quito, 1940). The most scholarly study of the anti-Alfaro school is Wilfrido Loor, *Eloy Alfaro*, 3 vols. (Quito, 1947).

40. See Pío Jaramillo Alvarado, *La Asamblea Liberal y sus aspectos políticos* (Quito, 1924), pp. 200–210, and *La doctrina liberal (hombres e ideas en el Ecuador)* (Quito, 1923), p. 62, and José María Velasco Ibarra, *Conciencia o barbarie: exégesis de la política americana* (Buenos Aires, 1938), p. 196. Some idea of the González Suárez policies may be obtained from Manuel María Polit Laso, ed., *Obras pastorales del Ilmo: Sr. D. Federico González Suárez*, 2 vols. (Quito, 1927, 1928).

41. See Albert B. Franklin, *Ecuador* (New York, 1943), p. 287.

42. Chavarría, "La desaparición," pp. 138–140, provides an excellent summary of Peru's economic development in the early twentieth century.

43. On the Italian colony see Jane Evelyn Morrall, "Italian Immigration to Peru: 1680–1914," Ph.D. diss., Indiana University, 1972. Rodrigo Zárate, *España y América: proyecciones y problemas derivados de la guerra* (Madrid, 1917), provides an indication of some of the activities of the Spanish colony in Peru.

44. Carl F. Herbold, Jr., "Peru," in Richard M. Morse, ed., *The Urban Development of Latin America, 1750–1920* (Stanford, 1971), p. 108.

45. For good coverage of this period see Emilio Romero, *Historia económica del Perú* (Buenos Aires, 1949), the standard work by Peru's leading economic historian, and Ernesto Yepes del Castillo, *Perú 1820–1920: un siglo de desarrollo capitalista* (Lima, 1972).

46. See Walter Gomez-D'Angelo, "Mining in the Economic Development of Bolivia, 1900–1970," Ph.D. diss., Vanderbilt University, 1973.

47. For a defense of the Montes diplomacy, written by the man who negotiated the treaty with Chile, see Alberto Gutiérrez, *El tratado de paz con Chile: breve comentario en respuesta al manifesto de la minoría parlamentaria residente en Sucre* (La Paz, 1904).

48. See J. Valerie Fifer, *Bolivia: Land, Location and Politics since 1825* (Cambridge, Eng., 1972), p. 70, Margaret Alexander Marsh, *The Bankers in Bolivia: A Study in American Foreign Investment* (New York, 1928), pp. 67–72, and

Alberto Ostria Gutiérrez, *Una obra y un destino: la política internacional de Bolivia después de la guerra del Chaco* (Buenos Aires, 1946), p. 40.

49. William L. Lofstrom, "Attitudes of an Industrial Pressure Group in Latin America: The *Asociación de Industriales Mineros de Bolivia, 1925–1935,*" M.A. thesis, Cornell University, 1968, p. 4.

50. Enrique Finot, *Nueva historia de Bolivia: ensayo de interpretación sociológico* (Buenos Aires, 1946), p. 339. On general economic conditions of the period see Moisés Ascarrunz, *El Partido Liberal en el poder,* 2 vols. (La Paz, 1917), Eduardo López Rivas, *Esquema de la historia económica de Bolivia* (Oruro, 1955), William L. Schurz, *Bolivia: A Commercial and Industrial Handbook* (Washington, 1921), and Paul Walle, *Bolivia, Its People and Its Resources, Its Railways, Mines and Rubber Forests,* trans. B. Miall (New York, 1914).

51. Marsh, *The Bankers,* p. 42.

52. Lofstrom, "Attitudes," p. 17.

53. Luis Peñalosa, *Historia económica de Bolivia,* 2 vols. (La Paz, 1947), II, 166, 171.

54. José Fellman Velarde, *Historia de Bolivia,* 3 vols. (La Paz, Cochabamba, 1968–1970), III, 38.

55. Quoted in Porfirio Díaz Machicao, *Saavedra, 1920–1925* (La Paz, 1954), p. 35.

56. The best brief account of the rise of the Patiño enterprises is Herbert S. Klein, "The Creation of the Patiño Tin Empire," I-AEA, 19 (1965), 3–23. Manuel Carrasco, *Simón I. Patiño, un procer industrial* (Paris, 1960) is uncritically favorable.

57. Peñalosa, *Historia económica,* II, 165, 171.

58. Klein, *Parties and Political Change in Bolivia, 1880–1952* (Cambridge, Eng., 1969), pp. 33–34.

59. Augusto Guzmán, *Historia de Bolivia* (La Paz, 1973), pp. 264–268.

60. Lofstrom, "Attitudes," p. 12.

61. Remigio Crespo Toral quoted in Robalino, *Los orígenes,* VII, 821. General information on economic conditions of the period is found in Reginald C. Enock, *Ecuador: Its Ancient and Modern History, Topography and Natural Resources, Industries and Social Development* (London, 1914), and Charles M. Pepper, *Report on Trade Conditions in Ecuador* (Washington, 1908).

62. See Luis Napoleón Dillon, *La crisis económico-financiera del Ecuador* (Quito, 1927), pp. 24, 31–34. Also useful on this matter are Alfredo Espinosa Tamayo, *Psicología y sociología del pueblo ecuatoriano* (Guayaquil, 1918), Víctor Emilio Estrada, *Money and Banking in Ecuador* (Guayaquil, 1925), and E. Riofrío Villagómez, *Manual de ciencia de hacienda y de derecho fiscal ecuatoriano*, 3 vols. (Quito, 1934), an excellent reference work on the functioning of the public treasury, 1830–1930.

63. Ernesto Niño, *El Ecuador ante las revoluciones proletarias* (Ambato, 1935), p. 151.

64. See Dillon, *La crisis*, pp. 46–49, Niño, *El Ecuador*, pp. 150–151, and Reyes, *Breve historia*, pp. 719–723.

65. This is a central theme developed by Casto Rojas in his *Cuestiones económicas y financieras* (La Paz, 1909).

66. See Liisa North, *Civil-Military Relations in Argentina, Chile, and Peru* (Berkeley, 1966), p. 24, and François Bourricaud, in Bourricaud and others, *La oligarquía en el Perú*, p. 36.

67. Bourricaud and others, *La oligarquía*, p. 62.

68. On the mestizo versus white aspects of the Liberal revolutions in Ecuador and Bolivia, respectively, see Alfredo Pareja Diez Canseco, *Historia del Ecuador*, 2 vols. (Quito, 1958), II, 23, and Gustavo Adolfo Navarro, *Ensayos y críticas: revoluciones bolivianas, guerras internacionales, y escritores* (La Paz, 1961), p. 28.

69. See Leopoldo Benites Vinueza, *Ecuador: drama y paradoja* (Mexico, 1950), p. 264.

70. Fellman Velarde, *Historia de Bolivia*, III, 120.

71. Mira Wilkins, *The Emergence of Multinational Enterprise: American Business Abroad from the Colonial Era to 1914* (Cambridge, Mass., 1971), pp. 201–202.

72. Ibid., p. 195. According to the same source, p. 110, the comparative figures for Mexico are $200 million in 1897 and $587 million in 1914; for Canada and Newfoundland, $160 million and $618 million; for Europe $131 million and $573 million.

73. Ibid., p. 191.

74. See David Spitz, *Patterns of Anti-Democratic Thought: An Analysis and a Criticism with Special Reference to the American Political Mind in Recent Times*, 2d ed. (New York, 1965), p. 157.

75. Arendt, *On Revolution* (New York, 1965), p. 133.

76. See Robert H. Wiebe, *The Search for Order, 1877–1920* (New York, 1967), esp. pp. 30–41, 77.

77. See Diez de Medina, *Franz Tamayo*, pp. 70–71.

78. Gutiérrez, *Notas y impresiones de los Estados Unidos* (Santiago de Chile, 1904), pp. 51, 53.

79. Paul C. Nagel, *This Sacred Trust: American Nationality 1798–1898* (New York, 1971), pp. 13, 26, 251.

80. Wiebe, *Search for Order*, p. 109.

81. Christopher Lasch, "The Anti-Imperialists, the Philippines, and the Inequality of Man," *Journal of Southern History*, 24 (August 1958), p. 319. See too Rubin F. Weston, *Racism in U.S. Imperialism: The Influence of Racial Assumptions on American Foreign Policy, 1893–1946* (Columbia, 1972), pp. 7 et passim.

82. Wilkins, *Multinational Enterprise*, p. 176. See also Eugene W. Burgess and Frederick H. Harbison, *Casa Grace in Peru* (Washington, 1954), viewing the firm in a highly favorable light.

83. See James Carey, *Peru and the United States, 1900–1962* (Notre Dame, 1964), pp. 21–23, Darío Sainte Marie, ed., *Perú en cifras* (Lima, 1945), pp. 217–220, and Wilkins, *Multinational Enterprise*, pp. 183–184.

84. Luis Alberto Sánchez, *Un sudamericano en norteamérica: Ellos y nosotros*, 2d ed. (Lima, 1968), p. 14.

85. F. Halsey, *Investments in Latin America and the British West Indies* (Washington, 1918), p. 322.

86. J. Fred Rippy, "British Investments in Paraguay, Bolivia and Peru," I-AEA, 5 (1953), pp. 43ff.

87. William S. Bollinger, "The Rise of the United States in the Peruvian Economy, 1869–1921," M.A. thesis, University of California, Los Angeles, 1971, p. 14. See also Dale William Peterson, "The Diplomatic and Commercial Relations between the United States and Peru from 1883 to 1918," Ph.D. diss., University of Minnesota, 1969.

88. Wilkins, *Multinational Enterprise*, p. 173.

89. On the rubber boom as it affected Bolivia and helped give rise to the dispute with Brazil over Acre see J. Valerie Fifer, "The Empire Builders: A History of the Bolivian Rubber Boom and the Rise of the House of Suárez," *Journal of Latin American Studies*, 2 (1970), 113–146.

90. On the diplomatic events involving the United States that led up to the treaty see Miguel Mercado Moreira, *Historia internacional de Bolivia*, 2d ed. (La Paz, 1930), pp. 112–146. See also Charles E. Stokes, Jr., "The Acre Revolutions, 1899–1903: A Study in Brazilian Expansionism," Ph.D. diss., Tulane University, 1974.

91. Fifer, *Bolivia*, pp. 129–130.

92. Leslie B. Rout, Jr., *Politics of the Chaco Peace Conference, 1935–1939* (Austin, 1970), p. 24.

93. For a typical attack on the Speyer Contract see José E. Rivera, *Los empréstitos extranjeras y la política americana* (La Paz, 1925).

94. Marsh, *The Bankers*, p. 79.

95. Fifer, *Bolivia*, p. 72.

96. See William Eleroy Curtis, *Between the Andes and the Ocean* (New York, 1907), p. 90.

97. Reyes, *Breve historia*, p. 680.

98. See Jorge Pérez Concha, *Eloy Alfaro, su vida y su obra* (Quito, 1942), pp. 183–186.

99. Alfaro, *Obras escogidas*, 2 vols. (Guayaquil, 1959), II, 182. See also the Jacinto Jijón y Caamaño prologue to the volume he edited, *Federico González Suárez, obras escogidas* (Quito, 1944), pp. xxx–xxxi, for an indication that the Archbishop of Quito believed that contact with Harman posed a threat not only to Ecuador's religion but also to its political independence.

100. Alfaro, *Obras escogidas*, II, 216.

101. Walter V. Scholes and Marie V. Scholes, "The United States and Ecuador, 1909–1913," TA, 19 (1963), 288.

102. July 19, 1902 letter from Harman, then in New York, to Alfaro, in the latter's *Obras escogidas*, II, 219.

103. March 30, 1907 letter of Emilio Estrada to Alfaro, in Robalino, *Los orígenes*, VII, 830.

104. Ibid., VII, 468.

105. For background see David H. Zook, Jr., "The Spanish Arbitration of the Ecuador-Peru Dispute," TA, 20 (1964), 359–375.

106. See Alfaro, *Obras escogidas*, II, 221–223, 367–371.

107. See Scholes and Scholes, "The United States and Ecuador," pp. 285–290.

108. Agustín Cueva, "¿Imperialismo o Panamericanismo? Protestas y amenazas del Secretario de Estado Mr. Lansing Contra la República del Ecuador," in *Biblioteca Ecuatoriana Mínima: juristas y sociólogos* (Quito, 1960), pp. 541–549. The article appeared originally in 1916.

109. Scholes and Scholes, "The United States and Ecuador," p. 290.

110. It is not surprising that Andean leaders became apprehensive about the dangers of U.S. hegemony, for precisely the same type of fear was manifested by some of the leading powers of Europe. See Richard M. Abrams, "United States Intervention Abroad: The First Quarter Century. A Review Article," AHR, 79 (1974), 81, C. Furnes, *The American Invasion* (London, 1902), F. M. McKenzie, *The American Invaders* (London, 1902), and W. T. Stead, *The Americanization of the World* (London, 1902).

111. See, for example, Guillermo Lora, *Historia del movimiento obrero boliviano*, 3 vols. (La Paz, 1967–1970), I, 134.

112. See A. Gutiérrez, *Notas y impresiones de los Estados Unidos*, p. 403.

113. Julio M. Matovelle, *Obras completas*, 2 vols. (Cuenca, 1930, 1934), II, 340.

114. See César Lévano, *La verdadera historia de la jornada de las ocho horas en el Perú* (Lima, 1963). Lévano's father, Delfín Lévano, played a key role in the 1919 strike.

115. Jaime Ponce G., "El sindicalismo boliviano: resumen histórico y perspectivas actuales," *Estudios Andinos*, I (1970), 33–35.

116. Carlos Manuel Tobar y Borgoño, "La protección legal del obrero en el Ecuador," *Biblioteca Ecuatoriana Mínima: juristas y sociólogos*, p. 570. The essay appeared originally in 1913. See too José Buenaventura Navas U., *Evolución social del obrero en Guayaquil, 1849–1920* (Guayaquil, 1920) and Costales and Costales, *Historia social de Ecuador*, IV, esp. 45, for indications of the attention that Ecuadoran intellectuals had begun to pay to the social problem.

117. Chavarría, "La desaparición," pp. 141–142.

118. See Adolfo Ballivián, *Congreso Financiero Panamericano: Bolivia, memorial e informe presentado por . . . delegado del gobierno y representante de las Cámaras de Comercio e Instituciones Bancarias Nacionales* (La Paz, 1915), p. 71, and Augusto Céspedes, *El dictador suicida: 40 años de historia de Bolivia* (Santiago de Chile, 1956), p. 44

119. Quoted in Eduardo Diez de Medina, *De un siglo al otro: memorias de un hombre público* (La Paz, 1955), p. 211.

120. F. Diez de Medina, *Franz Tamayo*, p. 174.

121. This was the message that Tobar y Borgoño had begun to spread in 1913. See his "La protección del obrero," p. 575.

7. Andean Political Establishments and Transition: The 1920s

1. Raúl Porras Barrenechea, *El sentido tradicional en la literatura peruana* (Lima, 1969), p. 51.

2. See Mark Van Aken, *Pan-Hispanism: Its Origin and Development to 1866* (Berkeley, Los Angeles, 1959).

3. See F. B. Pike, "Making the Hispanic World Safe from Democracy: Spanish Liberals and *Hispanismo*," RP, 33 (1971), esp. 308–309, 317.

4. See F. B. Pike, "Capitalism and Consumerism in Spain of the 1890s: A Latin Americanist's View," I-AEA, 26 (1973), esp. 23–24, 32–35.

5. Quoted in Manuel A. Capuñay, *Leguía: vida y obra del constructor del Perú* (Lima, 1952), p. 151.

6. See Carl Fredric Herbold, Jr., "Developments in the Peruvian Adminis trative System, 1919–1930: Modern and Traditional Qualities of Government under Authoritarian Regimes," Ph.D. diss., Yale University, 1973.

7. See F. B. Pike, *Hispanismo, 1898–1936: Spanish Conservatives and Liberals and Their Relations with Spanish America* (Notre Dame, 1971), pp. 176–177.

8. See F. B. Pike, *The Modern History of Peru* (London, 1967), p. 220.

9. See Peter F. Klarén, *Modernization, Dislocation, and Aprismo: Origins of the Peruvian Aprista Party, 1870–1932* (Austin, 1973), p. 48, and James L. Payne, *Labor and Politics in Peru: The System of Political Bargaining* (New Haven, 1965), p. 39.

10. See Stephen Jay Stein, "Populism and Mass Politics in Peru: The Political Behavior of the Lima Working Classes in the 1931 Presidential Election," Ph.D. diss., Stanford University, 1973, pp. 142–143.

11. Magali Sarfatti Larson and Arlene Eisen Bergman, *Social Stratification in Peru* (Berkeley, 1969), p. 9.

12. See Enrique Ravago Velarde, *Legislación del empleado dictada en el gobierno de Don Augusto B. Leguía* (Lima, 1928). A helpful bibliographical guide for this and other periods is Steve Stein and Carl Herbold, *Guía bibliografía para la historia social y política del Perú en el siglo XX, 1895–1960* (Lima, 1971).

13. Especially useful on Leguía's pre-*oncenio* background is René Hooper López, *Leguía* (Lima, 1964).

14. See Gary Richard Garrett, "The Oncenio of Augusto B. Leguía: Middle Sector Government and Leadership in Peru, 1919–1930," Ph.D. diss., University of New Mexico, 1973.

15. See Alcira Leiserson, *Notes on the Process of Industrialization in Argentina, Chile, and Peru* (Berkeley, 1966), pp. 24–25.

16. Thomas E. Davies, Jr., *Indian Integration in Peru: A Half Century of Experience, 1900–1948* (Lincoln, 1974), pp. 68–69. See too Howard L. Karno, "Augusto B. Leguía, the Oligarchy and the Modernization of Peru, 1870–1930," Ph.D. diss., University of California, Los Angeles, 1970, pp. 216, 258.

17. See Aníbal Ismodes Cairo, *Bases de una sociología del Perú*, 2 vols. (Lima, 1967), I, 208–209. The author contends Leguía thought that the new bourgeoisie and the old-guard oligarchy would remain in perpetual combat. Actually, Leguía may have anticipated the ultimate fusing of the two groups that actually occurred.

18. Davies, *Indian Integration*, p. 93, cautions that this fascinating hypothesis requires additional research before its validity can be fully established.

19. François Chevalier, "Official *Indigenismo* in Peru in 1920: Origins, Significance, and Socioeconomic Scope," in Magnus Mörner, ed., *Race and Class in Latin America* (New York, 1970), pp. 195–196.

20. See Porfirio Díaz Machicao, *Historia de Bolivia*, 5 vols. (La Paz, 1954–1958), I, *Saavedra, 1920–1925*, p. 78, a work exhibiting commendable impartiality but based upon research that is less than exhaustive. On the political infighting that split the Republicans at the beginning of the 1920s see Benigno Carrasco, *Hernando Siles* (La Paz, 1961), dealing with Siles before he came to the presidency.

21. See Roberto Prudencio, "Notas políticas y sociales: Bautista Saavedra, un intelectual en la políticia," *Kollasuyo*, no. 3 (1939), p. 60. Like Leguía, with whom many parallels can be suggested, Saavedra remains without an adequate biography.

22. See Saavedra, *Palabras sinceras: para una historia de ayer*, 2d ed. (La Paz, 1929), p. 105.

23. Prologue by Saavedra to M. Rigoberto Paredes, *Política parlamentaria de Bolivia: ensayo de psicología-colectiva*, 2d ed. (La Paz, 1908), pp. iv–v.

24. The nature of Saavedra's reformism is caught in Tomás M. Elío, *El socialismo en Bolivia: polémica y didáctica* (Cochabamba, 1921).

25. On Saavedra's conciliatory policy with the church see Filipe López Menéndez, *Compendio de la historia eclesiástica de Bolivia* (La Paz, 1965), pp. 234–236.

26. Frente de Izquierda Boliviano, *¡Hacia la unidad de las izquierdas bolivianas!* (Santiago de Chile, 1939), p. 6. On this subject see also Gastón Arduz Eguía, *Legislación boliviana del trabajo y de la previsión social* (La Paz, 1941), and Abraham Maldonado, comp., *Legislación social boliviana* (La Paz, 1957).

27. Herbert S. Klein, *Parties and Political Change in Bolivia 1880–1952* (Cambridge, Eng., 1969), p. 60.

28. See José Fellman Velarde, *Historia de Bolivia*, 3 vols. (La Paz, Cochabamba, 1968–1970), III, 110–111.

29. See Lee L. Lofstrom, "Attitudes of an Industrial Pressure Group in Latin America: The *Asociación de Industriales Mineros de Bolivia, 1925–1935*," M.A. thesis, Cornell University, 1968, p. 13.

30. See Margaret A. Marsh, *The Bankers in Bolivia: A Study in American Foreign Investment* (New York, 1928), p. 52, and Luis Peñalosa, *Historia económica de Bolivia*, 2 vols. (La Paz, 1947), II, 174–175.

31. See Víctor Paz Estenssoro, "Bolivia," in Luis Roque Gondra and others, *Pensamiento económico latinoamericano* (Mexico, 1945), pp. 62–63.

32. See Alberto Mendoza López, *La soberanía de Bolivia estrangulada* (La Paz, 1942), pp. 152–154.

33. Gustavo Adolfo Navarro, *Ensayos y crítica: revoluciones bolivianas, guerras internacionales, y escritores* (La Paz, 1961), p. 33. Useful on Siles is Díaz Machicao, *Historia de Bolivia*, II, *Guzmán, Siles, Blanco Galindo, 1925–1931* (La Paz, 1955).

34. On programs of the various political parties in Bolivia from the early 1880s to the mid-1940s see Alberto Cornejo S., *Programas políticos de Bolivia* (Cochabamba, 1949).

35. Siles tried to capitalize on the fact that the university reform movement was gathering momentum in Bolivia in the mid-1920s, after having manifested itself some five or six years earlier in Argentina, Peru, and other South American republics. See Manuel Durán Padilla, *La reforma universitaria en Bolivia* (Oruro, 1961).

36. See Faustino Suárez Arnez, *Historia de la educación en Bolivia* (La Paz, 1963), p. 291.

37. Quoted in J. Gonzalo Orellana, ed., *El Ecuador en cien años de independencia, 1830–1930*, 2 vols. (Quito, 1930), I, 136.

38. Luis Napoleón Dillon, *La crisis económico-financiera del Ecuador* (Quito, 1927), p. 147.

39. In 1927 the international price was one-third of what it had been in 1920. See Guillermo Peñaherrera, *Opúsculos para la historia*, 3 vols. (Quito, 1958), II, 7–9. On this period see also Alberto Azanza, "El presupuesto nacional a través de 115 años," *Boletín del Ministerio del Tesoro* (Quito), 5 (1946), 1–136, and Luis Alberto Carbo, *Historia monetaria y cambiaria del Ecuador desde época colonial* (Quito, 1953).

40. Joseph Grunwald and Philip Musgrove, *Natural Resources in Latin American Development* (Baltimore, 1970), pp. 331–332.

41. See Leopoldo Benites Vinueza, *Ecuador: drama y paradoja* (Mexico, 1950), p. 238, and José de la Cuadra, *El montuvio ecuatoriano: ensayo de presentación* (Buenos Aires, 1937), pp. 26–27.

42. See Alfredo Pareja Diez Canseco, *Historia del Ecuador*, 2 vols. (Quito, 1958), II, 370.

43. Óscar Efrén Reyes, *Breve historia general del Ecuador*, 6th ed. (Quito, 1950), p. 731.

44. Jaramillo, *La Asamblea Liberal y sus aspectos políticos* (Quito, 1924), p. xlvi.

45. See Alfredo Pérez Guerrero, *Ecuador* (Quito, 1948), pp. 116–117.

46. Belaúnde's ideas on the middle class are expressed in his *La crisis presente* (Lima, 1914) and *Meditaciones peruanas* (1917).

47. Tobar y Borgoño, "La protección legal del obrero en el Ecuador," *Biblioteca Ecuatoriana Mínima: juristas y sociólogos* (Quito, 1960), pp. 563–597.

48. Piedad Peñaherrera de Costales and Alfredo Costales, *Historia social del Ecuador*, 4 vols. (Quito, 1964–1971), IV, 9–10.

49. See PLE, *Programa de principios y de acción del Partido Liberal Ecuatoriano* (Quito, 1923).

50. See Jacinto Jijón y Caamaño, *Política conservadora*, 2 vols. (La Paz, Riobamba, 1929, 1934), II, 356, and Julio Tobar Donoso, *La Asamblea del Partido Conservador y su doctrina* (Quito, 1926).

51. Orellana, ed., *Ecuador cien años*, I, 135–137.

52. See Robert N. Seidel, "American Reformers Abroad: The Kemmerer Missions in South America, 1923–1931," *Journal of Economic History*, 32 (1972), 520–545.

53. See Miguel Ángel Zambrano, *Breve historia del Código del Trabajo Ecuatoriano, su génesis, elaboración y expedición* (Quito, 1962).

54. See Agustín Cueva, *Discurso del . . . , Presidente de la Asamblea Nacional del Ecuador, pronunciado en la sesión solemne del 17 de abril de 1929, en la que el Sr. Presidente Constitucional de la República, Dr. Dn. Isidro Ayora prestó la promesa previa al desempeño de su cargo* (Quito, 1929), pp. 19–20.

55. Dillon, *Crisis económica*, p. 308.

56. Joseph S. Tulchin, *The Aftermath of War: World War I and U.S. Policy Toward Latin America* (New York, 1971), p. 36.

57. December 30 statement of Román Paz, in Bolivia: Congreso, Cámara de Senadores, *Debates en el H. Senado Nacional sobre la concesión de un millón de hectáreas petrolíferas al Richmond, Levering Co. y la Standard Oil Co., Legislatura ordinaria de 1921–22* (La Paz, 1922), p. 248.

58. Quoted in Arthur P. Whitaker, *The United States and the Independence of Latin America, 1800–1830*, 2d ed. (New York, 1964), p. 43.

59. See Cleona Lewis, *America's Stake in International Investments* (Washington, 1938), p. 606, whose estimates are $2.29 billion for 1919 and $5.14 billion for 1929. According to *Private Investment in Latin America: Hearings before the Subcommittee on Inter-American Economic Relationships of the Joint Committee, Congress of the United States . . . January 14, 15 and 16, 1964* (Washington, 1964), p. 443, the total value of U.S. investments in 1929 stood at $5.25 billion, of which $1.6 was indirect (portfolio) and $3.63 was direct investment, in rounded figures.

60. Max Winkler, *Investments of United States Capital in Latin America* (New York, 1929), pp. 148–153.

61. Tulchin, *Aftermath of War*, p. 93. On the short-lived policy of State Department supervision over foreign loans see Joan Hoff Wilson, *American Business and Foreign Policy, 1920–1933* (Lexington, Ky., 1971).

62. Tulchin, *Aftermath of War*, p. 61.

63. See Richard M. Abrams, "United States Intervention Abroad: The First Quarter Century. A Review Article," AHR, 79 (1974), 96.

64. *Foreign Relations of the United States, 1925*, II (Washington, 1940), pp. 60–61.

65. See George Blanksten, *Ecuador: Constitutions and Caudillos* (Berkeley, 1951), p. 2, and Winkler, *Investments*, p. 136.

66. *Foreign Relations, 1920,* III (Washington, 1936), p. 364. For good general coverage see I. G. Bertram, "Development Problems in an Export Economy: A Study of Domestic Capitalists, Foreign Firms, and Government in Peru, 1919–1930," D.Phil. diss., Oxford University, 1974.

67. See Roger Marett, *Peru* (London, 1969), pp. 136–139.

68. Ronald J. Owens, *Peru* (London, 1963), p. 170.

69. Lewis, *America's Stake,* p. 382.

70. Pinelo, *The Multinational Corporation as a Force in Latin American Politics: A Case Study of the International Petroleum Company in Peru* (New York, 1973), p. 35. See also James Carey, *Peru and the United States* (Notre Dame, 1964), p. 78, Ilse Mintz, *Deterioration in the Quality of Foreign Bonds Issued in the United States* (New York, 1951), and U.S. Senate, Committee on Finance, *Sale of Foreign Bonds or Securities in the United States* (Washington, 1932).

71. Fellman Velarde, *Historia de Bolivia,* III, 104.

72. Marsh, *The Bankers,* p. 101. Klein, *Parties and Political Change,* pp. 79–80, places the issue in an objective perspective.

73. Fernando Diez de Medina, *Una polémica entre ... y Augusto Céspedes en torno a "40 años de la historia de Bolivia"* (Potosí, 1957), p. 32.

74. See Bolivia: Comisión Informativa de la Misión Kemmerer, *La Misión Kemmerer en Bolivia: proyectos e informes presentados al Supremo Gobierno* (La Paz, 1927), and Edwin Kemmerer, *Informe Kemmerer y proyectos de ley para la reorganización del Banco de la Nación Boliviana, y otros proyectos* (La Paz, 1927).

75. Marsh, *The Bankers,* p. 98. See also Herbert S. Klein, "American Oil Companies in Latin America: The Bolivian Experience," I-AEA, 18 (1964), 47–72, with excellent bibliographical references.

76. Bolivia: Congreso, Cámara de Senadores, *Debates,* pp. 176, 206–209. For accounts favorable to Iturralde written by Bolivian leftists see Moisés Alcázar, *El centinelo de petroleo* (La Paz, 1944), Sergio Almaráz, *Petroleo en Bolivia,* 2d ed. (La Paz, 1969), esp. pp. 86–104, and Amado Canelas O., *Petroleo: imperialismo y nacionalismo* (La Paz, 1963), esp. pp. 20–21.

77. See Carlos Montenegro, *Frente al derecho del estado el oro de la Standard Oil (El petroleo, sangre de Bolivia)* (La Paz, 1938), pp. 25–35.

78. See Pinelo, *The Multinational Corporation,* p. 13.

79. Peñalosa, *Historia económica de Bolivia,* II, 238–239.

80. See J. Valerie Fifer, *Bolivia: Land, Location, and Politics since 1825* (Cambridge, Eng., 1972), p. 246, Lofstrom, "Attitudes of an Industrial Pressure Group," pp. 19–20, and Marsh, *The Bankers*, p. 47.

81. Marsh, *The Bankers*, p. 4. The estimates made by Winkler, *Investments*, p. 80, appear considerably higher, but much of the amount he lists went into refunding.

82. Lewis, *America's Stake*, pp. 237–238, 583–584. For useful background material see W. F. C. Purser, *Metal-Mining in Peru, Past and Present* (New York, 1972).

83. Eugene W. Burgess and Frederick H. Harbison, *Casa Grace in Peru* (Washington, 1954), p. 3.

84. On this see Lewis Hanke, ed., *Do the Americas Have a Common History? A Critique of the Bolton Theory* (New York, 1964), and Arthur P. Whitaker, *The Western Hemisphere Idea: Its Rise and Decline* (Ithaca, 1954).

85. See Pedro Ugarteche, *La política internacional peruana durante la dictadura de Leguía* (Lima, 1930), pp. 20–33. Ugarteche's wrath is directed equally against the United States and Leguía.

86. See José Carrasco, *Bolivia's Case for the League of Nations* (London, 1920), Eduardo Diez de Medina, *El problema continental* (La Paz, 1921), Warren H. Kelchner, *Latin American Relations with the League of Nations* (Washington, 1929), and Miguel Mercado Moreira, *Historia internacional de Bolivia*, 2d ed. (La Paz, 1930), esp. p. 512.

87. On the background to Bolivian hopes that an understanding with the United States and Brazil would lead to restoration of a seaport see Emily S. Rosenberg, "World War I and 'Continental Solidarity,' " TA, 31 (1975), esp. 317–318.

88. Quoted in Alberto Ostria Gutiérrez, *Una obra y un destino: la política internacional de Bolivia después de la guerra del Chaco* (Buenos Aires, 1946), p. 323.

89. Díaz Machicao, *Historia de Bolivia*, I, 125–126.

90. See Ronald Bruce St. John, "Peruvian Foreign Policy, 1919–1939: The Delimitation of Frontiers," Ph.D. diss., University of Denver, 1970, and Joe Foster Wilson, "An Evaluation of the Failure of the Tacna-Arica Plebiscitary Commission," Ph.D. diss., University of Georgia, 1965.

91. See Alberto Gutiérrez, *El problema del Pacífico y la fórmula de solución del Secretario de Estado de los Estados Unidos: Documentos oficiales publicados por el Ministerio de Relaciones Exteriores de Bolivia* (La Paz, 1927).

92. See Orellana, ed., *Ecuador cien años*, I, 165–166.

93. See F. B. Pike, *Chile and the United States, 1880–1962* (Notre Dame, 1963), pp. 228–231. Quite properly the Chilean author Conrado Ríos Gallardo, *Chile y Perú: los pactos de 1929* (Santiago de Chile, 1959), pp. 292, 294–295, gives full credit to the useful, behind-the-scenes efforts of Secretary of State Kellogg to bring about a settlement. On this consult L. Ethan Ellis, *Frank B. Kellogg and American Foreign Relations, 1925–1929* (New Brunswick, 1961).

94. *Foreign Relations, 1928*, I (Washington, 1942), p. 532. Tending to confirm this appraisal are works by two of Leguía's political foes who in writing on the Tacna-Arica matter were equally scathing in their attacks on the dictator and on Washington: Alberto Ulloa Sotomayor, *El fallo arbitral del presidente de los Estados Unidos de América en la cuestión de Tacna y Arica* (Lima, 1925) and Pedro Ugarteche, *El Perú en la vida internacional americana* (Lima, 1927). A more balanced account is found in Arturo García Salazar, *Historia diplomática del Perú* (Lima, 1930).

95. Marett, *Peru*, p. 145.

96. This is a point insistently developed by Hooper López, *Leguía*. See esp. p. 170.

97. See Howard L. Karno, "Julio César Arana, Frontier Cacique in Peru," in Robert Kern and Ronald Dolkart, eds., *The Caciques: Oligarchical Politics and the System of Caciquismo in the Luso-Hispanic World* (Albuquerque, 1973), esp. pp. 95–98, Alberto Ulloa Sotomayor, *Posición internacional del Perú* (Lima, 1941), pp. 168–169, and José Zárate Lescano, *Historia militar del conflicto con Colombia de 1932* (Lima, 1965), p. 5. For background material see Fabio Lozano Torrijos (the Colombian signatory to the treaty), *El tratado Lozano-Salomón* (Mexico, 1934), and Evaristo San Cristóval, *Páginas internacionales: antecedentes diplomáticos del tratado Salomón-Lozano* (Lima, n.d.). Many Peruvians felt Washington was following a pro-Colombian policy in order to make amends for the 1904 intervention in Panama and to pave the way for the granting of oil concessions to U.S. companies. See Pablo E. Coletta, "William Jennings Bryan and the United States-Colombia Impasse, 1903–1921," HAHR, 47 (1967), 486–501, and Arthur P. Whitaker, *The United States and South America: The Northern Republics* (Cambridge, Mass., 1948), pp. 176–185.

98. Bryce Wood, *The United States and Latin American Wars, 1932–1942* (New York, 1966), pp. 170–171.

8. Aspiring Elites and Transition

1. Orrego, *Pueblo-continente*, 2d ed. (Buenos Aires, 1957), p. 67.

2. José Gaos, *Sobre Ortega y Gasset y otros trabajos de historia de las ideas en España y la América Española* (Mexico, 1957), p. 9.

3. Ortega y Gasset, *Man and Crisis*, trans. Mildred Adams (New York, 1962), p. 10.

4. Gaos, *Sobre Ortega*, p. 37.

5. On the Europeans see H. Stuart Hughes, *The Sea Change: The Migration of Social Thought, 1930–1965* (New York, 1975), p. 76. Along these lines, Edward Shils, "The Intellectuals and the Political Development of New States," in J. H. Kautsky, ed., *Political Change in Underdeveloped Countries* (New York, 1962) writes perceptively on the importance of Latin American intellectuals in introducing ferment into otherwise static societies.

6. Gabriel Cevallos García, *Reflexiones sobre la historia del Ecuador*, 2 vols. (Cuenca, 1957, 1960), I, 269. As early as 1912 the Peruvian intellectual and political leader Mariano H. Cornejo expressed the view that came to prevail in the 1920s. It was the destiny of Latin America, he wrote, to evolve not as North America, created only by Europeans, but as a universal America that would join the mysticism of the East with the energy and activity of the West. See his *Discursos* in Enrique Cuentas Ormachea and Manuel Suárez-Miraval, eds., *Ensayistas puñenos* (Lima, 1959), p. 91.

7. Quoted in Guillermo Francovich, *El pensamiento boliviano en el siglo XX* (Mexico, 1956), p. 64.

8. See Philip Rosenberg, *The Seventh Hero: Thomas Carlyle and the Theory of Radical Activism* (Cambridge, Mass., 1974), showing that in Carlyle's thought to be a hero meant to act courageously against social injustices and to be a hero-worshipper meant to become the "seventh hero," to join with a small band in following the leader in a revolution against the prevailing order.

9. Walter Struve, *Elites Against Democracy: Leadership Ideals in Bourgeois Political Thought in Germany, 1890–1933* (Princeton, 1973), pp. 249, 267, 276, 294. Among the writings of Hermann Keyserling popular in Andean America was his *Meditaciones sudamericanas*, trans. Luis López-Ballesteros y de Torres (Madrid, 1933). The English translation, by Theresa Duerr, bears the title, *South American Meditations: On Hell and Heaven in the Soul of Man* (New York, 1932).

10. See Robert Solomon, ed., *Nietzsche* (Garden City, 1973), p. 75.

11. Primo de Rivera, *Obras de . . . edición cronológico*, comp. Agustín del Río Cisneros, 6th ed. (Madrid, 1966), p. 787.

12. On the influence of Vasconcelos and his cosmic race theories, see José Luis Romero, *El pensamiento político de la derecha latinoamericana* (Buenos Aires, 1970), pp. 167–168. In 1925, the very year that his best-known work, *La raza cósmica*, appeared, Valconcelos was awarded the coveted title of Mentor of Peruvian Youth (Maestro de Juventud Peruana). See Luis Alberto Sánchez, *La literatura peruana*, 6 vols., 2d ed. (Asunción, 1950–1951), VI, 290.

13. See Talcott Parsons, *The Structure of Social Action*, 2 vols., 2d ed. (New York, 1968), I, 61, describing the positivist belief system.

14. See Augusto Salazar Bondy, *Historia de las ideas en el Perú contemporáneo*, 2 vols. (Lima, 1965), II, 256.

15. See H. Stuart Hughes, *Consciousness and Society: The Reorientation of European Social Thought, 1890–1930* (New York, 1958), pp. 119–120.

16. See Robert A. Nisbet, *The Sociology of Emile Durkheim* (New York, 1974), esp. pp. 156–165.

17. Delgado, *La formación espiritual del individuo*, 2d ed. (Lima, 1949), pp. 125–126. The work first appeared in 1933.

18. Velasco Ibarra, *Democracia y constitucionalismo* (Quito, 1929), pp. 112, 114. The work is dedicated to José Enrique Rodó, "with respect and love from a modest disciple." Perhaps the foremost Bolivian *pensador* to expound the view that only Catholicism could guarantee the hierarchical social order was Roberto Prudencio. For his final summation of this argument that he had been advancing since the 1920s see *Los vaolores religiosos* (La Paz, 1945).

19. See David Spits, *Patterns of Anti-Democratic Thought: An Analysis and a Critique with Special Reference to the American Political Mind in Recent Times*, 2d ed. (New York, 1965), p. 232.

20. See F. B. Pike, "Church and State in Peru and Chile since 1840," AHR, 73 (1967), 40.

21. See F. B. Pike, *Hispanismo, 1898–1936: Spanish Conservatives and Liberals and Their Relations with Spanish America* (Notre Dame, 1971), pp. 93–96, 370–371.

22. See Jacinto Jijón y Caamaño, *Política conservadora*, 2 vols. (Riobamba, Quito, 1929, 1934), II, 447.

23. Ibid., II, 491, 506–507. See too Julio Tobar Donoso, *Cooperativas y mutualidades* (Quito, 1942), comprised of articles first published in 1926 editions of *La Defensa*.

24. On the reaction in the United States see Aaron Abel, "The Reception of Leo XIII's Labor Encyclical in America, 1891–1919," RP, 7 (1945), 465–495.

25. Quoted in Pike, "Church and State," pp. 43–44. For a good analysis of Riva Agüero's writings see Fred Bonner, "José de la Riva-Agüero, Peruvian Historian," HAHR, 36 (1956), 490–502.

26. Some Marxists-Leninists did, of course, become Communists, often engaging thereafter in violent polemics with socialists who refused to do so. For

valuable general surveys, see Robert J. Alexander, *Communism in Latin America* (New Brunswick, 1957), and *Trotskyism in Latin America* (Stanford, 1973), Stephen A. Clissold, ed., *Soviet Relations with Latin America, 1918–1968: A Documentary Survey* (London, 1970), and Rollie E. Poppino, *International Communism in Latin America: A History of the Movement, 1917–1963* (New York, 1964). An excellent bibliography is Ronald H. Chilcote, *Revolution and Structural Change in Latin America: A Bibliography on Ideology, Development and the Radical Left, 1903–1965*, 2 vols. (Stanford, 1970).

27. José Carlos Mariátegui review of Miguel de Unamuno, *L'agonie du christianisme*, in *Libros y Revistas*, a supplement to the Lima review *Amauta*, no. 3 (September 1926), p. 3.

28. Jorge Crespo Toral, *El comunismo en el Ecuador* (Quito, 1958), p. 11.

29. Miguel Jorrín and John D. Martz, *Latin-American Political Thought and Ideology* (Chapel Hill, 1970), p. 276.

30. See Parsons, *Structure of Social Action*, II, 497.

31. See Erich Fromm, *Escape from Freedom*, 2d ed. (New York, 1965), p. 33, and *Marx's Concept of Man*, with a Translation of Marx's "Economic and Philosophical Manuscripts" by T. B. Bottomore (New York, 1961), p. v.

32. See Lukács, *History and Class Consciousness: Studies in Marxist Dialectics*, trans. Rodney Livingstone, 2d ed. (Cambridge, Mass., 1971). See too Daniel Bell, *The End of Ideology*, rev. ed. (New York, 1960), pp. 364–365.

33. Iberico, *El nuevo absoluto* (Lima, 1926), pp. 222–223.

34. Arze, *Sociografía del inkario: ¿Fue socialista o comunista el imperio inkaiko?* (La Paz, 1952), pp. 21–22.

35. Castro Pozo, *Del ayllu al cooperativismo socialista* (Lima, 1936), p. 211.

36. Samuel P. Huntington, *Political Order in Changing Societies* (New Haven, 1968), p. 336.

37. In *The Political Ideas of Marx and Engels*, vol. I, *Marxism and Totalitarian Democracy, 1818–1850* (Pittsburgh, 1974), Richard N. Hunt argues persuasively that the concept of elitist domination does not inhere in the ideology of Marx and Engels, although some have purported to encounter it there.

38. See Gerald H. Meaker, *The Revolutionary Left in Spain, 1914–1923* (Stanford, 1974), p. 305.

39. On Machajski, whose major works are unavailable in English translation, see Bell, *End of Ideology*, pp. 355–356, V. F. Calverton, ed., *The Making of*

Society (New York, 1937), and Max Nomad, *Apostles of Revolution* (New York, 1939).

40. Seymour Martin Lipset, *Revolution and Counter-revolution: Change and Persistence in Social Structures*, rev. ed. (Garden City, 1970), p. 263.

41. On the manner in which Marxism-Leninism was synthesized into Bolivian and Peruvian nationalism, respectively, see José Ortega, *Aspectos del nacionalismo boliviano* (Madrid, 1973) and Jesús Chavarría, "José Carlos Mariátegui, Revolutionary Nationalist: The Origins and Crisis of Modern Peruvian Nationalism, 1870–1930," Ph.D. diss., University of California, Los Angeles, 1967. On the popularity of Marxism-Leninism among Ecuadoran intellectuals see Oswaldo Hurtado, ed., *Dos mundos superpuestos: ensayo de diagnóstico de la realidad ecuatoriana* (Quito, 1969), esp. p. 226.

42. See Enrique Anderson Imbert, *Spanish American Literature: A History*, trans. John V. Falconieri (Detroit, 1963), p. 220, Salazar Bondy, *Historia de las ideas en el Perú*, I, 10–37, and Martin S. Stabb, *In Quest of Identity: Patterns in the Spanish American Essay of Ideas, 1890–1960* (Chapel Hill, 1967), esp. p. 110. See too chap. 5, n. 53.

43. See his *Anarquía*, 3d ed. (Santiago de Chile, 1940), p. 29.

44. Prada, "Propaganda y ataque," in *Pájinas libres* (Paris, 1894).

45. Prada, *Horas de lucha*, 2d ed. (Callao, 1924), pp. 68–69.

46. Ibid., pp. 28–29.

47. See Luis E. Aguilar, ed., *Marxism in Latin America* (New York, 1968), pp. 18–19. Works dealing with the extensive literature of Indianism (*Indigenismo*) in Andean America include: Mary Consuela Callaghan, "Indianism in Peru, 1883–1939," Ph.D. diss., University of Pennsylvania, 1951, Thomas M. Davies, Jr., *Indian Integration in Peru: A Half Century of Experience, 1900–1948* (Lincoln, 1974), P. J. Gold, "The Literature of the Indigenista Movement in the Andean Republics, 1919–1941," B. Litt. thesis, Oxford University, 1971, Hector Martínez, Miguel Cameo C., and Jesús Ramírez S., *Bibliografía indígena andina peruana, 1900–1968*, 2 vols. (Lima, 1969), Concha Meléndez, *La novela indianista en hispanoamérica* (Madrid, 1934), Rafael A. Reyeros, *Historia social del indio boliviano: "el pongueaje,"* rev. ed. (La Paz, 1963), Gonzalo Rubio Orbe, *Aspectos indígenas* (Quito, 1965), with an excellent bibliography of Ecuadoran Indianist literature, pp. 208–224, Antonio Sacoto, *The Indian in the Ecuadoran Novel* (New York, 1967) and *El indio en el ensayo de la América española* (New York, 1970).

48. On the dislike of Indians among lower-class coastal Peruvians, many of whom are "former Indians," see Baltazar Caravedo, Humberto Rotondo and Javier Mariátegui, *Estudios de psiquiatría social en el Perú* (Lima, 1963).

49. Two important novels in which local and U.S. capitalists are linked in responsibility for the seizure of Indian lands, thus forcing rural migration into urban centers, are Jorge Icaza, *Huasipungo* (Quito, 1935), trans. Bernard M. Dulsey as *Huasipungo: The Villagers* (Carbondale, 1964), and César Vallejo, *Tungsteno* (Lima, 1931).

50. Francovich, *El pensamiento boliviano*, p. 66.

51. *La justicia del Inca*, pp. 22–23.

52. Ibid., p. 11.

53. Ibid., p. 10.

54. Ibid., p. 8.

55. Ibid., p. 25.

56. Ibid., p. 81.

57. The major source of Mariátegui's writings is the *Ediciones Populares de Obras Completas*, launched with the publication in 1959 (Lima) of 10 volumes, several of which were second editions. Subsequent volumes have been added in 1969 and 1970. The *Ediciones Populares* contain valuable biographical studies and content analyses by leading Peruvian authorities on Mariátegui. *Siete ensayos de interpretación de la realidad peruana* (1928), Mariátegui's most famous work, is available in a splendid English translation by Marjory Urquidi, *Seven Interpretive Essays on Peruvian Reality*, with an introduction by Jorge Basadre (Austin, 1971). On Mariátegui and his publications see Guillermo Rouillón, *Bío-Bibliografía de José Carlos Mariátegui* (Lima, 1963). Jesús Chavarría's "José Carlos Mariátegui" is an excellent study, based on painstaking research and rich in its probing analysis. Also useful is John A. Kromkowski, "The Emergence and Ongoing Presence of José Carlos Mariátegui in Peru and in the Soviet Union," Ph.D., diss., University of Notre Dame, 1972.

58. See Estuardo Núñez, "José Carlos Mariátegui y su experiencia italiana," *Cuadernos Americanos*, 137 (1964) and his introduction to *Cartas de Italia*, 3 vols., in Mariátegui, *Ediciones Populares de Obras Completas* (Lima, 1969). See in addition two works by Robert Paris, "La Formation Ideologique de José Carlos Mariátegui," Ph.D. diss., University of Paris École Pratique des Hautes Etudes, 1969, and "El Marxismo de Mariátegui," *Aportes*, no. 17 (1970), 12–15, and also Harry E. Vanden, *Mariátegui: influencias en su formación ideológica* (Lima, 1975).

59. See Lukács' autobiographical preface to the 1967 ed. of his *History and Class Consciousness*, p. xxiii.

60. Fromm, *Marx's Concept of Man*, p. 63.

61. See John M. Baines, *Revolution in Peru: Mariátegui and the Myth* (Tuscaloosa, 1972), pp. 36–37.

62. Quoted in James L. Payne, *Labor and Politics in Peru: The System of Political Bargaining* (New Haven, 1965), p. 40.

63. Mariátegui, prologue to Luis E. Valcárcel, *Tempestad en los Andes* (Lima, 1927), pp. 33–34.

64. Mariátegui, "Defensa del marxismo," *Amauta*, 19 (1928), 10ff.

65. Mariátegui's concept of Inca socialism has been consistently, and with good reason, challenged. For one of the first instances of this see Jorge Basadre, "Marx y Pachacotec," *Nueva Revista Peruana* (Lima), 1 (1929), 16–22.

66. Baines, *Revolution in Peru*, p. 103.

67. On this see César Lévano, "Mariátegui, la voz del Perú integral," in Emilio Romero and Lévano, *Regionalismo y centralismo* (Lima, 1969), pp. 78–83.

68. See Carlos Núñez Anavitarte, *Mariátequi y decentralismo* (Cuzco, 1958).

69. On the González Prada influence see Robert E. McNicoll, "Intellectual Origins of Aprismo," *HAHR*, 23 (1943), 424–440. A judicious resumé and analysis of the massive liberature on Haya de la Torre and the APRA is Richard Lee Clinton, "APRA: An Appraisal," *JIAS*, 12 (1970), 288–297. F. B. Pike, "The Old and the New APRA in Peru: Myth and Reality," *I-AEA*, 18 (1964), 3–45, now strikes the author as excessively negative in appraising the controversial movement. The standard work in English presenting the APRA in a favorable light is Harry Kantor, *The Ideology and Program of the Peruvian Aprista Movement* (Washington, 1960). Some of the more important writings of Haya de la Torre, together with valuable editorial notes and introduction, are found in Robert J. Alexander, ed., *Aprismo: The Ideas and Doctrines of Víctor Raúl Haya de la Torre* (Kent, O., 1973). Helpful for understanding the rise of APRA is John Plank, "Peru: A Study in the Problems of Nation Forming," Ph.D. diss., Harvard University, 1959.

70. Quoted in Robert Michels, *Political Parties: A Sociological Study of the Oligarchical Tendencies of Modern Democracy*, trans. Eden and Cedar Paul (New York, 1915), p. 41.

71. Orrego, *Pueblo-continente*, pp. 108–109.

72. Haya de la Torre, quoted in Jeffrey Klaiber, "Religion and Revolution in Peru: 1920–1945," *TA*, 31 (1975), 307. Klaiber's treatment is placed in broader context in his "Religion and Reform in Peru, 1824–1945," Ph.D. diss., Catholic University of America, 1976, a revised and expanded version of which is a forthcoming publication of the University of Notre Dame Press.

73. Klaiber, "Religion and Revolution," p. 311. Mariátegui, too, had been much impressed by the favorite Peruvian manifestation of the suffering Christ, "El Señor de los Milagros," to which the most important annual religious festival in Peru is devoted. While Marxists like to claim him as exclusively theirs, some Peruvians find in Mariátegui a precursor of the Catholic social justice movement of the 1960s. See, for example, Antonio San Cristóbal-Sebastián, *Economía, educación y marxismo en Mariátegui* (Lima, 1960).

74. See James H. Meisel, *The Myth of the Ruling Class: Gaetano Mosca and the "Elite"* (Ann Arbor, 1958), p. 60.

75. Struve, *Elites*, p. 293.

76. Quoted in Michael T. Dalby and Michael S. Werthman, eds., *Bureaucracy in Historical Perspective* (Glenview, 1971), p. 30.

77. Krause, *Ideal de la humanidad para la vida*, trans. Julián Sanz del Río (Madrid, 1860), p. 102.

78. See Ignacio Campos, *Colloquios de Haya de la Torre*, 3 vols. (no date, no place, ca. 1971), containing reports on Haya's conversations with student groups in his classes at the Popular Universities, and Jeffrey Klaiber, S.J., "The Popular Universities and the Origins of Aprismo, 1921–1924," HAHR, 55 (1975), 693–715.

79. Stephen Jay Stein, "Populism and Mass Politics in Peru: The Political Behavior of the Lima Working Classes in the 1931 Presidential Election," Ph.D. diss., Stanford University, 1973, p. 369.

80. Ibid., pp. 334–342, 352.

81. Ibid., p. 312.

82. A related interpretation on the rise of APRA is presented by Liisa North, "The Origins and Growth of the APRA Party and Socio-Economic Change in Peru," Ph.D. diss., University of California, Berkeley, 1970.

83. Klarén, *Modernization, Dislocation, and Aprismo: Origins of the Peruvian Aprista Party, 1870–1932* (Austin, 1973), pp. 12–16.

84. See Julio Cotler, "Haciendas y comunidades tradicionales en un contexto de movilización política," *Estudios Andinos*, 1 (1970), 131, and José Matos Mar, "Las haciendas del valle de Chancay," in Henri Favre, Claude Collin-Delavaud, and Matos Mar, *La hacienda en el Perú* (Lima, 1967), pp. 346–347. Their interpretations reaffirm the findings of Klarén.

85. Klarén, *Modernization*, p. xviii.

86. Jaime Ponce García, "El sindicalismo boliviano: Resumen histórico y perspectivas actuales," *Estudios Andinos*, 1 (1970), 33.

87. Guzmán, *Historia de Bolivia* (La Paz, 1973), p. 214.

88. See Rengel, *Realidad y fantasía revolucionarias: polémica* (Loja, 1954), p. 35. On the plight of the Ecuadoran middle sectors, threatened by a rising proletariat and by a plutocracy, see also Juan Manuel Rueda, *Aspiraciones nacionales* (Quito, 1939).

89. Maldonado Estrada, *Bases del Partido Socialista Ecuatoriana: su declaración de principios, estatutos, y programa mínimo* (Quito, 1938), pp. 25–26.

90. Hughes, *The Sea Change*, pp. 130–131.

91. See Jorrín and Martz, *Latin American Political Thought*, p. 207, and J. L. Romero, *Pensamiento político de la derecha*, pp. 145–146. On Latin American populism see also Alistair Hennessy, "Latin America," in Ghita Ionescu and Ernest Gellner, eds., *Populism* (New York, 1969), esp. p. 46, and A. E. Niekerg, *Populism and Political Development in Latin America* (Rotterdam, 1974).

92. U.S. populism, as described in George McKenna, ed., *American Populism* (New York, 1974) is quite distinct from the Latin American variety. According to Irving Kristol, "Corporate Capitalism in America," *The Public Interest*, no. 41 (1975), p. 127, "populism is the constant fear and suspicion that power and/or authority, whether in government or out, is being used to frustrate 'the will of the people.'" In Andean America, populism rests on the view that private interests and power are being used to prevent government from directing the people in accordance with their "real" interests. Yet, there are some parallels between U.S. and Andean populists, for both have objected to selling primary goods in an international marketplace controlled by foreigners in league with local industrialists, bankers, and monopolists. On this strain of U.S. populism see Norman Pollack, *The Populist Response to Industrial America: Midwestern Populist Thought* (Cambridge, Mass., 1962) and Theodore Saloutos, *Farmer Movements in the South, 1865–1933* (Berkeley, Los Angeles, 1960).

93. Struve, *Elites*, p. 276.

94. Stein, "Populism and Mass Politics," p. 17.

95. For the degree to which Haya de la Torre himself expresses the Aprista desire for a patriarchal society controlled by paternalistic aristocrats and attributes part of the APRA's early success precisely to this stance see the Stein interview of December 12, 1970 with Haya, ibid., p. 385.

96. See Manuel Seoane, *Mirando a Bolivia con ojo izquierdo* (Buenos Aires, 1926), p. 79. On Haya's corporativism see his *El antimperialismo y el APRA*, 2d ed. (Santiago de Chile, 1936), p. 149, *La defensa continental* (Buenos Aires, 1942), pp. 78, 228–232, and *Y después de la guerra, ¿Que?* (Lima, 1946), pp.

246–247. See also Grant G. Hilliker, *The Politics of Reform in Peru: The Aprista and Other Mass Parties of Latin America* (Baltimore, 1970), p. 19, and Magali Sarfatti Larson and Arlene Eisen Bergman, *Social Stratification in Peru* (Berkeley, 1969), pp. 15–21.

97. Haya, *Antimperialismo*, p. 124.

98. See ibid., pp. 75–76, 138–139, 149, 153.

99. That it was not much more than lip service is indicated by Thomas M. Davies, Jr., "The Indigenismo of the Peruvian Aprista Party: A Reinterpretation," HAHR, 51 (1971), 626–645.

100. See Haya, *La defensa*, esp. p. 69–89, and Stabb, *In Quest of Identity*, pp. 121–123.

101. See Haya, *Antimperialismo*, pp. 177–178.

102. See Haya, *Por la emancipación de América Latina: Artículos, mensajes, discursos (1923–1927)* (Buenos Aires, 1927), p. 210, and L. A. Sánchez, *Un sudamericano en norteamérica: ellos y nosotros*, 2d ed. (Lima, 1968), pp. 12, 20, 32–33, 46.

103. *Un sudamericano*, pp. 39–40. For further insights on this topic see Linda Klein, "The Rhetorics of Yankeephobia: Anti-U.S. Sentiment in Spanish American Literature, 1783–1936," Ph.D. diss., Columbia University, 1971.

104. See *La justicia del Inca*, pp. 15–20.

105. These articles make up the bulk of his book *El antimperialismo*, in which Haya responded to the attacks of the Cuban Communist Julio Mella.

106. Ibid., p. 151.

107. See Stein, "Populism and Mass Parties," p. 228.

108. César Pacheco Vélez, *Menéndez Pelayo y Riva Agüero* (Lima, 1958) finds parallels between the Spanish conservative (1856–1912) and the Peruvian Arielist-turned-"Fascist."

9. Experiments with Reformism: The Depression and Wartime Years

1. Dora Mayer de Zulén, *El oncenio de Leguía*, 2 vols. (Callao, 1932), II, 51–52.

2. On the effects of the depression in Bolivia see Herbert S. Klein, *Parties and Political Change in Bolivia, 1880–1952* (Cambridge, Eng., 1969), p. 108, and Luis Peñalosa, *Historia económica de Bolivia*, 2 vols. (La Paz, 1947), II,

156–159, 175. Full information on the depression's impact on each of the Latin American republics is found in the League of Nations, *World Economic Report, 1932–33* (Geneva, 1934).

3. On New Deal experiments with corporativism see John A. Garraty, "The New Deal, National Socialism, and the Great Depression," AHR, 74 (1973), esp. pp. 912–915.

4. See Dick Steward, *Trade and Hemisphere: The Good Neighbor Policy and Reciprocal Trade* (Columbia, 1975).

5. Stimson and McGeorge Bundy, *On Active Service in Peace and War* (New York, 1948), pp. 182–183.

6. The best treatment of this topic, and of the Good Neighbor policy in general, is Bryce Wood, *The Making of the Good Neighbor Policy* (New York, 1961).

7. See *Foreign Relations of the United States, 1936,* V (Washington, 1954), p. 520.

8. The best treatment of the German menace, as it was perceived and actually existed, is Walton Frye, *Nazi Germany and the American Hemisphere, 1933–1941* (New Haven, 1968).

9. See *Foreign Relations, 1939,* V (Washington, 1957), pp. 141–147, and *1940,* V (Washington, 1961), pp. 1135–1146.

10. Ibid., *1941,* VII (Washington, 1962), pp. 535–548.

11. David Green, *The Containment of Latin America: A History of the Myths and Realities of the Good Neighbor Policy* (Chicago, 1971) and Lloyd Gardner, *Economic Aspects of New Deal Diplomacy* (Madison, 1964) tend to focus exclusively on the ambitions of Good Neighbor policy planners to provide growth opportunities for U.S. capitalism by increasing the economic dependence of Latin America. This interpretation is valid as far as it goes, but it ignores the considerations of self-interest that led many Latin Americans, of their own choice, to seek and to welcome increased dependence.

12. See the unpaginated introduction to the second edition of Manuel Seoane, *El gran vecino: América en la encrucijada* (Santiago de Chile, 1944). See too Haya de la Torre, *La defensa continental* (Buenos Aires, 1942), pp. 55–64, 186, 206, 209, and Luis Alberto Sánchez, *Un sudamericano en norteamérica: ellos y nosotros,* 2d ed. (Lima, 1968), pp. 299–301.

13. June 24, 1941 address of Berle, quoted in Green, *Containment of Latin America,* p. 82. See also Berle, *New Directions in the New World* (New York, 1940). On the objectives of employing public capital for international develop-

ment loans see Frederick Charles Adams, *The Export-Import Bank and American Foreign Policy, 1934–1939* (Columbia, 1976).

14. For a sympathetic study see Carlos Miró Quesada Laos, *Sánchez Cerro y su tiempo* (Lima, 1947). More objective is Orazio A. Ciccarelli, "The Sánchez Cerro Regimes in Peru, 1930–1933," Ph.D. diss., University of Florida, 1969. Extensive source materials have been compiled by Sánchez Cerro's close friend and political partisan, Pedro Ugarteche: *Papeles y recuerdos de un presidente del Perú*, 4 vols. (Lima, 1969–1970).

15. Alfredo Saco, *Síntesis aprista* (Lima, 1934), p. 114.

16. On the address see Jorge Guillermo Llosa, *En busca del Perú* (Lima, 1962), pp. 97–98. On APRA and foreign capital, as the issue was addressed during the 1931 campaign, see Stephen Jay Stein, "Populism and Mass Politics in Peru: The Political Behavior of the Lima Working Classes in the 1931 Presidential Election," Ph.D. diss., Stanford University, 1973, pp. 417–420. The conduct of Apristas at this time tends to bear out the analysis of Robin W. Winks, "On Decolonization and Informal Empire," AHR, 81 (1976), esp. 552–555. Winks argues that "anti-imperialism" often results simply from competition among local elites within a "colonial" country for the benefits to be derived from ties with capitalists of the "imperialistic" nation. He points also to the tensions in the "colonial" country arising from the desire of local elites to find an equilibrium with foreigners which will allow them to maintain domestic equilibrium between themselves and those they wish to maintain in positions of subordination.

17. See Stein, "Populism," pp. 467–478.

18. Ibid., p. 407.

19. Luis Heysen, *El comandante del Oropesa* (Lima, 1931), p. 24.

20. For a reliable study enhanced by maps and illustrations see Guillermo Thorndike, *El año de la barbarie, Perú 1932* (Lima, 1969).

21. *Foreign Relations, 1932*, V (Washington, 1948), pp. 359–360, and Bryce Wood, *The United States and Latin American Wars, 1932–1942* (New York, 1966), p. 245. See also Ronald Bruce St. John, "Peruvian Foreign Policy, 1919–1939: The Delimitation of Frontiers," Ph.D. diss., University of Denver, 1970, and Jose Zárate Lescano, *Historia militar del conflicto con Colombia de 1932* (Lima, 1965).

22. *Foreigns Relations, 1932*, V, 235, 270–315.

23. See Wood, *The United States*, p. 9.

24. Kermit E. McKenzie, *Comintern and World Revolution, 1928–1943: The Shaping of Doctrine* (New York, 1964) places these and similar ideological issues that plagued the international communist movement in their broader context.

25. See Ramiro Borja y Borja, *Derecho constitucional ecuatoriano*, 3 vols. (Madrid, 1950), II, 683.

26. Rafael Baraona, "Justicia social: una cooperativa agropecuaria en la sierra ecuatoriana," in José R. Sabogal Wiesse, ed., *La comunidad andina* (Mexico, 1969), pp. 154–155. For indications of the social problems that helped turn the Ecuadoran lower classes toward a political leader who spoke to them in a new way see Pablo Arturo Suárez, *Contribución al estudio de las realidades entre las clases obreros y campesinos* (Quito, 1934).

27. See Luis Robalino Dávila, *Los orígenes del Ecuador de hoy*, 8 vols. (Quito and Puebla, Mexico, 1949–1969), VII, 833. Velasco Ibarra harped incessantly on the theme that the liberalism-conservatism issue, as defined in its old terms, was dead. See his *Obra doctrinaria y práctica del gobierno ecuatoriano: Mensajes, discursos y declaraciones de prensa*, 2 vols. (Quito, 1956). The work also abounds in Velasco Ibarra's attacks, rude and often vulgar, against the oligarchy and against all political opponents.

28. See his *Democracia y constitucionalismo* (Quito, 1929), p. 233.

29. Velasco Ibarra, *Civilización o barbarie: exégesis de la política americana* (Buenos Aires, 1938), p. 30.

30. See Velasco Ibarra's reference to Maeztu in his *Democracia*, p. 106, and the José Rafael Bustamante prologue to this work, p. xi.

31. Ibid., p. 293.

32. The best full-length study of Velasco Ibarra and Velasquism is Georg Maier, "The Impact of Velasquismo on the Ecuadorian Political System," Ph.D. diss., Southern Illinois University, 1965.

33. Georg Maier, *The Ecuadorian Presidential Election of June 2, 1968: An Analysis* (Washington, 1969), p. 22.

34. On economic conditions see Víctor Emilio Estrada, *El problema económico del Ecuador en 1934*, 2 vols. (Guayaquil, 1934). Estrada drew up the economic plan for the first Velasco Ibarra administration.

35. See Leslie B. Rout, Jr., *Politics of the Chaco Peace Conference, 1935–1939* (Austin, 1970), p. 38.

36. Humberto Vásquez Machicado, *Facetas del intelecto boliviano* (Oruro, 1958), pp. 281–282.

37. Klein, *Parties and Political Change*, p. 152. Works which tend to exonerate Salamanca from the major share of blame in precipitating the Chaco War include David Alvéstegui, *Salamanca, su gravitación sobre el destino de Bolivia*, 4

vols. (La Paz, Cochabamba, 1957–1962), especially the third volume in which Salamanca's friend and long-time political partisan argues that the war exploded despite the president's sincere quest for peace, and Enrique Finot, *Nueva historia de Bolivia: ensayo de interpretación sociológica* (Buenos Aires, 1946), pp. 272–273. The defenders of the president make a strong case. Undoubtedly, blaming Salamanca for the war became the means whereby a great number of Bolivians who had themselves favored hostilities salved their consciences when the Chaco campaigns did not produce the hoped-for consequences.

38. Fernando Diez de Medina, *Franz Tamayo: hechicero del Ande*, 2d ed. (La Paz, 1941), p. 272.

39. Isaac Sandoval Rodríguez, *Nacionalismo en Bolivia: ensayo histórico-político* (La Paz, 1970), p. 125. A thorough account of the overthrow of Salamanca is found in Julio Díaz Arguedas, *Como fué derrocado el hombre símbolo, Salamanca: un capítulo de la guerra con Paraguay* (La Paz, 1957). On the president's troubled relations with his generals prior to his overthrow see Eduardo Arze Quiroga, ed., *Documentos para una historia de la guerra del Chaco: seleccionados del archivo de Daniel Salamanca*, 3 vols. (La Paz, 1951–1960).

40. J. Valerie Fifer, *Bolivia: Land, Location and Politics since 1825* (Cambridge, Eng., 1972), p. 217. For fuller coverage of the war see Porfirio Díaz Machicao, *Historia de Bolivia*, 5 vols. (La Paz, 1954–1958), III, *Salamanca, La Guerra del Chaco, Tejada Sorzano, 1931–1936,* and Hans Kundt, *Campaña del Chaco,* ed. and with an introduction by Raúl Tovar Villa (La Paz, 1961), in which the German-born general who was Bolivia's chief of staff at the outset of the war defends his conduct. A powerful indictment of the old order because of its behavior in the war is Augusto Céspedes' fictionalized account, *Sangre del mestizos: relatos de la Guerra del Chaco* (La Paz, 1936). See also Murdo J. MacLeod, "The Bolivian Novel, the Chaco War, and the Revolution," in James Malloy and Richard S. Thorn, eds., *Beyond the Revolution: Bolivia Since 1952* (Pittsburgh, 1971), 341–368.

41. See Peter Calvert, *Latin America: Internal Conflict and International Peace* (New York, 1969), p. 105.

42. Wood, *The United States*, p. 161.

43. Fernando Diez de Medina, *Una polémica entre . . . y Augusto Céspedes en torno a "40 años de historia de Bolivia"* (Potosí, 1957), p. 37, argues that the denomination should be civil-military socialism; for much of the socialist impulse came from the civilian disciples of Saavedra and Siles who exercised a strong influence over the military officers.

44. See Klein, *Parties and Political Change*, p. 245.

45. See Augusto Céspedes, *El dictador suicida: 40 años de la historia de historia de Bolivia* (Santiago de Chile, 1956), p. 148.

46. For refutation of the frequently made charge that Standard Oil was responsible for the Chaco War see Fifer, *Bolivia*, p. 220, Rout, *Chaco Peace Conference*, pp. 47–52, Harris Gaylord Warren, *Paraguay: An Informal History* (Norman, 1949), p. 294, Wood, *The United States*, p. 374, and David H. Zook, Jr., *The Conduct of the Chaco War* (New Haven, 1961), p. 80.

47. See Herbert Klein, "American Oil Companies in Latin America: The Bolivian Experience," I-AEA, 18 (1964), 47–72.

48. On the various charges that Bolivians brought against Standard Oil see Sergio Almaráz, *Petroleo en Bolivia*, 2d ed. (La Paz, 1969), pp. 86–185, Céspedes, *El dictador*, pp. 122, 151, Guillermo Francovich, *El pensamiento boliviano en el siglo XX* (Mexico, 1956), pp. 105–106, Alberto Mendoza López, *La soberanía de Bolivia estrangulada* (La Paz, 1942), pp. 98–118, and Carlos Montenegro, *Frente al derecho del estado el oro de la Standard Oil* (La Paz, 1938).

49. Vicente Mendoza López, *Las finanzas en Bolivia y la estrategía capitalista* (La Paz, 1940), p. 12. The author served as Busch's minister of the treasury (hacienda) in 1938 and helped set the regime's approach to socioeconomic problems.

50. The best account of the 1938 constitution is found in Ciro Félix Trigo, ed., *Las constituciones de Bolivia* (Madrid, 1958). Its social and labor provisions are discussed in Gastón Arduz Eguía, *Legislación boliviana del trabajo y de la previsión social* (La Paz, 1941).

51. See Laurence Duggan, "Background for Revolution," *Inter-American*, 9 (1946), pp. 16–17.

52. See Víctor Paz Estenssoro, "Bolivia," in Luis Roque Gondra and others, *Pensamiento económico latinoamericano* (Mexico, 1945), p. 66.

53. See Klein, *Parties and Political Change*, pp. 315–316.

54. Diez de Medina, *De un siglo al otro: memorias de un hombre público* (La Paz, 1955), p. 398. A good treatment of Busch is found in Díaz Machicao, *Historia de Bolivia*, IV, *Toro, Busch, Quintanilla, 1936–1940*.

55. Augusto Guzmán, *Historia de Bolivia* (La Paz, 1973), p. 334.

56. Mario A. Gutiérrez Pacheco, ed., *Verbo y espíritu de Unzaga* (La Paz, 1968), pp. 21–22. On Unzaga, see Enrique Achá Álvarez and Mario H. Ramos y Ramos, *Unzaga: mártir de América* (Buenos Aires, 1960), eulogizing the founder of the FSB. For essays written originally in 1953 by an important FSB leader who discusses the party's ideology see Gonzalo Romero, *Reflexiones para una interpretación de la historia de Bolivia* (Buenos Aires, 1960).

57. See Unzaga, "Mensaje de Falange Socialista Boliviana al pueblo de Bolivia," in Guillermo Lora, ed., *Documentos políticos de Bolivia* (La Paz, 1970), pp. 273–282.

58. On the early MNR see José Fellman Velarde, *Víctor Paz Estenssoro, el hombre y la revolución*, 2d ed. (La Paz, 1955), James M. Malloy, *Bolivia: The Uncompleted Revolution* (Pittsburgh, 1970), esp. pp. 111–126, and Luis Peñalosa C., *Historia del Movimiento Nacionalista Revolucionario, 1941–1952* (La Paz, 1963). On other leftist opposition groups during this period see Frente de Izquierda Boliviano, *¡Hacia la unidad de las izquierdas bolivianas!* (Santiago de Chile, 1939), an excellent exposition of the views of many Bolivian Marxists, generally attributed to José Antonio Arze, Guillermo Lora, *José Aguirre Gainsborg, fundador del P.O.R.* (La Paz, 1960), a valuable biography of the founder of a Trotskyite labor party, and José Ortega, *Aspectos del nacionalismo boliviano* (Madrid, 1973), esp. the concluding chapter which contains a good treatment of the literature of nationalism, 1932–1953.

59. Francovich, *Pensamiento*, pp. 83–84.

60. See chap. 4, n. 56, and Fausto Reinage, *Belzu: precursor de la revolución nacional* (La Paz, 1952).

61. See *Foreign Relations, 1937*, V (Washington, 1954), pp. 279ff, *1938*, V (1956), pp. 286–288, and *1939*, V (1957), pp. 313–334, and Wood, *Good Neighbor Policy*, pp. 189–194.

62. See the superb study by Cole Blasier, "The United States, Germany, and the Bolivian Revolutionaries, 1941–1946," *HAHR*, 52 (1972), 26–54. Also valuable is Emmett James Holland, "A Historical Study of Bolivian Foreign Relations, 1935–1946," Ph.D. diss., The American University, 1967.

63. See José Fellman Velarde, *Historia de Bolivia*, 3 vols. (La Paz, Cochabamba, 1968–1970), III, 305–306, and A. M. Schlesinger, Jr., *A Thousand Days: John F. Kennedy in the White House* (Boston, 1965), p. 171.

64. An excellent account of the 1939–1942 negotiations between the United States and Bolivia written by a stalwart of the Concordance—he served as Peñaranda's minister of foreign relations—who was one of the persons primarily responsible for propagating the myth of the MNR's Nazi affiliations is Alberto Ostria Gutiérrez, *Una obra y un destino: la política internacional de Bolivia después de la Guerra del Chaco* (Buenos Aires, 1946), esp. pp. 323–330. See too Cleona Lewis, *The United States and Foreign Investment Problems* (Washington, 1948), p. 155, and Díaz Machicao, *Historia de Bolivia, V, Peñaranda, 1940–1943*, pp. 45–61.

65. See Mervin L. Bohan, *Informe de la Misión de los Estados Unidos en Bolivia* (La Paz, 1942).

66. See Vicente Donoso Torres, *El estado actual de la educación en Bolivia: Informe de la Misión Magruder* (La Paz, 1943).

67. Fellman Velarde, *Historia*, III, 301. For a condemnation of the Villarroel government as fascist-dominated, written by an important figure in the Con-

cordance, see Pedro Zilveti Arce, *Bajo el signo de la barbarie* (Santiago de Chile, 1946).

68. See *Foreign Relations, 1944*, VII (Washington, 1967), p. 431.

69. Wilkie, *The Bolivian Revolution and U.S. Aid Since 1952* (Los Angeles, 1969), p. 21.

70. Fellman Velarde, *Historia*, III, 301.

71. The standard source on Bolivian demography for this period is Asthenio Averanga Mollinedo, *Aspectos generales de la población boliviana* (La Paz, 1956).

72. See E. Rebagliati, "Compulsory Social Security in Peru," *Bulletin of the Pan American Union*, 71 (1937), 284–287.

73. See David Chaplin, *The Peruvian Industrial Labor Force* (Princeton, 1967), p. 78. Good coverage is also provided by Allen Gerlach, "Civil-Military Relations in Peru: 1914–1945," Ph.D. diss., University of New Mexico, 1973.

74. See Gerardo Bedoya Sáez, "Historia de la labor gubermental en favor de los indígenas peruanos," *AI*, 2 (1941), 21–24.

75. See F. B. Pike, *The Modern History of Peru* (London, 1967), p. 276.

76. See Alcira Leiserson, *Notes on the Process of Industrialization in Argentina, Chile, and Peru* (Berkeley, 1966), pp. 32–34.

77. Borja y Borja, *Derecho constitucional*, II, 687. For a defense of the Páez dictatorship see Carlos Honorato Endara, *Desde el mirador de América: la dictadura y la patria nueva* (Quito, 1936), p. 14.

78. Páez, *Explico* (Quito, 1939), pp. 29–30.

79. On the Law of Communes and related aspects of Indian relations see César Cisneros y Cisneros, "Comunidades indígenas del Ecuador," *AI*, 9 (1949), esp. pp. 39–41, and *Demografía y estadística sobre el indio ecuatoriano* (Quito, 1948), an important pioneering study, Humberto García Ortiz, "Consideraciones acerca de una legislación indígena en el Ecuador," *AI*, 2 (1942), 25–27, Luis Monsalvo Pozo, "La figura social de los aborígenes del Ecuador," *AI*, 2 (1942), 35–42, and Gonzalo Rubio Orbe, *Aspectos indígenas* (Quito, 1965), pp. 102, 106, 125–128.

80. See Robert Bialek, *Catholic Politics: A History Based on Ecuador* (New York, 1963), esp. pp. 87–97, Juan Ignacio Larrea Holguín, *La Iglesia y el estado en el Ecuador: la personalidad de la Iglesia en el modus vivendi celebrado entre la Santa Sede y el Ecuador* (Seville, 1954), p. 96, Maier, *Ecuadorian Presidential Election*, pp. 43–45, J. Lloyd Mecham, *Church and State in Latin America*, 2d

ed. (Chapel Hill, 1966), pp. 155–156, and Julio Tobar Donoso, *Monografías históricos* (Quito, 1937), pp. 458–461.

81. See Alfredo Pareja Diez Canseco, *Historia del Ecuador*, 2 vols. (Quito, 1958), II, 422–423.

82. Ricardo A. Paredes, *El imperialismo en el Ecuador: oro y sangre en Portovelo* (Guayaquil, 1970) is a carefully documented, scholarly account of Ecuador's dealings during the 1930s with the South American Development Company. Paredes was a leading member of the Ecuadoran Communist party.

83. On the background to the clash see Georg Maier, "The Boundary Dispute between Ecuador and Peru," *American Journal of International Law*, 43 (1969), 28–48. A valuable account written by Ecuador's minister of foreign relations at the time of the Peruvian invasion is Julio Tobar Donoso, *La invasión peruana y el protocolo de Río: antecedentes y explicación histórica* (Quito, 1945).

84. Objective accounts are found in Wood, *The United States*, pp. 255–331, and David H. Zook, Jr., *Zarumilla-Marañón: The Ecuador-Peru Dispute* (New York, 1964).

85. Arroyo del Río defends his rule and attacks the succeeding Velasco Ibarra regime in *Bajo el imperio del odio*, 2 vols. (Bogotá, 1946).

10. Revolution in Bolivia, Muddling through Peru and Ecuador, 1945–1960

1. Haya de la Torre, *Y después de la guerra, ¿Qué?* (Lima, 1946), pp. 22–27.

2. January 9, 1945 communication of Walter Thurston to Cordell Hull, *Foreign Relations of the United States, 1945*, IX (Washington, 1969), p. 573.

3. Useful surveys of U.S.-Latin American relations following World War II include James C. Tillapaugh, "From War to Cold War: United States Policies Toward Latin America," Ph.D. diss., Northwestern University, 1973, and R. Harrison Wagner, *United States Policy Toward Latin America: A Study in Domestic and International Politics* (Stanford, 1970), stressing the importance of security rather than economic considerations.

4. See Laurence Duggan, *The Americas: The Search for Hemispheric Security* (New York, 1949), p. 117, and F. B. Pike, "Corporatism and Latin American-United States Relations," RP, 36 (1974), 150.

5. Quoted in David Green, *The Containment of Latin America* (Chicago, 1971), p. 277.

6. See *Private Investment in Latin America: Hearings Before the Subcommittee on Inter-American Economic Relationships of the Joint Committee, Con-*

gress of the United States, January 14, 15, and 16, 1964 (Washington, 1964), pp. 444–449.

7. See International Economic Consultants, Inc., "Commodity Problems in Latin America," in *United States-Latin American Relations*, Congress of the United States, Senate Committee on Foreign Relations (Washington, 1960), pp. 167–171. For a general treatment see Rodney Philip Bunker, "Inter-American Politics and the Recession of 1957–1958: Trade Linkages and Policy Change in the United States," Ph.D., diss., University of Notre Dame, 1972.

8. Quoted in W. W. Rostow, *Politics and the Stages of Economic Growth* (Cambridge, Eng., 1971), p. 189. On the parallels of Hamiltonian and ECLA analysis see Joseph Grunwald, "Some Reflections on Latin American Industrialization Policy," *Journal of Political Economy*, 78 (1970), Supplement, 826–856.

9. See Prebisch, *El desarrollo económico de la América Latina y algunos de sus principales problemas* (Lake Success, 1949), made available the following year in English translation.

10. See Joseph Grunwald and Philip Musgrove, *Natural Resources in Latin American Development* (Baltimore, 1970), pp. 25–29. For objective treatment of ECLA-Prebisch analysis see M. June Flanders, "Prebisch on Protectionism: An Evaluation," *The Economic Journal*, 74 (1964), 305–326, and Albert O. Hirshman, "Ideologies of Economic Development in Latin America," in Hirshman, ed., *A Bias for Hope: Essays on Development and Latin America* (New Haven, 1971), pp. 270–311, and Gustavo Lagos, *International Stratification and Underdeveloped Countries* (Chapel Hill, 1963).

11. See Pedro C. M. Teichert, *Economic Policy Revolution and Industrialization in Latin America* (Oxford, Miss., 1959), esp. p. 188.

12. See James Stanford Bradshaw, "The 'Lost' Conference: The Economic Issue in United States-Latin American Relations, 1954–1957," Ph.D. diss., Michigan State University, 1972.

13. Herbert Goldhamer, "The Nonhemispheric Powers in Latin America," in Luigi R. Einaudi, ed., *Beyond Cuba: Latin America Takes Charge of Its Future* (New York, 1974), pp. 173–174.

14. Plaza, *Problems of Democracy in Latin America* (Chapel Hill, 1955), p. 84.

15. Eisenhower, *The Wine is Bitter: The United States and Latin America* (Garden City, 1963), p. 205. For Beltrán's views at this time see his "Foreign Loans and Politics in Latin America," *Foreign Affairs*, 34 (1956), 297–304.

16. *The Wine is Bitter*, p. 206.

17. Quoted by R. H. Wagner, *United States Policy Toward Latin America*, p. 147.

18. See Peter Gold, "The *Indigenista* Fiction of José María Arguedas," *Bulletin of Hispanic Studies*, 50 (1973), 68.

19. See Luis E. Valcárcel, *La educación del campesino* (Lima, 1954), esp. pp. 6–11.

20. See, for example, José Antonio Arze, *Sociografía del inkario: ¿Fue socialista o comunista el imperio inkaiko?* (La Paz, 1952), esp. pp. iii–iv. The eminent Bolivian sociologist describes here how he came to reject his early views on the socialism of the Inca past and to recognize instead the dichotomized, two-culture nature of preconquest native civilization.

21. According to Ecuador's Gonzalo Rubio Orbe, "El Indio del Ecuador," AI, 9 (1949), 109, subjects of the Inca Empire were "cells" who lacked individualism and whose lives revolved about their collectivities.

22. Vicente Mendoza López quoted in Frente de Izquierda Boliviano, *¡Hacia la unidad de las izquierdas bolivianas!* (Santiago de Chile, 1939), p. 83.

23. Valcárcel, "Sumario del Tahuantinsuyo," originally published in a 1928 edition of *Amauta* and quoted in Arze, *Sociografía*, pp. 33–34. See too Valcárcel, *Del ayllu al imperio* (Lima, 1925), pp. 168, 184–185.

24. See M. Alberto Zelada, *El kollasuyo* (Sucre, 1937), p. 43.

25. Jaramillo, *El indio ecuatoriano*, 4th ed. (Quito, 1954), pp. 12–25. See also pp. 426–427 for Jaramillo's list of twenty important studies, published between 1915 and 1947, depicting the true nature of the Indians and refuting the "romantic" belief that the natives stood constantly ready to join in waging social revolution.

26. Otero, *Figura y caracter del indio: los ando-bolivianos*, 2d ed. (La Paz, 1954), pp. 138–140.

27. Larco, H., "El problema del Indio," in Valcárcel and others, *Hacia el despertar del alma indio* (Lima, 1929), pp. 53–74.

28. Castro Pozo, *Del ayllu al cooperativismo socialista* (Lima, 1936), p. 78.

29. See *El nuevo indio: ensayos indianistas sobre la sierra surperuana*, 2d ed. (Cuzco, 1937), pp. 27–30, 192.

30. Castro Pozo, "El 'ayllo' peruano debe transformarse en cooperativa agropecuaria," AI, 2 (1942), 15–16.

31. See Manuel Seoane, *Con el ojo izquierdo: mirando a Bolivia* (Buenos Aires, 1926), p. 118, and Valcárcel, "Supervivencias precolumbinas en el Perú," AI, 10 (1950), esp. p. 54.

32. See Valcárcel, Del ayllu al imperio, p. 171.

33. Castro Pozo, "Social and Economico-Political Evolution of the Communities of Central Peru," in Julian H. Steward, ed., Handbook of South American Indians, II, The Andean Civilizations (New York, 1963), p. 497.

34. See Thomas R. Ford, Man and Land in Peru (Gainesville, 1955), pp. 41, 46, 98–99, and Henry F. Dobyns, The Social Matrix of Peruvian Indigenous Communities (Ithaca, 1964), esp. pp. 13–22. See too Richard N. Adams, "The Community in Latin America: A Changing Myth," The Centennial Review, 6 (1962), 409–434, Richard Patch, "How Communal are the Communities?" (New York: American Universities Field Staff, Latin America, Peru, RWP-5-59), p. 9, and Bernard Mishkin, "The Contemporary Quechuas," in Steward, ed., Handbook of South American Indians, II, 411–470. Following George Foster's interpretations—Culture and Conquest: America's Spanish Heritage (Chicago, 1960)—José María Arguedas, Las comunidades de España y del Perú (Lima, 1968), p. 346, maintains that the communalism of the Indians derived largely from their experience within the Spanish colonial system.

35. Castro Pozo, "El 'ayllo'," esp. pp. 11–15.

36. See Alfredo Guillén Pinto, La educación del indio (La Paz, 1919), p. 131.

37. See Castro Pozo, Del ayllu al cooperativismo, pp. 273–275.

38. See Thomas M. Davies, Jr., Indian Integration in Peru: A Half Century of Experience, 1900–1948 (Lincoln, 1974), p. 128.

39. See Manuel María Marzal, "El Indio y la tierra en el Ecuador," AI, 23 (1963), 21.

40. See Sáenz, Sobre el indio peruano y su incorporación al medio nacional (Mexico, 1933) and Sobre el indio ecuatoriano y su incorporación al medio nacional (Mexico, 1933).

41. See Gonzalo Rubio Orbe, Aspectos indígenas (Quito, 1965), p. 302.

42. See Valcárcel, La educación del campesino, p. 11.

43. The most important agency in advancing the cause of respectable Indianism has been the Instituto Indigenista Interamericano, founded shortly after the first Congreso Indigenista Interamericano celebrated in 1941 at Pátzcuaro, Mexico. The periodical América Indígena (AI) is published by the Instituto.

44. See James Malloy, Bolivia: The Uncompleted Revolution (Pittsburgh, 1970), p. 98.

45. See José Fellman Velarde, Historia de Bolivia, 3 vols. (La Paz, Cochabamba, 1968–1970), III, 323–325, Herbert S. Klein, Parties and Political Change

in Bolivia, 1800–1952 (Cambridge, Eng., 1969), p. 384, Jaime Ponce G., "El sindicalismo boliviano: resumen histórico y perspectivas actuales," *Estudios Andinos*, 1 (1970), 40–41, and Steven S. Volk, "Class, Union, Party: The Development of a Revolutionary Union Movement in Bolivia (1905–1952)," *Science and Society*, 24 (1975), 26–43.

46. See Augusto Guzmán, *Historia de Bolivia* (La Paz, 1973), p. 278, and Klein, *Parties and Political Change*, p. 387. On the economic circumstances that contributed to a revolutionary situation see also Carter Goodrich, "Bolivia in Time of Revolution," in James Malloy and Richard Thorn, eds., *Beyond the Revolution: Bolivia since 1952* (Pittsburgh, 1971), pp. 3–24, and *The Economic Transformation of Bolivia* (Ithaca, 1955). Also helpful are United Nations, *Report of the United Nations Mission of Technical Assistance to Bolivia* (New York, 1951), the report of Dr. H. L. Keenleyside who headed a UN technical assistance mission to Bolivia in 1950, and United Nations, Economic Commission for Latin America, *El desarrollo económico de Bolivia* (Mexico, 1958).

47. Guzmán, *Historia*, p. 338.

48. See Grunwald and Musgrove, *Natural Resources*, pp. 94, 240.

49. See "Programa obrera" (1959) in Guillermo Lora, ed., *Documentos políticos de Bolivia* (La Paz, 1970), pp. 361–368.

50. Malloy, *Bolivia*, pp. 158–159, lists the three in this manner. "The first had a generally rightist reformist approach; the second, a revolutionary socialist approach; and the third, a pragmatic nationalist approach." Although differing slightly with Malloy's description, I am in general accord with his splendid study which is the best available source on the Bolivian revolution. Somewhat marred by its uncritically favorable viewpoint is Robert J. Alexander, *The Bolivian National Revolution* (New Brunswick, 1958). An excellent bibliographical survey is Charles W. Arnade, "Bolivia's Social Revolution: A Discussion of Sources," *JIAS*, 1 (1959), 341–352.

51. See Arturo Urquidi, *Bolivia y su reforma agraria* (La Paz, 1969), pp. 108–109. Fellman Velarde, *Historia*, III, 356, reports that 3 percent of the rural population owned 64 percent of all cultivated estates of more than twenty hectares.

52. See Rafael R. Reyeros, *Historia social del indio boliviano: "El pongueaje,"* rev. ed. (La Paz, 1963), pp. 10–11.

53. See Arturo Urquidi, *Las comunidades indígenas en Bolivia* (Cochabamba, 1970), pp. 17, 144–147. Guillermo Lora, *Historia del movimiento obrero boliviano*, 3 vols. (La Paz, 1967–1970), I, 34, sets the number of comunidades at only 1,500.

54. See George Jackson Eder, *Inflation and Development in Latin America: A Case History of Inflation and Stabilization in Bolivia* (Ann Arbor, 1968), pp.

74–75, Dwight B. Heath, "Bolivia: Peasant Syndicates Among the Aymaras of the Yungas: A View from the Grass Roots," in Henry A. Landsberger, ed., *Latin American Peasant Movements* (Ithaca, 1969), esp. pp. 175–177, and Malloy, *Bolivia*, pp. 188–215.

55. See Richard W. Wilkie review of Ernest Feder, *The Rape of the Peasantry: Latin America's Landholding System*, in HAHR, 53 (1973), 540, and Cornelius Zondag, *The Bolivian Economy, 1952–65: The Revolution and Its Aftermath* (New York, 1966), p. 147.

56. Valuable general studies of the Bolivian revolution's land reform that properly stress the diversity of its effects include William E. Carter, "Revolution and the Agrarian Sector," in Malloy and Thorn, *Beyond the Revolution*, pp. 233–269, Dwight B. Heath, Charles J. Erasmus, and Hans C. Buechler, *Land Reform and Social Revolution in Bolivia* (New York, 1970), Daniel Heyduk, *Huayrapampa: Bolivian Highland Peasants and the New Social Order*, CULASP (Ithaca, 1971), William J. McEwen and others, *Changing Rural Bolivia* (New York, 1969), and Peter R. Odell and David A. Preston, *Economies and Societies in Latin America: A Geographical Interpretation* (New York, 1973).

57. See William Léons, "Modelos cambiantes de organización laboral en una comunidad boliviana," *Estudios Andinos*, 1 (1970), esp. 58–59, and Madeline Barbara Léons and William Léons, "Land Reform and Economic Change in the Yungas," Malloy and Thorn, eds., *Beyond the Revolution*, pp. 269–301. On the colonization-commercialization approach of early land reform see Isaac Sandoval Rodríguez, *Bolivia y América Latina* (La Paz, 1969), pp. 29–30. On the prosperity in the Santa Cruz region resulting from colonization-commercialization programs see Zondag, *Bolivian Economy*, p. 156.

58. See Heath, "New Patrons for Old: Changing Patron-Client Relationships in the Bolivian Yungas," in Arnold Strickon and Sidney M. Greenfield, eds., *Structure and Process in Latin America* (Albuquerque, 1972), p. 110. See too Hans Buechler and Judith M. Buechler, *The Bolivian Aymara* (New York, 1971), Melvin Burke, "An Analysis of the Bolivian Agrarian Reform," Ph.D. diss., University of Pittsburgh, 1968, and "Land Reform in the Lake Titicaca Region," in Malloy and Thorn, eds., *Beyond the Revolution*, pp. 301–340, and William E. Carter, "The Ambiguity of Reform: Highland Bolivian Peasants and Their Land," Ph.D. diss., Columbia University, 1963. On land reform and new models of patron-client relationships in the Cochabamba valley, where mestizos of Quechua background predominate, see Jorge Erwin Dandler-Hanhart, "Politics of Leadership, Brokerage and Patronage in the Campesino Movement of Cochabamba, Bolivia," Ph.D. diss., University of Wisconsin, 1971. On the appearance of a patronage-clientage system in the colonization-commercialization projects of the Yungas see Madeline Barbara Léons, "Changing Patterns of Stratification in an Emergent Bolivian Community," Ph.D. diss., University of California, Los Angeles, 1966, and "Stratification and Pluralism in the Bolivian Yungas," in Walter Goldschmidt and Harry Hoijer, eds., *The Social Anthropology of Latin America* (Los Angeles, 1970), pp. 256–282.

59. See Daniel Heyduk, "Bolivia's Land Reform Hacendados," I-AEA, 27 (1973), esp. 88–90, 92–93.

60. Charles J. Erasmus, "Agrarian Reform vs. Land Reform: Three Latin American Countries," in Philip Bock, ed., *Peasants in the Modern World* (Albuquerque, 1969), p. 11. On the inability of the national government to establish control over ex-colonos see also Eder, *Inflation*, p. 33, and Samuel Huntington, *Political Order in Changing Societies* (New Haven, 1968), p. 33. According to Zondag, *Bolivian Economy*, p. 148, as of 1959 there existed only twenty-one cooperatives with 2,663 members.

61. Paz Estenssoro, *La revolución boliviana* (La Paz, 1964), p. 45.

62. On the manner in which Indian education programs were devised with the intention of keeping the natives as *campesinos* and impeding their migration to cities, see Lambros Comitas, "Educación y estratificación social en Bolivia," AI, 28 (1968), esp. 649.

63. See addresses of October 31 and December 31, 1952, in Paz Estenssoro, *Discursos y mensajes* (Buenos Aires, 1953), pp. 40–41, 49–50.

64. Carlos Montenegro, *Nacionalismo y coloniaje: su expresión histórica en la prensa de Bolivia*, 3d ed. (La Paz, 1953), p. 195.

65. Henry Landsberger, "The Labor Elite," in Seymour Martin Lipset and Aldo Solari, eds., *Elites in Latin America* (New York, 1967), esp. pp. 269, 298, is convincing as he argues that Paz Estenssoro succeeded on the whole in co-opting labor leadership and in isolating and rendering impotent the few labor theoreticians who stuck to their Marxist and Trotskyist guns. See too Robert J. Alexander, *Organized Labor in Latin America* (New York, 1965), p. 107.

66. Huntington, *Political Order*, pp. 309, 312.

67. Fernando Diez de Medina, *Bolivia y su destino, y ostros temas de la patria* (La Paz, 1962), p. 62.

68. *Discursos y mensajes*, p. 17.

69. Cornelius Zondag, *Problems in the Economic Development of Bolivia* (La Paz, 1956), pp. 169, 224.

70. The price per pound of tin, standing at $1.27 in 1950, was down to 91.8 cents in 1954. It rallied to 94.7 cents in 1955 and to $1.01 in 1956, only to fall back to 95 cents in 1958 before rising to $1.02 and $1.01 in 1959 and 1960. See Grunwald and Musgrove, *Natural Resources*, p. 204.

71. Zondag, *Bolivian Economy*, p. 83.

72. See discourses and writings of Óscar Unzaga de la Vega in Mario Gutiérrez Pacheco, ed., *Verbo y espíritu de Unzaga* (La Paz, 1968).

73. See Gonzalo Romero, *Reflexiones para una interpretación de la historia de Bolivia* (Buenos Aires, 1960), p. 175. The MNR, unconvincingly, attributed Unzaga's death to suicide, inspiring the rejoinder from Luis Belzu, *Así murió Unzaga de la Vega* (La Paz, 1961).

74. For an example of this type of Marxist criticism, see PIR, "Tesis política" (1956), in Lora, ed., *Documentos*, esp. pp. 462–464. For a good glimpse of the political ideologies of the different parties and factions during the period see Mario Rolón Anaya, *Política y partidos en Bolivia* (La Paz, 1966).

75. On the clash between proletariat and middle-sector interests, arising out of disagreement on the best way to apply populist programs resting on economism in an underdeveloped country, see the penetrating study by Melvin Burke and James Malloy, "Del populismo nacional al corporativismo nacional: el caso de Bolivia, 1952–1970," *Aportes*, no. 26 (1973), esp. 70–71.

76. See Charles D. Corbett, *The Latin American Military as a Socio-Political Force: Case Studies of Bolivia and Argentina* (Coral Gables, 1972), pp. 33–35.

77. See n. 44.

78. Eisenhower, *The Wine is Bitter*, p. 124.

79. See Eder, *Inflation*, p. 595.

80. Paz Estenssoro, *Discursos y mansajes*, pp. 44–45.

81. Eder, *Inflation*, p. 79. For an excellent study of the topic see Cole Blasier, *The Hovering Giant: U.S. Responses to Revolutionary Change in Latin America* (Pittsburgh, 1976), esp. pp. 128–150. Also useful is G. Earl Sanders, "The Quiet Experiment in American Diplomacy: An Interpretive Essay on United States Aid to the Bolivian Revolution," *TA*, 33 (1976), 25–49.

82. Eder, *Inflation*, p. ix.

83. Ibid., p. 605. James W. Wilkie, *The Bolivian Revolution and U.S. Aid Since 1952: Financial Background and Context of Political Decisions* (Los Angeles, 1969), p. 10, estimates that up to 1961, 47.2 percent of all dollars channeled into Bolivia through USAID programs went into economic expenditure. But this statistic covers the use of aid that Bolivia had received since 1942. The early aid programs were overwhelmingly oriented toward economic spending.

84. Wilkie, *Bolivian Revolution*, p. 12.

85. Fellman Velarde, *Historia*, III, 381. For a useful study of Bolivian foreign policy objectives during the 1952–1964 period, with many references to relations

with the United States, see Juan José Vidaurre, *Diez años de política internacional boliviana* (La Paz, 1964).

86. See Zondag, *Problems*, p. 121. For leftist criticism of the conditions under which U.S. petroleum firms returned to Bolivia see Sergio Almaráz Paz, *Petroleo en Bolivia*, 2d ed. (La Paz, 1969), pp. 285–362, and Amado Canelas O., *Petroleo: imperialismo y nacionalismo* (La Paz, 1963), p. 163.

87. Grunwald and Musgrove, *Natural Resources*, pp. 112–113.

88. Bustamante presents his side of the case in *Tres años de la lucha por la democracia en el Perú* (Lima, 1949).

89. On these events see two books by Víctor Villanueva Valencia: *El militarismo en el Perú* (Lima, 1962) and *La tragedia de un pueblo y de un partido: páginas para la historia del APRA* (Santiago de Chile, 1954).

90. See Serafino Romualdi, *Presidents and Peons: Recollections of a Labor Ambassador in Latin America* (New York, 1967), pp. 300–303.

91. Charles T. Goodsell, *American Corporations and Peruvian Politics* (Cambridge, Mass., 1974), p. 42.

92. For an important study showing how social security serves as an instrument of stratification in that it reflects and perpetuates power differentials among bargaining groups see Carmelo Mesa-Lago, "La estratificación de la seguridad social y el efecto de la desigualdad en América Latina: el caso peruano," *Estudios Andinos*, 3 (1973), 17–48.

93. James Payne, *Labor and Politics in Peru: The System of Political Bargaining* (New Haven, 1965), p. 51. See also David Chaplin, *The Peruvian Industrial Labor Force* (Princeton, 1967), p. 12 et passim, and, for an overview, Larry Larson, "Labor, Social Change, and Politics in Peru," Ph.D. diss., University of North Carolina, 1967.

94. See Elsa M. Chaney, "Women in Latin American Politics: The Case of Peru and Chile," in Ann Pescatello, ed., *Female and Male in Latin America: Essays* (Pittsburgh, 1973), pp. 104–105.

95. Adalberto J. Pinelo, *The Multinational Corporation as a Force in Latin American Politics: A Case Study of the International Petroleum Company in Peru* (New York, 1973), pp. 50–51.

96. See Erich Egner, "El crecimiento económico del Perú y sus obstáculos," *Revista de la Facultad de Ciencias Económicas y Commerciales de la Universidad Mayor de San Marcos*, 66 (1963), 46.

97. See De Gaulle, *Memoirs of Hope, Renewal and Endeavor*, trans. Terence Kilmartin (New York, 1971), p. 226.

98. Pinelo, *The Multinational Corporation*, p. 102, referring to the findings of sociologist Phillip Gillette, University of California, Los Angeles.

99. See Grunwald and Musgrove, *Natural Resources*, pp. 102, 366–368, 372, and Charles R. Gibson, *Foreign Trade in the Economic Development of Small Nations: The Case of Ecuador* (New York, 1971), pp. 176–177.

100. See George I. Blanksten, *Ecuador: Constitutions and Caudillos* (Berkeley, 1951), p. 64, and Jacques M. P. Wilson, *The Development of Education in Ecuador* (Coral Gables, 1970), p. 58.

101. See Georg Maier, *The Ecuadorian Presidential Election of June 2, 1968: An Analysis* (Washington, 1969), p. 44.

102. See Óscar Efrén Reyes, *Breve historia general del Ecuador*, 4th ed. (Quito, 1960), p. 785, and Lilo Linke, *Ecuador, Country of Contrasts* (London, 1954), pp. 30–31.

103. For background material and good insights on this troubled period see John Samuel Fitch III, "Toward a Model of the Coup d'État as a Political Process in Latin America: Ecuador 1948–1966," Ph.D. diss., Yale University, 1973.

104. The fact that Galo Plaza co-authored a study placing the United Fruit Company in a favorable light lent ammunition to those accusing him of collaborating with Yankee imperialism. See Stacy May and Plaza, *The United Fruit Company in Latin America* (New York, 1958). Unlike the situation in Central America, the United Fruit Company's role in Ecuador was fairly insignificant and confined largely to the marketing rather than the production of bananas. In the mid-1950s its share of Ecuador's total banana exports was barely over one-fifth.

105. See Plaza, *Problems of Democracy*, esp. p. 39.

106. John D. Martz, *Ecuador: Conflicting Political Culture and Quest for Progress* (Boston, 1972), p. 44.

107. See Velasco Ibarra, *Obra doctrinaira y práctica del gobierno ecuatoriano: mensajes, discursos y declaraciones de prensa*, 2 vols. (Quito, 1956), II, esp. 23–28, 160–169.

108. Martz, *Ecuador*, p. 72.

109. See Acción Revolucionaria Nacional Ecuatoriana, *El pensamiento de ARNE* (Quito, 1970), p. 18.

110. Ibid., pp. 15, 39–42, 76–78.

111. Ibid., p. 52.

112. Ibid., p. 157. On ARNE ideology see also Jorge Crespo Toral, *El comunismo en el Ecuador* (Quito, 1958) and Jorge Luna Yepes, *Visión política del Ecuador* (Madrid, 1950).

11. The Alliance for Progress and Andean Transitions, 1961–1968

1. "Soviet Bloc Latin American Activities and Their Implications for United States Foreign Policy," in *United States-Latin American Relations*, Congress of the United States, Senate Committee on Foreign Relations (Washington, 1960), pp. 696–697.

2. Critical accounts of the Alliance for Progress include Douglas A. Chalmers, ed., *Changing Latin America: New Interpretations of Its Politics and Society*, vol. 30, *Proceedings of the Academy of Political Science* (New York, 1973), and Simon G. Hanson, *Five Years of the Alliance for Progress: An Appraisal* (Washington, 1967). More sympathetic treatment is found in Richard B. Gray, ed., *Latin America and the United States in the 1970s* (Itasca, Ill., 1971), pp. 78–136, and Jerome Levinson and Juan de Onís, *The Alliance that Lost Its Way: A Critical Report on the Alliance for Progress* (Chicago, 1970).

3. For persuasive critiques of the prevailing liberal assumptions that helped lead to expanding U.S. activities in the underdeveloped areas see Guillermo O'Donnell, *Modernization and Bureaucratic Authoritarianism* (Berkeley, 1973) and Robert A. Packenham, *Liberal America and the Third World: Political Development Ideas in Foreign Aid and Social Science* (Princeton, 1973). Also useful is Travis C. McBride, "Social and Political Factors in United States Foreign Assistance Programs," Ph.D. diss., University of Oklahoma, 1967, dealing principally with Mexico and Peru.

4. Moore, *Social Origins of Dictatorship and Democracy: Lord and Peasant in the Making of the Modern World* (Boston, 1966), pp. 142–145. Fresh insights abound also in Moore, *Reflections on the Causes of Human Misery* (Boston, 1972).

5. Placing this diplomacy in its broader framework is Robert H. Terry, "Ecuadorean Foreign Policy, 1958–1968, As Reflected in the Organization of American States and the United Nations," Ph.D. diss., American University, 1972.

6. See Philip Agee, *Inside the Company: CIA Diary* (New York, 1975). Although this book, written as an exposé by a man who left the CIA in 1969 after having served since late 1960 in Ecuador and Uruguay, must be used with caution, its detailed description of agency activities in Ecuador is convincing. On AFL-CIO operations see Donald R. Torrence, "American Imperialism and Latin American Labor, 1959–1970: A Study of the Role of the Organización Interamericana de Trabajadores in the Latin American Policy of the United States," Ph.D. diss., Northern Illinois University, 1975.

7. For a perceptive analysis of the way in which bureaucratic infighting contributed to the general fultility of the Alliance for Progress see Abraham F. Lowenthal, "United States Policy Toward Latin America: 'Liberal,' 'Radical,' and 'Bureaucratic' Perspectives," LARR, 7 (1973), 3–25.

8. René Barrientos quoted in James W. Wilkie, The Bolivian Revolution and U.S. Aid Since 1952 (Los Angeles, 1969), p. 37.

9. See Juan Lechín Oquendo, Discurso inaugural del Secretario Ejecutivo de la Central Obrera Boliviana (La Paz, 1962), p. 57, and Paz Estenssoro, La revolución boliviana (La Paz, 1964), p. 32.

10. See DeLesseps S. Morison, Latin American Mission: An Adventure in Hemisphere Diplomacy (New York, 1965), pp. 243–246.

11. The percentage declined in the following year (1964) to 35.7. See Bolivia, Ministerio de Planificación y Coordinación, Estrategía socio-económico del desarrollo nacional, 2 vols. (La Paz, 1970), I, 49, 170.

12. See Cornelius H. Zondag, The Bolivian Economy, 1952–65: The Revolution and its Aftermath (New York, 1966), p. 114.

13. See "Tesis de Colquiri" (1964), in Guillermo Lora, ed., Documentos políticos de Bolivia (La Paz, 1970), p. 395.

14. Céspedes, Imperialismo y desarrollo (La Paz, 1963), p. 69.

15. See ibid., p. 62, and Cornelius H. Zondag, Problems in the Economic Development of Bolivia (La Paz, 1956), p. 28.

16. Diez de Medina, Bolivia y su destino, y otros temas de la patria (La Paz, 1962), p. 14. Good summaries of the situation in Bolivia and other Andean countries during the 1960s are found in Jorge Dandler, ed., Contradictions in the Andes: Bolivia, Chile and Peru (New York, 1975).

17. See Wilkie, The Bolivian Revolution, pp. 60–61.

18. Samuel P. Huntington, Political Order in Changing Societies (New Haven, 1968), p. 331. For leftist criticism of alleged U.S. responsibility for the strengthening of the military see Sergio Almaráz Paz, Requiem para una república (La Paz, 1969), esp. pp. 17–21, 82.

19. See William H. Brill, Military Intervention in Bolivia: The Overthrow of Paz Estenssoro and the MNR (Washington, 1967), esp. p. 31. Brill presents a far fuller account in "Military Civic Action in Bolivia," Ph.D. diss., University of Michigan, 1966.

20. See Charles D. Corbett, The Latin American Military as a Socio-Political Force: Case Studies of Bolivia and Argentina (Coral Gables, 1972), pp. 39–41.

21. Barrientos, "Ni revanchismo ni continuismo: la Nueva Bolivia," in Lora, ed., Documentos, pp. 545–567.

22. See Allen J. Ellender, Review of United States Government Operations in Latin America, United States Senate, Ninetieth Congress (Washington, 1967), pp. 216–217.

23. Melvin Burke and James M. Malloy, "Del populismo nacional al corporativismo nacional: el caso de Bolivia, 1952–1970," Aportes, no. 26 (1972), 85.

24. Jonathan Kandell, "Bolivians Discuss Gulf Gifts in Cynicism and Resentment," New York Times, May 27, 1975.

25. International Bank for Reconstruction and Development, International Development Association, Current Economic Position and Prospects of Bolivia (Washington, 1970), p. 17. See also Melvin Burke, comp., Estudios críticos sobre la economía boliviana (La Paz, 1973). For reliable coverage of the economic situation in Bolivia and elsewhere in Latin America, see Bank of London and South America, Ltd., Fortnightly Review, The Economist Para América Latina, published 1967–1970 by The Economist of London, and Quarterly Economic Review, Peru, Bolivia, Ecuador, published in London and prior to 1956 called the Three Monthly Economic Review, Peru, Bolivia, Ecuador.

26. See Federico Aguiló, "La transformación sindical en Bolivia," in José Prats and others, La transformación actual en América Latina y en Bolivia (Oruro, 1970), pp. 189–214, and John H. Magill, Labor Unions and Political Socialization: A Case Study of Bolivian Workers (New York, 1974), based on 1968 interviews with workers.

27. For a highly sympathetic account of Guevara's campaign in Bolivia see Richard Gott, Guerrilla Movements in Latin America (Garden City, 1972), pp. 397–481.

28. Salvado Romero Pittari, "Bolivia: sindicalismo campesino y partidos políticos," Aportes, no. 23 (1972), 75. See also Adrianne Aron Schaar, "Local Government in Bolivia: Public Administration and Popular Participation," in Dwight Heath, ed., Contemporary Cultures and Societies of Latin America, 2d ed. (New York, 1974), esp. pp. 499–500.

29. Romero Pittari, "Bolivia," p. 91.

30. See Martin C. Needler, Anatomy of a Coup d'Etat: Ecuador, 1963 (Washington, 1964), p. 1.

31. Ecuador, Junta Militar, Paz creadora y trabajo fecundo: mensaje a la nación ecuatoriana (Quito, 1965), p. 6.

32. George Pope Atkins, "La Junta Militar Ecuatoriana (1963–1966): Los militares latinoamericanos de nuevo tipo," Aportes, no. 24 (1972), 11–12.

33. Junta Militar, *Paz creadora*, pp. 94, 105–106.

34. Jacques M. P. Wilson, *The Development of Education in Ecuador* (Coral Gables, 1970), p. 9.

35. See Piedad Peñaherrera del Costales and Alfredo Costales, *Historia social del Ecuador*, 4 vols. (Quito, 1964–1971), IV, 81, and Charles R. Gibson, *Foreign Trade in the Economic Development of Small Nations: The Case of Ecuador* (New York, 1971), p. 128.

36. On the agrarian sector and attempts at land reform see David G. Basile, *Tillers of the Andes: Farmers and Farming in the Quito Basin* (Chapel Hill, 1974), Ralph L. Beals, *Community in Transition: Nayón, Ecuador* (Los Angeles, 1966), Comité Interamericana de Desarrollo Agrícola (CIDA), *Tenencia de la tierra y desarrollo del sector agrícola, Ecuador* (Washington, 1965), Muriel M. Crespi, "The Patrons and Peons of Pesillo: A Traditional Hacienda System in Highland Ecuador," Ph.D. diss., University of Illinois, 1968, Ernest Feder, *The Rape of the Peasantry: Latin America's Landholding System* (Garden City, 1971), esp. pp. 116–119, 154–163, 197–205, and Peter M. Gladhart, "Capital Formation of the Ecuadoran Frontier: A Study of Human Investment and Modernization in the Riobambenos Cooperative," mimeo., Department of Agricultural Economics, Cornell University Agricultural Experiment Station, New York State College of Agriculture and Life Sciences (Ithaca, 1972).

37. See Atkins, "La Junta Militar," pp. 16–20, and Wilson, *Development of Education*, pp. 8–9.

38. The best population study is John Van Dyke Saunders, *The People of Ecuador: A Demographic Analysis* (Gainesville, 1961).

39. Gibson, *Foreign Trade*, p. 259.

40. Cyrano Tama Paz, *Petroleo, drama ecuatoriano* (Guayaquil, 1970), p. 15.

41. On the AP program see Fernando Belaúnde Terry, *Peru's Own Conquest* (Lima, 1965).

42. An excellent description of the land reform program, in theory and practice, is found in James F. Petras and Robert LaPorte, Jr., *Cultivating Revolution: The United States and Agrarian Reform in Latin America* (New York, 1971), pp. 33–115. See also Solon Barraclough and Juan Collarte, eds., *El hombre y la tierra de América Latina* (Santiago de Chile, 1972), which includes coverage of Peru and Ecuador.

43. Belaúnde's approach was remarkably similar to one pioneered by Manuel Prado, 1939–1945, as described by Thomas M. Davies, Jr., "Indian Integration in Peru, 1820–1948: Overview," TA, 30 (1973), 203–205. It represents also an expansion on the Indian policy of Óscar Benavides (1933–1939) who had recognized the expediency of protecting the comunidades.

44. On the economic situation see Instituto Nacional de Planificación, *Plan de desarrollo económico y social, 1967–70,* 4 vols. (Lima, 1966–1967), International Development Association, *Recent Economic Performance and Policies of Peru* (Washington, 1966), and René Vandendries, "An Appraisal of the Reformist Development Strategy of Peru," in Robert E. Scott, ed., *Latin American Modernization Problems: Case Studies in the Crisis of Change* (Urbana, 1973), pp. 260–284.

45. See Adalberto J. Pinelo, *The Multinational Corporation as a Force in Latin American Politics: A Case Study of the International Petroleum Company in Peru* (New York, 1973), pp. 118–119. On Peruvian-U.S. relations in general see John Allen Peeler, "The Politics of the Alliance for Progress in Peru," Ph.D. diss., University of North Carolina, 1968, "U.S. Aid to Peru under the Alliance for Progress," prepared by the Peru Desk of the Department of State, in Daniel A. Sharp, ed., *U.S. Foreign Policy and Peru* (Austin, 1972), pp. 423–442, and *United States Relations with Peru,* Hearings before the Subcommittee on Western Hemisphere Affairs, U.S. Senate, Foreign Relations Committee, Ninety-first Congress (Washington, 1969).

46. A perceptive account of the Belaúnde regime and the difficulties that brought its fall is found in Jane S. Jaquette, *The Politics of Development in Peru,* CULASP (Ithaca, 1971), pp. 131–198.

47. See George M. Ingram, *Expropriation of U.S. Property in South America: Nationalization of Oil and Copper Companies in Peru, Bolivia and Chile* (New York, 1974).

48. See Mario Vázquez, *Hacienda, peonaje y servidumbre en los Andes peruanos* (Lima, 1961).

49. Julio Colter and Felipe Portocarrero, "Peru: Peasant Organizations," in Henry Landsberger, ed., *Latin American Peasant Movements* (Ithaca, 1969), p. 311. See also Henry F. Dobyns, Paul L. Doughty, and Harold D. Lasswell, eds., *Peasants, Power and Applied Social Change: Vicos as a Model* (Beverly Hills, 1964), p. 12, and Hugo Neira, *Cuzco: tierra y muerte* (Lima, 1964), stressing the rise of Quechua nationalism and the role of women in leading invasions around Cuzco. A valuable general account is Howard Handelman, *Struggle in the Andes: Peasant Mobilization in Peru* (Austin, 1975).

50. See Peter Howell Gore, *The Highland Campesino: Backward Peasant or Reluctant Pawn: A Study of the Social and Economic Factors Affecting Small Farm Modernization in Four Highland Ecuadorian Communities,* CULASP (Ithaca, 1971). Suggesting the broader setting of this topic are Leslie Ann Brownrigg, "The Role of Secondary Cities in Andean Urbanism: A Bibliographic Essay Exploring Urban Processes," Northwestern University, Center for Urban Affairs, Comparative Studies Program (1974), mimeo, and Norman E. Whitten, Jr., *Sacha Runa: Ethnicity and Adaptation of Ecuadorian Jungle Quichua* (Urbana, 1971).

51. See Joseph B. Casagrande, "Strategies for Survival: The Indians of High-land Ecuador," in Heath, ed., *Contemporary Cultures*, esp. pp. 94–95, and Manuel María Marzal, "El Indio y la tierra en el Ecuador," AI, 23 (1963), 7–30. For an indication of Indian unrest in northern Ecuador, contrasting to the gen-erally calm situation, see Muriel Crespi, "Changing Power Relations: The Rise of Peasant Unions on Traditional Ecuadorian Haciendas," *Cuadernos Americanos*, 44 (1971), 223–240. An excellent guide to the topic is University of Wisconsin, *Agrarian Reform in Latin America: An Annotated Bibliography* (Madison, 1974).

52. José Matos Mar, "¿Qué son los 'Comunidades de Indígenas'?" in Sebas-tián Salazar Bondy and others, *La encrucijada del Perú* (Montevideo, 1963), p. 57, correctly stresses the divergences among Indian comunidades. In some areas a full process of cultural change was well underway; in others the Indian settlements were virtually untouched by forces of transition. Some of the vast literature deal-ing with continuity and change among Peruvian Indians includes: Giorgio Alberti, *Inter-village Systems and Development: A Study of Social Change in Highland Peru*, CULASP (Ithaca, 1970), Wesley W. Craig, Jr., *From Hacienda to Com-munity: An Analysis of Solidarity and Social Change in Peru*, CULASP (Ithaca, 1967), John Theodore Fishel, "Politics and Progress in the Peruvian Sierra: A Comparative Study of Development in Two Districts," Ph.D. diss., Indiana Uni-versity, 1971, Raymond Frederic Hafer, "The People Up the Hill: Individual Progress Without Village Participation in Parimarca, Cajamarca, Peru," Ph.D. diss., Indiana University, 1971, Robert G. Keith and others, *La hacienda, la comunidad y el campesino en el Perú* (Lima, 1970), Charles D. Kleyemer, "Social Interaction Between Quechua Campesinos and Criollos: An Analytic Description of Power and Dependency, Domination and Defense, in the Southern Sierra of Peru," Ph.D. diss., University of Wisconsin, 1973, José Matos Mar, "Las ha-ciendas del valle de Chancay," in Henri Favre, Claude Collin-Delavaud, and Matos Mar, *La hacienda en el Perú* (Lima, 1967), Matos Mar and others, *Dominación y cambios en el Perú rural: la micro-región del valle de Chancay* (Lima, 1969), Solomon Miller, "The Hacienda and the Plantation in Northern Peru," Ph.D. diss., Columbia University, 1964, José R. Sabogal Wiesse, ed., *La comunidad andina* (Mexico, 1969), and William F. Whyte, "Rural Peru—Peasants as Activists," in Heath, ed., *Contemporary Cultures*, pp. 526–541.

53. See Julio Cotler, "Haciendas y comunidades tradicionales en un contexto de movilización política," *Estudios Andinos*, 1 (1970), pp. 127–134.

54. On the impact that some of the nuclear schools, initiated in the 1940s with the backing of U.S. technical assistance programs, had in raising the skills and expectations of Peruvian Indians see Facultad de Educación de la Universidad Nacional del Cuzco, *Problemas fundamentales de la educación nacional* (Lima, 1955), pp. 54ff, and Rolland G. Paulston, *Society, Schools and Progress in Peru* (Oxford, Eng., 1971), pp. 64–65, 79.

55. The "structural binds" terminology has been borrowed from F. LaMond Tullis, *Lord and Peasant in Peru: A Paradigm of Political and Social Change* (Cambridge, Mass., 1970).

56. See Charles P. Davignon, "A History of the Radio Schools of Peru (from Puno) from 1961 to 1969 and Their Contribution to Present and Future Education in Peru," Ph.D. diss., Catholic University of America, 1973, and Dan Chapin Hazen, "The Awakening of Puno: Government Policy and the Indian Problem in Southern Peru, 1900–1955," Ph.D. diss., Yale University, 1974.

57. On the importance of *forasteros* in bringing pressures for change in Puno see Edward Dew, *Politics in the Altiplano: The Dynamics of Change in Rural Peru* (Austin, 1969), esp. pp. 75–85.

58. On competition among political activists for Indian support see Susan C. Bourque, *Cholification and the Campesino: A Study of Three Peruvian Peasant Organizations in the Process of Societal Changes,* CULASP (Ithaca, 1971), pp. 47, 53–62, et passim, and P. A. Oakley, "*El pueblo lo hizo:* A Study of Communal Labour Practices in the Indigenous Communities of the Peruvian High lands and the Programme of *Cooperación Popular,* 1963–1968," Ph.D. diss., Liverpool University, 1972.

59. A particularly dramatic case of structural bind, which facilitated for a time the organizational and revolutionary activities of the Trotskyist Hugo Blanco, occurred in the La Convención valley near Cuzco. For accounts see Blanco, *Land or Death: The Peasant Struggle in Peru,* trans. Naomi Allen (New York, 1972), Gott, *Guerrilla Movements,* pp. 313–390, and Eric Hobsbawm, "A Case of Neo-Feudalism: La Convención, Peru," *Journal of Latin American Studies,* 1 (1969), 31–50. On the whole, the most reliable account is Wesley W. Craig, Jr., "Peru: The Peasant Movement of La Convención," in Landsberger, ed., *Latin American Peasant Movements,* pp. 274–295. On other attempts to parlay a structural bind into a Marxist-led revolution see Héctor Béjar, *Peru, 1965: Notes on a Guerrilla Experience,* trans. William Rose (New York, 1969). A valuable bibliographical survey is Leon G. Campbell, "This Historiography of the Peruvian Guerrilla Movement, 1960–65," LARR, 8 (1973), 45–70.

60. See Henry Dobyns, Paul Doughty, and Allen Holmberg, *Peace Corps Program Impact in the Peruvian Andes: Final Report* (Ithaca?, 1966?), mimeo. On other aspects of Peace Corps activity see Moritz Thomsen, *Living Poor: A Peace Corps Chronicle* (Seattle, 1969).

61. See Allan Holmberg, "Changing Community Attitudes and Values in Peru: A Case Study in Guided Change," in R. N. Adams and others, *Social Change in Latin America Today* (New York, 1960), pp. 63–107. On a notable experiment in community development carried out under Peruvian auspices see Óscar Núñez del Prado, with William Foote Whyte, *Kuyo Chico: Applied Anthropology in an Indian Community* (Chicago, 1973).

62. Henry Dobyns, *The Social Matrix of Peruvian Indigenous Communities* (Ithaca, 1964), p. 96.

63. See William P. Mangin, "The Indians," in Sharp, ed., *U.S. Foreign Policy and Peru,* p. 213.

64. See Gabriel Escobar M., *Organización social y cultural del sur del Perú* (Mexico, 1967), p. 211.

65. See Eugene A. Hammel, *Power in Ica: The Structural History of a Peruvian Community* (Boston, 1969), pp. 112–113.

66. See Solomon Miller, "Hacienda to Plantation in Northern Peru," in Julian H. Steward, ed., *Contemporary Change in Traditional Societies*, vol. III, *Mexican and Peruvian Communities* (Urbana, 1967), pp. 135–225.

67. Gibson, *Foreign Trade*, p. 67. For a broader treatment of the topic see David Parker Hanson, "Political Decision Making in Ecuador: The Influence of Business Groups," Ph.D. diss., University of Florida, 1971.

68. Leslie Ann Brownrigg, "Interest Groups in Regime Changes in Ecuador," I-AEA, 28 (1974), 7. On the autonomous entities of Ecuador see also Freeman J. Wright, *The Upper Level Public Administrator in Ecuador* (Quito, 1968). At the time of writing, Wright estimated the number of these entities at 1,300.

69. See Alfredo Mallet, "Trends in Latin American Social Security," in Stanley M. Davis and Louis Wolf, eds., *Workers and Managers in Latin America* (Lexington, Mass., 1972), pp. 143–145.

70. See Aníbal Ismodes Cairo, *Bases de una sociología del Perú*, 2 vols. (Lima, 1967), I, 191–192, and Larry Larson, "Labor, Social Change, and Politics in Peru," Ph.D. diss., University of North Carolina, Raleigh, 1967).

71. See Carlos A. Astiz, *Pressure Groups and Power Elites in Peruvian Politics* (Ithaca, 1969), pp. 67–68.

72. See Aldo Solari, "Secondary Education," in Lipset and Solari, eds., *Elites*, p. 459, and William Foote Whyte with Graciela Flores, "High-level Manpower for Peru," in Frederick Harbison and Charles A. Myers, eds., *Manpower and Education: Country Studies in Economic Development* (New York, 1965), pp. 52–53.

73. On a similar set of circumstances in Ecuador, see Emily M. Nett, "The Functional Elites of Quito," JIAS, 13 (1971), 112–121.

74. See Sara Michl, "Urban Squatter Organizations as a National Government Tool," in Francine F. Rabinovitz and Felicity Trueblood, eds., *Latin American Urban Research*, 3 vols. (Beverly Hills, 1971–1973), III, 164, Diego Robles Rivas, "Development Alternatives for the Peruvian *Barriada*," ibid., II, 235, and Margo L. Smith, "Domestic Service as a Channel of Upward Mobility for the Lower-Class Woman: The Lima Case," in Ann Pescatello, ed., *Female and Male in Latin America: Essays* (Pittsburgh, 1973), p. 193.

75. Wilson, *Development of Education*, p. 101.

76. Paulston, *Society, Schools and Progress*, p. 254.

77. Between 1950 and 1962 the Ecuadoran urban population increased from 28.5 to 36 percent of the total population, according to Gonzalo Rubio Orbe, *Población rural ecuatoriana* (Quito, 1966), p. 9; while between 1940 and 1962 the increase in Peru was from 34.5 to 47.4 percent, according to Carlos Delgado, "Metropolitan Policy for Squatter Settlements: Three Proposals Regarding Accelerated Urbanization Problems in Metropolitan Areas, the Lima Case," in John Miller and Ralph A. Gakenheimer, eds., *Latin American Urban Policies and the Social Sciences* (Beverly Hills, 1969), p. 274.

78. Neil W. Chamberlain, *Beyond Malthus: Population and Power* (New York, 1970), p. 30. On population issues see also David Chaplin, ed., *Population Policy and Growth in Latin America* (Lexington, Mass., 1971), Erik P. Eckholm, *Losing Ground: Environmental Stress and World Food Prospects* (New York, 1975), Terry L. McCoy, ed., *The Dynamics of Population Policy in Latin America* (Cambridge, Mass., 1974), and Nicolás Sánchez-Albernoz, *The Population of Latin America: A History*, trans. W. A. R. Richardson (Berkeley, 1974), a survey beginning with the Indian preagricultural society and concluding with projections that extend to the year 2000. See also n. 6, chap. 13.

79. Vandendries, "An Appraisal of the Reformist Development Strategy," p. 263, and Herbert Goldhamer, *The Foreign Powers in Latin America* (Princeton, 1972), p. 254.

80. Harold Lasswell, introduction to Richard H. Stephens, *Wealth and Power in Peru* (Methuchen, 1971), p. vi.

81. On the issue of industrialization and employment see Solon L. Barraclough, "Rural Development and Employment Prospects in Latin America," in Arthur J. Field, ed., *City and Country in the Third World: Issues in the Modernization of Latin America* (Cambridge, Mass., 1970), pp. 97–135. He establishes that a 3 percent increase in industrial output usually results in only a 1 percent increase in employment.

82. Magali Sarfatti Larson and Arlene Eisen Bergman, *Social Stratification in Peru* (Berkeley, 1969), p. 154. See also Victor E. Teckman, "Income Distribution, Technology and Employment in Developing Countries: An Application to Ecuador," *Journal of Development Economics*, 2 (1975), 49–80, United Nations, Economic Commission for Latin America, *Income Distribution in Latin America* (New York, 1971), and Richard Charles Webb, *Government Policy and the Distribution of Income in Peru, 1963–1973* (Cambridge, Mass., 1977).

83. Carlos Malpica, *Los dueños del Perú* (Lima, 1965) and César Augusto Reinaga, *Humanismo y economía* (Cuzco, 1966), esp. pp. 17–19, posit the existence of a united and cohesive oligarchy as of the mid-1960s. On the differing views among Peruvian researchers on this matter see the José Matos Mar introduction to François Bourricaud and others, *La oligarquía en el Perú*, 2d ed.

(Lima, 1971), pp. 9–12, and Larson and Bergman, *Social Stratification*, pp. 262–276.

84. The importance of this transition is the point most emphasized by Mauricio Solaún and Michael A. Quinn in their jointly authored book, *Sinners and Heretics: The Politics of Military Intervention in Latin America* (Urbana, 1974).

85. For a useful account of AFL-CIO activities not only in Peru but elsewhere in Latin America as well see Serafino Romualdi, *Presidents and Peons: Recollections of a Labor Ambassador in Latin America* (New York, 1967). The controversial nature of the AFL-CIO role is revealed in Carroll Hawkins, *Two Democratic Labor Leaders in Conflict: The Latin American Revolution and the Role of the Workers* (Lexington, Mass., 1973). The topic is placed within a broader framework by Adolf Sturmthal and James G. Scoville, eds., *The International Labor Movement in Transition: Essays on Africa, Asia, Europe and South America* (Urbana, 1973).

86. Céspedes, *Imperialismo y desarrollo*, p. 66.

87. On the impact of study abroad in nourishing frustration and militancy among aspiring elites see Robert F. Arnove, "Promoters of the U.S. Model in Latin American Universities, International Exchange Programs and the Peace Corps," in Richard R. Renner, ed., *Universities in Transition: The U.S. Influence in Latin American Education* (Gainesville, 1973), esp. p. 110.

88. See Joseph Grunwald, Miguel S. Wionczek, and Martin Carnoy, *Latin American Economic Integration and U.S. Policy* (Washington, 1972), p. 111, and *Private Investment in Latin America: Hearings Before the Subcommittee on Inter-American Economic Relationships of the Joint Committee*, Congress of the United States, January 14, 15, and 16, 1964 (Washington, 1964), pp. 15, 63, 379.

89. See David P. Calleo and Benjamin R. Rowland, *America and the World Political Economy* (Bloomington, 1973), pp. 163, 167–168.

90. Mira Wilkins, *The Emergence of Multinational Enterprise: American Business Abroad from the Colonial Era to 1914* (Cambridge, Mass., 1971), p. 66. The author is describing the thrust of U.S. investment in the developing nations of the world beginning in the 1890s. By the 1960s, North American private capital was adopting the same approach toward Latin America.

91. Eduardo Galeano, "Latin America and the Theory of Imperialism," in K. T. Fann and Donald C. Hodges, eds., *Readings in U.S. Imperialism* (Boston, 1971), p. 211.

92. Tomás Guillermo Elío, *Objectivos y proyecciones del acuerdo subregional andino: desarrollo e integración* (La Paz, 1970), p. 247.

93. See Alcira Leiserson, *Notes on the Process of Industrialization in Argentina, Chile, and Peru* (Berkeley, 1966), p. 79, and Aníbal Quijano, *Nationalism and Capitalism in Peru: A Study in Neo-Imperialism*, trans. Helen R. Lane (New York, 1971), p. 120.

94. Among the most moderate and persuasive writers subscribing to the economic drain theory is Keith Griffin. In his edited work *Financing Development in Latin America* (London, 1971), p. 243, he writes: Almost all the evidence we have suggests that international movements of capital, whether public or private, are a poor instrument for accellerated development." Also important in evaluating this situation is the fact that often direct foreign investment does not even involve capital movements but depends instead on mobilization of local capital in a process controlled by foreigners. See Stephen H. Hymer, *The International Operations of National Firms: A Study of Direct Foreign Investment* (Cambridge, Mass., 1976).

95. The terms are used by Susanne Bodenheimer in her brilliant Marxian analysis, "Dependency and Imperialism," in Fann and Hodges, eds., *Readings in U.S. Imperialism*, pp. 155–181. See too Irving Louis Horowitz, "The Norm of Illegitimacy: Toward a General Theory of Latin American Economic Development," in Field, ed., *City and Country in the Third World*, pp. 25–48.

96. Dos Santos, "La crisis de la teoría del desarrollo y las relaciones de dependencia en América Latina," in Helio Jaguaribe and others, *La dependencia político-económico de América Latina* (Mexico, 1970), p. 180. For an analysis of dependency theories see Werner Baer, "Import Substitution and Industrialization in Latin America: Experiences and Interpretations," LARR, 7 (1972), 95–122, C. Richard Bath and Dilmus James, "Dependency Analysis of Latin America: Some Criticisms," LARR, 11 (1976), 3–55, Michael J. Francis, "Dependency as a Theory of International Relations," mimeo., paper delivered at the International Studies Association Meeting, Washington, March 19, 1975, Joseph A. Kahl, *Modernization, Exploitation and Dependency in Latin America: Germani, González Casanova and Cardoso* (New Brunswick, 1976), James D. McBrayer, "External Economic Linkages and Political Instability in Latin America, 1949–1969," Ph.D. diss., Emory University, 1972, Ivar Oxaal, Tony Barnett, and David Booth, *Beyond the Sociology of Development: Economy and Society in Latin America and Africa* (London, 1975), James Rosenau, ed., *Linkage Politics* (New York, 1969), and Albert John Szymanski, "The Dependence of South America on the United States," Ph.D. diss., Columbia University, 1971.

97. Whyte with Flores, "High-level Manpower," p. 60. See too Luigi R. Einaudi and Alfred C. Stepan III, *Latin American Institutional Development: Changing Military Perspectives in Peru and Brazil*, A Report Prepared for the Office of External Research, Department of State, by the Rand Corporation (Santa Monica, 1971), pp. 21–24, L. N. McAlister, "Peru," in McAlister, Anthony P. Maingot, and Robert A. Potash, *The Military in Latin American Sociopolitical Evolution: Four Case Studies* (Washington, 1970), pp. 36–37, and Liisa North, *Civil-Military Relations in Argentina, Chile, and Peru* (Berkeley, 1966), p. 154.

98. See Carlos Astiz, *Pressure Groups and Power Elites*, pp. 142–145, and Astiz and José Z. García, "El ejército peruano en el poder: ¿contrainsurgencia, desarrollo, o revolución?" *Aportes*, no. 26 (1972), 16–17.

99. Stepan, "Commentary," in Julio Cotler and Richard R. Fagen, eds., *Latin America and the United States: The Changing Political Realities* (Stanford, 1974), p. 363. The emphasis is his. See too David F. Ronfeldt and Luigi Einaudi, "Prospects for Violence," in Einaudi, ed., *Beyond Cuba: Latin America Takes Charge of Its Future* (New York, 1974), pp. 42–43.

100. Einaudi and Stepan, *Latin American Institutional Development*, p. 123.

101. Address of Admiral Ramón Castro Jijón, in Ecuador, Junta Militar, *Con patriotismo sin temor: discursos políticos* (Quito, 1964), pp. 80–82.

102. General Juan Valasco Alvardo quoted in Víctor Villanueva, *¿Nueva mentalidad militar en el Perú?* (Buenos Aires, 1969), p. 65.

103. McAlister, "Peru," p. 30. See also Willard F. Barber and C. Neale Ronning, *Internal Security and Military Power: Counterinsurgency and Civic Action in Latin America* (Columbus, O., 1966).

104. Schumpeter, *Capitalism, Socialism and Democracy*, 2d ed. (New York, 1947), p. 138.

105. For a provocative analysis of the questioning of old beliefs, as the United States moves away from faith in individualism and the efficacy of interest-group pluralism and competition, see George G. Lodge, *The New American Ideology* (New York, 1975). Providing helpful perspective, Seymour Martin Lipset, "The Paradox of American Politics," *The Public Interest*, no. 41 (1975), esp. 161–163, notes that attacks against the "materialistic philistines concerned with bourgeois values" (associated in Europe with Catholic medieval conservatism, fascism, and forms of socialism, communism, and left-wing nationalism) have a lengthy history in the United States. See also Howard J. Wiarda, "The Latin Americanization of the United States," paper presented at the 1976 annual meeting of the American Political Science Association in Chicago, mimeo.

12. A New Era Emerges, 1968–1976

1. The polls through which these figures were derived are discussed in Donald R. Lesh, *A Nation Observed: Perspectives on America's World Role* (New York, 1974).

2. Robert W. Cox, "Labor and the Multinationals," *Foreign Affairs*, 54 (1976), 364, comments perceptively on the decline of the "cult of growth—unquestioned as recently as the early 1960s." The old faith that problems were resolvable or postponable through growth, "with differential payoffs to the contending parties in proportion to their relative strength," is giving way to the

realization that economic resources are no longer adequate to moderate social tensions and alleviate industrial conflict. For more extended development of the argument that the growth ethic of capitalism can no longer serve as an adequate sociopolitical control mechanism in U.S. society see Daniel Bell, *The Cultural Contradictions of Capitalism* (New York, 1976).

3. Walter Struve, *Elites Against Democracy: Leadership Ideals in Bourgeois Political Thought in Germany, 1890–1933* (Princeton, 1973), p. ix. Samuel Huntington, "The Democratic Distemper," *The Public Interest*, no. 41 (1975), 193–224, draws attention to an interesting complicating factor. While a questioning of traditional values (including, in the United States, democratic values) develops during a period of rapid social change, there is also a tendency among North Americans to reaffirm the democratic and egalitarian values of the American creed, resulting in the weakening of political control.

4. On the declining importance of Latin America in overall U.S. private investment see Warren Dean, "Latin American Golpes and Economic Fluctuations," University of Texas Institute of Latin American Studies Offprint Series, no. 104, p. 80, Abraham L. Lowenthal, "The United States and Latin America: Ending the Hegemonic Presumption," *Foreign Affairs*, 55 (October 1976), 199–214, and Osvaldo Sunkel, "Commentary," in Julio Cotler and Richard R. Fagen, eds., *Latin America and the United States: The Changing Political Realities* (Stanford, 1974), p. 119.

5. *New York Times*, October 26, 1974. The major study of the decline of the unilateral dominance of U.S. capital in Latin America is Herbert Goldhamer, *The Foreign Powers in Latin America* (Princeton, 1972). See also Robert W. Fontaine and James D. Theberge, eds., *Latin America's New Internationalism: The End of Hemispheric Isolation* (New York, 1976). For an excellent study of the rising Japanese influence in Peru see C. Harvey Gardiner, *The Japanese and Peru, 1873–1973* (Albuquerque, 1975). Among other topics, Gardiner considers the expansion of industry and commerce, technical assistance, immigration, cultural relationships, and diplomatic history.

6. *An Address by Secretary of State . . . before the Inaugural Session of the Conference of Tlatelolco, February 21, 1974*, News Release, Bureau of Public Affairs, Department of State, Office of Media Services, p. 2.

7. For an even-handed treatment of the multinationals see Raymond Vernon, *Sovereignty at Bay: The Multinational Spread of U.S. Enterprise* (New York, 1971) and Dolph Warren Zink, *The Political Risks for Multinational Enterprise in Developing Countries: With a Case Study of Peru* (New York, 1973). The most cogent defense of multinational enterprise is Mira Wilkins, *The Maturing of Multinational Enterprise: American Business Abroad from 1914 to 1970* (Cambridge, Mass., 1974). Provocative and often critical treatment is found in Richard J. Barnet and Ronald Müller, *Global Reach: The Power of the Multinational Corporations* (New York, 1975), Robert Gilpin, *U.S. Power and the Multinational Corporation: The Political Economy of Foreign Direct Investment* (New York, 1975), and Jon P. Gunnemann, *The Nation-State and the Trans-*

national Corporations in Conflict, with Special Reference to Latin America (New York, 1975).

8. On the "most-favored ally" policy see Octavio Ianni, "Imperialism and Diplomacy in Inter-American Relations," in Cotler and Fagen, eds., Latin America and the United·States, esp. pp. 45–51.

9. Luciano Martins, "The Policies of U.S. Multinational Corporations in Latin America," ibid., p. 383.

10. Velasco Alvarado, La revolución peruana (Buenos Aires, 1973), pp. 26, 66.

11. See Barry B. L. Auguste, The Continental Shelf: Practice and Policy of the Latin American States with Special Reference to Chile, Ecuador and Peru (Geneva, 1960), Richard Bath, "Latin American Claims on Living Resources of the Sea," I-AEA, 27 (1974), 59–85, David C. Edmonds, "The 200-Mile Fishing Rights Controversy: Ecology or High Tariffs?" ibid., 27 (1973), 3–18, Arthur D. Martínez, "The United States-Peruvian Territorial Waters Controversy: Juridical, Political, Economic, and Strategic Considerations," Ph.D. diss., University of California, 1974, J. R. V. Prescott, The Political Geography of the Oceans (New York, 1975), P. S. Rao, The Public Order of Ocean Resources: A Critique of the Contemporary Law of the Sea (Cambridge, Mass., 1975), John Temple Swing, "Who Will Own the Oceans?" Foreign Affairs, 54 (1976), 527–546, and Thomas Wolff, "Inter-American Maritime Disputes over Fishing in the Twentieth Century," Ph.D. diss., University of California, Santa Barbara, 1968.

12. Charles T. Goodsell, American Corporations and Peruvian Politics (Cambridge, Mass., 1974), p. 7.

13. José Matos Mar, "Dominación, desarrollos desiguales y pluralismo en la sociedad y cultura peruana," in Matos Mar and others, El Perú actual (Lima, 1970), pp. 16–17. See also Raymond F. Mikesell, Foreign Investment in Copper Mines in Peru and Papua, New Guinea (Baltimore, 1975).

14. See Kenneth A. Switzer, "The Andean Group: A Reappraisal," I-AEA, 26 (1973), 78–79.

15. See Luigi R. Einaudi, "Latin America's Development and the United States," in Einaudi, ed., Beyond Cuba: Latin America Takes Charge of Its Future (New York, 1974), pp. 222–223.

16. Shane J. Hunt, "Evaluating Direct Foreign Investment in Latin America," ibid., p. 160. See also William P. Avery and James D. Cochrane, "Innovation in Latin American Regionalism: The Andean Common Market," International Organization, 27 (1973), 181–223, Bases generales para una estrategía subregional de desarrollo: Bolivia, Colombia, Chile, Ecuador, Perú, 3 vols. (Cartagena, 1972), Joseph Grunwald, Miguel S. Wionczek, and Martin Carnoy, Latin American

Economic Integration and U.S. Policy (Washington, 1972), esp. pp. 25–26, 116–117, Kevin C. Kearns, "The Andean Common Market: A New Thrust at Economic Integration in Latin America," JIAS, 14 (1972), 225–249, Edward S. Milenky, "Development Nationalism in Practice: The Problems and Progress of the Andean Group," I-AEA, 26 (1973), 49–68, David Morawertz, *The Andean Group: A Case Study in Economic Integration Among Developing Countries* (Cambridge, Mass., 1974), and Robert N. Seidel, *Toward an Andean Common Market for Science and Technology* (Ithaca, 1974).

17. C. Fred Bergsten, "The Threat from the Third World," *Foreign Policy*, 11 (1973), 113. Fine essays on the foreign policies of Peru, Bolivia, and Ecuador that stress economic integration attempts of the 1960s and 1970s, written respectively by Thomas J. Dodd, E. James Holland, and Mary Jeanne Reid Martz, are found in Harold Eugene Davis, Larman C. Wilson, and others, *Latin American Foreign Policies: An Analysis* (Baltimore, 1975).

18. Velasco, *La revolución peruana*, p. 95. For a thoughtful explanation of why Third World countries have been turning against both U.S. capitalism and Soviet socialism see Peter L. Berger, *Pyramids of Sacrifice* (Garden City, 1976), pp. 40, 43–44. He concludes that in the Third World View, "Western 'monopoly capitalism' and Soviet 'state capitalism'" are now often lumped together as two sides of the same coin—a worthless coin, to boot." The search therefore is underway for alternative models of growth less rooted in materialism. For this reason Maoism for a time exercised a certain fascination.

19. Delgado, *Problemas sociales en el Perú contemporáneo* (Lima, 1971), p. 37. For the most detailed account of Peru's military revolution and the attempt to alter the political and socioeconomic structures of the country, see Abraham F. Lowenthal, ed., *The Peruvian Experiment: Continuity and Change under Military Rule* (Princeton, 1975). Lowenthal in his introductory essay stresses the military government's lack of popular support. The ensuing chapters by Julio Cotler, Richard Webb, David Collier, Susan C. Bourque and David Scott Palmer, Colin Harding, Robert S. Drysdale and Robert G. Myers, Shane Hunt, Peter Knight, and Jane S. Jaquette are based generally upon impressively exhaustive research. Hunt is especially perceptive in his treatment of direct foreign investment. Superior as a broad interpretive framework is David Chaplin, ed., *Peruvian Nationalism: A Corporative Revolution* (New Brunswick, 1976). Also impressive are David Collier, *Squatters and Oligarchs: Authoritarian Rule and Policy Change in Peru* (Baltimore, 1976), E. V. K. Fitzgerald, *The State and Economic Development: Peru Since 1968* (London, 1976), and David Scott Palmer and Kevin Jay Middlebrook, *Military Government and Corporativist Political Development: Lessons from Peru* (Beverly Hills, 1975).

20. Fellman, *El sentido de lo nacional en la teoría y en la prática* (La Paz, 1948), pp. 80–81.

21. See the fine study by David Scott Palmer, "Revolution from Above:" *Military Government and Popular Participation in Peru, 1968–1972*, CULASP (Ithaca, 1973), p. 5.

22. Frank Bonilla, "Cultural Elites," in Seymour Martin Lipset and Aldo Solari, eds., *Elites in Latin America* (New York, 1967), p. 250.

23. On the importance of civilians in the military government see Frederick M. Nunn, "Notes on the 'Junta Phenomenon' and the 'Military Regime' in Latin America, with Special Reference to Peru, 1968–1972," TA, 31 (1975), 237–252.

24. Velasco Alvarado, *La revolución peruana*, p. 56. For a good analysis of the populism of Peru's government see Julio Cotler, "Political Crisis and Military Populism in Peru," *Studies in Comparative International Development*, 6 (1970–1971), 95–113.

25. Robert E. Scott, "National Integration Problems," in Scott, ed., *Latin American Modernization Problems: Case Studies in the Crisis of Change* (Urbana, 1973), pp. 304–305.

26. Quijano, *Nationalism and Capitalism in Peru: A Study in Neo-Imperialism*, trans. Helen R. Lane (New York, 1971), p. 59.

27. See Mark O. Dickerson, "Peru Institutes Social Property as Part of Its 'Revolutionary Transformation,' " I-AEA, 29 (1975), 23–34, and Donald W. Pearson, "The Comunidad Industrial: Peru's Experiment in Worker Management," I-AEA, 27 (1973), 18.

28. See Robert E. Klitgard, "Observations on the Peruvian National Plan for Development, 1971–75," I-AEA, 25 (1971), 15.

29. See the March 1971 interview with minister of economy—and future president of Peru—General Francisco Morales Bermúdez, in Joseph S. Tulchin, ed., *Problems in Latin American History: The Modern Period* (New York, 1973), pp. 378–379.

30. See Jane S. Jaquette, *The Politics of Development in Peru*, CULASP (Ithaca, 1971), pp. 210–211.

31. Chaplin, *The Peruvian Industrial Labor Force* (Princeton, 1967), p. 15.

32. See Ozzie Simmons, "The Criollo Outlook in the Mestizo Culture of Coastal Peru," *American Anthropologist*, 57 (1955), 107–117.

33. On the influence of Yugoslavian models on the industrial community see Ismael Frías, *Nacionalismo y autogestión* (Lima, 1971), pp. 182–185. The concept of "communitarian property," associated most prominently with leftist elements of Christian Democracy, especially in Chile during the 1960s, undoubtedly exercised a more profound influence.

34. Velasco Alvarado, *La revolución peruana*, p. 123.

472

35. Delgado, *Problemas sociales*, p. 37.

36. See Scott, "National Integration," p. 347.

37. See David Chaplin, "Corporatism and Development in Peru," mimeo., paper presented at the conference on Development Strategies in the Third World, University of Notre Dame, April 11, 1975, p. 28. Palmer, "*Revolution from Above*," p. 123, estimates—only half in jest—that in some enterprises the arrival of full co-ownership is likely to be delayed by between 100 and 200 years. What is more, various sections of production enjoy legislative immunity from industrial community experiments.

38. For a discussion of the basic issues involved see T. R. Marshall, *Citizenship and Social Class and Other Essays* (Cambridge, Eng., 1950), esp. p. 80.

39. Pablo Macera, quoted in Shane Hunt, "The Economics of Haciendas and Plantations in Latin America," mimeo., Research Program in Economic Development, Woodrow Wilson School, Princeton University (October 1972), p. 6.

40. Carlos Astiz and José Z. García, "El ejército peruano en el poder," *Aportes*, no. 26 (1972), 26.

41. James M. Malloy, "Authoritarianism, Corporatism and Mobilization in Peru," in F. B. Pike and Thomas J. Stritch, eds., *The New Corporatism: Social-Political Structures in the Iberian World* (Notre Dame, 1974), p. 72.

42. Jaquette, *Politics of Development*, pp. 262–263.

43. See Carlos Delgado, "Metropolitan Policy for Squatter Settlements: Three Proposals Regarding Accelerated Urbanization Problems in Metropolitan Areas, the Lima Case," in John Miller and Ralph A. Gakenheimer, eds., *Latin American Urban Policies and the Social Sciences* (Beverly Hills, 1969), esp. pp. 276–295. See also Howard Handelman, "The Political Mobilization of Urban Squatter Settlements," *LARR*, X (1975), 35–72, for a good analysis of some of the abundant literature on the topic.

44. Henry A. Dietz, "Bureaucratic Demand-Making and Clientelist Participation: The Urban Poor in an Authoritarian Context," in James M. Malloy, ed., *Authoritarianism in Latin America* (Pittsburgh, 1976), p. 54. The author kindly made available an advance mimeo. copy of this essay and page reference is to it. See too Dietz, "Becoming a Poblador: Political Adjustment to the Urban Development in Lima, Peru," Ph.D., diss., Stanford University, 1974.

45. On substitution of *campesino* for the word Indian see Velasco Alvarado, *La revolución peruana*, pp. 12–13. On government attempts to establish control over rural comunidades see Howard Handelman, *Struggle in the Andes: Peasant Political Mobilization in Peru* (Austin, 1975), pp. 246–265, William Mangin, "The Indians," in Daniel Sharp, ed., *U.S. Foreign Policy and Peru* (Austin,

1972), esp. pp. 211–212, and Frits C. M. Wils, *Agricultural and Industrial Development in Peru: Some Observations on Their Interrelationship* (The Hague, 1972).

46. James F. Petras and Robert LaPorte, Jr., *Cultivating Revolution: The United States and Agrarian Reform in Latin America* (New York, 1971), p. 255. See also Paul R. Shaw, *Land Tenure and the Rural Exodus in Chile, Colombia, Costa Rica and Peru* (Gainesville, 1976).

47. John Kautsky, *The Political Consequences of Modernization* (New York, 1972), pp. 121–122, notes that reform of land tenure results in very tangible immediate satisfactions and thereby encourages political order in agricultural societies.

48. Quoted in Arturo. Barea, *Unamuno* (Cambridge, Eng., 1952), p. 23.

49. Tama Paz, *Petroleo, drama ecuatoriano* (Guayaquil, 1970), p. 51.

50. Georg Maier, *The Ecuadorian Presidential Election of June 2, 1968* (Washington, 1969), p. 71. On general economic conditions at the time see Junta Nacional de Planificación y Coordinación, *Plan ecuatoriano para el desarrollo de los recursos humanos*, 2 vols. (Quito, 1970), and Misión Andina, Ecuador, *Programa de acción inmediata, 1972–1973* (Quito, 1972).

51. Leslie Ann Brownrigg, "Interest Groups in Regime Changes in Ecuador," I-AEA, 28 (1974), 11.

52. See *New York Times*, December 9, 1974, and November 17, 1975.

53. Ibid., September 20, 1975.

54. "Informe a la Nación, por el General Alfredo Ovando Candia," in Guillermo Lora, ed., *Documentos políticos de Bolivia* (La Paz, 1970), p. 592.

55. International Bank for Reconstruction and Development, International Development Association, *Current Economic Position and Prospects of Bolivia* (Washington, 1970), p. i.

56. Sergio Almaráz, *Petroleo en Bolivia*, 2d ed. (La Paz, 1969), pp. 11–25, develops this thesis.

57. Scott, "National Integration," p. 384.

58. On the importance of Santa Cruz in the toppling of Torres see G. Richard Fletcher, "Santa Cruz: A Study of Economic Growth in Eastern Bolivia," I-AEA, 29 (1975), esp. 34–36.

59. Charles D. Corbett, *The Latin American Military as a Socio-Political Force: Case Studies of Bolivia and Argentina* (Coral Gables, 1972), p. 62.

60. See Laurence Whitehead, "El estado y los intereses seccionales: el caso boliviano," *Estudios Andinos*, 4 (1974–1975), 85–118, and "National Power and Local Power: The Case of Santa Cruz de la Sierra, Bolivia," in Francine F. Rabinovitz and Felicity Trueblood, eds., *Latin American Urban Research*, 3 vols. (Beverly Hills, 1971–1973), III, 39–40. A good overview is provided by Susan Eckstein, "Después de la Revolución: una comparación de México y Bolivia," *Estudios Andinos*, 4 (1974–1975), 5–38. On the situation in the countryside see William J. McEwen, *Changing Rural Society: A Study of Communities in Bolivia* (New York, 1975).

61. See the controversial book *De Torres a Banzer: diez meses de emergencia en Bolivia* (Buenos Aires, 1972), written during a Chilean exile by Jorge Gallardo Lozada, a cabinet member of the Torres administration who disappeared in Chile following the 1973 military overthrow of Salvador Allende. Subsequently, in June of 1976, Torres was murdered in Argentina in the course of rightist terrorism erupting after the military seized power in March.

62. See Goldhamer, *The Foreign Powers*, p. 247.

63. See *New York Times*, July 27, 1974, and September 28, 1975 (E3), and Latin American Center, University of California, Los Angeles, *Statistical Abstract of Latin America 1971*, ed. Kenneth Ruddle and Donald Odermann (1972), p. 89.

64. For valuable surveys see Frederick C. Turner, *Catholicism and Political Development in Latin America* (Chapel Hill, 1971), Brian H. Smith, S.J., "Religion and Social Change," LARR, 10 (1975), 3–34, and Ivan Vallier, *Catholicism, Social Control and Modernization in Latin America* (Englewood Cliffs, 1970).

65. On ONIS, see Michael Gregory Macaulay, "The Role of the Radical Clergy in the Attempt to Transform Peruvian Society," Ph.D. diss., University of Notre Dame, and Susan C. Bourque, *Cholification and the Campesino: A Study of Three Peruvian Peasant Organizations in the Process of Societal Changes*, CULASP (Ithaca, 1971), pp. 48–50, 64–105.

66. On the "prophetic Church" see Thomas C. Bruneau, "Power and Influence: Analysis of the Church in Latin America," LARR, 8 (1973), 25–52, and Luigi Einaudi, Michael Fleet, and Alfred Stepan, "The Changing Catholic Church," in Einaudi, ed., *Beyond Cuba*, esp. pp. 88–92. An excellent critique of the use of religion to achieve revolutionary ends is Gunter Lewy, *Religion and Revolution* (New York, 1974).

67. William Foote Whyte with Graciela Flores, "High-level Manpower for Peru," in Frederick Harbison and Charles Myers, eds., *Manpower and Education: Country Studies in Economic Development* (New York, 1965), p. 59. See also Federico Aguiló, *Sondeo de opinión sobre la Iglesia en Bolivia* (La Paz, 1968), dealing with opinions on the Catholic church as ascertained through extensive interviews.

68. See Isidoro Alonso and others, *La Iglesia en el Perú y Bolivia: estructuras eclesiásticas* (Madrid, 1961), esp. pp. 184–192, Macaulay, "The Role of the Radical Clergy," p. 78, Jaime Ponce García and Óscar Uzín Fernández, *El clero en Bolivia, 1968* (Cuernavaca, Mex., 1970), and Turner, *Catholicism and Political Development*, p. 195.

69. Manuel Vicente Villarán, quoted in Tulchin, ed., *Problems in Latin American History*, p. 361.

70. See Gustavo Gutiérrez Merino, an important Peruvian intellectual and ONIS leader, "Notes for a Theology of Liberation," *Theological Studies*, 31 (1970), 243–261.

71. Macaulay, "The Role of the Radical Clery," p. 541.

72. See Berger, *The Sacred Canopy: Elements of a Sociological Theory of Religion* (Garden City, 1967).

73. Chardin, *The Divine Milieu: An Essay on the Interior Life*, trans. D. M. MacKinnon and others (New York, 1965), p. 69.

74. See Zbigniew Brzezinski, *Between Two Worlds: America's Role in the Technetronic Era* (New York, 1970).

75. For interpretations assuming the inevitability of dominant-subordinate patterns in international relations see Marshall R. Singer, *Weak States in a World of Powers: The Dynamics of International Relationships* (New York, 1972), and Steven L. Spiegel, *Dominance and Diversity* (Boston, 1972). For general treatment of the changing parameters of relations between strong and weak, developed and developing countries see Guy F. Erb and V. Kallab, *Beyond Dependency: The Developing World Speaks Out* (Washington, 1975), Robert E. Gamer, *The Developing Nations* (Boston, 1976), G. K. Helleiner, ed., *A World Divided: The Less Developed Countries in the International Economy* (London, 1976), and G. Ramis, ed., *The Gap Between Rich and Poor Nations* (New York, 1972). For a defense of "interdependency," defined in such manner as to suggest that the poor nations are necessarily dependent upon a trickle-down from the expansion of economic life in the developed countries see Institute of Man and Science, *New Structures for Economic Interdependence* (Rensselearville, N.Y., 1975).

76. Rothschild, "Banks: The Coming Crisis," *The New York Review of Books*, May 27, 1976, pp. 16–22.

77. See Christopher Garbacz, *Industrialization under Economic Integration in Latin America* (Austin, 1971) and Edward S. Milenky, *The Politics of Regional Organization in Latin America: The Latin American Free Trade Association* (New York, 1973).

78. See Dale V. Slaght, "The New Realities of Ecuadorean-Peruvian Relations: A Search for Causes," I-AEA, 27 (1973), 3–14.

79. Strained relations with neighbor republics help account for the fact that in the 1963–1973 period, Peru, Bolivia, and Ecuador were among the Latin American countries spending the highest percentage of GNP on arms. These three republics, together with Brazil and Uruguay, spent between 2 and 4 percent of GNP on arms purchases, and were exceeded in Latin America only by Cuba, with a figure slightly above 5 percent. While the three Andean republics were among the leaders in arms purchases, the figures reveal that in recent years Latin America has not, on the whole, invested as much in military preparedness as is commonly assumed. See U.S. Arms Control and Disarmament Agency, *World Military Expenditures and Arms Trade: 1963–1973* (Washington, 1975).

80. For an excellent account of interpower rivalry involving Andean America prior to the overthrow of Allende, a period when leftist Chile and leftist Peru were aligned against conservative Brazil, see Weston Agor, "Latin American Inter-State Politics: Patterns of Cooperation and Conflict," I-AEA, 26 (1972), 19–33. On the situation following the September 1973 fall of Allende see Norman A. Bailey and Ronald M. Schneider, "Brazil's Foreign Policy: A Case Study in Upward Mobility," I-AEA, 27 (1974), 3–36, and R. H. Swansbrough, "Peru's Diplomatic Offensive," in R. G. Hellman and E. J. Rosenbaum, eds., *Latin America: The Search for a New International Role* (Beverly Hills, 1975).

81. Servan-Schreiber's book *The American Challenge*, appearing in Spanish translation as *El desafío americano* (Santiago de Chile, 1967), made a tremendous impact in Andean America. See also Philippe C. Schmitter, *Autonomy or Dependence as Regional Integration Outcomes: Central America* (Berkeley, 1972) for the argument that, contrary to expectations of proponents, regional integration has not deterred but has in fact increased foreign economic penetration.

82. An excellent general coverage of the pitfalls and possibilities of popular participation is found in Samuel P. Huntington and Joan M. Nelson, *No Easy Choice: Political Participation in Developing Countries* (Cambridge, Mass., 1976).

13. Epilogue: On Life and Culture in Postmodern Times

1. The major work in this new field is Edward O. Wilson's controversial *Sociobiology: The New Synthesis* (Cambridge, Mass., 1975).

2. See F. B. Pike and Blair R. Williamson, "Cultures and Organisms: Historical-Biological Perspectives of United States-Latin American Economic Affairs," I-AEA, 28 (1975), 45–76.

3. See Daniel Bell, *The Coming of Post-Industrial Society: A Venture in Social Forecasting* (New York, 1973), p. 240.

4. Wagar, "Religion, Ideology, and the Idea of Mankind in History," in Wagar, ed., *History of the Idea of Mankind* (Albuquerque, 1971), p. 196.

5. Karl Mannheim, *Man and Society in an Age of Reconstruction*, trans. Edward Shils (New York, n.d., from the London, 1940 ed.), p. 281.

6. See Michael E. Conroy, "Recent Research in Economic Demography Related to Latin America: A Critical Survey and Agenda," LARR, 9 (1974), 3–27, and T. Lynn Smith, *The Race Between Population and Food Supply in Latin America* (Albuquerque, 1976). See also n. 78, chap. 11.

7. See Philippe C. Schmitter, "Still the Century of Corporatism?" in F. B. Pike and Thomas J. Stritch, eds., *The New Corporatism: Social-Political Structures in the Iberian World* (Notre Dame, 1974), pp. 85–131.

8. Peter F. Drucker, "Pension Fund 'Socialism,'" *The Public Interest*, no. 42 (1976), p. 44, puts the matter this way: "No 'system' can create harmonious or even stable industrial relations and human relations. Industrial relations and human relations are not primarily macro-phenomena. They are primarily micro-phenomena—the results of the management of work by management and the management of the job by the worker. Both can be affected only at the workplace, by redefining the relationship of a specific worker to a specific job. The problems of work and job cannot be remedied by changing the 'system.'"

Index

Index

Index

Index

Index

Index

Mining: Peru, 153–154; Bolivia, 163–165, 287–292. *See also* Copper; Gold; Lead; Manganese; Silver; Tin

Ministry of Public Health, Labor and Social Security, Peru, 262

Ministry of Social Security and Labor, Ecuador, 191

Miscegenation, 77, 79

Mita, 52

MNR (*Movimiento Nacionalista Revolucionario*), and MNRistas, of Bolivia, 256–257, 258, 259–260, 268, 273, 280, 281–294, 301, 310–312, 314, 343, 358, 364, 366

Mollendo (Peru), 104, 154

Monarchy, 19, 124

Monroe Doctrine, 120, 126, 203, 341

Monroe, James, 195

Montalvo, Juan, 13, 34, 114, 116

Montaña, 69, 70

Montes, Ismael, 155, 164, 184, 195, 249, 250

Montevideo, seventh Pan American Conference of, 238

Montoneros, 83, 140

Montuvios, 74, 169, 188

Moore, Barrington, Jr., 305

Moquegua (Peru), 223

Morales Bermúdez, Francisco, 357–359

More, Paul Elmore, 211

Morse, Richard M., 10

Moscow, 218, 313

MSC (*Movimento Social Cristiano*), Ecuador, 301

Mugwumps, 200

Mulattoes, 95

Multinational corporations, 342, 372–373, 374

Mussolini, Benito, 187, 192, 260

National Agrarian Confederation, Peru, 355

National Assembly, Ecuador, 151, 152

National City Bank, New York, 164

National Crusade in Favor of the Indian, 187

National Inter-University Planning Office, Peru, 327

National Junta of Planning and Coordination, Ecuador, 316

National Office of Social Information, Peru, *see* ONIS

National System of Aid to Social Mobilization, *see* SINAMOS

Nationalist party (*Partido Nacionalista*), Bolivia, 187

Nationalist Revolutionary Movement, Bolivia, *see* MNR

Nationalization, 233–234, 252–253, 287–292, 356

Natural law doctrine, 42–43

Navarro, Gustavo Adolfo (pseud. Tristán Marof), 222–223, 225, 233, 251, 252, 256, 287, 292, 337

Nazis, and nazism, 257–258, 259

Nearing, Scott, 233

New York City, 162, 197, 199, 299, 345

New York Times, 346, 359

Nicaragua, 198, 233, 344

Nicolaus loan, 196–197

Nietzsche, Friedrich Wilhelm, 146, 208–209, 210, 227

Nitrate industry Peru, 92, 132, 356; Bolivia, 104, 131, 132

Nixon, Richard M., 274, 309, 339, 341

Nonintervention doctrine (1933, 1936), 238

Nueva Granada, republic of, 123–124; viceroyalty of, 48, 50, 51. *See also* Colombia

Nuevo indio, El, 277

OAS (Organization of American States), 275, 299, 310, 360

Obrajes, 50

Obrero, 327, 328

Ochenio, Peru, 295–296

Odría, Manuel A., and Odriistas, 295–297, 318–319

Odría, María Delgado de, 296

Office of General Supervision of Labor, Ecuador, 191

Olañeta, Casimiro, 98, 103

Olañetismo, 98, 99

Olmedo, José Joaquín, 108–109

488

Index

The American Foreign Policy Library

DATE DUE